AUTODESK® REVIT® ARCHITECTURE 2014

NO EXPERIENCE REQUIRED

D1374266

AUTODESK® REVIT® ARCHITECTURE 2014

NO EXPERIENCE REQUIRED

Eric Wing

AUTODESK.
Official Press

SYBEX®
A Wiley Brand

Senior Acquisitions Editor: Willem Knibbe
Development Editor: Richard Mateosian
Technical Editor: Alberto Malagón
Production Editor: Eric Charbonneau
Copy Editor: Tiffany Taylor
Editorial Manager: Pete Gaughan
Production Manager: Tim Tate
Vice President and Executive Group Publisher: Richard Swadley
Vice President and Publisher: Neil Edde
Book Designer: Franz Baumhackl
Compositor: Jeff Lytle, Happenstance Type-O-Rama
Proofreader: Rebecca Rider
Indexer: Ted Laux
Project Coordinator, Cover: Katherine Crocker
Cover Designer: Ryan Sneed
Cover Image: iStockphoto.com / Manuel Velasco

Dear Reader,

Thank you for choosing *Autodesk Revit Architecture 2014: No Experience Required*. This book is part of a family of premium-quality Sybex books, all of which are written by outstanding authors who combine practical experience with a gift for teaching.

Sybex was founded in 1976. More than 30 years later, we're still committed to producing consistently exceptional books. With each of our titles, we're working hard to set a new standard for the industry. From the paper we print on to the authors we work with, our goal is to bring you the best books available.

I hope you see all that reflected in these pages. I'd be very interested to hear your comments and get your feedback on how we're doing. Feel free to let me know what you think about this or any other Sybex book by sending me an email at nedde@wiley.com. If you think you've found a technical error in this book, please visit http://sybex.custhelp.com. Customer feedback is critical to our efforts at Sybex.

Best regards,

NEIL EDDE
Vice President and Publisher
Sybex, an Imprint of Wiley

To my offspring, Cassidy and Jacob. Thanks for waiting patiently on the weekends as I work away.

ACKNOWLEDGMENTS

Before I ever even pondered writing a technical book such as this one, I was the guy who bought them and studied them from the front to the back. This specific page, however, I always thought was somewhat superfluous…bordering on self indulgent. As I sit here now, after finishing 22 chapters, I can categorically say that the 750-word allotment only scratches the surface of the list of people close to me who have been tremendously inconvenienced by my unavailability and, conversely, by my temperament during the rare occasions when I was available. Of course, topping this list are my wife Jennifer and the kids; Cassidy and Jacob. You guys always come through for me, and there is no way I could have written a single chapter without your support; and yes, you get to go to Disney again like the last seven years!

Also, I'd like to thank Grandma and Baci for constantly watching and being with the kids.

On the technical side, thanks to Willem Knibbe for acquiring the book and working with me on my manuscript, and for his constant patience as I lumbered through each chapter. Thanks to Alberto Malagón for his thorough technical edits. Also, I would like to thank Richard Mateosian for keeping it all on track.

About the Author

Eric Wing lives in Syracuse, New York, with his family. He is the BIM services manager for C&S Companies, which is a full service engineering/architectural firm headquartered in Syracuse. Eric's degree is in construction; he earned it from Delhi University. In addition to writing this book, Eric has written *Autodesk® Revit® Architecture: No Experienced Required 2010, 2011, 2012,* and *2013* and *Revit Structure Fundamentals 2010,* and he co-wrote *Mastering Revit Structure 2009.* Eric is also the author of the *Learning Revit* video tutorial, the *Custom Stairs* video tutorial, and the *Revit Families* video tutorial. Eric is an adjunct instructor at Clarkson University, teaching BIM and IPD. In addition to his writing, Eric is a globally recognized speaker, consultant, and trainer. He is also a bass player in a Syracuse band called Jemba when time permits.

Contents at a Glance

CONTENTS

CHAPTER 12   Detailing   605

CHAPTER 13   Creating Specific Views and Match Lines   671

CHAPTER 14   Creating Sheets and Printing   687

CHAPTER 18   Site and Topography   821

CHAPTER 19   Rendering and Presentation   851

CHAPTER 20   Importing and Coordinating Models   875

INTRODUCTION

Why do you need a big, thick technical book? Well, it's true that the best way to learn is to just do it. But do you ever just *do* it and not fully *get* it? Books can serve either as the basis for learning or as supplements for your learning. No one book will teach you everything you need to know about a specific application, but you may never learn everything you need to know about an application without a book. When written appropriately, the book you purchase is there to start you off using good practices. If you have already begun, the book serves as a desktop reference. And last, a book can serve as confirmation that you're approaching an application in the correct manner.

The Autodesk® Revit® Architecture tool is no exception. Although this application has proven to be easy to learn and easy to get a feel for, it's still a deep, sometimes complicated application with many procedures that require step-by-step instructions to fully understand. And to be honest, some of these features just don't work in the real world.

This book has been written by an author who is "in the trenches" using Revit Architecture, Revit Structure, and Revit MEP simultaneously every day. So, yes, you could figure out all this information on your own, but sometimes it's nice to let someone else figure it out for you and pass that knowledge along to you in the form of a book.

Instead of lengthy paragraphs of text that ultimately lead to non-tangible information, this book addresses each subject in a step-by-step approach with more than 1,000 pictures and screenshots to make sure you're on track.

Also, this book also uses an actual project and relates to real-world scenarios. As you're following the step-by-step procedures in the book, you'll be encouraged to try many techniques on your own and also to embellish the procedure to fit your own needs. If you would rather stick to the instructions, this book allows you to do so as well. The book's project uses a five-story office building with a link (corridor) to a three-story multiuse building. The book's website provides the model (plus additional families) you'll need for each chapter so that you can open the book, jump to your chapter of interest, and learn something! In addition, this book is flexible enough that you can substitute your own project if you don't want to follow the book's examples.

Although it has around 1,000 pages, this book doesn't waste time and space with examples of other people's triumphs, but is designed for you to open it to any random page and learn something.

Who Should Read This Book

Revit Architecture 2014: No Experience Required. Does that mean that if you've used Revit, you won't find this book advanced enough? No. This book is designed for anyone who wishes to learn more about Revit Architecture. The book is also intended for architects, architectural designers, and anyone who is using a CAD-based platform to produce architectural-based drawings.

What You Need

BIM can be tough on hardware. This book recommends that you have 8 GB of RAM with a 4 GHz processor. You should also be running at least 1 GB for your graphics. If you're under these specifications (within reason), in some cases you'll be fine. Just realize, however, that when your model is loaded, your system may start slowing down and crashing.

All Revit applications are intended to run on a PC-based system. Windows 7 is recommended.

FREE AUTODESK SOFTWARE FOR STUDENTS AND EDUCATORS

The Autodesk Education Community is an online resource with more than five million members that enables educators and students to download—for free (see website for terms and conditions)—the same software used by professionals worldwide. You can also access additional tools and materials to help you design, visualize, and simulate ideas. Connect with other learners to stay current with the latest industry trends and get the most out of your designs. Get started today at www.autodesk.com/joinedu.

What Is Covered in This Book

Revit Architecture 2014: No Experience Required covers the full gamut of using the software and is organized as follows:

Chapter 1: The Autodesk Revit World   This chapter introduces you to the Revit Architecture 2014 interface and jumps right in to modeling your first building.

Chapter 2: Creating a Model   This chapter begins with placing walls, doors, and windows. It's designed to point you in the right directions in terms of using reference planes and all-around best practices.

Chapter 3: Creating Views   This chapter shows you how to navigate the Revit Project Browser and create new views of the model. Also, you'll learn how to create specific views such as elevations, sections, callouts, plans, and, our favorite, 3D perspectives.

Chapter 4: Working with the Autodesk Revit Tools   In this chapter, you'll learn how to use the everyday drafting tools needed in any modeling application. You'll become familiar with such actions as trim, array, move, and copy. Although it seems remedial, this is one of the most important chapters of the book. It gets you on your way to the "Revit feel."

Chapter 5: Dimensioning and Annotating   In this chapter, you'll learn how to annotate your model. This includes adding and setting up dimensions, adding and setting up text, and using dimensions to physically adjust objects in your model.

Chapter 6: Floors   Yes! Just floors. In this chapter, you'll learn how to place a floor. You'll also learn how to add materials to a floor and how to pitch a floor to a drain.

Chapter 7: Roofs   In this chapter, we'll discuss the ins and outs of placing roofs. You'll learn how to model flat roofs, sloping roofs, pitched roofs, and roof dormers. In addition, you'll learn how to pitch roof insulation to roof drains.

Chapter 8: Structural Items   In this chapter, you'll delve into the structural module of Revit Architecture. The topics we'll cover include placing structural framing, placing structural foundations, and creating structural views.

Chapter 9: Ceilings and Interiors   This chapter focuses predominately on interior design. Placing and modifying ceilings will be covered as well as adding specific materials to portions of walls and floors. You'll also learn how to create soffits.

Chapter 10: Stairs, Ramps, and Railings   This chapter focuses on the creation of circulation items. You'll learn how to create a simple U-shaped multistory staircase to start; then you'll move on to creating a custom winding staircase. From there, you'll learn how to create a custom wood railing. You'll add ramps to the model in this chapter, as well.

Chapter 11: Schedules and Tags   In this chapter, you'll start bringing the BIM into your model. This chapter focuses on adding schedules and adding annotation tags to specific objects and materials in your model. Most important, in this chapter you'll learn how your model is parameter driven and how these parameters influence the annotations.

Chapter 12: Detailing   In this chapter, you'll learn how to draft in Revit. The procedures allow you to draft over the top of a Revit-generated section or create your own drafting view independent of the model. You'll also learn how to import CAD to use as a detail.

Chapter 13: Creating Specific Views and Match Lines   In this chapter, you'll learn how to take advantage of the multitude of views you can create and how to control the visibility graphics of those views to create plans such as furniture and dimensional plans.

Chapter 14: Creating Sheets and Printing   This chapter explores how to produce construction documents using Revit. The procedures include creating a new drawing sheet, adding views to a sheet, creating a title block and a cover sheet, and plotting these documents.

Chapter 15: Creating Rooms and Area Plans   The focus of this chapter is creating rooms and areas. The procedures lead you through the placement of rooms, and you'll learn how to set the properties of those rooms. We'll also discuss how to create room separators and how to create gross area plans. This chapter also guides you through the creation of a color-fill floor plan.

Chapter 16: Advanced Wall Topics   This chapter focuses specifically on the creation of compound walls. By using the Edit Assembly dialog, you'll learn how to add materials, split walls, and add sweeps and reveals such as parapet caps, brick ledges, and brick reveals. Creating stacked walls is also addressed.

Chapter 17: Creating Families   This chapter focuses on the topic of creating families. The procedures start with a simple wall-sweep family and then move on to creating a door family with an arched header. You'll also learn how to create an in-place family.

Chapter 18: Site and Topography   In this chapter, you'll learn how to place a topographical surface into your model. We'll discuss how to control point-by-point elevations in your site. Splitting and then creating subregions to create swales and berms will be covered. You'll also learn how to utilize an imported CAD site plan and place a toposurface over the top of the CAD lines. And we'll explore rotating your project to true north.

Chapter 19: Rendering and Presentation   In this chapter, you'll learn how to use the Revit rendering tools built into the Revit GUI. This chapter also shows you how to create walkthroughs as well as solar studies.

Chapter 20: Importing and Coordinating Models   This chapter focuses on the ins and outs (pun intended) of importing and exporting CAD formats as well as linking Revit Structure models. The procedures include configuring CAD layering settings as well as linking and importing AutoCAD for plans and sections.

You'll also learn how to link Revit Structure and perform a Copy/Monitor operation as well as use Revit interference detection.

Chapter 21: Phasing and Design Options   This chapter explains how to create an existing floor plan and then moves through demolition into new construction. You'll also learn how to create alternates using design options.

Chapter 22: Project Collaboration   In this chapter, you'll learn how to use Revit in a multiuser environment. The procedures in the chapter will lead you through activating worksharing and then creating a central model. You'll move to creating local user files as well as saving to the central model and placing requests to relinquish.

Included with the book are Revit Architecture project files that follow along with the instructions. Each chapter has one or more actual Revit models that have been completed up to the point of the instruction in that specific chapter—or even that specific section of the chapter—to allow you to jump in at any moment. Also included with the book are custom families that accompany the lessons as well as additional families and projects that you can download as a bonus. You can download the accompanying files at www.sybex.com/go/revit2014ner.

Contacting the Author

As you're reading along, please feel free to contact me at ewing@cscos.com, and I will be glad to answer any question you have. In addition, if you would like me to come speak or train at your firm, feel free to give me a shout. You can visit my company's website at www.cscos.com and click the BIM link. You can also go directly to www.bimnation.com

Sybex strives to keep you supplied with the latest tools and information you need for your work. Please check the website at www.sybex.com/go/revit-2014ner, where we'll post additional content and updates that supplement this book if the need arises. Enter **Revit architecture** in the Search box (or type the book's ISBN—**9781118542743**), and click Go to get to the book's update page.

The Autodesk Revit World

I'm sure you've seen plenty of presentations on how wonderful and versatile this 3D Autodesk® Revit® Architecture revolution is. You may be thinking, "This all seems too complicated for what I do. Why do I need 3D anyway?"

The answer is: you don't need 3D. What do you do to get a job out—that is, after the presentation when you're awarded the project? First, you redraw the plans. Next comes the detail round-up game we have all come to love: pull the specs together and then plot. This is a simple process that works.

Well, it worked until 3D showed up. Now we have no real clue where things come from, drawings don't look very good, and getting a drawing out the door takes three times as long.

That's the perception, anyway. I've certainly seen all of the above, but I've also seen some incredibly coordinated sets of drawings with almost textbook adherence to standards and graphics. Revit can go both ways—it depends on you to make it go the right way.

One other buzzword I'm sure you've heard about is *Building Information Modeling (BIM)*. Although they say BIM is a process, not an application, I don't fully buy into that position. Right now, you're on the first page of BIM. BIM starts with Revit. If you understand Revit, you'll understand Building Information Modeling.

This chapter will dive into the Revit graphical user interface (GUI) and tackle the three topics that make Revit ... well, Revit.

▶ **The Revit interface**

▶ **The Project Browser**

▶ **File types and families**

The Revit Interface

Toto, we aren't in CAD anymore!

If you just bought this book, then welcome to the Revit world. In Revit, the vast majority of the processes you encounter are in a flat 2D platform. Instead of drafting, you're placing components into a model. Yes, these components have a so-called third dimension to them, but a logical methodology drives the process. If you need to see the model in 3D, it's simply a click away. That being said, remember this: there is a big difference between 3D drafting and modeling.

With that preamble behind us, let's get on with it.

First of all, Revit has no command prompt and no crosshairs. Stop! Don't go away just yet. You'll get used to it, I promise. Unlike most CAD applications, Revit is heavily pared down, so to speak. It's this way for a reason. Revit was designed for architects and engineers. You don't need every command that a mechanical engineer would need. An electrical engineer wouldn't need the functionality that an architect would require. In the new Revit 2014 interface, the functionality I just mentioned is available, but it's tucked away so as not to interfere with your architectural pursuits.

N O T E   The preceding paragraph is the longest one of the book. This book is designed to cut to the chase and show you how to use Revit Architecture in a step-by-step fashion without having to read through paragraph after paragraph just to find the answer you're seeking. Datasets are provided on the book's accompanying website (www.sybex.com/go/revit2014ner), but you can also use your own model as you go through the book. If you don't wish to read this book cover to cover, don't! Although I recommend going from front to back, you can use the book as a desk reference by jumping to a desired topic. The datasets will be added in phases to accommodate this type of usage. Either way, get ready to learn Revit!

You'll find that, as you get comfortable with Revit, there are many, many choices and options behind each command.

Let's get started:

1. To open Revit, click the icon on your desktop (see Figure 1.1), or choose Start ➢ All Programs ➢ Autodesk ➢ Autodesk Revit Architecture 2014 ➢ Autodesk Revit Architecture 2014 (see Figure 1.2).

F I G U R E 1 . 1 :   You can launch Revit Architecture from the desktop icon.

FIGURE 1.2: You can also launch Revit Architecture using the Windows Start menu (this illustration shows the Windows 7 operating system).

2. After you start Revit, you'll see the Recent Files window, as shown in Figure 1.3. The top row lists any projects on which you've been working; the bottom row lists any families with which you've been working. The column to the right allows you to view some tutorial videos. If you have time, I recommend investigating this feature.

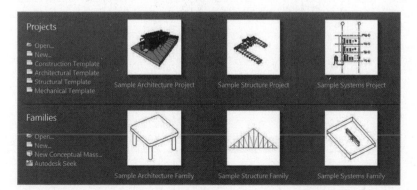

FIGURE 1.3: The Recent Files window lists any recent projects or families on which you've worked.

3. If you're firing up Revit for the first time, you'll see some sample projects, some sample families, and a getting started video. On the left side of the Projects and the Families categories, you're provided with choices for what type of project or family you would like to start (see Figure 1.4).

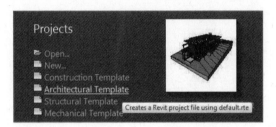

FIGURE 1.4:   You can create a new model or browse for an existing one.

4. In the upper-left corner of the Revit window, you'll see a big purple *R*. This is commonly known as the *Application Icon*. Click the purple *R*, and choose New ➢ Project.

5. The New Project dialog shown in Figure 1.5 opens. Click the Template File drop-down menu, and select Architectural Template. If you're a metric user, click the Browse button. This will open Windows Explorer. Go up one level, and choose the US Metric folder. Select the file called DefaultMetric.rte.

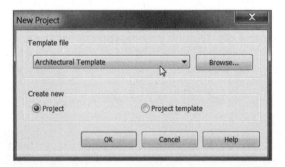

FIGURE 1.5:   The New Project dialog allows you to start a new project using a preexisting template file, or you can create a new template file.

Now that the task of physically opening the application is out of the way, we can delve into Revit. Revit has a certain feel that Autodesk® AutoCAD® converts, or MicroStation converts, will need to grasp. At first, if you're already a CAD user, you'll notice many differences between Revit and CAD. Some of these differences may be off-putting, while others will make you say, "I wish CAD did that." Either way, you'll have to adjust to a new workflow.

The Revit Workflow

This new workflow may be easy for some to adopt, whereas others will find it excruciatingly foreign. (To be honest, I found the latter to be the case at first.) Either way, it's a simple concept. You just need to slow down a bit from your CAD habits. If you're new to the entire modeling/drafting notion, and you feel you're going too slowly, don't worry. You do a lot with each click of the mouse.

Executing a command in Revit is a three-step process:

1. At the top of the Revit window is the Ribbon. A series of tabs is built into the Ribbon. Each tab contains a panel. This Ribbon will be your Revit launch pad! Speaking of launch pads, click the Wall button on the Architecture tab, as shown in Figure 1.6.

FIGURE 1.6: The Ribbon is the backbone of Revit.

2. After you click the Wall button, notice that Revit adds a tab to the Ribbon with additional choices specific to the command you're running, as shown in Figure 1.7. You may also notice that Revit places an additional Options bar below the Ribbon for even more choices.

You'll hear this throughout the book: always remember to look at your options. With no command prompt, the Options bar will be one of your few guides.

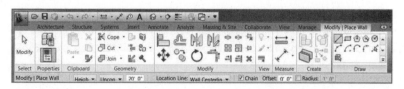

FIGURE 1.7: The Options bar allows you to have additional choices for the current command.

3. After you make your choices from the Ribbon and the Options bar, you can place the object into the view window. This is the large drawing area that takes up two-thirds of the Revit interface. To place the wall, simply pick a point in the window and move your pointer in the direction that you want the wall to travel. The wall starts to form. Once you see that, you can press the Esc key to exit the command. (I just wanted to illustrate the behavior of Revit during a typical command.)

Using Revit isn't always as easy as this, but just keep this basic three-step process in mind and you'll be OK:

1. Start a command.

2. Choose an option from the temporary tab or the Options bar that appears.

3. Place the item in the view window.

Thus, on the surface Revit appears to offer a fraction of the choices and functionality that are offered by AutoCAD (or any drafting program, for that matter). This is true in a way. Revit does offer fewer choices to start a command, but the choices that Revit does offer are much more robust and powerful.

Revit keeps its functionality focused on designing and constructing buildings. Revit gets its robust performance from the dynamic capabilities of the application during the placement of the items and the functionality of the objects after you place them in the model. You know what they say: never judge a book by its cover—unless, of course, it's the book you're reading right now.

Let's keep going with the main focus of the Revit interface: the Ribbon. You'll be leaning on the Ribbon extensively in Revit.

Using the Ribbon

You'll use the Ribbon for the majority of the commands you execute in Revit. As you can see, you have little choice but to do so. However, this is good because it narrows your attention to what is right in front of you.

When you click an icon on the Ribbon, Revit will react to that icon with a new tab, giving you the specific additional commands and options you need. Revit also keeps the existing tabs that can help you in the current command, as shown in Figure 1.8. Again, the focus is on keeping your eyes in one place.

In this book, I'll throw quite a few new terms at you, but you'll get familiar with them quickly. We just discussed the Ribbon, but mostly you'll be directed to choose a tab in the Ribbon and to find a panel on that tab.

To keep the example familiar, when you select the Wall button, your instructions will read: "On the Build panel of the Architecture tab, click the Wall button."

FIGURE 1.8: The Ribbon breakdown showing the panels

WHAT'S THAT TOOLBAR ABOVE THE RIBBON?

This toolbar is called the *Quick Access toolbar*. I'm sure you've seen a similar toolbar in other applications. It comes filled with some popular commands. If you want to add commands to this toolbar, simply right-click any icon and select Add To Quick Access Toolbar. To the left of this toolbar is the Revit Application Icon. Clicking this icon gives you access to more Revit functions that will be covered later in the book. One great icon that I like to have docked on the Quick Access toolbar is the Select Objects (or Modify) icon. I like to add this icon as shown in the following graphic.

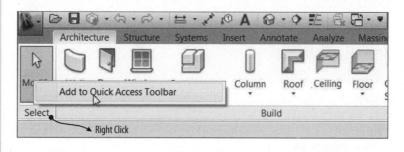

Now that you can see how the Ribbon and the tabs flow together, let's look at another feature in the Ribbon panels that allows you to reach beyond the immediate Revit interface.

The Properties Interface

When you click the Wall button, a new set of commands appears on the Ribbon. This new set of commands combines the basic Modify commands with a tab specific to your immediate process. In this case, that process is adding a wall.

You'll also notice that the Properties dialog near the left of the screen changes, as shown in Figure 1.9. The Properties dialog shows a picture of the wall you're about to place. If you click this picture, Revit displays all the walls that are available in the model. This display is called the Type Selector dropdown (see Figure 1.10).

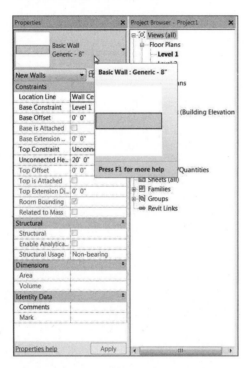

FIGURE 1.9: Click the Properties button to display the Properties dialog. Typically, the dialog is shown by default.

The objective of the next exercise is to start placing walls into the model:

1. Close Revit by clicking the close button in the upper-right corner.

2. Reopen Revit, and start a new project (Metric or Imperial).

3. On the Architecture tab, click the Wall button.

4. In the Properties dialog, select Exterior - Brick and CMU on MTL. Stud from the Type Selector.

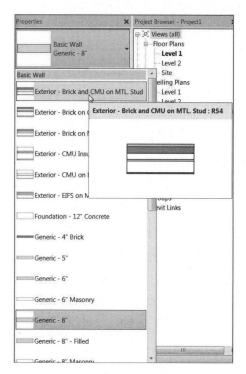

FIGURE 1.10:   The Properties dialog gives you access to many variables associated with the item you're adding to the model.

Element Properties

There are two different sets of properties in Revit: instance properties and type properties. Instance properties are available immediately in the Properties dialog when you place or select an item. If you make a change to an element property, the only items that are affected in the model are the items you've selected.

The Properties Dialog

As just mentioned, the Properties dialog displays the instance properties of the item you've selected. If no item is selected, this dialog displays the properties of the current view in which you happen to be.

New to Revit 2014, you have the ability to combine the Properties dialog with the adjacent dialog, which is called the Project Browser (we'll examine the Project Browser shortly). Simply click the top of the Properties dialog, as shown in Figure 1.11, and drag it onto the Project Browser. Once you do this, you'll see a tab that contains the properties and a tab that contains the Project Browser (also shown in Figure 1.11).

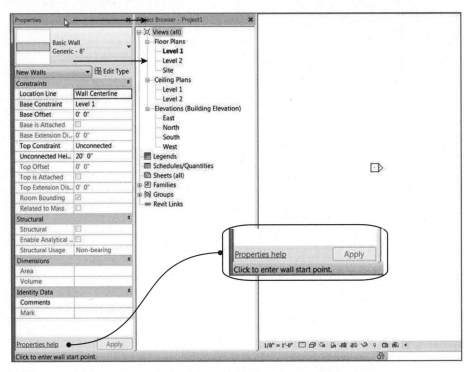

FIGURE 1.11: Dragging the Properties dialog onto the Project Browser

Let's take a closer look at the two categories of element properties in Revit.

Instance Properties

The items that you can edit immediately are called *parameters* or *instance properties*. These parameters change only the object being added to the model at this time. Also, if you select an item that has already been placed in the model, the parameters you see immediately in the Instance Properties dialog change only that item you've selected. This makes sense—not all items are built equally in the real world. Figure 1.12 illustrates the instance properties of a typical wall.

Type Properties

Type properties (see Figure 1.13), when edited, alter every item of that type in the entire model. To access the type properties, click the Edit Type button in the Properties dialog, as Figure 1.14 shows.

FIGURE 1.12: The instance properties change only the currently placed item or the currently selected item.

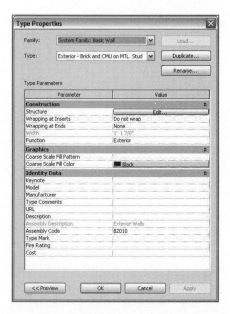

FIGURE 1.13: The type properties, when modified, alter every occurrence of this specific wall in the entire model.

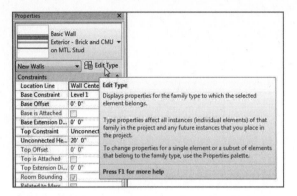

FIGURE 1.14:   The Edit Type button allows you to access the type properties.

At this point, you have two choices. You can either make a new wall type (leaving this specific wall unmodified) by clicking the Duplicate button at upper right in the dialog, or you can start editing the wall's type properties, as shown in Figure 1.15.

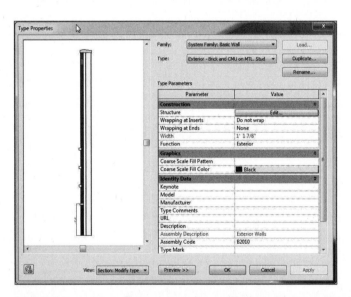

FIGURE 1.15:   The type properties modify the wall system's global settings. Click the Preview button at the bottom of the dialog to see the image that is displayed.

WARNING   I can't stress enough that, if you start modifying type properties without duplicating the type, you need to do so in a very deliberate manner. You can easily affect the model in unintended ways. We'll discuss the specifics of all the wall's type properties in Chapter 16, "Advanced Wall Topics."

Now that you've gained experience with the Type Properties dialog, it's time to go back and study the Options bar as it pertains to placing a wall:

1. Because you're only exploring the element properties, click the Cancel button to return to the model.

2. Back in the Options bar, find the Location Line menu. Through this menu, you can set the wall justification. Select Finish Face: Exterior (see Figure 1.16).

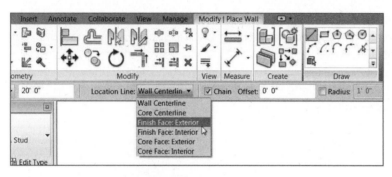

FIGURE 1.16: By selecting Finish Face: Exterior, you know the wall will be dimensioned from the outside finish.

3. On the Options bar, be sure the Chain check box is selected, as Figure 1.16 shows. This will allow you to draw the walls continuously.

4. The Draw panel has a series of sketch options. Because this specific wall is straight, make sure the Line button is selected, as shown in Figure 1.17.

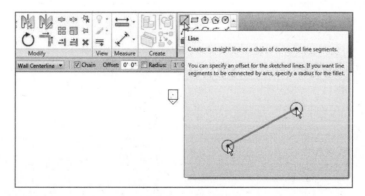

FIGURE 1.17: You can draw any shape you need.

Get used to studying the Ribbon and the Options bar—they will be your crutch as you start using Revit! Of course, at some point you need to begin placing items physically in the model. This is where the view window comes into play.

The View Window

To put it simply, "the big white area where the objects go" is the view window. As a result of your actions, this area will become populated with your model. Notice that the background is white—this is because the sheets you plot on are white. In Revit, what you see is what you get … literally. Line weights in Revit are driven by the object, not by the layer. In Revit, you aren't counting on color #5, which is blue, for example, to be a specific line width when you plot. You can immediately see the thickness that all your "lines" will be before you plot (see Figure 1.18). What a novel idea.

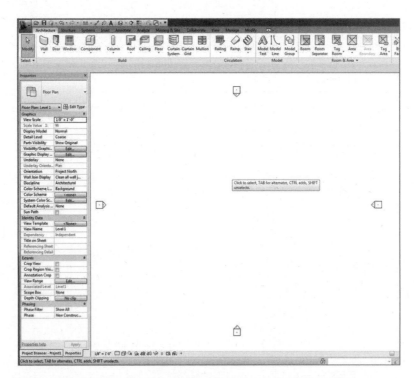

FIGURE 1.18:   The view window collects the results of your actions.

WARNING   Metric users should not type in mm or other metric abbreviations when entering amounts suggested in the exercises. Revit won't accept such abbreviations. Simply enter the number provided within the parentheses.

To continue placing some walls in the model, keep going with the exercise. (If you haven't been following along, you can start by clicking the Wall button on the Architecture tab. In the Properties dialog box, select Exterior - Brick and CMU on MTL. Stud. Make sure the wall is justified to the finish face exterior.) You may now proceed:

1. With the Wall command still running and the correct wall type selected, position your cursor in a location similar to the illustration in Figure 1.19. Pick a point in the view window.

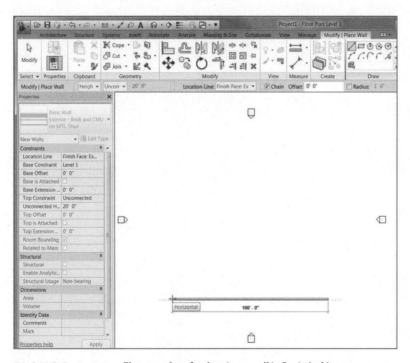

FIGURE 1.19:   The procedure for drawing a wall in Revit Architecture

2. With the first point picked, move your cursor to the left. Notice that two things happen: the wall seems to snap in a horizontal plane, and a blue dashed line locks the horizontal position. In Revit, there is no Ortho. Revit aligns the typical compass increments to 0°, 90°, 180°, 270°, and 45°.

3. Also notice the blue dimension extending from the first point to the last point. Although dimensions can't be typed over, this type of dimension is a temporary dimension for you to use as you place items. Type **100′** (30000mm), and press the Enter key. (Notice that you didn't need to type the foot mark (′) or mm. Revit thinks in terms of feet or millimeters. The wall is now 100′ (30000mm) long (see Figure 1.19).

4. With the Wall command still running, move your cursor straight up from the endpoint of your 100′-long wall. Look at Figure 1.20.

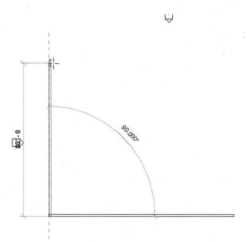

FIGURE 1.20:   How Revit Architecture works is evident in this procedure.

5. Type **80′** (24000mm), and press Enter. You now have two walls.

6. Move your cursor to the right until you run into another blue alignment line. Notice that your temporary dimension says 100′–0″ (30000.0). Revit understands symmetry. After you see this alignment line, and the temporary dimension says 100′–0″ (30000.0), pick this point.

7. Move your cursor straight down, type **16′** (4800mm), and press Enter.

8. Move your cursor to the right, type **16′** (4800mm), and press Enter.

9. Press the Esc key twice.

Do your walls look like Figure 1.21? If not, try it again. You need to be comfortable with this procedure (as much as possible).

F I G U R E   1 . 2 1 :   Working with Revit starts with the ability to work with the view window and learn the quirks and feel of the interface.

To get used to the Revit flow, always remember these three steps:

1. Start a command.

2. Focus on your options.

3. Move to the view window, and add the elements to the model.

If you start a command and then focus immediately on the view, you'll be sitting there wondering what to do next. Don't forget to check your Options bar and the appropriate Ribbon tab.

Let's keep going and close this building by using a few familiar commands. If you've never drafted on a computer before, don't worry. These commands are simple. The easiest but most important topic is how to select an object.

Object Selection

Revit has a few similarities to AutoCAD and MicroStation. One of those similarities is the ability to perform simple object selection and to execute common modify commands. For this example, you'll mirror the two 16′–0″ (4800mm) L-shaped walls to the bottom of the building:

1. Type **ZA** (zoom all).

2. Near the two 16′–0″ (4800mm) L-shaped walls, pick (left-click) and hold down the left mouse button when the cursor is at a point to the right of the walls but above the long, 100′–0″ (30000mm) horizontal wall.

3. You see a window start to form. Run that selection window down and to the left past the two walls. After you highlight the walls, as shown in Figure 1.22, let go of the mouse button, and you've selected the walls.

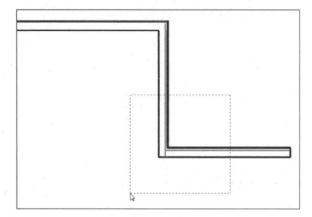

F I G U R E   1 . 2 2 :   Using a crossing window to select two walls

There are two ways to select an object: by using a crossing window or by using a box. Each approach plays an important role in how you select items in a model.

Crossing Windows

A *crossing window* is an object-selection method in which you select objects by placing a window that crosses through the objects. A crossing window always starts from the right and ends to the left. When you place a crossing window, it's represented by a dashed-line composition (as you saw in Figure 1.22).

Boxes

With a box object-selection method, you select only items that are 100 percent inside the window you place. This method is useful when you want to select specific items while passing through larger objects that you may not want in the selection set. A box always starts from the left and works to the right. The line type for a selection window is a continuous line (see Figure 1.23).

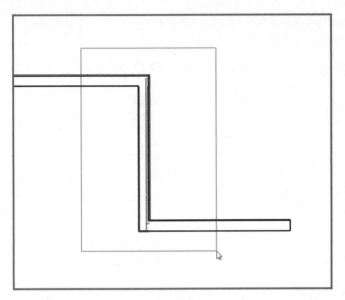

FIGURE 1.23: To select only objects that are surrounded by the window, use a box. This will leave out any item that may be partially within the box.

Now that you have experience selecting items, you can execute some basic modify commands. Let's begin with mirroring, one of the most popular modify commands.

Modifying and Mirroring

Revit Architecture allows you either to select the item first and then execute the command or to start the command and then select the objects to be modified. This is true for most action items and is certainly true for every command on the Modify toolbar. Try it:

1. Make sure only the two 16′–0″ (4800mm) walls are selected.

2. When the walls are selected, the Modify | Walls tab appears. On the Modify panel, click the Mirror – Draw Axis button, as shown in Figure 1.24.

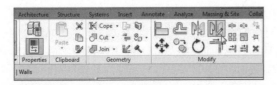

FIGURE 1.24: The Ribbon adds the appropriate commands.

3. Your cursor changes to a crosshair with the mirror icon, illustrating that you're ready to draw a mirror plane.

4. Make sure the Copy check box is selected (see Figure 1.25).

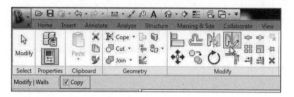

FIGURE 1.25:   There are options you must choose for every command in Revit.

5. Hover your cursor over the inside face of the 80′–0″ (24000mm)-long vertical wall until you reach the midpoint. Revit displays a triangular icon, indicating that you've found the midpoint of the wall (see Figure 1.26).

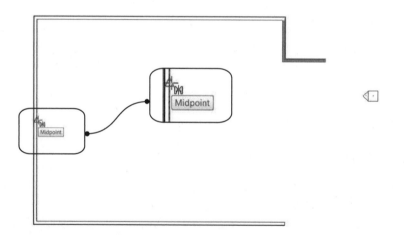

F I G U R E   1 . 2 6 :   Revit has snaps similar to most CAD applications. In Revit, you'll only get snaps if you choose the draw icon from the Options bar during a command.

6. When the triangular midpoint snap appears, pick this point. After you pick the point where the triangle appears, you can move your cursor directly to the right of the wall. An alignment line appears, as shown in Figure 1.27. When it does, you can pick another point along the path. When you pick the second point, the walls are mirrored and joined with the south wall (see Figure 1.28).

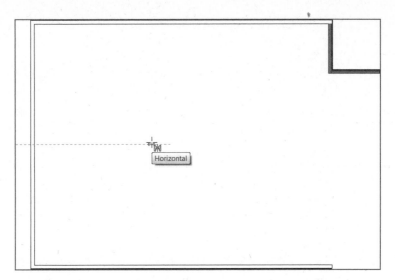

FIGURE 1.27: Mirroring these walls involves: (1) picking the midpoint of the vertical wall, and (2) picking a horizontal point along the plane.

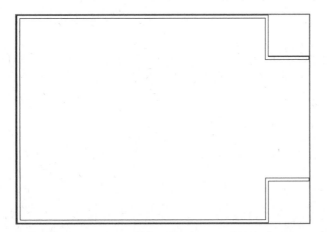

FIGURE 1.28: Your building should look like this illustration.

Now that you have some experience mirroring items, it's time to start adding components to your model by utilizing the items that you placed earlier. If you're having trouble following the process, retry these first few procedures. Rome wasn't built in a day. (Well, perhaps if they'd had Revit, it would have sped things up!) You want your first few walls to look like Figure 1.28.

Building on Existing Geometry

You have some geometry with which to work, and you have some objects placed in your model. Now Revit starts to come alive. The benefits of using Building Information Modeling (BIM) will become apparent quickly, as explained later in this chapter. For example, because Revit knows that walls are walls, you can add identical geometry to the model by simply selecting an item and telling Revit to create a similar item.

Suppose you want a radial wall of the same exact type as the other walls in the model. Perform the following steps:

1. Type **ZA** to zoom the entire screen.

2. Press the Esc key.

3. Select one of the walls in the model—it doesn't matter which one.

4. Right-click the wall.

5. Select Create Similar, as shown in Figure 1.29.

6. On the Modify | Place Wall tab, click the Start-End-Radius Arc button, as shown in Figure 1.30.

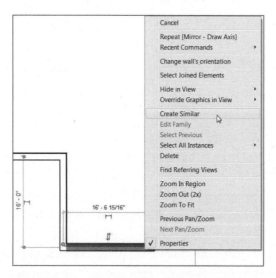

FIGURE 1.29: You can select any item in Revit and create a similar object by right-clicking and selecting Create Similar.

N O T E   When you right-click an item, you can choose to repeat the last command. You can now also select all items that are only in the current view.

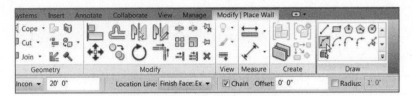

FIGURE 1.30: Just because you started the command from the view window doesn't mean you can ignore your options.

7. Again with the options? Yes. Make sure Location Line is set to Finish Face: Exterior (it should be so already).

8. With the wheel button on your mouse, zoom into the upper corner of the building and select the top endpoint of the wall, as shown in Figure 1.31. The point you're picking is the corner of the heavy lines. The topmost, thinner line represents a concrete belt course below. If you're having trouble picking the correct point, don't be afraid to zoom in to the area by scrolling the mouse wheel.

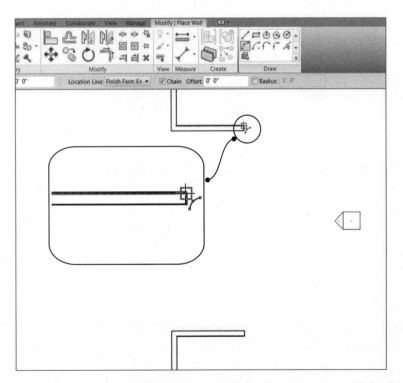

FIGURE 1.31: Select the top corner of the wall to start your new radial wall.

9. Select the opposite, outside corner of the bottom wall. Again, to be more accurate, you'll probably have to zoom in to each point as you're making your picks.

10. Move your cursor to the right until you see the curved wall pause. You'll see an alignment line and possibly a tangent snap icon appear as well. Revit understands that you may want an arc tangent on the two lines you've already placed in your model.

11. When you see the tangent snap icon, choose the third point. Your walls should look like Figure 1.32.

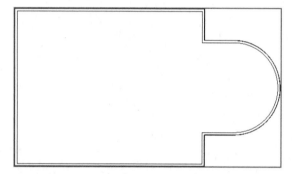

FIGURE 1.32: The completed exterior walls should look like this illustration.

Just because you've placed a wall in the model doesn't mean the wall looks the way you would like it to appear. In Revit, you càn do a lot with view control and how objects are displayed.

View Control and Object Display

Although the earlier procedures are a nice way to add walls to a drawing, they don't reflect the detail you'll need to produce construction documents. The great thing about Revit, though, is that you've already done everything you need to do. You can now tell Revit to display the graphics the way you want to see them.

The View Control Bar

At the bottom of the view window, you'll see a skinny toolbar (as shown in Figure 1.33). This is the View Control bar. It contains the functions outlined in the following list:

Scale   The first item on the View Control bar is the Scale function. It gets small mention here, but it's a huge deal. In Revit, you change the scale of a view by selecting this menu. Change the scale here, and Revit will scale annotations and symbols accordingly (see Figure 1.34).

Detail Level   The Detail Level allows you to view your model at different qualities. You have three levels to choose from: Coarse, Medium, and Fine (see Figure 1.35).

FIGURE 1.33:   The View Control bar controls the graphical view of your model.

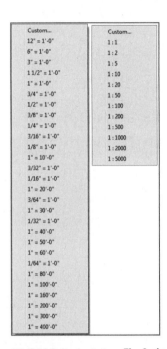

FIGURE 1.34:   The Scale menu allows you to change the scale of your view.

FIGURE 1.35:   The Detail Level control allows you to set different view levels for the current view.

If you want more graphical information with this view, select Fine. To see how the view is adjusted using this control, follow these steps:

1. Click the detail level icon, and choose Fine.

2. Zoom in on a wall corner. Notice that the wall components are now showing in the view.

 T I P When you change the view control in a view, it isn't a temporary display. You're telling Revit how you want to plot this view. The view you see on the screen is the view you'll see when it comes out of the plotter.

There are other items on the View Control bar, but we'll discuss them when they become applicable to the exercises.

The View Tab

Because Revit is one big happy model, you'll quickly find that simply viewing the model is quite important. In Revit, you can take advantage of some functionality in the Navigation bar. To activate the Navigation bar, first go to the View tab and click the User Interface button. Then go to the default 3D view, and make sure the Navigation bar is activated, as shown in Figure 1.36.

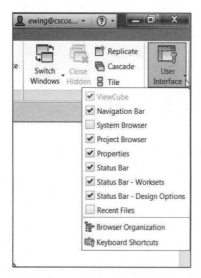

FIGURE 1.36: The View tab allows you to turn on and off the Navigation bar.

One item we need to look at on the Navigation bar is the steering wheel.

The Steering Wheel

The steering wheel allows you to zoom, rewind, and pan. When you click the steering wheel icon, a larger control panel appeard in the view window. To choose one of the options, you simply pick (left-click) one of the options and hold down the mouse button as you execute the maneuver.

To use the steering wheel, follow along:

1. Go back to Floor Plan Level 1, and pick the steering wheel icon from the Navigation bar, as shown in Figure 1.37.

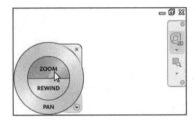

FIGURE 1.37: You can use the steering wheel to navigate through a view.

2. When the steering wheel is in the view window (as shown in Figure 1.37), left-click and hold Zoom. You can now zoom in and out.

3. Click and hold Rewind in the steering wheel. You can now find an older view, as shown in Figure 1.38.

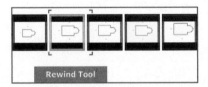

FIGURE 1.38: Because Revit doesn't include zoom commands in the Undo function, you can rewind to find previous views.

4. Do the same for Pan, which is found on the outer ring of the steering wheel. After you click and hold Pan, you can navigate to other parts of the model.

Although you can do all this with your wheel button, some users still prefer the icon method of panning and zooming. For those of you who prefer the icons, you'll want to use the icons for the traditional zooms as well.

When you're finished using the steering wheel, press Shift+W to close out.

Traditional Zooms

The next items on the Navigation bar are the good-old zoom controls. The abilities to zoom in, zoom out, and pan are all included in this function, as shown in Figure 1.39.

FIGURE 1.39: The standard zoom commands

Of course, if you have a mouse with a wheel, you can zoom and pan by either holding down the wheel to pan or wheeling the button to scroll in and out.

Thin Lines

Back on the View tab, you'll see an icon called Thin Lines, as shown in Figure 1.40. Let's talk about what this icon does.

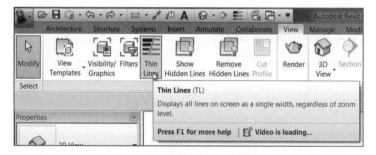

FIGURE 1.40: Clicking the Thin Lines icon lets you operate on the finer items in a model.

In Revit Architecture, there are no layers. Line weights are controlled by the actual objects they represent. In the view window, you see these line weights. As mentioned before, what you see is what you get.

Sometimes, however, these line weights may be too thick for smaller-scale views. By clicking the Thin Lines icon, as shown in Figure 1.40, you can force the view to display only the thinnest lines possible and still see the objects.

To practice using the Thin Lines function, follow along:

1. Pick the Thin Lines icon.

2. Zoom in on the upper-right corner of the building.

3. Pick the Thin Lines icon again. This toggles the mode back and forth.

4. Notice that the lines are very heavy.

The line weight should concern you. As mentioned earlier, there are no layers in Revit Architecture. This topic is addressed in Chapter 13, "Creating Specific Views and Match Lines."

3D View

The 3D View icon brings us to a new conversation. Complete the following steps, which will move us into the discussion of how a Revit model comes together:

1. Click the 3D View icon, as shown in Figure 1.41.

2. On the View Control bar, click the Visual Style button and choose Realistic, as shown in Figure 1.42.

FIGURE 1.41: The 3D View icon will be used heavily.

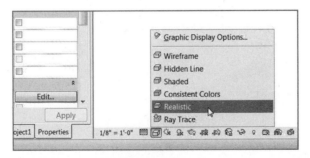

FIGURE 1.42: The Visual Style button enables you to view your model in color. This is typical for a 3D view.

3. Again on the View Control bar, select the Shadows On icon and turn on shadows, as shown in Figure 1.43.

W A R N I N G   A word of caution: if you turn on shadows, do so with care. This could be the single worst item in Revit in terms of performance degradation. Your model *will* slow down with shadows on.

Within the 3D view is the ViewCube. It's the cube in the upper-right corner of the view window. You can switch to different perspectives of the model by clicking the quadrants of the cube (see Figure 1.44).

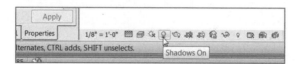

F I G U R E   1 . 4 3 :   Shadows create a nice effect, but at the expense of RAM.

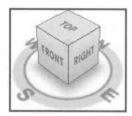

F I G U R E   1 . 4 4 :   The ViewCube lets you look freely at different sides of the building.

 T I P   The best way to navigate a 3D view is to press and hold the Shift key on the keyboard. As you're holding the Shift key, press and hold the wheel on your mouse. Now move the mouse around. You'll be able to view the model dynamically.

Your model should look similar to Figure 1.45.

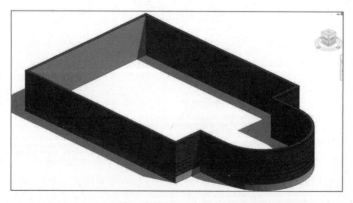

F I G U R E   1 . 4 5 :   The model with shadows turned on

Go back to the floor plan. Wait! How? This brings us to an important topic in Revit: the Project Browser.

The Project Browser

Revit is the frontrunner of BIM. BIM has swept our industry for many reasons. One of the biggest reasons is that you have a fully integrated model in front of you. That is, when you need to open a different floor plan, elevation, detail, drawing sheet, or 3D view, you can find it all right there in the model.

Also, this means your workflow will change drastically. When you think about all the external references and convoluted folder structures that make up a typical job, you can start to relate to the way Revit uses the Project Browser. In Revit, you use the Project Browser instead of the folder structure you used previously in CAD.

This approach changes the playing field. The process of closing the file you're in and opening the files in which you need to do work is restructured in Revit to enable you to stay in the model. You never have to leave one file to open another. You also never need to rely on external referencing to complete a set of drawings. Revit and the Project Browser put it all in front of you.

To start using the Project Browser, follow along:

1. To the far left of the Revit interface are the combined Project Browser and Properties dialogs. At the bottom of the dialogs, you'll see two tabs as shown in Figure 1.46. Click the Project Browser tab.

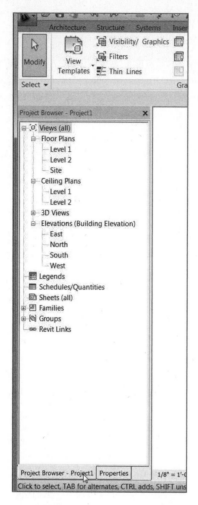

FIGURE 1.46:   The Project Browser is your new BIM Windows Explorer.

2. The Project Browser is broken down into categories. The first category is Views. The first View category is Floor Plans. In the Floor Plans category, double-click Level 1.

3. Double-click Level 2. Notice that the walls look different than in Level 1. Your display level is set to Coarse. This is because any change you make on the View Control bar is for that view only. When you went to Level 2 for the first time, the change to the display level had not yet been made.

4. In the view window, you see little icons that look like houses (see Figure 1.47). These are elevation markers. The elevation marker to the right might be in your building or overlapping one of the walls. If this is the case, you need to move it out of the way.

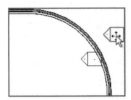

FIGURE 1.47: Symbols for elevation markers in the plan. If you need to move them, you must do so by picking a window. There are two items in an elevation marker.

5. Pick a box around the elevation marker. When both the small triangle and the small box are selected, move your mouse over the selected objects.

6. Your cursor turns into a move icon. Pick a point on the screen, and move the elevation marker out of the way.

7. In the Project Browser, find the Elevations (Building Elevation) category. Double-click South.

8. Also in the Project Browser, notice the 3D Views category. Expand the 3D Views category, and double-click the {3D} choice. This brings you back to the 3D view you were looking at before this exercise.

Now that you can navigate through the Project Browser, adding other components to the model will be much easier. Next you'll begin to add some windows.

WARNING   "Hey! What happened to my elevation?" You're in Revit now. Items such as elevation markers, section markers, and callouts are no longer just dumb blocks: they're linked to the actual view they're calling out. If you delete one of these markers, you'll delete the view associated with it. If you and your design team have been working on that view, then you've lost that view. Also, you must move any item deliberately and with caution. The elevation marker you moved in the previous exercise has two parts: the little triangle is the elevation, and the little box is the part of the marker that records the sheet number on which the elevation will wind up. If you don't move both items by placing a window around them, the elevation's origin will remain in its original position. When this happens, your elevation will look like a section, and it will be hard to determine how the section occurred.

Windows

By clicking all these views, you're simply opening a view (window) of the building, not another file that is stored somewhere. For some users, this can be confusing. (It was initially for me.)

When you click around and open views, they stay open. You can quickly open many views. There is a way to manage these views before they get out of hand.

In the upper-right corner of the Revit dialog, you'll see the traditional close and minimize/maximize buttons for the application. Just below them are the traditional buttons for the files that are open, as shown in Figure 1.48. Click the X to close the current view.

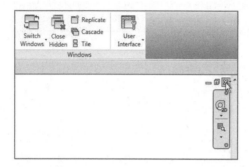

FIGURE 1.48: You can close a view by clicking the X for the view. This doesn't close Revit, or an actual file for that matter—it simply closes that view.

In this case, you have multiple views open. This situation (which is quite common) is best managed on the View tab. To use the Window menu, perform the following steps:

1. On the Window panel of the View tab, click the Switch Windows button, as shown in Figure 1.49.

2. After the menu is expanded, look at the open views.

3. Go to the {3D} view by selecting it from the Window menu and clicking the 3D icon at the top of the screen or by going to the {3D} view in the Project Browser.

FIGURE 1.49: The Switch Windows menu lists all the current views that are open.

4. On the Windows panel, click Close Hidden Windows.

5. In the Project Browser, open Level 1.

6. Go to the Windows panel, and select Tile Windows.

7. With the windows tiled, you can see the Level 1 floor plan along with the 3D view to the side. Select one of the walls in the Level 1 floor plan. Notice that it's now selected in the 3D view. The views you have open are mere representations of the model from that perspective. Each view of the model can have its own independent view settings.

8. Click into each view, and type **ZA**. Doing so zooms the extents of each window. This is a useful habit to get into.

You're at a safe point now to save the file. This also brings us to a logical place at which to discuss the different file types and their associations with the BIM model.

BUT I USED TO TYPE MY COMMANDS!

You can still type your commands. In the Revit menus, you may have noticed that many of the menu items have a two- or three-letter abbreviation to the right. This is the keyboard shortcut associated with the command. You can make your own shortcuts, or you can modify existing keyboard shortcuts—if you navigate to the View tab. On the Windows panel, click the User Interface button. In the drop-down menu, click the Keyboard Shortcuts button. Here you can add or modify keyboard shortcuts.

File Types and Families

Revit Architecture has a unique way of saving files and using different file types to build a BIM model. To learn how and why Revit has chosen these methods, follow along with these steps:

1. Click the save icon (see Figure 1.50).

2. In the Save As dialog, click the Options button in the lower-right corner (see Figure 1.51).

3. In the File Save Options dialog is a place at the top where you can specify the number of backups, as shown in Figure 1.52. Set this value to 1.

FIGURE 1.50:   The traditional save icon brings up the Save As dialog if the file has never been saved.

FIGURE 1.51:   The Options button in the Save As dialog lets you choose how the file is saved.

FIGURE 1.52:   The options in the File Save Options dialog box let you specify the number of backups and the view for the preview.

Revit provides this option because, when you click the save icon, Revit duplicates the file. It adds a suffix of 0001 to the end of the filename. Each time you click the save icon, Revit records this save and adds another file called 0002, leaving the 0001 file intact. The default is to do this three times before Revit starts replacing 0001, 0002, and 0003 with the three most current files.

4. In the Preview section, you can specify in which view this file will be previewed. I like to keep it as the active view. That way I can get an idea of whether the file is up to date based on the state of the view. Click OK.

5. Create a folder somewhere, and save this file into the folder. The name of the file used as an example in the book is NER.rvt. (NER stands for "No Experience Required.") Of course, you can name the file anything you wish, or you can even make your own project using the steps and examples from the book as guidelines.

Now that you have experience adding components to the model, it's time to investigate exactly what you're adding here. Each component is a member of what Revit calls a *family*.

UNDERSTANDING THE REVIT ARCHITECTURE FILE (.RVT)

The extension for a Revit Architecture file is .rvt. There are three separate Revit applications: Revit Architecture, Revit Structure, and Revit MEP. All three Revit applications share the same .rvt file extension. You can directly open a Revit file produced in any of these three applications. You don't need object enablers to read items that don't pertain to that discipline.

System and Hosted Families (.rfa)

A Revit model is based on a compilation of items called families. There are two types of families: system families and hosted families. A *system family* can be found only in a Revit model and can't be stored in a separate location. A *hosted family* is inserted similarly to a block (or cell) and is stored in an external directory. The file extension for a hosted family is .rfa.

System Families

System families are inherent to the current model and aren't inserted in the traditional sense. You can only modify a system family through its element properties in the model. The walls you've put in up to this point are system families,
for example. You didn't have to insert a separate file in order to find the wall
type. The system families in a Revit Architecture model are as follows:

Walls	Shafts
Floors	Rooms
Roofs	Schedules/quantity takeoffs
Ceilings	Text
Stairs	Dimensions
Ramps	Views

System families define your model. As you can see, the list pretty much covers most building elements. There are, however, many more components not
included in this list. These items, which can be loaded into your model, are
called hosted families.

Hosted Families

All other families in Revit are hosted in some way by a system family, a level, or a
reference plane. For example, a wall sconce is a hosted family in that, when you
insert it, it's appended to a wall. Hosted families carry a file extension of .rfa.
To insert a hosted family into a model, follow these steps:

1. Open the NER-01.rvt file or your own file.

2. Go to Level 1.

3. On the Architecture tab, click the Door button.

4. On the Modify | Place Door tab, click the Load Family button, as
   shown in Figure 1.53. This opens the Load Family dialog.

5. Browse to the Doors directory.
   Note that, if you're on a network, your directories may not be the
   same as in this book. Contact your CAD/BIM manager (or whoever
   loaded Revit onto your computer) to find out exactly where they may
   have mapped Revit.

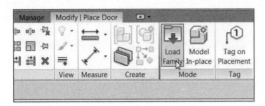

FIGURE 1.53:   You can load an .rfa file during the placement of a hosted family.

6. Notice that there is a list of doors. Select `Single-Raised Panel with Sidelights.rfa`, and click Open.

7. In the Properties dialog, click the Type Selector, as shown in Figure 1.54. Notice that in addition to bringing in the raised panel door family, you also have seven different types of the door. These types are simply variations of the same door. You no longer have to explode a block and modify it to fit in your wall.

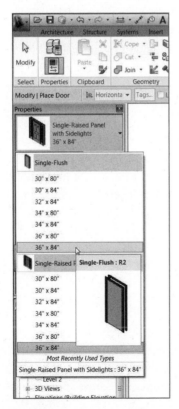

FIGURE 1.54:   Each family `.rfa` file contains multiple types associated with that family.

8. Select Single-Flush 36″ × 84″ (914mm × 2134mm), as shown in Figure 1.54.

9. Zoom in on the upper-left corner of the building, as shown in Figure 1.55.

FIGURE 1.55: Inserting a hosted family (.rfa)

10. To insert the door into the model, you must place it in the wall. (Notice that before you hover your cursor over the actual wall, Revit won't allow you to add the door to the model, as shown in Figure 1.55.) When your pointer is directly on top of the wall, you see the outline of the door. Pick a point in the wall, and the door is inserted. (We'll cover this in depth in the next chapter.)

11. Delete the door you just placed by selecting it and pressing the Delete key on your keyboard. This is just practice for the next chapter.

You'll use this method of inserting a hosted family into a model quite a bit in this book and on a daily basis when you use Revit. Note that when a family is loaded into Revit Architecture, there is no live path back to the file that was loaded. After it's added to the Revit model, it becomes part of that model. To view a list of the families in the Revit model, go to the Project Browser and look for the Families category. There you'll see a list of the families and their types, as Figure 1.56 shows.

The two main Revit files have been addressed. Two others are also crucial to the development of a Revit model.

Using Revit Template Files (.rte)

The .rte extension pertains to a Revit template file. Your company surely has developed a template for its own standards or will do so soon. An .rte file is simply the default template that has all of your company's standards built into it. When you start a project, you'll use this file. To see how an .rte file is used, follow these steps:

1. Click the Application button, and select New ➤ Project.

2. In the resulting dialog, shown in Figure 1.57, click the Browse button.

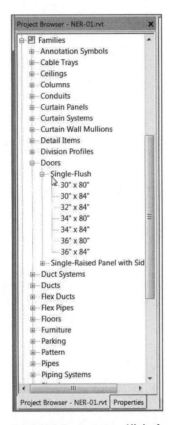

FIGURE 1.56: All the families are listed in the Project Browser.

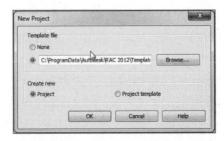

FIGURE 1.57: A new Revit model is based on an .rte template file.

3. Browsing throws you into a category with several other templates. You can now choose a different template.

4. Click Cancel twice.

Whenever you start a project, you'll use the .rte template. When you start a new family, however, you'll want to use an .rft file.

Using Revit Family Files (.rft)

The .rft extension is another type of template—only this one pertains to a family. It would be nice if Revit had every family fully developed to suit your needs. Alas, it doesn't. You'll have to develop your own families, starting with a family template. To see how to access a family template, perform these steps:

1. Click the Application button, and select New ➤ Family to open the browse dialog shown in Figure 1.58.

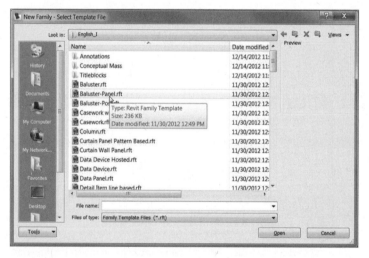

FIGURE 1.58:   The creation of a family starts with templates.

2. Browse through these templates. You'll most certainly use many of them.

3. Click the Cancel button.

Tempting? I know! We'll cover creating families thoroughly in Chapter 17, "Creating Families." As mentioned earlier, you'll reach a certain point when you run out of Revit-provided content. If you're feeling brave, go ahead and play around in one of the templates. You have nothing to lose (except time).

Are You Experienced?

Now you can...

- ☑ navigate the Revit Architecture interface, and start a model

- ☑ find commands on the Ribbon, and understand how this controls your options

- ☑ find where to change a keyboard shortcut to make it similar to CAD

- ☑ navigate through the Project Browser

- ☑ understand how the Revit interface is broken down into views

- ☑ tell the difference between the two different types of families, and understand how to build a model using them

Creating a Model

Now that you have a solid working knowledge of the Autodesk® Revit® Architecture interface and you understand how it differs from most other drafting applications, it's time to move on to creating the Revit model.

The first chapter had you add some exterior walls to the model, and this chapter will expand on that concept. You'll also be placing some of the components, such as doors, that were introduced in Chapter 1, "The Autodesk Revit World." Revit is only as good as the families that support the model.

To kick off the chapter, I'll focus on the accurate placement of interior and exterior walls. You also have a lot to learn about the properties of walls and how to tackle tricky areas where the walls just won't join together for you.

▶ **Placing walls**

▶ **Using reference planes**

▶ **Adding interior walls**

▶ **Editing wall joins**

▶ **Placing doors and windows**

Placing Walls

In Chapter 1, you placed some walls and then added exterior walls to the model. In this section, you'll add more walls to the model. Although adding walls to the model isn't difficult, you need to explore how to control these walls when adjacent items start moving around and corners get fussy. Also, I'll present proven methods to ensure accuracy so that I can keep you from starting down the wrong path.

Adding Exterior Walls

To continue with the perimeter of the building from Chapter 1, let's add some more exterior walls. The first few walls you added to the model were pretty basic in terms of layout. It would be nice to have only square geometry! The reality is, you're going to encounter walls at different angles and dimensions to which you can't just line up other walls. To get around this, you'll add what are called *reference planes* to help lay out the building. At the end of this section, your building's perimeter will look like Figure 2.1.

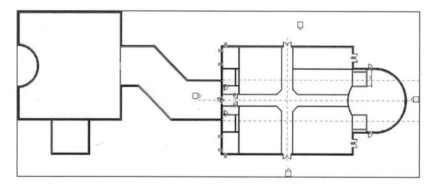

FIGURE 2.1: The footprint of your completed building

The objective of the next set of procedures is to establish some strong working points and then add walls along those guidelines. You'll also use these rules to make the necessary adjustments later in the section.

Using Reference Planes

Reference planes are construction lines that you can place in your model to establish center lines and to use as an aid for symmetrical geometry. If you add a reference plane in one view, it will appear in another. If you add one in a plan view, you can see that same plane in an elevation. This approach is a great way to build using a common reference. Also, reference planes, by default, don't plot.

N O T E   Metric users should not type in mm or other metric abbreviations when entering amounts suggested in the exercises. Revit won't accept such abbreviations. Simply enter the number provided within the parentheses.

The only drawback to reference planes is that they suffer from overuse. Try to use them only as what they are: a reference. To practice using reference planes, follow these steps:

1. Open the file you created in Chapter 1. If you didn't complete that chapter, open the file NER-02.rvt in the Chapter 2 directory, which you can download from the book's website at www.sybex.com/go/revit2014ner. (You can also use your own building if you choose.)

2. Go to Floor Plan Level 1 in the Project Browser (if you aren't there already).

3. On the Work Plane panel of the Architecture tab, click the Ref Plane button (all the way to the right), as shown in Figure 2.2.

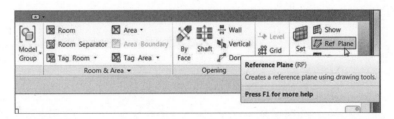

F I G U R E   2 . 2 :   The Ref Plane command is on the Architecture tab's Work Plane panel on the Ribbon.

N O T E   As you move through the exercises in this book, you'll discover that the Ref Plane command is also found elsewhere in the program.

4. Draw the reference plane through the center of the building, extending each end past the exterior walls. (Remember, this is a construction line. You can go long if you need to.) See Figure 2.3 for an idea of where the line should go. If you're having trouble locating the reference points for the start of the reference plane, make sure you're snapping to the midpoint of the walls. You can also type **SM** to snap to the midpoint of the wall.

5. Press Esc.

6. If the line isn't the length you want, you can stretch it. First select the line; at each end, you see blue grips. Simply pick (left-click) the grip, and stretch the reference plane to the desired length, as shown in Figure 2.3.

7. Start the Ref Plane command again.

8. On the Draw panel, click the Pick Lines icon, as shown in Figure 2.4.

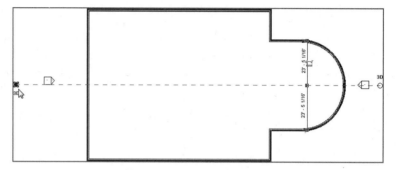

FIGURE 2.3: You can grip-edit reference planes to the required length.

FIGURE 2.4: Offsetting a reference plane

9. Set Offset to 15′–0″ (4500mm) (Imperial users, remember, you can type **15**, and metric users type **4500**), as shown in Figure 2.4.

10. Hover your pointer above the mid-reference plane. A blue alignment line appears either above or below.

11. Move your pointer up and down. See the alignment line flip? When it flips to the top, pick the middle line. Doing so adds the line to the top.

12. With the Ref Plane command still running, hover over the middle line again. This time, offset the alignment line down. Your plan should now look like Figure 2.5.

TIP   Notice that you didn't actually use the Offset command. Revit has the offset function built into most of the commands you'll be running. You just need to remember to look at your temporary tab and your Options bar, and you'll be fine.

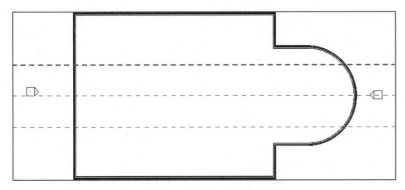

FIGURE 2.5:   Reference planes are used here to aid in the placement of walls.

Adding More Walls

Let's add some more walls. To do so, follow along with the next set of steps. (Before you start, here's a tip. In this procedure, you're going to add walls in a counterclockwise direction, so work in that manner. But keep in mind that Revit assumes you'll add walls in a clockwise manner. In the future, try adding the walls clockwise; doing so forces the exterior of the wall to the outside.) Okay, now back to adding walls:

1. Press the Esc key twice.

2. Select one of the exterior walls in the model, and right-click.

3. Select Create Similar. (You can still start the Wall command from the Architecture tab. If you do, make sure you select Basic Wall: Exterior - Brick And CMU On MTL. Stud.) Create Similar is also available on the Create panel of the Modify | Walls tab.

4. On the Options bar, make sure Location Line is set to Finish Face: Exterior.

5. Start drawing your new wall from the intersection of the west wall (the one on the left) and the upper reference plane, as shown in Figure 2.6. Make sure you're using the face of the wall and not the ledge below. The enlargement in Figure 2.6 can help you.

6. If the wall is starting on the wrong side of the reference plane, tap your spacebar to flip the wall to the correct side.

7. Making sure you have a horizontal line started, type **25 (7500mm)** and press Enter.

8. Press Esc.

9. Do the same for the other side. Your plan should now look like Figure 2.7.

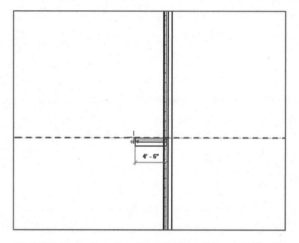

FIGURE 2.6: Drawing a single wall from a defined starting point

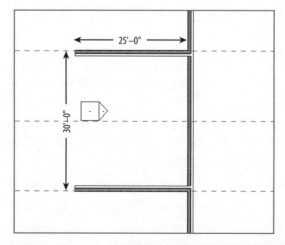

FIGURE 2.7: The two walls drawn here are 30′ (9000mm) from finish face to finish face.

10. Start the Wall command again if it isn't already running. Make sure the Chain check box is selected. This will allow you to keep drawing walls continuing from the last point of the previously drawn wall.

11. From the top 25′ (7500mm) wall, pick the corner of the finish face (again, the brick face and not the ledge below). The wall may be positioned in the wrong orientation, so tap the spacebar to flip it if it is.

12. Move your cursor up and to the left at a 135° angle (Revit snaps at 45° intervals).

13. When you move your cursor far enough in this direction, Revit picks up the north finish face of the building drawn in the previous procedure. After these two alignment lines appear, pick the point on the screen, as shown in Figure 2.8.

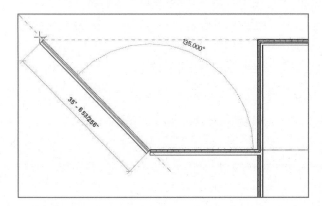

FIGURE 2.8:   Allow Revit to guide you in the placement of walls.

14. Draw a horizontal wall to the left 25′ (7500mm).

15. From the left point of that wall, draw a wall up 25′ (7500mm).

16. From the top of that wall, draw another wall to the left 80′ (24000mm).

17. Draw a wall down 25′ (7500mm).

18. On the Modify | Place Wall panel, click the Start-End-Radius Arc button, as shown in Figure 2.9.

19. Because the Wall command is still running, the next point to pick is the endpoint of the arc. Pick a point straight down at a distance of 30′–0″ (9000mm).

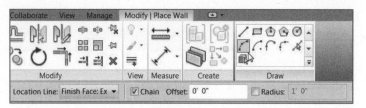

FIGURE 2.9: Draw a radial wall using the Start-End-Radius Arc method.

20. Move your pointer to the right until Revit snaps it to the tangent radius. (You may not get a tangent snap, but Revit will hesitate when you've reached the tangency.) After this happens, pick a point.

21. On the Draw panel, click the line button in the upper-left corner. This will allow you to draw a straight wall again.

22. Draw a wall straight down from the end of the arc 25′ (7500mm). (You'll have to press the spacebar to flip the wall.)

23. Draw a wall to the right 80′ (24000mm).

24. Draw a wall straight up 25′–0″ (7500mm).

25. Press Esc. Your building should look like Figure 2.10.

> If you're having trouble sketching the outline, remember to slow down. The next few walls will be a little tougher. You'll have to place them using the embedded offset function within the Wall command.

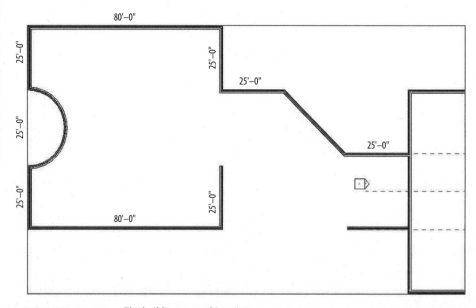

FIGURE 2.10: The building up to this point

26. Start the Wall command if it isn't running already.

27. On the Draw panel, click the Pick Lines icon, as shown in Figure 2.11.

FIGURE 2.11: The Pick Lines icon lets you add a wall by using an offset from another object.

28. On the Options bar, you'll see an Offset input. Type 30 (10000mm), and press Enter.

29. Move your cursor over the outside face of the wall, as shown in Figure 2.12. When you see the alignment line appear below the wall, pick the outside face.

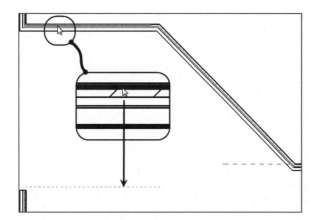

FIGURE 2.12: Adding a wall using the built-in offset function may take a few tries to get the method down.

30. Repeat the procedure for the angled wall. Make sure you offset the wall to the left (see Figure 2.13).

31. Click Modify.

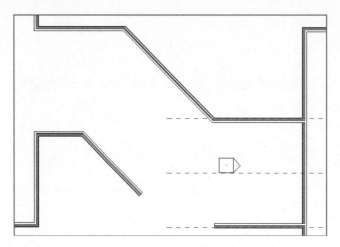

FIGURE 2.13:   Creating the bottom of the corridor

DID YOU SEE THAT?

See how Revit cleans up wall corners? It's almost like you're using an application that understands architecture!

Wall Adjustments

You've probably noticed that the walls are joining themselves together. This behavior is inherent to Revit. After the previous procedure, however, you're left with a gap between the bottom two walls. It's too wide for Revit to realize that these walls need to be joined. You can fix this by following these steps:

1. Pick the bottom diagonal wall. A number of blue icons and dimensions appear, as shown in Figure 2.14. Each of these icons plays a role in the adjustment of the wall.

2. On each end, you see a solid blue grip. Pick the right solid blue grip, and drag the wall down to meet the reference plane, as shown in Figure 2.15.

3. Select the horizontal wall to the right.

4. Pick the left blue grip, and drag this wall's end to the left until you hit the bottom corner of the diagonal wall, as shown in Figure 2.15. The two walls join together (see Figure 2.16).

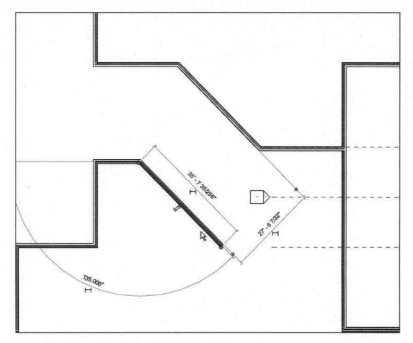

FIGURE 2.14: When you select a wall, you can make adjustments, such as stretching the ends, by picking the blue grips.

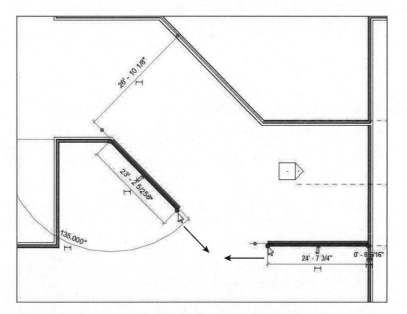

FIGURE 2.15: Stretching the wall using the blue grip

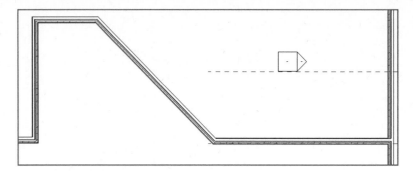

FIGURE 2.16: The walls are automatically joined when you pull the end of one into another.

5. You should add another part of the building. It's going to be a simple U-shape on the south end of the building. Select and right-click one of the exterior walls. Then, click Create Similar.

6. On the View toolbar, set the detail level to Coarse, as shown in Figure 2.17.

FIGURE 2.17: Sometimes, setting the graphic display to Coarse can make the placement of other walls easier.

7. On the Options bar, change Offset to 15′–0″ (4500mm).

8. Pick the midpoint of the south wall, as shown in Figure 2.18.

9. Draw the wall 25′ (7500mm) down from the south wall by typing 25 (7500mm) and pressing Enter.

10. After you pick the 25′ (7500mm) distance, move your cursor up, back toward the wall, as shown in Figure 2.19, resulting in a 25′ (7500mm)-long wall.

11. Set Offset to 0. Draw a wall across the front of the two walls, as shown in Figure 2.20. Make sure it's flipped in the right direction. You can determine this by switching back from Coarse to Fine detail. Click Modify.

    Your walls should look like Figure 2.20.

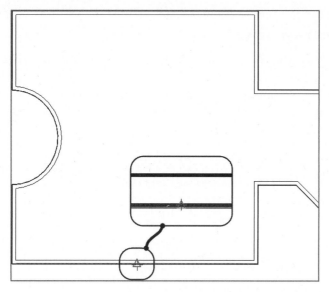

FIGURE 2.18: Adding the new walls requires picking the midpoint of this wall. Make sure Offset is set to 15′–0″ (4500mm) on the Options bar.

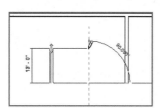

FIGURE 2.19: By using the Offset command as you draw walls, you can use one common centerline.

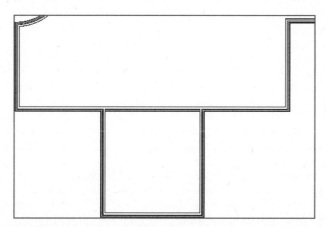

FIGURE 2.20: The completed walls for the south side of the building

Does It Measure Up?

In Revit, you can access the Measure function, which is the same as the Distance command in Autodesk® AutoCAD®. To verify whether your walls are placed at your chosen distances, click the Measure icon as shown here. After you measure the distance, the Options bar will show you the result. The Measure icon is also available on the Measure panel of the Modify tab.

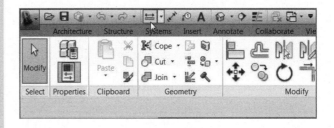

Adding Interior Walls

Interior walls are basically the same as exterior walls in terms of how they're placed in the model. This is a good thing. Luckily, you can be slightly more relaxed with the justification. Now that the building has a footprint, you can see more easily whether the walls need to be adjusted.

You'll start by laying out an elevator shaft and a stairwell, using an 8″ (200mm) CMU wall system. Follow these steps:

1. Open or make sure you're in Floor Plan Level 1. Zoom into the northeast corner of the building, as shown in Figure 2.21.

2. On the Architecture tab, click the Wall button.

3. In the Type Selector, select Generic - 8″ Masonry (Generic - 200), as shown in Figure 2.21.

4. For the starting point, pick the corner as shown in Figure 2.21. The wall will probably be in the wrong orientation, so if necessary, tap the spacebar to flip the wall's orientation.

5. Move your cursor downward, and type 12′ (3600mm). The wall will be 12′ long.

6. Move your cursor to the right, and type 10′ (3000mm).

7. Move your cursor back up the view, and pick the exterior wall.

8. Click Modify. You should have three walls that look like Figure 2.22.

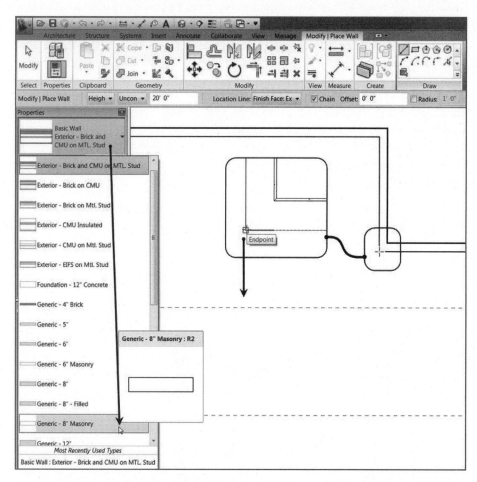

FIGURE 2.21: Start drawing the 8″ (200mm) CMU elevator shaft in the corner indicated here. Turn on Thin Lines if you need to.

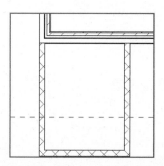

FIGURE 2.22:   The elevator shaft begins to take shape.

At this point, you have some walls in the model. It's time to look at ensuring that these walls are accurately placed, so you need to check the dimensions.

Using Temporary Dimensions to Gain Control of Your Model

After you place items in a model, you usually need to make some adjustments. Revit does a good job with this; however, there are some rules to which you need to adhere. The goal here is to have a clear 10′–0″ (3000mm) dimension on the inside faces of the shaft. At this point, you should assume that you don't. This is where temporary dimensions come into play. To start working with temporary dimensions, follow these steps:

1. Select the right, vertical CMU wall. A blue temporary dimension appears, as shown in Figure 2.23.

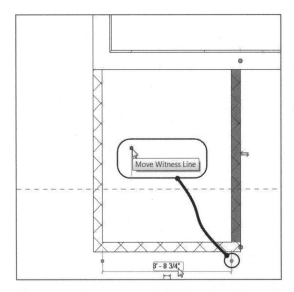

FIGURE 2.23: Temporary dimensions can be adjusted to measure from different wall faces by picking the witness-line grip.

2. On the temporary dimension, you see some blue grips. If you hover your cursor over one of them, a tooltip appears, indicating that this grip represents the witness line.

3. Pick the grip to the right side of the dimension. Notice that it moves to the outside face of the wall. Pick it again, and notice that it moves to the inside face. This is exactly where you want it.

4. The actual increment in the dimension is blue. Select the blue dimension, type **10′** (3000mm), and press Enter. The wall that was selected moves to accommodate the new increment, as shown in Figure 2.24.

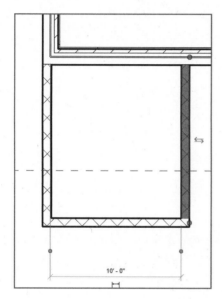

10′ - 0″

F I G U R E   2 . 2 4 :   The selected wall is the wall that will move when you type the new dimension.

Temporary Dimension Settings

Revit measures the default dimension for the temporary dimensions from the center of the walls—which is typically the last place from which you want to take the dimension. You can change some settings to fix this action:

1. On the Manage tab, click Additional Settings ➢ Temporary Dimensions, as shown in Figure 2.25.

2. In the Temporary Dimension Properties box, select Faces in the Walls group.

3. In the Doors And Windows group, select Openings, as shown in Figure 2.26.

62   Chapter 2 • Creating a Model

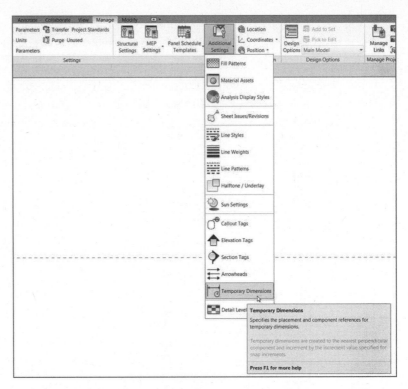

FIGURE 2.25: The Temporary Dimensions function lets you control where Revit measures the temporary dimensions.

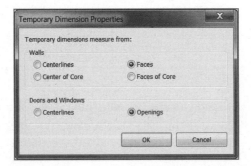

FIGURE 2.26: The most popular configuration for temporary dimensions

4. Click OK.

5. Select the south, horizontal wall.

6. To the right of the dimension, you see a small blue icon that also looks like a dimension. If you hover your mouse over it, a tooltip appears, indicating that you can make the temporary dimension permanent, as shown in Figure 2.27. When you see this tooltip, click the icon.

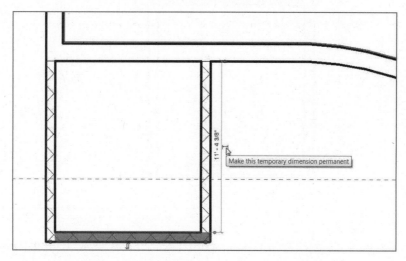

Make this temporary dimension permanent

FIGURE 2.27: You can make temporary dimensions permanent.

7. Press Esc.

8. Select the same wall again. Notice that the permanent dimension turns blue. You know that anything that turns blue in Revit can be edited. You can change this increment any time you wish.

9. Change the dimension to **12′ (3600**mm), and click out of the dimension text. The wall moves into position, and the dimension is now an even 12′ (3600mm).

You need one more shaft wall to create a separation between the exterior walls and the shaft, as shown in Figure 2.28. Perform these steps:

1. Select any CMU wall, and click Create Similar.

2. On the Draw panel, click the Pick Lines icon.

3. On the Options bar, type **10′ (3000**mm) in the Offset field.

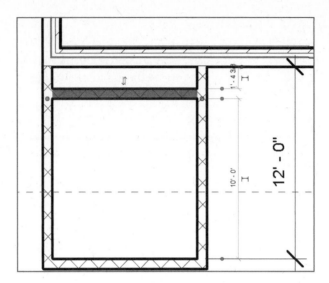

FIGURE 2.28: The shaft wall

4. On the Options bar, be sure Location Line is set to Finish Face: Interior.

5. Offset the south CMU shaft wall (from the inner line). Doing so separates the shaft from the exterior and creates a little chase.

6. Press Esc twice. Figure 2.28 shows the shaft wall. Make sure that you check your dimensions before proceeding.

The next task is to mirror these walls to the other side:

1. Pick a window around all the masonry walls (a window with your cursor, not an actual window).

2. On the Modify | Walls tab, click the Mirror ➢ Pick Axis button, as shown in Figure 2.29.

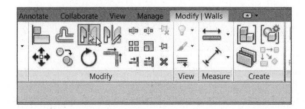

FIGURE 2.29: The Mirror ➢ Pick Axis command is activated when you have objects selected.

3. Pick the horizontal reference plane in the center of the building. Your walls are now mirrored, as shown in Figure 2.30.

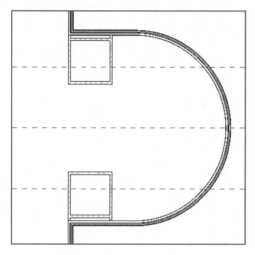

FIGURE 2.30:   The elevator shaft is now mirrored.

4. Save the model.

You're starting to get the hang of adding different wall types—but you aren't done yet. You still need to add quite a few interior partitions.

DID YOU SELECT TOO MUCH?

If you picked a window around all of your walls and have more items selected than you wish, you can press the Shift key on your keyboard and pick the item(s) you want to unselect. Doing so removes the item from the selection set. If the opposite happens and you want to add an item, press the Ctrl key and pick the item(s) you want to add. Your cursor will always appear with a plus or a minus sign, as shown here.

Placing Interior Partitions

The majority of your tasks in Revit involve placing interior partitions. Given the dimensional nature of placing these types of walls in Revit, you don't need to bother with reference planes as often as when you place the exterior walls.

Knowing that, creating interior partitions is somewhat easier than the exterior variety. With the exterior type, you must place partitions carefully, and constant double-checking is crucial. With interior partitions, you can typically get the wall where you think you need it. You can then go back and make adjustments without disturbing too many adjacent items. Not that you have to do it this way—you can be accurate to begin with—but life is all about second chances!

To start adding interior partitions, you'll add the necessary lavatory and egress and then fill the spaces with offices. When completed, this stage will look like Figure 2.31.

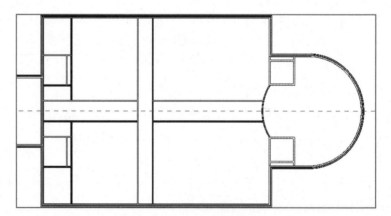

FIGURE 2.31:   The east side of the building with egress and lavatories

The objective of the next procedure is to begin adding interior partitions:

1. Make sure you're on Floor Plan Level 1.

2. On the Architecture tab, click the Wall button.

3. In the Type Selector, select Interior - 6 ⅛″ Partition (2-hr) (Interior – 135mm Partition (2-hr)).

4. For Height, choose Level 2 from the menu (if it isn't already the current selection).

5. For Location Line, choose Finish Face: Exterior.

6. On the Draw panel, click the Start-End-Radius Arc button (upper right in Figure 2.32).

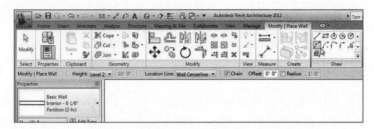

FIGURE 2.32: Choosing options should be old hat by now! The Start-End-Radius Arc button is at the upper right on the Ribbon.

7. Pick the lower-left corner of the upper CMU walls.

8. Pick the upper-left corner of the bottom CMU walls.

9. Move your cursor to the left, and specify a radius of 20′–0″ (6000mm), as shown in Figure 2.33.

10. Press Esc twice.

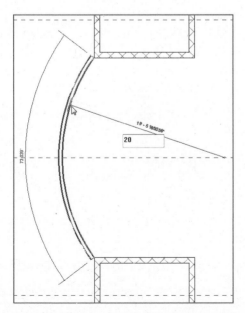

FIGURE 2.33: Drawing an arched radial wall requires a three-point method. It's similar to the Start-End-Direction command in AutoCAD.

You now need to add some corridor walls. You can do this using the center reference plane you established earlier:

1. If you aren't still in the Wall command, select and then right-click the radial wall, and then select Create Similar.

2. On the Draw panel, click the Line button.

3. For Location Line, choose Finish Face: Interior.

4. For Offset (on the Options bar), add a 4'–0" (1200mm) offset.

5. To start placing the wall, pick the intersection or endpoint of the center reference plane and the radial wall, as shown in Figure 2.34.

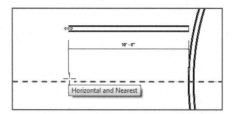

FIGURE 2.34: Drawing corridor walls using an offset can be a great timesaver.

6. Move your cursor to the left. Notice that the wall is being drawn, but at an offset of 4'–0" (1200mm) from the "line" you're drawing up the middle of the building (if it's in the opposite direction from what's shown in Figure 2.34, tap the spacebar to flip it).

7. For the second point of the wall, pick the intersection or endpoint of the vertical wall to the left.

8. Move your cursor back to the right. Notice that the other side of the wall is being drawn at a 4'–0" (1200mm) offset. This time, it's on the opposite side of the reference line.

9. Pick the intersection of the reference plane and the radial wall as the second point, as shown in Figure 2.35.

Let's clean up the gaps between the radial wall and the two corridor walls:

1. Make sure you aren't still in the Wall command by pressing Esc twice or by clicking the Modify button to the left of the Ribbon.

2. Select the top corridor wall. On the right end of the wall is a blue grip. Pick it, and drag the top corridor wall into the radial wall.

3. Repeat the step for the bottom wall (see Figure 2.36).

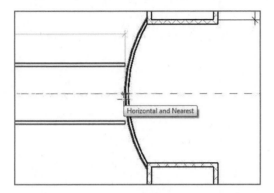

FIGURE 2.35: Completing the main corridor. You'll still have to drag the walls together to join them.

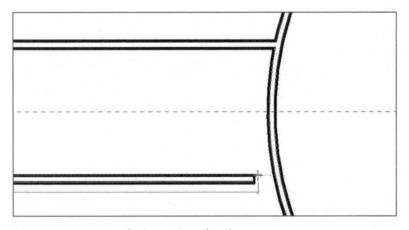

FIGURE 2.36: Getting a grip on the grips

The next step is to add the lavatories. These will show up at the west end (left side) of the building. Refer to Figure 2.37 for the dimensions, and follow along:

1. Select and then right-click one of the corridor walls, and select Create Similar from the menu.

2. Look at your options, and create the lavatories shown in Figure 2.37. All of the dimensions are taken from the finish inside face.

3. After you draw in the lavatory walls, mirror the walls to the other side of the building, as shown in Figure 2.38.

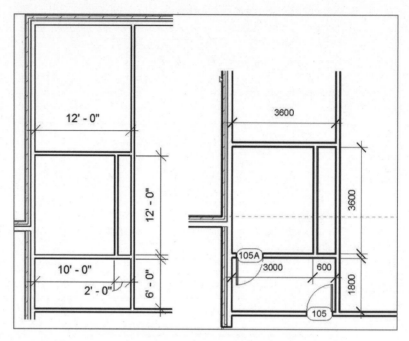

FIGURE 2.37:   The lavatory at the west side of the building

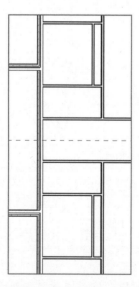

FIGURE 2.38:   Both the men's and women's lavatories

WARNING   Picking a grip on the end of a wall also means that you get a temporary dimension. Look at it! If it doesn't say 8′–0″ (2400mm) to the inside face of the corridor, you have a problem. It's much better to discover these discrepancies early in the design stage than to find out that you have a dimensional issue when the drawings are going out the door. If the increment isn't 8′–0″ (2400mm), first verify that the temporary dimension is going to the inside face. If not, pick the blue grip and move the witness line to the inside face of the walls. If the dimension is still off, move the witness line to the center reference plane. Now type 4′ (1200mm), and press Enter. Repeat the process for the other wall. Always check dimensions like this. The time you save could be your own!

You now need another corridor running north and south, as shown in Figure 2.39. The best way to approach this task is to add another reference plane and then add the walls in a fashion similar to the method applied to the east/west corridor. To open up the central area, you'll add 45° walls at 4′–0″ (1200mm). Follow these steps to add the new walls:

1. On the Work Plane panel of the Architecture tab, click Ref Plane.

2. Draw a reference plane from the midpoint of the top exterior wall to the midpoint of the bottom exterior wall.

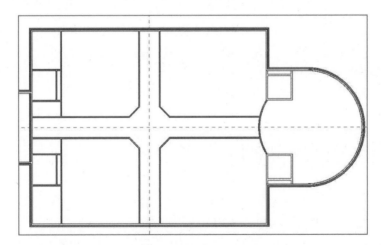

FIGURE 2.39:   This is the finished corridor layout.

3. Click the Measure Between Two References button. Make 100 percent sure that this is the center of the building. You're going to rely heavily on this line.

4. Start the Wall command.

5. On the Options bar, be sure Location Line is set to Finish Face: Interior and that Offset is 4'–0" (1200mm).

6. Pick the top intersection or endpoint of the reference plane and the exterior wall.

7. Draw the wall down to the bottom of the building.

8. Keeping the Wall command running, draw the other side of the corridor by picking the same two points along the reference plane. When you're finished, press Esc.

 T I P   Are the reference planes really necessary? No, they aren't. But using them is a good, sound approach to laying out your building. These lines will be used heavily throughout the life of your project.

You've created an area in the middle of the building where four walls intersect each other. You can now add 45° walls there to open the corridor at this area, as shown in Figure 2.40.

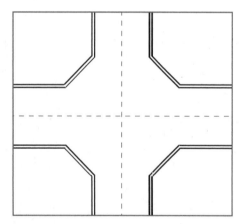

FIGURE 2.40: The corridor with the 45° walls added

---

1. Zoom into the intersection of the corridors.

2. On the Work Plane panel of the Architecture tab, click Ref Plane.

3. On the Draw panel, click the Pick Lines button, and change Offset to 4'–0" (1200mm).

4. From the finish inside face of the top, horizontal corridor wall, offset the reference plane up (see Figure 2.41).

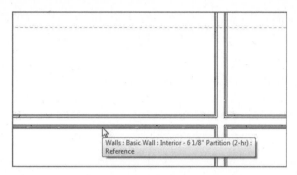

F I G U R E 2 . 4 1 : Adding yet another reference plane to the model. You'll delete this one.

 T I P It can be tricky to get the reference plane going in the correct direction. If the reference plane is being stubborn and is still trying to offset the line down, move your cursor up a little. The reference plane will change direction.

After you establish the reference plane, you can add the new wall. It can be as simple as drawing the wall in, but there are still a few little procedures of which you should be aware:

1. Start the Wall command.

2. On the Options bar, be sure the wall's Location Line is justified from Finish Face: Exterior.

3. Pick the intersection of the reference plane and the inside finished face (right face) of the left, vertical corridor wall (see Figure 2.42).

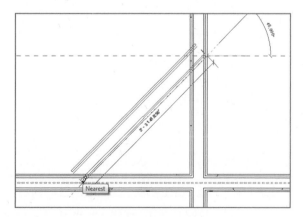

F I G U R E 2 . 4 2 : Adding the 45° wall

Chapter 2 • Creating a Model

4. After you pick the start point, move your cursor to the left and down at a 45° angle. (You can approximate the angle; Revit will snap you to the correct angle.)

5. At a 45° angle, pick the endpoint at a location within the horizontal, top corridor wall. When you're finished, press the Esc key twice. You may have to press the spacebar to get your wall flipped in the proper direction, as shown in Figure 2.42.

EYEBALLING WITH ACCURACY

You may notice that when you're using temporary dimensions, the increment always seems to snap to even increments. This is no accident. If you click the Snaps button on the Manage tab, you'll see values for Length Dimension Snap Increments and Angular Dimension Snap Increments. These values change based on the zoom percentage. The closer you zoom in, the smaller the increments get. You can also add to these values by typing a semicolon and adding a new increment to the end of the list, as shown here.

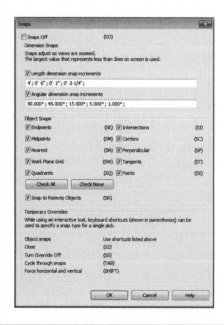

WARNING   If you proceed with assuming that these walls are a specific increment (4′ [1200mm]) from the inside face, you may be making a big mistake. Take distances after you add walls—especially if the walls aren't 90°.

The next task is to mirror the walls. This part will be easy because you put in those reference planes:

1. Select the 45° wall.

2. Pick Mirror Pick Axis from the Modify | Walls tab as shown in Figure 2.43.

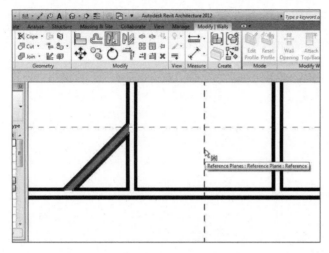

FIGURE 2.43: Using the Mirror command in conjunction with a reference plane is a good example of thinking ahead.

3. Pick the vertical reference plane, and voilà! The wall is mirrored

4. Select the two 45° walls, and mirror them around the horizontal reference plane. You should now have four 45° walls, as shown in Figure 2.44.

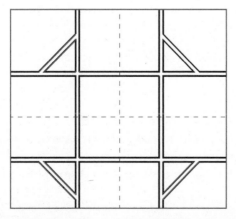

FIGURE 2.44: Stuck inside these four walls

5. Delete the temporary horizontal offset reference plane by selecting it and clicking the Delete button on the keyboard.

Now it's time for some further cleanup. Although all the modify commands will be featured in Chapter 4, "Working with the Autodesk Revit Tools," you can still use some here. You've already borrowed the Mirror command from that chapter. You might as well borrow the Split command too:

1. On the Modify panel of the Modify tab, click the Split Element button, as shown in Figure 2.45.

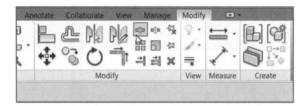

FIGURE 2.45: Using the Split Element command

2. Always look at the Options bar! Select the Delete Inner Segment option.

3. Pick a point along the top horizontal corridor wall near the intersecting 45° wall.

4. Pick the second point along the same wall, only on the opposite side (see Figure 2.46).

5. Repeat the process for the other three walls. You should now have an open central area for your corridor, as shown in Figure 2.47.

N O T E   If the Split Element command is giving you a splitting headache rather than splitting the walls, keep trying. We'll also cover this in Chapter 4. Commands such as Split Element require a different touch than the AutoCAD Break command.

Looking back, you've accomplished quite a bit. Laying out walls and then modifying them to conform to your needs is a huge part of being successful in Revit, but you aren't finished. The next few processes will involve dealing with different types of walls that merge together. Historically, merging walls has been an issue in modeling software. Although Revit tends to clean up these areas a little better than other modeling applications, you must still cope with some sticky areas. Let's create a sticky situation!

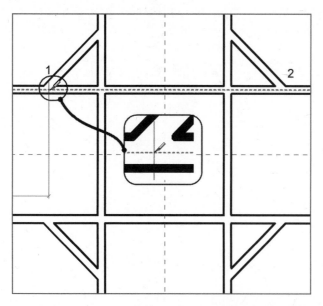

FIGURE 2.46:   Split the wall at two points. If you've selected Delete Inner Segment, the result is to eliminate the wall between the two points.

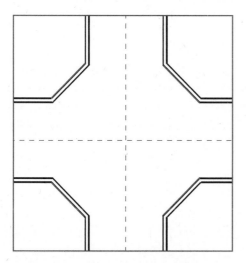

FIGURE 2.47:   The open corridor

Editing Wall Joins

A separate function in Revit deals with editing wall joins—specifically, the Edit Wall Joins command, which can come in quite handy. To get started, let's add more walls to an already busy corner of the building:

1. Zoom into the northeast corner of the building, as shown in Figure 2.48, and set the detail level to Fine.

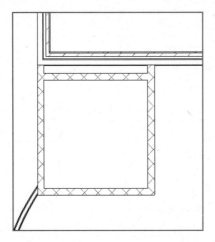

FIGURE 2.48: The northeast corner

2. Start the Wall command. Make sure it's the same 6 ⅛″ (153mm) two-hour partition you've been using.

3. With the Chain button off and Location Line set to Finish Face: Exterior, to start the wall, pick the intersection where the CMU wall abuts the finish inside face of the exterior wall (see Figure 2.49). Again, you can turn on Thin Lines to get a better view of what you're seeing.

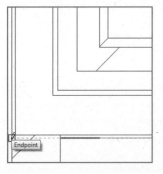

FIGURE 2.49: Adding to the mess in the corner

4. The wall may be flipped in the opposite direction from Figure 2.50. If it is, remember to press the spacebar; doing so flips it up to the proper orientation.

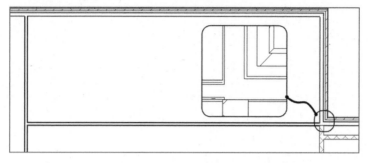

F I G U R E 2 . 5 0 :   The wall and the resulting intersection

5. Pick the second point of the wall at the corridor in the middle of the building. Press Esc twice. The intersection should look like Figure 2.50.

6. Zoom back in on the intersection. If the view doesn't resemble Figure 2.50 in terms of line weight, click the Thin Lines icon, as shown in Figure 2.51.

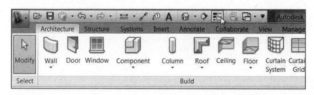

F I G U R E 2 . 5 1 :   Click the Thin Lines icon to see how the walls are joining together.

7. On the Geometry panel of the Modify tab, click the Wall Joins button, as shown in Figure 2.52.

8. Hover your pointer over the intersection. Revit displays a big box, as shown in Figure 2.53.

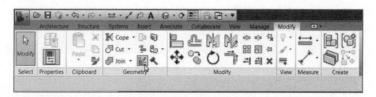

F I G U R E 2 . 5 2 :   You'll find the Wall Joins button on the Modify tab.

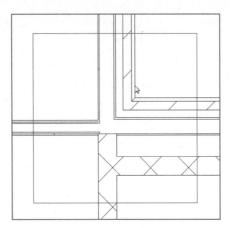

FIGURE 2.53: Choosing the intersection you wish to edit

9. Pick anywhere within the area. Doing so establishes that this is the intersection you wish to edit.

   After you pick the intersection, some additional lines appear. These lines expose how Revit is actually looking at the corner.

10. On the Options bar, you now see some choices for configuring this intersection. Select the Miter option, as shown in Figure 2.54. This option is the most popular. Click Modify.

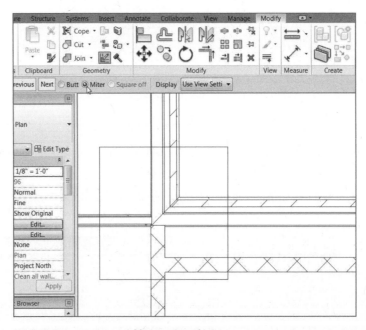

FIGURE 2.54: Adding a mitered join

Although a wall of this type would never have a 45° miter in real life, mitering the corner in Revit allows for a more uniform join between adjacent walls.

Displaying Wall Joins

Usually, in a plan view such as this, no wall joins are shown. Typically only the outside lines join, and an enlarged detail would show the specific construction methods. But in some cases, you want Revit to reveal this information. In Revit, you have two choices for the display (Figure 2.55):

Clean All Wall Joins   This option joins together the same materials in each wall, regardless of the wall type.

Clean Same Type Wall Joins   Stating the obvious, this option clean joins only within walls of the same type.

FIGURE 2.55:   Choosing a display option

The objective of the next procedure is to identify the difference between wall join types:

   1. Zoom in on the northwest corner of the east addition, as shown in Figure 2.56.

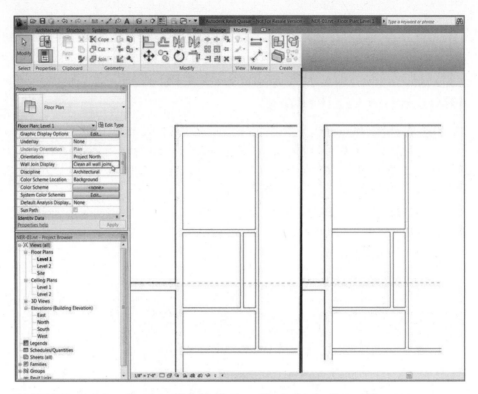

FIGURE 2.56:   Choosing a Wall Join Display option in the view's properties

2. Make sure Detail Level is set to Coarse.

3. In the Properties dialog, change Wall Join Display to Clean Same Type Wall Joins.

4. Observe the difference between the wall joins, as shown in Figure 2.56.

5. Save the model.

Disallowing Wall Joins

You must deal with another important item when walls join together. In some cases, you may not want walls to join automatically even if they're the same exact wall type. To learn how to prevent this behavior, follow along:

1. Change Detail Level to Fine.

2. Select the long, horizontal 6 ⅛″ (156mm) wall that comes into the corner, as shown in Figure 2.57. A blue grip appears to the right of the intersection. This represents where the wall's extents are located.

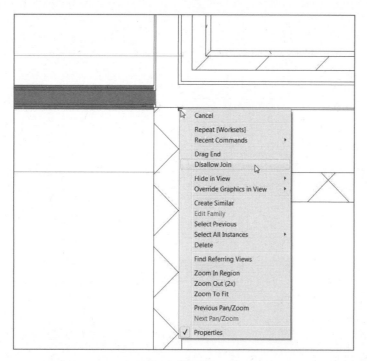

FIGURE 2.57: By right-clicking the wall's end grip, you can tell Revit to disallow that wall's join function.

3. Hover directly over the blue grip.

4. After the blue grip highlights, right-click.

5. Select Disallow Join (see Figure 2.57).

6. When the wall is unjoined, you can pick the same blue grip and slide the wall back to where you want it to terminate (see Figure 2.58).

7. After the wall slides into place, select it (if it isn't already selected).

8. Notice that there is an additional blue T-shaped icon. Hover your cursor over this icon; you can pick it to allow the walls to join back up, as shown in Figure 2.59.

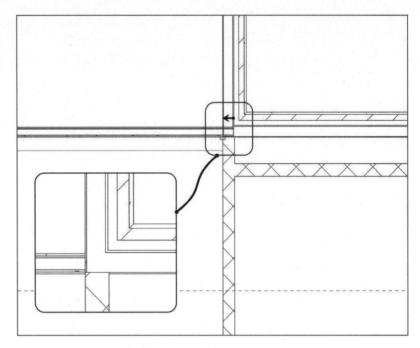

FIGURE 2.58:   Slide the wall back to abut the adjacent wall.

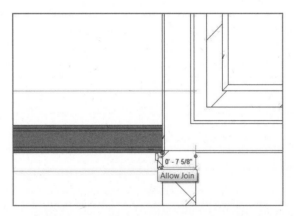

FIGURE 2.59:   Allowing the walls to join back up again

9. Click this icon to allow the join.

As mentioned earlier, your ability to edit wall joins can determine how quickly you start either liking or disliking Revit. This book took a few extra steps in the effort of joining walls, but the experience will carry through, project after project.

We need to investigate one more area before we leave this corner: the area within the chase. Suppose you don't want to run the gypsum into this area. This is a common situation that can cause people to have fits with Revit. Let's try to avoid those fits right now!

Editing the Cut Profile

A plan view is simply a section taken 4′–0″ (1200mm) up the wall from the finish floor. In Revit, you can manually edit the profile of any wall cut in plan. This is extremely useful if, for example, you need to take sections of drywall out of specific areas without creating or adding an entirely new wall. To do this, perform the following steps:

1. Zoom in on the right side of the elevator shaft at the intersection of the exterior wall, as shown in Figure 2.60.

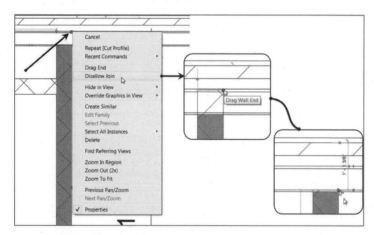

FIGURE 2.60: Pull the CMU out of the wall, disallow the join, and then drag it back into the face of the stud.

2. Select the east CMU wall, and right-click the blue grip on the endpoint of the wall.

3. Select Disallow Join (see Figure 2.60).

4. Pick the blue grip, and drag the wall end back to the face of the wall behind the gypsum.

5. On the Graphics panel of the View tab, click the Cut Profile button, as shown in Figure 2.61.

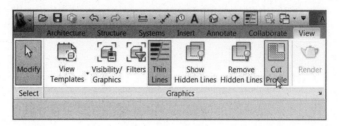

FIGURE 2.61: Click the Cut Profile button, and select the gypsum.

6. Pick the finish face of the exterior wall. You're selecting the gypsum layer to be cut out of the shaft.

7. You now need to draw a very short, vertical line from the inside face of the wallboard to the outside face, as labeled 1 and 2 in Figure 2.62. Press Esc.

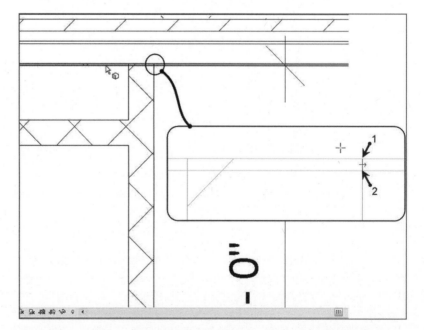

FIGURE 2.62: This line indicates where the wallboard will be cut. The blue arrow indicates the side of the material that will remain.

8. When the short line is drawn in, you see a blue arrow. This arrow indicates the side of the material you wish to keep. If you pick the arrow, it flips direction. Make sure it's pointing to the right.

9. What you see here is called Sketch Mode. Because you're finished sketching the cut profile, click Finish Edit Mode, as you can see in Figure 2.63. Figure 2.64 shows the final result.

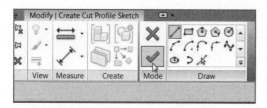

FIGURE 2.63: Clicking Finish Edit Mode finalizes the session and completes the command.

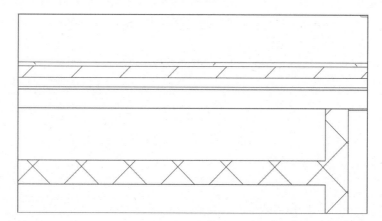

FIGURE 2.64: The finished wall with the drywall deducted from the core of the chase

NOTE   If you receive an error that says "Ends of the sketched loop don't lie on the boundary of the face being modified" when you're trying to finish the sketch, it's because you haven't drawn the line exactly from point to point. This line can't cross over, or be shy of, the material you're trying to split. If you're getting this error, select the magenta line. You'll see two familiar blue grips. Pick the grip that doesn't touch the face of the material, and drag it back.

Go through and do the same thing to the south side of the building, starting at the Edit Wall Joins section.

There are many more walls left to add, but we need to save something for Chapter 4. At this point, it sure would be nice to start adding some doors and windows to the model.

Placing Doors and Windows

Adding doors and windows is one of the easiest things you'll do in Revit. Finding the correct door or window becomes a bit harder. Creating a custom door or window takes time and patience. In this section, you'll focus on adding these items to the model. Chapter 17, "Creating Families," will drill down into the specifics of creating custom families.

Adding Doors

Placing a door in Revit can seem annoying and unnecessarily tedious at first. But like anything else in Revit, once you get the method down, you'll find your groove. Follow these steps:

1. Make sure you're in Floor Plan Level 1.

2. On the Architecture tab, click the Door button (see Figure 2.65).

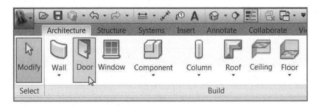

FIGURE 2.65: Adding a door

3. Make sure the Tag On Placement button is highlighted, as shown in Figure 2.66.

4. In the Type Selector, choose Single-Flush: 36″ × 84″ (M_Single-Flush 0915mm × 2134).

5. Move your cursor over to the south wall near the elevator shaft, as shown in Figure 2.66. Notice that if your cursor isn't within a wall,

you get the NO sign. Revit won't allow you just to place a door into space; a door is considered a hosted family and needs a wall into which it must be embedded.

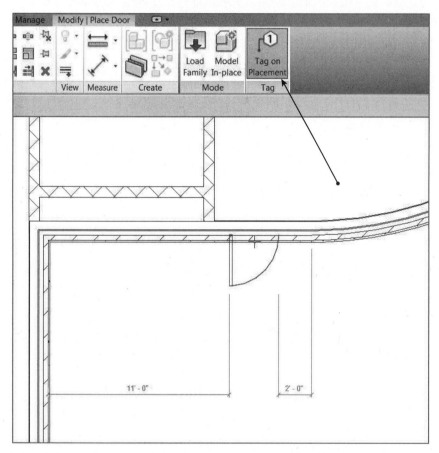

FIGURE 2.66: Placing a door always requires a host. Remember, you can press the spacebar to change the orientation, and move your cursor up and down to flip the direction.

6. After you get your cursor positioned approximately where Figure 2.66 shows it, move your pointer up and down. Notice that the door's direction changes. This is typical behavior for a door.

7. Press the spacebar. The door swing flips direction.

8. Make the door face outward and to the left, as shown in Figure 2.66. Then pick a point on the wall. If you accidentally put it in wrong, don't worry—you can fix it.

Notice that, when the door is placed, a tag appears with an automatic number. This happens when Tag On Placement is activated on the Tag panel in the Modify | Place Door tab. In Revit, after you place a door, you should press Esc twice and then go right back and select the door. Doing so highlights the door and activates a few different options. Follow these steps:

1. Click the Modify button at left on the Ribbon. Doing so disengages you from the Door command.

2. Pick the door you just added to the model. Notice the blue temporary dimensions. Let's make sure these dimensions are going where you want them:

   a. On the Settings panel of the Manage tab, click Additional Settings ➢ Temporary Dimensions, as shown in Figure 2.67.

   b. Make sure that Wall Dimensions are going to Faces and that Door Dimensions are going to Openings.

   c. Click OK.

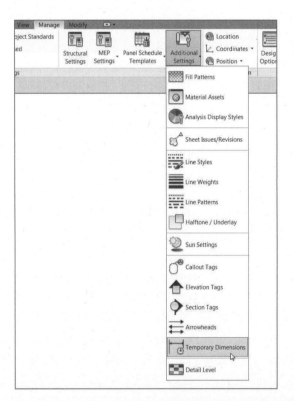

FIGURE 2.67: Select Additional Settings ➢ Temporary Dimensions.

YIKES, LOOK AT MY WALLS!

When you place a door or any opening into a compound wall, you need to tell Revit specifically how to wrap the materials. By default, Revit will stop the brick and any other finish right at the opening. Obviously, this usually isn't correct. The following steps guide you through wrapping materials at an insert:

1. Select the exterior wall.

2. In the Properties dialog, click the Edit Type button, as shown here:

3. In the drop-down menu that specifies Wrapping At Inserts, select Both.

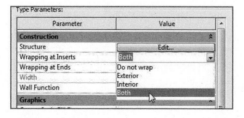

4. Click OK.

Now that you've configured the temporary dimensions the way you need them, you can start using them to manipulate the placement of your door:

1. Select the door again.

2. Move the left witness line of the left temporary dimension to the outside face of the CMU wall, as shown in Figure 2.68.

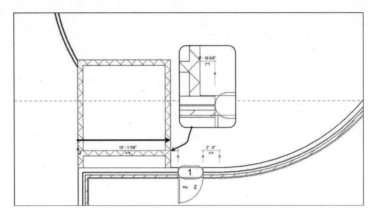

FIGURE 2.68: Moving the witness line to a more appropriate location

3. As you know, in Revit anything that turns blue can be edited. Click the blue dimension that extends from the CMU wall, drag it to the right of the elevator shaft, and change it to 1′–0″ (300mm) (see Figure 2.69).

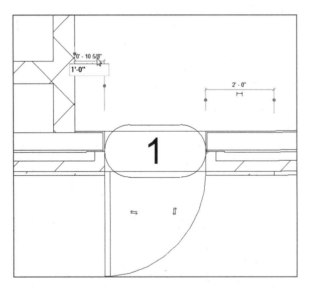

FIGURE 2.69: Changing the temporary dimension

Editing Door Tags

Let's concentrate on the tag now. The number contained within the "box" is an instance parameter. That means each door in the model will contain a unique number. When you place a door, this number will be added automatically. Revit knows not to duplicate this number. As each door is placed, Revit will assign the next sub-sequential number to the door. This number, of course, can be changed.

Follow along with the next exercise to see how to manipulate the door number:

1. Select the door (or the door tag).

2. Pick the number in the door tag.

3. Change the number to **101**.

4. With the door still selected, notice that you have flip arrows as well. If the door isn't in the orientation you see in the previous figures, click these arrows to flip the door.

5. Mirror this door and its tag about the building's horizontal center-line. Notice the number for the new door is 102.

Most items that are added to the Revit model can be selected and flipped using the same method. Also, selecting the items to be flipped and pressing the spacebar have the same effect.

Loading Families

It would be nice if the seven doors available in the Revit model were all you needed. They aren't, of course. Like most other CAD programs and applications that use building information modeling, Revit doesn't load every single component into the drawing or model. File size is just as much of a concern in Revit as it is in AutoCAD. If you need a different door, you have to go get it:

1. On the Architecture tab, click the Door button.

2. On the Modify | Place Door tab, click the Load Family button, as shown in Figure 2.70.

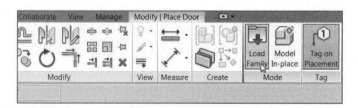

FIGURE 2.70: Click Load Family on the Mode panel.

3. Find the Doors directory, navigate to Double-Flush.rfa (M_Double-Flush.rfa), and click Open.

4. Select Double-Flush: 72″ × 84″ (M_Double-Flush 1830 × 2134) from the Type Selector.

5. Place the double doors in the wall, as shown in Figure 2.71. Click Modify.

> Normally, doors automatically find the center of the wall. But to make sure, you can type SM. Doing so tells Revit that you want to snap to the middle.

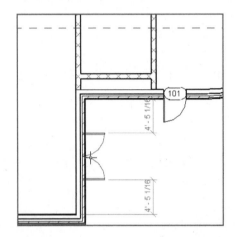

FIGURE 2.71: Placing the double doors

6. Mirror the door and tag using the center reference plane.

7. Add lavatory doors as shown in Figure 2.72, keeping all offsets 1′-0″ (300mm) away from the walls. Use Single-Flush: 36″ × 84″ (M_ Single-Flush 0915 × 2134).

8. Label them accordingly.

9. In the exterior wall that divides the east building from the corridor, add a Single Raised Panel With Side Lights: 36″ × 84″ (914mm × 2134mm) door centered on the opening.

10. Change the tag to read **100B**, as shown in Figure 2.73.

You need to add more doors and interior partitions, but they will be best suited for Chapter 4, where you can be more accurate. In the meantime, let's add some simple openings.

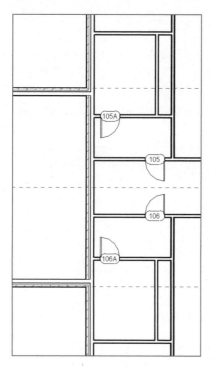

FIGURE 2.72: Adding lavatory doors. You'll have to renumber the tags.

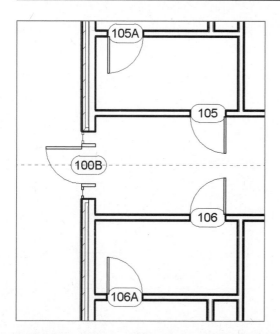

FIGURE 2.73: Adding a new corridor door. If this door isn't loaded into your model, you have to click the Load Family button on the Mode panel of the Modify | Place Door tab.

Placing Openings in Your Walls

I like to think of openings as doors in a sense. That is, you still need to insert something into a wall to create a void. This void can contain casing as well.

To add an opening to the model, run through these steps:

1. On the Architecture tab, click Component, as shown in Figure 2.74.

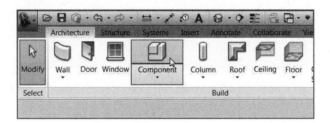

FIGURE 2.74:   Clicking Component on the Architecture tab

2. On the Modify | Place Component tab, click the Load Family button.

3. Browse to the Openings directory.

4. Find the file called Passage Opening-Elliptical Arch.rfa (M_Passage Opening-Elliptical Arch.rfa), and click Open.

5. Click the Edit Type button in the Properties dialog, as shown in Figure 2.75.

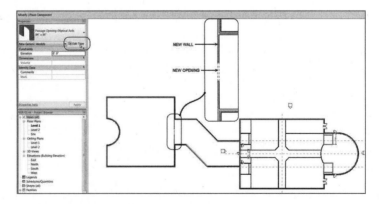

FIGURE 2.75:   The new opening

6. Click Duplicate in the Type Properties dialog.

7. In the Name dialog, name the opening 84″ × 84″ (2100mm × 2100mm), and then click OK.

8. Under Dimensions, change Width to 7′–0″ (2100mm).

9. Click OK. Then press Esc to clear the command.

10. Zoom into the area shown in Figure 2.75, and place an Interior - 6 ⅛″ Partition (2-hr) (Interior - 135mm Partition (2-hr)) wall as shown. This is the wall into which you'll place the opening.

11. On the Architecture tab, click Component, and place the opening into the wall as shown in Figure 2.75.

Add two more doors, and you'll be finished with this section:

1. On the Architecture tab, click Door.

2. In the Properties dialog, pick Double-Flush: 72″ × 84″ (M_Double-Flush 1830 × 2134).

3. Add the double doors to the ends of the vertical corridor, as shown in Figure 2.76.

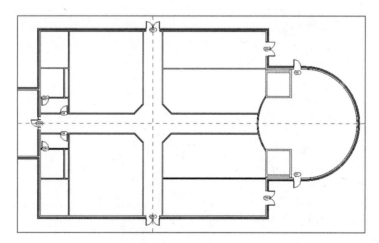

FIGURE 2.76:   Two new corridor doors

4. Label the doors **100C** and **100D**.

Again, there are many more doors and partitions that you can add to the model, but that will have to wait until Chapter 4. Let's move on to add some windows.

Adding Windows

Doors, windows, openings … it's all the same. When you have experience adding one, the others are just as easy.

The objective of the next procedure is to add some windows to the model:

1. On the Architecture tab, click the Window button, as shown in Figure 2.77.

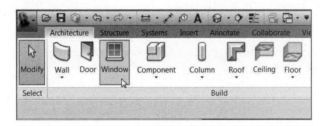

FIGURE 2.77: Adding a window is the same as adding a door.

2. Select the Fixed: 36″ × 72″ (M_Fixed 0915 × 1830) window from the Type Selector, and make sure the Tag On Placement button is active.

3. Add the window to the corner of the building, as shown in Figure 2.78. Be careful with the placement. If your cursor is toward the exterior of the wall, the window will be oriented correctly and the window tag will appear on the outside of the wall.

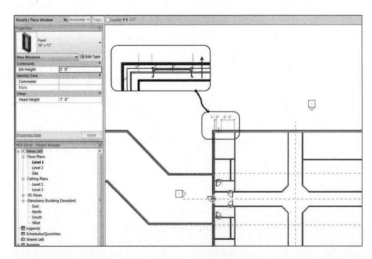

FIGURE 2.78: Depending on which side of the wall your cursor is on, you can add a window to the correct orientation.

4. Add two more windows to the west wall adjacent to the wall in which you just put the first window. Use your temporary dimensions to ensure that you're placing the windows at the increments shown in Figure 2.79. You'll have to place the windows and then use the temporary dimensions to move them to the proper dimensions in a similar manner to the first door you placed earlier in this chapter.

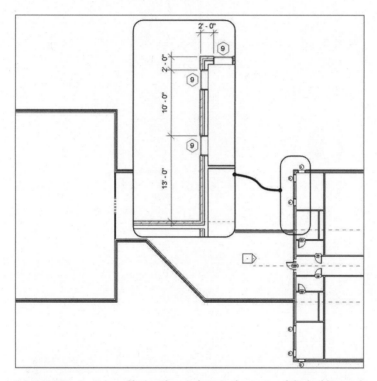

FIGURE 2.79: Placing the windows in the corner of the building and mirroring them

5. Mirror the windows and tags using the center horizontal reference plane (see Figure 2.79).

6. Select one of the placed windows. Notice the temporary dimensions and the flip arrows.

7. Change the tag to read **A.** (All of the windows are type A.)

8. You get a warning stating that you're changing a type parameter. Click Yes.

Now that the windows are in place, it's time to investigate how they're built by taking a look at their properties.

Window Properties

Again, just as with doors and openings, you can check the Element Properties to tweak the unit even further:

1. Select one of the windows.

2. In the Properties dialog, click the Edit Type button, as shown in Figure 2.80.

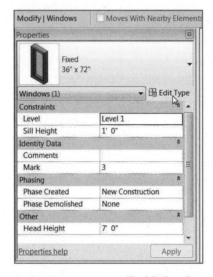

FIGURE 2.80:   The Edit Type button in the Properties dialog

   T I P   If you want to change an instance parameter (such as Sill Height) for every window in the model, you can. Knowing that an instance parameter only applies to one item, instead of picking just one window, you can pick a window, right-click, and choose Select All Instances. From there, you can change every window's parameters in the Properties panel because you had every window selected.

3. Scroll down until you see Type Mark. Notice that this value is set to A. This is the property you changed by typing the value into the tag in the model. Window tags read the Type Mark property by default, whereas door tags read Mark, which is an instance property. In either case, Revit works both ways. If you change a tag value in the model, it changes the parameter value in the tagged object or tagged family (see Figure 2.81).

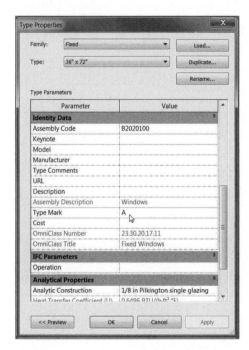

FIGURE 2.81: Changing a type parameter changes every window of that type.

Windows are among the most difficult items in Revit to use out of the box without any real customization. In Chapter 17, we'll dive into creating custom Revit windows. For now, however, remember the lessons learned in this chapter. They will go a long way.

Are You Experienced?

Now you can...

- ☑ place exterior walls
- ☑ place interior walls
- ☑ add reference planes
- ☑ join walls
- ☑ use the Split command
- ☑ edit a cut profile
- ☑ add doors
- ☑ add openings
- ☑ add windows

Creating Views

One of the strongest points of the Autodesk® Revit® Architecture platform is that it is one single model. This single model, however, has to be broken down into a tangible format that allows the user to navigate through a project. Chapter 1, "The Autodesk Revit World," and Chapter 2, "Creating a Model," featured the Project Browser (which is included in this chapter as well), but what is the Project Browser managing? Well, it's simply managing views of the model. The Browser also handles sheets, families, groups, links, and assemblies, but you'll use it to open and work with the properties of views more than anything else.

Here's an example: in the Project Browser, under Floor Plans, you'll usually see Level 1. This is a view of the model that just so happens to be a floor plan. Under Elevations (Building Elevation), you'll see East, North, South, and West elevations. These are exactly the same as the floor plans in the sense that they're just views of the model.

▶ **Creating and managing levels**

▶ **Adding sectional and elevation views**

▶ **Controlling your views for aesthetic values**

Creating Levels

This chapter focuses on the creation of views and their relationship to the model. You'll start with possibly the most important function in Revit: creating levels. The power of Revit comes with the single-model concept. By adding levels to a model, you also add floor plans. This two-way interaction is what makes Revit the BIM choice for many users.

As you wander through the floor plans in the Project Browser, you'll see Level 1 and Level 2. Not every job you'll work on will have only a Level 1 and a Level 2. Your task in this section is to create new levels that are appended to floor plans.

To follow along, open the model you've been working on, or go to `www.sybex .com/go/revit2014ner` and browse to the Chapter 3 folder. Open the file called `NER-03.rvt`. If you wish, you can use an actual project you're working on. You'll just have to replace any names and specific dimensions with ones that are applicable to your project. Perform these steps:

1. In the Project Browser, double-click the South elevation. It's located under Elevations (Building Elevation), as shown in Figure 3.1.

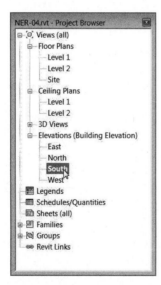

F I G U R E 3 . 1 :   Finding an elevation in the Project Browser

Notice at the right side of the building that there are two symbols with a datum at the end. These are elevation markers. Unfortunately, right now they're somewhat obscured by the exterior wall. Zoom in to this area, as shown in Figure 3.2.

T I P   As you progress through the next few steps, if you don't see what is shown in the next two figures, try zooming in more and repeating the instructions.

2. Select (left-click) Level 1. Note that you get several blue icons and a lock. Where the actual level line intersects the datum bubble, there is a hollow blue circle (grip), as shown in Figure 3.3, except that your view is slightly obscured by the wall. Move the bubble so you can see the grip clearly.

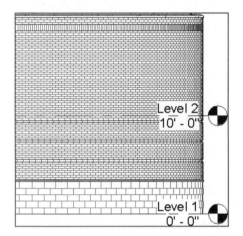

F I G U R E   3 . 2 :   When dealing with levels, it's a good idea to zoom in close so you can manipulate them.

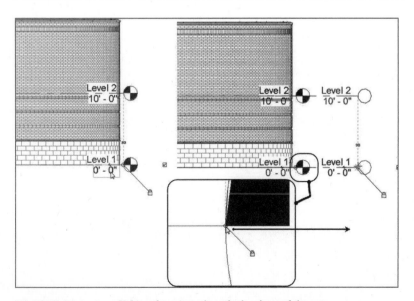

F I G U R E   3 . 3 :   Picking the grip to drag the level out of the way

3. Left-click (pick) the grip, and hold the pick button on the mouse. You can now drag the bubble to the right.

4. When you get to a point where the level marker is outside the building, pick a spot to place the bubble and the annotation.

5. Press Esc.

Now that the levels are physically in a position where you can work on them, you can start building on them.

Adding Levels

Adding an entirely new level in Revit Architecture is quite simple. However, you need to adhere to certain procedures in order to ensure that you add the levels correctly.

When you use the Level feature in Revit, you should follow two procedures. The first is to look at the Options bar after you start the command. The second is to click the Modify button or press Esc when you've finished. It's easy to get confused as to how Revit wants you to proceed with adding a level, and it's also easy to create multiple levels inadvertently. Remember, in Revit you're always in a command.

To add a level, follow along:

1. On the Datum panel of the Architecture tab, click the Level button, as shown in Figure 3.4.

FIGURE 3.4: Adding a level from the Datum panel on the Architecture tab

2. On the Draw panel on the Modify | Place Level tab, you see that you can either draw a line or pick a line, as shown in Figure 3.5. Make sure Pick Lines is selected.

FIGURE 3.5: Choosing the options for the Level command

3. On the Options bar, make sure the Make Plan View option is selected.

4. At the end of the Options bar is the Offset field. Type **10′** (3000mm), and press Enter. Basically the approach here is to pick Level 2 and create a new level that is offset 10′ (3000mm) above (see Figure 3.5).

5. With the options set, hover your cursor over Level 2.

When you come into contact with Level 2, a blue dotted line appears. If you move your cursor slightly above the Level 2 line, the blue alignment line appears above Level 2. If you inch your cursor slightly below Level 2, the blue alignment line appears below Level 2.

6. When you see the blue line appear above Level 2, pick the Level 2 line, as shown in Figure 3.6.

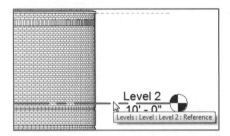

FIGURE 3.6: Waiting for the alignment to appear

 T I P You may notice that speeding through the commands as you may have done in Autodesk® AutoCAD® isn't helping you at all in Revit. In Revit, you may need to slow down a bit and let Revit "do its thing." After you get the hang of the Revit behavior, you can speed up again.

7. You should now have a Level 3 at 20′ (6000mm), as shown in Figure 3.7.

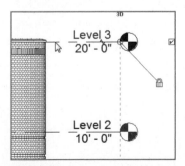

FIGURE 3.7: The completed Level 3. Remember, you're still in the Level command until you tell Revit to stop.

WARNING   Just because you've created a new level, this doesn't tell Revit to shut down the command. Notice that the Options bar is still active and the Pick Lines icon still has the focus. If you start clicking around in the view area, you'll create levels. Every time you pick a point on the screen, a new level will appear. Also, Revit doesn't care if you have a level on top of another level. This situation can get ugly fast.

8. With the Level command still running, create Levels 4, 5, 6, and 7. Your elevation should now look like Figure 3.8. Also, look at your Project Browser. It shouldn't have any levels other than Levels 1 through 7 and Site. You also have new levels under the Ceiling Plans category.

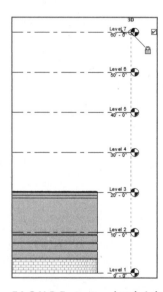

FIGURE 3.8:   Levels 1 through 7 are complete.

9. On the Select panel of the Ribbon, click the Modify button. You've safely terminated the Level command. (You could also press the Esc key on your keyboard to end the command.)

Now that you have some experience adding levels, it's time to investigate the physical level to see how it can be manipulated and modified.

Understanding the Composition of a Level

Levels have controls that enable the user to adjust the level's appearance. As stated throughout the book, when you select a family, multiple items turn blue. The blue color indicates that these items can be modified. Also, if the level bubbles are blue, that means there is a plan with which the level is associated. If the bubble is black, then no plan is associated. When you select a level, a few additional items will appear.

To investigate further, follow along:

1. Zoom in on Level 7.

2. Select Level 7 by picking (left-clicking) either the text or the level line. This puts the focus on the level line. Notice that the text turns blue. You know that any blue item can be modified (see Figure 3.9).

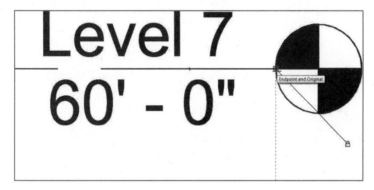

FIGURE 3.9:   The selected level

3. Click the blue Level 7 text field. This enables you to edit the name of the level.

4. Type **Parapet**, as shown in Figure 3.10, and press Enter.

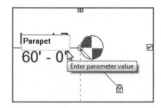

FIGURE 3.10:   Renaming the level

By renaming corre-
sponding views, you
tell Revit to keep the
level and its corre-
sponding view named
accordingly.

5. Revit asks whether you want to rename any corresponding views. Click Yes (see Figure 3.11). Level 7 is now the Parapet level, as shown in Figure 3.12.

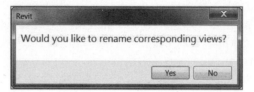

FIGURE 3.11: Click Yes to rename corresponding views.

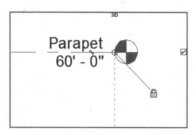

FIGURE 3.12: The renamed level

6. With the Parapet level still selected, click the 60′–0″ (18000mm) field.

7. Type **52′ (16600**mm), and press Enter. This physically drops the level to the true elevation.

You now have two slightly overlapping levels. This can be fixed by manipulating some of the controls that appear when you select the level.

Press the Esc key a few times to clear any commands that may be active, and then follow along:

Can't you just type
over the dimension? In
Revit, you can't have an
inaccurate increment.
If you type a new value
to any increment, the
model will change
to reflect this new
dimension.

1. Select the Parapet level (if it isn't still selected from the previous exercise).

2. The blue items light up. One of them is the choice to add an elbow, as shown in Figure 3.13. Click it, and Revit bends the level.

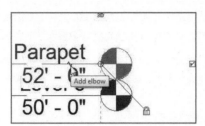

FIGURE 3.13:   You can add an elbow to the elevation marker.

3. Now that you've added the elbow, you need to move it. Notice the blue grip at each bend point. Pick the blue grip, as shown in Figure 3.14, and drag the Parapet level out of the level below.

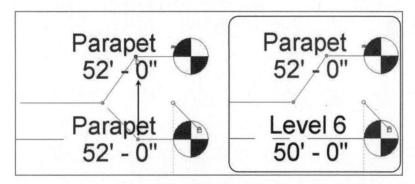

FIGURE 3.14:   Dragging the level to a new position by using the grips provided

4. The line of the level is still in the way. The two blue grips are still available: pick and drag the horizontal line out of the way of the Parapet text, as shown in Figure 3.15.

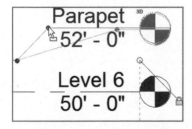

FIGURE 3.15:   Making the final adjustments to the level

Now that you've established the Parapet level, let's make modifications to Level 6. Luckily, the procedures is the same as when you made the modifications to the Parapet level:

1. Press Esc to clear any commands.

2. Select Level 6.

3. Pick the blue text that reads Level 6.

4. Rename it **Roof**.

5. Press Enter.

6. Click Yes to rename the corresponding views.

7. Press Esc. Your levels should look like Figure 3.16.

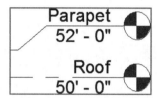

FIGURE 3.16:   The Roof and Parapet levels

Making Other Level Adjustments

We need to review three more adjustments before you can move on. As you may notice, the level lines are projected all the way to the other end of the east building. Only level heads and level data are displayed on the right side of the level line. You can control the other end of the level as well.

To follow along, pan over to the left side of the building, where the level lines seem to stop, as shown in Figure 3.17. Then perform these steps:

1. Select the Parapet level.

2. Pick the small blue box to the left of the level. Doing so turns on the level information at that end of the building (see Figure 3.17).

3. Turn on the Roof-level left-end bubble as well. Use the blue adjustment icons (elbow icons) to move the level out of the way (see Figure 3.18).

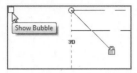

FIGURE 3.17:   You can click the box that appears, to turn on the level information at the other end of the building.

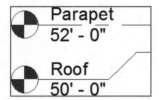

FIGURE 3.18:   Controlling the visibility of the levels at the other end

With the two upper levels established, you can constrain some walls up to these levels. Sometimes the best way to do this is to look at the model from a 3D view:

1. Click the Default 3D View icon on the Quick Access toolbar at the top of your screen, as shown in Figure 3.19.

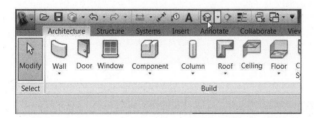

FIGURE 3.19:   Clicking the Default 3D View icon

2. The next step is to select all the walls you want to be extended to the Parapet level. In this case, only the east building will go all the way up to this level. Select the exterior and the elevator shaft walls, as shown in Figure 3.20. (Be sure to select all of the elevator shaft walls as well.) You must hold the Ctrl key to add to the selection. The walls turn blue when they're selected. You can also hover over one of the walls and press the Tab key. Once the walls are highlighted, pick a wall. All of the walls will be selected.

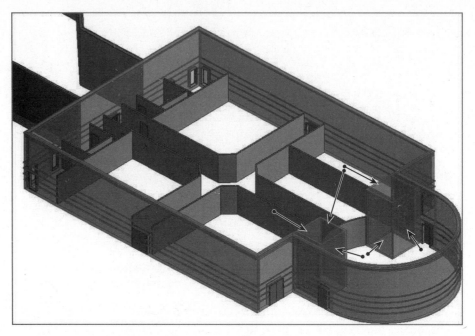

FIGURE 3.20:   Selecting the walls that extend to the Parapet level

3. In the Properties dialog, under the Constraints category, change Top
   Constraint to Up To Level: Parapet, as shown in Figure 3.21. Click
   Apply or move your cursor into the drawing window to set the property change. The walls should now extend to the Parapet level, as
   shown in Figure 3.22.

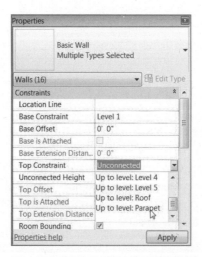

FIGURE 3.21:   Setting the top constraint to Up To Level: Parapet

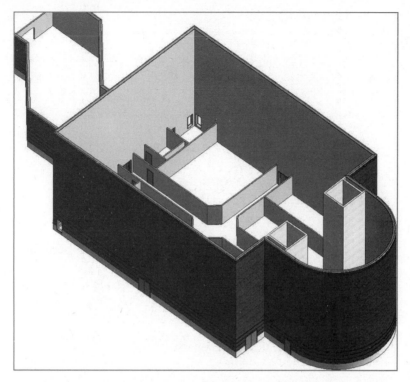

FIGURE 3.22: The walls on the east side of the building are now constrained to the Parapet level.

4. In the Project Browser, double-click the South elevation under Elevations (Building Elevation).

5. Start the Level command again.

6. Offset Level 4 up 4′ (1200mm). Remember, you're in the Level command. You must choose Pick Lines on the Draw panel. Also, you must specify an Offset value of 4′–0″ (1200mm) on the Options bar.

7. Offset another level up from the fourth level, 2′–0″ (600mm), and then press Esc to terminate the command.

8. Rename the 4′–0″ (1200mm) offset level **West Parapet**. Click Yes to rename corresponding views.

9. Rename the 2′–0″ (600mm) offset **West Roof** (see Figure 3.23), and click Yes to rename corresponding views. You'll have to add elbows to the levels to see the names and elevations.

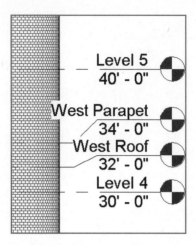

FIGURE 3.23: Adding two new levels for the west side of the building

See? Adding levels isn't all that hard. You just need to know how Revit wants you to do it. Now that you've added some levels, you can go back and configure how they're displayed:

1. For the two new levels, uncheck the Show Bubble check box to the *right* of the level lines by clicking the Hide Bubble check box.

2. Display the bubbles to the *left* side of the level line by selecting the Show Bubble check box. The level should now look like Figure 3.24 (you have to add those elbows again).

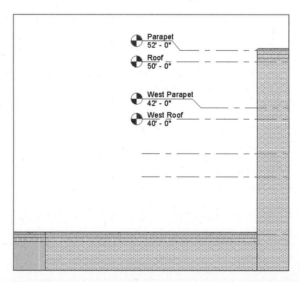

FIGURE 3.24: Using the display bubble toggles to switch the display to the appropriate side of the building

3. Staying focused on the left side of the building, select the West Parapet level.

4. Notice that some blue icons still appear. One of those icons reads 3D.

5. Pick (left-click) the 3D icon. It now reads 2D. The larger, hollow blue grip turns into a smaller, solid grip. You can now drag the level end without dragging the rest along with it. The 2D function also ensures that this modification doesn't affect other views (see Figure 3.25 and Figure 3.26).

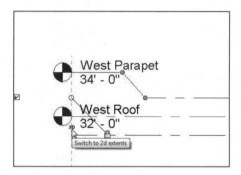

FIGURE 3.25: Turn off the 3D extents so you can drag the level end freely and without disturbing any other view.

FIGURE 3.26: The little blue grip enables you to drag the entire level.

6. Repeat the procedure for the West Roof level. Now both of the level ends are set for 2D extents. The blank ends at the right side are still set to 3D extents.

7. Select the West Parapet level, activating the grips.

8. Pick the blue grip, and drag the end to the left side of the building, approximately to the location shown in Figure 3.27. Notice that the two 2D lines are locked to one another.

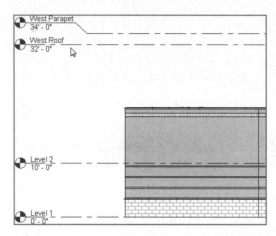

FIGURE 3.27:   You can drag the 2D level ends wherever you want them.

9. Drag the West Roof level to the left as well.

10. Turn on the left side for Levels 1 and 2.

11. Switch these levels to 2D, and drag them to align with the West Parapet and West Roof levels, as shown in Figure 3.27. (If you can't pick a level, hover over it with your cursor, and press the Tab key. When the level highlights, pick it.)

12. Add another level 2′ (600mm) above Level 3, and call it **Corridor Parapet**. Click Yes to rename corresponding views.

13. Turn on the level information on the left side.

14. Turn off the level information on the right side.

WARNING   On almost every project, you'll have to adjust a level's display in different views. Keep in mind that if the 3D button is left on, moving the level in the current view will also move it in other views—sometimes for the better and sometimes for the worse. Switching to 2D can eliminate aggravation.

15. On the left side, turn on the 2D extents.

16. Drag the left side of the line to an area approximately as shown in Figure 3.28.

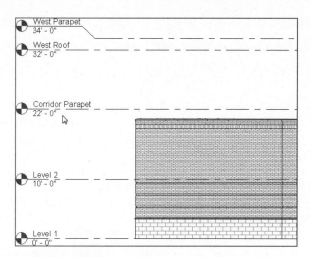

FIGURE 3.28: All the levels are in place for now.

Let's move these walls to their proper levels. Again, in this case it may be a little easier to go to a 3D view so you can get a good perspective on the results of constraining the tops of the walls. Perform the following steps:

1. Click the Default 3D icon on the Quick Access toolbar.

2. In the 3D view, select the west side of the building, excluding the corridor and the three walls to the south, as shown in Figure 3.29. You should have seven walls selected. To check this, look in the lower-right corner of the Revit window. You see a filter icon with the number 7 next to it. (You need to press and hold the Ctrl key for multiple selections.)

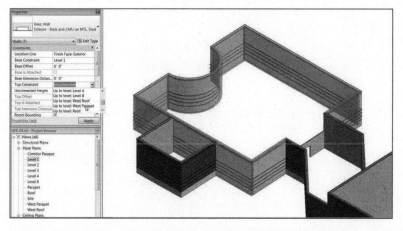

FIGURE 3.29: Selecting the west part of the building

3. In the Properties dialog, set Top Constraint to Up To Level: West Parapet. Click Apply or move your cursor into the view window.

4. In the 3D view, your walls should grow to meet the new constraints.

5. Press Esc.

6. Select the corridor walls as well as the three south walls whose tops remain unconstrained. (You may need to rotate the view to see everything.)

7. In the Constraints category of the Properties dialog, set Top Constraint to Up To Level: Corridor Parapet (see Figure 3.30).

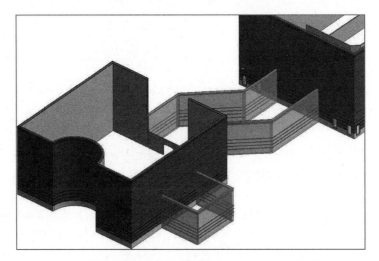

FIGURE 3.30: The final walls are constrained to the Corridor Parapet level.

8. Go back to the South elevation. Set the top constraints of the selected walls to Corridor Parapet, as shown in Figure 3.31.

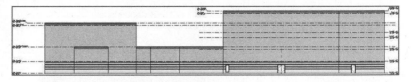

FIGURE 3.31: The final look of the building

9. Save the model.

Creating and Modifying Building Sections

As your model starts to develop, you'll begin to see areas that need further attention. (Certainly the area where the corridor hits the west building needs to be fixed.) This brings us to a good point. Sections in Revit Architecture, when placed into the model, not only help you build a set of construction documents but also help you work physically on the model. For example, you need to fix the east wall of the west wing. However, you don't have any good views established that focus directly on this area. This is the perfect place to add a section!

Adding a Building Section

To add a section and some important wall-modify commands, follow along:

1. Go to Level 1 Floor Plan, and zoom in on the area where the corridor meets the west wing of the building.

2. On the Create panel of the View tab, select Section, as shown in Figure 3.32.

FIGURE 3.32: The Section command is found on the Create panel of the View tab.

3. A section takes two picks to place into the model. You must first pick the point for the head; then you pick a point for the tail. To place the section as shown in Figure 3.33, first pick a point above the corridor and to the right of the vertical wall.

4. After you pick the first point, move your cursor straight down the view. When you're positioned directly below the bottom corridor wall, pick the second point (see Figure 3.33). If the section is facing the wrong way, that's fine. You'll fix that in a moment.

5. With the section placed, it looks like you need to flip it to face the wall you intended to modify. A few blue icons appear. You're interested in the icon that looks like two arrows. This is a *flip grip*. It's the same thing you saw in the doors and windows (see Figure 3.34).

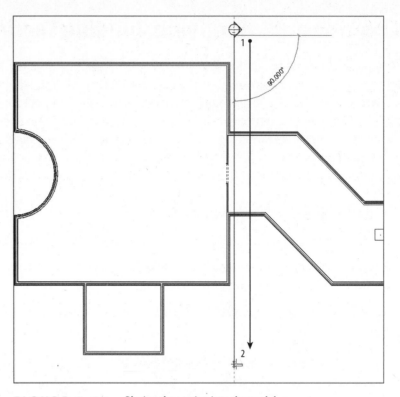

FIGURE 3.33:   Placing the section into the model

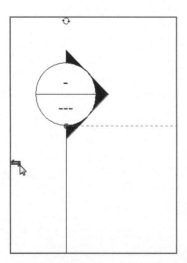

FIGURE 3.34:   After you select the section, you'll see the flip grip.

6. When you see the flip grip, pick it. It flips the section into the correct direction.

WARNING   I may be jumping ahead, but here's a word of caution: if you cut a section in Revit Architecture and then place detail components and draft over the top of that section, you're stuck. Don't flip or move the section after you've drafted over the top of it. The results will be bad. The walls will move, but your line work won't, leaving you with a mess.

With the section flipped in the correct direction, a dashed line forms a box around part of the model, as shown in Figure 3.35. This forms the view extents of the section. Anything outside of this box won't be shown.

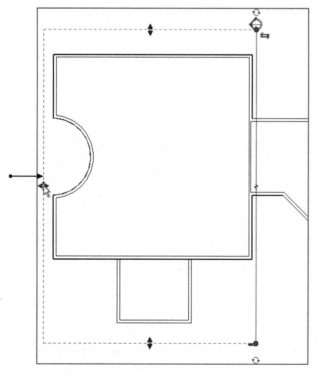

FIGURE 3.35:   You can control how deep into the building you want the section to appear.

7. The vertical dashed line (to the left) has a move arrow. Pick the move arrow, and drag the crop region into the area shown in Figure 3.35.

N O T E   If the section isn't selected, you need to select it. You must pick the line of the section, not the bubble. When you pick the line, the section is selected.

8. With the section still selected, notice the small, blue break icon in the middle of the section (see Figure 3.36). Pick the break line (it's called the Gaps In Segments icon). The section is now broken, and you have grips controlling the ends of the break lines (see Figure 3.36).

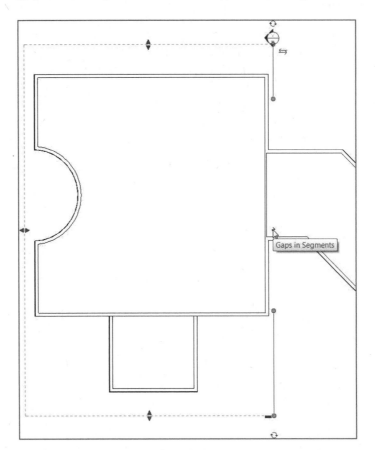

F I G U R E   3 . 3 6 :   Adding a gap in the section. You can move your grips to be the same as the figure.

9. At each end of the section is a blue icon that resembles a recycle symbol. This controls what the section head displays. By selecting this icon, you can choose to have a section head, a tail, or nothing. At the tail of the section, cycle through until you get a section head (see Figure 3.37).

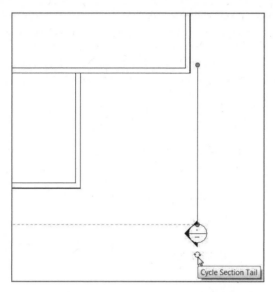

FIGURE 3.37:   Cycling through the display choices

With the section cut, it's time to open the view you've created. In the Project Browser, you now see a new category called Sections (Building Section). In this category is a view called Section 1. When you cut the section, you added a view to the project. This view carries its own properties and can be drafted over (see Figure 3.38).

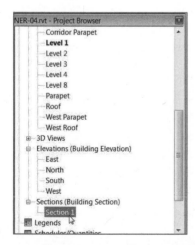

FIGURE 3.38:   The Project Browser with the new section

TIP   Be organized. Just because you're using BIM, that doesn't negate the need for basic organization. The first thing you should do when creating a section (or any new view, for that matter) is give it a name. If you don't, and you leave your sections as Section 1, Section 2, Section 3, and so on, you'll find yourself wasting a lot of time looking for the right view.

At this point, you need to name the section and open the view. You can also fix the gap in the wall while you're at it. Perform the following steps:

1. In the Project Browser, right-click Section 1.

2. Choose Rename from the context menu (see Figure 3.39).

FIGURE 3.39:   You can rename the view by right-clicking in the Project Browser.

3. Change the name of Section 1 to **West Corridor Section**.

4. Click OK.

5. Double-click the West Corridor Section in the Project Browser. Doing so opens the section. You can see the two corridor walls and the west wing beyond.

6. Chances are that the section looks great, but no levels are displayed. If you can't see your levels, open the south elevation.

7. Select a window around the west levels, as shown in Figure 3.40.

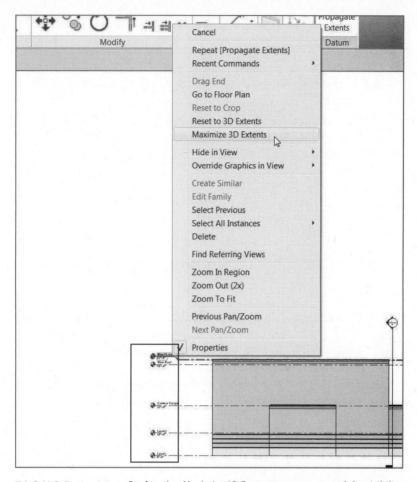

FIGURE 3.40: By choosing Maximize 3D Extents, you can control the visibility of the levels in other views.

8. With the levels selected, place your pointer directly on top of one of the levels, and right-click.

9. Select Maximize 3D Extents, as shown in Figure 3.40.

10. Go back to the West Corridor Section, and clean up the levels so they're to the right of the building and the Parapet level isn't overlapping the level below (see Figure 3.41).

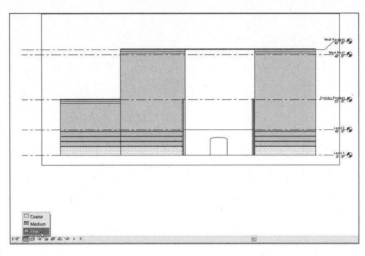

FIGURE 3.41:   On the View Control bar, set Fine as the detail level.

 NOTE   Notice that when you're adjusting the levels in the section, the 2D icon appears. This means any adjustments made here won't affect any other views. In a sectional view, Revit automatically makes the levels 2D. In an elevation view, however, Revit makes the levels 3D. If you want to make adjustments in an elevation, it's a good idea to turn these into 2D extents.

11. On the View Control bar, select Fine for the detail level, as shown in Figure 3.41. (Making adjustments like this to a view will become second nature to you very soon.)

Cutting a section is immensely helpful in terms of viewing the model from any perspective you want. To go even further, when you cut a section, you can also work on your model by modifying any item in the section.

Making Building Modifications in a Section

Now that you've had a good look at this side of the west wing, it's obvious that this wall needs to be repaired. In Revit Architecture, you can make a modification to a building in any view. This is good and bad. Just remember that everything you do has a downstream effect on the entire model.

The following procedure will guide you through making a modification to a wall's profile while in a section view:

1. In the Project Browser, find the West Corridor Section and open it by double-clicking the name West Corridor Section (if it isn't open already).

In Revit Architecture, you can also double-click the annotation that refers to the view you wish to open. For example, if you want to open the West Corridor Section, and you're in a plan, all you have to do is double-click the section bubble, and the view will open. If you're in the section, and you want to go back to a floor plan, you can double-click a datum bubble, and Revit will open that view.

2. In this section, select the east wall of the west wing, as shown in Figure 3.42.

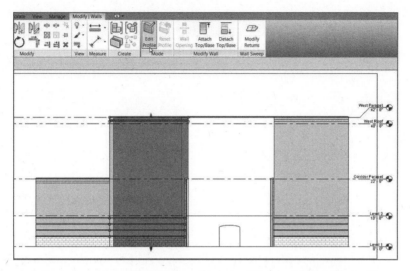

FIGURE 3.42: Selecting the wall to be modified, and clicking Edit Profile

3. After you select the wall, click the Edit Profile button in the Modify | Walls tab.

   You're presented with a magenta outline of the wall. This magenta outline can be modified to alter the wall's profile. On the Ribbon, Edit Profile has been added to the title of the Modify | Walls tab. This enables you to focus on the modification at hand.

After you select a wall, you can access options to modify that wall. Edit Profile is one of those options.

4. On the Draw panel of the Modify | Walls ➤ Edit Profile tab, select the Line button, as shown in Figure 3.43.

FIGURE 3.43: Adding additional lines to alter the wall's profile

5. With the Line command running, move your pointer to the vertical magenta line on the right where it intersects the Corridor Parapet level, as shown in Figure 3.44.

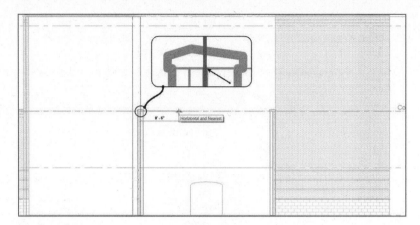

FIGURE 3.44: Revit aligns your cursor to levels, enabling you to sketch a new profile accurately.

6. When you see that you're snapped and aligned with the magenta line and the Corridor Parapet level, pick this point. Your line starts.

7. Draw the line to the right until you intersect with the centerline of the corridor wall, as shown in Figure 3.45.

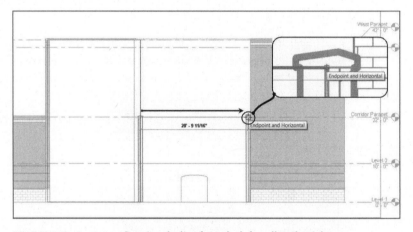

FIGURE 3.45: Drawing the line from the left wall to the right

8. When you see the snap icon appear, pick this point (see Figure 3.45).

9. Draw the line straight up the wall to the top. Make sure you don't snap to the top of the parapet cap. The point you want is to the top of the brick, as shown in Figure 3.46. (All you're doing here is sketching the profile of the wall.)

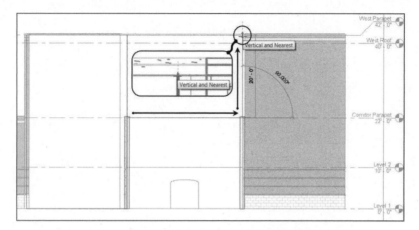

FIGURE 3.46: Drawing another line from Level 3 to the bottom of the Corridor Parapet level

10. Continue drawing the line from right to left, across the top of the wall. Snap to the endpoint of the wall to the left, as shown in Figure 3.47.

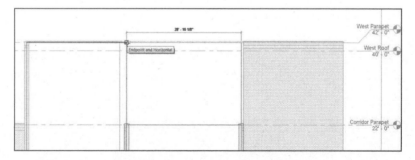

FIGURE 3.47: Drawing the line across the top

11. Press the Esc key, or click the Modify button on the Select panel.

12. Pick the vertical line to the left that goes from the bottom of the wall to the top.

13. Pick the top blue grip, and stretch the line down to Level 3.

14. You now have a closed loop, as shown in Figure 3.48.

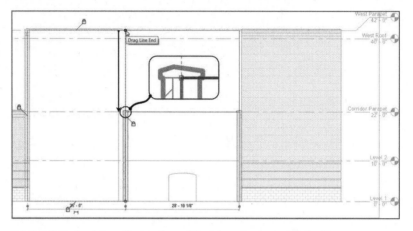

FIGURE 3.48:   Closing the wall by using grips to stretch the line

 WARNING   If you don't have a perfectly closed, continuous loop with your magenta lines, Revit won't allow you to proceed to finish altering the profile of this wall. Make sure you have no gaps, overlaps, or extra line segments aside from the six lines you need to form the wall's outline.

15. On the Wall panel of the Modify | Walls ➤ Edit Profile tab, click Finish Edit Mode, as shown in Figure 3.49. Your finished wall profile should look like Figure 3.50.

FIGURE 3.49:   Clicking Finish Edit Mode

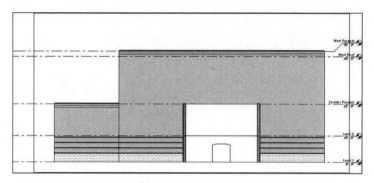

FIGURE 3.50: The finished wall profile

There is one thing left to do before you leave this section: select the two-hour fire-rated partition wall that is constrained only to Level 2. Now that you've opened up this area, the wall can go up to Level 3. To constrain the top of this wall to Corridor Parapet, follow along:

1. Select the internal (white) wall with the arched opening, as shown previously in Figure 3.50.

2. In the Properties dialog, change Top Constraint to Up To Level: Corridor Parapet, as shown in Figure 3.51.

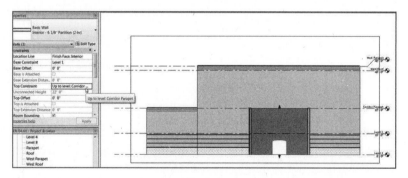

FIGURE 3.51: Choosing the properties to change a wall's constraints is becoming old hat!

3. The partition wall now meets the brick exterior wall.

4. In the Project Browser, double-click Level 3 Floor Plan view.

5. Change the detail level to Fine. (Remember, this option is on the View Control bar at the bottom of the screen.)

6. On the View tab, click the Section button.

7. Place a section as shown in Figure 3.52. Make sure the extents are similar to the figure.

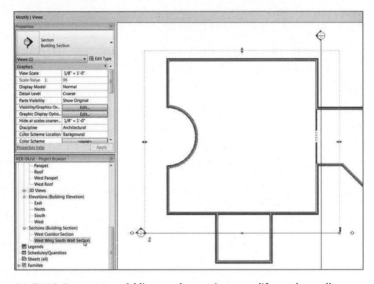

FIGURE 3.52:   Adding another section to modify another wall

8. In the Project Browser, right-click the new section and rename it **West Wing South Wall Section.** You'll use this section in Chapter 4, "Working with the Autodesk Revit Tools."

Adding entire building sections is a great way to break down the model quickly into large segments. Another type of section, a wall section, enables you to view smaller portions of the item being detailed.

Adding Wall Sections

A *wall section* is basically the same as a building section. The only difference is that, when you place a wall section, Revit holds the extents to a much smaller area. When you add a building section, Revit wants to extend to the farthest geometry. That being said, a wall section is usually placed to show only the item being cut but not the geometry beyond.

To place a wall section, follow this procedure:

1. Double-click Level 1 in the Project Browser.

2. On the View tab, pick the Section button (the same one you picked for the building section).

3. In the Properties dialog box, select Wall Section, as shown in Figure 3.53.

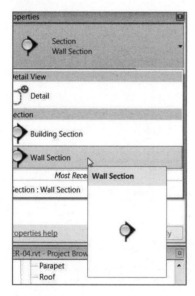

FIGURE 3.53: Changing the type of section from Building Section to Wall Section

 WARNING   If you're directed to go to a specific floor plan, and your view looks nothing like the one shown in the book, you need to make sure you aren't in a ceiling plan. Notice in the Project Browser that you have floor plans and ceiling plans. The two are quite different. Make sure you're in a floor plan.

4. Add the section through the corridor wall that was modified in the previous section of this chapter, as shown in Figure 3.54.

5. Right-click the new section in the Project Browser. It's in a category called Sections (Wall Section).

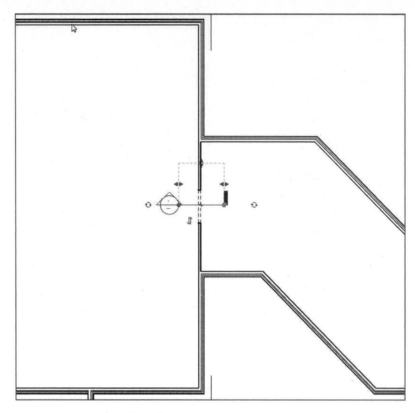

FIGURE 3.54:   The wall section in the plan

6. Select Rename.

7. Call the new section **Corridor Entry Section**. Click OK.

8. Open the Corridor Entry Section.

9. Change the scale to **1/2″ = 1′–0″** (1:20mm).

10. Change the detail level to Fine. Your section should look like Figure 3.55.

11. Save the model.

You're narrowing down the types of sections you can use, and it's time to venture into a specific type of section that can enable you to create a plan-section detail.

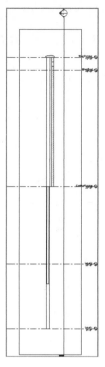

FIGURE 3.55: The finished wall section

Creating Detail Sections

There is a third type of section we need to discuss: the detail section. Revit refers to this type of section as a *detail view*, so that's how we'll start addressing it.

To add a detail section, perform the following steps:

1. Open the view called Corridor Entry Section (if you don't have it open already).

2. On the View tab, select Section (yes, the same section you've been using all along.)

3. In the Properties dialog box, select Detail View: Detail.

4. Place a section horizontally below the head of the opening, as shown in Figure 3.56. Make sure the section is flipped so it's looking downward.

5. In the Project Browser is a new category called Detail Views (Detail). Expand the tree, and you see your new detail. It's usually called Detail 0, depending on the number of details that have been added to the model previously.

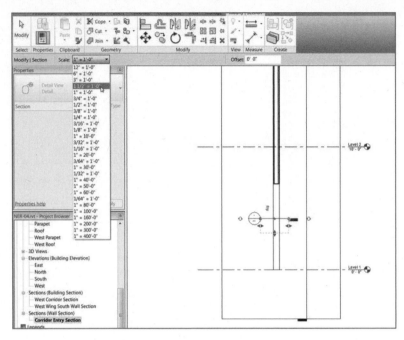

F I G U R E   3 . 5 6 :   Creating a plan section detail

6. Right-click Detail 0, and select Rename.

7. Rename the detail **Plan Detail at Corridor Opening**, and click OK.

8. Open the Plan Detail at Corridor Opening view.

9. Change the scale to **1′ 1/2″ = 1′–0″ (1:5mm)**.

With the detail open, you may be able to see only two dashed lines. This is because the crop region needs to be expanded, as explained in the next section.

Using Crop Regions

The border that surrounds the detail is called a *crop region*. It dictates the extents of the specific view you're in. You can adjust this crop region and use it to your advantage. To learn how to make adjustments to the crop region, follow these steps:

1. Select the window surrounding the detail, as shown in Figure 3.57.

2. You see four blue dot grips at the midpoint of each line. Pick the top grips, and stretch the top region up until you can see the opening jamb (see Figure 3.57).

3. Repeat the process for the bottom so you can see the entire opening.

4. With the crop region still selected, notice the break icons similar to the make-elbow icons in the level markers. Pick the break icon, as shown in Figure 3.58. Slice part of the section away, resulting in two separate cropped regions.

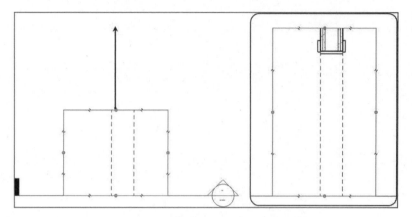

F I G U R E   3 . 5 7 :   **Stretching the crop region to view the detail**

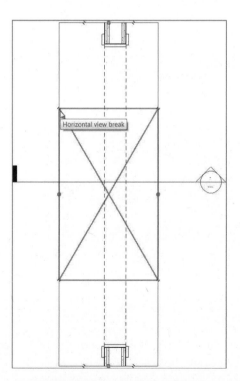

F I G U R E   3 . 5 8 :   **Splitting the section**

5. Within the cropped regions are blue move icons. If you don't see blue icons, as shown in Figure 3.59, you need to select the crop region again.

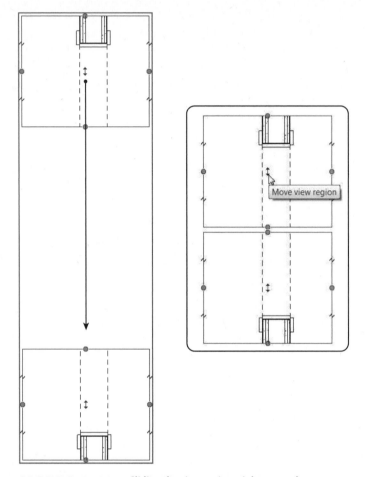

FIGURE 3.59:   Sliding the view regions tighter together

6. Slide the sections closer together by clicking the top icon and moving the section down. (Be careful; if you slide them too close together, you'll get a warning telling you that the two regions are being joined back to one.)

7. Save the model.

You now have nice control over how the details are shown. Let's go back and learn how to make the section marker more aesthetically pleasing.

Splitting a Section Segment

One more section item, and then you're finished! Sometimes you need to split (or *jog*) a section. You do this to show items that aren't necessarily in line with one another. You can accomplish this in Revit Architecture as follows:

1. Open the Level 1 floor plan.

2. On the View tab, click the Section button. (You can also grab a section from the Quick Access toolbar.)

3. In the Type Selector, select Building Section.

4. Pick a point above the corridor that connects to the east wing of the building for the section head, and then pick a point well below the bottom of the corridor, as shown in Figure 3.60.

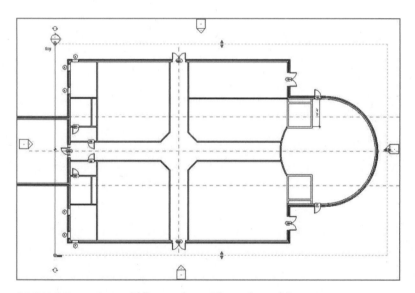

FIGURE 3.60: Adding another section to the model

5. In the Project Browser, find the section you just made and rename it **East Corridor Section**.

6. Select the new section marker.

7. On the Section panel of the Modify | Views tab, click the Split Segment button.

8. Pick a point along the section line just below the corridor, as shown in Figure 3.61.

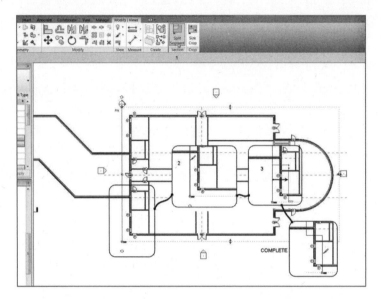

FIGURE 3.61: Jogging a section calls for splitting the segment.

9. Move your cursor to the right. A jog appears in the section; place the jog into the building. The section is now jogged into the building. Press Esc twice to clear the command.

Finally! You're finished with sections. Just remember that by adding a section to the model, not only are you preparing to build your construction documents, but you're also enabling access to specific elements, thus enabling you to make modifications you otherwise could not have made.

Creating Callouts

Creating an enlarged area of your model will be a task on every project you tackle. Luckily, in Revit Architecture, not only are callouts easy to add to your model but also directly link to the view to which they refer. This is crucial for project coordination. Another nice thing about callouts is that you can make modifications to the callout view independent of the host view from which you pull the information. The biggest change you make is the scale. Yes, your call-out can be at a different scale from the main floor plan.

Here's the procedure for adding callouts:

1. In the Project Browser, under Sections (Wall Section), open the Corridor Entry Section.

2. Find the View tab on the Ribbon.

3. On the View tab, click the Callout button, as shown in Figure 3.62.

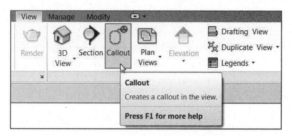

FIGURE 3.62:   The Callout button is located on the View tab.

4. Pick a window around the area where the corridor firewall meets the exterior wall with the brick façade, as shown in Figure 3.63.

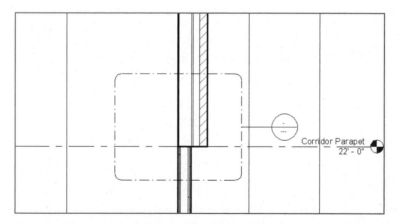

FIGURE 3.63:   The callout area is directly related to the view it's calling out.

5. In the Project Browser, there is a new Sections (Wall Section) item. Its name is Callout of Corridor Entry Section—which is fine just the way it is. Press Esc.

6. Select the callout you just added by picking any point along the line. A bunch of blue grips appear. These grips enable you to stretch the shape of the callout.

7. Pick the grip that connects the callout bubble to the leader coming from the callout window.

8. Drag the bubble to the location shown in Figure 3.64.

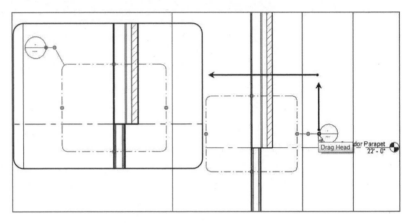

FIGURE 3.64: Adjusting callouts will be a common task.

9. Pick the blue midpoint grip on the leader and create an elbow, as shown in Figure 3.64.

10. In the Project Browser, find Callout of Corridor Entry Section under the Sections (Building Section) category, and open the view. (You can also double-click the callout bubble to open the view.)

11. With the section open, select the crop region, as shown in Figure 3.65.

12. Change the scale to **1′ 1/2″ = 1′– 0″** (1:5mm).
    After you select the crop region, you see an additional region that consists of a dotted line. This is called an *annotation region*, and it gives you a gutter in which to place text outside the area that is physically being cropped.

13. Type **WT**. This tiles the windows you have open.
    The callout window is selected in the Corridor Entry Section along with the crop region in your callout. That is because the two objects are one and the same (see Figure 3.66).

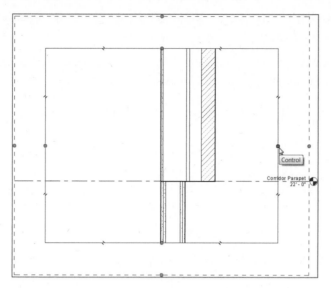

F I G U R E   3 . 6 5 :   Selecting the crop region

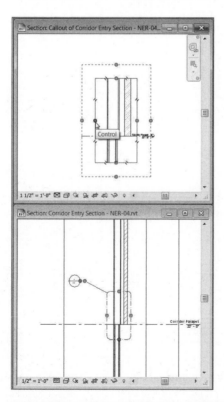

F I G U R E   3 . 6 6 :   Modify the crop region by selecting it and stretching the grip.

14. Stretch the crop region closer to the actual wall, as shown in Figure 3.66.

15. Save the model. You'll use this detail in future chapters to get the model ready for construction documents.

Now that you've created a callout for a detail, let's go to the plan and create some callouts there. It would be nice to have some typical lavatory callouts as well as a typical elevator callout:

1. In the Project Browser, go to Floor Plan Level 1. (It may need to be maximized because you tiled the windows in the previous exercise.) Make sure it's a floor plan, not a ceiling plan.

2. Zoom in on the area shown in Figure 3.67.

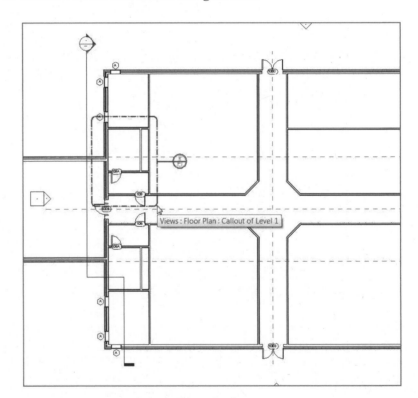

The crop region and the callout outline are the same. If you modify one, the other changes accordingly.

FIGURE 3.67: Creating a plan callout

3. On the View tab, select Callout.

4. Pick a window around the lavatory, as shown in Figure 3.67.

5. In the Project Browser, under the Floor Plans category, is Callout of Level 1. Right-click Callout of Level 1, and select Rename.

6. Rename it **Typical Men's Lavatory.**

7. Open the Typical Men's Lavatory view. Choose Zoom To Fit.

8. The detail level is set to Coarse. Change it to Fine. Note that the callout is placed under the category where it was created; you won't see a "callouts" category.

T I P   You may have noticed that you've been opening quite a few views. It's a good idea to close the views you don't need open, because they could slow you down a tad. To close views, choose Window ➤ Close Hidden Windows.

9. Save the model.

10. Open the Level 1 floor plan.

11. Create a callout for the women's room below the corridor (directly below the men's room).

12. Name the new callout **Typical Women's Lavatory.**

13. Create one more callout around the elevator shaft in the east wing, as shown in Figure 3.68.

14. Name the new callout **Typical Elevator Shaft.**

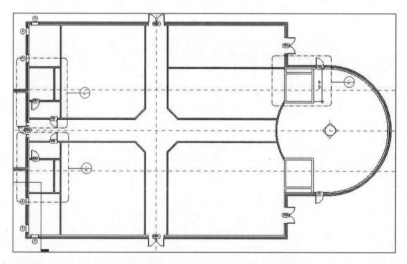

F I G U R E   3 . 6 8 :   The plan showing the three typical callouts

The boring views are out of the way! Let's create some perspective views of the model. Creating these views is just as easy but requires a specific procedure in which you'll take advantage of the camera function.

Creating and Modifying a Camera View

The camera view is the view with which you'll have by far the most fun. Revit Architecture seems to lend itself naturally to this type of view.

Taking a camera view essentially tells Revit to look at a certain area from a perspective vantage point. Like a section or a callout, such a view may never see the light of day in terms of going on a drawing sheet, but camera views are perfect to see how a model is coming along from a realistic point of view.

Adding a Camera View

To create a camera view, follow these steps:

1. Go to the Level 1 floor plan.

2. On the View tab, click the drop-down arrow in the 3D View button and select Camera, as shown in Figure 3.69. (You can also access this on the Quick Access toolbar.)

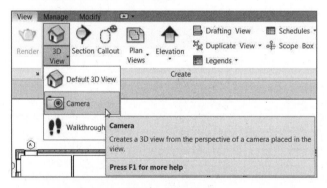

FIGURE 3.69: Adding a camera view

3. Pick a point in the main corridor of the east wing, and move your cursor to the left—down the hallway. You want to take a perspective view as if you were standing in the intersection of the two main corridors, as shown in Figure 3.70.

4. The second point you pick will specify how far the camera reaches into the building. Pick a point past the corridor doors, as shown in Figure 3.71.

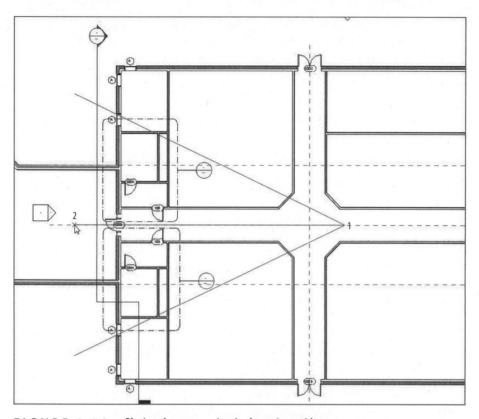

F I G U R E 3 . 7 0 :   Placing the camera view in the main corridor

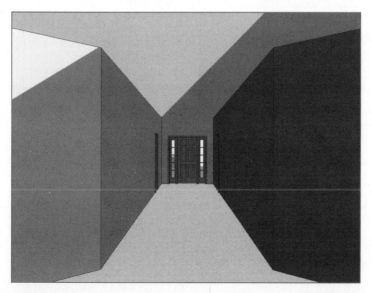

F I G U R E 3 . 7 1 :   The perspective view down the east wing corridor

5. Unlike when you're placing a section or a callout, Revit automatically opens the new 3D view. This doesn't mean it automatically has a useful name. In the Project Browser, you see a new view in the 3D Views category. It's called 3D View 1. Right-click 3D View 1, and name it **East Wing Corridor Perspective**.

6. On the View Control bar located at the bottom of the view, change Visual Style to Realistic.

7. Two buttons to the right is the Shadows button. For a perspective view, turning on shadows is OK if the view is relatively small. In this example, go ahead and turn them on.

When the camera is in place, you may find it difficult to modify at first. You can do quite a bit to the view, but the following section focuses on modifying the actual camera in the plan.

Modifying the Camera

After you place the camera in the model, Revit doesn't leave behind any evidence that the camera is there. If you need to make adjustments or see the location from which the view is being taken, perform the following steps:

1. Open the Level 1 floor plan.

2. In the Project Browser, right-click the East Wing Corridor Perspective view in the 3D Views category, and select Show Camera, as shown in Figure 3.72.

FIGURE 3.72: By finding the view in the Project Browser, you can tell Revit to show the camera in the plan.

The camera appears in the plan temporarily so you can see it. In the view, the camera icon is a triangle and a straight line. You can physically move the camera, and you can also adjust the grip on the midpoint of the triangle to swivel and to look farther into the model. Figure 3.73 shows the perspective view.

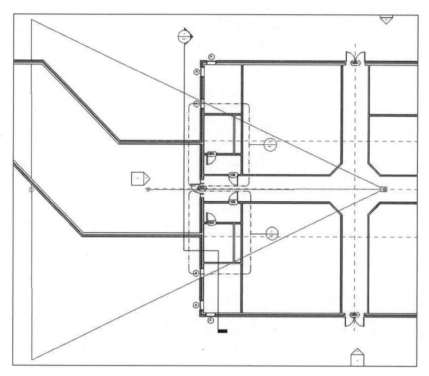

FIGURE 3.73: The perspective view

Creating an Elevation

I saved the best view—or at least, the most popular—for last. Elevations are essential for any project—so essential, in fact, that Revit provides four of them before you place a single wall into the model. The four shapes that represent houses that were in the model at the beginning of the book are elevation markers, as shown in Figure 3.74. These markers are typically handy but are most certainly now in the way. The first thing you need to do is to move one of them out of the way. The second thing you need to do is to create a few new ones!

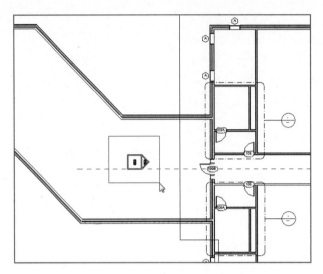

FIGURE 3.74:   The elevation marker is right in the way!

To start manipulating elevations, follow along:

1. Go to the Level 1 floor plan. In the eastern part of the corridor is an elevation. Yours may be in a slightly different location than the book's example, but it needs to be moved nonetheless (see Figure 3.74).

   You're about to move the elevation marker. To do so, however, you need to break down what an elevation marker comprises. It's actually two separate items: the square box is the elevation, and the triangle is the part of the marker that activates the view, as shown in Figure 3.75. To move this elevation marker, you must pick a window around both items and move them together. If you don't, the view will stay in its original location, leaving you wondering what is wrong with your elevation.

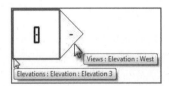

FIGURE 3.75:   The elevation marker is broken down into two pieces. You need to move both together by picking a window around the entire symbol.

2. Pick a window around the elevation marker. Make sure you aren't picking any other items along with it.

3. Move your mouse over the selection. Your cursor turns into a move icon with four move arrows, as shown in Figure 3.76.

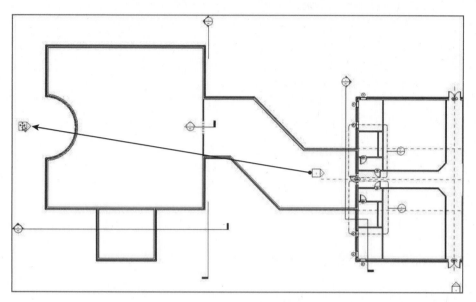

FIGURE 3.76: You can drag the elevation marker when the entire item is selected.

4. Drag the elevation marker to the west side of the building (see Figure 3.76).

Now that the elevation marker is out of the corridor, it's time to make a new one. To do so, make sure you're in the Level 1 floor plan and follow along:

1. On the View tab, click the Elevation button, as shown in Figure 3.77.

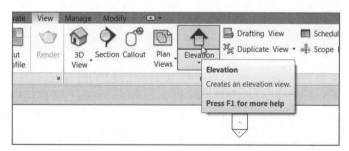

FIGURE 3.77: The Elevation button on the View tab

2. In the Type Selector, make sure Exterior Elevation is current.

3. Move your cursor around the perimeter of the building. Notice that the elevation marker follows the profile of the exterior walls. This is a great thing!

 WARNING   When you're creating an elevation of a radial wall or nonlinear item, be sure you know the exact angle at which you're placing the elevation marker. When you're in the elevation view, you may get a false sense of the true dimensions based on the view's perspective. Draw a reference plane if you need to, and then place the elevation on that plane.

4. Pick a place for the elevation, as shown in Figure 3.78, and press Esc to terminate the command.

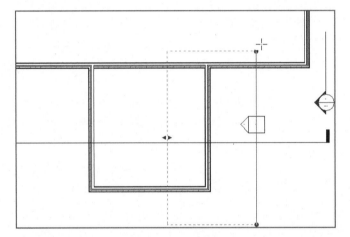

FIGURE 3.78:   The elevation is placed. You can select the view arrow and move the extents of the elevation into the building.

5. When the elevation is placed, select the triangle. You see the same extents window that you saw in the previous section (see Figure 3.78). This controls how deep into the model you're viewing, and it also shows you the length of the section. Because you placed this elevation up against a wall, Revit stops the extents of the elevation at that wall.

6. Pick the top grip, and stretch the elevation past the wall, as shown in Figure 3.78.

7. In the Project Browser under Elevations (Building Elevation) is a new elevation. Right-click it, and rename it West Wing Southeast Elevation.

8. Open the elevation.

9. On the View Control bar, change the scale to 1/4″ = 1′–0″ (1:50).

10. On the View Control bar, set the detail level to Fine. (You can also set these in the Properties dialog at any time.)

11. Save the model.

You've added a new exterior elevation. You can add an interior elevation as well. It's just as easy and much more fun!

Interior Elevations

The difference between an exterior elevation and an interior elevation is the same as the difference between a building section and a wall section. Both interior and exterior elevations are executed the same way: by selecting the View tab on the Design bar. The only difference is that you can make a choice between the two in the Type Selector in the Options bar. To add an interior elevation, perform these steps:

1. Go to the Level 1 floor plan.

2. On the View tab, click the Elevation button.

3. In the Type Selector, choose Elevation : Interior Elevation, and place it in the area shown in Figure 3.79.

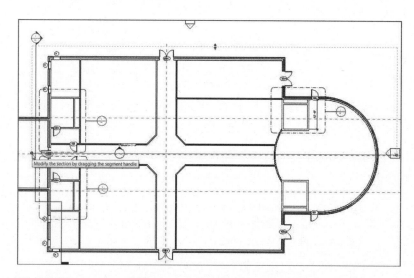

FIGURE 3.79: Adding an interior elevation and making the adjustments

4. Hover your cursor in the corridor near a point shown in the middle of Figure 3.79. Notice that when you move your cursor up, the arrow flips up. When you move your pointer down, the arrow flips down.

5. Make sure the arrow in the elevation target is pointing up, and then pick a point along the horizontal corridor, as shown at the right of Figure 3.79, to place the elevation. Once it's placed, press Esc to terminate the command.

6. After you place the elevation, select the arrow. Notice that the extents are outside the building. (This occurs in most cases. If it doesn't, you're good to go.) Select the elevation again and, on the left side, pick the blue grip and drag the left extent to the point shown at the left in Figure 3.79. Repeat the process for the right side as well.

7. In the Project Browser, there's a new elevation under the Elevations (Interior Elevation) category. Right-click the new elevation (Revit will call it Elevation 1 - a or something similar), and call it **East Wing Corridor North Elevation**.

8. Open the new view called East Wing Corridor North Elevation.

9. Notice that the crop region extends all the way up to the parapet. Select the crop region, and drag the top down to Level 2, as shown in Figure 3.80.

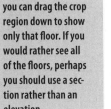

In the elevation's view, you can drag the crop region down to show only that floor. If you would rather see all of the floors, perhaps you should use a section rather than an elevation.

FIGURE 3.80: Stretching the grip down to crop the view

 N O T E   If you had floors already placed in the model, Revit would create the interior elevation so that it extended only to this geometry. Because you don't have floors, Revit doesn't know where to stop. If you happen to place an elevation without floors and put them in later, Revit won't make the adjustment. You'll have to adjust the interior elevation manually for the new floors.

Let's create some more elevations:

1. Go to Floor Plan Level 1. Zoom into the east wing entry area, as shown in Figure 3.81.

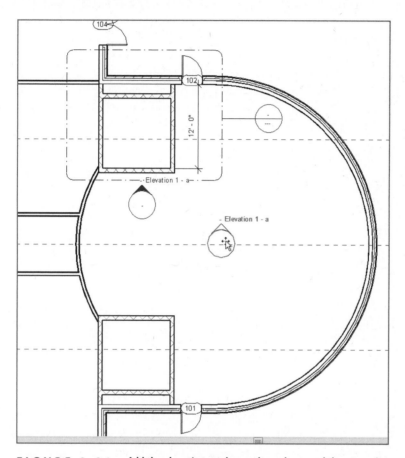

FIGURE 3.81: Add the elevation marker as shown here, and then move it to a new location.

2. On the View tab, click the Elevation button.

3. Place an elevation marker in an area similar to the one shown in Figure 3.81, and then move it to the center of the lobby.

T I P   Notice that when you're trying to place the elevation in the entry area, it seems to wander all over the place. This is because the elevation is trying to locate the radial geometry. The safest bet in this situation is to find a straight wall and aim the elevation at that wall. In this case, you should aim the elevation at the bottom of the elevator shaft. When the elevation marker is in place, you can then move it to where you need it to be.

4. With the elevation marker centered in the lobby, select the round bubble. Four blue boxes appear, as shown in Figure 3.82. These boxes let you turn on multiple views. Turn on all four views, as shown in Figure 3.82.

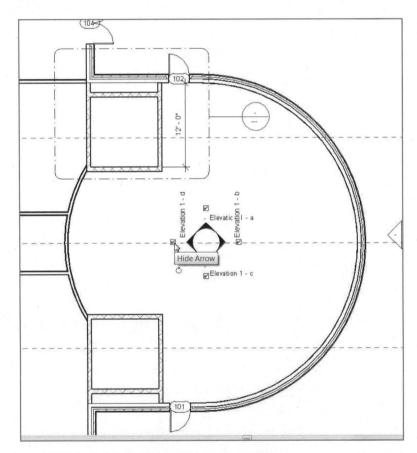

F I G U R E   3 . 8 2 :   Turn on all four views in the lobby.

With the four elevations turned on, you have some naming to do! Up to this point, you have been going to the Project Browser to rename the elevations. Let's explore another way to rename an elevation and to view its properties as well.

Elevation Properties

With each view comes a new set of properties. For example, when you made the perspective view of the corridor, you set Visual Style to Shaded, and you turned on shadows. Normally, in an interior elevation, you don't want to do this. Revit allows you to have separate view properties on a view-by-view basis.

To access the View Properties dialog, follow these steps:

1. On the interior elevation with the four arrows, select only the arrow facing up (north).

2. The Properties dialog provides a wealth of information about that view. You have a multitude of options as well. Find the View Name option under the Identity Data heading, and change it to **East Wing Entry North Elevation**, as shown in Figure 3.83.

> By changing the value in the Properties dialog, you are, in effect, changing the name in the Project Browser. Again, change something in one place, and it changes in another.

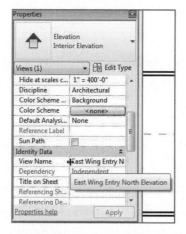

FIGURE 3.83: Changing the View Name setting to East Wing Entry North Elevation

3. Select the East Wing Entry North Elevation again. Notice that the view's extents are stretching past the entry atrium. Pick the blue grips at the end of the elevations, and bring them into the atrium area, as shown in Figure 3.84. Also, drag the view limit up to show the radial exterior wall (see Figure 3.84).

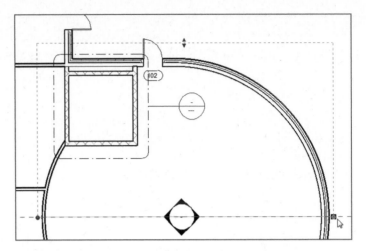

FIGURE 3.84: Making the adjustments to bring the view back into a reasonable range

---

4. Click the elevation arrow facing left (west).

5. Change View Name to **East Wing Entry West Elevation**.

6. Click the arrow facing down (south).

7. Change View Name to **East Wing Entry South Elevation**.

8. Click the arrow facing right (east).

9. Change View Name to **East Wing Entry East Elevation**.

10. Select each elevation, and adjust the view's extents as you did for the north elevation.

11. Save the model.

The actual view names appear in the plan. This is nice, but unfortunately it leaves no room for anything else other than the view. Plus, no construction documents have these names right in the plan (at least, none that I have ever seen). You can turn off this feature.

Now that you can place and modify annotations, let's delve into their physical properties.

Annotation Properties

Annotations all have properties you can modify. To change the elevation symbol properties, follow along:

1. On the Manage tab, click Settings ➢ Additional Settings ➢ Elevation Tags.

2. At the top of the Type Properties dialog, you see Family: System Family: Elevation Tag. Below that is Type. Change Type from 1/2″ (13mm) Square to 1/2″ (13mm) Circle (see Figure 3.85).

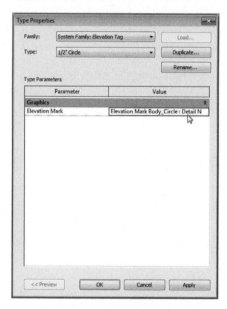

FIGURE 3.85: Modifying the properties for the elevation markers

3. In Type Parameters, under Graphics, change Elevation Mark to Elevation Mark Body_Circle : Detail Number.

4. Click OK.

5. Save your work.

6. Zoom back in on the elevation markers. They should look like Figure 3.86.

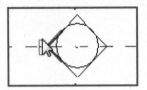

FIGURE 3.86:   The revised, less-obtrusive elevation markers

NOTE   It's Revit time! No longer will you see "dumb" placeholder information in a tag. When you create your construction documents and put these views on sheets, Revit will automatically fill out tags with the correct information. To take it one step further, you can tell Revit not to print these annotations if the views they represent aren't on a sheet.

The ability to add elevations is a must. As you can see, physically adding an elevation is simple. It does, however, take practice to manipulate elevations to look the way you want.

Are You Experienced?

Now you can...

- ☑ create levels and constrain walls to stretch or shrink if the level's elevation information changes in any way

- ☑ cut wall sections and building sections through the model

- ☑ create detail views, allowing you to add plan sections through a wall or a building section

- ☑ create a callout view, and control the crop region

- ☑ add a camera to the model, giving the user a nice perspective of a certain area

- ☑ create interior and exterior elevations within the model

Working with the Autodesk Revit Tools

You can get only so far when allowing a computer application to place architectural components into a model. At some point, the application needs to be flexible enough to enable users to employ their own sets of drafting and modifying tools, thus providing architects and designers with the freedom to create their own architecture and construction procedures. The Autodesk® Revit® Architecture program does provide the basic modify and edit commands, which are quite common in other drafting applications such as AutoCAD® and Microstation, but Revit does this with a little more flair and some differences in procedure as compared to a 2D drafting application.

▶ **The basic edit commands**

▶ **The Array command**

▶ **The Mirror command**

▶ **The Align tool**

▶ **The Split Element command**

▶ **The Trim command**

▶ **The Offset command**

▶ **Copy/Paste**

▶ **Creating the plans**

The Basic Edit Commands

In this chapter, you'll learn how to use the geometry you've already placed in the model to build an actual working plan. As you manipulate the plan, all of the other views you made in Chapter 3, "Creating Views," will reflect those changes. You'll start with the edit commands.

 N O T E   As with the previous chapters, it's important that you become comfortable with the material in this chapter. If you're still not comfortable with the first few chapters, I recommend reviewing them now. You may pick up something you missed the first time around and have a "light bulb" moment.

You aren't going to get very far in Revit without knowing the edit commands. Up to this point, we have been avoiding the edit commands with a few exceptions. There will be some overlap in some of the chapters, because many aspects of Revit span multiple topics.

The basic commands covered in this section are Move, Copy, and Rotate. Then, in the following sections, you'll move on to Array, Mirror, Align, Split Element, Offset, Copy/Paste, and Trim. Each command is as important as the next at this stage of the game. Some are obvious, whereas others can take some practice to master.

The first command, Move, is one you'll recognize from previous chapters. Move is probably the most heavily used command in Revit.

The Move Command

The Move command is generally used to create a copy of an item while deleting the original item.

 N O T E   Metric users should not type in mm or other metric abbreviations when entering amounts suggested in the exercises. Revit won't accept such abbreviations. Simply enter the number provided within the parentheses.

Begin by finding the model you're using to follow along. If you haven't completed the previous chapter procedures, open the file called NER-4.rvt found at the book's website, www.sybex.com/go/revit2014ner. Go to the Chapter 4 folder to find the file.

To use the Move command, perform the following steps:

1. Go to Level 1 under the Floor Plans category in the Project Browser.

2. Zoom in on the west wing.

3. Select the south wall of the bump-out at the south side of the west wing, as shown in Figure 4.1.

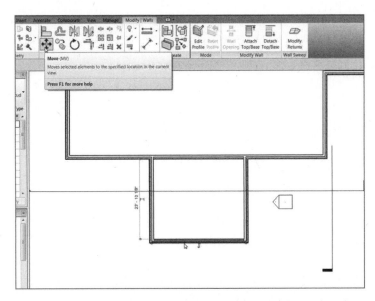

FIGURE 4.1: Select the wall to be moved. The Move button now appears on the Ribbon.

4. On the Modify | Walls tab is the Move button (see Figure 4.1); click it.

5. Now that the Move command is running, you see some choices on the Options bar:

    Constrain   If you select Constrain, you can move only at 0, 90, 180, or 270 degrees.

    Disjoin   If you select Disjoin, then when you move the wall, any walls that are joined to it won't be affected by the move. The wall will lose its join.

6. To start moving the item, you must first pick a base point for the command. Pick a point somewhere toward the middle of the wall, as shown in Figure 4.2.

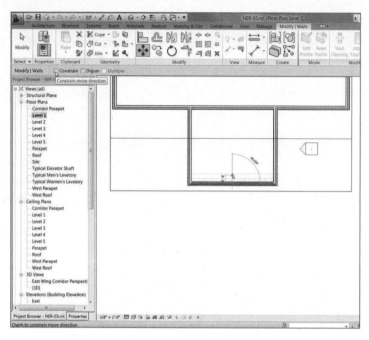

FIGURE 4.2: Choices on the Options bar. The first point has been picked, and the wall is being moved up.

7. After you pick this point, move your cursor straight up. You see a blue dimension. At this point, you have two choices: you can either eyeball the increment, or you can type the increment you want (see Figure 4.2).

8. Type in the value 2′–6″ (750mm), and press Enter. The wall moves 2′–6″ (750mm). Notice that the adjacent walls move with it. In Revit, there is no stretch command (see Figure 4.3).

TIP   Revit will accept a few different values for feet and fractional inches. For example, instead of typing **2′–6″** (which Revit will accept), you can type **2 6**. Just make sure you have a space between the 2 and the 6. Revit will accept that value. If there are fractional increments, you can type **2 6 1/2**, and Revit will accept the value. Or you can type **2′–6 1/2″**.

> You may be thinking, "But I used to type my commands!" Well, you still can in Revit. If you type **MV**, Revit launches the Move command.

Now that Move is officially in the history books, it's time to move on to Move's close cousin: the Copy command.

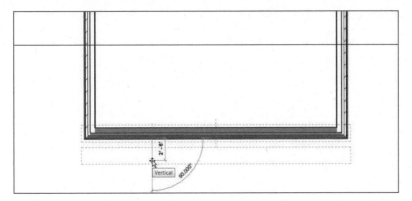

FIGURE 4.3:   Moving the wall 2′–6″ (750mm) also means that any adjoining walls will be adjusted along with it.

The Copy Command

When you need to make duplicates of an item, Copy is your go-to player. The Copy command works like the Move command, except that it leaves the initial item intact. You can also create multiple copies if necessary.

To start using the Copy command, follow along:

1. Make sure you're still in Floor Plan Level 1.

2. Zoom and pan so you're focused on the east wing, as shown in Figure 4.4.

3. Select the right corridor wall (see Figure 4.4).

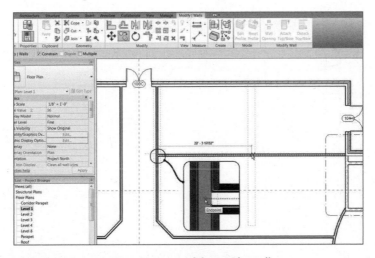

FIGURE 4.4:   Creating a copy of the corridor wall

4. Click the Copy command on the Modify | Walls tab.

5. On the Options bar, check the Constrain toggle.

6. Zoom in on the wall close to the midpoint of the selected wall and the intersection of the horizontal wall that divides this portion of the building (see Figure 4.4).

7. If you hover your cursor in the center of the wall (not near the actual finish faces, but the core of the wall), you see a blue dotted centerline indicating that you've found the center of the wall. (If you're having difficulty picking the item, change the detail level to Coarse.)

   Also, if you move your cursor to the right a little, you can position it so that it picks up the horizontal wall's centerline. After you pick up the horizontal wall's centerline, the centerline for the vertical wall will disappear. This is fine.

   When you see that you're snapped to the endpoint of the horizontal wall, pick the point (see the previous figure).

8. Move to the right until you pick up the midpoint of the horizontal wall. When you do, pick that point. If the midpoint doesn't appear, type 22'–3" (6675mm) or type SM for Snap Mid.

9. Mirror the two walls to the south side of the corridor, as shown in Figure 4.5. The ends of the walls don't meet. This is fine—you'll modify these walls with the Trim command in a moment.

10. Save the model.

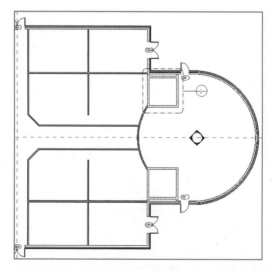

FIGURE 4.5:   The two walls copied, segmenting the spaces north and south of the corridor

The next step is to rotate an item. Although the Rotate command is a simple concept, Revit does have unique processes involved in this command.

The Rotate Command

The Rotate command enables you to change the polar orientation of an item or a set of items. This command may take a little practice to understand. The good thing, however, is that when you have experience with the Rotate command, you'll be better at other commands that share a similar process.

To use the Rotate command, follow along:

1. Open the Level 1 floor plan.

2. Zoom in on the radial portion of the west wing, as shown in Figure 4.6.

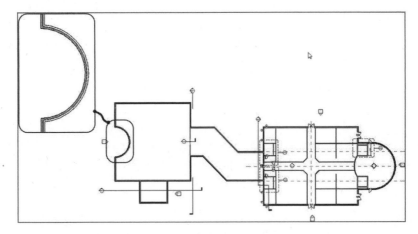

FIGURE 4.6:   The radial portion of the west wing

3. You're going to add a new reference plane and rotate it by 45°. To do so, click Ref Plane in the Work Plane panel in the Architecture tab (see Figure 4.7).

4. In the Draw panel, click the Line button (it should be set current by default).

5. For the first point, pick the center point of the radial wall, as shown in Figure 4.7.

6. For the second point, pick a point horizontally to the right, outside the radial wall (again, see Figure 4.7).

7. Press Esc twice, or click Modify.

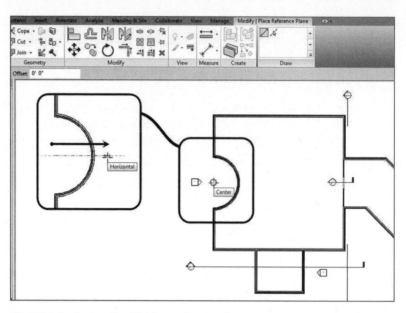

FIGURE 4.7: Establishing a reference plane

TIP In Revit, sometimes finding the correct snap can be difficult. To overcome this, you can type the letter **S** followed by the first letter of the snap you wish to use. For example, if you wanted to snap to the center of the arc wall, you would start the Ref Plane command (any command works here, but I'm using a reference plane as an example), type **SC**, place the cursor over the arc until the snap marker appears, and then click. This will snap to the center.

WARNING Before you rotate, be careful. Figure 4.7 shows the second point extended past the radial wall, and that is where you generally want it. However, watch out for your snaps. When you pick the second point, be sure to zoom in on the area, ensuring that you aren't inadvertently snapping to the wrong wall.

Now that you've added the reference plane, you can rotate it into place. (Yes, you could have just drawn it at a 45° angle, but you're practicing the Rotate command here.) Follow these steps:

1. Select the reference plane you just drew.

2. On the Modify tab, click the Rotate button, as shown in Figure 4.8.

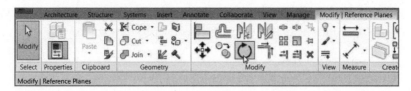

FIGURE 4.8: The Rotate command is active for the specific item you've selected.

3. After you start the Rotate command, look back at the reference plane. Notice the blue dot in the middle of your line. Revit always calculates the center of an object (or group of objects) for the rotate point (see Figure 4.9).

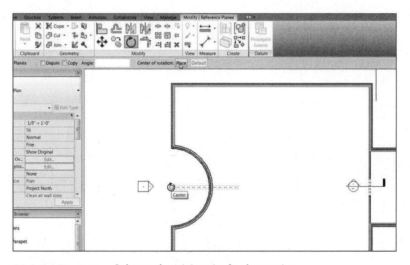

FIGURE 4.9: Relocate the origin point for the rotation.

4. On the Options bar, click the Place button, and select the end point of the reference plane. A temporary rotate icon appears, indicating that you can now move the blue dot (see Figure 4.9).

5. With the rotate origin in the correct location, it's rotate time! If you swivel your cursor around the reference plane, a line forms from the rotate origin to your cursor. This indicates that the origin is

You can start the Rotate command by typing **RO**, selecting the item(s) to rotate, and then pressing the spacebar or Enter to place the rotation icon.

established. Now you need to pick two points. The first point you pick must be in line with the object you're rotating. In this case, pick a point at the right endpoint of the reference plane, as shown in Figure 4.10.

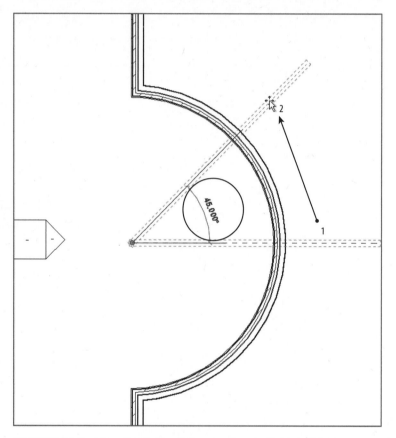

FIGURE 4.10: To rotate an item, you must specify two points.

6. When you move your cursor up, you see an angular dimension. When that angular dimension gets to 45°, pick the second point (see Figure 4.10).

7. Press Esc.

ROTATE OPTIONS

While you're in the Rotate command, don't forget that you have options. The most popular option is to create a copy of the item you're rotating, as shown here:

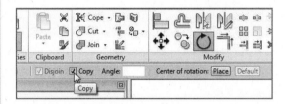

Another popular option is to specify an angle. This can be difficult, because the correct angle may be the opposite of what you think, resulting in your having to undo the command and then redo the rotation with a negative (–) value.

As you're well aware, you'll use the Rotate command quite frequently. Now that you have some experience with the Rotate command and know how Revit wants you to move the pivot point, the next command—Array—will be easy for you to grasp.

The Array Command

When you need to create multiple duplicates of an item or a group of items, the Array command is the logical choice. The Array command in Revit functions in a fashion similar to the Rotate command. The similarities of the Array command also extend to the Array command in AutoCAD. You have two basic choices:

▶ *Radial*, which enables you to array an item around a circle or an arc

▶ *Linear*, which enables you to array an item in a straight line or at an angle

Let's look at the radial array first.

Radial Array

A *radial array* is based on a radius. If you need items to be arrayed in a circular manner, the radial array is your best choice. Again, after you start the Array command, don't ignore the Options bar. It will guide you through most of the command.

To start using a radial array, follow these steps:

1. Select the 45° reference plane.

2. On the Modify | Reference Planes tab, click the Array button, as shown in Figure 4.11.

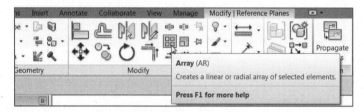

FIGURE 4.11:   Select the item to be arrayed first, and then click the Array button on the Modify | Reference Planes tab.

3. With the Array command active, some choices become available on the Options bar, as shown in Figure 4.12. For this procedure, click the Radial button.

FIGURE 4.12:   Setting the options for the Radial array

4. Select the Group And Associate check box.

5. Set Number to 4.

6. Click the Move To: Last button.

7. With the options set, focus your attention on the object being arrayed. Notice the familiar rotate icon.

I DON'T WANT TO MOVE ANYTHING!

The Move To: Last and the Move To: Second choices are somewhat misleading. You aren't actually "moving" anything. If you choose Move To: Last, for example, Revit places an additional item in the last place you pick, keeping the first item intact. Revit then divides the space between the two items evenly based on the number of items you specify in the options. If you specify four items, Revit still has two items left to divide.

If you choose Move To: Second, Revit places an additional item at the second point picked (just as with Move To: Last), but this time Revit adds additional items beyond the second item. The overall distance is calculated by the distance between the first two items.

8. On the Options bar, click the Place button. It's located next to the Origin label, as shown in Figure 4.13.

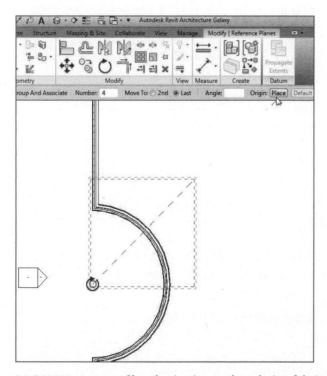

FIGURE 4.13:   Place the pivot icon on the endpoint of the item being arrayed.

9. Click the center/endpoint of the reference plane (see Figure 4.13).

10. With the pivot point in place, specify two points for the array. The first point will be a point along the angle of the item being arrayed. The second point will be a point along the angle on which you want to end.

11. Pick the endpoint of the reference plane you're arraying.

12. Move your cursor down until you see 90°. Then pick the second point (see Figure 4.14).

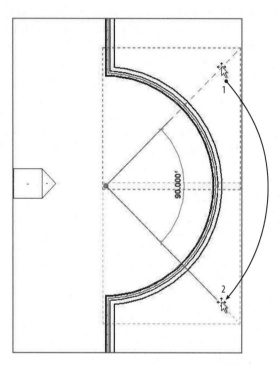

FIGURE 4.14:   Specifying the two angles for the radial array

13. Click (that is, left-click) off into another part of the view. This establishes the array. You should have four reference planes at this point, similar to Figure 4.15.

14. Select (left-click) one of the reference planes. You see a large, dashed box surrounding the reference plane, and a temporary arc dimension with a blue number 4 at the quadrant. It may be obscured by the arc, as it is in Figure 4.15, but it's there nonetheless.

15. Click the number 4.

16. Change the count to **5**. Press Enter, or click outside the array count field to set the change.

17. You now have five reference planes, as shown in Figure 4.16.

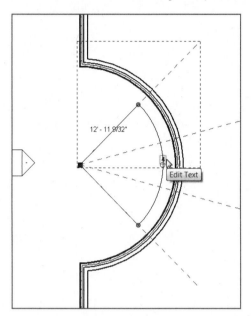

FIGURE 4.15: After the array is created, select one of the arrayed members. Notice that you can change the count.

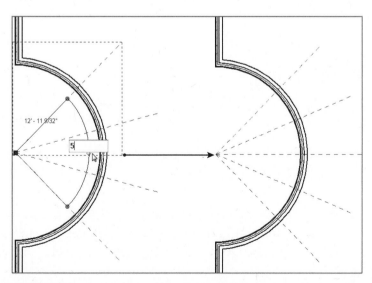

FIGURE 4.16: You can control the number of items in an array group after you create the array.

Getting the hang of radial arrays may take a few projects. The next array type, the linear array, follows the same concept as the radial array, but it's more straightforward. Yes, pun intended.

Linear Array

You may wish to create an array along a line, and you can do this in Revit. When you create a *linear array*, you enjoy the same flexibility that you have with a radial array.

The objective of this procedure is to create an array of windows along the north and south wall, on the west side of the building's west wing. To do this, you'll first need to establish two strong reference planes.

To learn how to use the Linear array command, follow along:

1. Zoom in on the northwest section of the west wing, as shown in Figure 4.17.

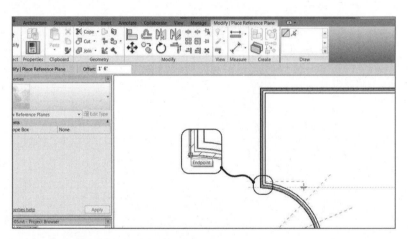

F I G U R E   4 . 1 7 :   Creating the reference plane

2. Add two reference planes. You'll use these reference planes to establish the ends of your window array. Go to the Ref Plane command on the Work Plane panel of the Architecture tab.

3. On the Draw panel, keep the Line icon active and add an offset of 1'–6" (450mm)—Imperial users, remember that you can just type 1 6—on the Options bar.

4. Pick the corner of the radial wall, where it intersects the straight wall, for the first point of the reference plane, as shown in Figure 4.17.

5. Pick a second point similar to that shown in Figure 4.17 to finish the reference plane.

6. With the Ref Plane command still running, repeat the procedure for the top of the wall. You want to pick the top, outside face of brick, avoiding the concrete ledge below, as shown in Figure 4.18.

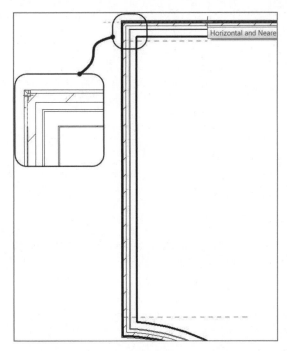

FIGURE 4.18:   The two reference planes are established.

Now you need to add a window based on the bottom reference plane. This window will then be arrayed up the wall to meet the northern reference plane. Here are the steps:

1. On the Architecture tab, click the Window button.

2. Change Element Type to Fixed: 24″ × 72″ (610mm × 1829mm).

3. Place the window approximately where it's shown in Figure 4.19. You have to move the window in alignment with the reference plane.

If you're drawing the reference plane and it keeps going above the wall (as opposed to below the wall), you can tap the spacebar as you're drawing. Doing so flips the side of the wall on which the plane is being drawn.

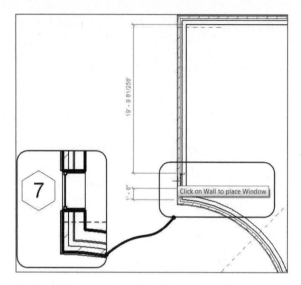

FIGURE 4.19:   Adding the window to be arrayed

4. Press the Esc key.

5. Select the window.

6. On the Modify | Windows tab, click the Move button.

7. Move the window from the bottom, outside corner down to the reference plane, as shown in Figure 4.20.

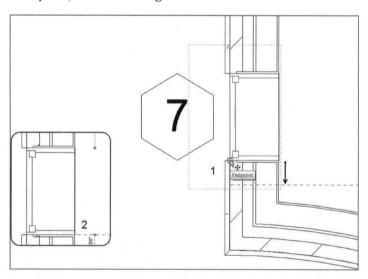

FIGURE 4.20:   Moving the window into position

8. Press Esc.

9. Zoom out until you can see the entire wall.

10. Select the window you just inserted into the wall.

11. On the Modify | Windows tab, click the Array button.

12. On the Options bar, select Linear, as shown in Figure 4.21.

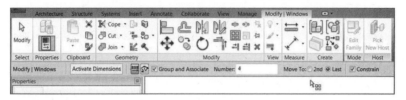

FIGURE 4.21: Choosing the linear array options

13. Select the Group And Associate check box (if it isn't already selected).

14. For Number, enter 4.

15. Select Move To: Last.

16. Pick the top endpoint of the bottom window.

17. Move your cursor up the wall, and pick a point perpendicular to the top reference plane, as shown in Figure 4.22.

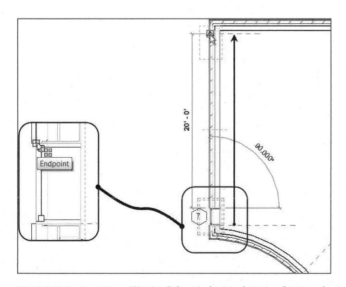

FIGURE 4.22: "Moving" the window to the top reference plane

18. After you pick the second point, you'll have to wait a moment; then Revit evenly fills the void with the two additional windows. Revit also gives you the option of adding more windows. Enter a value of 5, and press Enter (see Figure 4.23).

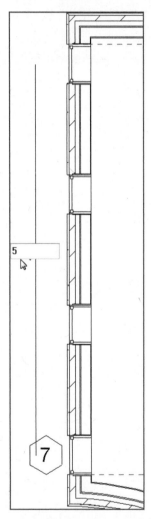

FIGURE 4.23: Changing the number of items in the array. You can always come back to the arrayed group and change this value at any time.

N O T E   After your items are grouped and arrayed, you can still move the end item. Not only can you move the end item in the direction of the array, but you can move it laterally to the array, causing a step in the array.

With the array completed, it's time to duplicate your efforts on the other side of the radial portion of this wall. As in CAD, at this point you have a few choices. You can repeat the Array command, copy the items, or mirror the items.

The Mirror Command

The Mirror command works exactly as expected: it makes a copy of an object or a group of objects in the opposite orientation of the first item(s). The crucial point to remember is that you'll need to specify a mirror *plane*.

Although you simply couldn't avoid using this command in previous chapters, we need to address and explore the Mirror command officially. The most useful aspect of the Mirror command is that if reference planes already exist in the model, you can pick these planes to perform the mirror, as opposed to sketching a new plane around which to mirror.

The objective of the following example is to mirror the windows to the south side of the west wall:

1. Zoom in on the windows you arrayed in the previous exercise.

2. Select the windows starting from the upper-left corner to the lower-right corner, as shown in Figure 4.24. Remember, you can look at the bottom-right corner of the Revit window to verify that you have five windows selected.

T I P   Oops! You selected the wall. That's okay. You don't need to press Esc and start your selection over. Simply hold down the Shift key and select the wall. It will become deselected.

3. On the Modify | Windows tab, click the Mirror - Pick Axis button, as shown in Figure 4.25.

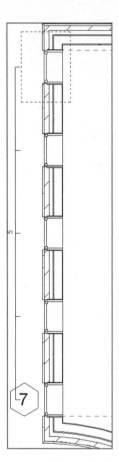

FIGURE 4.24:   Selecting the items to be mirrored. Make sure you don't select the wall in which the windows reside.

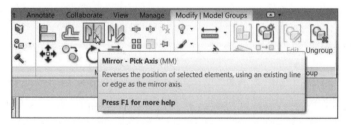

FIGURE 4.25:   The Mirror buttons appear when you select an item.

4. Position your cursor over the center reference plane that is part of the Radial array. When you pause, a tooltip indicates that you're about to select the reference plane. When you see this tooltip, select the reference plane, as shown in Figure 4.26.

5. Zoom out to check the placement of the windows. Don't assume that everything went as planned. Your Level 1 floor plan should resemble Figure 4.27.

N O T E   If the mirror went wrong or you aren't comfortable with the results, use the Undo button and try again. Now is the time to practice!

> When you pick the reference plane, Revit mirrors the entire group of windows.

The two straight walls have windows, and it's time to array some windows within the radial portion. The problem is, when you insert a window along a radius, you can't snap it to the intersection of the reference plane and the wall. This is where the Align tool becomes critical.

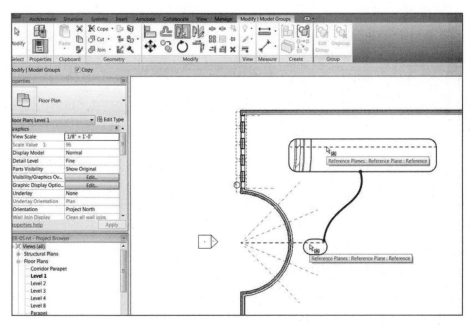

F I G U R E   4 . 2 6 :   The line you're going to pick is the reference plane shown here.

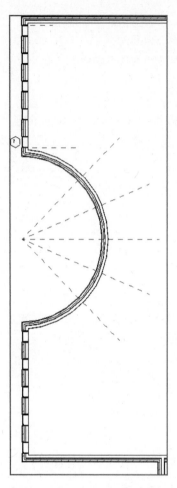

FIGURE 4.27:   The finished west wall

The Align Tool

You'll find yourself in situations where two items need to be aligned with one another. The Align command is a great tool for accomplishing this task. It's one of the most useful tools in Revit, and you'll use it extensively. Overuse of this command isn't possible! Because Align is a tool, you don't have to select an item first for this function to become available. You can select Align at any time.

To practice using the Align tool, follow along:

1. Zoom in on the radial portion of the west wall, as shown in Figure 4.28.

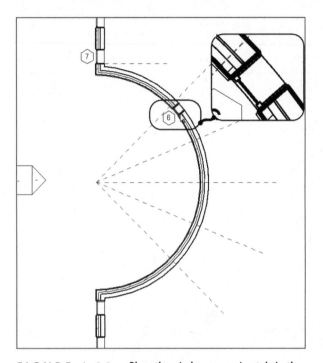

FIGURE 4.28: Place the window approximately in the area shown here.

2. On the Architecture tab, click the Window button.

3. In the Type Selector, choose Fixed: 16″ × 72″ (406mm × 1829mm).

4. Place the window in the radial wall in a location similar to that shown in Figure 4.28. Don't attempt to eyeball the center of the window with the reference plane. As a matter of fact, purposely misalign the window.

5. On the Modify | Place Window tab, click the Align button, as shown in Figure 4.29.

6. The Align tool needs you to select two items. First select the item you want to *align to*; pick the reference plane as shown in Figure 4.30.

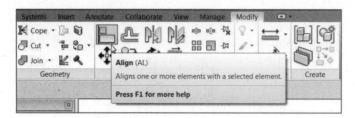

FIGURE 4.29:   Click the Align button on the Modify | Place Window tab.

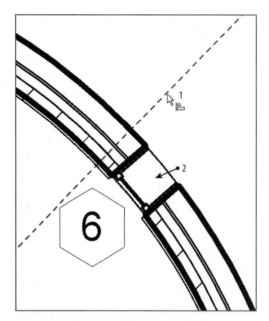

FIGURE 4.30:   Choosing the items for alignment. Remember that you must first choose the item you want to align to.

7. Now you need to pick a point on the window: the centerline of the window. By looking at the window, you won't see this line. Hover your cursor over the middle of the window, and a centerline becomes highlighted. When you see this centerline, pick the window.

   The window moves into alignment with the reference plane, as shown in Figure 4.31.

8. Press Esc, and then select the window.

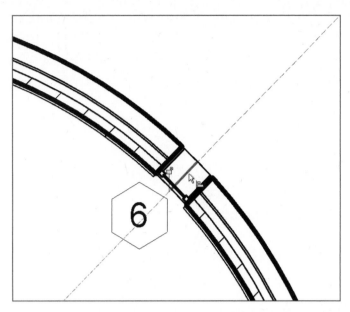

FIGURE 4.31: The window is now in alignment with the reference plane.

9. Pick the Array button on the Modify | Windows tab.

10. Create a radial array of the windows with a count of five (total). You remember how, right? The only thing I want you to do differently is to uncheck Group and Associate on the Options toolbar. We'll discuss groups in Chapter 22, "Project Collaboration."

N O T E   Adding reference planes and working in a controlled environment is very typical of Revit Architecture. You establish a reference plane, add a component, and then execute a command such as Array, Copy, or Move. Although it may seem like quite a few steps, you're now accurately and deliberately placing items in your model. The accuracy you apply here will propagate itself throughout the project in terms of elevations, sections, and drawing sheets.

Let's practice more with the Align tool. It's one of the most important modify tools in the Revit arsenal, and I don't want to understate its usefulness. Follow along with these steps:

1. Zoom in to the end of the corridor in the east wing of the building, as shown in Figure 4.32.

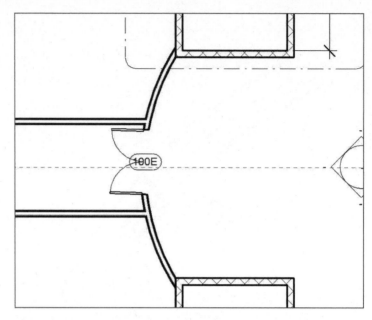

FIGURE 4.32:   Adding a double door to the east wing corridor

2. On the Architecture tab, click the Door button.

3. Place a Double Flush: 72″ × 84″ (1829mm × 2133mm) door in the radial corridor wall, as shown in Figure 4.32. As when you placed the window along the reference plane in the preceding procedure, don't try to eyeball the correct alignment; you want to misalign the door on purpose.

4. Renumber the door 100A.

5. On the Modify panel, click the Align button.

6. Pick the horizontal reference plane.

7. Pick the centerline of the door. When the reference plane is aligned, pause for a moment without pressing Esc. You see a little blue padlock. If you can't see it, zoom out a little. You can use this function to lock the alignment.

Another nice feature of the Align command is that, after your alignment is complete, you can physically lock the items together, allowing the two aligned items to move as one.

Locking an Alignment

After you've aligned the items, you'll notice that small, blue padlock icon I just mentioned. In Revit, you can lock items together using the Align tool. This is good and bad. It's great in the sense that, if the center reference plane moves for whatever reason, the door will also move. It's bad in the sense that, if the door moves, the center reference plane will also move.

When you align an item and lock it, be sure this is what you want to do. It's simple: pick the padlock icon, as shown in Figure 4.33. You're now aligned and locked to the center reference plane.

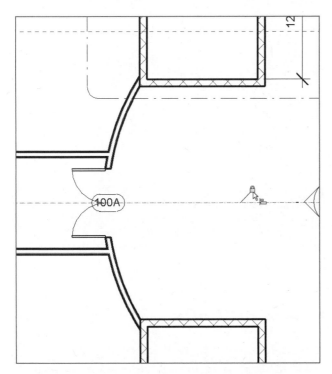

FIGURE 4.33: The door is now aligned and locked.

There will also be times when two items are already aligned, and you just want to lock the items together. To do this, you must still use the Align command to access the lock option:

1. Zoom in to the west side of the east wing at the corridor intersection.

2. Start the Align command.

3. Pick the centerline of the door at that end of the corridor.

4. Pick the center reference plane.

5. Pick the blue padlock to lock the doors to the center reference plane (see Figure 4.34).

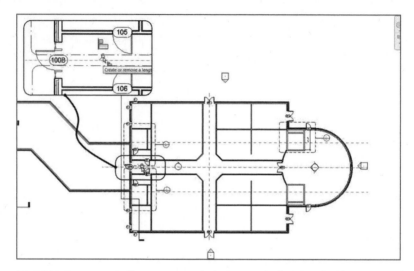

FIGURE 4.34:   You can create a locked constraint by using the Align command even if the items were in alignment to begin with.

Now that the Align command is out of the way, you can move on to the next item on the Modify tab: the Split Element command.

The Split Element Command

The Split Element command is the equivalent of the Break command in AutoCAD. You can use the Split Element command on walls and when you edit an element in Sketch Mode.

The objective of this procedure is to cut a notch out of a wall by using the Edit Profile function:

1. In the Project Browser, open the Sections (Building Section) called West Wing South Wall Section, as shown in Figure 4.35.

2. Select the wall beyond, as shown in Figure 4.36.

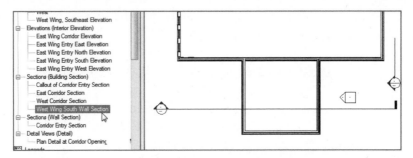

FIGURE 4.35: Open the section called West Wing South Wall Section.

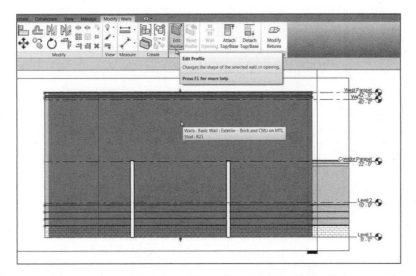

FIGURE 4.36: Select the wall beyond, and click the Edit Profile button on the Modify | Walls tab.

3. On the Modify | Walls tab, click the Edit Profile button (see Figure 4.36).

   After you select the Edit Profile option, you're put into Sketch Mode. You know you're in Sketch Mode because your Ribbon now has a Mode panel with Finish Edit Mode and Cancel Edit Mode options that you must select to return to the full model. Also, the wall you've selected now consists of four magenta sketch lines, and the rest of the model is shaded into the background.

4. On the Modify | Walls ➢ Edit Profile tab, click the Split Element button, as shown in Figure 4.37.

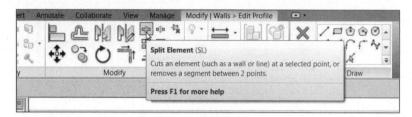

FIGURE 4.37: Select the Split Element button on the Modify | Walls ➢ Edit Profile tab.

5. Look at your Options bar. Notice that you can specify that you want to delete the inner segment. Select the Delete Inner Segment check box, as shown in Figure 4.38.

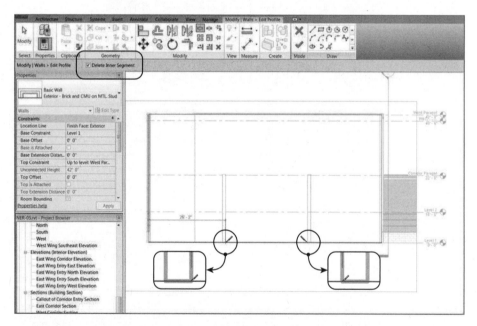

FIGURE 4.38: To remove a segment of a line, you must use the Split Element command and select Delete Inner Segment from the Options bar.

6. Pick the intersection of the bottom magenta sketch line and the inside face of the left wall for the first split point (see Figure 4.38).

7. Pick the intersection of the bottom magenta sketch line and the inside face of the right wall (see Figure 4.38).

You Can Also Add a Gap

There is a second split option. The Split With Gap function enables you to split an item and choose the size of the gap segment.

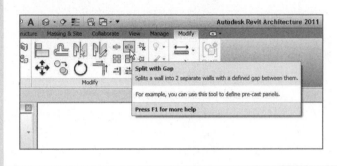

After you pick these points, the magenta sketch line is segmented. Now you need to add more lines to the sketch. To do this, leave the Split Element command and follow along by using the sketch tools on the Draw panel:

1. On the Draw panel of the Modify | Walls ➢ Edit Profile tab, click the Pick Lines icon, as shown in Figure 4.39.

2. Pick the inside face of the left wall (item 1 in Figure 4.39).

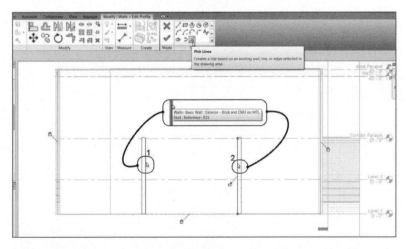

FIGURE 4.39: Tracing the walls to form a notch. This is done by selecting the Pick Lines icon and picking the walls.

3. Pick the inside face of the right wall (item 2 in Figure 4.39).

4. In the Offset field on the Options bar, add **1′-0″** (300mm).

5. Select the Corridor Parapet level, and offset the line down, as shown in Figure 4.40.

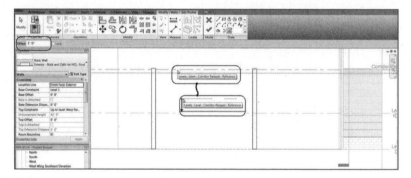

FIGURE 4.40:   Offsetting the Corridor Parapet level down 1′-0″ (300mm)

The next step is to get the magenta lines to form a continuous loop. This means there can be no gaps or overlapping lines. Each line starts exactly where the last line ends:

1. Press Esc.

2. Pick (left-click) the horizontal magenta line that is offset from the Corridor Parapet level.

3. On each end is a round, blue grip. Pick each grip, and stretch the line to the intersection of the vertical magenta lines, as shown in Figure 4.41.

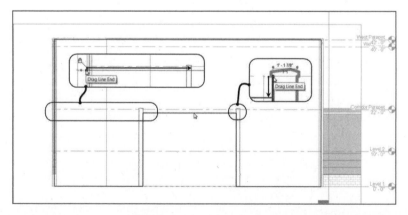

FIGURE 4.41:   Modifying the sketch lines by stretching the grips to form a continuous loop

4. Select the left, vertical magenta line, and stretch the top grip down to the intersection of the horizontal magenta line (see Figure 4.41).

5. Select the right, vertical magenta line, and stretch the top down to the horizontal magenta sketch line. You should now have a continuous loop (see Figure 4.41).

6. On the Mode panel of the Modify | Walls ➤ Edit Profile tab, click the Finish Edit Mode button, as shown in Figure 4.42.

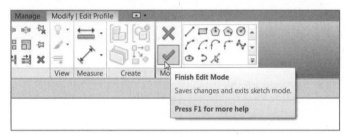

FIGURE 4.42: Click Finish Edit Mode to get back to the model.

7. Go to a 3D view to check out your model, as shown in Figure 4.43. You can either click the Default 3D View button on the Quick Access toolbar or pick the {3D} view from the Project Browser.

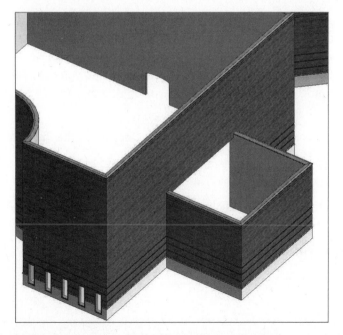

FIGURE 4.43: The building in 3D up to this point

REVIT WANTS IT CLEAN!

As mentioned earlier, if you click Finish Edit Mode and Revit gives you a warning, as shown in this graphic, you *must* be sure you have no overlapping lines or gaps in your sketch. Revit is quite unforgiving and won't allow you to proceed.

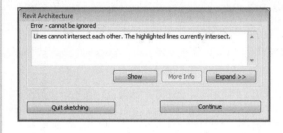

The next set of procedures focuses on basic cleanup using the Trim command. Although you can accomplish a lot with this single command, you must get used to a certain Revit method.

The Trim Command

Anytime you need to cut or extend an item, you'll use the Trim command. In any design-based application, you won't get very far without this command. Similar to the Split Element command, you can use the Trim command on walls and in Sketch Mode. As mentioned earlier, however, you need to understand specific procedures to be comfortable using this command.

To use the Trim command, follow along:

1. Go to Level 1 under the Floor Plans category in the Project Browser.

2. Zoom in on the east wing. Two walls extend beyond their destination. These walls need to be trimmed.

3. On the Modify tab, click the Trim/Extend Single Element button, as shown in Figure 4.44.

4. Zoom in on the area, as shown in Figure 4.45.

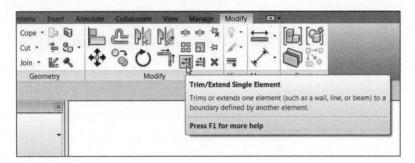

FIGURE 4.44: Click the Trim/Extend Single Element button on the Modify tab.

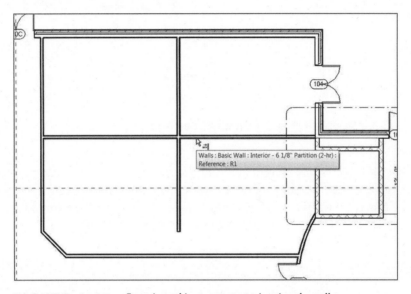

FIGURE 4.45: Zoom in to this area to start trimming the walls.

5. To trim the vertical wall back to the horizontal wall, you must first pick the wall that you want to trim. In this case, select the south face of the horizontal wall (see Figure 4.45).

6. Now you must pick a point along the vertical wall. The trick here is that you must pick a point on the side of the wall that you want to *keep*. Pick a point along the vertical wall above (north of) the horizontal wall, as shown in Figure 4.46. After you do, the wall is trimmed back.

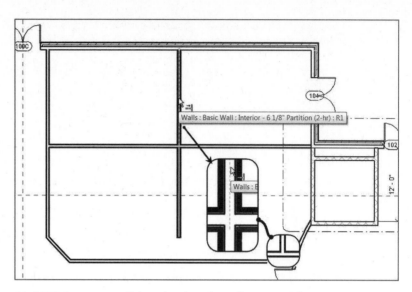

FIGURE 4.46:   Pick a point along the wall you want to keep.

7. Press Esc to terminate the command.

You may not always want to trim an item. Often, you need to elongate an item to reach a destination point. In the drafting world, this procedure is better known as *extend*. The process for using the Extend feature is similar to the Trim command. First, however, you must select the wall to which you want to extend an object, and then select the object to be extended:

1. Zoom in on the south part of the east wing.

2. On the Modify tab, click the Trim/Extend Single Element button.

3. Pick the south corridor wall. This is the wall to which you want to extend.

4. Pick the vertical wall that doesn't quite intersect. Press Esc, and your walls should now look like Figure 4.47.

5. Save the model.

There is one more command to examine that is used in the day-to-day modification of a Revit model. Most of the commands you've used to place items in the model have had the Offset command built into the options of that specific procedure. The next section focuses on offsetting items by using the stand-alone Revit Offset command.

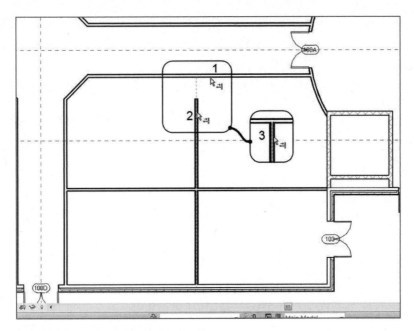

FIGURE 4.47:   The finished walls

The Offset Command

The Offset command enables you to create a copy of a linear item at a specified distance. As mentioned earlier, the need to offset an item crops up much less often in Revit Architecture than in a conventional drafting application. This is because, in Revit, most commands provide offset functionality as an option. Sometimes, however, you need the good old Offset command.

To get used to using the Offset command, follow these steps:

1. Zoom in on the west part of the east wing. This is the area where the restrooms are located (see Figure 4.48). The objective is to offset the vertical wall that is to the right of the restrooms, to the middle of the open space.

2. On the Modify panel of the Modify tab, click the Offset button, as shown in Figure 4.48.

3. On the Options bar, click the Numerical button.

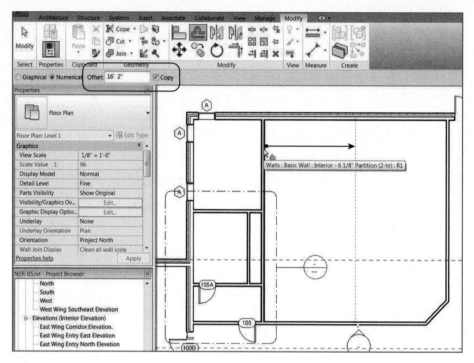

FIGURE 4.48: Choosing your options, and picking the wall to be offset

4. Enter 16′–2″ (4850mm) in the Offset field.

5. Make sure Copy is selected.

6. Hover your cursor over the wall to the right of the lavatory, as shown in Figure 4.48. A dashed alignment line appears to the right of the wall.

7. Pick the wall. The new wall should be in the middle of the large room.

8. Repeat the process for the walls south of the corridor. Your interior should resemble Figure 4.49.

WARNING   Be sure your math is correct. After you offset an item, use the Measure command. I've mentioned this before, and I will mention it repeatedly throughout this book! You'll be glad you measured now, rather than later.

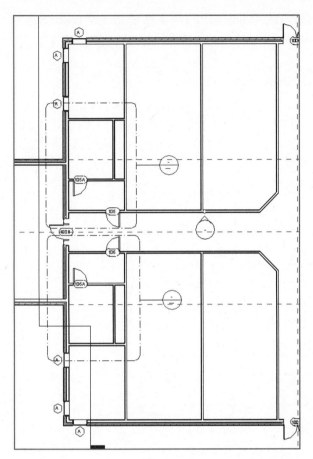

FIGURE 4.49: Completing the floor plan by using the Offset command will be a common procedure.

This concludes our discussion of Offset. Because this floor plan consists of items you want to repeat on other floors, you can now explore how to do this by using the Copy/Paste command from Windows.

Copy/Paste

Yes, this is the actual Microsoft Windows Copy/Paste function. In Revit Architecture, you'll use this feature quite a bit. There is no better way to complete a space or a layout on one level and then use that layout on another level than by copying the geometry.

To practice using the Copy/Paste function, you'll select the two lavatories on Level 1, copy them to the Windows Clipboard, and paste them to the remaining floors:

1. Zoom in to the east wing of the building.

2. Select the walls, door, and windows that define both bathrooms. Also select the corridor walls and the radial corridor wall at the east end of the building. Be sure to select the internal doors as well. These selections are shown in Figure 4.50.

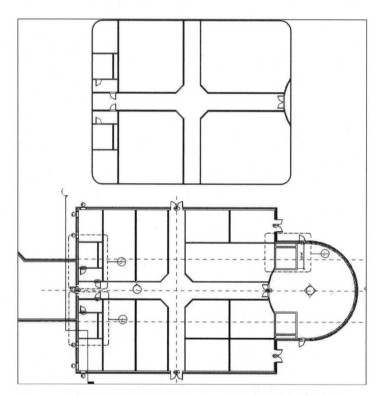

FIGURE 4.50: Selecting the items to be copied to the Clipboard

3. Choose Copy To Clipboard from the Clipboard panel of the Modify | Multi-Select tab (or press Ctrl+C).

4. Go to a 3D view.

5. On the Clipboard panel of the Modify | Multi-Select tab, expand the Paste tool and then click Aligned To Selected Levels, as shown in Figure 4.51.

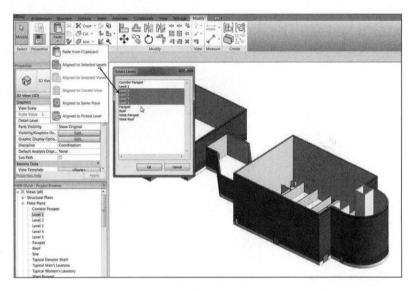

FIGURE 4.51: The Select Levels dialog box enables you to choose the levels to which you're pasting the information.

6. In the next dialog box, hold down the Shift key and select Floor Plan: Levels 2 through 5 (see Figure 4.51).

7. Click OK.

Your model should look like Figure 4.52. If it doesn't, go back and try the procedure again. If you did get it wrong, you can right-click and choose Select Previous. That way, you don't have to pick around all over again.

N O T E   Just because you copied and pasted identical items doesn't mean they're linked in any way. If you move, edit, or delete any of the original walls, the new walls you pasted won't be affected.

The last section in this chapter focuses on actual practice. You now have five floors in the east wing alone, and you must add a layout to them. You also need to add a layout to the west wing.

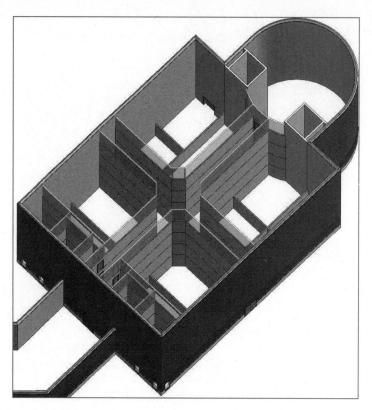

FIGURE 4.52:   The east wing is starting to come together.

You Must Heed the Warning!

While pasting elements, if you see a Warning dialog box indicating that you've just created a duplicate and that double counting will occur, stop and undo the paste. Determine why Revit issued that warning. Did you already paste these elements to this level? Sometimes the tops of the walls are above the higher level. You can check this as well.

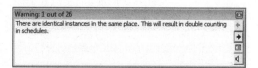

Creating the Plans

Now that you've added walls, doors, and windows, you can begin to combine this experience with your knowledge of the basic Revit editing commands. In the previous section, you *started* to lay out your floor plans.

You can follow along with the book's examples up to floor 3. You can then create your own plans for floors 4 and 5.

To start building a floor plan to be copied to other levels, follow these steps:

1. In the Project Browser, go to Level 1 under Floor Plans.

2. Add walls, doors, openings, and windows to resemble Figure 4.53. These doors and windows can be any type you like. If your model varies slightly from the example in the book, don't be concerned.

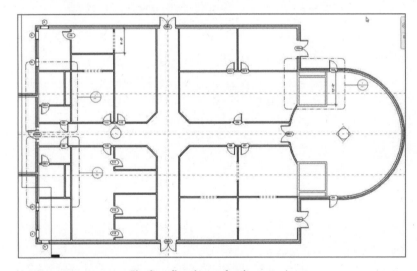

FIGURE 4.53: The first-floor layout for the east wing

3. In the Project Browser, go to Floor Plan Level 2.

4. Press Esc to clear any selection.

5. In the Properties dialog box, set Underlay to None, as shown in Figure 4.54. (Underlay is simply the floor below. You can set your underlay to any floor you'd like.)

FIGURE 4.54: Switch Underlay from Level 1 to None.

6. Set Detail Level to Fine.

7. Create a floor plan layout similar to Figure 4.55. Make all of the dimensions as even and as round as possible. Use all the commands and functions you've learned up to this point.

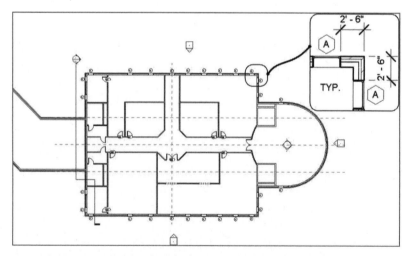

FIGURE 4.55: The layout for Level 2. Try to make the dimensions as even as possible, consistent with what is shown here.

8. Select the windows on Level 2, go to a 3D view and, using Copy and Paste ➤ Aligned to Selected Levels, align them all the way to Level 5. This way, you know your windows are aligned, and you can follow this procedure in your room layout for each floor (see Figure 4.56).

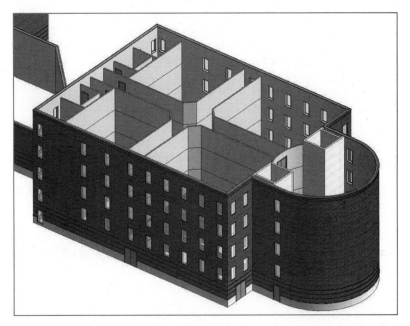

FIGURE 4.56: Using Copy/Paste, align the windows to the higher floors. This will influence your floor layout for each level.

WARNING   When you use Copy/Paste, you may get the same duplicate value warning mentioned earlier. If you do, stop and undo. Make sure you aren't pasting windows over other windows.

9. Go to Level 3, and create a floor plan similar to Figure 4.57. You can do this by using Paste ➤ Aligned To Selected Levels from Level 1. The floor plans are identical, other than the wall configuration in the northwest corner.

10. Go to Level 4, and create your own floor plan. The book will give no example. You're on your own!

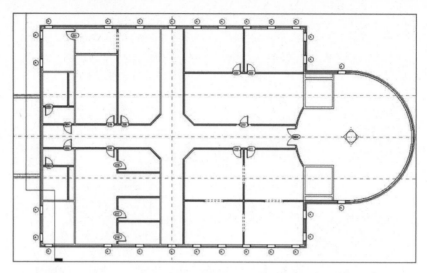

FIGURE 4.57: Level 3: This floor plan was mostly copied from Level 1, with the exception of the northwest corner.

11. Create one more floor plan for Level 5. Again, design your own layout. Be as creative as you wish.

12. Save the model.

If you got through that last procedure and you're happy with the results, you're well on your way to being efficient in Revit. This is because you just created a floor plan on your own. These last few steps were provided to prove that Revit can be quite intuitive when approached with a little experience.

If you aren't comfortable with your results in this section, that's okay. I had an uncomfortable feeling the first time I did this, as well. Take a deep breath, and go back through the steps where you think you got lost. Feel free to send me an e-mail if you have questions or concerns. My e-mail address is provided in the front of this book.

Are You Experienced?

Now you can...

- ☑ use common editing commands to alter the appearance of your model

- ☑ use reference planes to establish good, accurate methods of layout

- ☑ array items, and change the count, length, and radius if needed

- ☑ align items and keep them constrained

- ☑ use locks to constrain the alignment of one element to another

- ☑ split items to remove a segment or to turn one item into two

- ☑ use the Copy and Paste ➢ Aligned To Selected Levels commands to create multiple floors that are similar in layout

Dimensioning and Annotating

This chapter focuses on giving you the ability to dimension and annotate a model. After the novelty of having a really cool model in 3D wears off, you need to buckle down and produce some bid documents. This is where the Autodesk® Revit® Architecture program must prove its functionality. You should ask yourself, "Can Revit produce drawings consistent with what is acceptable according to national standards and—more important—my company's standards? And, if so, how do I get to this point?" These are the questions that owners and managers will be asking you. If you're an owner or a manager, then you should be asking yourself these questions.

▶ **Selecting and applying dimensioning**

▶ **Using dimensions as a layout tool**

▶ **Placing text and annotations**

Dimensioning

The answers to the questions I listed begin with dimensioning and annotations. This is where you can begin to make Revit your own. Also, in this chapter you'll find that dimensions take on an entirely new role in the design process.

I think you'll like dimensioning in Revit. It's almost fun … almost. Before you start, however, let's get one thing out of the way: you can't alter a dimension to display an increment that isn't true. Hooray! As you go through this chapter, you'll quickly learn that when you place a dimension, it becomes not only an annotation but a layout tool as well.

The Dimension command has six separate types: Aligned, Linear, Angular, Radial, Arc Length, and Diameter. Each is important in adding dimensions to a model, and each is covered separately in this section.

Let's get going. To begin, open the file in which you've been following along. If you didn't complete the example in Chapter 4, "Working with the Autodesk Revit Tools," go to the book's website at www.sybex.com/go/revit2014ner. From there you can browse to Chapter 5 and find the file called NER-05.rvt.

Aligned Dimensions

The most popular of all the Revit Architecture dimensions is the Aligned option. You'll use this type of dimension 75 percent of the time.

An aligned dimension in Revit enables you to place a dimension along an object at any angle. The resulting dimension aligns with the object being dimensioned. A linear dimension, in contrast, adds a dimension only at 0°, 90°, 180°, or 270°, regardless of the item's angle.

 N O T E   Metric users should not type in mm or other metric abbreviations when entering amounts suggested in the exercises. Revit won't accept such abbreviations. Simply enter the number provided within the parentheses.

To add an aligned dimension, perform these steps:

1. Go to the Level 1 floor plan.

2. Zoom in on the east wing of the building.

3. On the Annotate tab, click the Aligned button, as shown in Figure 5.1.

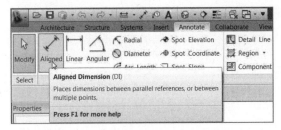

FIGURE 5.1: Starting the Aligned Dimension command from the Annotate tab

4. On the Options bar are two drop-down menus with some choices, as shown in Figure 5.2. Make sure Wall Faces is selected.

FIGURE 5.2: The Options bar for the Dimension command. Notice the Options button.

5. The next menu lets you pick individual references or entire walls. Select Entire Walls.

6. At far right on the Options bar is an Options button, which allows you to make further choices when selecting the entire wall. Click the Options button.

7. In the Auto Dimension Options dialog box, select Intersecting Walls (see Figure 5.3). Don't select any other item. Click OK.

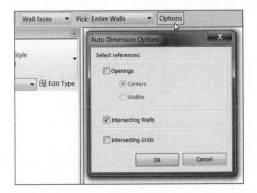

FIGURE 5.3: The Auto Dimension Options dialog box

8. Zoom in on the north wall, as shown in Figure 5.4.

9. Pick (left-click) the north exterior wall. Notice that the dimensions are completely filled out.

10. Pick a point (to place the dimension) approximately 8' (2400mm) above the north wall (see Figure 5.4).

11. In true Revit form, you're still in the command unless you tell Revit you don't want to be so. In this case, click the Options button on the Options bar (the same one you clicked before).

12. Deselect the Intersecting Walls option in the Auto Dimension Options dialog box, and click OK.

13. Pick (left-click) the same wall. You now have a dimension traveling the entire length of the building.

14. Move your cursor above the first dimension string you added. Notice that the dimension clicks when it gets directly above the first string.

15. When you see the dimension snap, pick that point (see Figure 5.5).

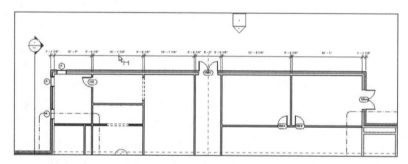

FIGURE 5.4: By choosing the Entire Walls option, you can add an entire string of dimensions in one click.

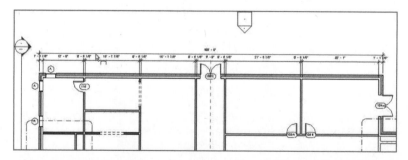

FIGURE 5.5: Adding a major dimension by turning off the Intersecting Walls choice in the Auto Dimension Options dialog box

In many cases, you'll need the ability to pick two points to create a dimension. What a world it would be if everything were as easy as the dimension string you just added. Unfortunately, it isn't.

Creating Aligned Dimensions by Picking Points

Nine times out of ten, you'll be picking two points to create a dimension. This is usually quite simple in Revit—until you get into a situation where the walls are at an angle other than 90°. In a moment, you'll explore that issue, but for now, let's add some straight dimensions:

N O T E   Before you get started, note that this procedure isn't easy. If it does come easily to you, great! If not, don't get discouraged. Keep trying.

1. Zoom in on the northeast portion of the east wing, as shown in Figure 5.6.

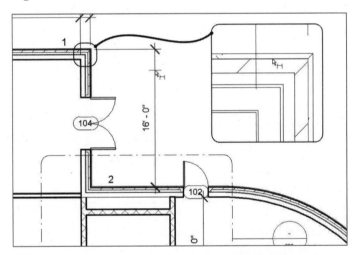

FIGURE 5.6:   Placing the dimension by picking two objects

2. On the Annotate tab, click the Aligned button if it isn't selected already.

3. On the Options bar, choose Individual References from the Pick menu, as shown previously in Figure 5.2, and do the following:

   a. Pick the north wall marked 1 in Figure 5.6.

   b. Pick the horizontal wall that ties into the radial wall, marked 2 in Figure 5.6.

   c. Place the dimension about 8′ (2400mm) to the right of the vertical wall, as shown in Figure 5.6.

4. With the Aligned Dimension command still running, do the following:

   a. Pick the outside face of the northern wall.

   b. Pick the centerline of the door, as shown in Figure 5.7, but don't press Esc or terminate the command.

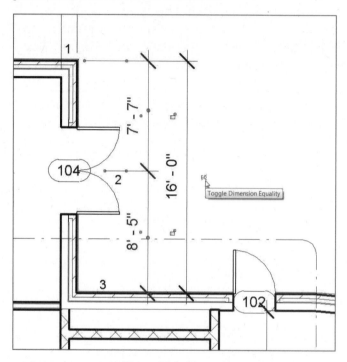

FIGURE 5.7:   Adding a dimension string manually

   c. Pick the horizontal wall that ties into the radial wall, marked 3 in Figure 5.7.

   d. Pick a point inside (to the left of) the first dimension (see Figure 5.7). This places the dimension string and finalizes the session.

   WARNING   When you add a string of dimensions, you must not stop and then resume the dimension string in the middle of the command. As you'll see in a moment, when you add dimensions in a continuous line, you can do a lot in terms of making adjustments to the objects you're dimensioning.

The actual dimension values are blue. You also see a blue EQ icon with a slash through it (see Figure 5.7).

5. Click the blue EQ button, as shown in Figure 5.8. If the door was not exactly centered, this will force the door to move to an equal distance between the two walls.

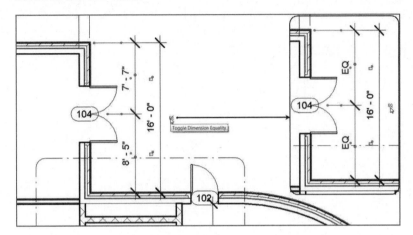

FIGURE 5.8: You can use the dimension string to move the door by clicking the EQ button.

6. Press Esc twice, or click Modify.

Sometimes you may want to display the dimensions rather than the EQ that Revit shows as a default. To do so, follow along:

1. Select the dimension.

2. Right-click.

3. Choose EQ Display (this deselects the option), as shown in Figure 5.9.

The dimensions will now show an increment.

Pretty cool. I should address one last item involving aligned dimensions: how do you dimension along an angle?

Dimensioning an Angle

No, not an *angel*, an angle. Adding this type of aligned dimension isn't the easiest thing to do in Revit. This is why I'm addressing the process as a separate item in this book. Here are the steps:

1. Zoom in on the 45° corridor area (the portion of the east building where the corridors meet), as shown in Figure 5.10.

2. On the Annotate tab, click the Aligned button on the Dimension panel.

Another way to tell Revit how to display dimensions is to select the dimension and then look at the properties. Here you'll be given additional choices.

3. On the Options bar, be sure Pick is set to Individual References.

4. Hover your pointer over the inside face of the brick in the angled wall (see Figure 5.10).

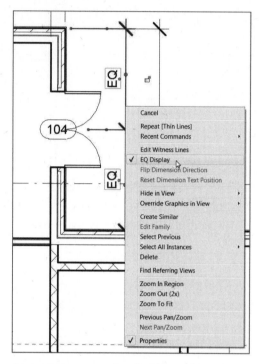

FIGURE 5.9: Toggle off the EQ Display.

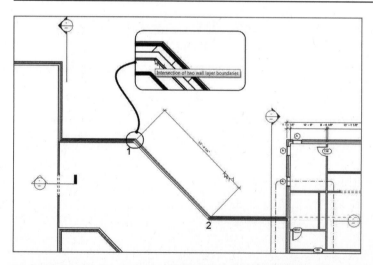

FIGURE 5.10: Press the Tab key to select the point shown.

5. Tap the Tab key until you see the square grip appear. You can also look down to the lower-left corner: the status bar gives you some guidance, as well.

N O T E   By tapping the Tab key, you tell Revit to filter through different points. When you arrive at the square grip, Revit can dimension the angled wall.

6. When the square grip appears, pick it (see Figure 5.10).

7. Move to the other intersection of the angled wall.

8. Hover your cursor over this core intersection, as shown in Figure 5.11.

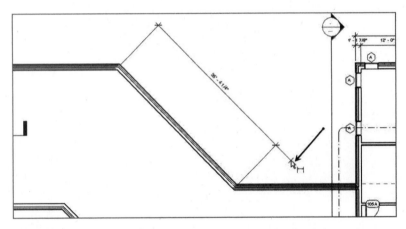

FIGURE 5.11:   Picking the second point along the wall and placing the dimension

9. Tap the Tab key until you see the same square grip.

10. Pick the square grip.

11. Now the dimension is following your pointer. Pick a third point about 8′ (2400mm) away from the angled wall (see Figure 5.11).

12. On the left end of the Ribbon, click the Modify button. This ends the command.

Unfortunately, you had to dimension to the core of the wall. This is the last place from which you would ever need to take a dimension. The dimension needs to be stretched to the outside/finished face of the brick, as you'll see next.

Editing the Witness Line

Every dimension in Revit Architecture has its own grip points when selected. This is similar to most CAD applications. Two of these grips control the witness line. The *witness line* is the line "attached" to the item being dimensioned. Because you had to take this dimension from the core of the wall, the witness lines need to be dragged to the outside face of the brick. Follow these steps:

1. Select the angled dimension. The blue grips appear.

2. On the left side of the dimension, pick and hold the grip in the middle of the dimension line, as shown in Figure 5.12.

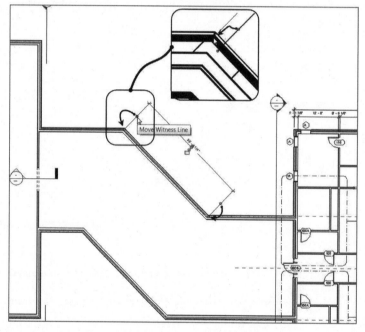

FIGURE 5.12: Dragging the witness line's grip

3. Drag the blue grip to the outside face of the brick. You'll know you're in the right spot because you'll see a small dot appear, as shown in the magnified segment of Figure 5.12.

4. Repeat the procedure for the other side.

Trust me—this is worth practicing now, before you get into a live situation. If you've already run into this, you know exactly what I mean.

Let's look at one more procedure for tweaking an aligned dimension: overriding a dimension's precision.

Overriding the Precision

When you dimension a wall at an angle such as this, the dimension usually comes out at an uneven increment. In most cases, you don't want to override every dimension's precision just to make this one, lone dimension read properly. In this situation, you want to turn to the dimension's Type Properties:

1. Select the angled dimension.

2. In the Properties dialog, click the Edit Type button, as shown in Figure 5.13.

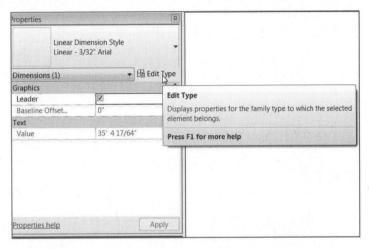

FIGURE 5.13: Clicking the Edit Type button to begin creating a new dimension style

3. Click the Duplicate button, as shown in Figure 5.14.

4. In the Name dialog box that opens, name the new dimension style **Linear - 3/32" Arial - 1/4" precision.** For metric users, it's **Linear - 2mm Arial-10mm precision.** Click OK.

5. Scroll down to the Text category. Near the bottom is a Units Format row with a button that displays a sample increment. Click it (see Figure 5.14).

6. In the Format dialog box, deselect the Use Project Settings option.

7. Choose To The Nearest 1/4" (To The Nearest 10) from the Rounding drop-down menu (see Figure 5.15).

8. Click OK twice. Note the new value on the dimension at the angled wall.

Although aligned dimensions will bear the brunt of your dimensioning, there are plenty of other dimension types for you to use.

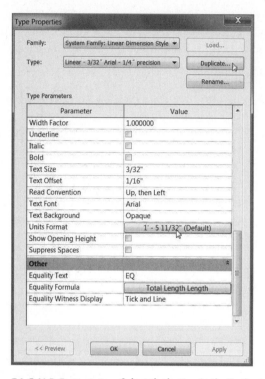

FIGURE 5.14: Select the button in the Text category to access the dimension's precision.

FIGURE 5.15: Changing the dimension's precision. Note some of the other available choices.

Linear Dimensions

Linear dimensions are used less frequently than most of the other dimensions. Unlike Autodesk® AutoCAD®, in which linear dimensions are the go-to dimensions, they're on the bench for most of the game in Revit. The best use for a linear dimension is to put a straight dimension across nonlinear (angled) geometry, as follows:

1. Zoom back in on the corridor area.

2. On the Annotate tab, click the Linear button. Notice that you can't select the entire wall. That option has been taken away. Instead, Revit requires you to pick a point.

3. Move your cursor over the inside corner, at the bottom intersection of the corridor. Make sure you're exactly over the exterior intersection of the brick. You'll know you're there when the blue dot appears, as shown in Figure 5.16.

4. When you see the dot, pick the corner.

5. Pick the same spot on the other end of the wall, as shown in Figure 5.17. When you pick the second corner, the dimension follows your cursor in a straight direction.

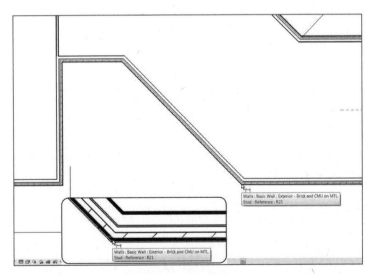

FIGURE 5.16: Select the finished exterior corner of the brick. You'll see a small blue dot appear, indicating that you can pick the start of the dimension.

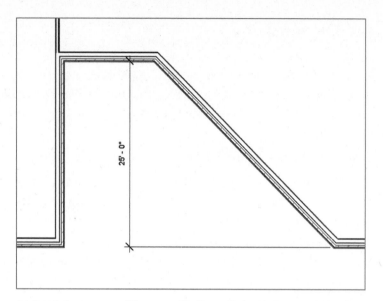

FIGURE 5.17: When you add a linear dimension to an angled wall, you get a straight dimension.

6. Move your cursor to the left, approximately 8′ (2400mm) past the first point you picked, and pick the third point to place the dimension (see Figure 5.17).

Aligned and linear dimensions are the two dimension styles that pertain to straight dimensioning. The next three dimension procedures add dimensions to angled and radial geometry.

Angular Dimensions

Angular dimensioning comes close to needing no introduction at all, but I'll introduce it anyway. Angular dimensions are used to calculate and record the angle between two items. These two items are usually walls. You'll add an angular dimension to your lovely corridor walls in the following steps:

1. Zoom back in on the corridor if you aren't there already.

2. On the Dimension panel, click the Angular button, as shown in Figure 5.18.

3. For the first wall, pick the finished, inside face of the angled corridor wall, which is marked 1 in Figure 5.18.

4. Pick the finished, inside face of the north corridor wall, marked 2 in Figure 5.18.

5. Move your cursor to the left about 8' (2400mm), and place the dimension marked 3 in Figure 5.18.

6. Press Esc.

7. Repeat the steps for the bottom of the corridor.

8. Add the rest of the dimensions, as shown in Figure 5.19. This completes the dimensioning of the corridor area.

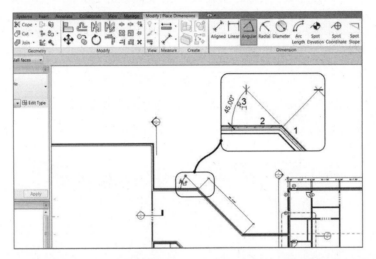

FIGURE 5.18: Placing an angular dimension involves picking two walls and then a point to place the dimension.

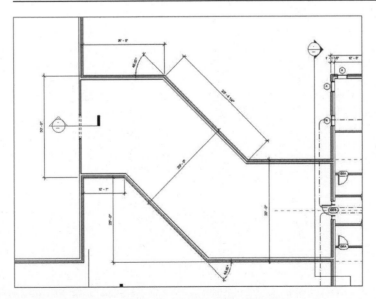

FIGURE 5.19: Finish placing the corridor dimensions.

If you would like to place the dimensions in different locations, feel free to do so. The next set of dimensions pertains to radial geometry. You can finally get out of this corridor!

Radial Dimensions

Keep in mind that you can add an angular dimension to physically change the angle of the items being dimensioned. Use caution, however, and be sure the correct items are being moved when you alter the angle.

Radial dimensions are used to, well, measure the radius of an item. You're lucky that Revit knows you're adding a radial dimension to a building component. This means the many different choices provided by a CAD application are taken away, leaving just the basics.

The following procedure will lead you through adding a radial dimension:

1. Zoom in on the east radial entry in the east wing.

2. On the Annotate tab, click the Radial button.

3. Pick the outside face of the radial wall, as shown in Figure 5.20.

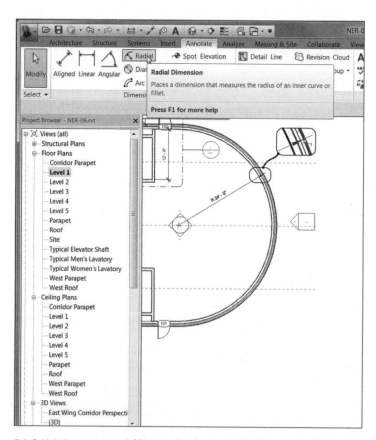

FIGURE 5.20: Adding a radial dimension is about as straightforward as it gets.

4. Place the radial dimension somewhere that makes sense. If your model looks like Figure 5.20, you may proceed. If it doesn't, go back and try again.

5. Pan all the way to the west radial end of the west wing, as shown in Figure 5.21.

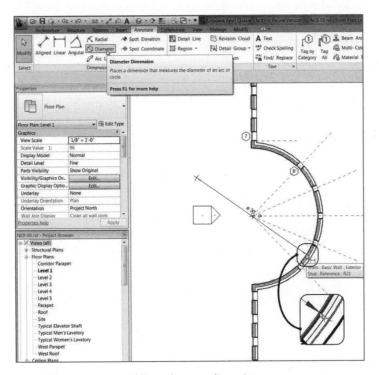

FIGURE 5.21: Adding a diameter dimension

6. On the Annotate tab, click the Diameter button, as shown in Figure 5.21.

7. Dimension to the finished outside face of the brick, and place your dimension in a location similar to that shown in Figure 5.21.

WARNING   All too often, you can easily dimension from the wrong reference point. This book uses a wall with a concrete ledge below the brick in order to emphasize that you need to be very deliberate in how and where you choose your references for dimensions. Don't be afraid to zoom in and out as you add dimensions.

If you're careful in how you add a radial dimension, you'll find this process quite simple. The next type of dimension, however, can be a little tricky.

Arc Length Dimensions

Measuring the length of an arc is a handy capability that was added back in the 2009 release. I have found the arc length dimension extremely useful in locating items such as windows along an arc. That is, in fact, what you need to do in the west wing of the building.

The following procedure will lead you through adding an arc length dimension:

1. Zoom in on the west radial entry of the west wing, as shown in Figure 5.22.

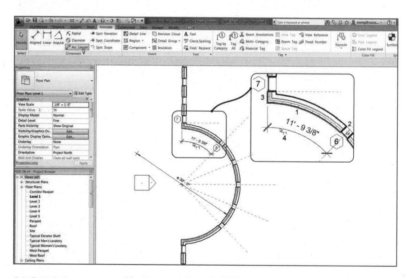

FIGURE 5.22: Placing an arc length dimension involves four separate picks.

2. On the Annotate tab, click the Arc Length button, as shown at upper left in Figure 5.22.

3. Pick the finish face exterior face of the brick on the radial wall marked 1 in Figure 5.22.

4. Pick the centerline of the uppermost window in the radial wall, marked 2. The NO symbol won't change, but you'll be able to pick the window centerline.

5. Pick a point along the exterior face of brick that runs along the vertical intersecting wall, marked 3 in Figure 5.22.

6. Pick a point at which to place the dimension, marked 4.

Let's try it again. This time the dimension will be taken from the first window (the one you just dimensioned) to the second window. The process is exactly the same:

1. On the Annotate tab, click the Arc Length button if you aren't still in the command.

2. Pick the exterior face of the brick along the radial wall.

3. Pick the first window's centerline again.

4. Pick the second window's centerline.

5. Pick a point to place the dimension (see Figure 5.23).

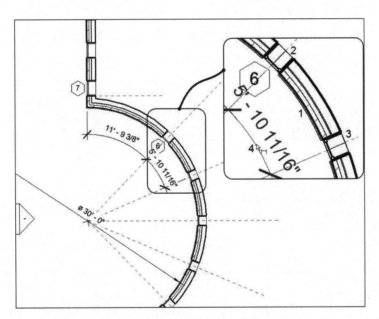

FIGURE 5.23: Adding a second arc length dimension

Now that you have experience adding dimensions to record the placement of items, it's time to see how you can physically use dimensions as a layout tool.

Using Dimensions as a Layout Tool

When it comes to dimensions, using them as a layout tool is my favorite topic. "Okay, fine," you may say. "I can do that in CAD." Well, not quite. You see, in Revit you can't alter a dimension to reflect an increment that isn't accurate. You can, however, select the item you're dimensioning and then type a new number in the dimension. At that point, the item you're dimensioning will move. The result is an accurate dimension.

The first task you need to explore is how to constrain a string of dimensions equally. You were exposed to this task earlier in the chapter, but now let's really dig in and gain some tangible experience using this tool.

For this procedure, you'll add some more walls to the west wing and then constrain them by using the EQ dimension function:

1. In the Project Browser, go to the Level 1 floor plan (not a ceiling plan!).

2. Zoom in to the west wing of the building.

3. Draw two interior-partition (2-hr) corridor walls, as shown in Figure 5.24.

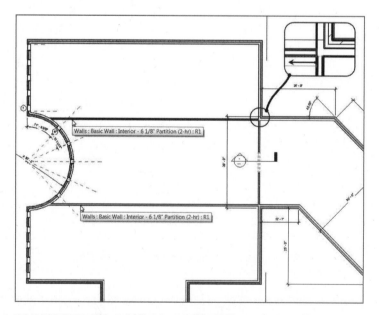

FIGURE 5.24:   Adding two corridor walls

4. Draw five more walls, as shown in Figure 5.25. They don't have to be an equal distance from one another.

WALLS KIND OF STICKY?

If you don't intend to draw continuous lines, check out the Options bar and uncheck the Chain button. This allows you to draw separate walls with just two clicks.

5. On the Annotate tab, click the Aligned button (see Figure 5.26).

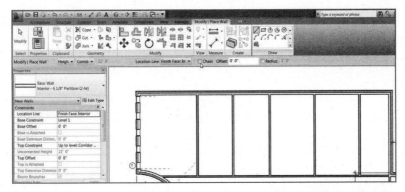

FIGURE 5.25: Place these walls as quickly as possible, and don't worry about their spacing.

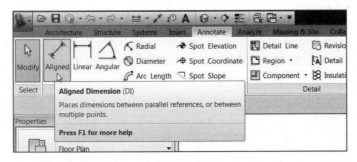

FIGURE 5.26: Changing the options for the dimension

6. On the Options bar, be sure Justification is set to Center Of Core.

7. Zoom in on the left exterior wall, as shown in Figure 5.27.

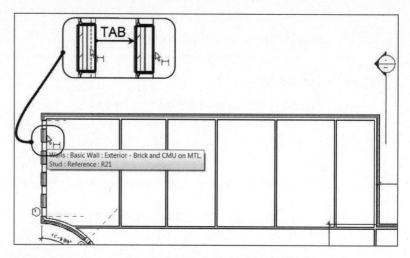

FIGURE 5.27: Press the Tab key to filter to the desired reference of the wall.

8. Hover your pointer over the wall. Do you notice that Revit is trying to locate the center of the wall? In this instance, you don't want this (even though you just told Revit to do that). You want Revit to start this dimension string by using the interior face of the finished wall. To do this, hover your pointer over the inside face of the wall (see Figure 5.27).

9. Tap the Tab key until Revit highlights the inside face of the wall.

10. Pick the inside face of the wall.

11. Move your cursor to the right until you pass over the first interior wall. Notice that the core centerline of the interior is highlighted, as shown in Figure 5.28. When you see this, pick the wall.

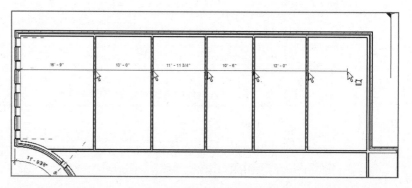

FIGURE 5.28: Adding a string of dimensions to the interior walls

W A R N I N G   Just as when you equally constrained the door in the previous procedure, you need to keep the Dimension command running. If you press Esc, undo the last dimension and start over.

12. After you pick the first interior partition, move to the right and pick the center of the next wall.

13. Repeat the procedure until you get to the last wall (see Figure 5.28).

When you reach the exterior wall to the right, you'll encounter the same issue as in steps 8–9. You want this string of dimensions to go to the inside face, not the core of the exterior wall. To finally finish the dimension string, go through the following procedure:

1. Hover your cursor over the inside face of the wall, and tap the Tab key until the inside face of the wall becomes highlighted, as shown in Figure 5.29.

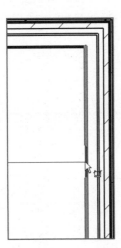

F I G U R E   5 . 2 9 :   Press Tab to locate the inside face of the wall.

2. When you locate the inside face, pick it.

3. Move your cursor up the view. The entire dimension string follows.

4. Placing a dimension in Revit is a little awkward, but you'll get the hang of it. You need to pick a point away from the last dimension in the string, as shown in Figure 5.30, almost as if you're trying to pick another item that isn't there. When you do this, the dimension will be in place.

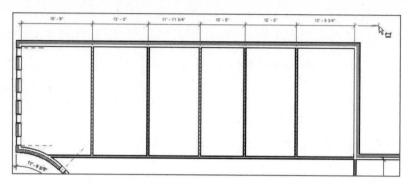

FIGURE 5.30: Pick a point away from the last dimension to place the string.

With the dimension string in place, let's move these walls so they're equal distances from one another. After you placed the dimension string, the familiar blue icons appeared. You can use them as follows:

If you placed the dimension string and then escaped out of the command, that's fine. You can simply select the string of dimensions again, and you'll be back in business.

1. Find the EQ icon in the middle of the dimension string, and pick it. The slash through it is now gone, and the walls have moved, as shown in Figure 5.31.

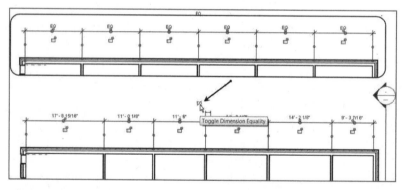

FIGURE 5.31: Before and after the EQ icon is selected

2. Press Esc twice to release the selection and exit the Aligned Dimension command.

Because these walls are constrained always to be equal, if one wall is moved, these five interior partitions will always maintain an equal relationship to one another—that is, as long as this dimension string is still associated with the walls.

In Revit Architecture, you can choose to keep the walls constrained or to use the dimension only as a tool to move the walls around.

Constraining the Model

Choices you make early in the design process, such as constraining a model, can either greatly benefit or greatly undermine the project's flow. As you gain more experience using Revit Architecture, you'll start hearing the term *overconstrained*. This is a term for a model that has been constrained in so many places that any movement of the model forces multiple warnings and, in many cases, errors that can't be ignored.

Given that, how you choose to constrain your model is up to you. You'll learn how to constrain (and, of course, *un*constrain) your model in this section, but deciding when and where to constrain your model will vary from project to project.

Unconstraining the Walls

The string of equal dimensions you now have in place has created a constraint with these walls. To unconstrain them, follow along:

1. Select the dimension string.

2. Press the Delete key on your keyboard.

3. Revit gives you a warning, as shown in Figure 5.32. You must choose whether to unconstrain the elements.

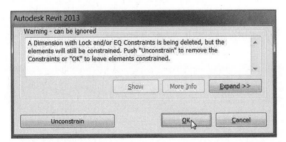

FIGURE 5.32: A Revit warning pertaining to the constraint of the walls

If you click the Unconstrain button, the EQ dimension will disappear as well as any constraint on the walls. If you move the exterior wall, the newly spaced walls won't reposition themselves.

OUT OF SIGHT, OUT OF MIND

In CAD, you type **E** and then press Enter to delete an item. This is no longer a good idea. If you do this to an item in Revit Architecture, you'll remove that element only from the current view—not from the entire model. You're better off either selecting the item and pressing the Delete key or selecting the item and clicking the Delete icon, as shown in this image.

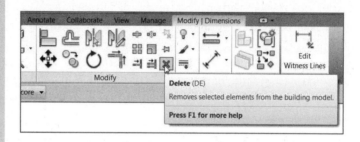

4. Click OK. You'll learn how to unconstrain these walls via a different method.

5. Select one of the interior walls that were part of the EQ dimension string.

6. The EQ icon appears. Click it to release the constraint set for the walls (see Figure 5.33). You're now free to move around the building. (Note that the EQ icon may be hiding behind a wall in the middle of the array. Zooming out will make the icon larger and easier to pick.)

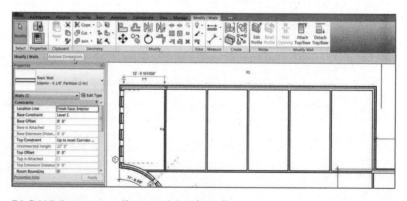

FIGURE 5.33: Unconstraining the walls

N O T E Sometimes, when you select an item that is being constrained, the dimensions are already activated and the Options bar doesn't provide the Activate Dimensions button. If you don't see the Activate Dimensions button on the Options bar for this example, your dimensions have been activated already.

T I P Notice in the figure the anchor icon to the left of the dimensions. You use this icon to determine which wall will remain stationary. You can move the anchor icon to any of the items involved in the constraint. For example, if you click and drag the anchor to the middle partition and then move one of the other constrained walls, the middle partition will stay in place while the other walls move an equal distance to the right and left of the anchored wall.

Now that you have experience with dimension equality constraints, it's time to learn about a different type of constraint that involves locking items together at a distance.

Locking a Dimension

At times you may want always to hold a dimension, no matter what else is going on around it. You can do this by physically adding a dimension to an item and then locking that dimension in place. For example, if you want to lock the middle space to a specific dimension, you simply add a dimension and lock it down. Sound easy? It is!

1. On the Annotate tab, click the Aligned button.

2. In the Properties dialog, select the Linear - 3/32″ Arial - 1/4″ Precision dimension style, as shown in Figure 5.34.

3. On the Options bar, change the alignment to Wall Faces.

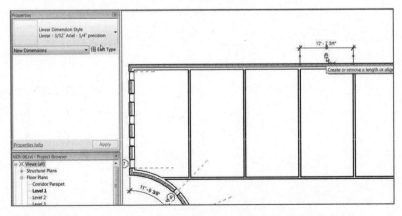

F I G U R E 5 . 3 4 : You can add a dimension and lock the distance between two items.

4. Pick the inside faces of the two middle partitions, as shown in the upper-left corner of Figure 5.34.

5. After you place the dimension, a blue padlock icon appears. Pick it. It should change to a locked padlock icon. When it does, press Esc twice or click Modify to terminate the command.

6. Select the left wall that has been dimensioned.

7. Move the wall to the right 2′ (600mm). Notice that the right wall moves as well. If you get a "constraints are not satisfied" message, you need to go back and un-EQ the five walls.

8. Click the Undo button, as shown in Figure 5.35.

9. Delete the dimension.

10. When you get the warning, click the Unconstrain button.

11. Save the model.

12. Add doors and windows to the plan, as shown in Figure 5.36. They can be any type of door or window you choose—just try to keep them similar to the ones in Figure 5.36. Also, placement doesn't matter. You'll adjust this in the next procedure.

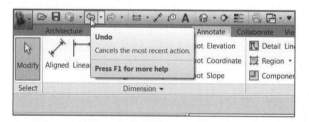

FIGURE 5.35: Click the Undo button.

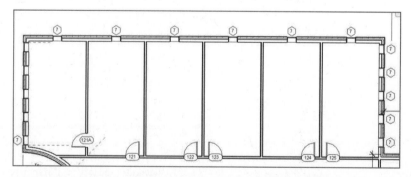

FIGURE 5.36: Adding doors and windows to the floor plan

In the next section, you'll start using dimensions as a tool to move elements around physically. Although this might seem like an exercise in futility, the practice is relevant to what you'll encounter in future projects.

Using Dimensions to Move Objects

As I have mentioned before, you can't type over a dimension and cause the value in that dimension to be inaccurate. Revit does provide tools to get around this. When you add a dimension and select the object being dimensioned, the dimension turns blue. This is a temporary dimension, which can be edited. Consequently, the object being dimensioned will move.

The objective of this procedure is to select an item and modify the temporary dimension, in effect moving the object:

1. Zoom in on the left side of the west wing, as shown in Figure 5.37.

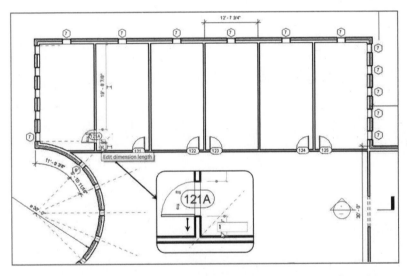

FIGURE 5.37:   When you type a different value, the temporary dimension moves the object.

2. Select the door (see Figure 5.37). There is a blue dimension on each side of the door. These are temporary dimensions.

3. Pick the blue text in the lower temporary dimension (see Figure 5.37). The text might be obscured by the wall, but if you hover over it, it will activate, and then you can select it.

4. Type 1 (300). For Imperial users, this is the equivalent of 1′–0″ (300 mm). The door moves.

5. Press the Esc key to release the door.

This procedure used a temporary dimension that appeared when you selected the item. After you edited the dimension, it went away. In the next procedure, you'll add a permanent dimension and do the same thing:

1. On the Annotate tab, select the Aligned button.

2. Place a dimension between the door and the wall, as shown in Figure 5.38.

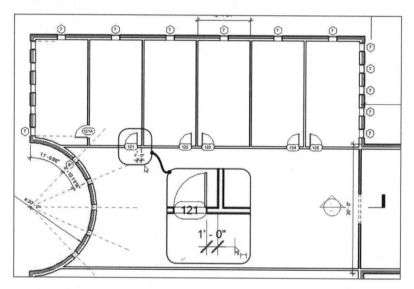

FIGURE 5.38:   Placing a dimension

3. Press the Esc key twice.

4. Select the door shown in Figure 5.39. The dimension turns small and blue: it's ready to be modified.

5. When the dimension turns blue, select the text and type 6″ (150mm). The door adjusts to the 6″ (150mm) increment.

6. Press the Esc key, or click anywhere in open space to clear the selection.

7. Select the dimension.

8. There is a blue grip just underneath the text. Pick the grip, and move the text out from between the extension lines, as shown in Figure 5.40. Revit places a *leader* (an arrow line extending from the model to your text) in the text.

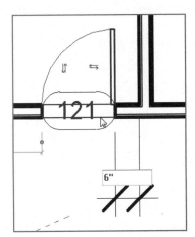

FIGURE 5.39: Making adjustments with the actual dimension

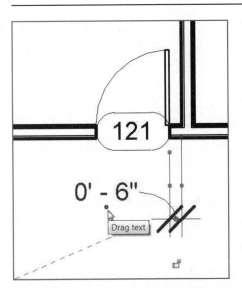

FIGURE 5.40: By grip-editing the text, you can slide it to a cleaner location. Revit automatically places a leader from the text to the dimension line.

The process of using dimensions to move objects takes some getting used to. The next procedure delves into making further modifications to dimensions and provides a nice fail-safe procedure embedded within the Dimension Properties.

Using Dimension Text Overrides

Although I just told you that you can't override a dimension, the following steps get around that problem. In many cases, you may want text or, more commonly, a prefix or a suffix within a dimension. You can do all three in Revit Architecture:

1. Select the 6″ (150mm) dimension.

2. The text turns blue. As you know, blue means this item is editable in Revit. Pick the text. You should see a dialog box like the one in Figure 5.41.

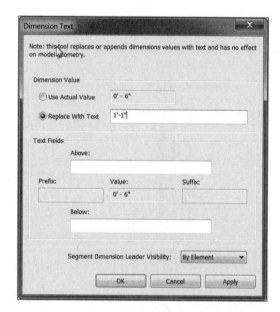

FIGURE 5.41: The Dimension Text dialog box

3. Under Dimension Value, click Replace With Text.

4. Type 1′–1″ (325mm), and press Enter.

5. You get an Invalid Dimension Value message, as shown in Figure 5.42. Revit won't allow you to do such a foolish thing. Click Close.

The fact that Revit displays temporary dimensions lends itself to another common process: the double-check. All you need to do in Revit Architecture is select any item, and the temporary dimensions will appear. (If not, remember to click Activate Dimensions on the Options bar.) You can simply look at the dimension.

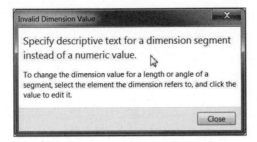

FIGURE 5.42: Any numeric value triggers a warning in Revit. You simply can't type a value over a dimension.

6. In the Dimension Text dialog box, select Use Actual Value.

7. Under Suffix, type **TYP.**, as shown in Figure 5.43.

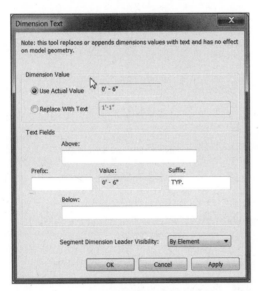

FIGURE 5.43: Under Dimension Value, choose Use Actual Value, and type TYP. as the suffix.

8. Click OK.

As a closing practice for dimensioning, move the rest of the doors along this wall to a 6″ (150mm) increment from the finished, inside face of the wall to the door opening. Also, dimension the floor plan as shown in Figure 5.44 and Figure 5.45.

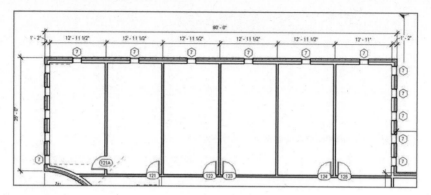

FIGURE 5.44: The dimensional layout for the north part of the west wing

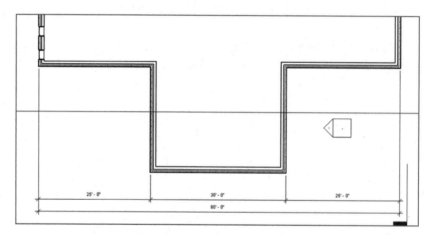

FIGURE 5.45: The dimensional layout for the south part of the west wing

Placing Text and Annotations

Text in Revit Architecture is a love/hate relationship for every Revit user. You'll love text because it automatically scales with the view's scale. You'll hate it because the text editor is something of a throwback from an earlier CAD application. Either way, the procedure for adding text doesn't change with your feelings toward it.

The objective of this procedure is simply to add text to the model, format it, and then add and format a leader:

1. In the Project Browser, go to the Level 1 floor plan.

2. Zoom in on the east wing's radial entry area, where the elevator shafts are located, as shown in Figure 5.46.

3. On the Text panel of the Annotate tab, click the Text button, as shown in Figure 5.47.

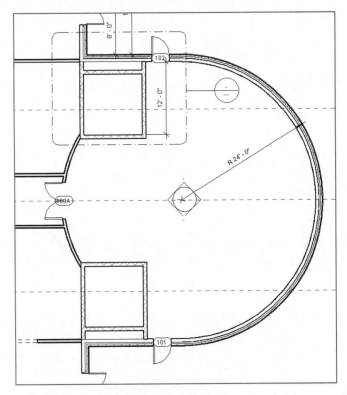

FIGURE 5.46: The radial entry

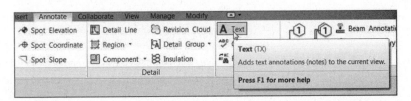

FIGURE 5.47: Click the Text button on the Text panel of the Annotate tab.

4. In the Type Selector, select Text : 3/32″ (2) Arial.

5. On the Format panel, you have choices for a leader. For this example, click the No Leader button. It's the button with the *A* on it, as shown in Figure 5.48.

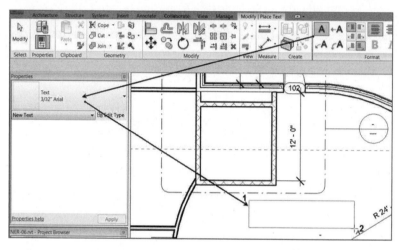

FIGURE 5.48:   Placing text

6. To place the text, you can pick a point or drag a window. Left-click at the point marked 1 in Figure 5.48. Keep the button down.

7. Drag the cursor to the point marked 2, and release the button.

8. Type **CMU SHAFT WALL**.

9. Click a point in the view outside the text box. You now have a note in the model. The text wraps to fit the size of the window you dragged.

10. Press the Esc key twice, or click Modify.

11. Select the text.

12. On the Format panel, review the choices you have to add a leader to the text.

13. Click the Add Left Side Straight Leader button, as shown in Figure 5.49. This option adds a leader to the left end of the text.

14. By clicking the grips and moving the text around, configure the text and the leader to resemble Figure 5.49.

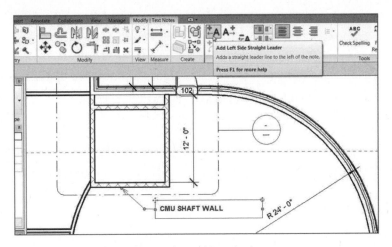

FIGURE 5.49: Adding and stretching a leader

Adding Leader Text

You can add text to a model by placing a leader first and then adding the text within the same command. Although in Revit you can add leaders to all text, you can choose to add text to a model with or without a leader.

The objective of the following steps is to place text with a leader:

1. On the Text panel of the Annotate tab, click the Text button.

2. On the Format panel, click the Two Segments button, as shown in Figure 5.50.

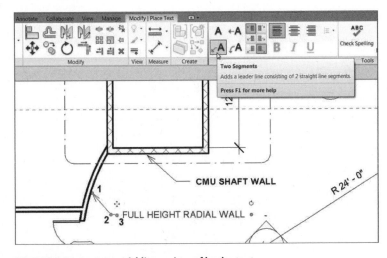

FIGURE 5.50: Adding a piece of leader text

3. Pick a point near the radial wall, marked 1 in Figure 5.50.

4. Pick a second point similar to the point marked 2.

5. Pick a third point just to the right of the second, marked 3.

6. Type **FULL HEIGHT RADIAL WALL**.

7. Click an area outside the text.

Now that you can add text to a model, let's investigate how to modify the text after you add it. You'll begin with the arrowhead on the end of the leader.

Changing the Leader Type

It almost seems as though Revit uses the ugliest leader as a default, forcing you to change it immediately. The large arrowhead you saw in Figure 5.50 isn't the only one Revit provides—had that been the case, Revit might have never have gotten off the ground!

To change the arrowhead that Revit uses with a text item, follow this procedure:

1. On the Text panel of the Annotate tab is a small arrow pointing down and to the right, as shown in Figure 5.51. Click it to open the Type Properties.

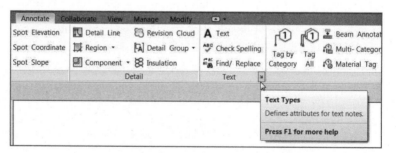

FIGURE 5.51: Accessing the Type Properties

2. Change the Leader Arrowhead parameter to Arrow Filled 15 Degree, as shown in Figure 5.52.

3. Click OK. You've changed a type parameter.

That's a handsome-looking arrowhead, as shown in Figure 5.53. The next item to address is how to modify the placement of text after you add it to the model.

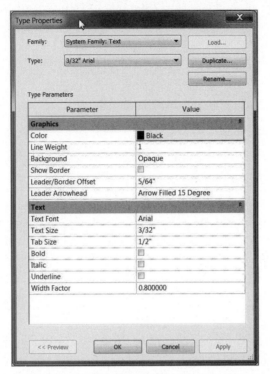

FIGURE 5.52: Changing that ugly arrow

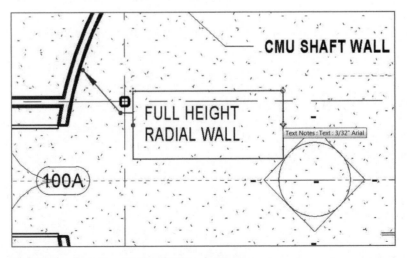

FIGURE 5.53: Configuring the arrowhead

Modifying the Text Placement

With any text item in Revit, you can select the text in your model, and you'll see grips for adjusting text: two grips on the text box, two on the leader, and a rotate icon.

Your next objective is to modify the text placement and to make the necessary adjustments:

1. Select the text you just added to the model.

2. Pick the right blue grip.

3. Stretch the text window to the left until it forces the text to wrap, as shown in Figure 5.53.

Observe the rotate icon. You don't need to rotate the text here, but notice that it's there, for future reference.

Modifying the placement of text is a straightforward process. Changing the actual font and size of the text in a model is another story and requires further investigation.

Changing Text Properties

Of course, you can change the font used for text. You can also change the text's height and width. Keep in mind, however, that the text height you specify is the actual text height you want to see on the sheet. You no longer have to multiply the desired text height to a line-type scale. Revit understands that text is scaled based on the view's scale.

To modify the text appearance, run through the following procedure:

1. Pick the Text Types arrow in the corner of the Text panel, as you did when you changed the leader type.

2. Click the Duplicate button.

3. Call the new text 3/16″ Tahoma (3.5mm Tahoma).

4. Click OK.

5. Change the Text Font setting to Tahoma.

6. Change the Text Size setting to **3/16″** (3.5mm), as shown in Figure 5.54.

7. Change the Width Factor setting to 0.8.

8. Click OK.

FIGURE 5.54: Changing the text values in the Type Properties dialog box

You've now successfully created a text style. (Of course, this large, non-uniform text isn't proper in this context.) You can use your new type easily:

1. Start the Text command.

2. In the Type Selector, verify that your new text is in the list.

Revit doesn't use an SHX font. As a matter of fact, SHX can't be used at all in Revit. It was invented by Autodesk, but it works only with AutoCAD. Keep this in mind when you're setting up your company's templates. If you're using an SHX font, you'll need to find an alternate font or allow Revit to convert it to Arial. If you don't, this will cause issues in text formatting.

Are You Experienced?

Now you can...

☑ add a multitude of different types of dimensions to your model simply by altering the options associated with the Dimension command

☑ equally constrain items in a model by adding a string of dimensions and clicking the EQ button

☑ use your dimensions as a layout tool, keeping the items constrained even after the dimension is deleted

☑ add text to a model by starting with either a leader or a paragraph of text

☑ change the text type and arrowhead type for leader text

Floors

It's going to be hard to convince you that floors are easy when an entire chapter is dedicated to this lone aspect of Autodesk® Revit® Architecture software. Well, floors *are* easy. I'm devoting an entire chapter to the subject because we need to address a lot of aspects of floors.

▶ **Placing a floor slab**

▶ **Building a floor by layers**

▶ **Splitting the floor materials**

▶ **Pitching a floor to a floor drain**

▶ **Creating shaft openings**

Placing a Floor Slab

Adding a floor to a model is quite simple, but in Revit Architecture, you're truly modeling the floor. That means you can include the structure and the finish when you create your floor. When you cut a section through the floor, you get an almost perfect representation of your floor system and how it relates to adjacent geometry, such as walls.

Floors, of course, are more than large slabs of concrete. Therefore, in this chapter you'll also be introduced to creating materials, and you'll learn how to pitch these materials to floor drains. You'll examine how to create sloped slabs as well.

The first area you'll explore is how to place a slab into your model. It's as simple as it sounds, but you must follow certain steps, which I'll outline next. As you've learned up to this point, in Revit Architecture you do need to add items the way Revit wants you to add them, or you'll probably generate errors—or, worse, inaccuracies in your model.

Creating the Slab

To begin, open the file on which you've been following along. If you didn't complete Chapter 5, "Dimensioning and Annotating," go to the book's web page at www.sybex.com/go/revit2014ner. From there you can browse to Chapter 6 and find the file called NER-06.rvt.

 NOTE   Metric users should not type in mm or other metric abbreviations when entering amounts suggested in the exercises. Revit won't accept such abbreviations. Simply enter the number provided within the parentheses.

The objective of the following procedure is to create a floor slab to be placed into the model:

1. In your Project Browser, go to the Level 1 floor plan.

2. Zoom in to the west wing.

3. On the Architecture tab, click the Floor button, as shown in Figure 6.1.

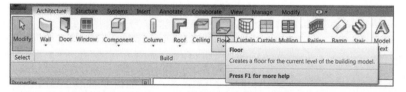

FIGURE 6.1:   The Floor button on the Architecture tab

4. Switch to the Properties dialog. Make sure Floors is the current selection, as shown in Figure 6.2.

5. At upper right in the dialog, click the Edit Type button (see Figure 6.3).

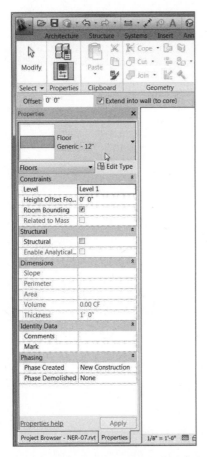

FIGURE 6.2: Changing the focus of the properties

You're now accessing the Type Properties. This means any change you make here will affect every slab of this type in the entire model.

TIP   At this point, you should always either create a new floor system or rename the current one. This will avert much confusion down the line when you have a floor called Generic - 12″ (Generic 300mm), and it's actually a 6″ (150mm) concrete slab on grade.

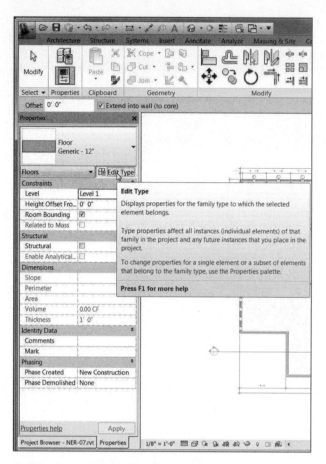

FIGURE 6.3: Clicking the Edit Type button to begin creating a new floor slab type

6. Click the Rename button, as shown in Figure 6.4.

7. Call the floor system **6″ Slab on Grade (150mm Slab on Grade)**; see Figure 6.4.

8. Click OK.

9. Change Function to Exterior, as shown in Figure 6.5.

10. In the Structure row, click the long Edit button (see Figure 6.5).

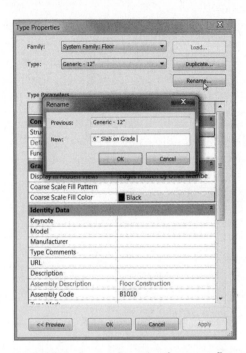

FIGURE 6.4:   Renaming the current floor type. You'll never have a Generic 12″ (300mm) floor in your model, so it's a good idea not to keep this floor type around.

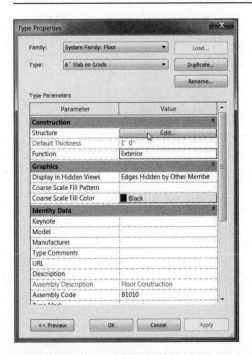

FIGURE 6.5:   Clicking the Edit button to access the structure of the floor

The term *layer* may throw you off a bit. Revit uses layer here to describe a component of the floor. This is not to be confused with an Autodesk® AutoCAD® layer.

You're now in the Edit Assembly dialog box. This is where you can specify a thickness for your slab. You can add layers of materials here as well.

In the middle of the Edit Assembly dialog box is a large spreadsheet-type field that is divided into rows and columns. The rows are defined by a structural component and include a boundary above and below the structure. It's the Structure row in which you're interested here:

1. The Structure row is divided into columns. Click in the Material column within the Structure row, as shown in Figure 6.6.

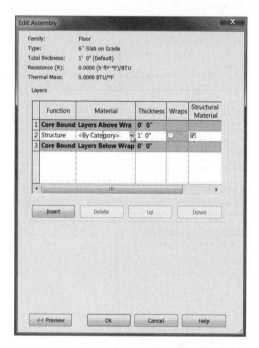

FIGURE 6.6: By clicking in the Material cell within the Structure row, you can access the Material Browser.

2. A small […] button appears when you click in the Material cell. This button indicates that you'll be given a menu if you click it. Click the […] button to open the Material Browser.

3. You can now choose a material from the menu. Scroll down until you arrive at Concrete, Cast-In-Place Gray, and select it.

4. Make sure the Graphics tab is current, as shown in Figure 6.7. You can display two different hatches: a sand hatch will be visible for floor plans, and a concrete hatch will be visible for sections (see Figure 6.7). These hatches allow a filling region to designate specific materials graphically.

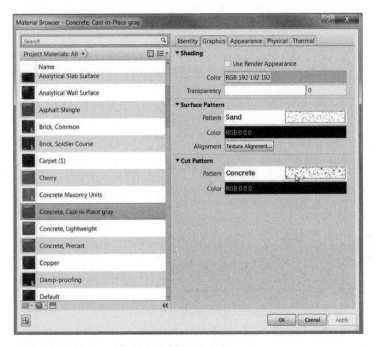

FIGURE 6.7: The Material Browser

5. Make sure Concrete, Cast-In-Place Gray is still selected, and click OK.

6. Back in the Edit Assembly dialog box, the Thickness column is directly to the right of the Material column. Currently the value in the Structure Row is 1′–0″ (300mm). Click into the cell, and change the value to 6″ (150mm).

TIP Imperial users, if you just type **6** and press Enter, you'll wind up with a slab 6′–0″ thick. Be sure to add the inch mark (″) after the 6. The value needs to read 0′–6″.

7. Click OK.

8. Click OK again to get back to the model.

Now that the slab type has been created, you can place an instance into the model. Notice that the Modify | Create Floor Boundary tab is in Sketch Mode. You'll now proceed to sketch the slab in place.

Sketching the Slab

You'll have to adjust to the way Revit wants you to proceed with the Create Floor Boundary tab; you're basically limited to the choices provided in this menu. Not to fear, you should have plenty of choices, but you'll still need to get a feel for how Revit works.

Here's what needs to happen: you must draw the perimeter of the slab into the model. This is basically a slab on grade, so you'll pour the concrete to the inside, finished face of the wall. You won't worry about a control joint between the wall and the slab at this point.

Picking Walls

The best way to add a slab is to use the Pick Walls button as much as possible (see Figure 6.8). In doing so, you tell Revit that this edge of slab needs to move if this wall moves. Pick Walls is the default Draw option.

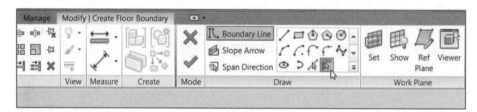

FIGURE 6.8: Picking walls ensures that that edge of your slab will move if the wall moves.

Let's start sketching the slab:

1. In the Modify | Create Floor Boundary tab, click the Pick Walls button, as shown in Figure 6.8, if it isn't already picked.

2. With the Pick Walls tool running, hover your mouse over the inside face of the wall.

3. After the wall becomes highlighted and you're sure you're on the inside of the wall, pick it (see Figure 6.9).

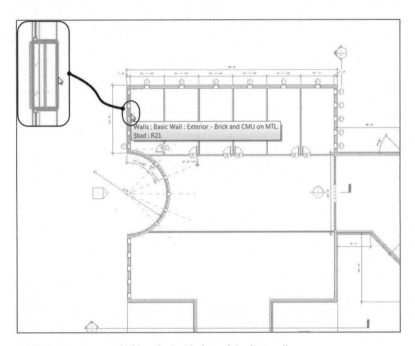

FIGURE 6.9:   Picking the inside face of the first wall

4. With the inside face of the wall picked, you need to move on to the next wall. Pick the inside face of the north wall.

  Notice that, as you pick the walls, a magenta *sketch line* appears on the inside face of the walls. This is another indicator telling you whether you're on the correct side of the wall. The first line has two parallel lines, one on each side. These indicate the slab direction for structural decking.

5. Keep picking the walls, as shown in Figure 6.10. You need to have a continuous loop—no gaps and no overlaps.

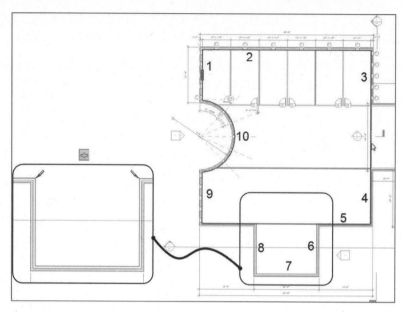

FIGURE 6.10:   Selecting the walls

6. Apply some basic modify commands as well. To clean the lower-right corner, use the Trim command. For the bottom line where the jog occurs, use the Split Element command. (Make sure the Delete Inner Segment button is selected on the Options bar.)

7. After you've picked the perimeter of the west wing, click Finish Edit Mode on the Modify | Create Floor Boundary tab, as shown in Figure 6.11. It may be a good idea to check out your model in 3D after making floors just to make sure nothing went wrong. (I constantly have to do that.)

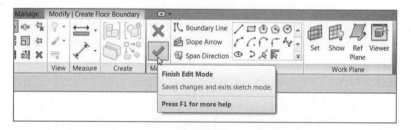

FIGURE 6.11:   Clicking Finish Edit Mode to finalize the floor sketch

WATCH WHAT YOU PICK!

As you pick the walls to place your edge of slab, be careful. If you don't pick the inside face, there is a chance that Revit will try to extend the slab to the core of the wall. Also, make sure the Extend Into Wall core option is unselected. This will help keep the edge of slab where you intend it to be. If you zoom in to the area that you're picking, an alignment line will appear. Make sure this line is where you want it, as shown in the following image:

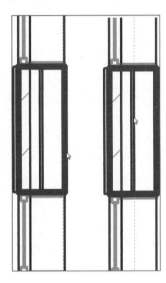

PICKY, PICKY, PICKY!

I'll keep repeating this, but if you get the error message shown here saying that your lines are overlapping, that means your lines are in fact overlapping. You *must* have a single, closed loop. Click the Show button to zoom in on the offending area.

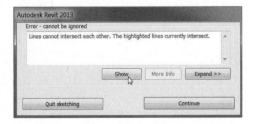

After you finish the floor, you'll have plenty of opportunity to practice adding floors in this model. You need to add a floor to the corridor as well as the west wing. Follow these steps:

1. Zoom in to the corridor, as shown in Figure 6.12.

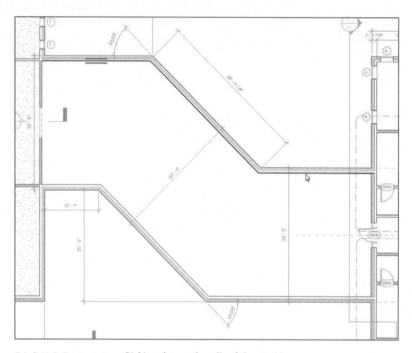

FIGURE 6.12:   Picking the north walls of the corridor

2. On the Architecture tab, start the Floor command.

3. In the Modify | Create Floor Boundary tab, click the Pick Walls button.

4. Uncheck Extend Into Wall.

5. Pick the three north walls of the corridor. Remember to keep the blue line to the inside face (see Figure 6.12).

USING FLIP ARROWS

If you accidentally pick the wrong place in the wall, that's okay. Flip arrows appear as you place lines. Realize that a previous line is wrong? Press Esc, and then select the magenta line—a flip arrow will appear. Pick the flip arrow, and the magenta line will flip back to the correct face of the wall, as shown in the following graphic. Also, if other sketch lines are on the wrong face, this one flip will take care of any connected sketch lines.

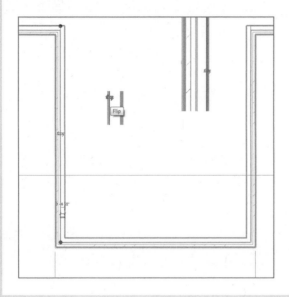

6. Revit may not let you pick the wall to add the east edge of the slab. If you do, the magenta line will go either to the core centerline or to the opposite face of the wall. At this point, click the Pick Lines button on the Modify | Create Floor Boundary tab, as shown in Figure 6.13.

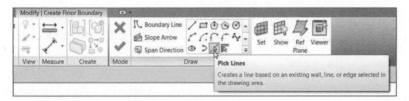

FIGURE 6.13: Sometimes you'll need to click the Pick Lines button to select the edge of the slab. If you have to resort to this, however, the slab edge won't move if the wall does.

7. Pick the face of the east wall, as shown in Figure 6.14.

8. On the Draw panel, click the Pick Walls button.

9. Pick the south corridor walls. (Remember to keep the magenta line to the inside of the corridor.)

10. Pick the west wall of the corridor. This time you want to be sure the magenta line is to the left of the wall. This will ensure that the two slabs meet. If not, you may need to move the line manually (see Figure 6.15).

When you pick the west wall of the corridor, you may find that Revit won't let you pick the opposite face of the wall. Simply click the inside face of the wall, and then move the magenta line to the opposite face of the wall by dragging it.

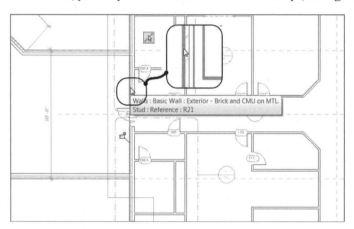

FIGURE 6.14: Picking the face of the east wall. The line will run past the corridor. That's okay; you'll trim it in a moment.

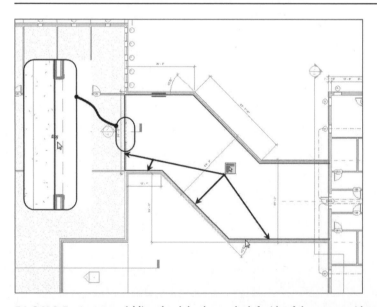

FIGURE 6.15: Adding the slab edge to the left side of the west corridor wall

Now that you understand the process of adding sketch lines to the model, you can start to look into how to clean up the sketch so you can finish.

Using Trim to Clean Up the Sketch

With the lines placed, you need to make sure you don't have any gaps or overlaps. And you do. To fix these gaps and overlaps, you'll use the basic modify commands from Chapter 5.

The east wall has a giant gap at the bottom and an overlap at the top. The command you need to use here is the Trim command:

1. Pick the Trim/Extend To Corner button from the Modify panel, as shown at the top of Figure 6.16. Then click the portions of the two lines you want to keep. This removes the excess from the corner.

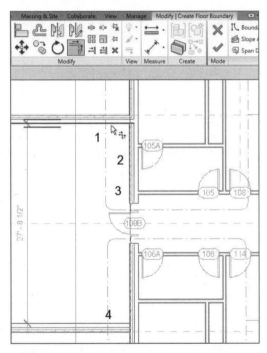

FIGURE 6.16: Pick the magenta lines in the numbered order illustrated in the figure.

2. With the corners successfully trimmed, click Finish Edit Mode.

When Revit allows you to finish the sketch, your west wing and corridor should have a continuous slab underneath them, as shown in Figure 6.17.

> While you create the floor boundary, you can access the basic editing commands such as Trim, Split Element, and Offset that work for sketching.
>
>

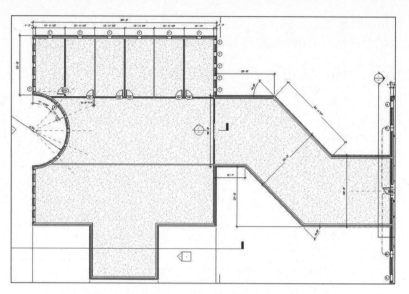

F I G U R E 6 . 1 7 :   The two slabs under the west wing and the corridor

  T I P   I hope you don't get an error stating that lines are overlapping. If you do, keep going with the Trim/Extend To Corner command. You may need to investigate each corner. You may also want to consider whether you've accidentally placed double lines along a wall. This can be easy to do when you're picking walls.

It's time to add a slab under the east wing. Go ahead and try it on your own. Look at these directions only if you get lost:

1. Zoom in on the east wing.

2. On the Architecture tab, click the Floor button.

3. In the Modify | Create Floor Boundary tab, click the Pick Walls button.

4. Pick the exterior walls of the east wing.

5. Trim any gaps or overlaps that occur in the corners, as shown in Figure 6.18. Also, pay special attention to the radial entry; it can be tricky.

6. Click Finish Edit Mode.

Now that you have a nice slab on the first floor, you need to add some more slabs to the rest of the levels. The trick with the slabs on upper levels is that they must extend into the core of the walls. This is where Revit can get sticky. Follow along with the next section, and let's work out this issue together.

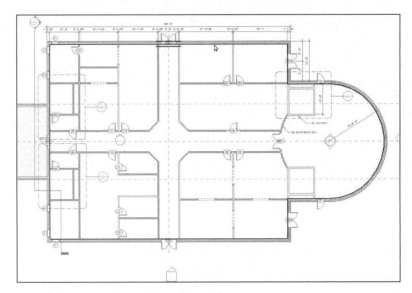

FIGURE 6.18: Adding a slab to the east wing

Building a Floor by Layers

As mentioned in the previous section, the term *layer* doesn't equate to an AutoCAD layer. It does, however, equate to layers of materials used to design a floor system. When you create a floor system in Revit Architecture, you should do it with the mindset of how a floor is actually constructed. You can also specify which material in the floor will stop at an exterior wall and which will pass through to the core.

In this section, you'll build on your experience of creating a floor. With the concrete slab in place, you'll start adding materials to create a floor finish.

Adding Materials

Your objective is to create a floor system with a structure and a finish material. You'll also design the floor to interrupt the exterior framing, while letting the brick façade pass from grade to parapet. Let's get started:

1. In the Project Browser, go to the Level 2 floor plan. (Remember not to go to the Level 2 ceiling plan.)

2. In the View Control bar (located at the bottom of the view window), be sure the detail level is set to Fine.

3. On the Architecture tab, click the Floor button.

4. In the Properties dialog box, click the Edit Type button.

5. Click the Duplicate button.

6. Call the new floor **6″ concrete with 1″ Terrazzo** (see Figure 6.19). For metric users, it's **150mm concrete with 25mm Terrazzo**.

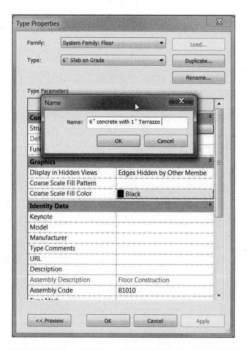

FIGURE 6.19: Duplicating the existing floor

7. Click OK.

8. In the Structure row, click the Edit button, as shown in Figure 6.20.

FIGURE 6.20:   Clicking the Edit button in the Structure row

You're now in the Edit Assembly dialog box, as you were in the previous procedure. The objective is to add 1″ (25mm) Terrazzo flooring to the top of the 6″ (150mm) concrete.

Adding a Layer

To add the additional material, you must understand how the Edit Assembly dialog box is broken down. Because you want to add a material to the top of the slab, you need to click above the concrete and insert a new layer, as follows:

1. In the Layers field are three rows. Each row has a corresponding number. Click the number 1. This is the top row that reads Core Boundary | Layers Above Wrap (see Figure 6.21).

2. Under the Layers field, click the Insert button, as shown in Figure 6.21.

3. The new layer is added. The field is now divided into columns. The first column is Function, which is currently set to Structure. This cell is a drop box containing the other available functions. Click the drop-box arrow, and select Finish 1 [4] (see Figure 6.22).

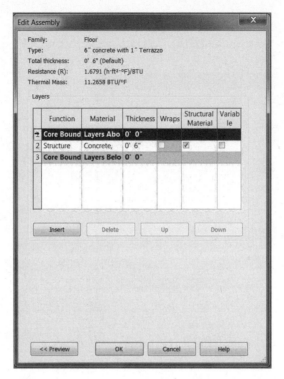

FIGURE 6.21: Inserting a new layer for the Terrazzo

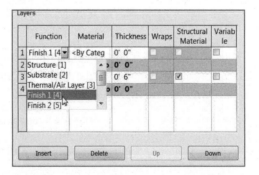

FIGURE 6.22: Choosing a layer function

4. Click in the Material cell for the new Layer 1.

5. Click the [...] button.

6. In the Material Browser, type **terrazzo** as shown in Figure 6.23. Your Terrazzo material appears. When it does, select it, and click OK.

7. Scroll down, and double-click Terrazzo (see Figure 6.23).

8. Find the Terrazzo material in the top portion, select it, and click OK.

9. Click OK.

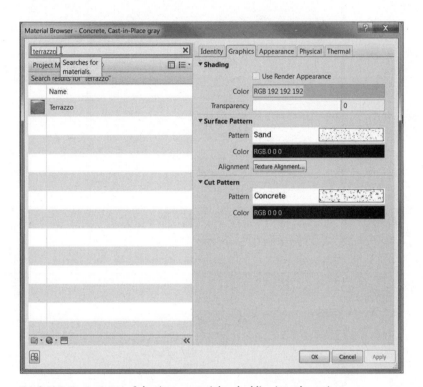

FIGURE 6.23: Selecting a material and adding it to the project

10. In the Thickness column, enter 1″ (25mm). Imperial users, make sure you're typing 1 inch and not 1 foot (see Figure 6.24).

11. At far right in the rows in the Layers field are Variable check boxes. Select Variable for the Structure row, as shown in Figure 6.25. This will enable you to slope the top of the slab if need be. Only the layer that is set to be variable will actually slope. Any layer that is on top of this variable layer will be pitched.

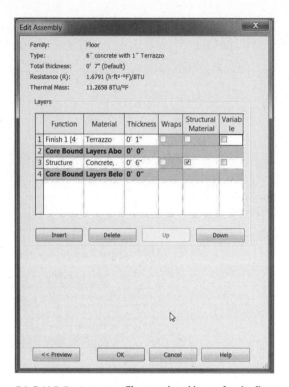

FIGURE 6.24: The completed layers for the floor system

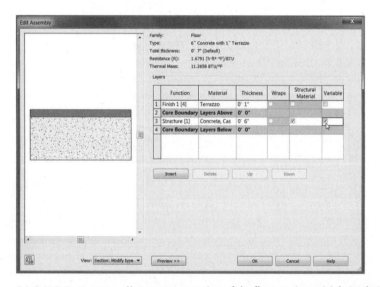

FIGURE 6.25: You can see a preview of the floor section as it's being built.

12. At the bottom of the Edit Assembly dialog box, click the Preview button. A graphic preview of your floor appears in a sectional view (see Figure 6.25).

13. Click OK twice to get back to the model.

Great job. You now have a floor with a finish material on it!

Now you can place your new floor into the model. Remember that you're on the second floor. When you place the slab, you want it to extend directly into the wall core. To do so, follow along:

1. Click the Pick Walls button on the Draw panel. You'll pick every exterior wall in the east wing except the radial wall.

2. Start picking walls, as shown in Figure 6.26. Do *not* pick the radial wall at the east entry.

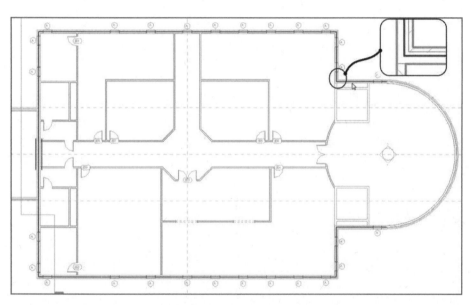

FIGURE 6.26: Picking the core centerline of the exterior walls, except the radial east wall

3. On the Draw panel, click the Line button.

4. Draw a line from the endpoint of the magenta line at the north wall of the east entry (see 1 in Figure 6.27) to the endpoint of the magenta line in the south wall (see 2 in Figure 6.27).

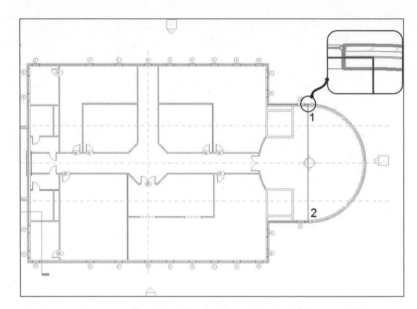

FIGURE 6.27: Sketching a line for the east portion of the entry slab

5. On the Modify | Create Floor Boundary tab, click Finish Edit Mode.

6. Revit begins asking you questions. First it asks whether you want to attach the walls that go up to Level 2 to the bottom of the floor. You *do* want to do this; this cuts the interior walls down to meet the bottom of the floor. Any change in the floor's thickness will alter the tops of the wall. Click Yes, as shown in Figure 6.28.

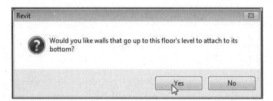

FIGURE 6.28: Click Yes to attach the walls to the floor's bottom.

7. The next message pertains to the exterior walls. Revit asks whether you would like to cut the section out of the walls where the slab is intersecting. In this case, you do, so click Yes in the message box, as shown in Figure 6.29.

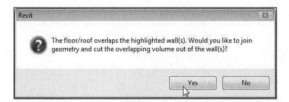

FIGURE 6.29: Click Yes if you want to cut overlapping volumes out of the exterior walls.

NOTE As these messages come up, Revit usually does a good job of highlighting the relevant items in the model. Get into the habit of looking past the messages to see what items in the model are being highlighted.

With the second floor in place, you can now add it to the floors above. To do so, you can use the Copy/Paste Aligned feature you used in Chapter 3, "Creating Views." Try to do this on your own. If you don't remember how, or if you skipped Chapter 3, follow these steps:

1. Select the floor in Level 2 if it isn't still selected. (It's easiest to select the floor at the east edge.)

2. On the Modify | Floors tab, click the Copy To Clipboard button on the Clipboard panel, as shown in Figure 6.30.

A good indication that you've successfully copied the floor to the Clipboard is that the Paste icon directly to the right of the Copy icon becomes activated.

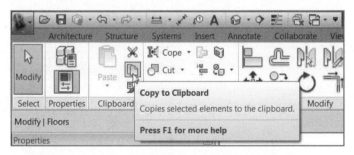

FIGURE 6.30: Clicking the Copy To Clipboard button

3. Go to the default 3D view, as shown in Figure 6.31.

4. From the Paste flyout on the Clipboard panel of the Modify tab, click Aligned To Selected Levels, as shown in Figure 6.32.

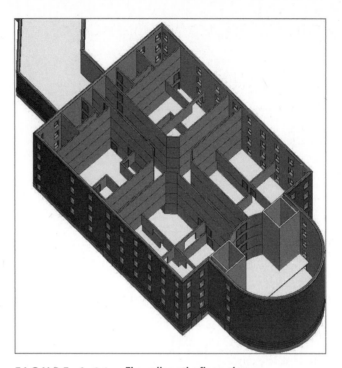

F I G U R E   6 . 3 1 :   The walls on the floors above

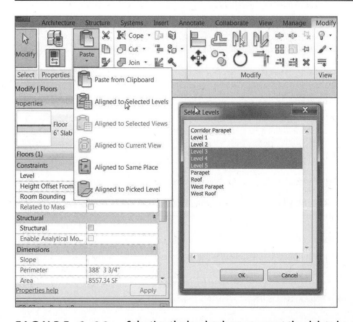

F I G U R E   6 . 3 2 :   Selecting the levels where you want the slab to be copied

5. The Select Levels dialog box appears, where you'll choose the levels to which you want to paste your floor. Choose Levels 3, 4, and 5 (see Figure 6.32; use Ctrl to select more than one level).

6. Click OK. The floors are pasted to the specified levels, as shown in Figure 6.33.

Note that if Selected Levels isn't available, Selected Views will be. This is because you selected an annotation such as a window tag or a door tag. You can pick Selected Views to achieve the same results.

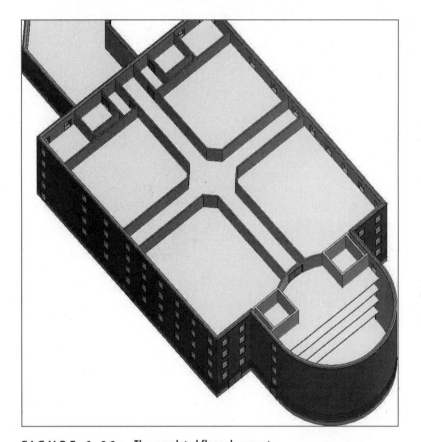

FIGURE 6.33:   The completed floor placement

Notice that the fifth-level floor isn't joined to any of the walls. This is because, when you pasted the floor to this level, Revit didn't prompt you to cut the overlapping geometry from the exterior walls. To fix this, follow these steps:

1. After the floors have been pasted, select the fifth-level floor, as shown in Figure 6.34.

2. On the Modify | Floors tab, click the Edit Boundary button.

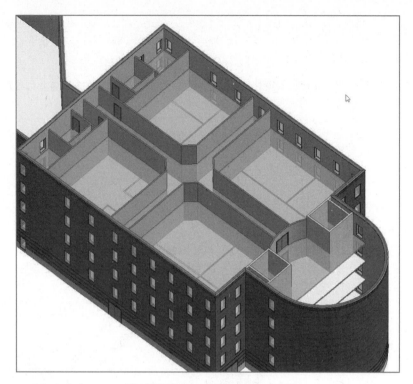

FIGURE 6.34:   The fifth floor is now cutting the walls.

3. On the Mode panel of the Modify | Floors ➤ Edit Boundary tab, click Finish Edit Mode.

4. Click Yes to attach the walls that go up to this floor's bottom.

5. Click Yes to cut the overlapping volume out of the walls. Figure 6.34 shows that the walls are now being cut by the slab.

6. Repeat steps 1 through 5 for floors 4 and 3.

7. Save the model.

Not too bad. You have a full building with floors placed. Now you'll drill into these floors (literally) and see how you can make them perform to your specifications.

Your next task is to create different floor materials for a few specific areas such as the restrooms. You'll then pitch the restroom floors to floor drains.

Splitting the Floor Materials

If you have a floor that includes a slab, and you have a single material of, say, vinyl composition tile (VCT) for the entire surface, won't that cause a problem in the restrooms? Better yet, suppose the floor is carpeted. Carpet never seems to perform well around a toilet!

Adding an Alternate Material

The goal of this procedure is to create a new material layer for the first-floor slab and then specify a new material for the restrooms. Follow these steps:

1. In the Project Browser, go to the Level 1 floor plan and then zoom in to an area of the east wing similar to the area shown in Figure 6.35.

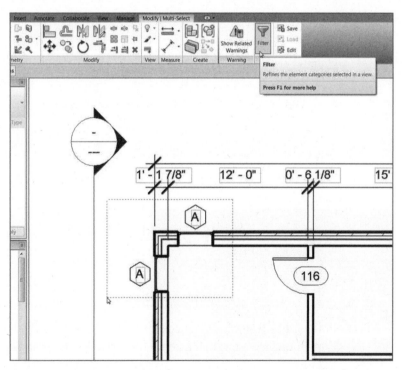

FIGURE 6.35:   To select the slab, you'll find it easier to pick an entire area and filter the floor.

2. Drag a right-to-left selection window around the corner of the build-ing, as shown in Figure 6.35.

3. On the Modify | Multi-Select tab, click the Filter button (see Figure 6.35).

4. In the Filter dialog box, click the Check None button, as shown in Figure 6.36.

FIGURE 6.36: Deselect all the elements, and then select Floors.

5. Select the Floors option (see Figure 6.36), and click OK.

6. With the floor selected, click Edit Type in the Properties dialog box.

7. Click Rename.

8. Call the floor 6″ Slab on Grade with 1″ Finish (150mm Slab on Grade with 25mm Finish).

9. Click OK.

10. Click the Edit button in the Structure row, as shown in Figure 6.37.

11. In the Edit Assembly dialog box, click the 1 button to the left of the Core Boundary item that is above the Structure layer, as shown in Figure 6.38.

12. Click the Insert button (see Figure 6.38).

13. Select Finish 1 [4] from the Function drop-down list.

14. Click in the Material cell.

15. Click the […] button.

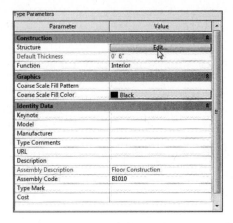

FIGURE 6.37: Editing the structure of the slab

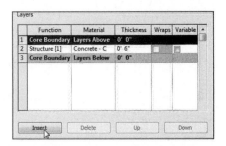

FIGURE 6.38: Adding a new layer

16. Search for Carpet (1), and click OK.

17. Give the material a thickness of **1″** (25mm).

18. In the Structure 1 row, select the Variable check box, as shown in Figure 6.39.

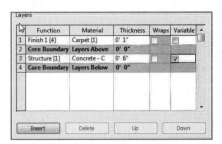

FIGURE 6.39: Adding the new material

19. Click OK twice.

20. Press Esc.

Now that you have experience adding a new material layer to the floor (you've done it twice in this chapter), you can specify a different material for the various rooms.

Splitting and Painting

Adding a new material to a floor is a two-part procedure. To specify an alternate material in an area, you must first split the floor's face. Then you can add (or paint) the desired material to that area.

The objective of the next two procedures is to add an alternate material to the restrooms. Follow along:

1. Zoom in on the lavatory north of the corridor.

2. On the Geometry panel of the Modify tab, click the Split Face button, as shown in Figure 6.40.

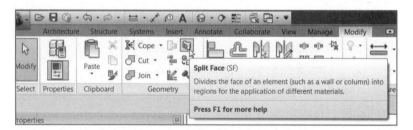

FIGURE 6.40:   The Split Face button is located on the Geometry panel of the Modify tab.

3. Move your cursor into the lavatory area, as shown in Figure 6.41.

4. Notice the little cube at your cursor. Hover the cursor over the wall shown in Figure 6.41. You should get a tooltip telling you that you're directly over the floor. When you see this indication, pick the floor.

5. After you select the floor, you need to draw three lines around the inside face of the lavatory walls. To do so, on the Draw panel of the Modify | Split Face ➢ Create Boundary tab, make sure the Line button is selected.

6. Draw the three lines shown in Figure 6.42 (you may have to trim and extend the lines).

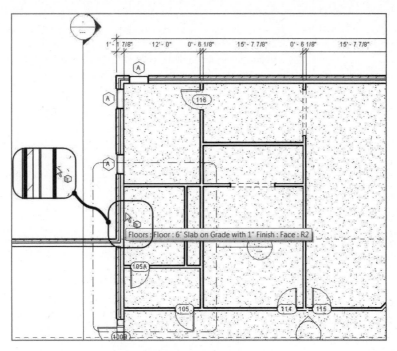

FIGURE 6.41:   Finding the edge of the floor

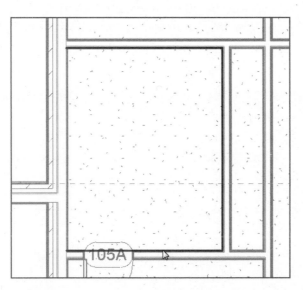

FIGURE 6.42:   Placing the three split lines around the perimeter of the lavatory

W A R N I N G   Because the line you're splitting is up against the edge of the slab, the actual floor's edge serves as one of the split lines. When you're adding the three additional lines, you must be snapped to the edge of the floor. There can be no overlaps or gaps.

7. On the Modify | Split Face ➤ Create Boundary tab, click Finish Edit Mode.

   The lavatory area should now be split.

Although it appears as if nothing happened, you just can't see it. The next series of steps will change the material of the region. At this point, it will become obvious that there is a different material.

SAVE YOUR MODEL!

Crashing has been a way of life since we got off the drafting boards and booted the first CAD station. Although the Revit material catalog is now more robust, it isn't the most stable addition to Revit. Do yourself a favor and save your model before you click that Paint button.

The floor is split, and it's time to add the new material to this room. This procedure is almost like adding a hatch to an area in AutoCAD. Here are the steps:

1. On the Geometry panel of the Modify | Split Face tab, click the Paint button, as shown in Figure 6.43.

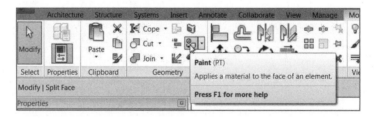

F I G U R E   6 . 4 3 :   The Paint button on the Geometry panel

2. From the material list, select Tile, Mosaic, Gray from the menu, as shown in Figure 6.44.

3. With the Material Browser still on the screen, move your cursor over the region you just created. Notice the material icon next to your cursor, as shown in Figure 6.45. The tooltip identifies the face region.

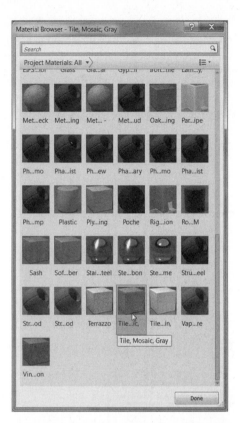

F I G U R E 6 . 4 4 :   Finding the correct material

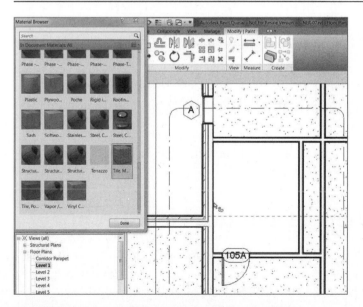

F I G U R E 6 . 4 5 :   Filling the region with the new material

TIP   If you don't see the Paint icon next to the cursor when you hover over the region as shown, simply click a point anywhere on the screen, and the icon will appear. You can then proceed to paint the floor.

4. When you see the perimeter of the small region you created around the inside of the lavatory, pick a spot. The area fills with the new material (see Figure 6.46). Click Done to close the Material Browser.

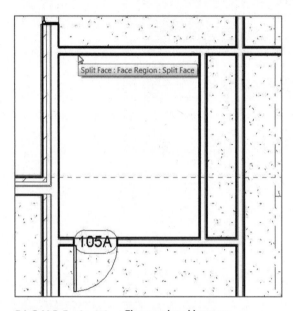

FIGURE 6.46:   The completed lavatory

5. Do the same thing to the lavatory south of the corridor. If you get stuck, go back through the steps.

6. Save your model.

Next you'll create a pitched floor situation. In some cases, this is an easy procedure. In others, it isn't.

Pitching a Floor to a Floor Drain

Sure, it's the responsibility of the plumbing engineer to specify what floor drains to use, but it's generally the responsibility of the architect to specify where they'd like the floor drain. That being said, let's move on to creating a pitched floor area in the restrooms. Because you have five floors with which to work, let's go up to the second floor and start pitching some slabs!

The objective of this procedure is to add points in the surface of the slab in order to pitch to a drain:

1. In the Project Browser, double-click the Level 2 floor plan. (Make sure you aren't in the Level 2 ceiling plan.)

2. Zoom in on the lavatory areas, as shown in Figure 6.47.

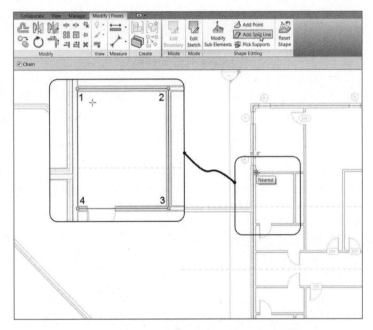

FIGURE 6.47: Drawing a split frame around the inside of the lavatory

3. Select the floor.

4. The Modify | Floors tab shows several choices. In the Shape Editing panel, click the Add Split Line button (see Figure 6.47).

5. On the Options bar, click the Chain button.

6. Draw lines along the finished inside face of the lavatory (see Figure 6.47). As always, there can be no gaps or overlaps.

THANK YOU, REVIT 2014!

New to Revit 2014, you can now pick an element by its face. When selecting floors and (when we get to it) ceilings, you used to have to pick a large window and then filter your selection. You don't have to do that now. Make sure the Select Elements By Face button is active, as shown in the graphic.

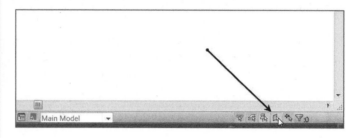

 N O T E   Yes, it's true that the snapping feature is tedious at best when you're using the Split Line command. Be patient. You'll basically need to get as close to the face of the wall as possible before you pick the point. This is one case where you'll need to eyeball the exact pick points.

With the split lines drawn, you've isolated the lavatory area from the rest of the floor. Now you can pitch the floor in this area without affecting the rest of the floor. The pitch will extend only as far as the split lines.

To create a drop in the floor, follow these steps:

1. On the Architecture tab, click the Model Lines button (see Figure 6.48).

2. Draw a line from the midpoint of the restroom's right wall to the left 3'–0" (900mm), as shown in Figure 6.48.

3. Press Esc twice.

4. Select the floor. (Remember the Filter dialog box.)

5. On the Modify | Floors tab, click the Add Point button, as shown in Figure 6.49.

6. Pick the endpoint of the line you just drew (see Figure 6.49).

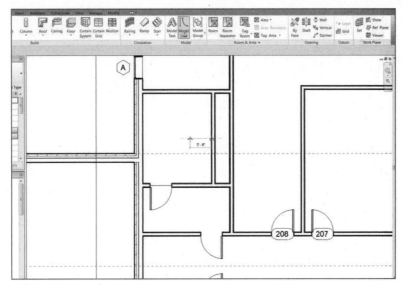

FIGURE 6.48: Drawing a line to establish the point to where the floor will slope

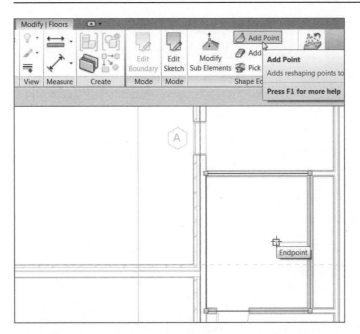

FIGURE 6.49: Picking the endpoint of the line

7. Press Esc once. This puts you in Modify Sub Elements Mode. You'll know you're in this mode by the icon next to your pointer, as shown in Figure 6.50.

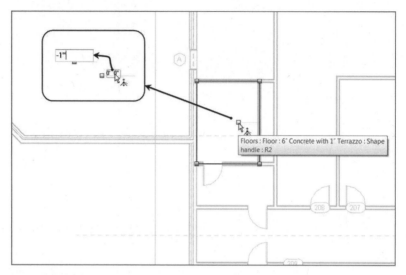

FIGURE 6.50: Dropping the elevation of the drain down 1″ (25mm) from the surface of the floor

8. Pick the point you just placed into the model. The point turns red, and a blue elevation appears. As you know, any blue item is modifiable. Click the 0′–0″ (0mm) value, and change it to -1″ (-25mm)— Imperial users, negative 1 inch.

9. Press Enter. Revit drops that area of the floor and adds the slope lines as if you drafted them in.

10. Press Esc twice.

11. Delete the line you drew as a guideline.

12. Save the model.
    See Figure 6.51: does your floor look like this? If not, go back and see where you went wrong.

13. Repeat the steps to add a pitch to the lavatory south of the corridor.

14. Save the model (see Figure 6.52).

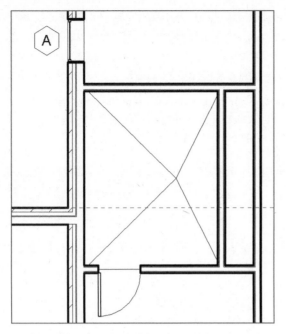

FIGURE 6.51:   The final slab in the restroom

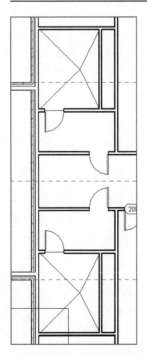

FIGURE 6.52:   Both lavatories are pitched and ready to have fixtures added.

Now that you have experience in creating and placing floors, as well as pitching a floor in a specific area, let's look at one more item: shaft openings.

CAN I ERASE THIS AND START OVER?

Often, you may need to clear shape edits of the entire slab and start over. You can do this by selecting the floor and clicking the Reset Shape button on the Options bar, as shown here:

Creating Shaft Openings

To create a shaft opening, you just create a void through your model. This void, however, can conform to walls that are set in the model. The elevator shaft walls, for instance, will define the outside edge of your shaft opening. You may notice that the floors you added to the model are indiscriminately running uninterrupted, straight through the shafts. You need to void the floor. Also, the good thing about creating a shaft opening is that if you create another floor, the shaft will be cut out automatically.

First you need to create two more levels. You need a subterranean level (T.O. Footing) and a penthouse level, through which you'll extend the elevator shaft. Follow these steps:

1. In the Project Browser, go to the South elevation.

2. On the Datum panel of the Architecture tab, click the Level button.

3. On the Draw panel, click the Pick Lines button, and set an offset of 10′–0″ (3000mm), as shown in Figure 6.53.

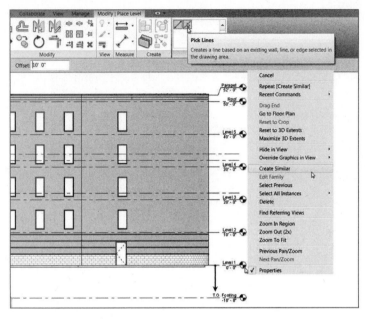

FIGURE 6.53: Adding a new Top of Footing level

4. Hover your cursor over Level 1. Make sure the alignment line is below Level 1. When you see the alignment line, pick Level 1. You now have a new level at -10′–0″ (-3000mm).

5. Click the Modify button on the Select panel to terminate the command.

6. Pick the level that is set to -10′–0″ (-3000mm), and rename it **T.O. Footing** (see Figure 6.53).

7. Click Yes when Revit prompts you to rename corresponding views.

The next step is to select the CMU elevator shaft walls and modify their properties so the bottoms are extended down to the top of the footing:

1. Go to a 3D view.

2. Select all of the east entry elevator CMU walls. Remember to press and hold the Ctrl key as you select the walls.

3. In the Properties dialog box, in the Constraints category, set Base Constraint to T.O. Footing, as shown in Figure 6.54.

To select all of the CMU walls, you can select one, right-click, and then click Select All Instances ➢ In Entire Project. Be careful, though; if there are other objects of the same type in the model, they will become selected as well.

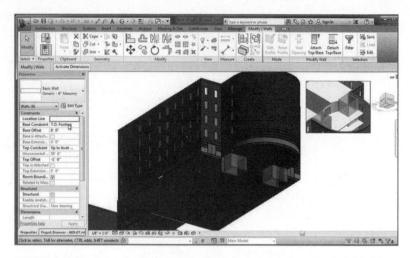

FIGURE 6.54:   In the Properties dialog box, change Base Constraint to T.O. Footing.

4. Click Apply.

With the bottom established at the correct level, it's time to add the shaft:

1. Go to the Level 1 floor plan. (Note that it doesn't matter which floor you're in when you place a shaft opening.)

2. On the Architecture tab, click the Shaft button in the Opening panel, as shown in Figure 6.55.

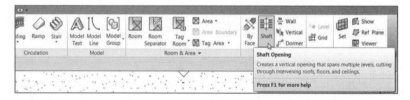

FIGURE 6.55:   Clicking the Shaft button on the Architecture tab

3. On the Modify | Create Shaft Opening Sketch tab, click Pick Walls, as shown in Figure 6.56.

4. Pick the walls shown in Figure 6.56. Notice that you can have more than one shaft opening in the same command.

5. Use the Line button on the Draw panel to draw the line across the inside face of the exterior wall.

6. Use the Trim command to clean up any corners (see Figure 6.56).

7. Mirror the lines you just drew up to the other shaft.

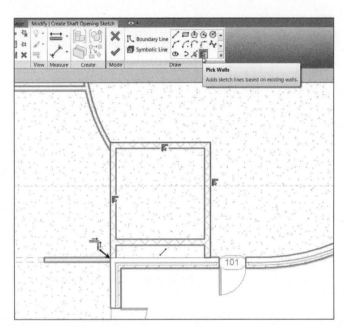

FIGURE 6.56: Adding the magenta lines to form the shaft opening to the outside of the CMU walls

With the perimeter established, it's time to choose which floors this opening will extend to. Just because you picked the CMU walls, this doesn't mean a base and a top height have been established. Follow these steps:

1. In the Properties dialog box, make sure Shaft Openings is selected, as shown in Figure 6.57.

2. In the Properties dialog, set Base Constraint to T.O. Footing.

3. Set Top Constraint to Up To Level: Roof.

4. Set Top Offset to -1′–0″ (-300mm); this keeps the roof from having two giant square holes in it.

5. Click Apply. Figure 6.57 shows the settings.

6. On the Modify | Create Shaft Opening Sketch tab, click the Symbolic Line button. This will allow you to sketch an opening graphic into the shaft.

7. Draw an X in both openings, as shown in Figure 6.58.

8. Click Finish Edit Mode.

FIGURE 6.57: Setting the properties of the shaft opening

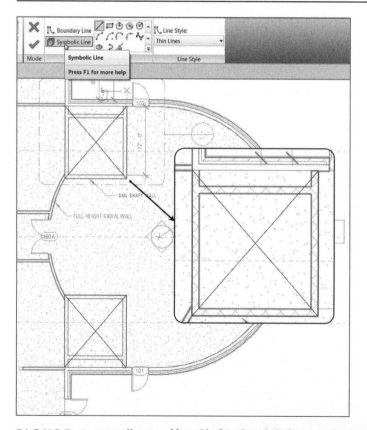

FIGURE 6.58: You can add any "drafting" symbolic lines you deem necessary.

The floor is now voided from the openings. Go to a 3D view, and look down the shafts. They're wide open, as shown in Figure 6.59. The symbolic lines you drew will appear in the floor plans only.

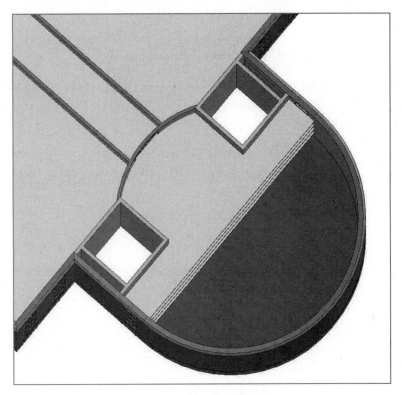

FIGURE 6.59:   The completed shafts as seen in 3D

 N O T E   A shaft opening voids only floors and roofs. Any other geometry, such as walls and structural framing, isn't voided. You need to modify these elements on a piece-by-piece basis.

Now that you know how to pitch floors, you can begin using Revit for its unique capabilities. Also, you're better prepared to move to the next chapter, which focuses on creating roofs.

Are You Experienced?

Now you can...

☑ add a floor to your model by using the building's footprint as a guide and by picking the walls and drawing lines

☑ add additional floors to higher levels by using the Copy/Paste Aligned method of quickly repeating the geometry up through the building

☑ add a specific, alternate material to different parts of the floor by using the Split Face command in conjunction with the paint materials function

☑ split a floor into segments, and add additional points to set a negative elevation for pitching to floor drains

☑ create a shaft opening that will cut out any new floor slab

☑ use symbolic lines within a shaft opening to indicate the opening

Roofs

Roofs come in all shapes and sizes. Given the nature of roofs, there is a lot to think about when you place a roof onto your building. If it's a flat roof, pitch is definitely a consideration. Drainage to roof drains or scuppers is another concern. But how about pitched roofs? Now you're in an entirely new realm of options, pitches, slopes, and everything else you can throw at a roof design. Also, there are always dormers that no pitched roof can live without! Do the dormers align with the eaves, or are they set back from the building?

▶ **Placing roofs by footprint**

▶ **Creating a sloping roof**

▶ **Creating roofs by extrusion**

▶ **Adding a roof dormer**

Placing Roofs by Footprint

This book can't address every situation you'll encounter with a roof system, but it will expose you to the tools needed to tackle these situations yourself. The techniques you'll employ in this chapter start with the concept of adding a roof to the model by using the actual floor-plan footprint. As with floors, you'll also build the roof's composition for use in schedules, quantities, and material takeoffs.

The command you'll probably use most often when working with roofs is the one to place a roof by footprint. Essentially, you'll create a roof by using the outline of the building in the plan view. There are three roof types you'll place by using a footprint:

▶ A flat roof (okay, no roof is actually flat, but you get the point)

▶ A gable roof, which has two sides that are sloped and ends that are left open

▶ A hip roof, which has all sides sloped

You have only these options while placing a roof by footprint because you're looking at the roof in the plan, which limits your ability to place a roof with non-uniform geometry. Later in the book, you'll explore doing just that, but for now let's start with placing a flat roof by using the footprint of the east wing.

Flat Roofs by Footprint

To begin, open the file in which you've been following along. If you didn't complete Chapter 6, "Floors," go to the book's web page at www.sybex.com/go/revit2014ner. From there, you can browse to Chapter 7 and find the file called NER-7.rvt.

 N O T E   Metric users should not type in mm or other metric abbreviations when entering amounts suggested in the exercises. The Autodesk® Revit® Architecture platform won't accept such abbreviations. Simply enter the number provided within the parentheses.

The objective of this procedure is to create a flat roof by outlining the building's geometry in the plan. Follow along:

1. In the Project Browser, double-click the Roof view in the Floor Plans section (be careful not to click Roof in the Ceiling Plans).

2. Zoom in to the east wing.

3. In the view Properties, find the Underlay row and select None from the menu, as shown in Figure 7.1.

FIGURE 7.1: Changing the view's Underlay to None

4. Click the Apply button if it's not already active.

5. Select all of the CMU walls again.

6. Set Top to Up To Level: Roof.

7. Set Top Offset to -1'-0" (-300mm).

8. On the Architecture tab, click Roof ➢ Roof By Footprint, as shown in Figure 7.2.

9. On the Modify | Create Roof Footprint tab, be sure the Pick Walls button on the Draw panel is selected, as shown at right in Figure 7.3.

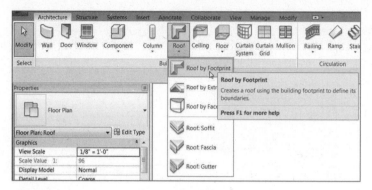

FIGURE 7.2: Clicking Roof By Footprint on the Architecture tab of the Design bar

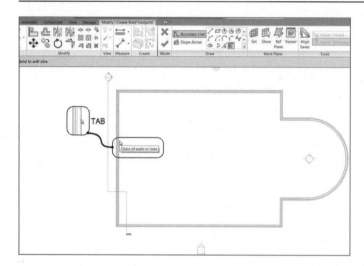

FIGURE 7.3: Adding a sketch line to the perimeter of the building by picking walls

10. On the Options bar, deselect Defines Slope.

11. On the Options bar, make sure Overhang is set to 0′–0″ (0mm).

12. Deselect Extend Into Wall Core (if it's selected).

13. Hover your pointer over the leftmost vertical wall. When it becomes highlighted, press the Tab key on your keyboard. All the perimeter walls highlight. When they do, pick (left-click) anywhere along the wall. This places a magenta sketch line at the perimeter of the building (see Figure 7.3).

14. On the Modify | Create Roof Footprint tab, click Finish Edit Mode.

15. Go to a 3D view, as shown in Figure 7.4.

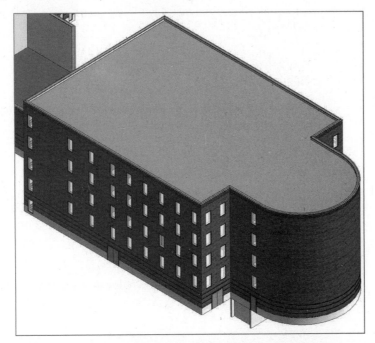

FIGURE 7.4: The roof has been added. You still have a lot of work to do, though.

With the roof added, step 1 is out of the way. Now you need to create a roof system. You'll do this the same way you created your floor system in Chapter 6.

Creating a Flat Roof System

Although you can use this system for a pitched roof, the steps for a flat roof system differ slightly. In Revit Architecture, there are two ways to look at a roofing system. One way is to create it by using all the typical roof materials and a large space for the structural framing. In this book, I don't recommend that approach. Creating a roof by using only the roofing components is necessary, but adding the structure will lead to conflicts when the actual structural model is linked with the architectural model. Also, it's hard for the architect to guess what the depth of the structural framing will be. In Revit, you want each component to be as literal and as true to the model as possible. The second way to look at a roofing system, as you're about to explore, is to build the roof in a literal sense—that is, to create the roof as it would sit on the structural framing by the structural engineer.

The objective of this procedure is to create a roof system by adding layers of materials. Follow these steps:

1. Select the roof. (If you're having trouble selecting the roof, remember the Filter tool.)

2. In the Properties dialog box, click Edit Type.

3. Click Duplicate.

4. Call the new roof system 4″ **Insulated Concrete Roof (100mm Insulated Concrete Roof).**

5. Click OK.

6. Click the Edit button in the Structure row.

7. Change the material of Structure 1 to Concrete, Lightweight. (You do this by clicking in the cell and then clicking the […] button. You can then select the material from the menu.) After the material is selected, click OK.

8. Change the structure Thickness to 4″ (100mm), as shown in Figure 7.5.

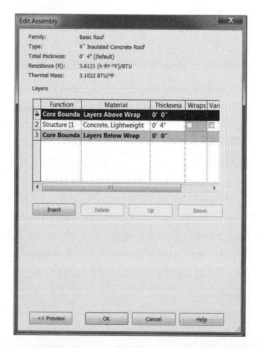

FIGURE 7.5: Changing the material and adding a layer

9. Insert a new layer above the core boundary. (You do this by clicking the number on the left side of the Layers Above Wrap row and clicking the Insert button below the Layers section, as shown in Figure 7.5.)

10. Change the function of the new layer to Thermal/Air Layer [3].

11. Click in the Material cell.

12. Click the […] button to open the Material Browser.

13. Select Rigid insulation for the material.

14. Click OK.

15. Change Thickness to 4″ (100mm).

16. Click the Variable button. When you modify the roof, this insulation layer will warp, enabling you to specify roof drain locations.

17. Insert a new layer above Insulation.

18. Give it a Function of Finish 1 [4].

19. Select Roofing - EPDM Membrane for the Material.

20. Click OK.

21. Change Thickness to 1/4″ (6mm), as shown in Figure 7.6.

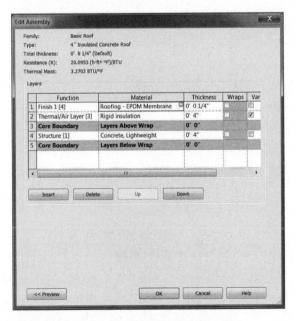

FIGURE 7.6: The completed roof system

22. Click OK.

23. Click OK again to get back to the model.

24. Press Esc or click in open space to clear the roof selection.

Phew! That was a long procedure. It was worth it, though. You'll be using this process a lot in Revit Architecture.

For the next procedure, you'll add some roof drain locations and then taper the insulation to drain to those locations.

TAKE A LOOK

It's always a good idea to keep the preview window open when you modify the roof system. If you look toward the bottom of the Edit Assembly dialog box, you'll see a Preview button, as shown in the following illustration. Click it, and you can see the roof as it's being constructed.

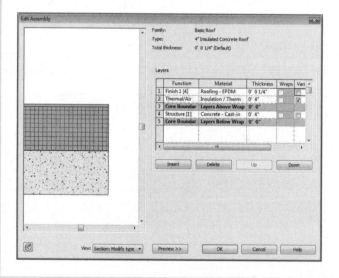

Tapering a Flat Roof and Adding Drains

If you went through the floor procedure in Chapter 6, you'll see that the process for tapering a roof is similar to pitching a floor. You may have also noticed that creating a roof system is identical to creating a floor system.

To taper the roof insulation, you must first divide the roof into peaks and valleys and then specify the drain locations based on the centering of these locations. Follow along:

1. In the Project Browser, make sure you're in the Roof floor plan.

2. Select the roof. (You may have to use the Filter tool.)

TIP   Even when you do successfully select the roof, you may not be able to tell. The roof doesn't seem to highlight. When the roof is selected, the Options bar shows the Modify icons. Also, look in the top of the Properties dialog box—it should read Basic Roof : 4″ Insulated Concrete Roof.

3. Click the Add Split Line button, as shown in Figure 7.7.

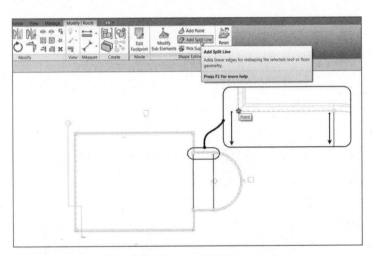

FIGURE 7.7:   Start splitting the radial portion of the roof.

4. Draw lines from the points shown in Figure 7.7.

5. Press Esc.

6. Select the roof.

TIP   The Chain tool is nice, but make sure it's deselected if you only want to draw single items.

T I P   One really nice thing about modifying the roof is that now, to select the roof, all you need to do is pick one of the ridgelines.

7. Click the Add Point button, as shown in Figure 7.8.

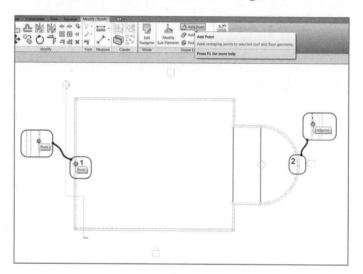

FIGURE 7.8:   Click the Add Point button, and add the two points.

8. Add two points at the midpoints marked 1 and 2 in Figure 7.8.

9. Click the Add Split Line button, and draw a ridge across the entire length of the building from point 1 to point 2, as shown in Figure 7.9.

10. Press Esc twice, or click Modify. Then, on the Architecture tab, click Ref Plane, as shown at upper right in Figure 7.10.

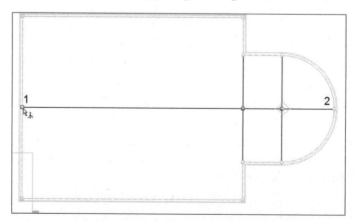

FIGURE 7.9:   Drawing a new ridge between the two points

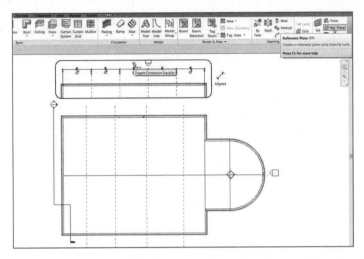

FIGURE 7.10: Add a dimension string to the reference planes shown here.

11. Draw four reference planes spaced approximately the same as in Figure 7.10.

12. On the Annotate tab, click the Aligned Dimension button.

13. Add a dimension string starting at the exterior wall to the left and ending at the exterior wall to the right (see Figure 7.10).

14. Click the blue EQ icon. This equally constrains the reference planes.

15. Press Esc twice, or click Modify to terminate the command.

16. Select the roof.

17. Click Add Split Line, as shown in Figure 7.11. Make sure to clear the Chain option.

18. Draw four ridges at the intersections of the reference planes (see Figure 7.11).

19. Press Esc.

20. Change Visual Style to Wireframe.

21. On the Annotate tab, click the Detail Line button.

22. Draw a diagonal line between the two points shown in Figure 7.12.

23. Click Modify, and then select the roof.

24. Click the Add Point button.

Chapter 7 • Roofs

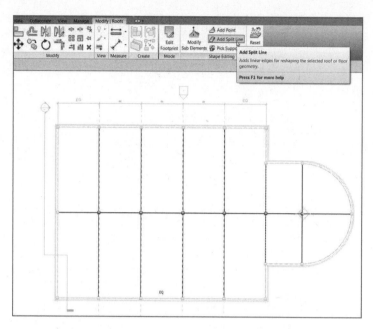

F I G U R E 7.11: The ridges are in. All that is left is to create some points and start tapering the roof.

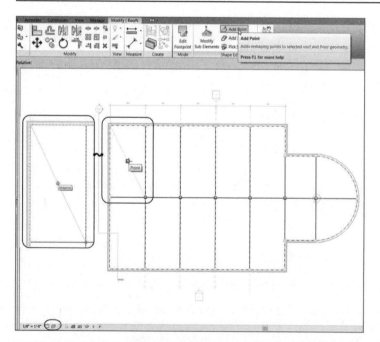

F I G U R E 7.12: Adding a temporary line

25. Pick the midpoint of the diagonal line.

26. There is a node where you picked the point. To access the node, click the Modify Sub Elements button on the Shape Editing panel, as shown in Figure 7.13.

27. Pick the point you just added. A blue elevation appears, as shown in Figure 7.14. Click the elevation, and type -3″ (-75mm).

28. Press Esc twice.

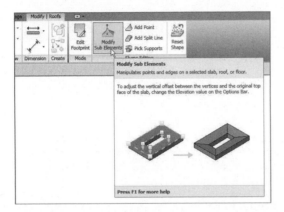

FIGURE 7.13: Click the Modify Sub Elements button to gain access to the points on the roof.

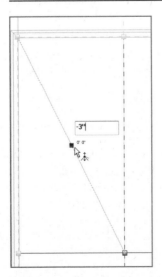

FIGURE 7.14: Click here to taper the roof to this point.

This process tapers the insulation only in this bay, as shown in Figure 7.15. The objective now is to do the same thing for every bay. Because you can't copy a point, you need to move the temporary line to the next bay and add a new point.

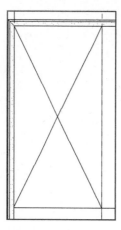

FIGURE 7.15: **The taper is in place.**

Follow along to create another taper:

1. Move the diagonal line (which you drew as a reference) to the next bay to the right.

2. Select the roof.

3. Click the Add Point button.

4. Click the Modify Sub Elements button, and add a point to the midpoint of the line.

5. Type -3″ (-75mm) in the blue elevation. The roof tapers.

6. Move the line to the next bay, and repeat the process.

N O T E   As you're adding additional lines in this section, remember that I'm merely recommending that you use the Move tool. At this point, you have enough experience either to draw in the lines or to use any tool you've studied thus far.

7. Complete every bay.

8. Add points to the radial area as well.

9. Delete the dimensions, the reference lines, and the detail lines.

10. Change Visual Style back to Hidden.

11. Your roof should look like Figure 7.16 when you've finished.

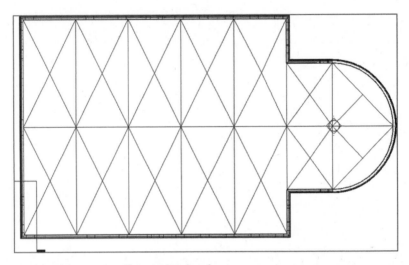

F I G U R E 7 . 1 6 :   **The completed roof**

To further investigate how this roof works, and to illustrate the benefits of using this approach rather than drafting the lines, let's cut a section through the roof and see how the detail looks:

1. On the Create panel of the View tab, click the Section button.

2. Add a section through the roof, as shown in Figure 7.17.

3. In the Type Selector, make sure the type of section is a building section, and change View Scale to 3/4″ = 1′–0″ (1:20mm).

4. Change Detail Level to Fine.

5. Change the View Name option (under Identity Data) to Roof Taper Section (see Figure 7.18).

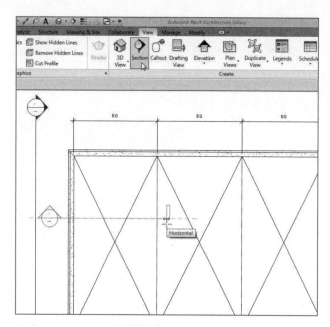

FIGURE 7.17:   Adding a section through the roof at this point

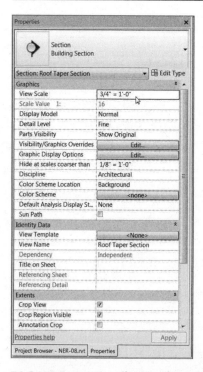

FIGURE 7.18:   Changing the properties of the section

6. Click the Apply button.

7. Double-click the section head (or find the section called Roof Taper Section in the Project Browser).

8. Adjust the crop region so you're looking only at the roof area, as shown in Figure 7.19. Zoom to fit.

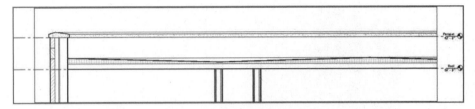

FIGURE 7.19: By adding the points to the roof, you now have an almost perfect section.

This concludes modeling a flat roof. You can now move on to creating a pitched roof. Again, although these types of roofs can be easy to add in the beginning, more work will be required to get them exactly the way you want them.

THE PROOF IS IN THE ROOF!

This is a perfect example of why the Revit approach to design documentation is the way to go. Although the sloping of the slab may have seemed tedious, in reality it didn't take much longer than it would have if you had drafted those lines in a CAD application. But now, to produce a section, all you need to do is to cut one. Also, if you change the location or the depth of the roof pitch, your lines in the plan will be accurate, as will your section.

Pitched Roofs by Footprint

You'll add a pitched roof in a manner identical to the way you added the flat roof. The only real difference is that each magenta sketch line will need more attention before you finish the sketch. But after tapering the roof's insulation, this will be a cakewalk.

You'll place the pitched roof over the corridor. The problem with the corridor is that you used a wall system with a parapet cap. This isn't the best wall system to receive a pitched roof. First you'll change to a simpler wall system, as follows:

1. Go to a 3D view of the model.

2. Select the six corridor walls, as shown in Figure 7.20.

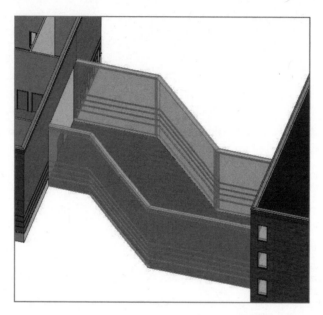

FIGURE 7.20:   Select the six walls to be modified.

3. In the Properties dialog box, click the Edit Type button.

4. Click the Duplicate button.

5. Call the new wall system **Exterior - Brick and CMU on MTL. Stud (No Parapet)**.

6. In the Structure row, click the Edit button.

7. In the Edit Assembly dialog box, make sure the Preview button is selected and the view is set to Section, as shown at the bottom of Figure 7.21.

8. Click the Sweeps button (see Figure 7.21).

9. In the Wall Sweeps dialog box, you see three sweeps. The top sweep is the parapet cap. Select sweep 1 (Parapet Cap), and click the Delete button, as shown in Figure 7.22.

10. Click OK three times.

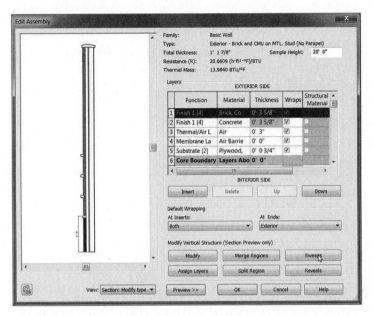

FIGURE 7.21:   Without the Preview button selected and set to Section, you can't modify the parapet sweep.

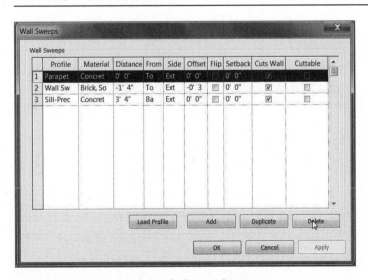

FIGURE 7.22:   Deleting the Parapet Cap sweep

Remember, your preview must be in Section: Modify Type for all the buttons to be active.

Your corridor walls should look exactly the same, but they're now void of the concrete parapet cap.

N O T E   Although you have pretty good experience with walls up to this point, Chapter 16, "Advanced Wall Topics," is dedicated to the advanced concepts and creation of wall systems.

It's time to add the roof to the corridor. Because the walls your roof will bear on are now correct, the rest will be a snap! Here are the steps:

1. Go to the Level 3 floor plan. (This is the roof level for your corridor.)

2. On the Architecture tab, choose Roof ➤ Roof By Footprint.

3. On the Draw panel, make sure the Pick Walls button is selected.

4. On the Options bar, make sure the Defines Slope button is selected.

5. Type 1' (300mm) in the Overhang field.

6. Pick the six walls that compose the corridor, as shown in Figure 7.23.

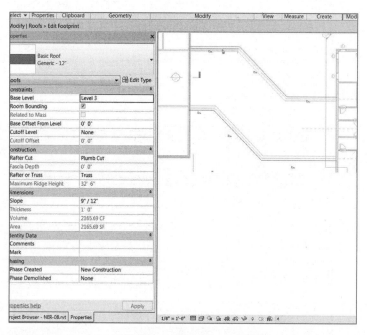

FIGURE 7.23:   Pick these walls for the roof's footprint.

With the easy walls out of the way, let's create the gable ends. You should still be in Pick Walls Mode. This is okay, but there are a few things you need to change on the Options bar. Follow these steps:

1. Click the Boundary Line button on the Draw panel if it isn't still active.

2. On the Draw panel again, click the Pick Lines icon, as shown in Figure 7.24.

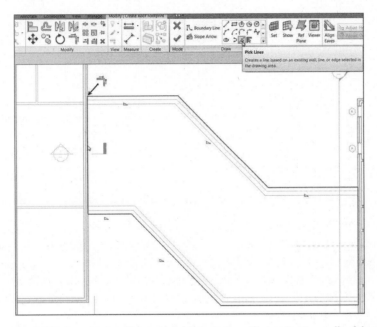

FIGURE 7.24: You must pick lines to trace the terminating walls of the roof.

3. On the Options bar, deselect Defines Slope.

4. For the offset, enter 0.

5. Pick the east wall of the west wing and the west wall of the east wing (see Figure 7.24).

It's cleanup time! Of course, the magenta lines are overlapping at the long walls. This is okay—you're an expert at the Trim command by now, especially in Sketch Mode:

1. On the Modify | Create Roof Footprint tab, select the Trim/Extend To Corner command, as shown in Figure 7.25.

As you pick the walls, notice that you now have an overhang. This overhang obviously needs to extend to the outside of the walls. Just be conscious of this as you pick the walls, and watch your alignment lines as you proceed.

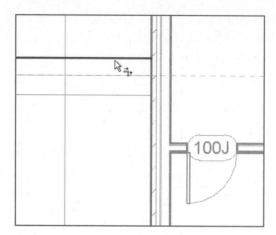

FIGURE 7.25:   Using the Trim command in conjunction with the roof sketch

2. Trim the intersections that overlap. There are four of them (see Figure 7.25).

3. On the Mode panel, click Finish Edit Mode, and go to a 3D view.

One ugly roof, huh? Welcome to the world of pitched roofs in Revit. You'll get the roof you want—you just need to add two roofs here. You'll understand this process, but it's going to involve patience and trial and error!

To fix this roof, you simply have to make two separate roofs and join them together. This is a common procedure for the more complicated roof systems in Revit. Here are the steps:

1. If you aren't in Level 3, go there now, and select the roof.

2. On the Modify | Roofs tab, click the Edit Footprint button, as shown in Figure 7.26.

3. Delete every line other than the three shown in Figure 7.27.

4. On the Draw panel, click the Line button.

5. Draw a diagonal line between the endpoints of the two lines, as shown in Figure 7.28. Make sure the Defines Slope button isn't selected.

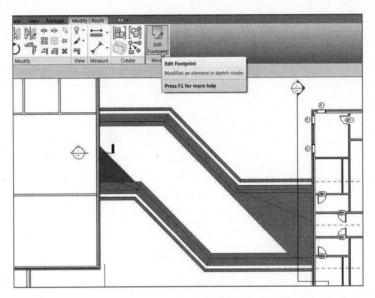

F I G U R E 7 . 2 6 :   Selecting the roof and clicking the Edit Footprint button

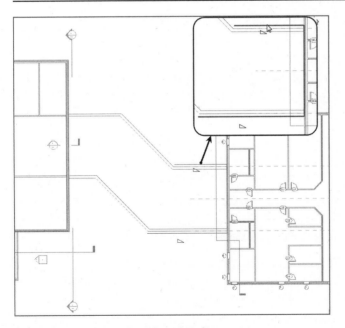

F I G U R E 7 . 2 7 :   Keep these three lines.

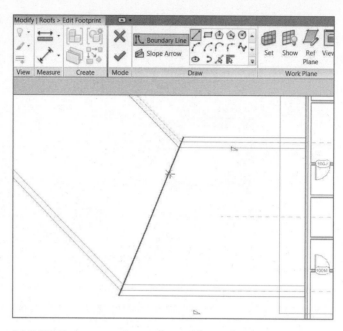

FIGURE 7.28: Draw a diagonal line as shown.

6. On the Modify | Roofs ➤ Edit Footprint tab, click Finish Edit Mode. The roof displays. It still looks funny, but you'll take care of that soon by altering the view range to make the view deep enough to display the ridge of the new roof.

7. Start the Roof ➤ Roof By Footprint command again on the Architecture tab. You can also select the roof, and click Create Similar on the Modify | Roofs tab that is currently active.

8. On your own, sketch the roof shown in Figure 7.29. Make sure the lines along the walls are defining a slope. The lines that represent the ends of the roof don't slope.

9. To add the line that matches the roof to the right, make sure the Boundary Line button is selected on the Draw panel and that Pick Lines is selected as well. Now simply pick the roof to the right, and the line appears.

10. Review Figure 7.29 to see if your sketch matches. You should have six lines total, and the right and the left ends should not have a slope.

11. On the Modify | Create Roof Footprint tab, click Finish Edit Mode.

12. Go to a 3D view. Does your roof look like Figure 7.30?

> If you accidentally add a line with (or without) a slope, that's fine. You can change it. First press Esc (to clear the command), and then select the line that needs to be changed. On the Options bar, you can select (or deselect) Defines Slope.

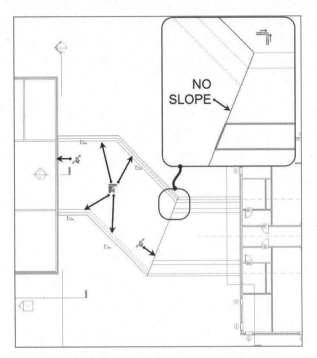

FIGURE 7.29: The new outline of the second roof

FIGURE 7.30: The corridor roof in 3D

When you've success-
fully mitered a corner
and are ready to move
to the next, nothing
indicates that you can
safely pick another
corner. You don't need
to keep trying to trim.
When you see that the
walls are at a miter,
you can pick the next
intersection. When
you've finished all four,
press Esc.

You don't always have
to modify the wall's
mitering. This exercise
is a special situation
in which the corners
won't attach to the
roof properly unless
you do so. There's really
no explanation for
why and when this will
occur. Just know that
you have some tools
under your belt to get
out of these real-life
situations.

The walls need some help! They're indiscriminately poking up through the roof. Let's do some wall cleanup. First, you need to force the walls to use a mitered join at the 45° intersections. The following procedure shows you how:

1. Go to the Level 1 floor plan.

2. Zoom in to the wall intersection, as shown in Figure 7.31.

3. On the Modify tab, click the Wall Joins button (see Figure 7.31).

4. Move your cursor over the intersection. A box forms around the corner. When you see this box, pick the wall.

5. On the Options bar, click the Miter radio button. The walls are now
   joined at a miter.

6. Perform this procedure at all four corners.

You can now attach the tops of the walls to the bottom of the roof, as follows:

1. Go back to a 3D view, and select one of the corridor walls.

2. On the Modify | Walls tab is an option to attach the top or base of the
   wall, as shown in Figure 7.32. Click the Attach Top/Base button.

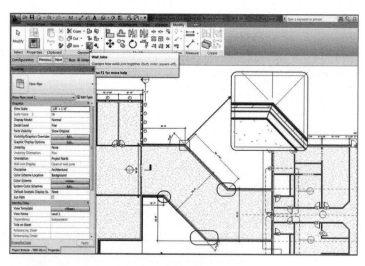

FIGURE 7.31:   Modifying the walls' corners

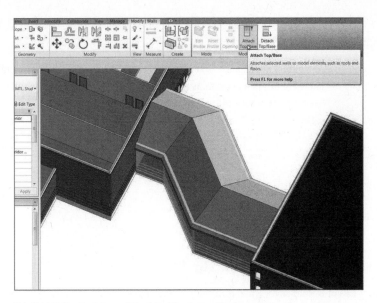

FIGURE 7.32:   Attaching the top or the base

3. Pick the roof that the wall is under. The wall no longer sticks up past the roof.

4. Perform steps 1 through 3 for each corridor wall. When you're finished, your corridor roof should be magnificent, just like Figure 7.33.

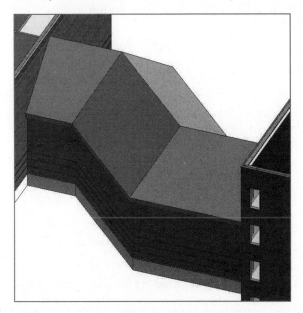

FIGURE 7.33:   The completed corridor roof

But I Got This Warning!

Sometimes Revit doesn't like you hacking up its perfectly fine walls. The warning shown in this image pertains to the soldier course in the wall. Because the walls are now lower than that elevation, Revit is kind enough to tell you.

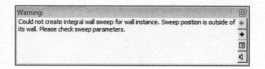

Viewing a Sloped Roof in the Plan

Back in Level 3 (the level in which the corridor roof resides), you're having a view problem: the roof is showing up only to the cut plane for that level. This can't be. There is a procedure to correct this, called a *plan region*. Here are the steps:

1. Go to the Level 3 floor plan.

2. On the View tab, choose Plan Views ➤ Plan Region, as shown in Figure 7.34.

3. On the Draw panel, click the Rectangle button, as shown in Figure 7.35.

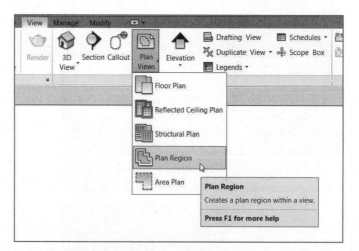

FIGURE 7.34: Using a plan region enables you to alter the view range in a specified area of a plan.

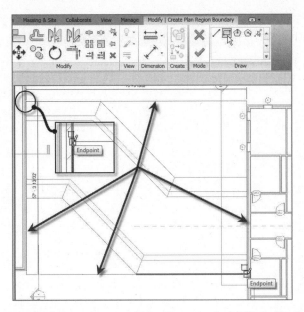

FIGURE 7.35: Creating the rectangle that forms the perimeter of the plan region

4. Draw a rectangle around the corridor (see Figure 7.35). Be sure to snap to the exact points where the roof meets the taller walls on the east and west wings.

5. In the Properties dialog box, click the Edit button in the View Range row (see Figure 7.36).

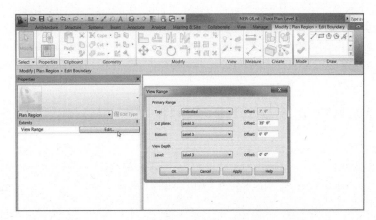

FIGURE 7.36: Setting the View Range for the plan region

6. In the View Range dialog box, set Top to Unlimited and Level 3 Cut Plane Offset to 35′–0″ (**11500**mm), as shown in Figure 7.36.

7. Click OK.

8. On the Modify | Create Plan Region Boundary tab, click Finish Edit Mode.

   You can now see the roof in its entirety, as shown in Figure 7.37.

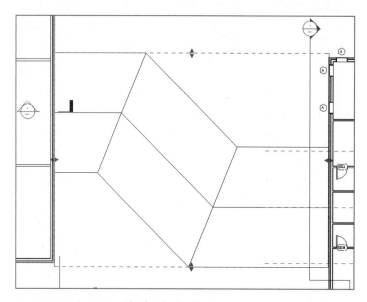

FIGURE 7.37:   The finished roof plan

There is one more kind of roof to add. It will be a flat roof that has a slope in a single direction. Although you can do this by simply creating a roof with one edge specified as a pitch, at times you'll want a roof sloped at an odd direction that can't be handled by angling a roof edge.

Creating a Sloping Roof

To begin the process of creating a sloping roof, you'll cap off the west wing of your building. The exterior walls used for the perimeter need to be altered. You're already a pro at this, so let's start right there:

1. Go to a 3D view.

2. Select the west wing exterior walls (see Figure 7.38).

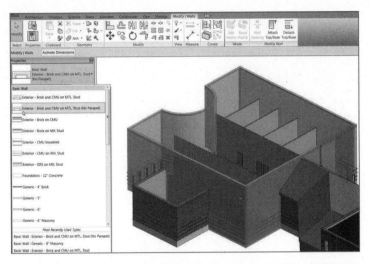

FIGURE 7.38: Changing the walls to Exterior - Brick And CMU On MTL. Stud (No Parapet)

3. In the Type Selector, select Exterior - Brick And CMU On MTL. Stud (No Parapet), as shown in Figure 7.38.

4. In the Project Browser, go to the West Roof floor plan.

5. On the Architecture tab, choose Roof ➢ Roof By Footprint.

6. On the Draw panel, verify that the Pick Walls button is selected.

7. On the Options bar, deselect Defines Slope.

8. Type 1′ (300mm) for the Overhang value.

9. Move your cursor over a wall. Make sure the overhang alignment line is facing outside the walls to the exterior.

10. Press the Tab key. All the walls are selected.

11. Pick the wall. The magenta lines are completely drawn in. Your sketch should look like Figure 7.39.

Now it's time to set the slope. The objective here is to slope the roof starting at the northeast corner (as the low point) and ending at the southwest corner (the high point). You do this by adding a slope arrow, as follows:

1. On the Draw panel, click the Slope Arrow button, as shown in Figure 7.40.

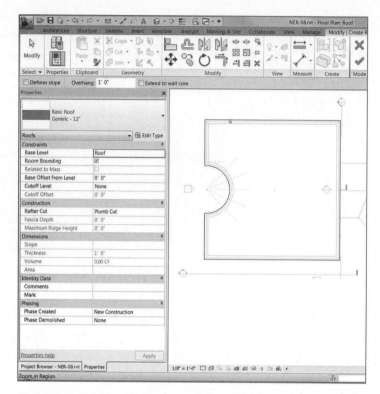

FIGURE 7.39:   The perimeter of the roof is set.

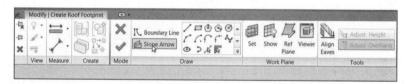

FIGURE 7.40:   Clicking the Slope Arrow button on the Draw panel

2. Pick the corner at upper right and then the corner at lower left, as shown in Figure 7.41.

3. Press Esc.

4. Select the slope arrow you just added to the model.

5. In the Properties dialog box, under Constraints, change Specify to Slope.

6. Under Dimensions, change Slope to **3″ / 12″** (250 / 1000mm), as shown in Figure 7.42.

7. Click Finish Edit Mode on the Modify | Create Roof Footprint tab.

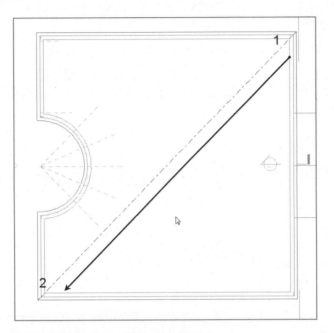

FIGURE 7.41: Adding the slope arrow

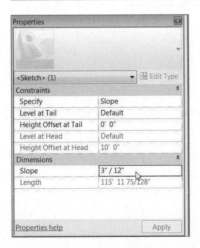

FIGURE 7.42: Changing the Slope Arrow properties

Again, you have a view range issue. You can see only the corner of the roof that sits below the cut plane. You can change that with the view range:

1. Press Esc to display the view properties in the Properties dialog box.

2. Scroll down the list until you arrive at the View Range row. When you do, click the Edit button.

3. In the View Range dialog box, under Primary Range, set Top to Unlimited.

4. Set the Cut Plane Offset to 40′ 0″ (12000mm), as shown in Figure 7.43.

FIGURE 7.43: Setting the view range

5. Change the rest of the settings to reflect Figure 7.43.

6. Click OK. You can see the entire roof.

7. Go to a 3D view. You now have a cool, sloping roof, as shown in Figure 7.44.

Of course, there is a wall issue. You can attach most of the walls to the roof simply by selecting them and attaching the tops. But you'll have to modify the profile for one wall, as follows:

1. In the 3D view, select all of the exterior west wing walls, excluding the one on the east side that is west of the corridor. (You can see it in Figure 7.45.)

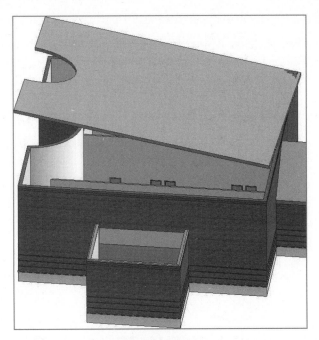

FIGURE 7.44: The sloping roof

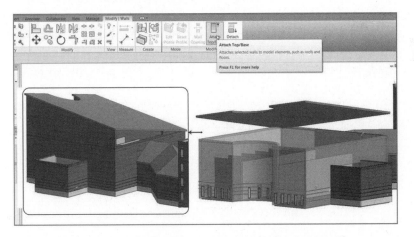

FIGURE 7.45: Attaching the tops of the walls to the sloping roof

2. On the Modify | Walls tab, select Attach Top/Base.

3. Pick Top from the Options bar (it's all the way to the left).

4. Pick the sloping roof (see Figure 7.45).

5. In the Project Browser, go to the section called West Corridor Section.

6. Select the wall that doesn't attach to the roof.

7. On the Mode panel, click Edit Profile.

8. Trace the roof with the Line tool. Be sure you delete the magenta line that established the top of the wall.

9. On the Sketch tab, click Finish Edit Mode. All of the walls are now joined to the roof. This would be a good time to check out the roof in 3D just to make sure the results are pleasing to you.

10. Save the model.

The next item to tackle will be creating a roof by extrusion. This is where you can design a custom roof.

Creating Roofs by Extrusion

Creating a roof by extrusion is almost always done in an elevation or a section view. The concept is to create unique geometry that can't be accomplished by simply using a footprint in a plan. A barrel vault or an eyebrow dormer comes to mind, but there are literally thousands of combinations that will influence how your roofs will be designed.

To get started, the last roof left to be placed is the south jog in the west wing of the model. This is the perfect area for a funky roof!

The first thing to do is to change the three walls defining the jog to the Exterior - Brick And CMU On MTL. Stud (No Parapet) wall type:

1. Go to a 3D view.

2. Select the three walls that compose the jog in the south wall (see Figure 7.46).

3. From the Properties dialog box, switch these walls to Exterior - Brick And CMU On MTL. Stud (No Parapet), as shown in Figure 7.46.

4. Go to the Level 1 floor plan.

5. On the View tab, click the Elevation button.

6. In the Properties dialog box, be sure that the elevation is a Building elevation (you're given the choice in the drop-down menu at the top of the dialog box).

7. Place the elevation as shown in Figure 7.47.

8. Open the elevation you just created.

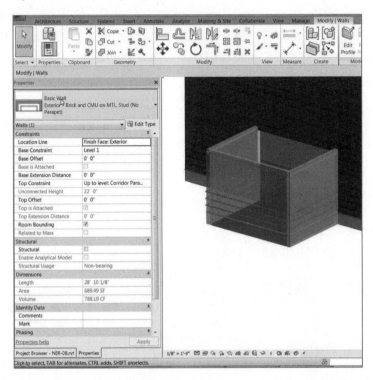

FIGURE 7.46: Changing the wall types as you have been doing all along

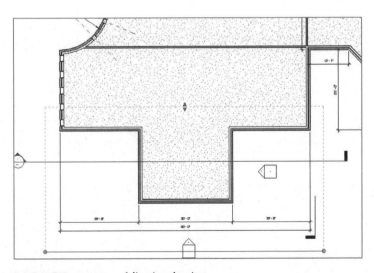

FIGURE 7.47: Adjusting the view

After you place the elevation, you'll have no idea where the view is extended to. Is it to the end of the building? You just don't know. If you pick the elevation arrow (the part of the elevation marker), you can then grip-edit the elevation to see what you need.

9. Pick the view extents (the blue grips at the ends of the elevation), and drag them in so that you can see only the west wing.

10. Make sure you pull the view depth window back to see the wall beyond (see Figure 7.47).

11. Change View Scale to 1/2″ = 1′–0″ (1:20mm).

12. Change Detail Level to Fine.

13. Change View Name to **South Entry Elevation**.

14. Click the Apply button.

15. On the Architecture tab, click the Ref Plane button; then, in the Draw panel, click the Pick Lines button.

16. Set Offset to 1′–6″ (450mm).

17. Pick the southernmost wall, and offset the reference plane away from the building (see Figure 7.48).

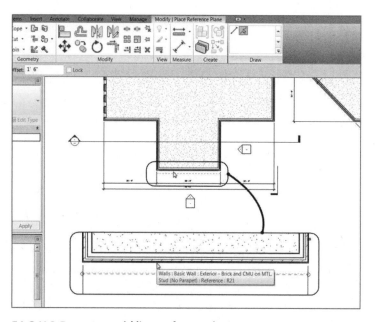

FIGURE 7.48: Adding a reference plane

18. Press Esc twice, or click Modify to clear the command.

19. Select the reference plane.

20. In the Properties dialog box, change the name to **South Entry Overhang**.

21. Click Apply.

22. Open the elevation called South Entry Elevation.

The importance of the reference plane that you just added becomes obvious at this point. You needed to establish a clear starting point for the roof you're about to add. Because the roof will be added in an elevation, Revit doesn't know where to start the extrusion. This reference plane will serve as the starting point. Naming reference planes is the way you can use them when they aren't visible in the view. Continue with these steps:

1. On the Architecture tab, choose Roof ➤ Roof By Extrusion, as shown in Figure 7.49.

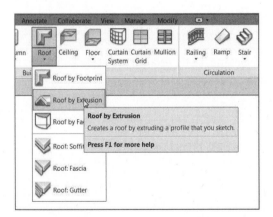

F I G U R E   7 . 4 9 :   The Roof ➤ Roof By Extrusion command

2. When you start the command, Revit asks you to specify a reference plane. Select Reference Plane: South Entry Overhang from the Name drop-down list, as shown in Figure 7.50.

FIGURE 7.50: Selecting the South Entry Overhang reference plane

3. Click OK.

4. In the next dialog box, change the Level setting to Level 3, and click OK.

5. In the Work Plane panel, click Ref Plane, as shown in Figure 7.51, and then click the Pick Lines button.

6. Offset a reference plane 3′–0″ (900mm) to the left and to the right of the exterior walls, marked 1 and 2 in Figure 7.51.

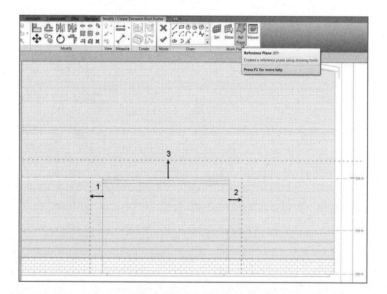

FIGURE 7.51: Adding reference planes to use as construction lines

7. Offset a reference plane 4'–0" (1200mm) up from the top of the wall, as marked 3 in Figure 7.51.

8. In the Properties dialog box, select Roofs from the drop-down list, and then click the Edit Type button.

9. Click Duplicate.

10. Change the name to **Canopy Roof**.

11. Click the Edit button in the Structure row.

12. In the Edit Assembly dialog box, change the structure thickness to 4" (100mm), as shown in Figure 7.52.

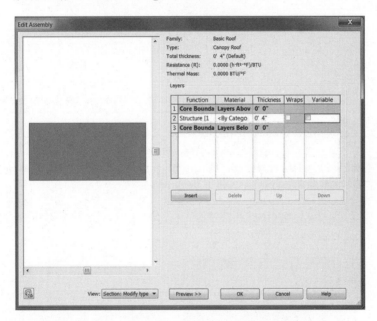

FIGURE 7.52: Changing the thickness of the canopy roof

13. Click OK twice to get back to the model.

It's time to put the actual roof into the model. So far, you've been using great discipline in terms of setting reference planes and creating a separate roof for this canopy. Try to make this a habit! Follow along:

1. On the Draw panel of the Modify | Create Extrusion Roof Profile tab, click the Start-End-Radius Arc button, as shown in Figure 7.53.

2. Draw an arc from the points shown in Figure 7.53.

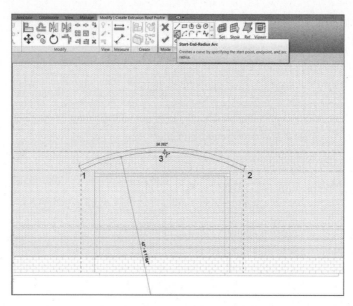

F I G U R E   7 . 5 3 :   Drawing an arc, which will define the outside face of the roof

T I P   When you're adding a roof by extrusion, you need to draw only one line. The thickness is defined in the roof you're using. After you click Finish Edit Mode, the 4″ (100mm) thickness will be added to the bottom.

3. In the Properties dialog box, set Extrusion End to -2′–0″ (-600mm), as shown in Figure 7.54.

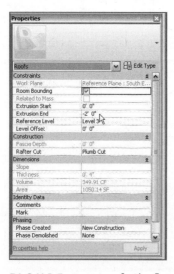

F I G U R E   7 . 5 4 :   Setting Extrusion End

4. Click Finish Edit Mode.

5. Go to a 3D view. Your roof should look like Figure 7.55.

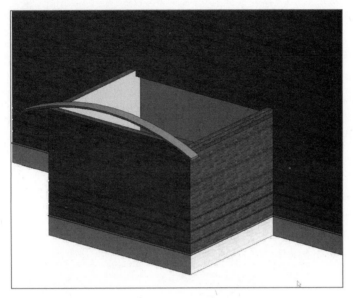

FIGURE 7.55:   The almost completed canopy roof

There is just one thing left to do, and it's pretty obvious: you need to attach the roof to the wall. This can be done in one command:

1. On the Modify tab, click the Join/Unjoin Roof button, as shown in Figure 7.56.

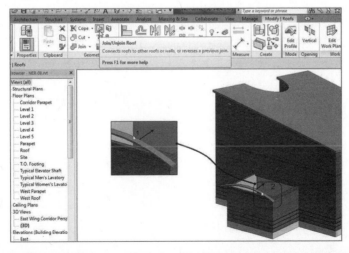

FIGURE 7.56:   Picking the roof and the wall to join the two together

2. Pick the top, back arc on the canopy roof, as shown in Figure 7.56.

3. Pick the wall into which the roof needs to terminate (see Figure 7.56).

4. Your roof should look like Figure 7.57. Select the three walls below the roof.

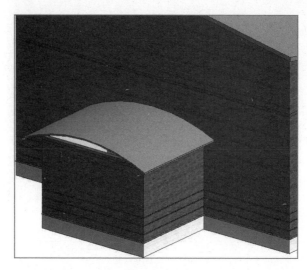

FIGURE 7.57: The completed canopy

5. On the Modify | Walls tab, click the Attach Top/Base button.

6. Select the canopy roof.

The walls are now joined to the roof, as shown in Figure 7.58.

All of the conventional roofing systems have been added. Let's move on and add some dormers. This process will require the use of a collection of the tools with which you've gained experience up to this point.

Adding a Roof Dormer

The best way to add a roof dormer is to modify an existing roof. You certainly have plenty of those in this model, so there should be no shortage of roof surfaces you can chop up into dormers.

To begin adding a roof dormer, follow along:

1. Go to the Level 3 floor plan.

2. Zoom in on the corridor roof.

3. Select the corridor roof, as shown in Figure 7.59.

Picking the wall is easier said than done, mostly because it's hard to tell whether you're picking the correct wall. Simply hover your pointer over the wall until the entire face becomes highlighted. When you see this, pick the wall. The roof will then extend to the wall.

4. On the Modify | Roofs tab, click the Edit Footprint button.

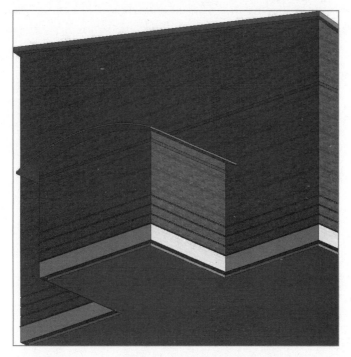

FIGURE 7.58: The walls are now attached to the roof.

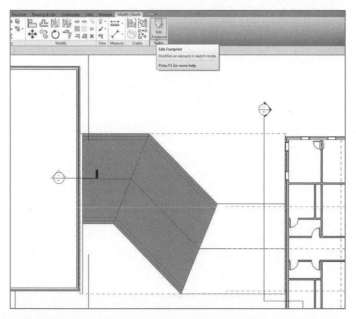

FIGURE 7.59: Selecting the roof to be modified

You're now in the Sketch Mode for this roof.

The procedure to modify the roof is reminiscent of climbing up on an actual roof and adding a dormer:

1. On the Modify | Roofs ➤ Edit Footprint tab, select the Split Element button, as shown in Figure 7.60.

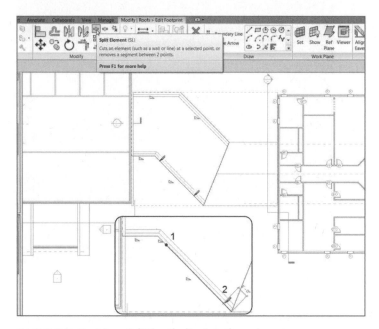

FIGURE 7.60:   Splitting the line into three pieces

2. On the Options bar, deselect Delete Inner Segment.

3. Pick two points on the roof edge (see Figure 7.60).

4. The two points are an even 4′ (1200mm) in from each edge.

5. Press Esc twice.

6. Select the middle line.

7. On the Options bar, deselect Defines Slope.

With the length of the dormer established, you need to indicate to Revit that you want it to be a gable-end dormer. You do this by adding slope arrows:

1. On the Draw panel, click the Slope Arrow button.

2. For the first point of the slope arrow, click the endpoint of the first point you split (marked 1 in Figure 7.61).

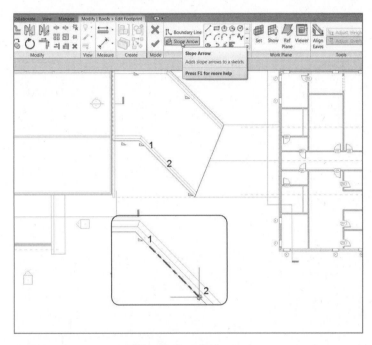

FIGURE 7.61:   Adding the first slope arrow

3. For the second point of the slope arrow, pick the endpoint of the same line (see Figure 7.61).

4. Add a second slope arrow coming from the opposite side of the ridge-line, as shown in Figure 7.62.

5. Press Esc twice.

6. Select both slope arrows.

7. In the Properties dialog box, under Constraints, change Specify to Slope.

8. Under Dimensions, keep the slope at 9″ / 12″ (750/1000mm) (see Figure 7.63).

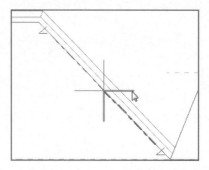

FIGURE 7.62: Adding a second slope arrow

FIGURE 7.63: Changing the values of the slope arrows

9. Click Finish Edit Mode.

10. Go to a 3D view to check out the dormer. It should look identical to Figure 7.64.

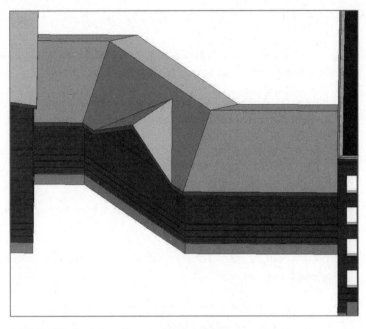

F I G U R E   7 . 6 4 :   The completed roof dormer

Adding roof dormers takes some practice to become efficient. If you don't feel confident that you can add a roof dormer on your own, feel free to either go back through the procedure or find another place in the building to add a second dormer.

N O T E   Notice in the 3D view that the wall followed the modification in the roof. This is because you attached the wall to the roof back when you added the roof to the corridor. The walls have no choice but to comply!

Are You Experienced?

Now you can...

☑ place different types of roofs, including flat roofs, pitched roofs, and unconventional sloping roofs, using the footprint of your building

☑ analyze tricky areas, and make multiple roofs if needed instead of relying on a single roof to flex and conform to the situation at hand

☑ edit wall joins to allow walls to attach to roofs after they're created

☑ design different roof systems based on their functionality

☑ create a tapered roof plan using a variable material in the roof system

☑ create a roof by extrusion by setting work planes and using them to lay out a custom roof

☑ create a roof dormer by editing an existing roof and adding slope arrows to indicate a gable end

Structural Items

Well, we can't avoid the topic of structure forever. Because you need to consider your structure from pretty much the beginning of the project, I had better add it to the first half of the book before we get too carried away!

▶ **Adding structural grids**

▶ **Adding structural columns**

▶ **Using structural framing**

▶ **Understanding foundation systems**

▶ **Adding structural footings**

▶ **Using structural views**

Adding Structural Grids

The Autodesk® Revit® Architecture 2014 program marks the first time that the full Revit Architecture, Structure, and MEP applications are blended together into one complete application with no separate, stand-alone applications for the different trades. This gives you, the architect, the same full spectrum of structural tools as your structural consultant. How far you delve into the structural design of your projects is between you and your structural consultant.

This chapter explores the structural world by presenting the basic functions of structural architecture. The first item you'll tackle is usually the first item in the model: structural grids. Although you add structural grids line by line, you'll soon discover that these grids are just as smart as the rest of Revit. The starting point for all things structural is most certainly the grid. In Revit, you'll quickly find that placing a structural grid into a model isn't a complicated task. Grids are essentially placed one line at a time. Those lines you place, however, have intelligence. For example, if you place a vertical grid line called A and then place a horizontal grid line called 1 that intersects with A, you'll have a grid location. If you place a column at that intersection, the column will assume a new property called Location. That location is—you guessed it—A-1.

Let's get started. To begin, open the file in which you've been following along. If you didn't complete the previous chapter, go to www.sybex.com/go/revit2014ner, browse to Chapter 8, and find the file called NER-08.rvt.

Placing a Grid

Placing a grid means drawing grid lines one by one. You can copy grids to speed up placement, and array them if the spacing is regular. This task sounds tedious, but it's a welcome change from other applications that force you to create an entire, rectangular grid, at which you have to keep picking until it resembles your layout. Grids are like snowflakes: no two are the same.

 N O T E   Metric users should not type in mm or other metric abbreviations when entering amounts suggested in the exercises. Revit will not accept such abbreviations. Simply enter the number provided within the parentheses.

To place a grid, follow these steps:

1. In the Project Browser, go to the Level 1 floor plan. (Make sure you aren't in the Level 1 ceiling plan.)

2. Zoom in to the east wing's radial entry.

3. The Datum panel that holds the Level and Grid tools appears on both the Architecture and Structure tabs. On the Datum panel of the Structure tab, click the Grid button, as shown in Figure 8.1.

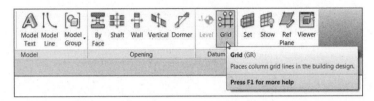

FIGURE 8.1:   The Grid button on the Datum panel of the Structure tab

4. On the Draw panel of the Modify | Place Grid tab, click the Pick Lines icon, as shown in Figure 8.2.

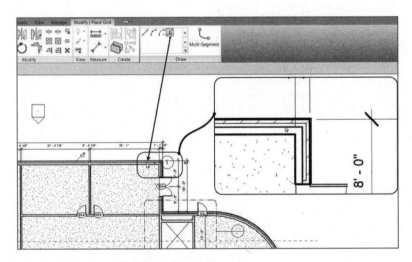

FIGURE 8.2:   Your first column grid

5. Pick the centerline of the north wall (see Figure 8.2).

6. The grid bubble needs to be moved. Press Esc twice, or click Modify (to clear the command), and select the grid bubble. Notice the round blue grip similar to that in Figure 8.3.

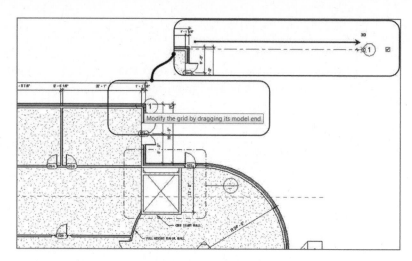

FIGURE 8.3:   Examining the column grid grips

7. Pick that round blue grip, and drag the column bubble to the right about 50′ (15,000mm), as shown in Figure 8.4.

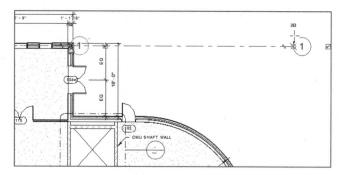

FIGURE 8.4:   Dragging the column bubble to the right

Notice that a column grid has functionality similar to that of levels, right down to the grips.

8. On the Datum panel, click the Grid button again.

9. On the Draw panel, click the Pick Lines icon if it's not picked already.

10. Pick the core centerline of the interior wall that terminates at the exterior wall, as shown in Figure 8.5.

11. Drag the right end of the line to align with grid 1. It snaps weakly. After you move your line to the length of grid 1, pick the second point. An alignment line appears.

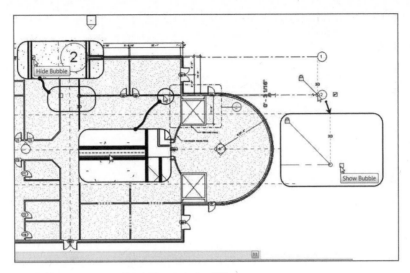

FIGURE 8.5: Adding the second grid line

T I P   Alignment lines, however useful, can be tricky to get to display. The percentage of your zoom has an effect. If you aren't getting the alignment lines, simply zoom back (or in) a small amount, and they will appear.

12. If the grid bubble doesn't appear on the right side as shown, but rather on the left side, find the blue check box on the right side of grid 2 and pick it. Doing so turns on the grid head.

13. On the left side of grid 2 are a grid bubble (see Figure 8.5) and the same blue check box. Click the check box to turn of the grid head at this location.

14. Press Esc.

Being able to pick lines is certainly an advantage, but you won't always be in a situation where you have geometry in place to do so. In the following procedure, you'll add grid 3 by picking two points:

1. Click the Grid button on the Architecture tab.

2. On the Draw panel, select the Line icon.

3. Pick a point along the center reference plane, as shown in Figure 8.6.

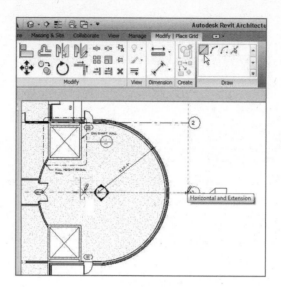

FIGURE 8.6:   Adding grid 3 at the center of the building

4. Pick a second point in alignment with grid 2 (see Figure 8.6).

5. Add grids 4 and 5 to the exact opposite ends of the east wing (see Figure 8.7).

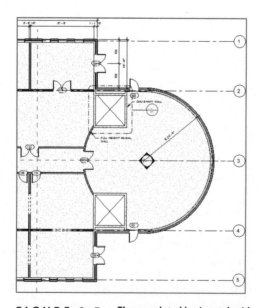

FIGURE 8.7:   The completed horizontal grids

You need to add two more grids at 45° angles. This will be as easy as drawing lines. The objective here is to manipulate the grids to read the appropriate numbering:

With grid lines, you can still copy, rotate, move, and mirror. Remember this when you're placing grids.

1. On the Architecture tab, click the Grid button if it's not selected already.

2. Pick the center of the radial wall.

 TIP   If you can't find the center of the radial wall, simply type **SC** (snap center) and then hover over the radial wall. When the center snap appears, pick that point.

3. Draw the line at a 45° angle until you're beyond the radial wall, as shown in Figure 8.8.

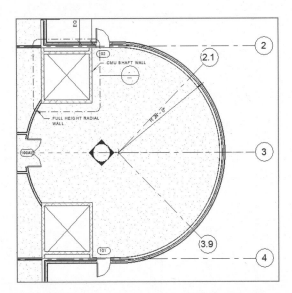

FIGURE 8.8:   Adding two additional grids and renumbering them

4. Click in the bubble for the angled grid, and rename the grid line **2.1**. You can do this while placing grids. Click outside the grid number field to enter the change.

5. Draw another grid line at a 45° angle in the opposite direction.

6. Renumber it to read **3.9** (see Figure 8.8).

N O T E   In many instances, you'll encounter elevation markers and other annotation items that get in the way. You can move these items, but be careful. After you move an item, open the referring view to make sure you didn't disturb anything.

You need two more horizontal column lines that span the length of the building. You'll number these lines 2.10 and 3.1. They will run centered on the corridor walls. To do this, you'll use the Pick Lines icon on the Draw panel. Here are the steps:

1. On the Architecture tab, click the Grid button if it's not selected already.

2. On the Draw panel, click the Pick Lines icon.

3. Pick the core centerline of the north corridor wall, as shown in Figure 8.9.

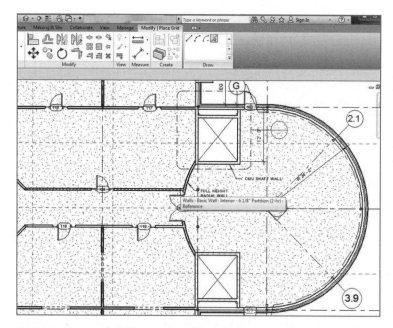

F I G U R E   8 . 9 :   Adding a column line to the north corridor wall

4. Pick the blue grip at the end of the line, and stretch it to align with the already-placed bubbles, as shown in Figure 8.10.

5. Click the Show Bubble button if necessary.

6. Rename the grid **2.10** (see Figure 8.10).

7. Zoom to the other end of the grid line, and deselect the Show Bubble check box if necessary.

8. Repeat the process for the south corridor wall, adding an additional grid line numbered **3.1**, as shown in Figure 8.11.

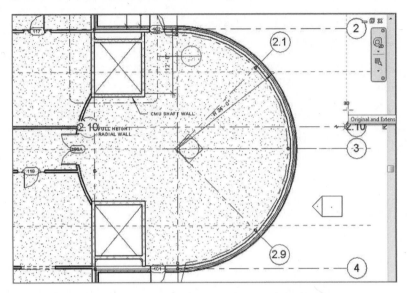

FIGURE 8.10: Dragging the line and turning on the bubble so you can rename the grid 2.10

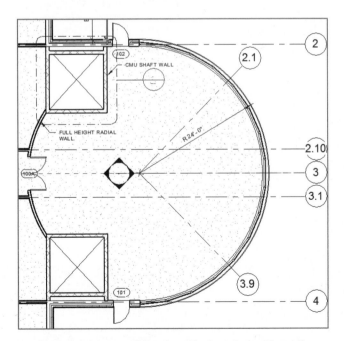

FIGURE 8.11: Adding the grids along the corridor walls

The grids are laying out okay, but it looks like you should make some adjustments to move the bubbles apart a little. You can do this by adding an elbow to the grid's end.

Adding Elbows

As with levels, you can add a break in the line of the grid, allowing you to make adjustments as if the grid were an arm with an elbow. Follow along:

1. Click Modify. Select grid 2.10.

2. Several blue grips appear. Pick the one that appears as a break line, as shown in Figure 8.12.

3. Picking this break line adds an elbow to your grid line, as shown in Figure 8.13.

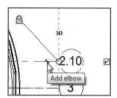

FIGURE 8.12:   Clicking the Add Elbow grip after selecting the grid

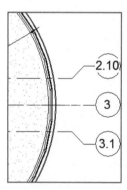

FIGURE 8.13:   The cleaned-up grid bubbles

4. Repeat the procedure for grid 3.1. Your grids should now look like Figure 8.13.

5. Save the model.

N O T E   Notice that the bubble was broken, and it was moved up and out of the way. This won't always happen. In most cases, the grid will move in the wrong direction. You can then select the blue grips and move the bubble in the direction you intended.

It's now time to add the vertical grids. This will be a simple process until you get to the radial entry area. At that point, you'll need to do some additional manipulating of the grid.

Adding Vertical Grids

The only real issue with adding vertical grids is the numbering versus lettering issue, because Revit continues the sequencing from the horizontal grids. Make sure that when you add your first grid going in the opposite direction, you renumber (or rename) the first occurrence of the grid.

The objective of the next procedure is to create a grid pattern running vertically across the view:

1. Zoom out so you can see the entire east wing.

2. On the Datum panel of the Architecture tab, click the Grid button.

3. On the Draw panel of the Modify | Place Grid tab, click the Pick Lines icon.

4. Pick the centerline of the west exterior wall of the east wing (see Figure 8.14).

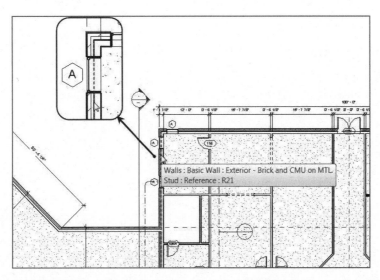

F I G U R E   8 . 1 4 :   Adding the first vertical grid by picking the centerline of the exterior wall

5. When you pick the wall, the grid is added, but it doesn't have the name or number you want. You'll change that. But first, pick the round blue grip and drag the bubble up past the dimensions, as shown in Figure 8.15.

6. Press Esc.

7. Select the new vertical grid.

8. Click in the bubble, and rename it **A**, as shown in Figure 8.16.

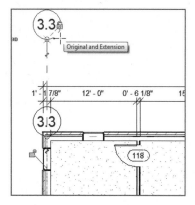

FIGURE 8.15:   Dragging the new bubble out of the wall

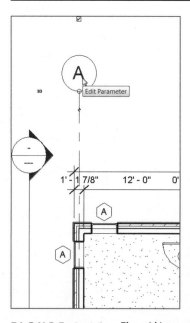

FIGURE 8.16:   The grid is now named A.

Next you'll duplicate this grid. Because you have an arsenal of modify commands under your belt, the best way to duplicate this grid is to copy it, as shown in the following steps:

1. Select grid A.

2. On the Modify | Grids tab, click the Copy button, as shown at the top of Figure 8.17.

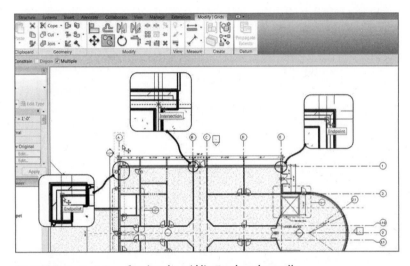

F I G U R E 8 . 1 7 :   Copying the grid line to the other walls

3. On the Options bar, make sure the Multiple check box is selected, as shown at upper left in Figure 8.17.

4. Pick a base point along the grid line within the wall (see Figure 8.17).

5. Copy grid A to the wall centerlines (see Figure 8.17). The grid lines auto-sequence as you go.

6. Press Esc twice.

7. Start the Grid command again.

8. On the Draw panel, be sure the Line button is selected.

9. Pick a start point at the endpoint of the radial wall, where it intersects with the straight wall, as shown near the bottom of Figure 8.18.

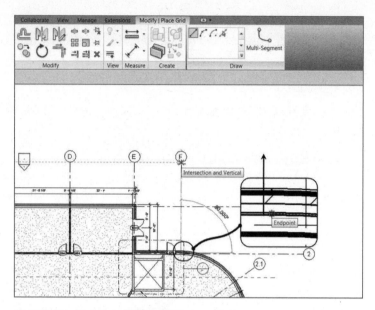

FIGURE 8.18: Adding grid F

10. Pick the second point in line with the adjacent grid bubbles (see Figure 8.18).

11. Press Esc.

12. Pick the grip on the bottom of the line, and drag it down past the south part of the radial wall.

The next step is to add the grid to the radial entry area. This won't be as easy as simply picking a wall's centerline. The trick is to establish a reference point to place the grid and, subsequently, a column.

Adding a Radial Grid Line

Sometimes you have to think outside the box. Literally. Because you have radial geometry with which you must contend, you need to add a radial grid as follows:

1. Zoom in on the radial entry of the east wing.

2. Click the Grid button on the Architecture tab, if the Grid command isn't currently running.

3. On the Draw panel, click the Pick Lines button, as shown in Figure 8.19.

4. Type in an Offset value of **6"** (**150**mm) on the Options bar.

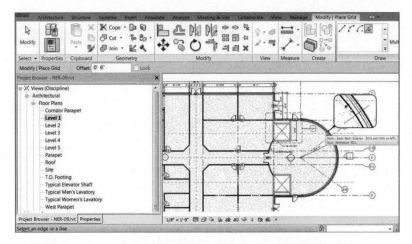

FIGURE 8.19:   Adding a grid line offset from the finish inside face

5. Pick the finished, inside face of the radial wall (see Figure 8.19). Make sure the alignment line indicating where the grid will go is on the inside of the wall.

6. The grid bubble lands in a congested area. Fix this by adding an elbow and adjusting the bubbles, as shown by grid G near the top of Figure 8.20.

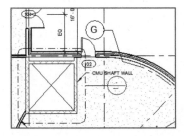

FIGURE 8.20:   Adding bubbles to the radial grid line, and adjusting their placements with elbows

One last thing you need to do is to make sure the grids extend all the way to the west side of the east building. This will play a major role when you start placing columns. Follow along:

1. Select grid 1.

2. Pick the grip icon to the left of the grid line.

3. Drag the grid to the left, past the west wall.

4. Repeat the procedure for grids 2, 2.10, 3.1, 4, and 5.

5. Repeat the procedure, stretching the vertical grids south. This will include grids A, B, C, D, and E. If you drag the lower end of grid A down, the copied grids B, C, D, and E will move with it. Make the lower end of grid F snap into alignment with the others.

I think you get the picture on adding grids. In the next procedure, you'll begin adding columns to these grid intersections. To do so, you'll explore the Structure tab on the Ribbon.

Adding Structural Columns

The hard part is over. Determining where to put the columns is more difficult than physically placing them in the model. But of course there are rules to follow, as well as rules you need to bend in order to accomplish the results you want to see.

This next series of procedures includes adding structural components to the model and placing framing systems in areas where a structural engineer may defer to the architect for structural integrity, given the design intent. (Try using that phrase in a meeting.)

To add columns to the model, follow this procedure:

1. In the Project Browser, go to the Level 1 floor plan.

2. Zoom in to the radial entry area in the east wing.

3. On the Structure tab, choose Column ➤ Structural Column, as shown in Figure 8.21. This tool is also on the Architecture tab.

4. Click the Load Family button, as shown in Figure 8.22.

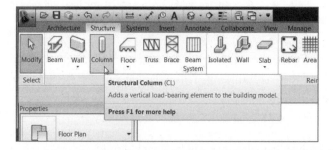

FIGURE 8.21:   Column ➤ Structural Column on the Structure tab of the Ribbon

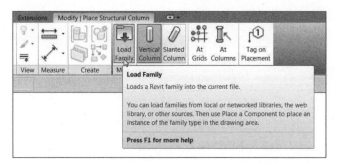

FIGURE 8.22: You can click the Load Family button to add additional columns to your project.

5. Browse to US Imperial ➤ Structural Columns ➤ Steel (or Metric ➤ Structural ➤ Columns ➤ Steel).

6. In the Steel folder, browse to HSS-Hollow Structural Section-Column.rfa (or M_HSS-Hollow Structural Column.rfa).

7. Double-click HSS-Hollow Structural Section-Column.rfa (or M_HSS-Hollow Structural Column.rfa). A dialog opens, enabling you to select the type, as shown in Figure 8.23.

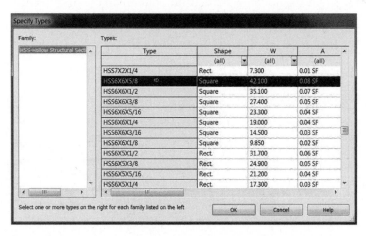

FIGURE 8.23: Select HSS-Hollow Structural Section-Column.rfa, and choose the HSS6×6×5/8 (HSS152.4×152.4×12.7) type.

8. Select the HSS6×6×5/8 (HSS152.4×152.4×12.7) column.

9. Click OK.

10. On the Options bar, make sure Height is set to Roof, as shown in Figure 8.24.

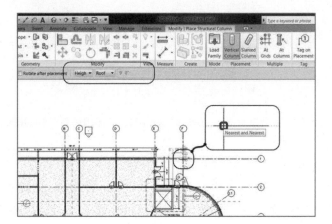

FIGURE 8.24:   Placing the column at grid intersection F-1

11. Place the column at grid intersection F-1.

12. Press Esc twice.

13. Choose Column ➤ Structural Column on the Architecture tab.

14. Place a column at grid intersection F-2. Before you place this column, be sure Height is set to Roof.

15. Place another column at grid intersection F-G (see Figure 8.25).

16. Click Modify.

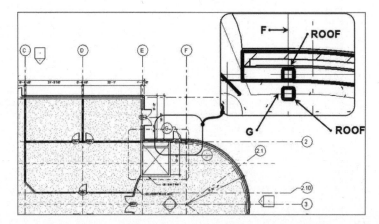

FIGURE 8.25:   Placing the two additional columns

17. Select the column you just placed (column F-G).

18. In the Properties dialog, make sure Top Level is set to Up To: Roof, as shown in Figure 8.26 (just to check).

N O T E   Notice that Column Location is set to F-G. This is important because, if the column is offset from one of these lines, Revit still considers the column to be at that column location, but with an offset dimension.

19. Mirror the three columns to the opposite side of the entry, using column line 3 as the reference plane.

20. Save the model.

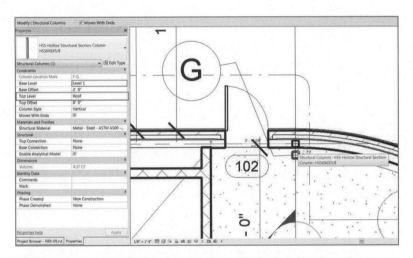

F I G U R E 8 . 2 6 :   Setting the column's top level to extend to the roof

Let's add some full-height columns at the rest of the grid locations. You'll begin with the radial grid and then place the rest of the columns in the walls of the exterior and the corridor. Here are these steps:

1. On the Structure tab, click the Column button.

2. On the Options bar, be sure Height is set to Roof.

3. Hover your cursor over grid intersection G-2.1. You can see the column, but it's at the wrong orientation.

4. Press the spacebar on your keyboard, and the column rotates to align with the grid, as shown in Figure 8.27.

> Because you rotated the first column, notice that, as you follow the radius, the column rotates on its own.
>

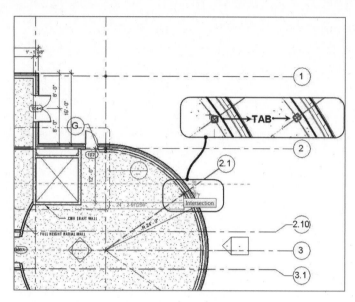

FIGURE 8.27: Placing and rotating a column

5. When the column is aligned, pick the intersection. The column is placed.

6. Repeat the steps for columns 3 and 3.9.

Now you'll place columns in the main part of the wing. Place a column at every grid location. Note that you must stretch the column lines to the left side of the wing. You should also turn on the grid bubbles at the west and south sides of the building, as shown in Figure 8.28.

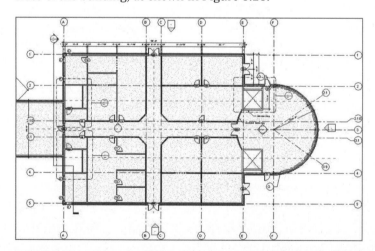

FIGURE 8.28: Extend the grids, and turn on the bubbles at each end.

To add columns by intersection, follow these steps:

1. Start the Structural Column command.

2. On the Modify | Place Structural Column tab, click the At Grids button on the Multiple panel, as shown in Figure 8.29.

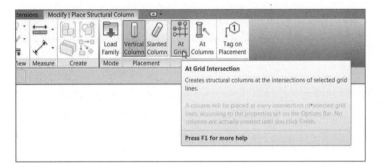

FIGURE 8.29: Using the Place Column At Grids function

3. Pick a window around the rectangular portion of the east wing (from right to left), as shown in Figure 8.30.

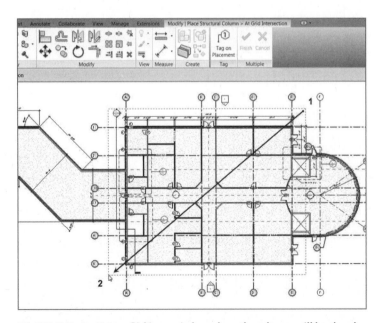

FIGURE 8.30: Picking a window where the columns will be placed

4. The Modify | Place Structural Column ➤ At Grid Intersection tab changes to allow you either to finish or cancel. After you have the window placed, click the Finish button on the Multiple panel, as shown at the top of Figure 8.30.

5. Press Esc.

Quite a few columns are placed. You'll need to move some of them, including the four columns in the corridor intersection area. Revit will still locate each column at a grid intersection, but it will add the offset in the column's properties.

To move the columns and create a column offset, follow these steps:

1. Zoom in to the middle of the east wing at the corridor intersection.

2. Select the two columns at the left of the corridor, as shown in Figure 8.31.

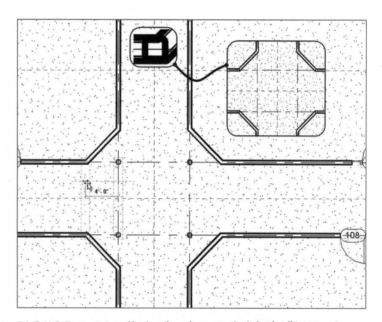

FIGURE 8.31:   Moving the columns to the left 4'–0" (1200mm)

3. Move the columns 4'–0" (1200mm) to the left (see Figure 8.31).

4. Repeat the same procedure for the other two columns (see Figure 8.32).

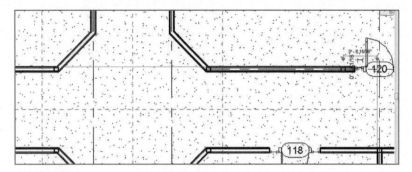

FIGURE 8.32: Adjustments such as moving a column will be necessary quite often.

5. Zoom in to the door shown in Figure 8.32.

6. Move the column to the left 4′–0″ (1200mm).

7. Thank your structural engineer for allowing this. The engineer is extremely understanding.

8. Save the model.

That's enough on columns for now. It's time to move on to adding some structural framing. You'll add framing primarily in the canopy areas surrounding the east entry of the east wing.

Using Structural Framing

Although you won't create much structural framing in Revit Architecture, you'll need to add framing in a few areas. Canopies with light structural framing are certainly one area that could call for the architect to wander over to the structural side of the fence.

To begin adding structural framing, follow along:

1. In the Project Browser, go to the Level 2 floor plan.

2. Zoom in to the radial entry area.

3. Select columns F-1 and F-5 (these are the columns outside the building).

4. In the Properties dialog, set Top Level to Level 2. (This makes the columns disappear for a moment.)

5. Press Esc.

6. In the Properties dialog, scroll down to the View Range row and click the Edit button (see Figure 8.33).

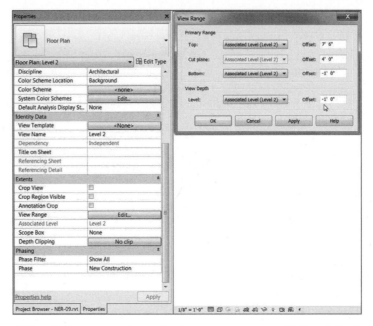

FIGURE 8.33: Setting the view range so you can see below the level

7. In the dialog that opens, in the Primary Range section, set Bottom Offset to -1'–0"(-300mm).

8. For View Depth, set Level Offset to -1'–0" (-300mm), as shown in Figure 8.33.

WARNING Be careful! Remember that when you make an adjustment to the view range, you're changing the view range for the entire view. Be sure you aren't inadvertently causing items on other floors to appear in the rest of the current view.

9. Click OK. You can now see the column.

Next you'll place the structural framing. Make sure you're zoomed in to the northeast corner of the east wing. Here are the steps:

1. On the Structure panel of the Structure tab, click the Beam button, as shown in Figure 8.34.

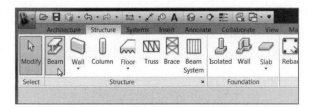

FIGURE 8.34: The Beam button on the Structure panel of the Structure tab

2. Click the Load Family button.

3. Browse to Structural ➤ Framing ➤ Steel.

4. Select HSS-Hollow Structural Section.rfa (or M_HSS-Hollow Structural Column.rfa). Click Open.

5. In the Specify Types dialog, select HSS6×6×5/8 (HSS152.4×152.4× 12.7), and click OK.

6. Pick the first point at column E-1, which is buried in the corner of the wall.

7. Pick the second point at exterior column F-1, as shown in Figure 8.35.

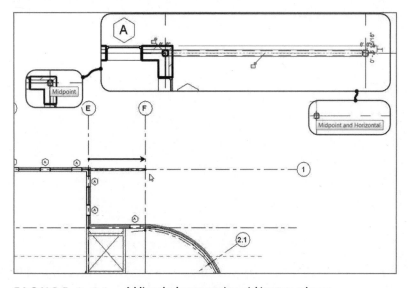

FIGURE 8.35: Adding the beam requires picking two columns.

I CAN'T SEE MY GRIDS!

If your grids aren't showing up on the second floor, do the following:

1. Go back to Level 1.

2. Select all of your grids.

3. Click the Propagate Extents button.

4. Select the floors on which you want to see your grids.

8. With the Beam command still running, pick the exterior column (F-1) and then column F-2, as shown in Figure 8.36.

9. Press Esc.

10. Draw a beam 6″ (150mm) off the finish face of the wall, starting at the top beam and ending on column line 2, as shown in Figure 8.37. (This beam will later be supported by the framing within the building.)

 N O T E   Revit may think you're bearing a beam on a nonbearing wall. If you're asked to make this wall bearing, click Make Wall Bearing.

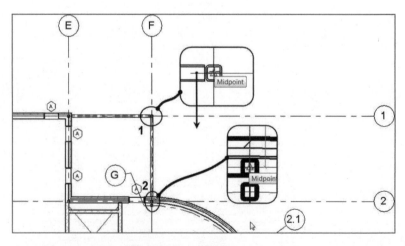

FIGURE 8.36:   Adding the second beam

11. In the View Control bar, change Visual Style to Wireframe. This allows you to see the beam within the wall you're about to draw.

12. Draw another beam from left to right, inside the wall, as shown in Figure 8.38.

13. Save the model.

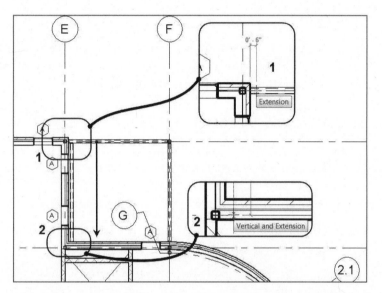

FIGURE 8.37: Adding a beam 6″ (150mm) off the face of the wall to column line 2

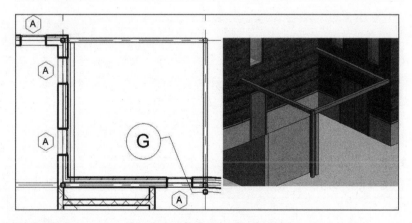

FIGURE 8.38: Completing the framing for the canopy

WHY IS IT CUTTING BACK THE BEAMS?

Well, that's an inherent function of Revit. If you draw your framing to and from beam centerlines, Revit will keep the connection points in the correct locations but will trim back the beam for you. You can adjust these cutbacks by using the Beam/Column Joins tool from the Geometry panel of the Modify tab.

Now let's add some filler beams. In Revit Architecture, you can add a beam system that is controlled by a specified spacing. After the system is in place, you can control the properties for the duration of the project.

Adding a Beam System

Although adding beam systems in Revit is much more crucial for structure, it's useful for architecture as well. Having the ability to space a framing system equally can be quite advantageous.

To create a beam system, follow along with this procedure:

1. On the Structure panel of the Structure tab, click the Beam System button, as shown in Figure 8.39.

2. Make sure the Automatic Beam System button is picked, as shown in Figure 8.40.

3. Click the Tag On Placement button (see Figure 8.40).

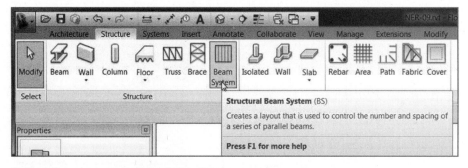

FIGURE 8.39: The Beam System button

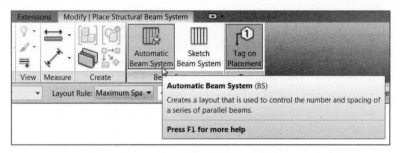

FIGURE 8.40: Selecting the Automatic Beam System and Tag On
Placement options

4. On the Options bar, make sure HSS6×6×5/8 (HSS152.4×152.4×12.7) is the Beam Type selection.

5. Change Layout Rule to Maximum Spacing, as shown in Figure 8.41. Set the distance field to 4′–0″ (1200mm).

6. Change Tag Style to Framing.

N O T E   The support you pick first determines the direction in which the beams will run. Notice the double lines in the horizontal beam? They indicate the direction of the beam system. If you want to change this direction, click the Beam Direction button on the Draw panel.

7. Hover your cursor over the top, horizontal beam, as shown in Figure 8.42. Notice the green dashed lines: this is where your beams will be placed.

8. When you see the green lines, pick the top beam, and your framing is placed (see Figure 8.43).

FIGURE 8.41: Setting the maximum spacing and the tag style on the Options bar

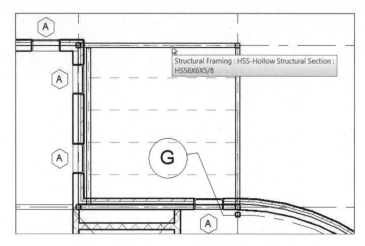

FIGURE 8.42:   Getting ready to place the framing system

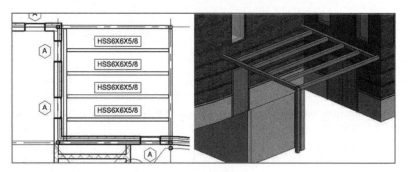

FIGURE 8.43:   The framing of the canopy

9. Click Modify. Mirror the canopy to the other side of the radial entry. Be careful not to mirror the columns accidentally.

10. You may receive the same message about bearing a structural member on a nonbearing wall. Click the Make Wall Bearing button.

By using the Beam System command, you can easily and quickly add multiple occurrences of framing members. In some cases, however, you need non-uniform members on a different plane, such as lateral bracing.

Adding Bracing

It would be nice to add a rod to the top of this canopy at an angle. You can accomplish this by using the Brace command. To do so, you'll need to load the rod (considered a family in Revit) into the model.

To use the Brace command, first add the rod family to your model:

1. Go to the Insert tab on the Ribbon.

2. Click the Load Family button.

3. Browse to Structural ➢ Framing ➢ Steel, and open the file Round Bar.rfa (or M_Round Bar.rfa).

4. Go to the North elevation in the Project Browser. Notice that grid lines A–F are visible in this view—very useful!

5. In the Properties panel for the North elevation, change Detail Level to Fine and Visual Style to Shaded.

6. Zoom in on the east canopy.

7. On the Structure panel of the Structure tab, click the Brace button, as shown in Figure 8.44.

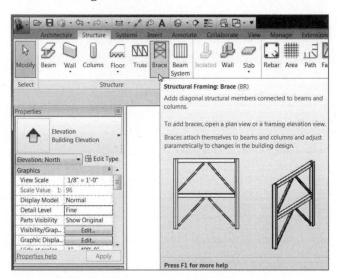

FIGURE 8.44:   The Brace button on the Structure tab

8. Revit displays a dialog asking you to specify a work plane. In the Name drop-down list, select Grid : 1, as shown in Figure 8.45, and then click OK.

9. Verify that Round Bar: 1″ (M_Round Bar 25) is the current framing member in the Type Selector.

10. Draw a diagonal bar, as shown in Figure 8.46. (I'll let you eyeball this one, or you can make the top offset a specific increment.)

FIGURE 8.45: Specifying Grid : 1 as the work plane for the bracing

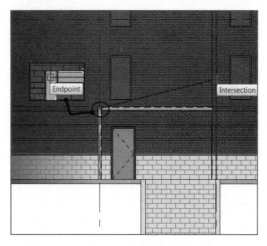

FIGURE 8.46: Adding the rod at an angle

11. Go to the Level 2 floor plan.

12. On the Quick Access toolbar, click the Section button.

13. Place the section along column line F, as shown in Figure 8.47, starting at point 1 and ending at point 2.

14. Open the section.

15. Rename the section **Framing at North East Canopy.**

16. Change Detail Level to Fine and Visual Style to Shaded.

17. On the Structure panel of the Structure tab, click the Brace button.

18. Choose Grid : F as the work plane. Click OK.

19. Draw a diagonal rod between the points shown in Figure 8.48, and press Esc.

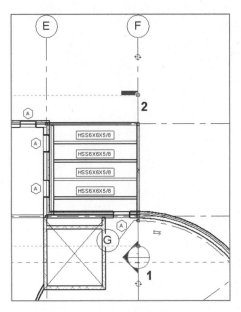

FIGURE 8.47: Cutting a section through the framing

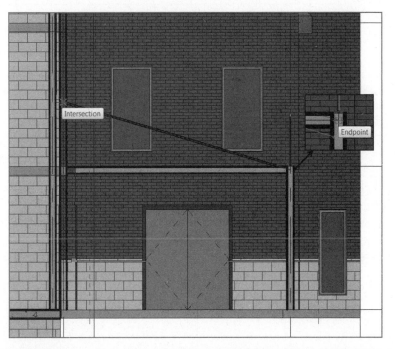

FIGURE 8.48: Finding the points along the column and beam to attach the rod

20. See Figure 8.49 to compare your rods to those in the book.

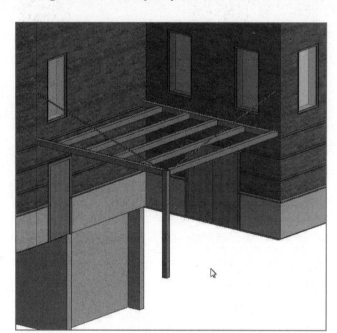

FIGURE 8.49:   Isometric of the bracing

21. Mirror the rods to the other canopy. You can open the East elevation to do so.

 N O T E   If you receive a warning about a circular reference chain, click Unjoin Elements.

22. Save the model.

That pretty much covers it for framing. The next section will bring you underground into the foundation. Although the structural engineer usually specifies the foundation system, architects must have access to foundation tools to place concrete foundation walls as well as to strip and isolate footings and piers. The next section addresses these topics.

Understanding Foundation Systems

The first question that arises while addressing structural foundations is, "What if the architect places a foundation in the model, and then the structural engineer places one in their model?"

What will happen is the structural engineer will use a method called Copy/Monitor, whereby the engineer takes the architect's foundation and makes it their own. The engineer is then free to alter the foundation. This method is addressed fully in Chapter 20, "Importing and Coordinating Models."

This section focuses on creating foundation walls. Although adding this type of wall is similar to adding architectural walls, there are a few things you need to be aware of.

For now, let's add a foundation and deal with coordination later. The task before you is to create a foundation wall constructed of 18″ (450mm) of solid concrete. To proceed, follow these steps:

1. Go to the Level 1 floor plan.

2. Click the Wall ➤ Wall: Structural button on the Structure tab. The same tool is on the Architectural tab.

3. In the Type Selector, in the Properties dialog, select Generic 8″ Masonry (Generic – 200mm).

4. Click the Edit Type button.

5. Click the Duplicate button.

6. Name the new wall 18″ Concrete (450mm Concrete).

7. Click OK.

8. Just under the Wall Function row is the Coarse Scale Fill Pattern row. Change the hatch to Concrete by clicking the […] button and selecting Concrete from the menu. Click OK.

9. Click the Edit button in the Structure row.

10. In the second row in the Layers chart, click in the Material cell.

11. Click the […] button.

12. Find Concrete – Cast-in-Place Gray, and select it.

13. Click OK.

14. Change Thickness to 1′–6″ (450mm) by typing 1(space) 6, as shown in Figure 8.51.

15. Click OK twice.

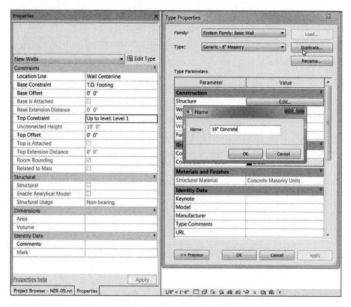

FIGURE 8.50: Adding a structural wall

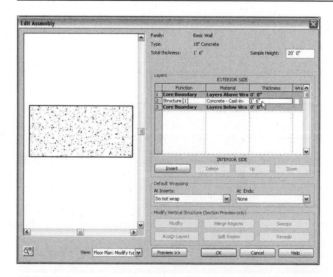

FIGURE 8.51: Changing the Material and Thickness settings

You're about to place a wall under this level. This view is currently set not to show anything below this level, forcing you to alter the view range.

To modify the view range, follow these steps:

1. Press Esc twice, and then scroll down to View Range in the Properties dialog and click the Edit button.

2. For Primary Range, set Bottom Offset to -1'–0" (-300mm).

3. For View Depth, set Level Offset to -1'–0" (-300mm).

4. Click OK.

5. Start the Structural Wall command again.

6. On the Draw panel, click the Pick Lines icon.

7. Foundation walls are placed top down, so Depth rather than Height appears on the Options bar. Make sure Depth is set to T.O. Footing and Justification is set to Wall Centerline.

8. Pick the centerline of the exterior wall, as shown in Figure 8.52.

9. Pick every exterior wall in all three sections of the model.

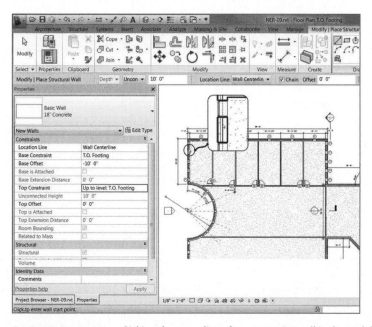

FIGURE 8.52: Picking the centerline of every exterior wall in the model. This includes the corridor and both wings.

Your 3D model should look like Figure 8.53. Get into the habit of viewing the model in 3D—especially when you can't see exactly where the walls are being placed in the plan.

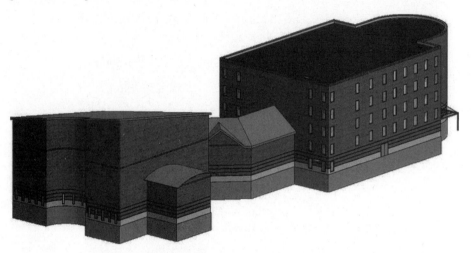

FIGURE 8.53:   The foundation walls

Now you can travel into the ground and check out how your walls are joining. Some cleanup will be involved:

1. In the Project Browser, double-click the T.O. Footing floor plan.

2. Zoom in to the east wing area, where the north elevator meets the foundation wall. There is an issue: the walls are funky, as shown in Figure 8.54.

3. Select the left masonry elevator shaft wall.

4. Drag the end blue grip of the wall out so that it abuts the foundation wall.

5. The masonry wall to the right needs to be joined to the foundation wall. To do this, click the Join Geometry button on the Modify tab, as shown in Figure 8.55.

6. Pick the foundation wall.

7. Pick the masonry wall. The masonry wall is notched back for the foundation.

8. Repeat the procedure for the south elevator. The condition may be slightly different from that of the north elevator, but the process to fix it is the same.

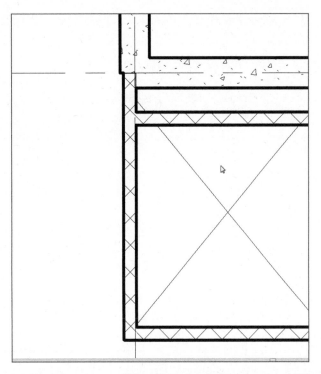

FIGURE 8.54: The walls aren't behaving as you would like them to.

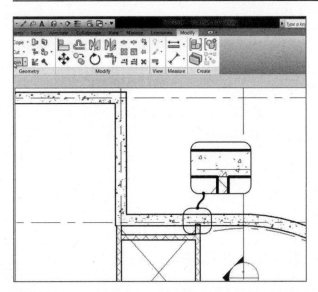

FIGURE 8.55: Joining the walls so the foundation walls terminate as expected

Moving to the west wing, you need to fix one wall. You'll use the Split command, as follows:

1. Zoom in on the area, as shown in Figure 8.56.

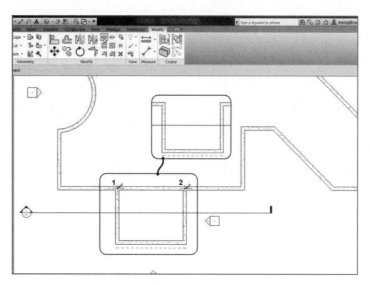

FIGURE 8.56: Splitting the foundation wall to follow the profile of the wall above

2. On the Modify tab, click the Split Element button (see Figure 8.56).

3. On the Options bar, click the Delete Inner Segment check box (see Figure 8.56).

4. Pick the points marked 1 and 2 in Figure 8.56, and press Esc twice.

Now that the foundation walls are in place, let's think about what these walls are bearing on. Revit Architecture has tools to add footings to the bottom of the walls.

Adding Structural Footings

If you're going as far as placing structural foundation walls, you might as well continue and place footings under them, right? Luckily, this isn't a difficult task.

Before you begin adding structural footings to the plan, you need to acknowledge that, by default, this view isn't set up to see objects that are physically below its level. To correct this, you must alter the view range of this specific plan. Follow these steps:

1. Make sure you're still in the T.O. Footing plan.

2. In the Properties dialog, go to the View Range row and click Edit.

3. Set Primary Range Bottom to Unlimited.

4. Set View Depth Level to Unlimited, as shown in Figure 8.57.

FIGURE 8.57: Again with the view range!

5. Click OK.

6. On the Foundation panel of the Structure tab, click the Wall button, as shown in Figure 8.58.

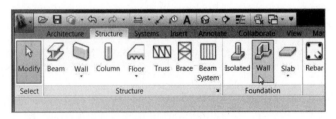

FIGURE 8.58: Adding a wall foundation

Just because this specific foundation is labeled Wall doesn't mean it's a wall. It's labeled Wall because it's a continuous (strip) footing that has a wall bearing on it.

At the top of the Properties dialog, it says Bearing Footing - 36″ × 12″ (900mm × 300mm). This is a little big for your purposes, so let's make a new footing:

1. In the Properties dialog, click the Edit Type button.

2. Click Duplicate.

3. Call the new footing element **Bearing Footing - 30″ × 12″** (Bearing Footing - 750mm × 300mm).

4. Click OK.

5. Change the Width setting to **2′–6″** (750mm), as shown in Figure 8.59.

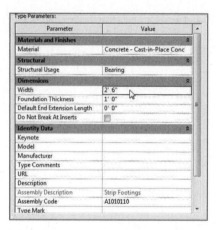

FIGURE 8.59: Changing the width

6. Click OK again to get back to the model.

7. Start picking walls. This footing will be centered under each wall you pick. Ignore the elevator shaft walls.

8. When you're finished picking the walls, go to a 3D view to make sure all the foundations are covered, as shown in Figure 8.60.

When all the footings are in place, you can see that you need to focus on the elevator shafts. Because an entire foundation mat is required under the elevators, you can use a structural slab.

Structural Slabs

Structural slabs are basically thick floors. The one you're about to use is a solid concrete floor 12″ (300mm) thick. Of course, Revit doesn't have something this thick built in the library, so you'll take this opportunity to make one. Here are the steps:

1. Go to the T.O. Footing floor plan.

> If you hover your cursor over a wall and press the Tab key, Revit selects all connecting walls, allowing you to add the bearing footing literally in two clicks.

2. Zoom in to the elevator area.

3. On the Foundation panel of the Structure tab, choose Slab ➤ Structural Foundation: Slab, as shown in Figure 8.61.

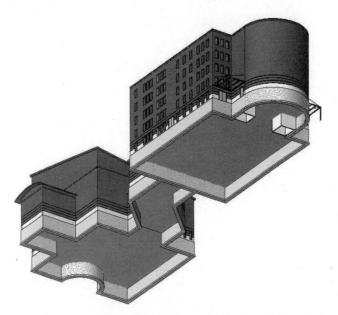

FIGURE 8.60: Doing a 3D investigation to see whether the footings are all in place

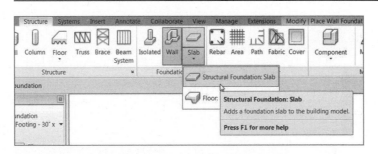

FIGURE 8.61: Choosing Structural Foundation: Slab

4. In the Properties panel, click Edit Type.

5. Click Duplicate.

6. Call the new slab **12" Elevator Slab (300mm Elevator Slab)**.

7. Click OK.

8. Click the Edit button in the Structure row.

9. In the Layers field, change Thickness to 1′–0″ (300mm), as shown in Figure 8.62.

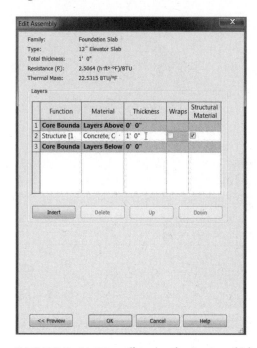

FIGURE 8.62: Changing the structure thickness

10. Click OK twice to get back to the model.

11. On the Draw panel, verify that the Pick Walls button is selected.

12. On the Options bar, set Offset to 1′–0″ (300mm).

13. Pick the three elevator shaft walls, as shown in Figure 8.63.

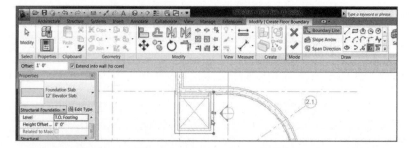

FIGURE 8.63: When picking the elevator shaft walls, be sure to include the 1′–0″ (300mm) offset.

14. Set Offset back to 0.

15. Select the Pick Lines button. Verify that the offset is 0.

16. Pick the inside of the exterior foundation wall.

Now that the perimeter is set, it's time to trim the edges to make sure you have a continuous, closed loop:

1. On the Modify panel, click the Trim/Extend To Corner button.

2. Trim any overlapping corners, as shown in Figure 8.64.

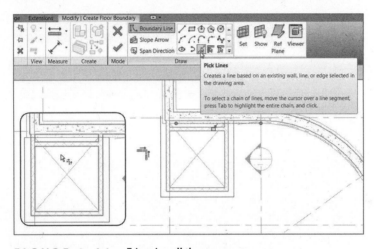

FIGURE 8.64: Trimming all the corners

3. On the Floor panel to the right of the Create Floor Boundary tab, click Finish Edit Mode.

4. Repeat the process for the south elevator.

5. Go to a 3D view.

6. If your slabs look more like a strip footing, as shown in Figure 8.65, hover your cursor over the inside of one of the foundations until the elevator shaft openings are highlighted.

7. Select the elevator shaft openings.

8. In the Properties dialog, change Base Offset to 0.

Your view should look like Figure 8.66.

FIGURE 8.65: Selecting the elevator shafts to remove the base offset in the Properties dialog

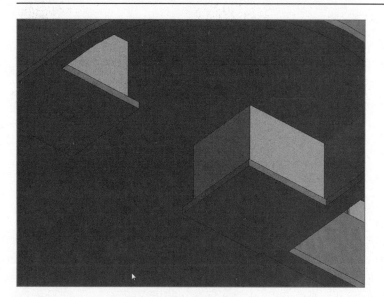

FIGURE 8.66: The finished elevator pads

With the footings mostly in place, you can think about placing piers and spread footings in the foundation. Luckily, as you're soon to discover, you already know how to do this.

Piers and Spread Footings

Piers and pilasters, simply put, are concrete columns. This is how Revit sees these items, and the following is the easiest placement method. A nice thing about this technique is that the grids are in place as well as the steel columns that bear on them. The only real trick is deciding which plan to put them in.

The objective of the next procedure is to add pilasters to support the columns bearing on them. Follow these steps:

1. Return to the T.O. Footing plan.

2. On the Structure panel of the Structure tab, click the Column button.

3. On the Insert tab, click the Load Family button, as shown at the top of Figure 8.67.

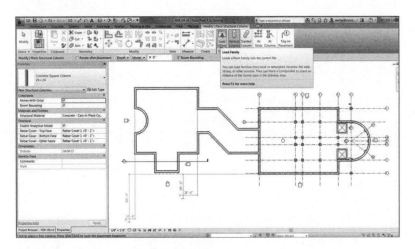

FIGURE 8.67:   Starting to place piers

4. Browse to Structural ➢ Columns ➢ Concrete.

5. Pick the file called Concrete-Square-Column.rfa (M_Concrete-Square-Column.rfa).

6. Click Open.

7. In the Type Selector, select the 24×24 (600 × 600mm) column. Verify that Height is set to Level 1.

8. Begin placing columns at the grid intersections, as shown in Figure 8.67. Using At Grids can speed up your work.

9. Press Esc, and then go to Level 1.

10. Zoom in to the corridor.

11. Move the piers under the columns that you moved before.

12. Do the same for the pier under the doorway, as shown in Figure 8.68.

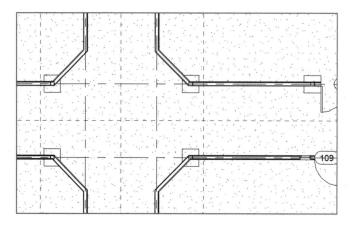

FIGURE 8.68:   Making the necessary adjustments

13. Delete columns, footings, and piers D-1 and D-5.

Now you'll add the spread footings under the piers. This process is almost identical to the previous one:

1. Go back to the T.O. Footing floor plan.

2. On the Foundation panel of the Structure tab, select the Isolated Foundation button.

3. No structural foundations are loaded into the project, so click Yes.

4. Browse to Structural ➤ Foundations.

5. Select the file called `Footing-Rectangular.rfa` (`M_Footing-Rectangular.rfa`).

6. Click Open.

7. In the Properties dialog, click the Edit Type button.

8. Click Duplicate.

9. Call the new footing 36″ × 36″ × 12″ (900mm × 900mm × 300mm).

10. Click OK.

11. Change Width to 36″ (900mm).

12. Change Length to 36″ (900mm).

13. Change Thickness to 12″ (300mm).

14. Click OK.

15. Add these footings to each pier. The At Columns option on the Multiple panel works like At Grids and will speed up your work.

16. Your foundation plan should resemble Figure 8.69.

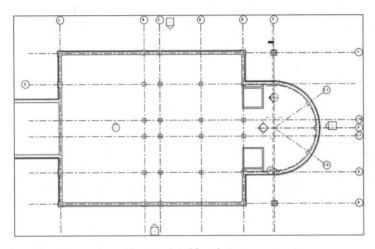

FIGURE 8.69:   The completed foundation

Having a foundation in place in an architectural plan can be both good and bad. It can be bad because structural items begin appearing in places you may not want to see them. The last procedure of the chapter involves isolating the structure from the architecture.

Using Structural Views

By creating a structural view, you essentially duplicate an architectural view and hide the nonessential items in that view. Sound easy? That's because it is! But before you get started, you're going to remove some structural views that Revit provided for you.

To create structural views, follow these steps:

1. In the Project Browser, find the Structural Plans category.

2. Select all the structural plans in that category, right-click, and select Delete to delete the plans.

Continue as follows:

1. In the Project Browser, go to Floor Plans, right-click T.O. Footing, and select Duplicate View ➤ Duplicate With Detailing, as shown in Figure 8.70. The new view opens.

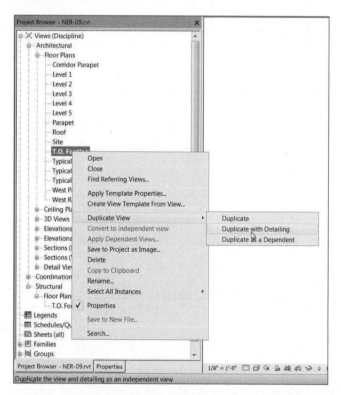

FIGURE 8.70:   Selecting Duplicate View a Duplicate With Detailing

2. Rename the view called Copy of T.O. Footing to T.O. Footing Structural Plan.

3. In the Discipline category of the View Properties, select Structural from the list, as shown in Figure 8.71. The sections disappear.

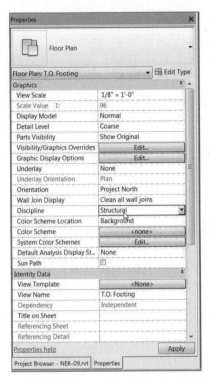

FIGURE 8.71: Changing Discipline to Structural

4. In the Project Browser, right-click Views (All), as shown in Figure 8.72.

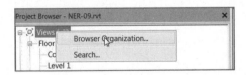

FIGURE 8.72: Right-clicking in the Project Browser

5. Select Browser Organization.

6. Select the Discipline option, as shown in Figure 8.73, and then click OK.

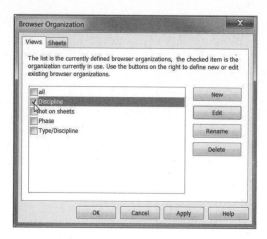

FIGURE 8.73: Selecting Discipline

Now the Project Browser is broken into categories. This will be helpful for large projects with a mix of structure and architecture.

This is getting easy! Let's make the Level 1 architectural plan truly architectural, as follows:

1. Open the Level 1 floor plan (architectural).

2. Scroll down to View Range.

3. Click the Edit button in the View Range row.

4. Change both the Bottom and View Depth offsets to 0.

5. Click OK.

The foundation information is no longer displayed in the Level 1 floor plan.

Although the last part of this chapter was short, it's a nice look into the Project Browser, and it shows how you can begin to get organized. If you would like more practice, go into the Project Browser on your own and organize it the way you'd like.

Are You Experienced?

Now you can...

☑ place a structural grid in your model by using the architectural walls as a reference

☑ add additional grids at a radius or by sketch where needed

☑ add columns to the grid lines

☑ add columns at an offset, keeping the relationship to the grid inter-section intact

☑ add structural beams to the model

☑ add structural beam systems, which can follow centering rules or equal-distance spacing

☑ use the Brace command to create brace framing to be used for both architectural appointments and structural bracing

☑ create entire foundation systems complete with foundation walls, piers, and spread footings

☑ organize the Project Browser to show your model broken into disciplines

☑ change a view's discipline to Structural

Ceilings and Interiors

Now that the exterior shell is up and the rooms are basically laid out, it's time to start considering the interiors. As it stands, you have a bunch of rooms with the same wall finish, the same floor finish, and no ceilings to speak of. The restrooms don't have any fixtures, and the other rooms are going to be useless without furniture.

Another issue is that you don't have any separate views such as furniture plans or finish plans. This chapter dives into all these items—and then some!

▶ **Creating ceilings**

▶ **Creating ceiling openings and soffits**

▶ **Adding interior design**

▶ **Adding alternate floor materials**

Creating Ceilings

Placing a ceiling is quite easy; the hard part is finding the view in which to do it. As you've probably noticed, the Project Browser is divided into categories. The categories for plans are Floor Plans and Ceiling Plans. Whereas floor plans show the views standing at that level looking down, ceiling plans show the view standing at that level looking up. In the Autodesk® Revit® Architecture platform, you're looking at a true reflected ceiling plan.

 N O T E   Metric users should not type in mm or other metric abbreviations when entering amounts suggested in the exercises. Revit will not accept such abbreviations. Simply enter the number provided within the parentheses.

To begin, open the file on which you've been following along. If you didn't complete Chapter 8, "Structural Items," go to the book's web page at www.sybex.com/go/revit2014ner. From there, you can browse to Chapter 9 and find the file called NER-09.rvt. Then, continue with these steps:

1. Go to the Level 1 ceiling plan, as shown in Figure 9.1 (remember, this is a ceiling plan, not a floor plan).

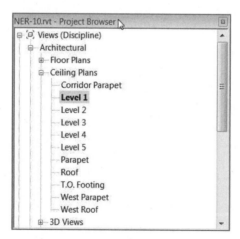

F I G U R E   9 . 1 :   The Ceiling Plans category

2. On the Architecture tab, click the Ceiling button, as shown in Figure 9.2.

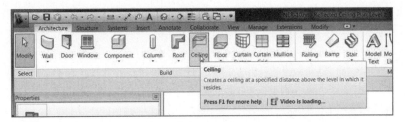

FIGURE 9.2:   The Ceiling button on the Architecture tab of the Ribbon

3. With the Ceiling command active, choose $2' \times 4'$ ACT System (600mm × 1200mm Grid) from the Type Selector, as shown in Figure 9.3.

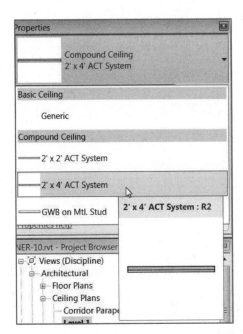

FIGURE 9.3:   The available ceiling types listed in the Type Selector

4. Hover your mouse over the room shown in Figure 9.4. Notice that the perimeter is outlined in red. This indicates that the ceiling has found at least four walls you can use as a layout.

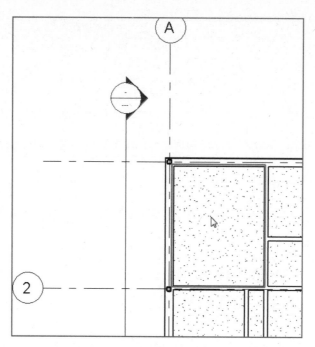

FIGURE 9.4:   The Ceiling command finds bounding items such as walls.

5. When you see the red outline, pick a point in the middle of the room. Your ceiling should now look like Figure 9.5.

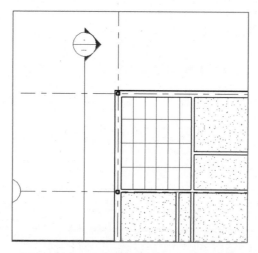

FIGURE 9.5:   Placing the 2 × 4 tiled ceiling

6. Have at it! Add a ceiling to every room in the east wing except the bathrooms, east radial entry, and, of course, the elevator shafts, as shown in Figure 9.6.

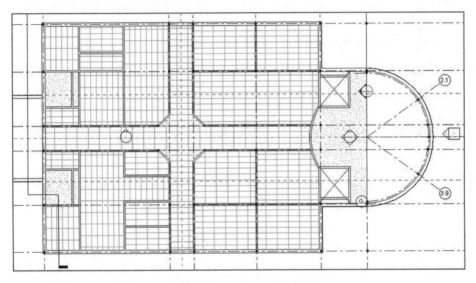

FIGURE 9.6:   Adding 2 × 4 ACT ceilings to the specified rooms

7. With the Ceiling command still running, select Compound Ceiling : GWB On Mtl. Stud from the Type Selector.

8. Pick the bathrooms (not the chases) and the hallway.

9. Press Esc.

NOTE   If you notice that some of the grids are running in the wrong direction, don't worry. You'll change that in a moment.

That was just too easy! Too good to be true, right? All right, it was. You always have to make adjustments to this type of item. You probably noticed that you had no control over the direction in which the grids were running. Also, you have no clue as to the height of these ceilings. Let's start modifying the ceilings.

Transferring Project Standards

At times, you won't have the system families you need to carry out the task at hand. Ceiling types seem to be the number-one system family to be inadvertently deleted from a model before being used. If you find that you don't have the ceiling types shown earlier, do the following:

1. Click the Application icon and choose New ➢ Project.

2. In the New Project dialog box, click OK to start a new project using the default template.

3. On the View tab, click Switch Windows in the Windows panel, and select Reflected Ceiling Plan from the fly-out to get back to the No Experience Required project.

4. On the Manage tab, click Transfer Project Standards in the Settings panel.

5. In the Select Items To Copy dialog box (see the following graphic), click the Check None button.

6. Click Ceiling Types.

7. Click OK.

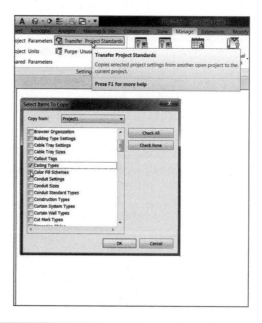

Modifying Ceiling Grids

To be honest, a ceiling consists of nothing more than a basic hatch pattern applied to a material. Actually, everything in Revit is a basic hatch pattern applied to a material. That sure does make it easy to understand!

The one unique thing about hatch patterns in Revit is that you can modify them onscreen. That means you can move and rotate a hatch pattern. That also means you can move and rotate a grid pattern. Let's give it a shot:

1. Press Esc or Modify to cancel the command you're in.

2. Pick a ceiling grid line, as shown in Figure 9.7. (Make sure you're zoomed in close enough to make the Rotate command active.)

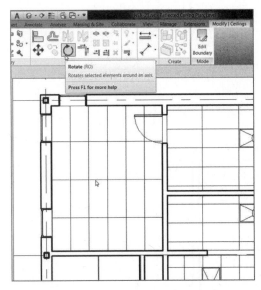

FIGURE 9.7: Select one of the grids, and click the Rotate button.

3. On the Modify | Ceilings tab, click the Rotate button (see Figure 9.7).

4. Rotate the grid 45° by using the two-pick method, as shown in Figure 9.8.

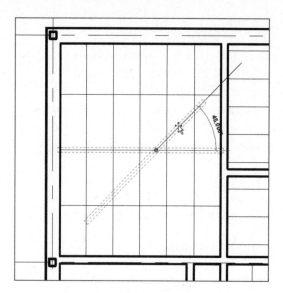

FIGURE 9.8:   The rotate process

Your ceiling should now look like Figure 9.9.

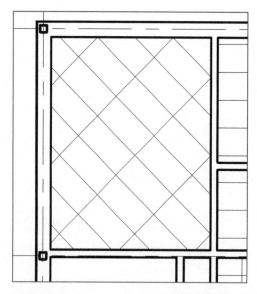

FIGURE 9.9:   The ceiling at a 45° angle

Now that the ceiling is in, let's look at the ceiling's properties before you go too far. As a matter of fact, it's a good idea to investigate the ceiling's properties before you place it in the model.

Setting Ceiling Element Properties

As I mentioned earlier, ceilings are set up in a fashion similar to floors. So it stands to reason that you'll see many similar properties.

Before you get started, let's make some modifications to the west wing. The objective of this procedure is to add a hard ceiling with metal framing, gypsum, and a ¾″ (18mm) cherry finish. To do so, however, you need to modify some of the walls:

1. Go to a 3D view of the model.

2. Select the sloped roof that covers the west wing, as shown in Figure 9.10.

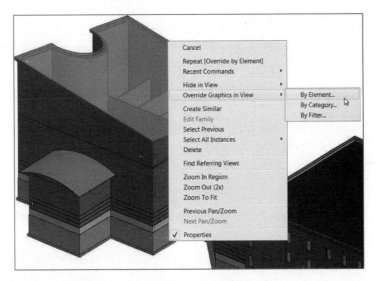

FIGURE 9.10:   Selecting the roof and right-clicking

3. Right-click.

4. Select Override Graphics In View ➤ By Element (see Figure 9.10).

5. In the View-Specific Element Graphics dialog box, select the small downward-pointing arrow in the Surface Transparency row, and slide Transparency to 50 percent. See Figure 9.11.

6. Click OK. The roof is now transparent by 50 percent.

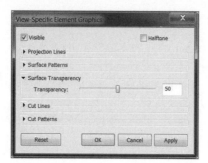

FIGURE 9.11: The View-Specific Element Graphics dialog box

THIS THING IS HAUNTED!

You can set an object to be ghosted—that is, semi-transparent—on the fly with the Transparent option. This helps especially with roofs and floors.

> Rotating a ceiling grid is a good example of the hatch functionality in Revit. You can rotate and move hatch patterns whether they're ceilings, brick, or any other pattern you need to manipulate.

You made the roof transparent because some of the walls have to be attached to the roof. It's much easier to attach the walls in a 3D view. But to do so, you need to see the walls on which you'll be working:

1. Select the wall shown in Figure 9.12.

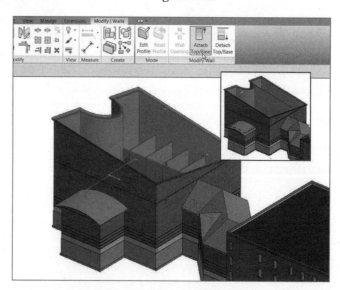

FIGURE 9.12: Attaching the wall to the roof

2. On the Modify | Walls tab, click the Attach Top/Base button.

3. Pick the roof.

Your wall should look like Figure 9.12.

The next step is to constrain the partition walls in this area to Level 3. The ceilings you'll add to these rooms will be much higher than those in the rest of the building. Follow these steps:

1. While still in a 3D view, select the partitions shown in Figure 9.13.

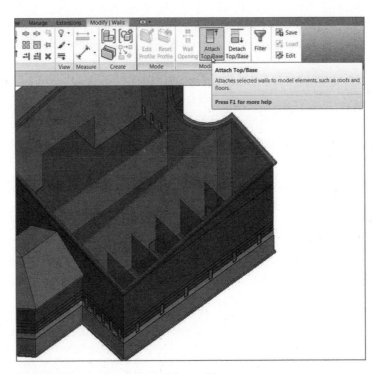

FIGURE 9.13: Selecting the partitions

2. In the Properties dialog box, set the Top constraint to Up To Level: Level 3.

3. The walls are now constrained to Level 3.

4. Select the roof that is transparent, right-click, select Override Graphics In View ➤ By Element, click the Reset button, and then click OK.

5. Go to Level 1 under Ceiling Plans.

The next procedure is a tad off the beaten path, but it fits squarely within this process. Because you've specified the walls in this area to be of a greater height than the rest of the walls in the model, you're obviously adding ceilings higher than 8'–0" (2400mm). This poses a problem in terms of the Level 1 ceiling plan view range.

Creating a Plan Region

Sometimes you'll need to set your view range in a specific area that differs from the view range in the plan as a whole. In this example, you'll add a ceiling at 14'–6" (4350mm) above the finish floor. If you do this with the current view range settings, Revit won't display the ceiling. If you modify the view range for the entire view, you'll see the 14'–6" (4350mm) ceilings, but you won't see the regular 8'–0" (2400mm) ceilings in the rest of the building in that view.

In the following procedure, you'll create a region that has a different view range as compared to the view range in the Level 1 ceiling plan:

1. In the Project Browser, make sure you're in the Level 1 ceiling plan.

 WARNING   Double-check to be absolutely sure you aren't in a floor plan. You want to be in the ceiling plan! If you don't see the ceilings you placed earlier, you're in the wrong view.

2. Zoom in to the west wing.

3. On the View tab, select Plan Views ➢ Plan Region, as shown in Figure 9.14.

4. On the Draw panel, click the Pick Lines button, as shown at the top of Figure 9.15.

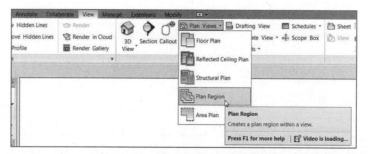

FIGURE 9.14:   The Plan Region option on the Create panel of the View tab

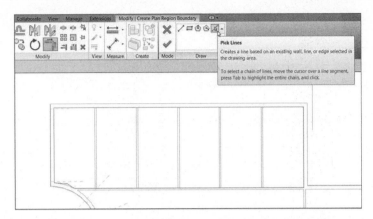

FIGURE 9.15: Defining the limits of the plan region by drawing a rectangle around a specific area

5. Pick the inside, finished face of the exterior walls around the north portion of the west wing (see Figure 9.15).

6. For the lower-left corner, draw a couple of straight lines, as shown in Figure 9.15. (Unfortunately you can't have radial perimeter lines in a plan region.)

Notice that the View tab has now switched to the Modify | Create Plan Region Boundary tab. You need to define the view range for this region:

1. In the Properties dialog box, click the Edit button in the View Range row.

2. In the View Range dialog box, set Top to Level 3.

3. Set Cut Plane Offset to **14′–6″** (4350mm).

4. Set Bottom Offset to **7′–6″** (2250mm).

5. Set View Depth Level to Level 2 with an Offset value of **16′–0″** (4800mm), as shown in Figure 9.16.

6. Click OK.

7. On the Mode panel, click Finish Edit Mode.

You now have a plan region. Although it may not seem as though you did anything in the plan, when you place a ceiling at 14′–6″ (4350mm), you'll be able to see it.

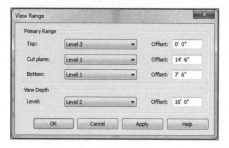

FIGURE 9.16:   Configuring the view range for the crop region

 N O T E   The dotted line you see represents the border of the plan region. Although these borders can get annoying (especially if you collect several plan regions), I recommend that you keep them turned on. It's helpful to know where a plan region is in the model, and it's more important for others to know that there is a plan region in that area. Also, these borders won't plot.

With the plan region in place, you can now place a ceiling at a higher distance from the finish floor. Because you're going to the trouble of placing a high ceiling, you might as well make the ceiling something special.

Creating a Custom Ceiling

So what do you do if your ceiling isn't an acoustical tile ceiling or a gypsum system? This is Revit! You make a new one.

As mentioned earlier, creating a ceiling is similar to creating a floor or a roof. The Properties dialog boxes are exactly the same. This procedure guides you through the process of creating a custom ceiling:

1. Be sure that you're in the Level 1 ceiling plan, and zoom in on the northwest room.

2. On the Architecture tab, click the Ceiling button.

3. In the Type Selector, select GWB On Mtl. Stud. To the right and below the picture of the ceiling is the Edit Type button. Click it (see Figure 9.17).

4. Click Duplicate.

5. Name the new ceiling **Wood Veneer on Metal framing**, and then click OK.

6. In the Structure row, click the Edit button, as shown in Figure 9.18.

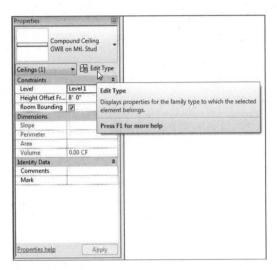

FIGURE 9.17: Clicking the Edit Type button after choosing the GWB On Mtl. Stud ceiling type

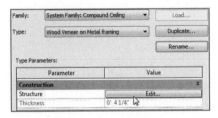

FIGURE 9.18: Clicking the Edit button in the Structure row to gain access to the ceiling's structural composition

7. In the Layers field, as shown in Figure 9.19, click row 4. This is the Finish 2 [5] Gypsum Wall Board row. The entire row should be highlighted in black when you have it selected properly.

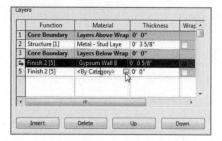

FIGURE 9.19: Clicking the button in the Material cell

8. Just below the Layers field is the Insert button. Click it.

9. Click the Down button to move the new row to the bottom.

10. Change the function from Structure to Finish 2 [5].

11. Click in the Material cell, and click the […] button (see Figure 9.19).

12. In the top of the Material Browser dialog, type **Cherry**, as shown in Figure 9.20.

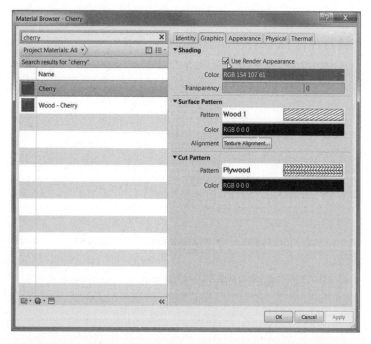

FIGURE 9.20: Selecting and configuring the material for the ceiling

13. In the Material Editor dialog to the right, click the field next to Pattern in the Surface Pattern category. The field contains the word <none>.

14. A new dialog opens. Scroll down until you see the Wood 1 pattern, and select it. Click OK.

15. Below the Surface Pattern category, expand the Cut Pattern category. Change the Pattern field to Plywood. Click OK. (See Figure 9.20.)

16. In the Shading category, click the Use Render Appearance box (see Figure 9.20.

17. In the Material Browser, click OK.

18. Change the Layer 5 thickness to 3/4″ (18mm).

19. Click OK twice.

20. In the Properties dialog box, change Height Offset From Level to 14′–6″ (4350mm), as shown in Figure 9.21.

21. Place the ceiling in the room shown in Figure 9.21.

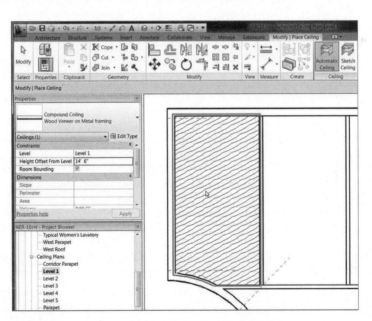

FIGURE 9.21: The cherry-veneered plywood ceiling

N O T E   Don't get discouraged if your final result isn't the same as shown in the figure. You took 21 steps to get to this wonderful cherry ceiling; any one of those steps could have gone wrong. Going back through the steps and retracing your path is something you may be doing quite often until you get used to the program. But remember, you're now set up for plans, sections, and even 3D views and renderings by completing one small task!

For the adjacent rooms, add the same ceiling. You can keep the same height. You can follow along with these steps, but I encourage you to try to put in the ceilings from memory:

1. In the Project Browser, be sure you're in the Level 1 ceiling plan.

2. On the Architecture tab, click the Ceiling button.

3. In the Change Element Type menu on the Element panel, find the ceiling called Compound Ceiling : Wood Veneer On Metal Framing. (It will probably be the current selection.)

4. In the Properties panel, set the height above the floor to 14′–6″ (4350mm).

5. Pick the rooms shown in Figure 9.22. When you've finished, press Esc a couple of times or click Modify to clear the command.

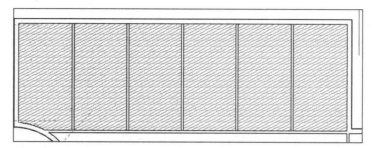

F I G U R E 9 . 2 2 :   The north row of rooms will receive cherry ceilings.

Now that you have experience placing ceilings and creating custom ceiling systems, it's time to start adding features. The first items that come to mind are lighting fixtures, but you need to go back even further and figure out how to "cut holes" in the ceilings and add soffits.

ADDING A CEILING IN EMPTY SPACE

Note that you can add a ceiling to a model even if there are no walls defining an enclosed space. To do this, start the Ceiling command in the typical manner by clicking the Ceiling button on the Architecture tab. When the Ceiling command starts, click the Sketch Ceiling button on the Ceiling tab, as shown in the following graphic. This will enable you to simply draft the ceiling boundaries.

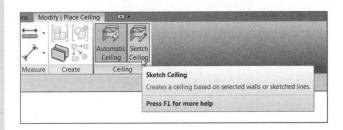

Creating Ceiling Openings and Soffits

Unless you're in a residential dwelling, a prison, or a subway, you can look up and notice that a ceiling is merely serving as a host for electrical, mechanical, and architectural components. Very seldom will you find a ceiling that doesn't require a modification in some capacity. This section of the chapter deals with this issue, starting with creating a ceiling opening.

Creating a Ceiling Opening

The objective of the next procedure is to cut an opening into a ceiling, into which you'll drop a soffit later:

1. Open the Level 1 ceiling plan.

2. Zoom in to the wood ceilings in the west wing, as shown in Figure 9.23.

3. Select the ceiling in the northwest corner of the building, and click the Edit Boundary button.

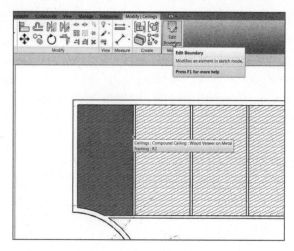

FIGURE 9.23:   Clicking the Edit Boundary button on the Modify | Ceilings tab

 TIP   Ceilings can be difficult to select. If you hover your cursor over the perimeter of the ceiling, you'll see it highlight. If the wall or some other overlapping geometry highlights instead, tap the Tab key on your keyboard to filter through until you find the ceiling. When the ceiling highlights, pick it.

4. Click the Ref Plane button on the Work Plane panel, as shown in Figure 9.24.

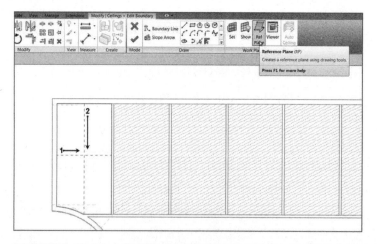

FIGURE 9.24:   Drawing two reference planes to create a center intersection

5. Draw two reference planes (see Figure 9.24). Be sure to snap to the midpoints of the magenta sketch lines.

6. Press Esc a couple of times or click Modify to clear the Ref Plane command.

7. On the Draw panel, click the Boundary Line button. You see an expanded list of sketch choices. Pick the Circle choice, as shown in Figure 9.25.

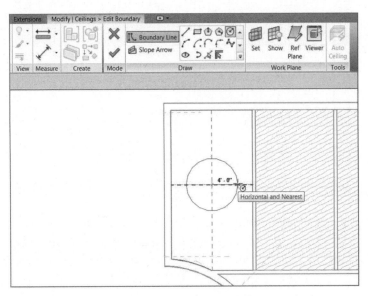

FIGURE 9.25: Sketching a 4′–0″ (1200mm) radius circle

8. Draw a 4′–0″ (1200mm) radius circle at the intersection of the reference planes (see Figure 9.25).

9. On the Mode panel, click Finish Edit Mode.

10. Verify that your ceiling looks like Figure 9.26.

With the cutout in place, you need to think about closing this feature with a soffit and, perhaps, another ceiling.

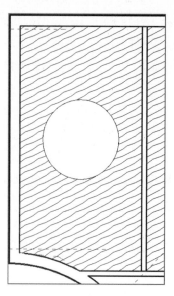

FIGURE 9.26: There's a hole in my ceiling!

Creating a Soffit

Soffits are nothing more than walls with a base offset. This makes sense if you think about it. If your floor level moves, you certainly want the distance from the finish floor to the bottom of the soffit to remain consistent. This one is going to be easy! Here are the steps:

1. On the Architecture tab, click the Wall button.

2. In the Type Selector, select Basic Wall : Interior - 3 1/8″ Partition (1-hr) (79mm), as shown in Figure 9.27.

3. In the Properties dialog box, set Base Offset to 14′–0″ (4200mm), as shown in Figure 9.28.

4. Set Top Constraint to Up To Level: Level 3 (see Figure 9.28).

You're now ready to place the soffit. You'll add it to the radial hole in the ceiling. If you had nothing to guide you, you would need to draw the wall physically by using the Arc Sketch function. In this case, you can simply pick the radial portion of the ceiling opening:

1. With the Wall command still running, click the Pick Lines icon on the Draw panel.

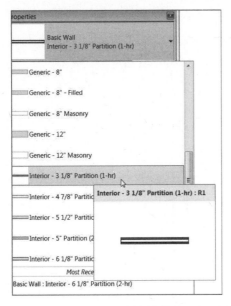

FIGURE 9.27:   Basic Wall : Interior - 3 1/8″ Partition (1-hr) (79mm)

Parameter	Value	
Constraints		
Location Line	Finish Face: Interior	
Base Constraint	Level 1	
Base Offset	14' 0"	
Base is Attached	☐	
Base Extension Distance	0' 0"	
Top Constraint	Up to level: Level 3	
Unconnected Height	6' 0"	
Top Offset	0' 0"	
Top is Attached	☐	
Top Extension Distance	0' 0"	
Room Bounding	☑	
Related to Mass	☐	

Instance Parameters - Control selected or to-be-created instance

FIGURE 9.28:   Setting Top Constraint and Base Offset

2. Mouse over the radial ceiling opening. A blue alignment line appears. Make sure it's to the inside of the opening, and then press the Tab key twice.

3. The entire circle is selected, and the blue alignment line is facing the inside of the hole (see Figure 9.29). When you see this, pick a point to the inside of the hole.

4. Press Esc twice, or click Modify.

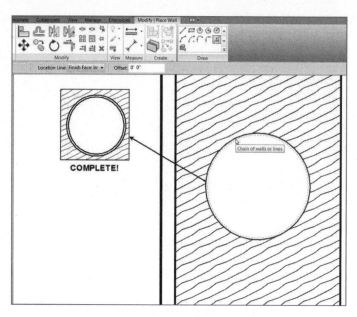

FIGURE 9.29:   Creating one cool soffit

Your soffit is complete.

Next you'll add a secondary ceiling to the inside of the soffit. This procedure is carried out exactly as it was when you added a ceiling to the entire room:

1. In the Project Browser, go to the Level 1 ceiling plan, and zoom in on the ceiling with the soffit if you aren't there already.

2. On the Architecture tab, click the Ceiling button.

3. Select Compound Ceiling : Wood Veneer On Metal Framing (if it isn't the current selection).

4. Click the Edit Type button.

5. Click Duplicate.

6. Call the new ceiling **Mahogany Veneer on Metal Framing**, and then click OK.

7. Click the Edit button in the Structure row.

8. Click in the bottom layer's (5) Material column, and click the […] button to change the material that is now Cherry, as shown in Figure 9.30.

Revit will allow you to add the wall only as a 180° arc. You'll need to pick each side of the circle to accomplish a full 360° soffit.

▶

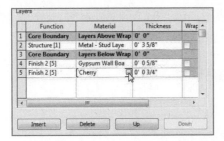

FIGURE 9.30: Click the button to change the material.

9. In the Material Browser, type **mahogany** in the search box, as shown in Figure 9.31.

10. Now that Mahogany is current, make sure you're on the Graphics tab, and make the values match Figure 9.32.

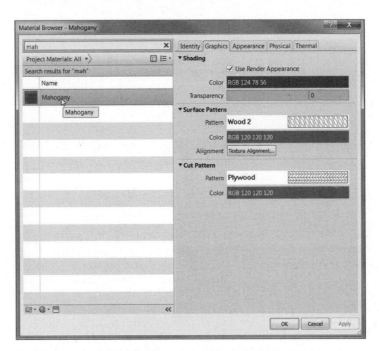

FIGURE 9.31: Adding a new material to the project

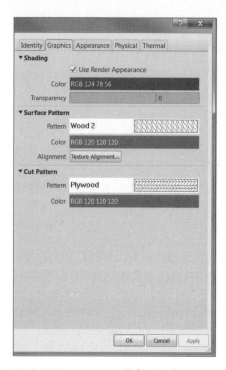

FIGURE 9.32: Making mahogany

You won't be able to see the ceiling at the lower elevation, so stop picking in the middle of the circle! As a matter of fact, if you picked inside the circle more than once, undo back to the point before you started picking in the circle—you probably have several overlapping ceilings.

11. Click OK twice.

12. Click OK one more time to get back to the model.

13. In the Properties dialog box, change Height Offset From Level to 14′–1″ (4225mm).

14. Place the ceiling inside the soffit. Press Esc, or click Modify.

You need to adjust your plan region. It has to be set so the cut plane is either below or equal to 14′–1″ (4225mm) so you can see the lower ceiling:

1. Pick the dotted rectangle surrounding the rooms. This is the plan region.

2. On the Modify | Plan Region tab, click the View Range button.

3. Change the Offset value for the cut plane to 14′–1″ (4225mm).

4. Click OK.

Your ceiling plan should look like Figure 9.33.

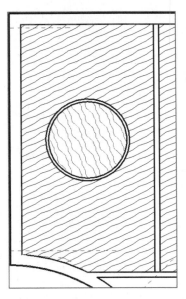

FIGURE 9.33: The completed ceiling

NEVER ASSUME ANYTHING!

They say you should never assume anything, and in this case "they" are right! Let's add a section through this entire row of rooms to gain a perspective on what is going on here:

1. On the View tab, click the Section button.

2. Cut a horizontal section through the entire side of the building, as shown here:

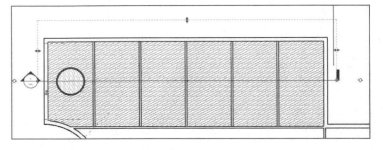

3. Select the section if it isn't still selected.

(Continues)

NEVER ASSUME ANYTHING!   *(Continued)*

4. In the Properties dialog box, change Detail Level to Fine.

5. Change the name to **Section at West Training**. (Yes, these are eventually going to be training rooms.)

6. Open the new section. You now have a clear perspective of what is going on with this area.

You're getting there with this ceiling, that's for sure! The only task left is to add some light fixtures.

Adding Light Fixtures to Ceilings

Adding lighting fixtures to a Revit Architecture model isn't a difficult task, but you must follow a few guidelines to achieve success in installing lighting. For example, you must work with the Ribbon to find a face in which to insert the component:

1. Go to the Level 1 ceiling plan where you've been adding the wood ceilings.

2. On the Architecture tab, click the Component button, as shown in Figure 9.34.

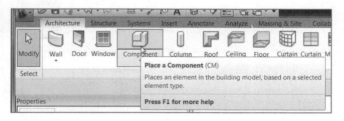

FIGURE 9.34:   Click the Component button on the Architecture tab.

3. On the Mode panel of Modify | Place Component, click Load Family, and then browse to Lighting ➢ Architectural ➢ Internal ➢ Pendant Light – Disk.

4. Open the file Pendant Light - Disk.rfa (M_Pendant Light - Disk.rfa).

5. Place the light approximately in the center of the radial mahogany soffit (you'll have to move it in a second).

6. Press Esc twice.

7. Select the fixture.

8. Click the Move button.

9. Type SC (this means Snap Center).

10. Pick a point in the center of the fixture.

11. Type SC again.

12. Hover your cursor over one of the inside radial walls. A center snap appears. Pick the radial wall. Your fixture should snap to the center of the soffit (see Figure 9.35).

 N O T E   There are no snaps when you're trying to place most components. You'll have to place the fixture and then move it into position. Needless to say, this is an extra step.

13. Open the section called Section At West Training. Notice that the light fixture is in the exact location where you expect it to be.

14. Select the fixture.

15. Click the Copy button on the Modify Lighting Fixtures tab.

16. On the Options bar, be sure the Multiple button is selected.

17. Copy the fixture 3′–0″ (900mm) to the right and 3′–0″ (900mm) to the left (see Figure 9.36).

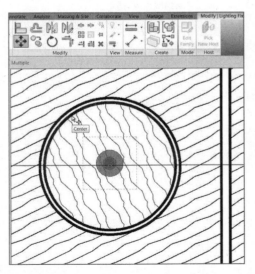

FIGURE 9.35: Moving the fixture to the correct location

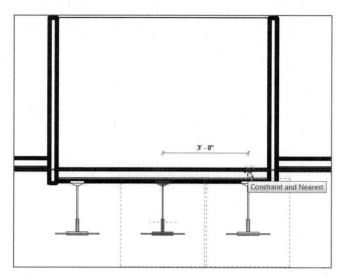

FIGURE 9.36: Copying the fixture in the section

The main point of having you open a section to copy the fixture is to illustrate that you're now in a full modeling environment. When you switch back to the plan, you'll see that the fixtures have been placed. In later chapters, you'll learn that the act of simply pacing fixtures in the model will also add line items to schedules.

YIKES, THIS ISN'T TO OUR STANDARDS!

Yes, the default line thicknesses are hideous. For now, you can click the Thin Lines icon to scale back the thickness of the lines, as shown here:

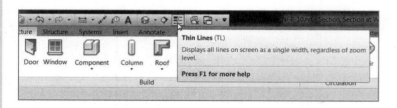

Now let's make some more fixtures:

1. In the Project Browser, go to the Level 1 ceiling plan.

2. Zoom in on the radial soffit. You see the two new fixtures.

3. Select the right and left fixtures.

4. Click the Rotate command on the Modify | Lighting Fixtures tab.

5. On the Options bar, make sure Copy is selected.

6. Rotate the fixtures 90° to create a total of five fixtures, as shown in Figure 9.37.

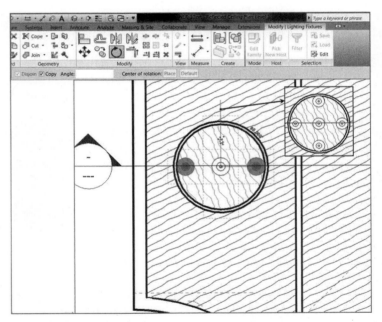

FIGURE 9.37: You're now copying and rotating as if you were in flat, 2D Autodesk AutoCAD® software.

 N O T E   Notice that the fixtures overlap the gypsum soffit. This is because you're actually standing on Level 1 looking up. Revit Architecture has finally taken the confusion out of the reflected ceiling-plan mystery.

Now that you have experience dealing with ceilings, let's start working on some interior design. Ceilings are a part of this, but what about wall treatments, trims, and architectural millwork? These items will be covered in the next section.

Adding Interior Design

Congratulations! You've arrived at possibly the most difficult subject when it comes to 3D modeling. Why is that? Well, for starters, this is the area where nothing is easy in terms of shape, configuration, and, for some projects, the sheer amount of millwork and detail. For example, suppose you want a crown molding at the ceiling where it intersects the walls. And suppose you need the same crown at the radial soffit. Of course, the floors and walls aren't the same material, and you need to add furniture as well.

I can go on and on listing the complications you'll face here, so let's just jump in. The first part of the process is adding plumbing fixtures and furniture.

Adding Plumbing Fixtures and Furniture

Adding a desk follows the same procedure as adding a light fixture. Notice, though, that when you added the light fixture, it "knew" that it was supposed to be hosted by the ceiling. It's important to note that most furniture isn't hosted by a floor; it's hosted by a level. This becomes very important if you have a floor system offset from a level. Your furniture will ignore the floor and stick to the level with which it's associated.

To begin, you'll have to knock out the less glamorous, but all too important, task of adding bathroom fixtures:

1. In the Project Browser, go to the Level 1 floor plan (floor plan, not ceiling plan).

2. Zoom in on the lavatory area, and turn off the thin lines mode, as shown in Figure 9.38.

3. As you can see, there is a callout of this area. Double-click the callout bubble to open the view called Typical Men's Lavatory.

 NOTE   Now that you're more experienced with Revit, you can see the benefit of having named this view something understandable at this stage in the game.

4. With the Typical Men's Lavatory view opened, you can start adding fixtures. On the Insert tab, click the Load Family button.

5. In the Imperial Library (or Metric) directory, browse to the Plumbing/Architectural/Fixtures/Water Closets/ folder.

6. Select the file called Toilet-Commercial-Wall-3D.rfa (M_Toilet-Commercial-Wall-3D.rfa), and click Open.

7. Go to the Architecture tab, and click the Component button.

8. If you see a dialog box asking whether you want to load a plumbing fixture tag, click No.

9. In the Type Selector, make sure the 15″ Seat Height (380mm Seat Height) toilet is selected.

10. Place it along the north wall approximately 6″ (150mm) from the west wall, as shown in Figure 9.39.

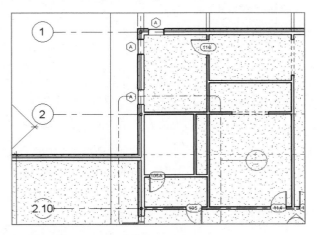

FIGURE 9.38:   The lavatory area

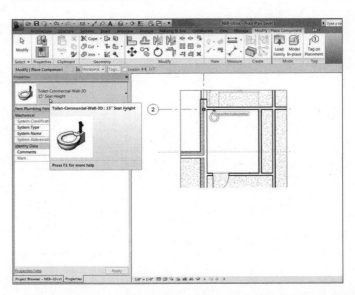

FIGURE 9.39:   Placing the 15″ (381mm) Seat Height toilet 6″ (150mm) from the west wall, along the north wall

Because you're not designing a military barracks from the 1960s, you need some stalls. Unfortunately, Revit doesn't provide any stalls out of the box, but this book you bought does! To add toilet stalls to the model, go to the book's web page at www.sybex.com/go/revit2014ner. From there, you can browse to the Chapter 9 folder and find these files:

▶ Toilet Stall-Accessible-Front-3D.rfa

▶ Toilet Stall-Accessible-Side-3D.rfa

▶ Toilet Stall-Braced-3D.rfa

▶ Grab Bar.rfa

▶ Double Sink - Round.rfa

Download the files to the location where you keep all your Revit families. Then, follow along with the procedure:

1. On the Insert tab, click Load Family.

2. Browse to the location where the new families are kept and select the new files; then click Open. They're loaded into your project.

3. On the Architecture tab, click the Place A Component button.

4. Select Toilet-Stall-Accessible-Front-3D 60″ × 60″ Clear.

5. Pick the corner of the bathroom, as shown in Figure 9.40.

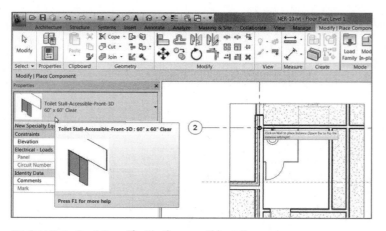

FIGURE 9.40: Placing the accessible stall

T I P   If you're having difficulty placing the stall directly in the corner, place it at any location along the north wall and then move it to the corner so that it looks like the figure.

The next step is to copy the toilet and add another stall. It would be nice if the family just fit, but this isn't a perfect world!

1. Copy the toilet to the right 6′–2 ½″ (1862mm).

2. On the Architecture tab, click the Place A Component button.

3. Select Toilet Stall – Braced – 3D 59″ × 60″ Clear.

4. Click Edit Type.

5. Click Duplicate.

6. Name the new stall type **54″ × 60″ Clear (1350 × 1500mm Clear)**. Set the width to 4′–6″ (1350mm), and click OK.

7. Place the stall in the model (see Figure 9.41).

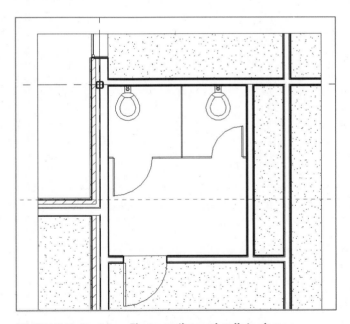

F I G U R E 9 . 4 1 :   The two toilets and stalls in place

T I P   You may have to press the spacebar as you place the stall to flip it into the correct position. Again, if you're having difficulty placing the stall directly in the corner, you can place it along the north wall at any location and then either align or move the stall into the correct position.

With the toilets and the stalls in place, you need to add a grab bar to the accessible stall. Again, Revit doesn't provide this content. You need to either make this component yourself (this is covered in Chapter 17, "Creating Families") or use the one from the book that you downloaded with the bathroom stalls.

To add a grab bar, follow these steps:

1. Zoom in on the accessible stall, as shown in Figure 9.42.

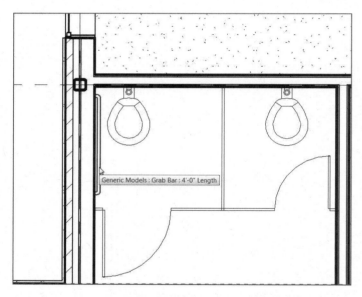

Generic Models : Grab Bar : 4'-0" Length

F I G U R E   9 . 4 2 :   Adding the grab bar family to the wall

2. Click the Place A Component button.

3. Select Grab Bar 4'–0" (1200mm) Length.

4. Place the grab bar along the wall (see Figure 9.42).

N O T E   As you place the grab bar, it will look like it's going to be embedded into the studs of the wall. Don't worry. After you pick the point where you want the grab bar, it will move to the finished face of the wall.

N O T E   Remember, although it kind of feels like you're just sticking blocks into your model, these are all 3D parametric parts. This grab bar, for all you know, is 6'–0" above the ground or sitting on the floor. To adjust this, you don't have to cut a section or go to a 3D view. You can simply select the grab bar and, in the Properties dialog box, set Elevation to 2'–0".

Because you're in the men's room, you need to add some urinals. You can fit two before you start getting too close to the sink area and the guy standing next to you:

1. On the Insert tab, click the Load Family button.

2. Browse to Plumbing Fixtures ➢ Architectural ➢ Urinals.

3. Select the file called `Urinal-Wall-3D.rfa` (`M_Urinal-Wall-3D.rfa`).

4. Click Open.

5. Click the Component button, and place two urinals about 6" (150mm) away from the front of the stall, with a 1'–0" (300mm) space between the two, as shown in Figure 9.43.

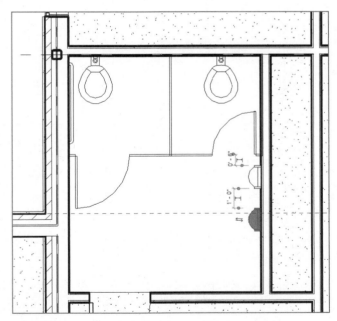

F I G U R E   9 . 4 3 :   Adding the urinals to the men's room

What a relief to get those urinals in! The next step is to install a sink with two stations in the bathroom. To do this, you can use the double sink you loaded from the book's website:

1. On the Architecture tab, click the Place A Component button if it isn't still running.

2. In the Type Selector, find the family called Double Sink - Round 24″ Depth (Double Sink - Round 600mm Depth).

3. Place it in the corner, as shown in Figure 9.44.

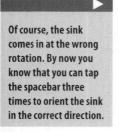

Of course, the sink comes in at the wrong rotation. By now you know that you can tap the spacebar three times to orient the sink in the correct direction.

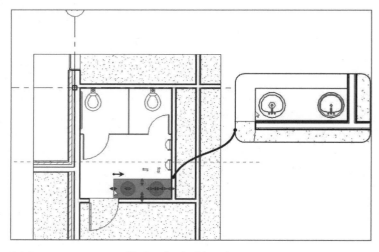

FIGURE 9.44: Placing the double sink

If your door is 12″ (300mm) from the left wall, then you have a problem, don't you? Luckily you're using an application that allows you to stretch a component dynamically.

4. Select the sink.

5. Click the leftmost stretch grip, and slide the sink to be flush with the door opening (see Figure 9.44).

The women's room is the same size, and it will have two stalls and a sink. Create the mirrored layout shown in Figure 9.45.

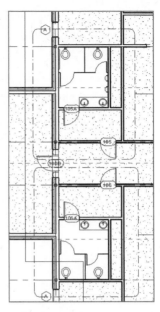

FIGURE 9.45:   Completing the women's room

With the first-floor bathrooms done, let's move to some of the actual rooms and offices to furnish them. The first thing you need to do is add lighting to the ceilings.

Adding Parabolic Troffers

As you're starting to see, the procedure for adding a component doesn't change based on the component you're adding. This is great news. Adding a troffer, however, is slightly different. You do need to be in a ceiling plan, and you do need to specify the face of the ceiling.

At this point, you may be good enough at adding these fixtures to simply look at the following figures and add the lights yourself. Or, if you desire a little help, follow these steps:

1. In the Project Browser, go to the Level 1 ceiling plan. (Notice that you're going to a ceiling plan, not a floor plan.)

2. Zoom in on the northwest corner of the east wing, as shown in Figure 9.46.

If you mirror the stalls, they will go haywire. You'll need to add them separately.

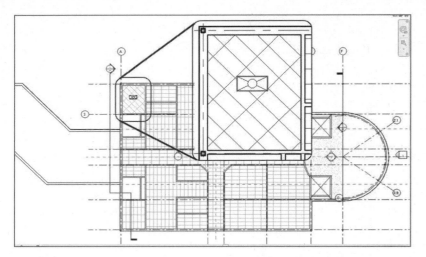

FIGURE 9.46:   Placing a light in a ceiling. You'll align it to the grid in a moment.

3. On the Insert tab, click the Load Family button.

4. Browse to the `Lighting Fixtures` folder.

5. Select the file called `Troffer Light - 2 X4 Parabolic.rfa` (`M_Troffer Light Parabolic Rectangular.rfa`).

6. Click Open.

7. Click the Place A Component button; then place the fixture in your ceiling (see Figure 9.46).

8. Click the Align button on the Modify tab, as shown in Figure 9.47.

9. Align the light fixture to the grid in both directions (see Figure 9.47).

10. Copy the light to the locations shown in Figure 9.48.

11. Add lights to the rest of the rooms in the east wing, as shown in Figure 9.48. It's quickest to place a single light horizontally and one vertically, align them to the grids, and then make multiple copies.

12. In the Properties dialog box, click the View Range button.

13. Set the cut plane to 4′–0″ (1200mm).

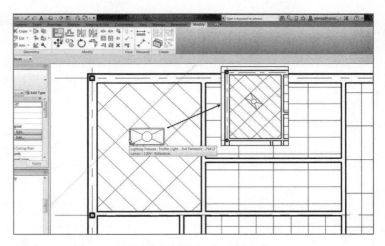

FIGURE 9.47:   Aligning the fixture to the grid

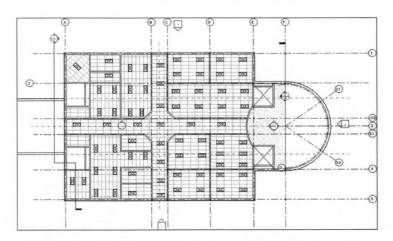

FIGURE 9.48:   Adding lights to the rest of the ceilings

Next, you need to illuminate the corridors. This can be done by adding a set of wall-mounted sconces, as follows:

1. Browse to the Level 1 floor plan.

2. On the Insert tab, click Load Family.

3. Browse to the Lighting/Architectural/Internal folder.

4. Select the file called Sconce Light - Uplight.rfa. (M_Sconce Light - Uplight.rfa).

5. Add the sconce to the corridor wall, as shown in Figure 9.49.

6. Add sconces to the walls of the hallways as appropriate, as shown in Figure 9.50.

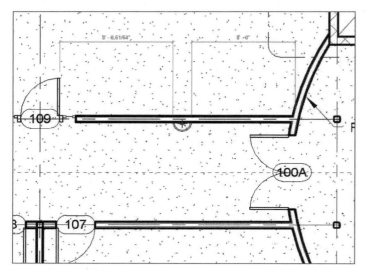

FIGURE 9.49:   Adding a sconce

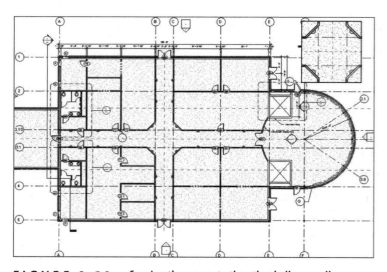

FIGURE 9.50:   Copying the sconce to the other hallway walls

7. In the Project Browser, double-click the 3D view called East Wing Corridor Perspective. This gives you a good idea of how the up-lighting influences the corridor (see Figure 9.51).

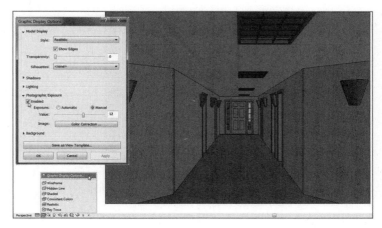

FIGURE 9.51:   Looking at the hallway in a perspective view

8. On the View Control toolbar, click the Visual Style Icon, and choose the Graphic Display Options choice at the top of the dialog, as shown in Figure 9.51.

9. For Photographic Exposure, check the Enabled box to turn on the exposure.

Well, that corridor is looking great! It's time now to begin looking into the offices and also to see whether you can complete a kitchen area.

Adding Casework and Furniture

Adding casework and furniture is the easiest part of this chapter—that is, if you like the casework and furniture that comes right out of the Revit box. Something tells me this isn't going to be adequate. For this chapter, you'll be using the out-of-the box items, but in Chapter 17, you'll make some custom millwork families.

To add some office furniture, follow along:

1. Select the Level 1 floor plan.

2. Zoom in to the northeast corner office, as shown in Figure 9.52.

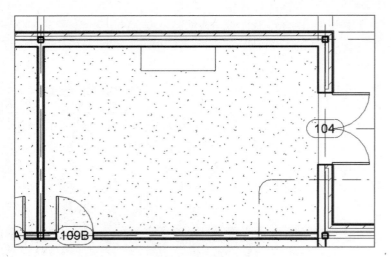

FIGURE 9.52:   Placing the credenza desk into the first office

3. On the Insert tab, click the Load Family button.

4. Browse to the `Casework/Base Cabinets` folder, and select the following item:

   ▶ `Base Cabinet-4 Drawers.rfa` (`M_ Base Cabinet-4 Drawers.rfa`)

5. Browse to the `Furniture/Seating` folder, and open the following:

   ▶ `Chair-Executive.rfa` (`M_Chair-Executive.rfa`)

6. Browse to the `Furniture/Storage` folder, and open the following:

   ▶ `Credenza.rfa` (`M_Credenza.rfa`)

   ▶ `Entertainment Center.rfa` (`M_Entertainment Center.rfa`)

   ▶ `Shelving.rfa` (`M_Shelving.rfa`)

7. Click the Place A Component button; then, in the Type Selector, select Credenza 72″ × 24″ (1830 × 610mm).

8. Place the credenza desk into the room, as shown near the top of Figure 9.52.

9. On the Architecture tab, click the Place A Component button if the command isn't still running.

10. From the Type Selector, select Chair-Executive, and place it in front of the credenza, as shown in Figure 9.53.

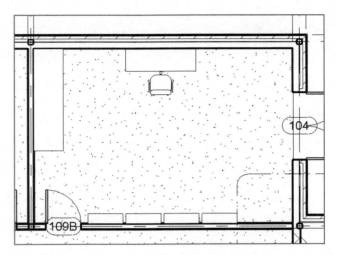

FIGURE 9.53: Adding furniture to the office

11. In the Type Selector, select the Entertainment Center 96″ × 84″ × 30″ (2743 × 2134 × 762mm) and place it in the corner (see Figure 9.53).

12. Place four 36″ (915mm) shelving units across the south wall, as shown near the bottom of Figure 9.53.

At this point, it's a good idea to take a perspective shot of this office to see if the space is developing the way you were envisioning. Although you may never put this perspective view onto a construction document, it's still a great idea to see what is going on:

1. On the View tab, select 3D View ➤ Camera.

2. Pick a point in the northeast corner.

3. Pick a second point beyond the southwest corner, as shown in Figure 9.54. The new view opens. You'll probably want to stretch the crop boundaries.

4. In the Project Browser, right-click the new 3D view, and call it **Perspective of Corner Office**.

5. See Figure 9.55 to get an idea of how to stretch the window to show more of the perspective.

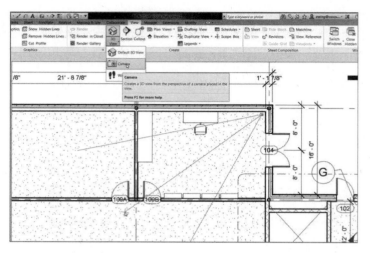

FIGURE 9.54:   Adding a camera (perspective view) to the corner office

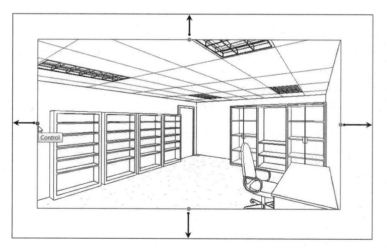

FIGURE 9.55:   The perspective of the corner office. If your entertainment unit is backward, you'll have to go back to the plan to rotate it.

It's time for a kitchen! This is such a nice office that there seems to be a need for a break area right outside. You wouldn't want your esteemed executive to have to walk very far for a cup of coffee or a snack.

To get started, you'll load some countertops and cabinets:

1. On the Insert tab, click the Load Family button.

2. Browse to the Casework folder.

3. Load the following families. You'll have to choose from the appropriate folders in the Casework directory:

   ▶ Base Cabinet-2 Bin.rfa

   ▶ Base Cabinet-Double Door & 2 Drawer.rfa

   ▶ Base Cabinet-Double Door Sink Unit.rfa

   ▶ Base Cabinet-Filler.rfa

   ▶ Base Cabinet-Single Door & Drawer.rfa

   ▶ Counter Top-L Shaped w Sink Hole 2.rfa

   ▶ Upper Cabinet-Double Door-Wall.rfa

4. Load the file Corner Base Filler.rfa from the Chapter 9 directory on the book's website.

5. Open the Level 1 floor plan. Zoom in on the kitchen area, as shown in Figure 9.56.

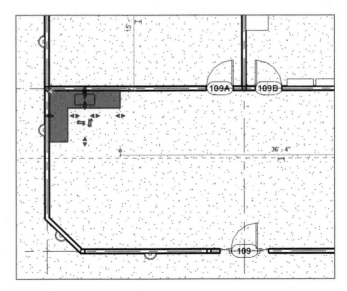

FIGURE 9.56: Adding the countertop

6. Add the countertop (see Figure 9.56).

7. Press Esc twice.

8. Select the countertop.

9. Select the stretch arrows, and stretch the leg of the counter to the end of the wall, as shown in Figure 9.57.

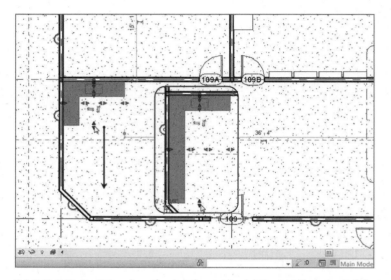

FIGURE 9.57: Lengthening the counter leg to meet the corner of the wall

10. Add the Base Cabinet-Double Door Sink Unit 30″ (900mm) under the sink hole in the north leg of the counter.

11. Align the base unit under the sink.

You now have a counter and a sink base. The problem is that you have no idea how high these items are or what they really look like. That's okay—this is Revit. You just need to create two elevations for these items, as follows:

1. On the Create panel on the View tab, click the Elevation button.

2. Add an interior elevation looking north, as shown in Figure 9.58.

3. Select the elevation marker, and turn on the elevation looking west (see Figure 9.58).

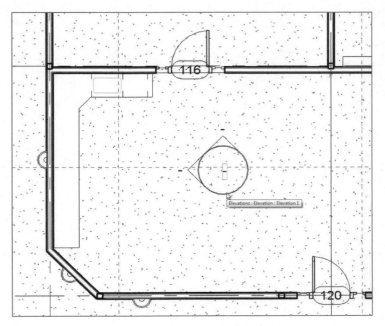

Elevations : Elevation : Elevation 1

FIGURE 9.58: Adding elevations to aid in design

4. Rename the north elevation **Kitchen North**.

5. With the elevation marker still selected, click the check box to the west, and rename the west elevation **Kitchen West**.

With the elevations in, you can flip back and forth to make sure you're putting items in the right places and to get a good idea of how your cabinet run looks.

The remainder of the procedure involves adding the rest of the cabinets. Let's do it!

1. On the Architecture tab, click the Place A Component button.

2. From the Type Selector, select Base Cabinet - Single Door & Drawer 24″ (600mm).

3. Place the base cabinet to the right of the sink cabinet.

4. Press Esc twice, or click Modify; then open the Kitchen North elevation. Does your elevation look like Figure 9.59?

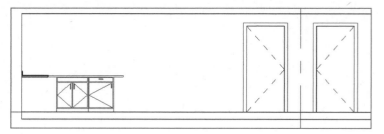

FIGURE 9.59:   The elevation of the cabinet run

5. Go back to the Level 1 floor plan.

6. Place a Base Cabinet Double Door & 2 Drawer 36″ (900mm) in the position shown in Figure 9.60.

7. Press Esc twice, or click Modify; then select the Kitchen West elevation.

8. Move the base cabinet so there is a 1″ (25mm) counter overhang, as shown in Figure 9.61.

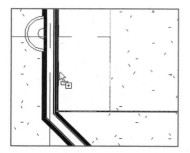

FIGURE 9.60:   Placing the 36″ (900mm) double-door, two-drawer base cabinet

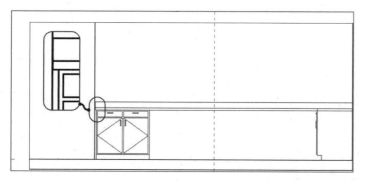

FIGURE 9.61:   The 1″ (25mm) overhang on the end

9. Copy the base cabinet to the right three times (four total cabinets), as shown in Figure 9.62.

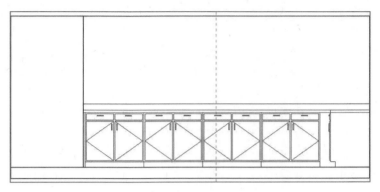

FIGURE 9.62:   The base cabinet run

10. Go back to Level 1, and click the Place A Component button.

11. Find Corner Base Filler.

12. Place it in the model on the side of the base cabinet, as shown in Figure 9.63.

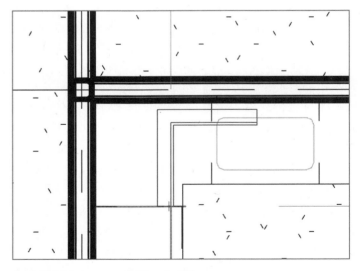

FIGURE 9.63:   Adding the filler

13. Select the filler.

14. Stretch the grips until the filler resembles Figure 9.64.

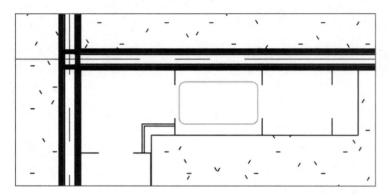

FIGURE 9.64:   The completed corner

The bases are done! Let's add some wall cabinets to the kitchen.

1. On the Architecture tab, click the Place A Component button.

2. In the Type Selector, select Upper Cabinet-Double-Door-Wall 36″ (900mm).

3. Place the wall cabinet in the model, as shown in Figure 9.65. (Don't worry too much about aligning it to the cabinet below. You'll align it in elevation.)

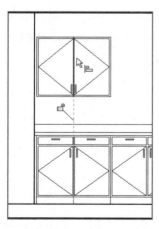

FIGURE 9.65:   Adding the wall cabinet

4. Open the Kitchen West elevation.

5. Click the Align button on the Modify tab.

6. Align the wall cabinet to the base cabinet, as shown in Figure 9.66.

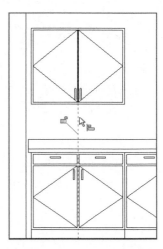

FIGURE 9.66: Aligning the wall to the base

7. Copy the wall cabinet to the right three times (for four total cabinets).

8. Save the model.

Your cabinets should look like Figure 9.67.

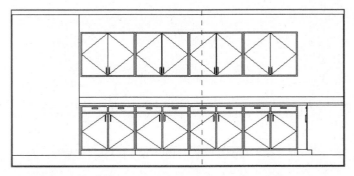

FIGURE 9.67: The finished west wall of the kitchen

Now that the kitchen is in place, it would be nice to add a tile floor only to that area. You can accomplish this without having to add extra floors to the model. You can simply split the face of the floor that is already there and add an additional material.

Adding Alternate Floor Materials

Carpeting doesn't perform well in kitchens. This is information you already know. What you don't know is how to add tile to a carpeted floor system without having to cut the existing floor and start piecing in sections of alternate materials. That's what you'll learn to do in this section.

Separating the Floor

You have a floor area targeted for a new material, and the following procedure guides you through the steps:

1. Open the Level 1 floor plan. Click the Split Face button on the Modify tab, as shown in Figure 9.68.

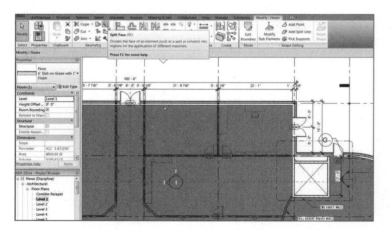

FIGURE 9.68: Clicking the Split Face button, and selecting the slab edge

2. Select the entire floor. This may require finding the edge of the floor along an exterior wall (see Figure 9.68).

3. Click the Line button on the Draw panel. Draw a continuous line around the kitchen, as shown in Figure 9.69.

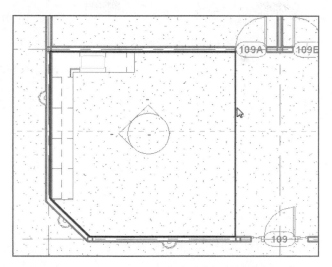

FIGURE 9.69: Drawing the perimeter of the alternate floor material

4. On the Modify | Split Face ➤ Create Boundary tab, click Finish Edit Mode.

N O T E Remember, you can't have any overlapping lines or gaps while adding your magenta sketch lines.

Although it doesn't seem like it, you have split the kitchen from the rest of the floor. Next you'll apply a material to the kitchen. The first step will be to create a suitable material to use.

Creating a Tile Material

There is one tile material in this model, but it would be beneficial to create a new one with 12″ (300mm) square tiles. This procedure takes the place of using hatching in a conventional drafting situation.

Follow this procedure to create a new material:

1. On the Manage tab, click the Materials button, as shown in Figure 9.70.

2. In the Material Browser, type **tile** in the search field at the top of the dialog, as shown in Figure 9.71, scroll down, and select Tile, Porcelain, 4in (100mm).

3. In the Material Editor, click Use Render Appearance under Shading, as shown in Figure 9.72. Click done, and then click OK.

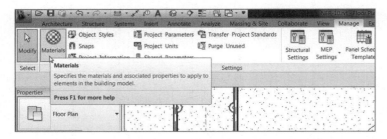

FIGURE 9.70: Clicking the Materials button on the Manage tab

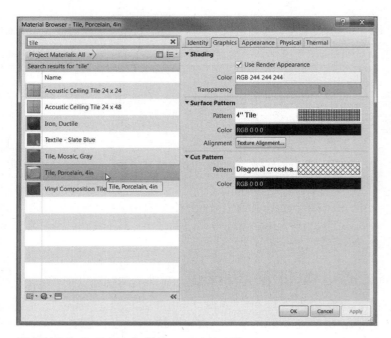

FIGURE 9.71: Grabbing some sweet tile

FIGURE 9.72: Mapping out the rendering and the shading appearance

The new material is locked, loaded, and ready to spill onto the floor! To do this, you'll paint to apply the new material to the kitchen. Follow along:

1. Click the Paint button on the Geometry panel of the Modify tab, as shown in Figure 9.73.

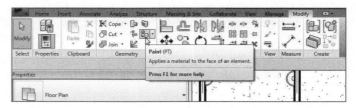

FIGURE 9.73:   The Paint button

2. Select Tile, Porcelain, 4in from the Material Class drop-down list, as shown in Figure 9.74.

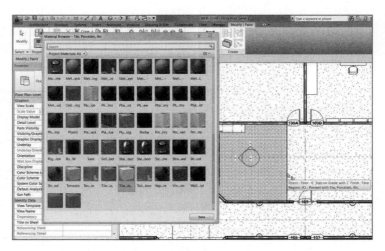

FIGURE 9.74:   Selecting porcelain tile

3. Place your paint icon over the edge of the kitchen floor until the region becomes highlighted.

4. Pick the floor. Your new tile appears. Click OK in the Materials dialog box.

Phew! You're gaining a good amount of experience in terms of adding components and making the interior of the building conform to your design. If you think about it, you've done nothing here that is out of the ordinary. You're simply replacing everyday drafting routines with modeling routines. What a way to go!

Because there is quite a bit of building left, go ahead and load up this model with components. If you get stuck anywhere, go back and find the procedure that pertains to your problem.

Are You Experienced?

Now you can...

- ☑ add ceilings to a room as well as create new ceilings and modify them to suit your needs

- ☑ transfer ceilings from other projects by using the Transfer Project Standards function

- ☑ add soffits to your model by using a typical wall and offsetting the base

- ☑ create a plan region so you can see elements at different elevations without disturbing the rest of the view

- ☑ add components such as bathroom fixtures, office furniture, and lighting to your model

- ☑ create subregions in which to specify alternate flooring, thus allowing you to avoid hatching

Stairs, Ramps, and Railings

A whole chapter just for stairs, ramps, and railings? You bet! If you think about it, there could be hundreds of combinations of stair and railing systems. As a matter of fact, you very seldom see two sets of stairs that are exactly the same. Kind of like snowflakes, aren't they? Okay, they're nothing like snowflakes! But you get the point.

▶ **Creating stairs by using the Rise/Run function**

▶ **Creating a winding staircase**

▶ **Creating a custom railing system**

▶ **Creating custom stairs**

▶ **Adding ramps**

Creating Stairs by Using the Rise/Run Function

To begin, this chapter will address the makings of a staircase—from commercial stairs to those with a more residential feel with wood members, balusters, and spindles. During this procedure, you'll see how the Autodesk® Revit® Architecture software brings stairs together. After you create a common staircase, you'll move on to winding stairs, custom railings, and, of course, ramps.

Before you begin, I should mention that there are some stair-related features (or lack of features) in Revit you'll love, and some you won't. As you create the stairs, keep in mind that Revit can't always provide enough functionality to re-create every type of stair you may encounter.

N O T E   Throughout this book, you'll have the opportunity to download custom families from the book's website.

In this section, you'll focus on creating a staircase by using the traditional Rise/Run method. Then I'll discuss modifying the boundary of the stairs, which allows you to create a more unusual shape than that provided out of the box.

N O T E   Metric users should not type in mm or other metric abbreviations when entering amounts suggested in the exercises. Revit will not accept such abbreviations. Simply enter the number provided within the parentheses.

To begin, open the file on which you've been following along. If you didn't complete Chapter 9, "Ceilings and Interiors," go to the book's web page at www.sybex.com/go/revit2014ner. From there you can browse to the Chapter 10 folder and find the file called NER-10.rvt.

The objective of the following procedure is to create a staircase using the Rise/Run method:

1. In the Project Browser, go to the Level 2 floor plan.

2. Zoom in on the radial entry in the east wing, as shown in Figure 10.1.

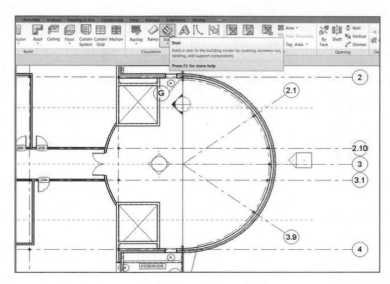

FIGURE 10.1:   Click the Stair button on the Circulation panel of the Architecture tab.

3. On the View Control bar, change Visual Style to Hidden Line.

4. On the Circulation panel of the Architecture tab, click the Stair button (see Figure 10.1).

5. You're put into Sketch Mode for the stairs you're about to design, as shown in Figure 10.2.

FIGURE 10.2:   The Modify | Create Stair tab, Sketch Mode

6. On the Components panel of the Modify | Create Stair tab, make sure the Run button and the Straight button are checked (see Figure 10.2).

7. In the Properties dialog, change Base Level to Level 1.

8. Change Top Level to Level 2.

9. Change Multistory Top Level to Level 5 (see Figure 10.3).

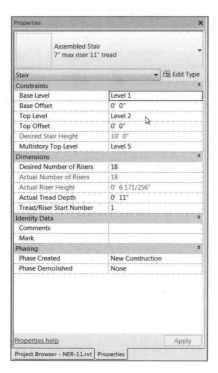

FIGURE 10.3:   Changing the Element Properties of the stairs

 NOTE   By setting the base to Level 1 and the top to Level 2, you give Revit the dimensions it needs to calculate the rise of the stairs. When you add the multistory height, Revit takes the calculation from Levels 1 and 2 and applies that increment up to the additional floors. Be warned, however, that if the floor-to-floor dimension changes in one of these levels, you'll have a problem. You'll then have to create a new staircase starting at the offending level.

10. Pick the intersection of the floor edge and grid 3.1 for the first point of the stairs. This spot is labeled 1 in Figure 10.4.

11. See also this book's web page at www.sybex.com/go/revit2014ner. From there you can browse to the Chapter 10 folder and find the video called _Creating Stairs by Run.mp4.

12. Move your cursor to the right. A faint display indicates that you have a certain number of risers created and a certain number remaining.

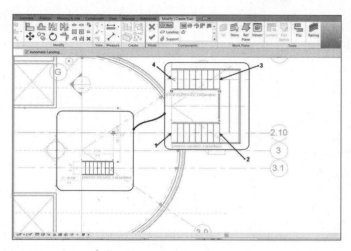

FIGURE 10.4:   Laying out the stairs

13. When you see that nine risers have been created with nine risers remaining, pick the spot labeled 2 in Figure 10.4.

14. Move your cursor straight up (north) until you get to the grid intersection labeled 3 in Figure 10.4. When you see this, pick the third point.

15. Move your cursor to the left—all the way past the floor landing. Revit reports that you have 18 risers created and 0 remaining (see Figure 10.4).

16. When the second leg is completed, pick the last point. Revit draws both legs as well as the landing (see Figure 10.4).

With the basic layout completed, it's time to examine the perimeter of the stairs. If you're looking for any architectural design outside of the basic box that you get when you place a staircase, you'll want to edit the boundary.

Modifying Boundaries

With the main stairs in place and laid out, you can now start modifying the profile. Given that this is a five-tiered, multilevel staircase, the boundary will be somewhat limited—but not to the point that you can't make something pop out of your design.

To modify the boundary, follow along:

1. Select the landing, as shown in Figure 10.5.

2. Click the Convert button (see Figure 10.5).

3. When you see the warning that you may be doing irreversible damage, click Close to dismiss it.

4. With the landing still selected, click the Edit Sketch button, as shown in Figure 10.6.

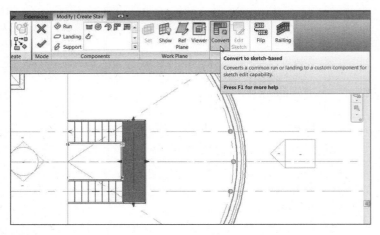

FIGURE 10.5:   The Convert button

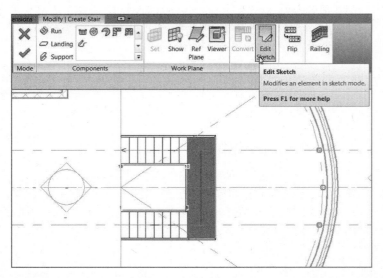

FIGURE 10.6:   The Edit Sketch button

5. On the Draw panel, click the Start-End-Radius Arc button, as shown in Figure 10.7.

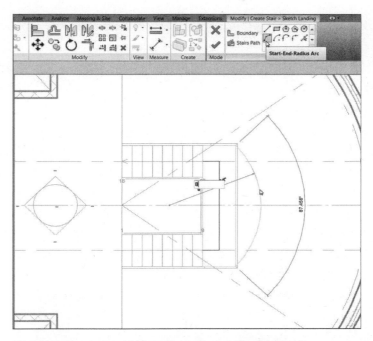

FIGURE 10.7:   Add a radius to the outside of the landing.

6. Draw an arc on the outside of the landing at an 8′–0″ (2400mm) radius (see Figure 10.7).

With the radius drawn in, it's important to pause at this point. What you have here is an extra line. Similar to when you're sketching a floor, if you have any overlapping line segments or gaps, Revit won't let you continue. Also, if you have any extra lines, Revit won't let you continue.

Let's clean up the stairs:

1. Click Modify or press the Esc key twice, and then select the straight green line at the outside of the landing.

2. Press the Delete key on your keyboard. The line is removed. Your stairs should look exactly like Figure 10.8.

3. Click the Finish Edit Mode button, as shown in Figure 10.9.

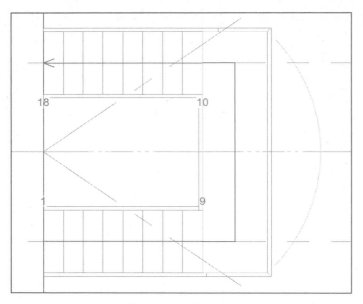

FIGURE 10.8:   The completed boundary

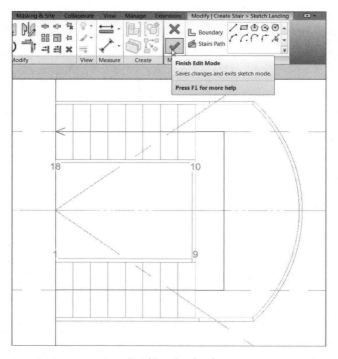

FIGURE 10.9:   Finishing the sketch

Now you can select the railing system to use. Out of the box, Revit provides only four choices. You'll select one of those choices for this staircase, but you'll add to the list later in this chapter.

Configuring Railings

Revit provides a small number of railing systems as a default. You can choose one of these five railings to apply to the staircase during the Sketch Mode of the stairs.

Follow this procedure to apply a railing to the stairs:

1. On the Modify | Create Stair tab in Sketch Mode, click the Railing button, as shown in Figure 10.10.

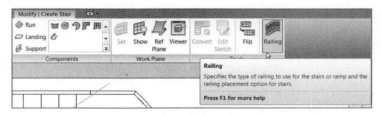

FIGURE 10.10: Click the Railing button.

2. In the Railing dialog, from the drop-down, select Guardrail - Pipe, as shown in Figure 10.11.

FIGURE 10.11: Select Guardrail - Pipe and the Stringer radio button.

3. Under Position, select the Stringer radio button (see Figure 10.11). Doing so hosts the railing to the stringer.

4. Click OK. With the railings in place, you're on your way to completing this staircase. As a matter of fact, round one is finished.

5. To complete the stairs, click Finish Edit Mode on the Modify | Create Stair tab.

6. Close the warning that states that the rail is non-continuous.

7. Go to Level 1. Your stairs should look like Figure 10.12.

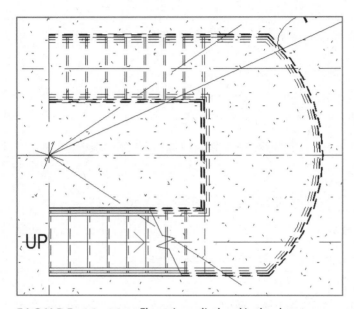

FIGURE 10.12: The stairs as displayed in the plan

Normally, when you're dealing with a large, multistory staircase, you should check it out in 3D to make sure all went as planned. This case is no exception! Here are the steps:

1. Click the Default 3D View button on the Quick Access toolbar.

2. In the 3D view, zoom in on the radial entry.

3. Select the radial wall. It becomes transparent.

Examine your stairs (see Figure 10.13).

Here's a problem: the railing just stops dead at the bottom of stringer. This may have been acceptable practice around the time, say, when the wheel was still on the drawing board. You need some kind of Americans with Disabilities Act (ADA) compliance at the bottom of the stairs. To accomplish this, follow along with the next procedure.

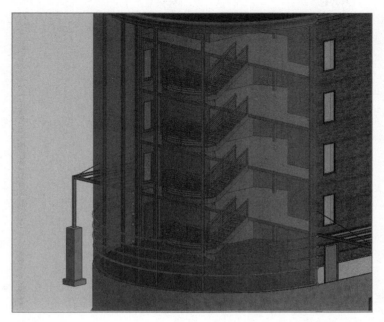

FIGURE 10.13: The stairs in 3D with the radial entry temporarily transparent

To begin, go to the book's web page, browse to the Chapter 10 folder, and find the file called ADA-Pipe.rfa. You can then download it to your computer. Now perform these steps:

1. On the Insert tab, click the Load Family button.

2. Browse to the directory where you stashed the family you just downloaded, and load ADA-Pipe.rfa into your model.

3. Go to the Level 1 floor plan.

4. Zoom in on the bottom of the stairs.

5. On the Work Plane panel of the Architecture tab, click the Ref Plane button.

6. Offset a reference plane 9 1/2″ (237mm) to the left of the bottom riser (see Figure 10.14).

7. Draw another reference plane from the center line of the bottom railing to the left about 2′–0″ (600mm) (see Figure 10.14).

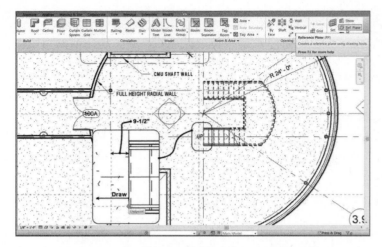

FIGURE 10.14: Add two reference planes as indicated here.

8. On the Architecture tab, click the Place A Component button.

9. In the Properties dialog, select ADA - Pipe.

10. Press the spacebar once to rotate the family into place so that it's oriented as shown in Figure 10.15.

11. Place the family at the intersection of the two reference planes (see Figure 10.15), and then press Esc twice or click Modify.

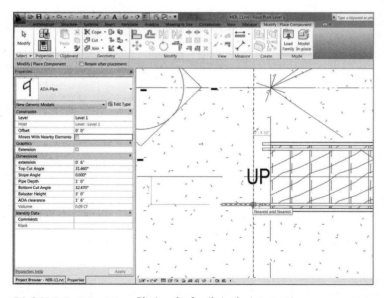

FIGURE 10.15: Placing the family in the intersection

Extending the Railings

You've added a family to finish the stairs at the bottom. The next step is to extend the railings on the stairs to meet the new family. There is one obstacle, though: the railing on the stairs already has an ending post. The trick is to remove the default ending post and replace it with the custom ADA post you just loaded into your model.

The objective of the next procedure is to extend the railings on the stairs to the ADA posts you just added to the model:

1. In the plan, select the bottom railing, as shown in Figure 10.16. Make sure you aren't selecting the stairs.

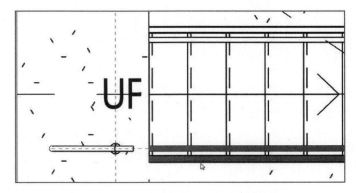

FIGURE 10.16:   Selecting the railing, not the stairs

2. In the Properties dialog, click the Edit Type button.

3. Click Duplicate.

4. Call the new railing **Entry Stair Railing**.

5. Click OK.

6. In the Baluster Placement row, click the Edit button, as shown in Figure 10.17.

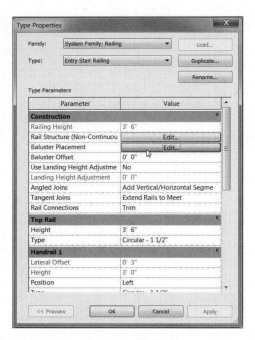

FIGURE 10.17: Click Edit next to Baluster Placement.

At the bottom of the Edit Baluster Placement dialog is a Posts category. In the Posts category is an option to place a post at the start, end, or corner of the railing. Follow along:

1. For Start Post (1) and End Post (3), type -6″ (-150mm) for the base offset, as shown in Figure 10.18.

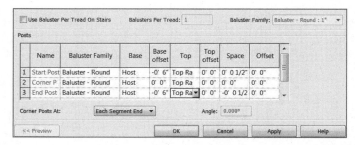

FIGURE 10.18: Setting the offset allows the post to extend to the floor where needed.

2. Click OK twice.

3. Select the railing on the inside of the stairs.

4. Change its type to Entry Stair Railing.

It's time to stretch the railing on the stairs to meet up with the family. This procedure is best done in a plan view, where you can see exactly how far you need to stretch the railing:

1. Select the bottom (south) railing.

2. On the Modify | Railings tab, click the Edit Path button.

3. Stretch the magenta line to the point shown in Figure 10.19.

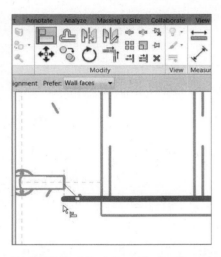

FIGURE 10.19:   Aligning the end of the railing to the new family

4. For the first alignment, pick the back edge of the family you loaded, as shown in Figure 10.19.

5. Pick the magenta railing line. (When you hover over the magenta line, you'll see an endpoint icon. When you do, click it.) The magenta line extends to the family (see Figure 10.19).

6. Click Finish Edit Mode.

7. Go to the default 3D view to make sure the railings align (see Figure 10.20).

Notice that the line seems off center. Don't worry about this—it will line up when you finish the sketch.

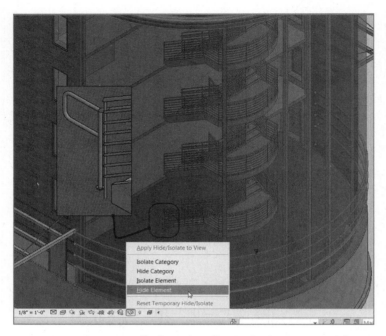

FIGURE 10.20: Check out the railing in 3D to ensure proper alignment.

8. Select the radial brick wall.

9. On the View Control bar, click the Temporary Hide/Isolate Element button, as shown in Figure 10.20.

10. Select Hide Element (see Figure 10.20).

11. When you're done marveling at your fantastic landing, click the Temporary Hide/Isolate Element button again, and select Reset Temporary Hide/Isolate.

It would be nice if this were the only place that this railing extension needed to go. The rest of the procedure will step you through the process of adding this extension to the inside railing and then copying it up to the other levels:

1. Return to the Level 1 plan view. Select the ADA - Pipe family you added to the model.

2. Click the Mirror - Pick Axis button, as shown in Figure 10.21.

3. Pick the grid 3.1, and your family is mirrored.

4. Select the inside railing.

5. On the Modify | Railings tab, click the Edit Path button.

6. Click the Align button.

7. Align the magenta line with the ADA - Pipe family, as shown in Figure 10.22.

FIGURE 10.21:   Mirroring the family

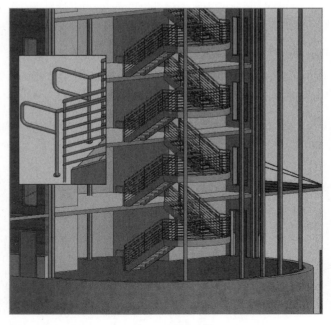

FIGURE 10.22:   The copied families

8. Press Esc twice, and then select both families.

9. On the Modify | Generic Models tab, click the Copy To Clipboard button on the Clipboard panel (the third panel from the left).

10. Choose Paste ➤ Aligned To Selected Levels, at the upper left on your screen.

11. Pick Levels 2, 3, and 4, and then click OK. Does your staircase look like Figure 10.22?

It's getting close, but it seems as though there is nothing keeping people from falling off the second, third, fourth, and fifth levels! I don't know about you, but I think this is the perfect place to put a separate railing and tie it into the existing stair railing.

Landing Railings

Railings, of course, can be drawn independently from a stair. Tying the railing into the stair, however, requires a little more patience. That being said, it becomes obvious that Revit reflects the real world when it comes to railings. If you have a railing that is difficult to build, it will probably be difficult to model. Also, if you arrive at an intersection that can't be physically accomplished in the field, then guess what? You'll struggle trying to get it into Revit.

To add some railings at the landings and tie them into the stair railings, follow these steps:

1. In the Project Browser, go to the Level 2 floor plan.

2. On the Architecture tab, click the Railing button, as shown in Figure 10.23.

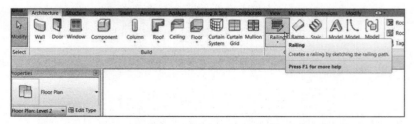

FIGURE 10.23: Click the Railing button on the Circulation panel of the Architecture tab.

3. Make sure Type is set to Handrail Pipe.

4. In the Properties dialog, click the Edit Type button.

5. Click the Duplicate button.

6. Call the new railing **Handrail - Pipe - Horizontal Railing**.

7. Click the Edit button next to the Baluster Placement choice.

8. Select None for the Start and End posts under the Posts category, as shown in Figure 10.24.

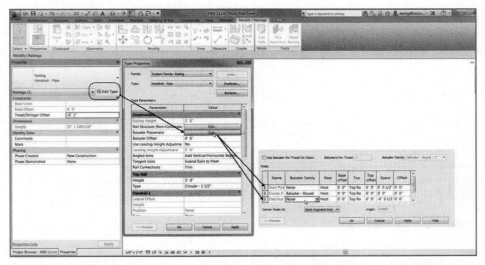

FIGURE 10.24: Configuring the default settings for the railing type Handrail - Pipe - Horizontal Railing

9. Click OK twice.

10. Pick a point at the intersection of the reference plane and the south wall, as shown in Figure 10.25.

11. Click the Preview button on the Options bar (see Figure 10.25).

12. Pick the intersection of the reference plane and the ADA - Handrail (see Figure 10.25).

13. Click Finish Sketch.

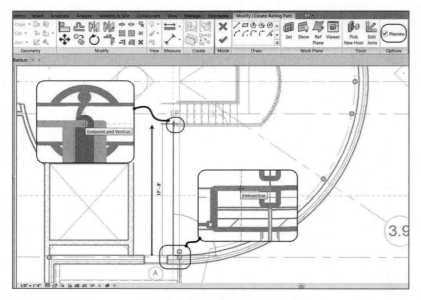

FIGURE 10.25:   Sketching the path of the railing

    N O T E   You can have only one continuous railing at a time. If there are gaps in the railing, it won't work. For example, the second floor needs three separate railings.

The next step is to add the ADA railing extensions to the north leg of the stairs and to create a railing between the two stair sections. This process can be a tad tricky, but once you get the progression, you'll see why it needs to be done in the following manner:

1. Still on the second floor, select the two ADA - Pipe families, and click the Mirror - Pick Axis button as shown in Figure 10.26.

2. Mirror the two families about the building's center reference plane.

3. Select the inside railing on the staircase.

4. Click Edit Path on the Modify | Railings tab.

5. Extend the railing to the front edge of the ADA family, exactly the same way you did for the south leg of the staircase (see Figure 10.27).

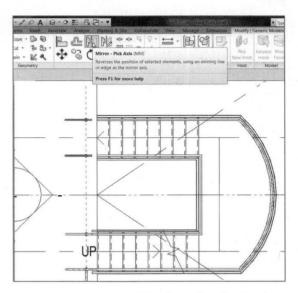

FIGURE 10.26: Mirroring and configuring the two railing extensions

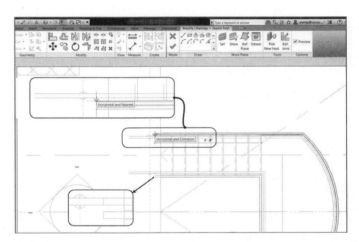

FIGURE 10.27: Creating a relationship between the stairs, the landing, and the handrail

6. Click Finish Edit Mode.

7. Repeat the procedure for the outside railing, as shown in Figure 10.27.

Let's add a railing to the center and the north side of the landing. This should be pretty easy:

1. Start the Railing command.

2. Make sure Handrail - Pipe - Horizontal Railing is the current railing.

3. Draw a line down 1'–0" (300mm) from the intersection of the upper-south ADA railing extension and the reference planes, as shown in Figure 10.28.

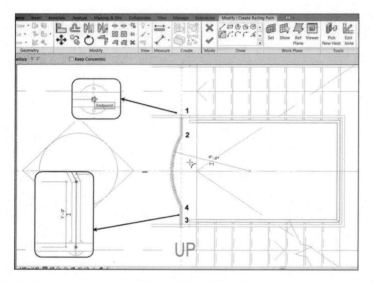

FIGURE 10.28:   Creating the middle railing

4. Draw a line up 1'–0" (300mm) from the top ADA railing extension on the south leg of the stairs (see Figure 10.28).

5. On the Draw panel, click the Start-End-Radius Arc button (see Figure 10.28).

6. Draw a 4'–0" (1200mm) arc from the endpoints of the top and bottom lines (see Figure 10.28).

7. Click Finish Sketch.

8. Draw another railing, as shown in Figure 10.29.

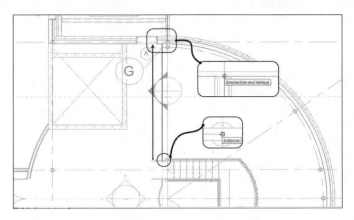

FIGURE 10.29: Creating the northern railing

What you need to do now is add this configuration to the third, fourth, and fifth floors. The fifth floor, however, will need to have a configuration change:

1. Select the middle railing, the two ADA railing extensions, and the northern railing, as shown in Figure 10.30.

2. On the Modify | Multi Select tab, click the Copy To Clipboard button (see Figure 10.30).

3. Click Paste ➢ Aligned To Selected Levels, as shown in Figure 10.31.

4. Paste the items to Level 3 through Level 5.

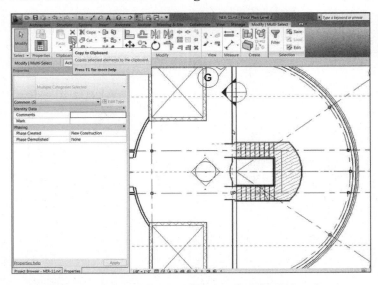

FIGURE 10.30: Copy the selected items to the clipboard.

5. Go to Level 5.

6. Change Detail Level to Fine.

7. Delete the middle railing, and make the south railing extend to the ADA post, as shown in Figure 10.32.

FIGURE 10.31:   Paste ➢ Aligned to Selected Levels

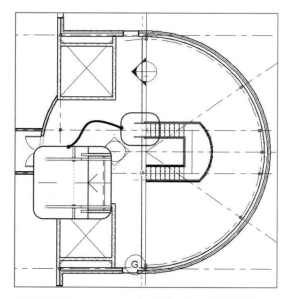

FIGURE 10.32:   Reconfiguring the fifth floor

8. Go to a 3D view, and select the radial brick wall to make it transparent. Check out your stairs, as shown in Figure 10.33.

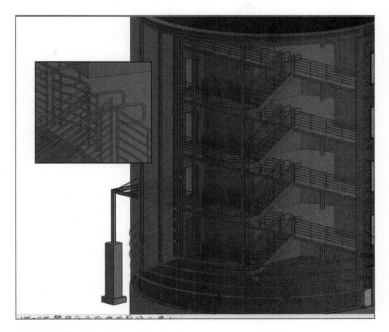

FIGURE 10.33: Check out your awesome stairs!

Phew! You've built a set of stairs. The good thing is that it's one sweet staircase. The bad thing is that you used all the default layouts and materials. Next, we'll get into some more complicated shapes and styles.

Creating a Winding Staircase

Before you get started, you should know that you'll create this staircase by using the separate stair components. You can try to make a winding staircase by using the Run function, similar to the one you used earlier; but in many cases (especially when you run into an existing staircase in either a renovation project or an addition), you may need to draft the stairs and then model over the top of the drafting lines. What? Drafting in Revit? Of course. How else can you expect to get anything done?

The first thing you'll need to do is make modifications to the floor in a specific area to create a landing. Follow along:

1. In the Project Browser, go to the Level 2 floor plan.

2. Zoom in on the area between the corridor and the east wing, as shown in Figure 10.34.

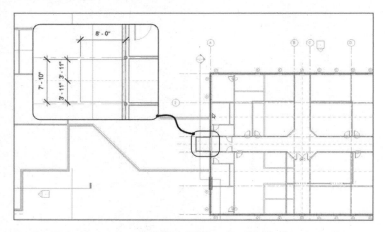

FIGURE 10.34: Creating a landing. You'll add a door in a moment.

3. Select the Level 2 floor in the east wing.

4. Click the Edit Boundary button on the Mode panel of the Modify | Floors tab.

5. Sketch a landing that is 8′–0″ (2400mm) long × 7′–10″ (2350mm) wide (see Figure 10.34). Center it on the reference plane.

6. Click Finish Edit Mode on the Mode panel. If you're asked if you want to attach the walls to the bottom of the floor, click Yes.

With the landing in place, you can now copy a door up to this level. To do this, you'll go to the first floor and copy the door that resides there. You can do this on your own, or you can follow along with these steps:

1. In the Project Browser, go to the Level 1 floor plan.

2. Select door 100B.

3. Copy the door to the clipboard (click Copy To Clipboard on the Clipboard panel).

4. Choose Paste ➢ Aligned To Selected Levels.

> You may have to pick a window around the entire area and then click the Filter button on the Ribbon. From there, you can select only Floors.

5. Select Level 2, and click OK.

6. In the Project Browser, go back to Level 2. The door and the landing are in place.

Next you'll create a winding set of stairs. The first task is to lay out the shape in the plan using simple drafting lines. The second step is to model over the lines you added, by using various stair tools as follows:

1. Select the Annotate tab.

2. Click the Detail Line button, as shown in Figure 10.35.

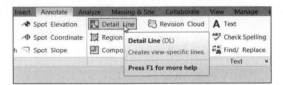

FIGURE 10.35:   Click the Detail Line button on the Annotate tab.

3. On the Draw panel, click the Start-End-Radius Arc button, as shown in Figure 10.36.

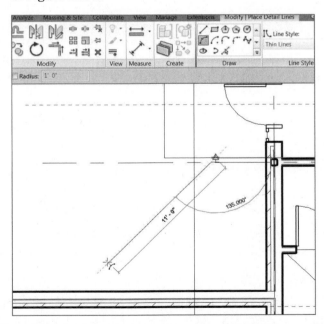

FIGURE 10.36:   With the Start-End-Radius Arc button, first start at the midpoint of the landing and then go southwest at an angle of 135° and a distance of 11′–0″ (3300mm).

4. For the first point of the arc, pick the midpoint of the landing (see Figure 10.36).

5. Move your cursor down, at 135° from the first point you just picked.

6. Extend your cursor 11′–0″ (3300mm), as shown in Figure 10.36, and then click to set the second point.

7. To form the arc, move your cursor to the right until the radius snaps into place. When it does, pick the point as shown in Figure 10.37.

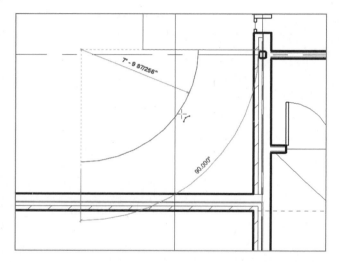

FIGURE 10.37:   Picking the third point to form the arc. It will be tangent upon the first two points you picked.

8. Press Esc.

9. On the Draw panel, click the Pick Lines icon.

10. On the Options bar, add an increment of 2′–0″ (600mm) to the Offset field (see Figure 10.38).

11. Offset the center arc to the right and then to the left, forming a 4′–0″ (1200mm) overall winder, as shown in Figure 10.38.

12. Press Esc.

13. Click the Line tool, make sure Offset is set to 0, and then draw a straight line at each end of the arcs, as shown in Figure 10.39.

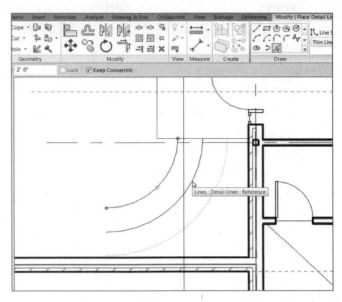

FIGURE 10.38: Adding two more arcs based on the centerline of the first

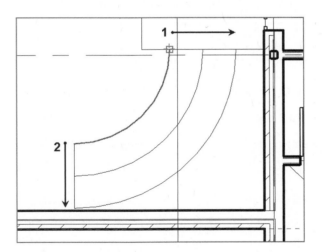

FIGURE 10.39: Adding a straight line at each end of the arcs

Okay, take a breather. Compare the examples in the book to what you have.
Are you close? If not, go back and investigate.

N O T E Get used to this drafting thing; it's still very much a part of BIM, regardless of whether people say you can't draft in Revit!

The next step is to make an array of the straight lines you just added. These lines will wind up being the guidelines for your risers:

1. Press Esc, and then select the smaller arc, as shown in Figure 10.40.

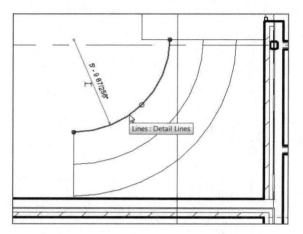

F I G U R E   1 0 . 4 0 :   Selecting the smaller arc

2. In the Properties dialog, select Center Mark Visible.

3. Select the line at the left end of the arcs, as shown in Figure 10.41.

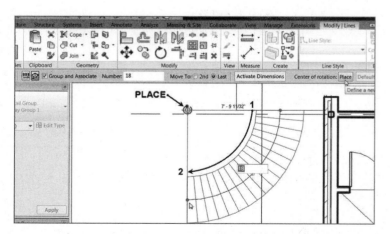

F I G U R E   1 0 . 4 1 :   Arraying the line to create your own treads

4. Click the Array button on the Modify | Lines tab.

5. On the Options bar, be sure Radial is selected.

6. Make sure Group And Associate is selected.

7. Type 18 for the number.

8. Click Move To: Last on the Options bar. (Remember that you aren't actually moving this line; you're simply copying it to the last place in the array.)

9. Click the Place button next to the Origin category on the Options bar, and pick the center of the arc.

10. Pick a point along the first line (the one at lower left).

11. Pick the second point along the upper-right line.

Your array is complete. Check out Figure 10.42 to see how the finished stairs will look.

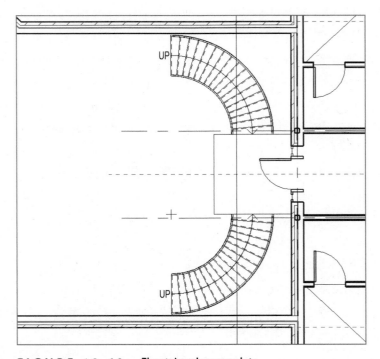

FIGURE 10.42: The stairs when complete

Now you can begin modeling the stairs. This procedure is nothing more than tracing the lines you've already added to the model. To do this, you'll use the available tools that you haven't touched in the previous staircase. Follow along:

1. On the Architecture tab, click the Stairs button.

2. In the Properties dialog, change Base Level to Level 1.

3. Change Top Level to Level 2.

4. Click Edit Type.

5. Click Duplicate.

6. Call the stairs **Corridor Entry Stairs.**

7. Click OK.

8. In the Construction category, click the cell to the right of Run Type. It contains the text 2″ (50mm) Tread 1″ (25mm) Nosing ¼″ (6mm) Riser. When you click in the cell, you see a […] button. Click it.

9. Choose Cherry for Tread Material.

10. For Riser Material, do the same.

11. Under the Treads category, select Front, Left, and Right for the Apply Nosing Profile row.

12. Click OK.

13. Scroll down to the Supports category, and change Right Support from Stringer (Closed) to Carriage (Open).

14. Click into Carriage - 2″ Width (50mm) to the right of Right Support Type.

15. Click the small […] button to the right of the cell.

16. Change Material to Mahogany. Click OK.

17. Change Left Support to Carriage (Open).

18. Add Mahogany as the material to the Carriage - 2″ Width. Your Properties dialog should look like the one shown in Figure 10.43.

19. Click OK to get back to the model.

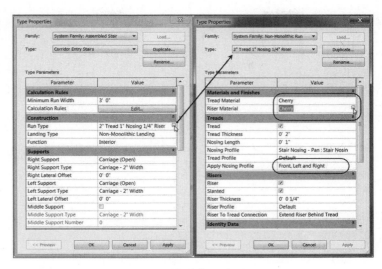

FIGURE 10.43: Customizing the stairs

It's time to add the stairs to the model. To do this, you'll first sketch the boundary:

1. On the Modify | Create Stairs tab in Sketch Mode, click the Create Sketch button, as shown in Figure 10.44.

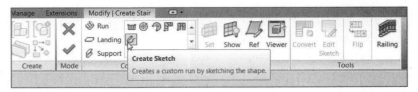

FIGURE 10.44: Click the Create Sketch button.

2. On the Draw panel, click the Pick Lines icon.

3. Pick the two arcs defining the outside of the stairs. Green arcs are copied directly on top of them.

4. On the Draw panel, click the Riser button, as shown in Figure 10.45.

5. On the Draw panel, click the Pick Lines icon.

6. Pick all of the lines you arrayed. This includes the bottom and the top lines (see Figure 10.46).

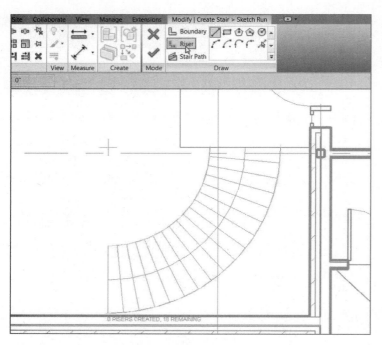

FIGURE 10.45:   Click the Riser button.

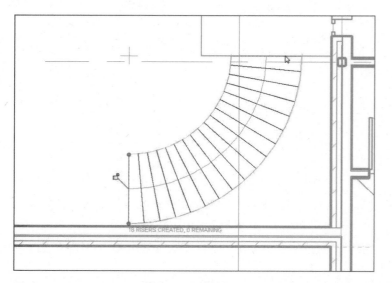

FIGURE 10.46:   Picking the detail lines to lay over the stair components

7. Click the Stair Path button.

8. Click the Pick Lines button.

9. Pick the centerline of the staircase.

10. Click Finish Edit Mode on the Mode panel.

11. Click the Railing button.

12. Change the railing to Handrail - Pipe, make sure the position is set to Treads, and click OK.

13. Click the Finish Sketch button (the green checkmark).

With the stairs roughed in, you need to get a better look at them. If you use the default 3D view, you need to turn off way too many items to see your stairs. Let's add a perspective view, just to see what's going on here!

If you're confident about adding your own perspective view, go ahead and put one in and name it **East Entry from Corridor**. If not, follow along with these steps:

1. In the Project Browser, go to the Level 1 floor plan.

2. On the View tab, click the 3D View ➤ Camera button.

3. Pick the first point shown in Figure 10.47.

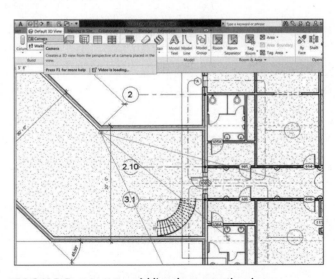

FIGURE 10.47: Adding the perspective view

4. Pick the second point shown in Figure 10.47.

5. In the Project Browser, find the new perspective view, and rename it **East Entry from Corridor.**

6. In the perspective view, turn on Realistic. (It's located on the View Control bar at the bottom of the view.)

7. Check out the view (see Figure 10.48)!

FIGURE 10.48: Looking nice

The next series of steps involves mirroring the stairs to the other side of the landing. Then, of course, you need to add a landing railing so people don't just walk out the door and off the ledge:

1. Go to the Level 2 floor plan in the Project Browser.

2. Select the stairs and the railings, as shown in Figure 10.49.

N O T E   To select only the stairs and the railings, you can pick a window around the entire set of lines, groups, railings, and stairs. From there, you can click the Filter button on the Ribbon, and select only Stairs And Railings.

3. On the Modify | Multi-Select tab, click the Mirror ➤ Pick Mirror Axis button, as shown in Figure 10.50.

4. Pick the center reference plane. (I told you this thing would come in handy.)

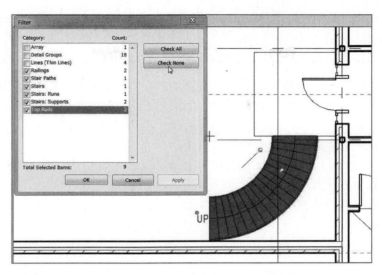

FIGURE 10.49: Selecting the items to be mirrored

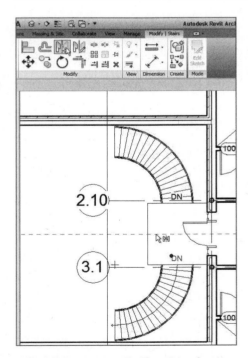

FIGURE 10.50: The mirrored stairs

Your stairs are now mirrored to the other side of the landing (see Figure 10.50).

Let's tie in the railings. If you're feeling up to the challenge, try it on your own by using the railing Handrail - Pipe. If not, just follow along with these steps:

1. On the Architecture tab, click the Railing button.

2. In the Type Selector, change the type to Handrail - Pipe, as shown in Figure 10.51.

3. On the Draw panel, click the Pick Lines icon, as shown in Figure 10.52.

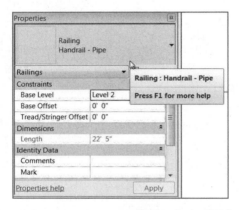

FIGURE 10.51: Setting the landing handrail type

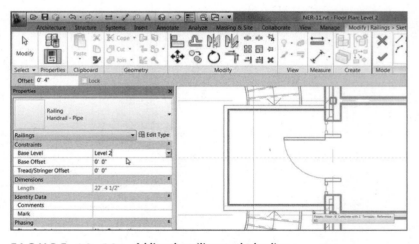

FIGURE 10.52: Adding the railings to the landing

4. Set Offset to 4″ (100mm).

5. Pick the landing lines to offset in the railing (see Figure 10.52).

6. After the offsets are complete, click the Line icon on the Draw panel, as shown in Figure 10.53. Set Offset to 0.

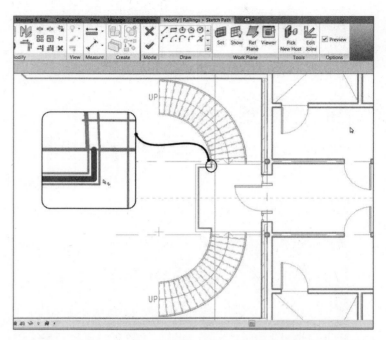

FIGURE 10.53: Connecting the landing railing to the stair railing

7. Draw the lines extending from the midpoint snap of the stair railing to the landing railing (see Figure 10.53).

8. Trim the corners so your railings look like Figure 10.53.

9. On the Mode panel, click Finish Edit Mode.

10. You may have to flip the railing by selecting it and then clicking the Flip arrow. Your railing should look like Figure 10.54.

11. Add two more railings between the stairs and the brick wall. Your stairs should look like Figure 10.55.

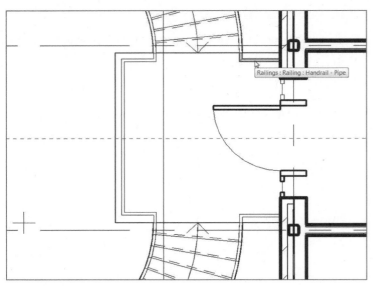

FIGURE 10.54:   The railing on the landing

FIGURE 10.55:   The completed landing

Remember, you must create only one railing at a time. If you try to do more than one continuous line, Revit won't let you proceed. Try creating one short railing and mirroring it.

Great! You're getting there. Now you'll see how a staircase and the accompanying railings come together. For example, it sure would be nice to have a railing with spindles or, better yet, panels added to it. Also, a nice half-round bullnose would improve your staircase. The next section will focus on this concept.

Stair and Railing Families

Similar to the model as a whole, stairs and railings comprise separate families that come together to form the overall unit. Although stairs and railings are considered a system family (a family that resides only in the model), they still rely heavily on hosted families to create the entire element.

The next procedure will involve loading separate families into the model and then using them in a new set of stairs and railings that you'll create in the west wing:

1. In the Project Browser, go to the Level 3 floor plan and change Detail Level to Fine.

2. Zoom in on the west wing.

3. On the Architecture tab, click the Floor button.

4. In the Properties dialog, click the Edit Type button.

5. Select the 6″ (152mm) concrete with 1″ (25mm) Terrazzo floor system from the Type drop-down list, as shown in Figure 10.56.

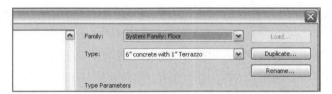

FIGURE 10.56: You must add a floor at the Level 3 floor plan for the stairs to have a landing.

6. Click OK.

7. On the Draw panel, click the Pick Walls button.

8. Pick the walls, and make sure the lines are set to the core centerline, as shown in Figure 10.57.

9. When picking the south wall, set Offset to 5′–0″ (1500mm) in the Options bar (see Figure 10.57).

T I P   Again, make sure you have no gaps or overlapping lines. Use the Trim/Extend Single Element command to clean up the lines to look like the figure.

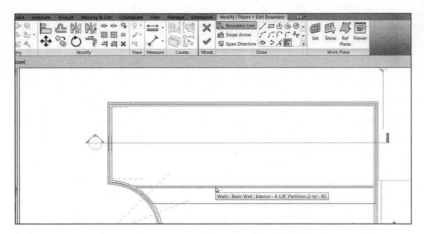

FIGURE 10.57: Adding the floor outline to the walls. Be sure to offset the line 5′–0″ (1500mm) from the south wall. This will be the stair landing.

10. Once the sketch lines are in place, trim the corners and click Finish Edit Mode on the Mode panel.

11. Revit asks if you want to attach the walls that go up to this floor's bottom. Click No.

12. Revit asks if you want to cut the overlapping volume out of the walls. Click Yes.

Your floor is now in place. The next item you'll tackle is creating a completely custom railing system.

Creating a Custom Railing System

Next you'll load the components that make up your stairs. Although Revit makes an attempt to supply you with some families, in this case you'll download the families included with this book by going to the book's web page at www.sybex.com/go/revit2014ner. From there, browse to the Chapter 10 folder and find the following files:

▶ 6210 (2-5_8).rfa

▶ landing.rfa

▶ post.rfa

▶ raised panels.rfa

▶ spindle.rfa

▶ stair nosing.rfa

To get started, you need to load the families into your model so they're available when it comes time to assemble your new railing. If you remember how to do this, go ahead and load all the families that you just downloaded from the web page. If you need some assistance, follow these steps:

1. On the Insert tab, click Load Family.

2. Find the files that you downloaded from the web page.

3. Select all of them, and click Open to load them.

4. Save the model.

The next step is to create a new railing and add some of these items to it:

1. In the Project Browser, find the Families category and expand it, as shown in Figure 10.58.

FIGURE 10.58: The railing family called Handrail - Rectangular

2. Find the Railings category, and expand it.

3. Find Handrail - Rectangular, and double-click it (see Figure 10.58).

4. Click Duplicate.

5. Call the new railing **Wood Railing with Spindles**.

6. Click OK.

7. Click OK again.

8. In the Project Browser, under the Families category, scroll down until you see Top Rail Type, as shown in Figure 10.59.

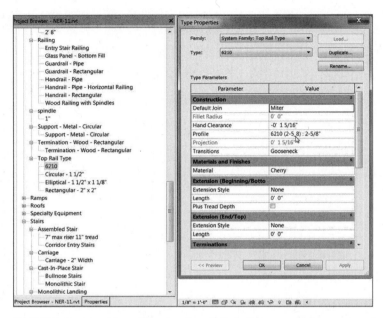

FIGURE 10.59: Changing the rail. Note that you can add as many rails as you wish. Here, you're adding only one.

9. Double click the Circular - 1 1/2″ (38mm) Top Rail Type.

10. Click Duplicate.

11. Change the name to **6210**, and click OK.

12. Change Profile to **6210 (2-5_8) : 2 5/8″ (67mm)**.

13. Change Transitions to Gooseneck.

14. Change Material to Cherry.

15. Click OK.

16. Under the Families category in the Project Browser, double-click Wood Railing With Spindles, located in the Railing directory.

17. Scroll down, and change Top Rail Type to 6210.

18. Click OK.

19. Click the Edit button in the Baluster Placement row.

20. In the Main Pattern area, change Baluster Family to Spindle: **1″** (25mm) (see Figure 10.60).

21. Just below the Main Pattern area is the Use Baluster Per Tread On Stairs option. Select it, as shown in Figure 10.61.

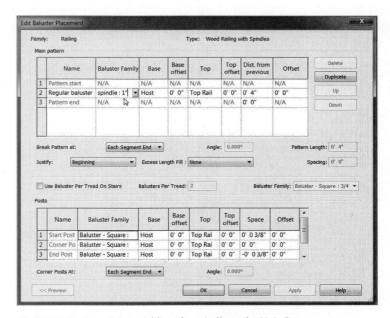

FIGURE 10.60: Adding the spindle to the Main Pattern area

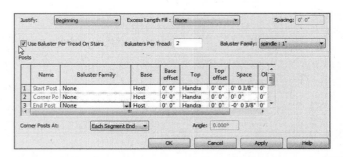

FIGURE 10.61: Specifying two balusters per tread and no actual posts

22. To the right is the Balusters Per Tread field. Specify two balusters per tread (see Figure 10.61).

23. Change Baluster Family to Spindle: 1″ (25mm), as shown in Figure 10.61.

24. In the bottommost field is the Posts category. Change each of the three Posts to None. Your spindles are all you need (see Figure 10.61).

25. Click OK twice.

You may or may not have noticed that you didn't get the opportunity to change the baluster's material as you did with the railing. This action must be done in the family itself, as follows:

1. In the Project Browser, the Spindle category is just below Railing, as shown in Figure 10.62. Expand Spindle to expose the 1″ (25mm) family.

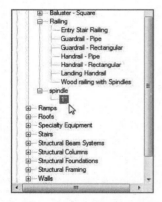

FIGURE 10.62:   Finding the Spindle : 1″ family to access the material

2. Double-click the 1″ (25mm) to open its Type Properties dialog.

3. Find the Material row, click into the <By Category> field, and click the […] button.

4. Change Material to Cherry.

5. Click OK twice.

This completes the railing setup. Once you add it to the stairs, however, some tweaking will certainly be required. The next step is to customize the stairs themselves.

Creating Custom Stairs

This is the third staircase you've created in the same chapter, so you've certainly have gained some experience regarding the placement of stairs and railings into the Revit model. You're also becoming familiar with the stair and railings dialogs. This last procedure will tie all of that together.

Let's create that staircase:

1. On the Architecture tab, click the Stairs button.

2. In the Properties dialog, make sure you choose Cast-In-Place Stair Monolithic Stair, as shown in Figure 10.63, and click the Edit Type button.

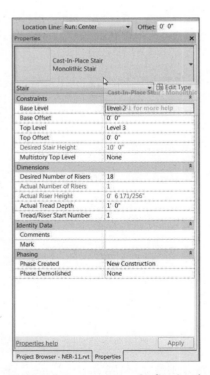

FIGURE 10.63: Configuring the stairs. As you can see, you have quite a few options.

3. Click Duplicate.

4. Call the new staircase **Custom Bullnose Stairs**.

5. Click OK.

6. Under Construction, next to Run Type, click into the ¾″ Nosing cell and then click the […] button.

7. Apply the nosing profile to Front, Left, and Right.

8. Select the Riser check box.

9. Change the riser thickness to 3/4″ (19mm).

10. For Riser To Tread Connection, choose Extend Tread Under Riser.

11. Change Monolithic Material to Mahogany.

12. Under Treads, make sure Treads are turned on.

13. Change Tread Material to Mahogany.

14. Change Riser Material to Mahogany.

15. Change the Nosing Profile to **stair nosing : stair nosing**.

16. Click OK.

17. Click the 7″ (178mm) Thickness cell next to Landing Type, and click the […] button to the right.

18. Click Duplicate.

19. Call the new landing 1′–0″ (300mm) **Mahogany Landing**.

20. Change Monolithic Thickness to 1′–0″ (300mm).

21. Change Monolithic Material to Mahogany.

22. Click OK.

23. Click OK again.

It's time to configure some of the layout properties. These will allow you to calculate the rise/run count as well as some basic offsets you'll need:

1. In the Properties dialog, set Base Level to Level 1.

2. Set Base Offset to 6 5/8″ (152mm), as shown in Figure 10.64.

3. Set Top Level to Level 3. (Yes, this is going to be one long staircase!)

FIGURE 10.64: The Base Offset value is set to 6 5/8″ (152mm).

The next step is to place this monster into the model. Although you didn't specify a multistory staircase, you'll need multiple landings to give your visitors a breather as they travel up the stairs. This layout will require a little more care in the initial planning stage:

1. On the Work Plane panel, click the Ref Plane button.

2. Click the Pick Lines button, and then offset a grid, as shown in Figure 10.65.

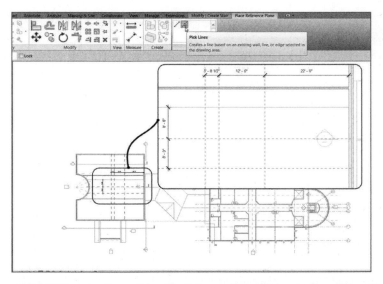

FIGURE 10.65: Using dimensions to lay out the centerlines of the stairs

The nice thing about using reference planes while in Sketch Mode is that they will disappear once you finish the sketch. If you need to go back and edit the stairs, the reference planes will appear again!

3. Click the Railing button.

4. Change the railing type to Wood Railing With Spindles, and make sure Position is set to Treads. Click OK.

5. On the Modify | Create Stairs tab in Sketch Mode, click the Run button.

6. Draw your stairs as shown in Figure 10.66. (Pick the points as the figure is sequenced.)

7. Verify that your plan looks like Figure 10.67.

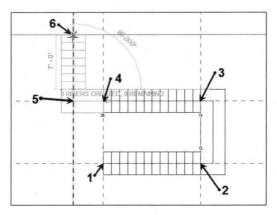

FIGURE 10.66: Picking the intersections of the reference planes to determine where the stairs will go

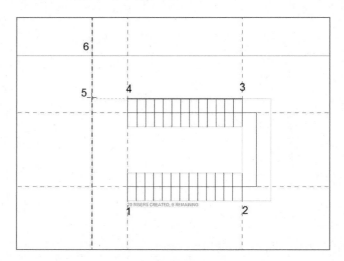

FIGURE 10.67: The stairs in place

8. Click Finish Sketch. Your stairs should look like Figure 10.68.

9. Go to a 3D view to check out the stairs. They should resemble Figure 10.69.

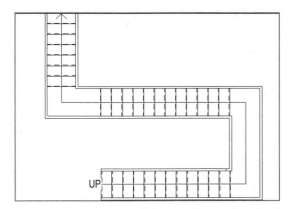

FIGURE 10.68: The stairs as shown in plan

FIGURE 10.69: The stairs as shown in 3D. Notice the nice bullnose and the railings.

The next step (pun intended) is to add a landing to the bottom of the stairs. This requires creating a family. Although we will cover creating families in Chapter 17, "Creating Families," this one has been created, and you've downloaded the families needed to create this step in the stairs.

Adding a Custom Landing

You left the 6 ⅝" (152mm) offset for the bottom tread because you need to introduce your own version of how that bottom tread should look. As mentioned earlier, this family has been loaded. If you haven't already loaded the family, go to www.sybex.com/go/revit2014ner. From there, browse to the Chapter 10 folder and find the Landing.rfa and Post.rfa files. After you've loaded the families, proceed with these steps:

1. In the Project Browser, go to the Level 1 floor plan.

2. On the Architecture tab, click the Place A Component button.

3. In the Type Selector, find and select the Landing family.

4. As you're inserting the family, press the spacebar to rotate the landing into the correct position.

5. Place the landing under the last tread at the point shown in Figure 10.70.

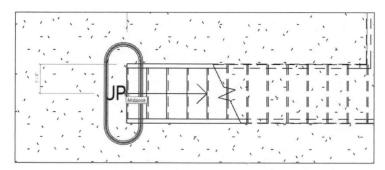

FIGURE 10.70: Placing the landing

6. Press Esc twice.

7. Select the landing.

8. In the Properties dialog, change Tread Material to Cherry.

9. Change Base Material to Mahogany, and click OK (see Figure 10.71).

The next task is to add a post.

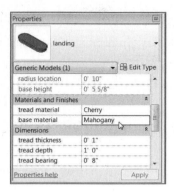

FIGURE 10.71: Changing the landing material to match the theme of the staircase

Adding a Gooseneck

In this style of railing system, it would be nice to have a gooseneck to catch the railing as it slopes downward and spiral it into the post. Of course, Revit doesn't have families for this built in, but this book does! If you didn't download the post family earlier in this chapter, go to the book's web page, browse to the Chapter 10 folder, and find the Post_up.rfa file. After you download it and load it into the model, follow these steps:

1. In the Project Browser, go to the Level 1 floor plan, and zoom in on the landing area, as shown in Figure 10.72.

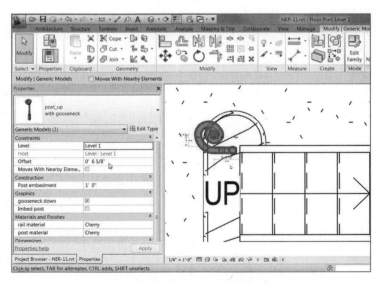

FIGURE 10.72: Placing the post with the gooseneck

2. On the Architecture tab, click the Place A Component button.

3. In the Properties dialog, select Post_up With Gooseneck.

4. As you're placing the post, press the spacebar twice to flip it into the correct orientation, as shown in Figure 10.73.

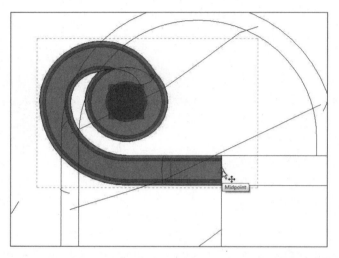

FIGURE 10.73:   Moving the post to align with the stair railing

5. Place it on the landing slightly away from the stair railing (see Figure 10.73).

6. Select the post, and change Offset to **6 5/8″ (152mm)** in the Properties dialog.

 N O T E   If the end of the post seems to be clipped in the plan, you need to adjust the view range in the Properties dialog. Right now, the 4′–0″ (1200mm) clip plane may be a tad too low. To fix this, find the View Range row in the Properties dialog and click the Edit button. In the View Range dialog, adjust Cut Plane Offset to 4′–6″ (1250mm).

7. Select the post again (if it's not still selected).

8. Click the Move button.

9. Move the post from the midpoint of the post's end to the midpoint of the stair railing's end, as shown in Figure 10.73.

10. Select the post again (if it's not selected already).

11. In the Properties dialog, go to the Materials And Finishes category and change materials for both the rail and the post to Cherry.

12. Mirror the post to the other railing.

In 3D, your landing should now look like Figure 10.74.

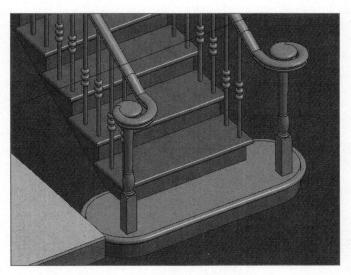

FIGURE 10.74: The completed landing

Adding a Railing to the Landing

Let's add the railing to the Level 3 balcony. Compared to that landing you just did, this is going to be a snap! If you feel as though you have the experience required to add your own landing railing, go ahead and take a shot at it. If not, follow these steps:

1. In the Project Browser, go to Level 3.

2. Zoom in on the stairs.

3. Right-click one of the railings on the stairs, and click Create Similar.

4. Sketch a railing that is 4″ (100mm) in from the face of the landing, as shown in Figure 10.75.

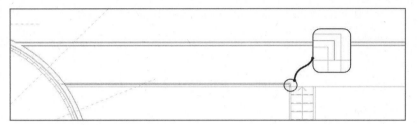

FIGURE 10.75:   Adding the railing. This process is becoming old hat!

5. Make sure you have a "leg" tied into the stair railing (see Figure 10.75).

6. On the Railing panel, click Finish Edit Mode.

7. Repeat the procedure on the other end (see Figure 10.76).

FIGURE 10.76:   Both railings are in place.

 N O T E   To repeat the procedure on the other end, you can either mirror the railing you just put in and then edit it to reach the far end of the landing, or you can start the Railing command and do it again. I recommend mirroring the railing, selecting the new railing, and then selecting Edit Path from the Modify | Railings tab. You can then grip-edit the right end to meet the wall. This assures you that the railing will be aligned with the railing on the stair.

The last step is to add a raised-panel stile and rail system along the third-floor wall.

Adding a Raised-Panel Stile and Rail System

The first thing you'll need to do is to add an entrance to the large Level 3 training room. The corridor will then receive a custom line-based, raised-panel family:

1. In the Project Browser, go to the Level 3 floor plan.

2. On the Architecture tab, click the Door button.

3. In the Properties dialog, select Single-Raised Panel With Sidelights : 36″ × 84″ (86mm × 2134mm).

4. Place it in the corridor wall aligned with the stairs, as shown in Figure 10.77.

5. Copy the door 10′–0″ (3000mm) to the right (see Figure 10.77).

6. On the View tab, click the Elevation button.

7. In the Change Element Type menu in the Properties dialog, select Interior Elevation.

8. Pick a point, as shown in Figure 10.78; then press Esc.

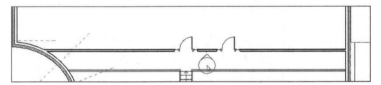

FIGURE 10.77: Pick the point as shown for the elevation.

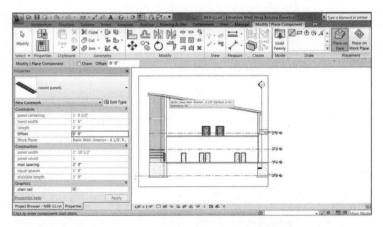

FIGURE 10.78: Picking the far wall to establish a work plane

9. In the Project Browser, right-click the new elevation, and rename it **West Wing Balcony Elevation.**

10. Open the West Wing Balcony elevation.

11. Stretch the crop region so that you can see the entire west wing.

12. On the Architecture tab, click the Place A Component button.

13. Scroll down the Type Selector list until you find Raised Panels (see Figure 10.78).

14. In the Work Plane dialog, make sure Pick A Plane is selected, and then click OK.

15. Pick the far wall (see Figure 10.78). If you don't have the raised panel family, you can download it at the book's web page; it's called Raised Panel.rfa. Once it's downloaded and loaded into the model, proceed with the next step.

16. On the Modify-Place Component tab, click the Place On Work Plane button, and pick the base point shown in Figure 10.79.

17. Pick the second point.

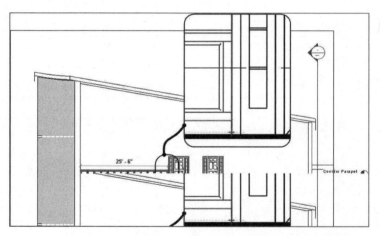

FIGURE 10.79: Adding the line-based, raised-panel family

NOTE   If you can't seem to pick the points specified in Figure 10.79, go ahead and pick two points close to the area indicated in the figure. After you place the line-based family, you can select it and grip-edit the ends to extend to the wall's edges as shown in the figure. Also, if the panels are too high, simply move them down to the floor or align them after the panels are in place.

18. Start the Place A Component command again, if it's not already running, and add the raised-panel family between the two doors and to the right. This completes the raised panels for this level.

19. Select all of the raised panel families on this floor (remember to hold the Ctrl key to add to the selection).

20. In the Materials And Finishes category of the Properties dialog, change the frame material to Cherry.

21. Change Panel Material to Mahogany. See Figure 10.80.

22. Change Visual Style to Realistic. Your elevation should look like Figure 10.81.

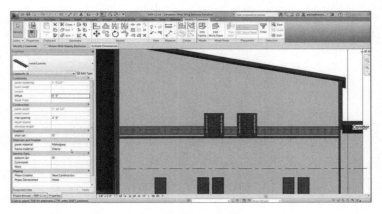

FIGURE 10.80:   Changing the material

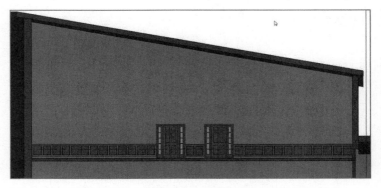

FIGURE 10.81:   The finished raised-panel, line-based family

Wow! That was quite a bit about stairs. If you take anything away from this chapter, it should be the knowledge that stairs don't come easy, but you can create any staircase if you know you'll need to create families.

The last section of this chapter focuses on adding ramps to the model. As far as Revit procedures go, ramps are the kid sister to stairs.

Adding Ramps

When you think of a ramp in Revit, think of a one-tread, one-rise staircase at a $\frac{1}{12}$ pitch. A ramp is placed in the model exactly the same way as a set of stairs. You still have the run method, and you can still sketch the ramp by using a boundary.

That being said, let's start placing a ramp in your model:

1. In the Project Browser, go to the Level 1 floor plan.

2. Zoom in on the radial entry of the east wing at grid intersection F-5 (see Figure 10.82).

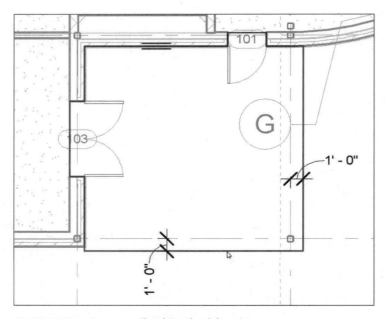

FIGURE 10.82: Sketching the slab perimeter

3. You need to create a flat landing, so, on the Architecture tab, click the Floor button.

4. Click Edit Type in the Properties dialog.

5. Select Generic - 12″ (305mm) Filled.

6. Click Duplicate.

7. Call the new floor **Exterior Concrete Slab**.

8. Click OK.

9. Click the Edit button in the Structure row.

10. Change Structure [1] Material to Concrete - Cast-In-Place Concrete.

11. Change Thickness to 6″ (150mm).

12. Click OK twice to get back to the model.

13. Place the concrete at the points shown in Figure 10.82.

 W A R N I N G   Make sure you're using Pick Lines Mode and are picking the outside face of brick. That extra line represents the water table above this floor's level.

14. When the slab is in place, click the Finish Edit Mode button.

15. Click No in the next dialog.

Now you can add the ramp. You'll set the ramp's properties for the top to Level 1, and the bottom will also be at Level 1 but with an offset:

1. On the Architecture tab, click the Ramp button, as shown in Figure 10.83.

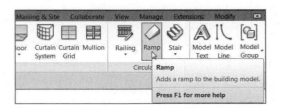

F I G U R E   1 0 . 8 3 :   Click the Ramp button on the Architecture tab.

2. In the Properties dialog, click Edit Type.

3. Click Duplicate.

4. Call the new ramp **Exterior Concrete Ramp**.

5. Click OK.

6. Give it a **6″** (**150**mm) thickness.

7. Change Function to Exterior.

8. For the ramp material, click the […] button, and specify Concrete - Cast-In-Place Concrete, as shown in Figure 10.84.

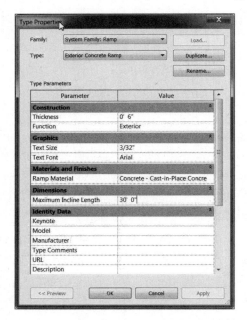

FIGURE 10.84: Modifying the Type Properties

9. Notice that Maximum Incline Length is set to the ADA standard of 30′–0″ (10000mm).

10. In the Other category, notice Ramp Max Slope is set to $\frac{1}{12}$.

11. Click OK.

12. In the Properties dialog, set Base Level to Level 1.

13. Set Base Offset to -2′–6″ (-750mm), as shown in Figure 10.85.

14. Set Top Level to Level 1.

15. Set Width to 5'–0" (1500mm) (see Figure 10.85).

16. On the Draw panel, click the Run button.

17. In the model, click the first point for the ramp, similar to the point shown in Figure 10.86. (You have to place the point near the midpoint. Revit doesn't allow you to snap while in Sketch Mode.)

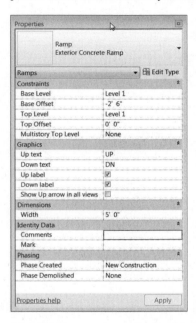

FIGURE 10.85: Setting the properties

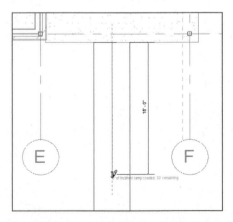

FIGURE 10.86: Pick the first point on the landing, and then move your cursor down 15'–0" (4500mm).

18. Move your cursor down the view (south) 15'–0" (4500mm), as shown in Figure 10.86. (You'll see the temporary dimension.)

19. Pick a point about 6'–0" (1800mm) below the end of the ramp, in alignment with the right boundary, as shown in Figure 10.87. After you pick the second point, the view should read "30' (10000mm) of inclined ramp created, 0 remaining."

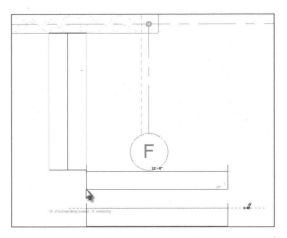

FIGURE 10.87: The second leg of the ramp

20. Move your cursor to the right until the ramp stops (see Figure 10.87).

21. On the Modify | Create Ramp tab in Sketch Mode, click the Railing Type button.

22. Select Handrail - Pipe in the Railing Type dialog that opens.

23. Click OK.

24. Click Finish Edit Mode.

25. Select the entire ramp (including the railing).

26. Move the ramp so that the midpoint of the top of the ramp meets the midpoint of the landing slab.

You may notice immediately that the ramp is sloping in the wrong direction. Also, you need to tie the railings into the slab. If you would like to pick around and see how to do these things on your own, go right ahead. Otherwise, follow along:

1. Select the ramp.

2. Pick the small blue arrow—this flips the direction of the ramp.

3. On the Architecture tab, click the Railing button.

4. In the Properties dialog, click Edit Type, change the type to Handrail - Pipe, and click OK.

5. Draw a railing 8″ (200mm) in from the slab edge, as shown in Figure 10.88.

It's best if you keep moving your cursor past the ramp, even knowing the end of the ramp has stopped. This ensures that the entire ramp has been put in place.

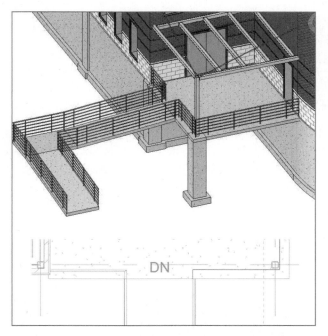

FIGURE 10.88: Adding the railing just as you've been doing this entire chapter

6. Mirror the slab, the ramp, and the railing to the other side of the building, as shown in Figure 10.89.

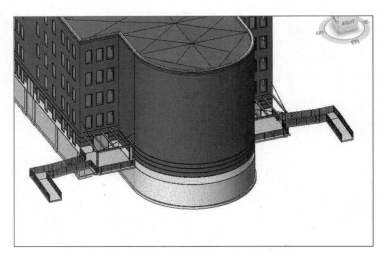

FIGURE 10.89: The two ramps

7. Save the model.

Creating ramps is necessary in almost every project. Some will be easier than others, and, at times, they may try your patience. Keep at it, and before long you'll have the experience you need to feel confident in creating ramps.

Are You Experienced?

Now you can...

- ☑ create stairs with the conventional method by using the Run command to generate the height and length you need

- ☑ create stairs by first laying out the geometry by placing line work in the model, and then tracing over the lines with the stair components

- ☑ determine the difference between the boundary and the riser when you need to sketch the stair profile

☑ load necessary components used to customize stairs and railings such as railing types, spindles, posts, and landings

☑ use separate components and access them in the Project Browser to place materials

☑ configure railings based on the baluster placement and the railing placement as used in the Element Properties of the railing

☑ determine how to tie a railing into a stair railing by using offsets and by aligning the railing sketch with the stairs

☑ add a line-based, raised-panel family to complete millwork items

☑ create ramp landings and create the actual ramp

☑ determine the length of the ramp based on the rise and run of the slope

Schedules and Tags

To begin, I want to clarify something specific for the people who have been using Autodesk® AutoCAD® Architecture software: you don't need to tag an item in order for it to appear in a schedule in the Autodesk® Revit® Architecture platform. You can't really just draft a schedule either. But this isn't a bad situation to be in. Say, for example, that you have a typical door schedule. Wouldn't it be nice to add a door to the model and have that door automatically show up in the schedule?

▶ **Creating schedules**

▶ **Creating material takeoffs**

▶ **Creating key legends and importing CAD legends**

▶ **Adding tags**

▶ **Creating custom tags**

▶ **Keynoting**

Creating Schedules

Revit allows you to schedule an item instantly based on a database. A door, for example, already has most of the information you need built into it. Didn't it seem funny that when you placed a door in the model, it was automatically tagged with a sequential door number? This is the power of BIM. We're now going beyond 3D.

Schedules don't stop at doors and windows in Revit. You can schedule almost any item that goes into the model. Along with schedules comes the ability to quantify materials and areas. You can even create a schedule for the sole purpose of changing items in the model. In Revit, it's always a two-way street.

The first topic we'll tackle is creating the most common of the schedules in architecture: the door schedule. When you get this procedure down, you'll be off and running.

The good news is that you have most of the information you need to create a multitude of schedules. The bad news is that Revit-produced schedules may not look like your company's schedules at all. Before we go further, it's important to note that some of you will be able to get a perfect duplication of your company's standard schedules; some of you won't. Those of you who don't will have to get as close as possible to your standards and, at that point, know that sometimes the cost of doing BIM isn't in the pocket but at the plotter.

Given that, let's get started. I think you'll find that creating and using schedules is a wonderful experience. You're about to learn how to save hours upon hours of work, all the while maintaining 100 percent accuracy.

Adding Fields to a Schedule

To begin, open the file on which you've been following along. If you didn't complete the previous chapter, go to the book's web page at www.sybex.com/go/revit2014ner. From there, you can browse to the Chapter 11 folder and find the file called NER-11.rvt. The following procedure focuses on creating a door schedule. Grab a cup of coffee or power drink, and follow along:

1. In the Project Browser, go to the Level 1 floor plan.

2. On the Create panel of the View tab, click the Schedules ➤ Schedule/Quantities button, as shown in Figure 11.1.

3. The next dialog box, as shown in Figure 11.2, allows you to choose which item you would like to schedule. Select Doors, and click OK.

4. The next dialog lets you add the fields (parameters) required for your schedule. The first field you'll add is Mark. To do this, select Mark in

the Available Fields area to the left, and click the Add button in the middle of the dialog to move the Mark field to the right, as shown in Figure 11.3.

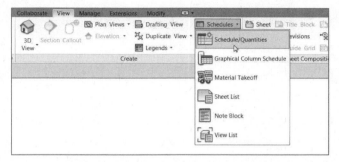

FIGURE 11.1: Click the Schedule/Quantities button on the View tab.

FIGURE 11.2: Select Doors, and click OK.

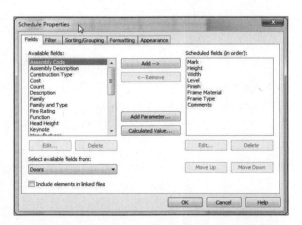

FIGURE 11.3: Adding the fields to produce a door schedule

5. Add the rest of the following fields using the same method (see Figure 11.3):

  ▶ Height

  ▶ Width

  ▶ Level

  ▶ Finish

  ▶ Frame Material

  ▶ Frame Type

  ▶ Comments

6. Click OK. Your schedule should be similar to Figure 11.4.

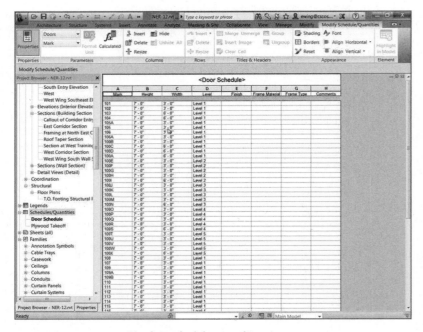

FIGURE 11.4: The door schedule up to this point

The next step is to start organizing your data in your preferred display format. You have a long way to go, but when you're finished, you can use this schedule over and over again.

N O T E   A schedule doesn't have to be placed on a drawing sheet. Many times, you'll produce a schedule so that you can manipulate data without having to search for it in the model.

Sorting and Grouping

Because Revit is a database, think of building a schedule as creating a query in a database, because that's exactly what you're doing. By creating a sort, you can begin to see your doors in groups and have a tangible understating of where you are. Let's get started:

1. Because you never use lowercase lettering, click into the header and title rows and change the names to all capital letters, as shown in Figure 11.5.

2. Select the rows that contain the headers from COMMENTS to MARK. Do this by clicking into the COMMENTS cell and dragging your cursor to the left.

3. With the cells highlighted, click the Shading button (see Figure 11.5).

4. Change the shading to the gray basic color shown in Figure 11.5.

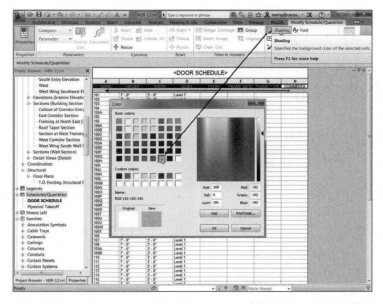

F I G U R E   1 1 . 5 :   Edit all the field names, and change the shading of the row.

5. In the Properties dialog is an Other category. Here you can return to the Schedule Properties dialog. Click the Edit button in the Sorting/Grouping row, as shown in Figure 11.6.

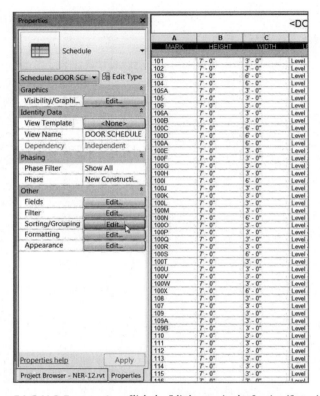

FIGURE 11.6: Click the Edit button in the Sorting/Grouping row.

6. On the Sorting/Grouping tab of the Schedule Properties dialog, set Sort By to Level.

7. Select the Header option.

8. Select the Footer option.

9. Select Title, Count, And Totals from the Sort By drop-down list (see Figure 11.7).

10. Click OK.

11. Save the model.

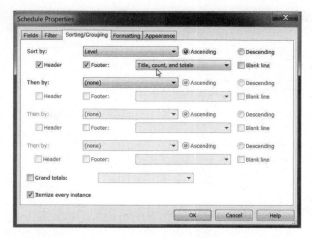

FIGURE 11.7: Sorting the schedule by level

The next step is to group the header information the way you would like it. Most schedules include groups such as Frame Material and Frame Type. You'll create similar groupings.

Controlling Headers

Although this step isn't crucial to producing an accurate, readable schedule, it's important in the attempt to get this Revit-produced schedule to look like the schedule you've been using for years in CAD. The objective of this procedure is to combine the header content into smaller groups under their own header, similar to what you can do in a spreadsheet.

To begin controlling the schedule headers, follow these steps:

1. In the Project Browser, open DOOR SCHEDULE (if you don't already have it open).

   At the top of the schedule are the title (DOOR SCHEDULE) and the headers (which include MARK, HEIGHT, WIDTH, and LEVEL, among others), as shown in Figure 11.8. Focus your attention here.

2. The goal is to combine MARK, HEIGHT, WIDTH, and LEVEL into a group under one header called DOOR INFORMATION. To do this, click the LEVEL cell, and drag your cursor to the left. You're selecting all four cells.

3. When the cells are selected, click the Group button on the Headers panel.

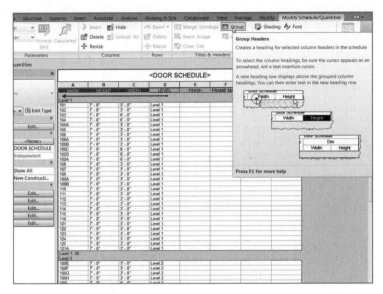

FIGURE 11.8: Click and drag across the four cells to activate the Group button.

 TIP Sometimes, when you're picking the first cell to do this task, you'll accidentally click into the cell. You don't want this. If this keeps happening, click into the LEVEL cell, and then click just below the cell into the gray area. Doing so selects the cell the way you want it. You can now pick the cell and drag your cursor to the left to highlight all the cells.

4. Click into the new cell, and type **DOOR INFORMATION**.

It would be nice if the defaults in Revit were all caps, but they aren't. The next procedure will rename some of the headers, but it won't change any values:

1. Click in the MARK header (see Figure 11.9), and change it to **DOOR NUMBER**.

\<DOOR SCHEDULE\>							
A	B	C	D	E	F	G	H
	DOOR INFORMATION				FRAME INFORMATION		
DOOR NUMBER	HEIGHT	WIDTH	FLOOR	FINISH	FRAME MATERIAL	FRAME TYPE	COMMENTS
Level 1							
101	7' - 0"	3' - 0"	Level 1	PT			
102	7' - 0"	3' - 0"	Level 1	PT			
103	7' - 0"	6' - 0"	Level 1				
104	7' - 0"	6' - 0"	Level 1				
105A	7' - 0"	3' - 0"	Level 1				
105	7' - 0"	3' - 0"	Level 1				
106	7' - 0"	3' - 0"	Level 1				
106A	7' - 0"	3' - 0"	Level 1				
100B	7' - 0"	3' - 0"	Level 1	WD			

FIGURE 11.9: Adding the new header and changing the descriptions

2. Change the LEVEL header to **FLOOR**.

3. Select the cells FRAME MATERIAL and FRAME TYPE.

4. On the Options bar, click Group in the Headers panel.

5. Call the new header **FRAME INFORMATION** (see Figure 11.10).

			<DOOR SCHEDULE>				
A	B	C	D	E	F	G	H
	DOOR INFORMATION				FRAME INFORMATION		
MARK	HEIGHT	WIDTH	FLOOR	FINISH	FRAME MATE	FRAME TYPE	COMMENTS
Level 1							
101	7' - 0"	3' - 0"	Level 1				
102	7' - 0"	3' - 0"	Level 1				
103	7' - 0"	6' - 0"	Level 1				
104	7' - 0"	6' - 0"	Level 1				
105A	7' - 0"	3' - 0"	Level 1				
105	7' - 0"	3' - 0"	Level 1				
106	7' - 0"	3' - 0"	Level 1				

FIGURE 11.10: The groups are complete.

Now it's time to begin filling out some of the blank fields. This is where you can increase productivity by using schedules. Instead of going door by door in the model, you have a list of every door right in front of you!

Modifying Elements in a Schedule

In Revit, data flows in multiple directions. When you created a schedule, the data from the doors flowed into the schedule to populate it. Now you'll ask Revit to collect data that you input into the schedule to flow into the doors.

To learn how to populate the schedule, follow along with the procedure:

1. In the Project Browser, open DOOR SCHEDULE (if it isn't open already).

 N O T E   Note that Door Schedule is now DOOR SCHEDULE in the Project Browser. This is because you renamed the title in the schedule—proof that you're dealing with bidirectional information.

2. Click into the FINISH cell for door number 101.

3. Type **PT** (for paint).

4. Click in the FINISH cell below the one you just changed.

5. Click the menu arrow, and notice that PT is in the list. Click PT (see Figure 11.11).

	A	B	C	D	E	F	G	H
<DOOR SCHEDULE>								
	MARK	DOOR INFORMATION			FINISH	FRAME INFORMATION		COMMENTS
		HEIGHT	WIDTH	FLOOR		FRAME MATE	FRAME TYPE	
Level 1								
	101	7' - 0"	3' - 0"	Level 1	PT			
	102	7' - 0"	3' - 0"	Level 1				
	103	7' - 0"	6' - 0"	Level 1	PT			
	104	7' - 0"	6' - 0"	Level 1				
	105A	7' - 0"	3' - 0"	Level 1				
	105	7' - 0"	3' - 0"	Level 1				
	106	7' - 0"	3' - 0"	Level 1				
	106A	7' - 0"	3' - 0"	Level 1				
	100B	7' - 0"	3' - 0"	Level 1				
	100C	7' - 0"	6' - 0"	Level 1				

FIGURE 11.11: When you start filling out the fields in a schedule, the items become available in the list for future use.

6. Save the model.

Let's see how this affected the actual doors in the model and perhaps find a door that needs to be tagged with a WD (wood) finish:

1. In the Project Browser, open the Level 1 floor plan.

2. Zoom in on the door between the corridor and the east wing, as shown in Figure 11.12.

3. Select the door.

4. In the Properties dialog, scroll down to the Materials And Finishes category, and find Finish.

5. Click in the Finish field, and type **WD** (see Figure 11.12).

6. Click the Apply button at the bottom of the Properties dialog.

7. Open the door schedule. Notice that door 100B has a WD finish.

8. Save the model.

In the interest of not getting carried away with the mundane process of filling out the entire schedule, note that this process is applicable for every field in this type of schedule. The main takeaway is that you can populate a schedule by either changing the data in the schedule itself or by finding the scheduled component and changing it there, such as a door or window.

If you click the menu drop-down arrow in the Finish field, you'll see that PT is available. The schedules and the actual doors are linked together.

N O T E   Also, it's worthwhile to note that if you click any row in the schedule, the Element panel has a Highlight In Model tool that essentially does the same thing as right-clicking.

The next step is to further modify the appearance of the schedule on which you're working. You can then begin using this schedule to focus on a specific group of doors and change them based on a filter.

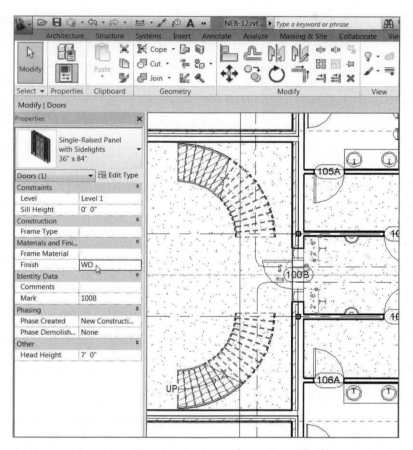

FIGURE 11.12:   Changing the property of an element in the model does the same thing as changing the element in the schedule.

Modifying the Schedule's Appearance

As it stands, not everyone uses the same fonts, headers, and linework around the border of the schedule. Although the usefulness of this next procedure won't be evident until Chapter 14, "Creating Sheets and Printing," it's applicable at this point in the book.

The objective of this procedure is to examine what font this schedule is using, as well as the line weights and spacing applied to the schedule. To learn how to adjust the appearance of a schedule, follow along:

1. In the Project Browser, open DOOR SCHEDULE (if it isn't open already).

2. In the Properties dialog, click the Edit button for Appearance.

3. On the Appearance tab of the Schedule Properties dialog are two categories: Graphics and Text. In the Graphics category, click Outline and select Medium Lines, as shown in Figure 11.13.

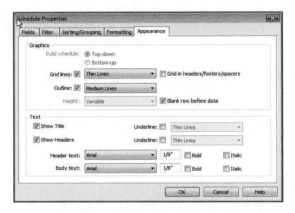

FIGURE 11.13: Configuring the schedule's appearance

USING THE SCHEDULE TO FIND A COMPONENT

In some cases, while you're filling out the schedule, you may not be sure which item you're looking at. Because schedules are "live," you can find a component from the schedule. To do this, follow these steps:

1. In the schedule, right-click door 114.

2. Select Show, as shown here:

(Continues)

Revit zooms in on the door and even gives you choices to find other views:

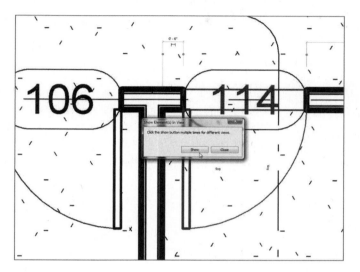

3. **Click Close.**

4. **Close the view, and go back to the schedule.**

---

4. In the Text category, make sure Show Title and Show Headers are selected (see Figure 11.13).

5. Click OK.

Your schedule doesn't change one bit! You've simply created a situation where the appearance of the schedule won't be apparent until you literally drag it onto a drawing sheet.

Adding a Schedule to a Sheet

Although adding a schedule to a sheet is a topic for Chapter 14, the process is so easy that you'll go ahead and do it now. Not to let the cat out of the bag or anything, but you'll enjoy how sheets come together in Revit. Perform the following steps:

1. In the Project Browser, find the Sheets (All) category, as shown in Figure 11.14. Coincidentally, it's located directly below Schedules/ Quantities.

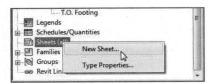

FIGURE 11.14: Creating a new sheet

HEY, THIS LOOKS FAMILIAR

You may have noticed that each time you open the properties of the schedule and click the Edit button next to a corresponding row (in this case, the Appearance row), you're only jumping to a specific tab of the Schedule Properties dialog. Each schedule category can be accessed in one dialog, as shown in the following image:

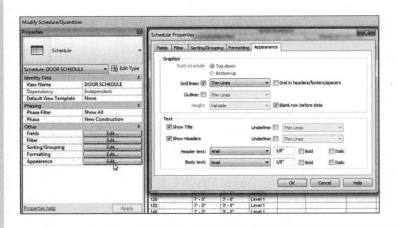

2. Right-click Sheets (All).

3. Select New Sheet (see Figure 11.14).

4. Select E1 30 × 42 Horizontal, as shown in Figure 11.15, and click OK.

5. You now have a new sheet containing a blank title block, as shown in Figure 11.16.

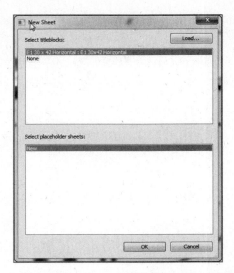

FIGURE 11.15: Using a sample title block

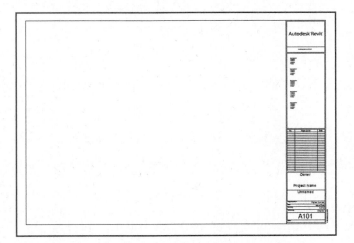

FIGURE 11.16: A new sheet, ready to be populated

The next objective is to click and drag the schedule onto the sheet. If the schedule fits, this is literally the easiest thing to do in Revit:

1. In the Project Browser, find DOOR SCHEDULE.

2. Click it, but don't double-click it—pick it and hold down the left mouse button.

3. With the left mouse button pressed, drag the schedule onto the sheet. You can place it anywhere you see fit (see Figure 11.17).

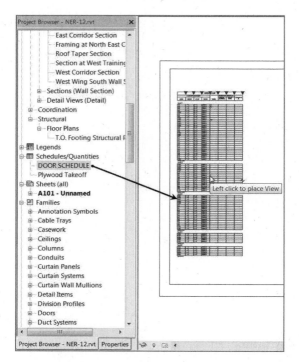

FIGURE 11.17: Clicking and dragging the schedule onto the sheet

4. When you've moved your cursor to the correct position, release the mouse button. If the bottom hangs over the sheet, that's okay—you'll fix it in a minute.

5. Notice the blue break grip located halfway up the schedule. This is the same type of grip that is used in grids, levels, and sections. Pick it, as shown in Figure 11.18.

6. With the schedule split in two, you can see that it fits onto the sheet quite nicely. With the schedule still selected, notice the blue grip at lower left, as shown in Figure 11.19. Pick the grip, and drag. You can slide the schedule so that the length of each side adjusts up and down evenly.

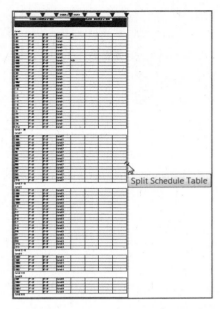

FIGURE 11.18: You can split the schedule into two (or more) sections.

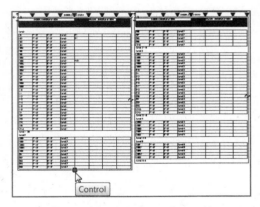

FIGURE 11.19: You can make further adjustments to the schedule by picking the round blue grip.

7. Zoom in on the top of the schedule, as shown in Figure 11.20, and select the schedule.

8. There are blue triangle-shaped icons at each cell in the title and the header. Pick the one on the COMMENTS column, and drag it to the right. The COMMENTS header is now readable.

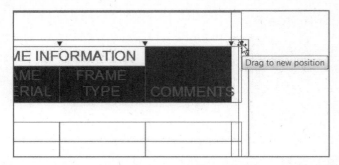

FIGURE 11.20: Pick the triangle grip to give the COMMENTS field some more room.

You can make two more adjustments to the schedule after you place it onto a sheet. They involve rotating and joining the two columns back together:

1. Select the schedule (if it isn't already selected).

   On the Modify | Schedule Graphics tab, there is a Rotation On Sheet menu on the Options bar, as shown at upper left in Figure 11.21. You don't need to change the rotation—just note that it's there.

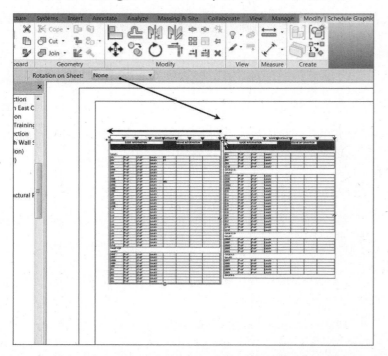

FIGURE 11.21: You can rotate the schedule on the sheet, and you can also join the columns back together if you need to.

2. Also notice the blue move grips in the upper-left corners of the schedules. If you pick one and drag the column back over the top of the other, the columns automatically join back together (see Figure 11.21).

3. Save the model.

To nail down the concept, let's create a window schedule. If you like, go ahead and make one on your own. You can compare it to the one in the book when you've finished to see if you got it right. If you would rather go step by step, that's fine too! Just follow along:

1. On the View tab, click the Schedules ➢ Schedule/Quantities button. Note that you can also right-click Schedules in the Project Browser to create a new schedule.

2. In the next dialog, select Windows, and click OK.

3. In the Schedule Properties dialog, add the following fields (see Figure 11.22):

   ▶ Type Mark

   ▶ Type

   ▶ Width

   ▶ Height

   ▶ Sill Height

   ▶ Level

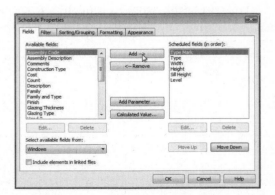

FIGURE 11.22: Adding fields to the schedule

4. Go to the Sorting/Grouping tab, as shown in Figure 11.23.

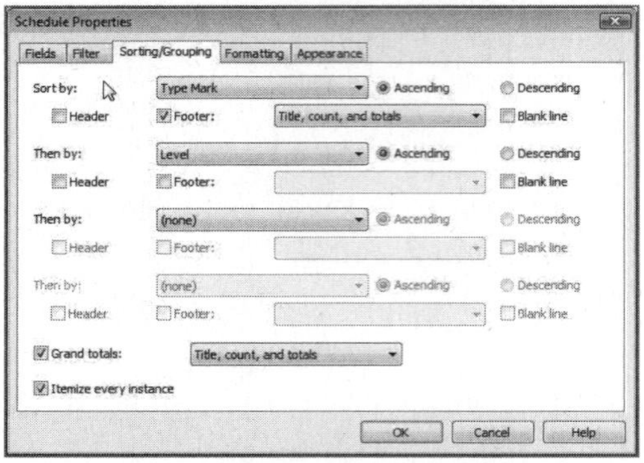

FIGURE 11.23: Specifying the settings for your window schedule

5. Sort by Type Mark.

6. Add a footer, with Title, Count, And Totals selected.

7. Choose Level from the Then By drop-down list.

8. Select the Grand Totals option.

9. Select Title, Count, And Totals.

10. Select the Itemize Every Instance option. (It should be checked by default; see Figure 11.23.)

11. Click OK to get to the schedule and see the results.

Sometimes, you may want to sort items based on a field but not actually display that field. You can do this as follows:

1. Select a cell in the Level column, as shown in Figure 11.24.

2. Click the Hide button. This hides the column.

3. Save the model.

N O T E   It's worth noting that you can create a schedule before you add any information to the model. You can then add this schedule to a sheet and save the entire file as a template. Whenever you start a new project, these schedules will start filling themselves out and will already be on sheets.

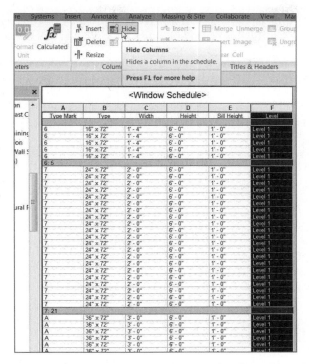

FIGURE 11.24:   You can hide a column but still have Revit sort the schedule based on the hidden information.

Phew! I think you get the picture. If you like, feel free to create a bunch of schedules on your own. Practice does make perfect.

Let's venture now into creating a material takeoff. It would be a shame to have all these computations go unused!

Creating Material Takeoffs

Creating a material takeoff is similar to creating a schedule. The only difference is that you're breaking down components and scheduling the smaller pieces. For example, as you know, you can make a schedule of all the doors in the model—you just did that. But with a material takeoff, you can quantify the square footage of door panels or glass in the doors. To take it a step further, you can do material takeoffs of walls, floors, and any other building components you want to quantify.

The objective of this procedure is to create three different material takeoffs: one for the walls, one for the floors, and one for the roofs. Let's get started:

1. On the View tab, click Schedules ➤ Material Takeoff, as shown in Figure 11.25.

2. In the New Material Takeoff dialog, select Walls, as shown in Figure 11.26.

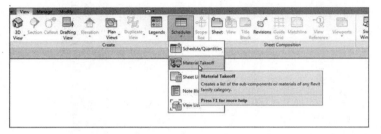

FIGURE 11.25: To add a new material takeoff, you can go to the View tab.

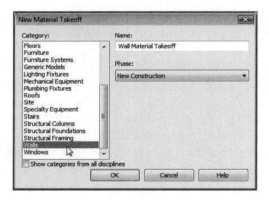

FIGURE 11.26: Select Walls in the New Material Takeoff dialog.

3. Click OK.

4. In the next dialog, add the following fields (see Figure 11.27).

   ▶ Material: Area

   ▶ Material: Name

   ▶ Count

5. Select the Sorting/Grouping tab.

6. Sort by Material: Name.

7. Add a footer.

8. Choose Title, Count, And Totals from the menu, as shown in Figure 11.28.

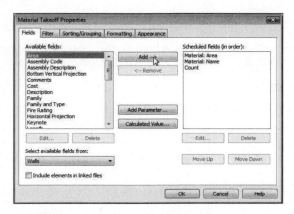

FIGURE 11.27: Adding the materials

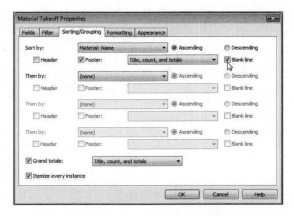

FIGURE 11.28: Configuring the parameters for the schedule

9. Select the Blank Line option.

10. At the bottom of the dialog box, select Grand Totals.

11. Choose Title, Count, And Totals from the menu.

12. Select the option Itemize Every Instance (see Figure 11.28).

13. Click OK.

The next step is to begin taking some totals on your own. The first thing you can do is have Revit automatically format a column to produce an independent total; then, you can break out this takeoff and drill in to more specific line-item totals:

1. In the Properties dialog, click the Edit button next to the Formatting row to bring up the Material Takeoff Properties dialog, shown in Figure 11.29.

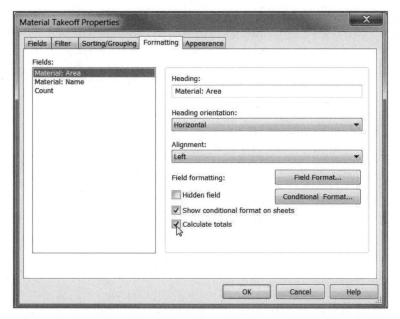

FIGURE 11.29: On the Formatting tab, you can specify Calculate Totals for the Material: Area option.

2. In the field to the left, select Material: Area (see Figure 11.29).

3. On the right, select Calculate Totals (see Figure 11.29).

4. Click OK.

You now have a total area at the bottom of your takeoff groups, as shown in Figure 11.30.

The next step is to break this takeoff into smaller, more specific takeoffs. When you do this, you can provide your own calculations based on almost any formula you need.

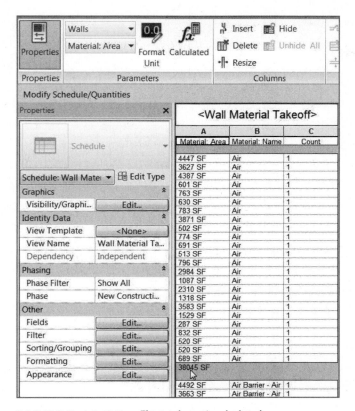

FIGURE 11.30: The total area is calculated.

Creating a Calculated Value Field

The objective here is to create separate schedules for plywood and gypsum by adding a new variable to the schedule that contains a formula you create. Yes, it's as hard as it sounds; but after you get used to this procedure, it won't be so bad! Perform the following steps:

1. In the Project Browser, right-click Wall Material Takeoff, and select Duplicate View ➤ Duplicate, as shown in Figure 11.31.

2. Right-click the new view in the Project Browser, and select Rename.

3. Rename it **Plywood Takeoff**.

4. In the Properties dialog, click the Edit button in the Filter row.

5. For Filter By, choose Material: Name.

6. In the menu to the right, select Equals from the list.

7. In the field below Material: Name, select Plywood, Sheathing (see Figure 11.32).

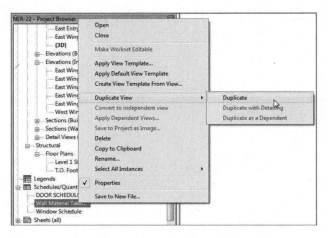

FIGURE 11.31: Duplicating the schedule

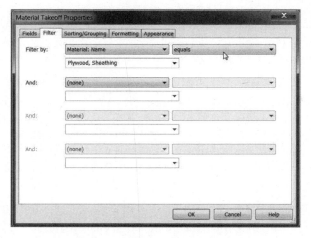

FIGURE 11.32: Filtering based on material

8. Click OK.

Your takeoff should look like Figure 11.33.

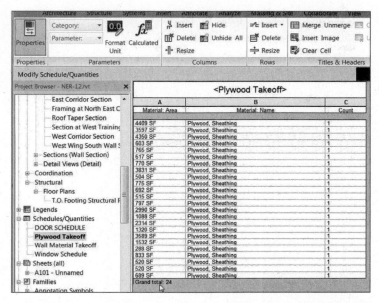

FIGURE 11.33: The takeoff is filtered based only on plywood, sheathing.

The next step is to break down the plywood into 4×8 sheets. You'll need to add a formula based on the square footage given by Revit divided by 32 square feet to come up with the plywood totals:

1. Open the Plywood Takeoff schedule in the Project Browser (if it isn't already).

2. In the Properties dialog, click the Edit button in the Fields row.

3. On the Fields tab in the Material Takeoff Properties dialog, click the Calculated Value button, as shown in Figure 11.34.

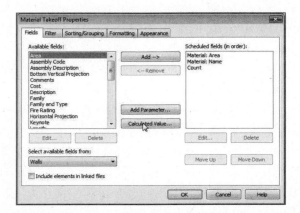

FIGURE 11.34: Click the Calculated Value button in the middle of the dialog.

4. For the name, enter **Number of Sheets**.

5. Make sure Discipline is set to Common.

6. Make sure Type is set to Number (see Figure 11.35).

7. Add the following formula: **Material: Area / 32 SF** (metric users type this formula: **Material: Area / 2.88 SF**).

8. Click OK.

9. Click the Formatting tab, as shown in Figure 11.36.

> You must type the fields being used exactly as they're displayed. For example, the formula: Material: Area must be typed exactly as specified in terms of spacing and capitalization. All formulas in Revit are case sensitive. You can also click the [...] button to add the available fields.

FIGURE 11.35: Changing the calculated values

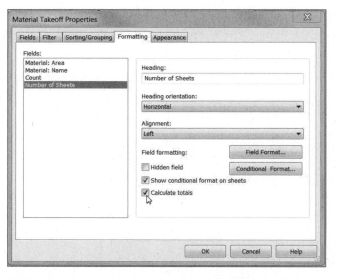

FIGURE 11.36: Selecting the Calculate Totals option

10. Select the new field called Number of Sheets.

11. In the Field Formatting section, select Calculate Totals (see Figure 11.36).

12. Click the Field Format button.

13. Deselect Use Default Settings, as shown in Figure 11.37.

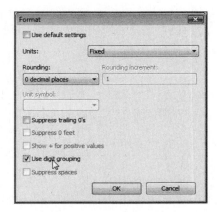

FIGURE 11.37: Overriding the units to allow this field to round

14. Change Units to Fixed.

15. Make sure Rounding is set to 0 Decimal Places.

16. Select Use Digit Grouping (see Figure 11.37).

17. Click OK.

18. Select the Sorting/Grouping tab.

19. At the bottom, select the Grand Totals option if it isn't selected already.

20. Click OK.

Your material takeoff should resemble Figure 11.38.

<Plywood Takeoff>			
A	B	C	D
Material: Area	Material: Name	Count	Number of Sheets
4409 SF	Plywood, Sheathing	1	138
3597 SF	Plywood, Sheathing	1	112
4350 SF	Plywood, Sheathing	1	136
603 SF	Plywood, Sheathing	1	19
765 SF	Plywood, Sheathing	1	24
617 SF	Plywood, Sheathing	1	19
770 SF	Plywood, Sheathing	1	24
3831 SF	Plywood, Sheathing	1	120
504 SF	Plywood, Sheathing	1	16
775 SF	Plywood, Sheathing	1	24
692 SF	Plywood, Sheathing	1	22
515 SF	Plywood, Sheathing	1	16
797 SF	Plywood, Sheathing	1	25
2990 SF	Plywood, Sheathing	1	93
1088 SF	Plywood, Sheathing	1	34
2314 SF	Plywood, Sheathing	1	72
1320 SF	Plywood, Sheathing	1	41
3589 SF	Plywood, Sheathing	1	112
1532 SF	Plywood, Sheathing	1	48
288 SF	Plywood, Sheathing	1	9
833 SF	Plywood, Sheathing	1	26
520 SF	Plywood, Sheathing	1	16
520 SF	Plywood, Sheathing	1	16
689 SF	Plywood, Sheathing	1	22
Grand total: 24			1,185

FIGURE 11.38:   The finished plywood material takeoff

Wow! Not too bad for only drawing a bunch of walls. As you can see, using the scheduling/material takeoff feature of Revit adds value to this application. Well, the value doesn't stop there. You can use the same functionality to create legends and drawing keys as well.

Creating Key Legends and Importing CAD Legends

Here's the problem with Revit. At some point, you'll need to add a component to the model that isn't associated with anything. Say, for example, you have a door that you would like to elevate on a sheet with the door schedule. You sure don't want that door included in the schedule, and you sure don't want to have to draw a wall just to display it. This is where creating a key legend comes into play.

Adding Legend Components

The objective of the following procedure is to create a key legend, adding elevations of doors that are used in the model. As it stands, a legend can mean any number of things. It can be a list of abbreviations, it can be a comprehensive numbering system keyed off the model itself, or it can be a graphical representation of items that have already been placed into the model for further detailing and coordinating. Another special aspect of legends is that a single legend may need to be duplicated on multiple sheets in a drawing set. You don't know it yet, but this is a problem for Revit. By creating a legend, however, you can get around this issue.

Follow these steps to create a door-type legend:

1. On the View tab, click the Legends ➤ Legend button, as shown in Figure 11.39. You can also right-click Legends in the Project Browser and pick New Legend.

2. The next dialog wants you to specify a scale. Choose 1/4″ = 1′–0″ (1:50mm). This is fine for now (see Figure 11.40).

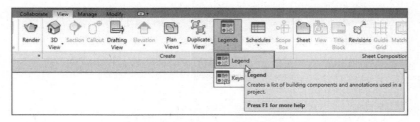

FIGURE 11.39:   Click the Legends a Legend button on the View tab.

FIGURE 11.40:   Choose 1/4″ = 1′–0″ (1:50mm).

3. Call the view **Door Type Legend.**

4. Click OK.

Congratulations! You now have a blank view. This is actually a good thing. Think of it as a clean slate where you can draft, add components, and throw together a legend.

OTHER FUNCTIONS HAVE BEEN ACTIVATED

Without knowing it, you've made some tools available that we haven't explored yet. You'll start to learn that Revit knows the type of view you happen to be in at present. Some commands are available in one view, but they may not be in the next. Keep this in mind as you venture through Revit and become frustrated that a command isn't working. You usually just need to switch views.

The next step is to begin adding components. You'll need to go to the Annotate tab for this:

1. Go to the Detail panel of the Annotate tab.

2. Click the Component ➤ Legend Component button, as shown in Figure 11.41.

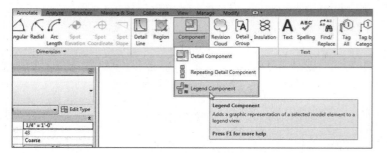

FIGURE 11.41:   Clicking the Legend Component button

3. In the Options bar, choose Doors : Single-Raised Panel with Sidelights : 36″×84″, as shown in Figure 11.42.

4. Change the view to Elevation : Front.

5. Pick a point to place the elevation.

6. With the command still running, you can place another instance.

7. Change the view to Floor Plan. Place another instance of the door just above the elevation, as shown in Figure 11.43. Revit provides a snap line on the left side for alignment.

8. In the Options bar, be sure Host Length is set to 6′–0″ (1800mm) (see Figure 11.43).

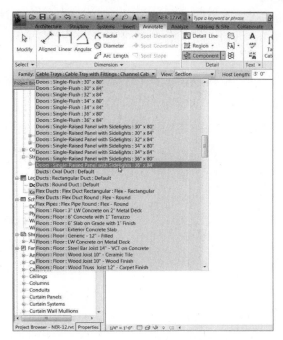

FIGURE 11.42: Changing the options for the legend

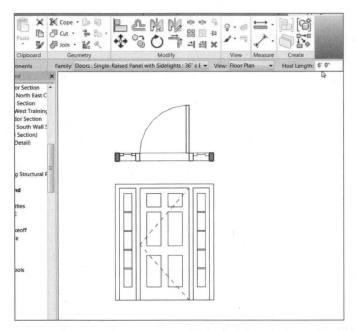

FIGURE 11.43: Placing two instances of the same door for the legend

9. With the command still running, place a Doors : Double-Flush : 68″ × 84″ to the right of the first door. Make sure View is set to Elevation : Front.

10. Place the corresponding plan view just above the door. Make sure Host Length is set to 6′–0″ (1800mm) (see Figure 11.44).

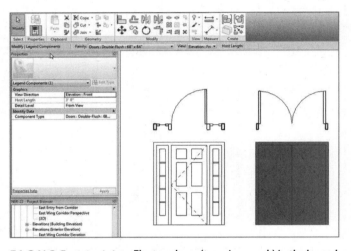

FIGURE 11.44:   The two doors (two views each) in the legend

The next step is to add some text in an attempt to label the doors. These items can't be labeled, which can be a disadvantage to breaking away from the model. This is basically a dumb sheet. Follow along:

1. On the Text panel, click the Text button.

2. Make sure the text style is Text: 3/32″ Arial and that the leader is set to None, as shown in Figure 11.45.

3. Place some text centered under each door elevation, and label the doors **Type A** and **Type B** (see Figure 11.45).

4. Save the model.

It's nice to have accurate blocks available based on what you've added to your model up to this point. By using the Revit method of building a legend like this, you're removed from the horror of stealing old legends from other jobs. I think we all know what a nightmare this turns into when they aren't accurate. Plus, in Revit, you have a library of the doors you're using right at your fingertips. They don't have to be managed or updated constantly. They will always be there, and they will always be accurate.

Next, you'll create a symbol legend; that is, you need to make a sheet that contains all your typical symbols. This task will be carried out in a similar manner.

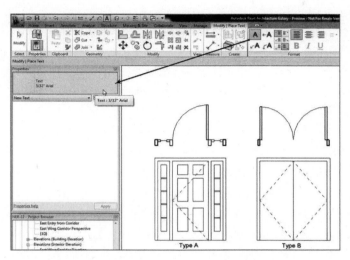

FIGURE 11.45: Placing text underneath the doors

Adding Symbols to a Legend

As mentioned earlier, adding symbols to a legend is similar to creating a door legend. The only difference is that you'll add your typical symbols as they appear on the sheets. Every company has a sheet like this. I'm sure yours does, too.

The first objective is to create this legend from scratch using the Revit tools. The second objective is to import your legend from CAD (which I'm sure you have). After you complete the two procedures, you can decide which approach is best for your firm.

Using the Revit Symbols

To use the Revit-provided symbols, you'll create a new legend view, and you'll use the Annotate tab to insert the typical components. If you're feeling brave, go ahead and make a symbol key on your own. You can follow the figures to make sure you're adding the expected components. If you would rather follow along with the procedure, let's get started:

1. On the View tab, click the Legends ➢ Legend button.

2. Set the scale to 1/4″ = 1′–0″ (1:50mm).

3. Call the new legend **Symbol Legend**.

4. Click OK.

5. On the Symbol panel of the Annotate tab, click the Symbol button, as shown in Figure 11.46.

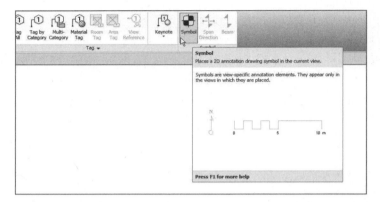

FIGURE 11.46: Clicking the Symbol button on the Annotate tab

6. In the Type Selector, select Callout Head.

7. Place the callout head into the view (see Figure 11.47).

8. With the Symbol command still running, place a door tag directly underneath the callout head, as shown in Figure 11.48.

9. Place a Room Tag With Area.

10. Place a View Title (see Figure 11.48).

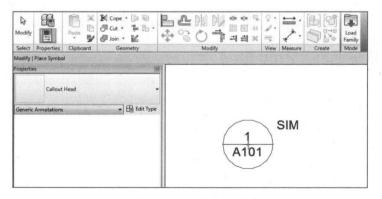

FIGURE 11.47: Placing the callout head

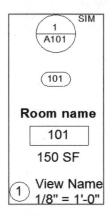

FIGURE 11.48: Populating the legend

The next step is to add some notes to indicate what you just added to the legend. Again, you won't be tagging the items—you're merely placing text and leaders:

1. On the Text panel of the Annotate tab, click the Text button.

2. On the Modify | Place Text tab, click the One Segment button, as shown in Figure 11.49.

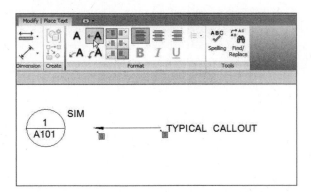

FIGURE 11.49: Adding the text to the legend

3. Pick two points for the leader, and type **TYPICAL CALLOUT** (see Figure 11.49).

4. Add the following notes to the rest of the symbols (see Figure 11.50):

    ▶ TYPICAL DOOR TAG

    ▶ TYPICAL ROOM TAG

    ▶ TYPICAL VIEW TITLE

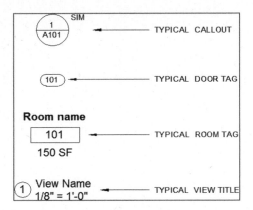

FIGURE 11.50: Adding descriptive text

Now you'll place a box around the items and draw three equal lines to make a grid. You do this by strictly drafting lines, as the following procedure shows:

1. On the Annotate tab, click the Detail Line button, as shown in Figure 11.51.

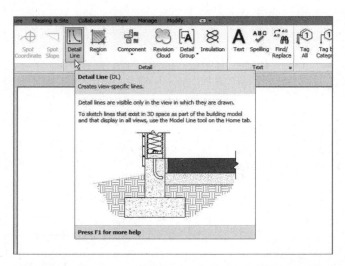

FIGURE 11.51: Click the Detail Line button on the Annotate tab.

2. In the Properties dialog, be sure Thin Lines is selected, as shown in Figure 11.52.

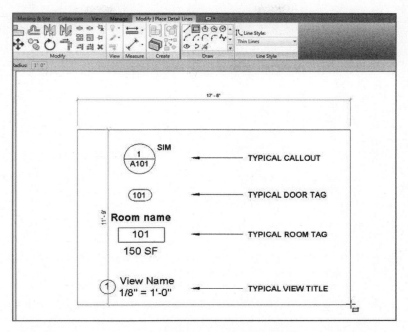

FIGURE 11.52: Adding the linework around the symbols and text

3. On the Draw panel, click Rectangle (see Figure 11.52).

4. Draw a rectangle around the symbols and the text (see Figure 11.52).

5. On the Draw panel, click the Line button.

6. Draw three horizontal lines in the box. They don't have to be equally spaced, but they should separate the symbols.

7. Place a dimension string starting at the top of the rectangle (to the first line you drew), to the second line, to the third, to the fourth, and then to the bottom of the rectangle.

8. Click the EQ button on the dimension string.

9. Move the symbols and the text to the proper positions (see Figure 11.53).

10. Delete the dimensions.

11. Click OK in the next dialog.

12. Save the model.

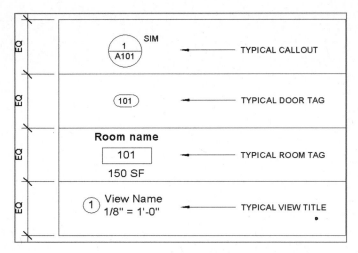

FIGURE 11.53: Draw the horizontal lines, and then equally constrain them using the Dimension command.

Now that you have experience with creating legends using strictly Revit components and lines, it's time to investigate how you can use a premade AutoCAD legend as an import.

Importing AutoCAD Legends

Just because you've switched to Revit doesn't mean you must throw away over a decade of work regarding typical details and legends. Revit accepts AutoCAD and MicroStation .dwg and .dgn files just fine. Of course, there will be some tweaking, but when you get the process down, I think you'll rely heavily on this functionality.

The objective of the following procedure is to create a new legend view and then import an existing AutoCAD legend into the view. To get started, go to the book's web page at www.sybex.com/go/revit2014ner. From there, you can browse to Chapter 11 and find the file called Interior Partition Legend.dwg. Place the drawing file on your system in a place where you can retrieve it later. Now perform the following steps:

1. On the View tab, click the Legends ➢ Legend button.

2. Call the new legend **Interior Partition Legend**.

3. Make the scale 1″ = 1′–0″ (one inch equals one foot) (1:10mm), and click OK.

4. On the Insert tab, click Import CAD, as shown in Figure 11.54.

5. Find the AutoCAD .dwg file called Interior Partition Legend.dwg.

WARNING   Don't click Open until you're instructed to do so. We need to look at several items in the Import CAD Formats dialog that have a crucial effect on the imported graphics.

6. At the bottom of the Import CAD Formats dialog, notice that you have a few choices (see Figure 11.55):

> **Colors**   Change Colors to Black And White.
>
> **Layers**   Make sure Layers is set to All. You'll be able to manipulate the AutoCAD layers after you bring the .dwg file into Revit.
>
> **Import Units**   Import Units should be set to Auto-Detect. In Chapter 18, "Site and Topography," you'll import a site. At that point, you'll have to modify this choice; but for now, leave it as Auto-Detect.
>
> **Positioning**   Leave Positioning as Auto - Center To Center.

7. Click Open.

FIGURE 11.54:   Importing CAD formats

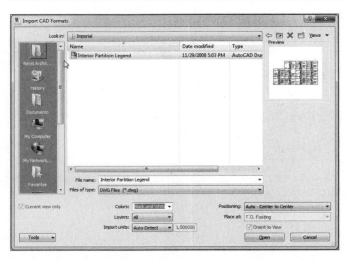

FIGURE 11.55:   The Import CAD Formats dialog. Be deliberate when importing a CAD file by choosing the options at the bottom of the dialog.

After you import the CAD file, it may be zoomed off the view so that you can't see it. Follow this procedure to zoom the CAD import into view and manipulate the data:

1. Type **ZA** (to zoom all).

2. You can now see the import. Select it.

3. On the Modify | Interior Partition Legend.dwg tab, in the Import Instance panel, click the Query button, as shown in Figure 11.56.

4. Select the line shown in Figure 11.56.

5. After you select the line, Revit reports information to you about that line. You're also given the chance to delete the layer. Click Delete, as shown in Figure 11.57.

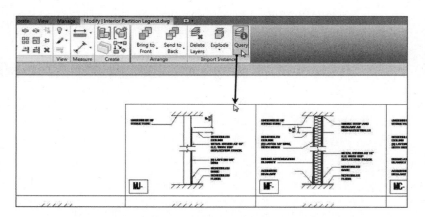

FIGURE 11.56: Clicking the Query button in the Import Instance panel

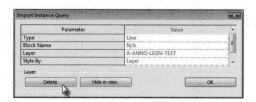

FIGURE 11.57: You can query items in the CAD import. You can also delete items.

6. Click OK. All of the lines on that layer are gone.

7. Press Esc twice.

W A R N I N G   Be careful when you delete layers. Revit isn't like AutoCAD. When you delete a layer in Revit, any object that happens to be on that layer is deleted as well. You can easily delete objects inadvertently.

The next step is to fix some of the text that didn't quite wrap correctly. You need to explode the import so that it's broken down into Revit lines and objects:

1. Select the import again.

2. On the Modify | Interior Partition Legend.dwg tab, click Explode ➤ Full Explode, as shown in Figure 11.58.

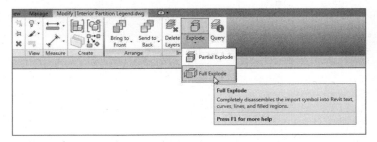

FIGURE 11.58:   Click the Full Explode button on the Modify | Interior Partition Legend.dwg tab.

 N O T E   The difference between Full Explode and Partial Explode is that a partial explode breaks the import down to the next level of blocks. For example, if a block was included in the drawing file, such as a column bubble, then a partial explode would break down the import but leave the column bubble as a block. When you do a full explode, you're exploding every object in the import—blocks and all.

3. Select the text METAL STUDS AT 16" O.C. WITH TOP DEFLECTION TRACK for the ME- detail.

4. Pick the grip to the right, and drag the text box to the right until the text wraps into the correct position, as shown in Figure 11.59.

5. Do the same for the other details that have improperly wrapped text.

6. Save the model.

 N O T E   You may ask, "How did Revit know what line weights to use for my import?" This is a great question. You can configure the import/export settings to translate AutoCAD colors to Revit line weights. If you're using standard AIA layering, you'll have very little problem with this translation. If not, you may have some work to do. In Chapter 12, "Detailing," you'll configure this file.

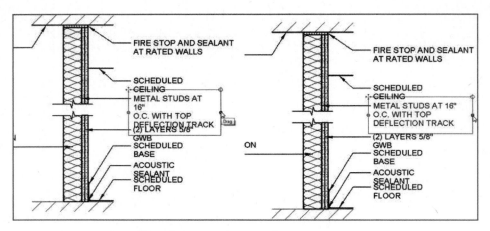

FIGURE 11.59:   Fixing the improperly wrapped text

Now that you have experience with keys, let's move on to learn how tags work in Revit, and why we address them along with schedules.

Adding Tags

You're halfway through the book, and you've probably noticed that some subjects, such as tags, were brushed over in earlier chapters. Tags simply can't be avoided because they come in automatically with many items. But a mystery surrounds them. Where do they come from, how does Revit know what tag to associate with what element, and how the heck do you make Revit tags look like your tags?

You can almost see a tag as a "window" looking into the item itself. A tag allows you to pull a parameter out of an item and put that parameter onto the drawing in a physical sense. Given that, tags are how you label things.

To start, let's concentrate on the simple and then move to the more complex. First, you'll learn how to add a tag that wasn't added automatically.

Adding Tags Individually

As you may have noticed, not everything you placed in the model received a tag—especially many of the doors and windows that you copied to different floors. The objective of the following procedures is to add tags to individual objects. The first type of tag will be by category.

Tagging by Category

Tagging an item by category means that when you start the Tag command, it looks for an entire object to tag with the loaded tag that was created specifically for that object:

1. In the Project Browser, go to the Level 2 floor plan.

2. Zoom in on the area where the corridor meets the east wing, as shown in Figure 11.60.

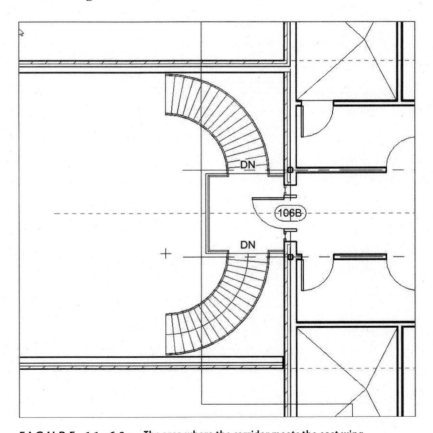

FIGURE 11.60:   The area where the corridor meets the east wing

3. On the Tag panel of the Annotate tab, click the Tag By Category button, as shown in Figure 11.61.

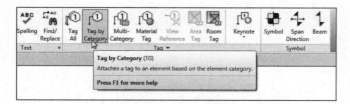

FIGURE 11.61:   Click Tag By Category on the Annotate tab.

4. On the Options bar, deselect the Leader option.

5. Pick the door shown in Figure 11.62. Your tag is added.

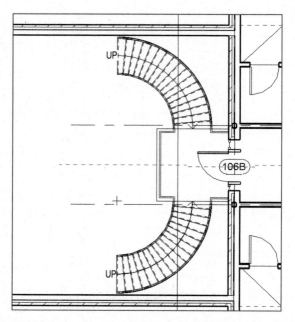

FIGURE 11.62:   Tagging the door. Be sure you deselect Leader on the Options bar.

Adding tags to doors is a straightforward concept. Keep in mind, however, that doors and windows are certainly not the only taggable items in Revit.

Tagging Walls

Tagging walls is almost as automatic as tagging doors and windows. The only difference is that when you tag a wall, the tag is initially blank.

To learn how to tag a wall, follow along with this procedure:

1. In the Project Browser, go to the Level 2 floor plan if you aren't there already.

2. Zoom in on the east wing.

3. Click the Tag By Category button.

4. Make sure the Leader button is checked.

5. Pick the wall indicated in Figure 11.63.

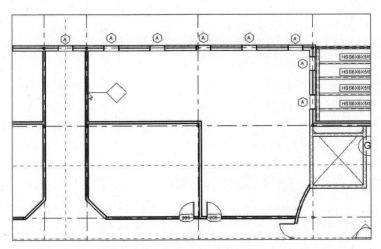

FIGURE 11.63: Picking one of the corridor partitions to tag

6. Many times, you won't have a tag loaded for this specific type of item. If that situation occurs, you'll get the message shown in Figure 11.64. If you want to load a tag, click Yes to do so. If you don't, proceed to step 14.

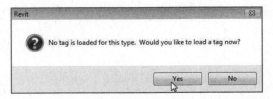

FIGURE 11.64: When you try to tag an item without a specific tag type loaded, this dialog prompts you to load the tag.

7. In the Load Family dialog, select Annotations ➤ Architectural ➤ Wall Tag.rfa.

8. Click Open.

9. On the Options bar, click the Leader option so the tag is leadered into the wall.

10. On the Architecture tab in the title bar of the Tag panel is a pull-down arrow. Click the Loaded Tags button (see Figure 11.65).

11. In the Tags dialog, scroll down to Walls, as shown in Figure 11.66.

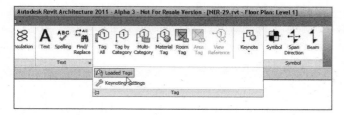

FIGURE 11.65: Click Loaded Tags.

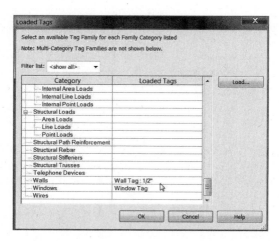

FIGURE 11.66: Changing the default tag for walls to Wall Tag : 1/2″

12. In the Loaded Tags cell for Walls, pick Wall Tag : 1/2″.

13. Click OK.

14. Pick the wall again. You now have a wall tag.

15. Press Esc twice.

16. Select the new wall tag (it's blank).

17. Notice the blue items. Click the blue question mark in the tag.

18. Call it **MC-1**, as shown in Figure 11.67.

The Tag By Category button is also located on the Quick Access toolbar.

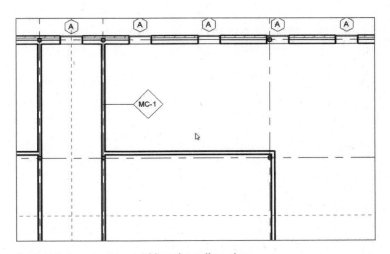

FIGURE 11.67: Adding the wall tag data

19. Click Yes in response to the warning that you're changing a type parameter.

20. Press Esc.

21. Click Tag By Category on the Annotate tab.

22. Pick any other corridor partition in the floor. This time the tag is automatically placed with the appropriate MC-1 tag filled out.

Suppose you would like to tag a number of the same items in one shot. Revit lets you do this by using the Tag All command.

Using the Tag All Command

The Tag All command is a favorite among Revit users. One of the most common examples of using this command is when you Copy/Paste Aligned multiple items to higher-level floors. You'll almost always miss a few tags, or even all of the tags. This is where Tag All comes into play.

The objective of this next procedure is to find the Tag All feature and tag many items in one shot:

1. In the Project Browser, go to the Level 4 floor plan.

2. Notice that many doors and windows aren't tagged. (If for some reason all the doors and windows are tagged, select the tags and delete them for this procedure.)

But Where Is That Information Stored?

When you modify this type of tag, it's generally the type mark that carries the data. To see the location of the type mark, select any one of the interior partitions, and click Edit Type in the Properties dialog. In the Type Parameters, you can scroll down to find Type Mark, as shown in the following image:

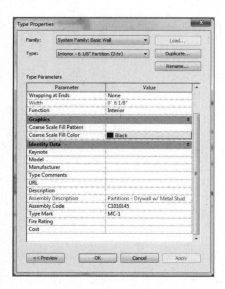

This information is also tied into the schedule. As you're selecting fields to add to the schedule, you're selecting from the same list that Revit used to tag items in the model. This is the definition of BIM: the right information is used in the right places.

3. On the Annotate tab, click the Tag All button, as shown in Figure 11.68.

FIGURE 11.68: The Tag All button on the Annotate tab

4. In the Tag All Not Tagged dialog, click Door Tags.

5. Hold the Ctrl key, and select Window Tags. This specifies that every door and window in the view is about to receive a tag.

6. Make sure the All Objects In Current View radio button is selected (see Figure 11.69).

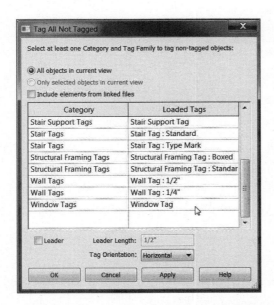

FIGURE 11.69: Selecting door and window tags

7. Click Apply.

8. Click OK.

It almost goes without saying that Tag All is quite a valuable tool. Another valuable tool is the ability to reach into a component and tag specific material within the component.

Tagging by Material

Tagging By Material may be one of the most underused commands in all of Revit. The reason is that most people think of a tag as, well, a tag—a drawn box containing some abbreviations or letters. That's too bad, because you can also use tags as a means to place notes. Tagging an item's material is one way of doing just that.

The objective of the following procedure is to create a material description and then place a tag pursuant to that note:

1. In the Project Browser, go to the Level 1 floor plan.

2. Zoom in on the kitchen area in the east wing.

3. On the Tag panel of the Annotate tab, click the Material Tag button, as shown in Figure 11.70.

FIGURE 11.70:   The Material Tag button on the Tag panel

4. You may get the message stating that no material tag family is loaded into the model. If so, click the Yes button to load one.

5. Browse to Annotations ➢ Architectural ➢ Material Tag.rfa.

6. Click Open.

7. Place your cursor over the tile floor, as shown in Figure 11.71. The tag reads "Porcelain tile, 4″, white." When you see this tag, pick a point on the tile floor, and then place the note to the right, as shown in the figure.

8. Press Esc twice, or click Modify.

9. Select the tag.

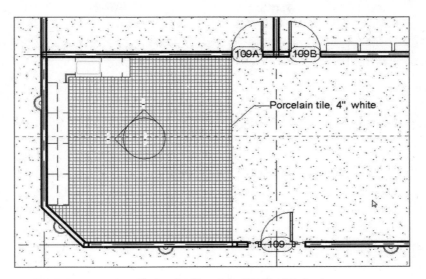

FIGURE 11.71:   Placing the "Porcelain tile, 4″, white" note

10. In the Properties dialog, click Edit Type.

11. Change Leader Arrowhead to Arrow Filled 15 Degree, as shown in Figure 11.72.

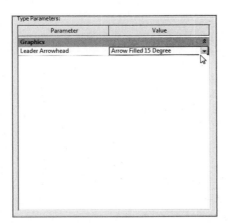

FIGURE 11.72:   Changing the leader arrowhead is one of the first things you'll probably have to do.

12. Click OK to reveal the leader. Yes, that looks much better.

The next topic we'll explore is where these tags come from and how you can create your own. Notations and symbols are the basis for maintaining graphical standards. If you simply use the examples given to you by Revit, you'll have a set of drawings that look very generic and immediately turn off your design team.

Creating Custom Tags

As mentioned before, templates very much drive how Revit works. Creating families is a prime example of this. To create a custom tag, you must first create a family and then load it into your drawing. The tag you'll create is a casework tag. Revit does provide one, but yours needs to be smaller (based on scale), and it needs a box surrounding it.

To learn how to create a custom tag from scratch, follow along:

1. Click the Application button, and select New ➤ Family.

2. Browse to the Annotations folder.

3. Select the Generic Tag.rft file.

4. Click Open.

Welcome to the Family Editor! The first thing you may notice is the large block of text in the middle of the view that says, "Note: Use Settings | Family Categories to set the tag's category. Insertion point is at intersection of ref planes. Delete this note before using."

This is a great note, and you need to start by taking its advice:

1. Select the note, and click the Delete button (or press the Delete key on your keyboard).

2. Click the Family Category And Parameters button, as shown in Figure 11.73.

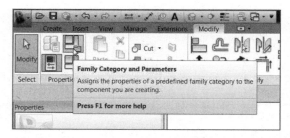

FIGURE 11.73: The Family Category And Parameters button

3. In the Family Category And Parameters dialog, select Casework Tags, as shown in Figure 11.74.

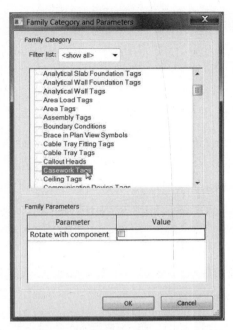

FIGURE 11.74: Selecting Casework Tags

4. Click OK.

Notice that the Ribbon has changed. The only items available are designed to aid you in the creation of a family. There are many buttons that we'll get to in Chapter 17, "Creating Families," but for now, you're interested in the Label button:

1. In the Text panel on the Create tab, click the Label button, as shown in Figure 11.75.

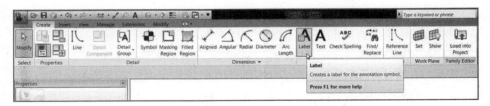

FIGURE 11.75: Clicking the Label button

2. Click the Edit Type button in the Properties dialog.

3. Click Duplicate.

4. Call the new label **1/16″ (1.5mm)**.

5. Click OK.

6. In the Text category, change Text Size to **1/16″ (1.5mm)**.

7. Change Width Factor to 0.8.

8. Click OK.

9. In the model, place the tag directly on the intersection of the reference planes (you'll have to eyeball the placement).

10. In the Edit Label dialog, select Type Mark from the list to the left.

11. In the middle of the Edit Label dialog, click the Add Parameter(s) To Label button. The Type Mark parameter should appear in the right field, as shown in Figure 11.76.

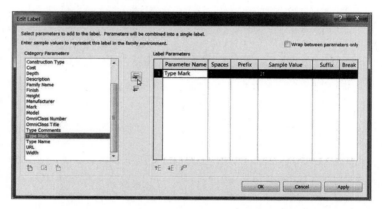

FIGURE 11.76:   Adding the Type Mark parameter

12. Click OK.

13. Press Esc twice.

The label has been added. It's small, but it's there. The next step is to draw a rectangle around this text. The following procedure describes how:

1. On the Create tab, Detail panel, click the Line button, as shown in Figure 11.77.

2. On the Draw panel, click the Pick Lines icon.

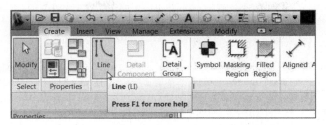

FIGURE 11.77: Click the Line button to start sketching the box.

3. On the Options bar, change the Offset value to 1/16″ (1.5mm).

4. Zoom into the label, and then offset the horizontal reference plane up 1/16″ (1.5mm) and down 1/16″ (1.5mm), as shown in Figure 11.78.

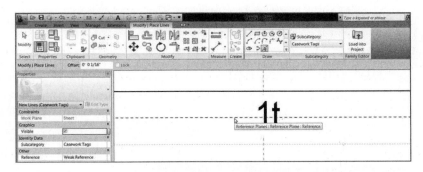

FIGURE 11.78: Offsetting the horizontal reference plane up and down

5. On the Options bar, change the Offset value to 1/8″ (3mm).

6. Offset the vertical reference plane to the left and to the right 1/8″ (3mm), as shown in Figure 11.79.

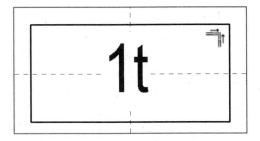

FIGURE 11.79: Creating the box

7. Trim the four corners.

8. Press Esc.

9. Save the file as **Casework Tag.rfa**. Make sure you save the file in a location where you can find it later.

10. On the Family Editor panel, click the Load Into Project button, as shown in Figure 11.80.

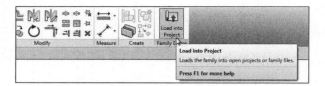

FIGURE 11.80:   Loading the family into your project

WHICH ONE DO I CHOOSE?

If you have more than one model open (other than this family), you'll see a dialog asking you to select the file into which you wish to load the family. If this happens, select NER-11.rvt (or the file on which you're working), as shown here:

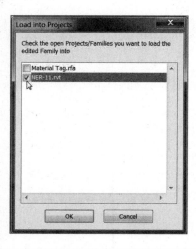

With the new tag loaded into the project, you can now use it. Because it's a casework tag, you need to find some casework to label, as follows:

1. In the Project Browser, go to the interior elevation called Kitchen North. You can also go to the Level 1 floor plan and zoom in on the kitchen. From there, double-click the elevation marker pointing at the north leg of the kitchen.

2. Zoom in on the cabinets, as shown in Figure 11.81.

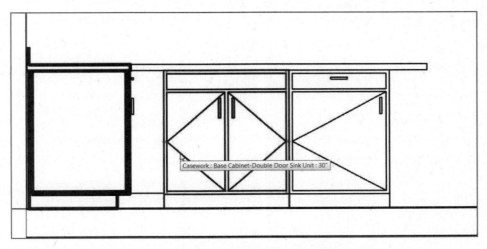

Casework : Base Cabinet-Double Door Sink Unit : 30"

FIGURE 11.81: Picking the base cabinet with two doors and one drawer

3. On the Tag panel on the Annotate tab, click the Tag By Category button.

4. On the Options bar, deselect Leader.

5. Pick the base cabinet with two doors and one drawer (see Figure 11.81).

6. Move the tag underneath the cabinet.

7. Select the question mark in the tag. (You'll see it once you select the tag.)

8. Rename the tag **B2D1D**, as shown in Figure 11.82, and then click Yes.

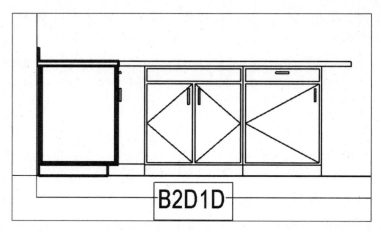

FIGURE 11.82: Renaming the tag

Because this is an annotation family, the size changes with the fluctuation of the scale. If you change the scale from 1/8″ (1:100mm) to 1/4″ (1:50mm), the tag will shrink by half. To do this, follow along:

1. On the View Control toolbar, change the scale from 1/8″ = 1′–0″ (1:100mm) to 1/4″ = 1′–0″ (1:50mm), as shown in Figure 11.83.

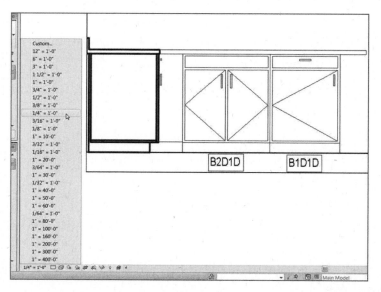

FIGURE 11.83: Changing the scale, and adding a second tag to the base cabinets

2. Move the tag up so it's closer to the cabinet.

3. Add another tag to the cabinet to the right.

4. Call it **B1D1D** (see Figure 11.83).

As you can see, this is a huge step beyond inserting a block in a 2D drafting application and filling out an attribute that has nothing to do with the actual element it's labeling. In addition, the scaling feature works wonders when it comes time to create elevations and enlarged views.

The next topic to explore is creating a tag that will work in any situation you need—sort of a multipurpose tag.

Using Multi-Category Tags

If you think about it, you used a door tag for the doors, a window tag for the windows, and a wall tag for the walls. Jeepers! How many different tags do you need to complete a set of construction documents? Well, in Revit, you can create a multi-category tag. This will be the same tag (aesthetically) that identifies a common property in any element.

Unfortunately, Revit doesn't provide a sample multi-category tag, so you'll have to make one. The objective of the next set of procedures is to create a new multi-category tag and then use it on various furniture items.

As mentioned earlier, you should create any new family by using a template. Doing so will ensure that you're using the correct data, so the family will behave as expected. This is what you're doing right now:

1. Click the Application button, and then choose New ➢ Family.

2. In the Annotations folder, locate the file called Multi-Category Tag.rft.

3. Open the Multi-Category Tag.rft template.

4. Because you've started the family by using a template, the Ribbon has changed. On the Create panel, click the Label button.

5. Pick the point at the intersection of the two reference planes.

6. In the Edit Label dialog, add the Family Name and Type Name parameters, as shown in Figure 11.84.

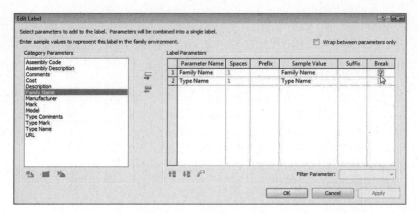

FIGURE 11.84: This time you're adding two parameters. By selecting the Break check box, you tell Revit to stack the parameters.

7. In the Family Name row, select the Break check box (see Figure 11.84).

8. Click OK.

9. Click the Application button, and select Save As ➤ Family. Place the file somewhere you can find it later.

10. Call the new tag **Multi-Category Tag**.

11. On the Family Editor panel, click Load Into Project.

12. In the NER-11 project (or whatever project name you're in at present), go to the Level 1 floor plan and zoom in on the northeast office in the east wing.

13. On the Annotate tab, click the Multi-Category button on the Tag panel, as shown in Figure 11.85.

FIGURE 11.85: The Multi-Category button on the Tag panel

14. On the Options bar, select the Leader option, as shown in Figure 11.86.

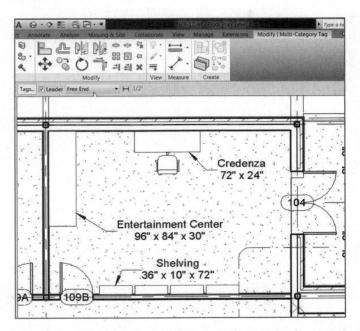

FIGURE 11.86: Adding the multi-category tag to the entertainment unit. Make sure you adjust the tag to show the information unobscured.

15. Again, on the Options bar, select Free End (see Figure 11.86).

16. Hover your mouse over the furniture items shown in the room in Figure 11.86. The tag reports the information for any item over which you hover. Pick the entertainment unit to the left of the room, and then pick two points to the right of the unit.

17. Click Modify. Select the tag you just placed into the model.

18. Click the Edit Type button.

19. For Leader Arrowhead, select Arrow Filled 15 Degree.

20. Click OK.

21. Using the grips on the tag, move it out of the way, and adjust the leader so it looks like the one in Figure 11.86.

22. Add another tag to the credenza located on the north wall. Adjust this tag as well (see Figure 11.86).

23. Add one more tag to the shelving on the south wall of the room, and adjust the leader so it looks acceptable (again, see Figure 11.86).

Using multi-category tags is a great way to label a model. It's nice because you don't need specific tags for the various elements. These items could have been different types of furniture and casework. As long as they have a family name and a type name, the label tag will work.

Another way to record items in a model is by adding keynoting. This procedure is done in conjunction with a schedule. The last section of this chapter will focus on this procedure.

Keynoting

Keynoting has been used in construction documents dating back to the Pharaohs. Okay, maybe not that far back, but you get the point. Revit does a nice job in terms of tracking keynotes. The only issue is that nothing comes pre-keynoted in Revit. That is, a keynote value needs to be assigned to each item. If your company uses keynoting, you'll have to assign a keynote to every item in Revit in your template.

That being said, let's break down keynoting and start learning how to add keynotes to your model. You can add three different types of keynotes to a model: keynote by element, by material, and by user.

Keynoting by Element

Keynoting by element means you select an object and place the keynoted text. This procedure is the same as when you tag an object, except that this time the information you're reporting is actually a Construction Specifiers Institute (CSI)-formatted keynote or a standard for your installation location.

Before you get started on this exercise, make sure there is a keynote.txt file to which Revit is pointing. Then follow along:

1. On the Annotate tab, click the small down arrow next to the word *Tag*.

2. Click Keynote Settings.

3. Make sure you're mapped to C:\ProgramData\Autodesk\RVT 2014\ Libraries\US Imperial\RevitKeynotes_Imperial_2004.txt (RevitKeynotes_Metric.txt), as shown in Figure 11.87.

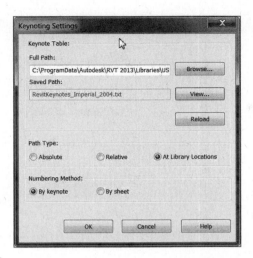

FIGURE 11.87:   Mapping the Keynote.txt file

To use the keynoting by element function, follow this procedure:

1. In the Project Browser, go to the Level 1 floor plan.

2. Zoom in on a hallway sconce lighting fixture.

3. On the Tag panel of the Annotate tab, select Keynote ➢ Element Keynote, as shown in Figure 11.88.

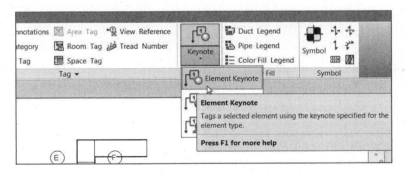

FIGURE 11.88:   Select Keynote ➢ Element Keynote.

 N O T E   If no keynote tag is loaded, click Yes in the subsequent dialog, and browse to Annotations ➢ Keynote Tag.rfa.

N O T E   At this point, it's up to you to determine which style of keynoting your firm uses. Do you keynote the plans with the CSI number, with the keynote description, or with a combination of the number and the description? Either way, you'll be making a keynote schedule with these items in a list.

4. In the Type Selector, click Keynote Tag ➤ Keynote Text, as shown in Figure 11.89.

5. Pick the wall sconce shown in Figure 11.90.

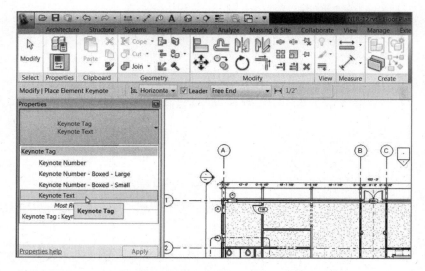

FIGURE 11.89:   Choosing Keynote Tag ➤ Keynote Text

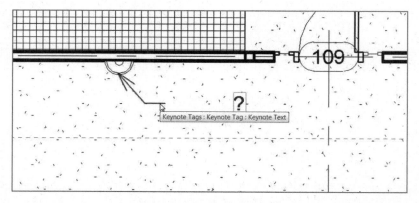

FIGURE 11.90:   Placing the leadered keynote

6. Pick a second point for the leader line.

7. Pick a third point to place the keynote text (see Figure 11.90).

Because no keynote has been assigned to this family, you can specify one now. Revit lets you specify keynoting information by either assigning the information through the Properties dialog or by placing a keynote tag, after which Revit will prompt you to specify the missing information.

After you pick the third point, Revit displays the Keynotes menu shown in Figure 11.91. Follow these steps to place the keynote value into the sconce family:

1. Scroll to Division 26 Electrical, and click the plus sign.

2. Go to the group 26 51 00 Interior Lighting.

3. Go to the group 26 51 00.B2 Wall Mounted Incandescent Fixture, as shown in Figure 11.91.

FIGURE 11.91: Selecting the proper keynote value for the sconce

4. Click OK.

5. Drag the text to the right to see the arrow and the note clearly.

6. On the Tag panel of the Annotate tab, select Keynote ➢ Element Keynote again.

7. Pick another wall sconce, and place the keynote. Notice that this tag is consistent throughout.

8. Click Modify. Select the tag.

9. In the Properties dialog, click Edit Type. Change Leader Arrowhead to Arrow Filled 15 Degrees.

The next style of keynoting allows you to specify an alternate keynote for an element. To begin, you'll physically open the keynote text file and add some custom notes.

Keynoting by User

Sometimes you'll need a completely custom keynote. Although you should try to stick to the CSI formatting, there will always be reasons to add your own. The first thing we need to look at is how to customize the Keynote list:

1. Save your model, and close out of Revit Architecture completely.

2. Using a text editor, open the file `C:\ProgramData\Autodesk\RAC 2014\Libraries\US Imperial\RevitKeynotes_Imperial_2004.txt` (`RevitKeynotes_Metric.txt`).

Note that your path may be different, especially on a company network.

 W A R N I N G   Before you start typing, be aware that when you need a separator between texts, you must press the Tab key. If you don't, the code won't work. Also, before you do this, be sure to make a copy of the original file.

---

3. Scroll down the list until you find the note 06 43 00.B1 ¾" Plywood Treads And Risers 06 43 00 (06430.B1 19mm Plywood Treads and Risers 06430).

4. Click at the end of the note, press Enter to start a new line, and add the row 06 43 00.B2 Custom Hardwood Stairs 06 43 00 (06430.B2 Custom Hardwood Stairs 06430) (see Figure 11.92).

5. Save the file as **Revit Keynotes Custom.txt**, and close the text editor.

6. Open Revit Architecture.

7. Open your project file.

8. Go to the Keynote settings, and browse to the new .txt file.

9. In the Project Browser, go to the Level 1 floor plan.

10. On the Tag panel of the Annotate tab, click Keynote ➤ User Keynote.

11. Pick the stairs, as shown in Figure 11.93.

FIGURE 11.92: Adding the row 06 43 00.B2 Custom Hardwood Stairs 06 43 00

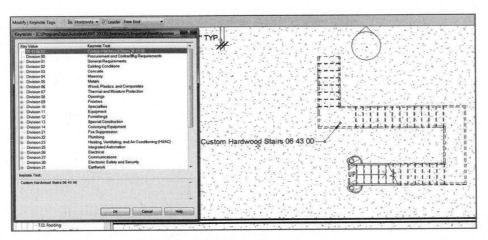

FIGURE 11.93: Picking the stairs to place the keynote

12. In the Keynotes dialog box, your new keynote is at the top of the list (see Figure 11.93).

13. Pick the new keynote.

14. Click OK.

The stairs now have a custom keynote.

You have every kind of tag imaginable placed in your model, but you need to create one more legend to close the chapter: a keynote legend.

Creating Keynote Legends

Creating keynote legends is similar to creating schedules. Sometimes there is a fine line between what a schedule is and what a legend is. Keynotes almost seem to fall between these two concepts. Either way, follow this procedure to create a keynote legend:

1. On the View tab, click Legends ➤ Keynote Legend.

2. The name Keynote Legend is fine, so click OK in the dialog that appears.

3. In the Keynote Legend Properties dialog, only two fields are available, and they're both added to the legend. All you need to do is click OK, and the legend is created (see Figure 11.94).

Keynote Legend	
Key Value	Keynote Text
06 43 00.B2	Custom Hardwood Stairs 06 43 00
26 51 00.B2	Wall Mounted Incandescent Fixture

FIGURE 11.94: The new keynote legend

Well, that was easy! As mentioned before, if the data is there, it isn't hard to create a query such as this to display the information.

One more item to address is where Revit looks for information regarding keynotes: in the settings listings.

Keynote Settings

To find the keynote settings, on the Annotate tab, click the drop-down arrow on the bottom of the Tag panel. This will allow you to click the Keynoting Settings button to open the Keynoting Settings dialog, as shown in Figure 11.95.

FIGURE 11.95: Keynoting Settings displays where the keynotes are configured.

Although you aren't going to change anything, it's noteworthy that the default path is by library location. This is good because when you upgrade Revit and have a custom keynote file, you can move it to the same directory, and Revit will read it into the model.

By specifying Numbering Method as By Keynote, you'll share only one keynote legend. If you specify By Sheet, you can then drag the legend onto multiple sheets, and only the keynotes that are visible on that specific sheet will be included in the legend. We'll cover this process in further detail in Chapter 14.

As you can see, many items can be tagged, keynoted, and scheduled. If you feel that you could use more practice, go ahead and create some more schedules, tags, and keynotes.

Are You Experienced?

Now you can...

☑ **create several different types of schedules**

☑ **add custom fields to the schedules that calculate values**

☑ **create material takeoffs that give you up-to-the-second information as you add items to the model**

☑ **create legends by using a blank view and basically drafting items into the model**

☑ import AutoCAD-generated data to create a legend that looks exactly like your CAD

☑ create drawing sheets, add a schedule, and manipulate a schedule to fit on the sheet

☑ add tags to the model in addition to the tags that were automatically added when you placed the components

☑ place tags that reach into a component and display different materials

☑ create custom tags to display any information

Detailing

Simply put, if detailing doesn't work, then you'll use the Autodesk®
Revit® Architecture software only as a schematic design application. It's
imperative that you can detail efficiently in Revit. When firms fail in their
attempt to use Revit, it's because of detailing. In fact, many who have bought
this book may jump straight to this chapter. And why is that? It's because
many people (including me) buy into the concept of really cool 3D perspectives and one-button modeling.

▶ **Working with line weights**

▶ **Drafting on top of the detail**

▶ **Adding notes**

▶ **Creating blank drafting views**

Working with Line Weights

When you understand Revit, you find out immediately that the real hurdle in getting it to work lies in the detailing. Sure, you can cut sections and create callouts, but how do you add that fine level of detailing needed to produce a set of documents that you're willing to stamp and sign? This chapter addresses the issues surrounding detailing.

The first thing that comes to mind when dealing with CAD standards is line weights, right? In AutoCAD® it's layers, in MicroStation it's levels, but on paper, it's line weights that control 75 percent of a company's standards. As you'll learn in this chapter, Revit can be a good 2D drafting application as well. As you learn how to control line weights in the 3D elements, you can also control line weights, well, line by line.

 N O T E   Metric users should not type in mm or other metric abbreviations when entering amounts suggested in the exercises. Revit will not accept such abbreviations. Simply enter the number provided within the parentheses.

To begin, open the file on which you've been following along. If you didn't complete the previous chapter, go to the book's web page at www.sybex.com/go/revit2014ner. From there, you can browse to the Chapter 12 folder and find the file called NER-12.rvt.

The objective of this procedure is to format the line weights and to see where and how they're read by Revit:

1. In the Project Browser, open the building section called Roof Taper Section. Zoom in to the wall at the left.

2. Notice that the perimeters of the walls and the roof are extremely heavy in contrast to the finer lines that divide the submaterials. This is what you'll change. On the Settings panel of the Manage tab, click the Object Styles button at left on the Ribbon, as shown in Figure 12.1.

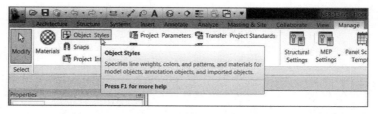

FIGURE 12.1:   Object Styles is located at left on the Manage tab.

3. In the Object Styles dialog is a list of every object category available in Revit. The first items you want to change are the roofs. In the Category column, scroll down until you see Roofs, as shown in Figure 12.2.

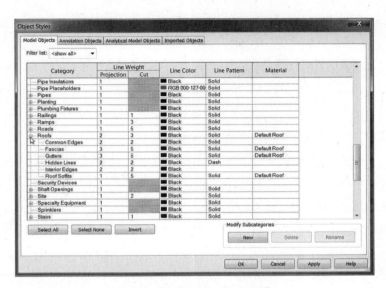

FIGURE 12.2: Changing the object line weights

Glancing up at the headers that describe the columns, you see the Line Weight column. This column is divided into two sections: Projection and Cut. The Projection column controls the line weights of objects as they're viewed in plan or elevation. The Cut column controls the line weights as they're shown in section. So, to reiterate, *projection* means plan and elevation, and *cut* means section. Your objective is to modify the line weight for both the cut and the projection of the roof.

4. In the Roofs row, change the Cut value to 3 (see Figure 12.2).

5. Click the plus sign next to Roofs to expand the category.

6. All the sub-elements are shown, and you can control the line weights accordingly. Change the Cut value of Fascias to 5.

7. Change the Cut value for Gutters to 5.

8. Change the Cut value for Roof Soffits to 5 (again, see Figure 12.2).

9. Find Floors, and change Cut Line Weight to 3.

10. Find Walls, and change Cut Line Weight to 3.

11. Click OK, and you'll see the change to your outline (see Figure 12.3).

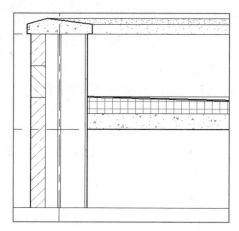

FIGURE 12.3:   Your section's outline should begin looking a lot better.

IT'S TEMPLATE TIME!

Many of the procedures covered in the first section of this chapter lend them-selves well to the topic of standards and templates. You need to change the line weights of objects in a Revit template.

Drafting on Top of the Detail

As mentioned before, Revit provides a good number of 2D details that you can insert at any time. When Revit doesn't have the component you need, you can always create one. It isn't that hard to do.

In this section, you'll physically create a detail. The procedures you'll apply consist of adding detail components, linework, and filled regions, and doing some good old-fashioned drafting!

Using Predefined Detail Components

The first procedure focuses on inserting predefined detail components. The great thing about this is that you'll do nothing you haven't done repeatedly throughout this book—it's just a matter of finding the right button to get started:

1. Make sure you're still in the detail called Roof Taper Section.

2. On the Detail panel of the Annotate tab, click Component ➤ Detail Component, and then click the Load Family button as shown in Figure 12.4.

3. Browse to the Detail Items directory. (It's located in the US Imperial Library directory.)

4. Open the Div 01-General folder.

5. Click the file called Break Line.rfa.

6. Click Open.

7. In the Type Selector of the Properties dialog, be sure Break Line is selected, as shown in Figure 12.5.

8. Press the spacebar twice. (This flips the break line into the correct orientation.)

9. Pick a point similar to the one shown in Figure 12.5.

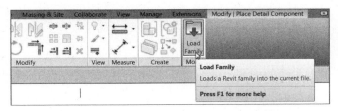

FIGURE 12.4: The Load Family button on the Mode panel of the Modify | Place Detail Component tab

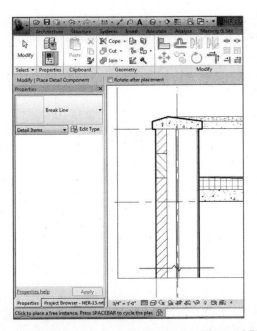

FIGURE 12.5: Placing the break line and flipping the component

The next step is simply to start drafting. As mentioned earlier, you're only going to get so far with 3D modeling before you have to take matters into your own hands and draft. You can approach this in Revit by taking the parts of the detail you want to keep and hiding the rest. After you hide portions of the detail, it's time to begin adding your own ingredients, such as detail components and lines.

THIS FLIPPIN' BREAK LINE IS BACKWARD!

If you forgot to flip the break line as you were inserting it and it's masking the wrong region, that's okay. Press Esc, and then select the break line. Now you can press the spacebar twice to flip the break line, as shown in the following image:

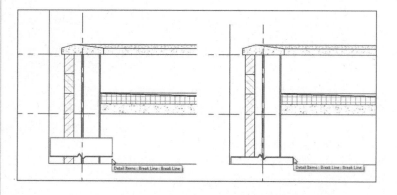

Masking Regions

To let you hide portions of the detail, Revit has added a nice feature called a *masking region*. Instead of wrestling with items over which you ultimately have little or no control, you can hide these items to make way for your detailing.

To learn how to apply a masking region, follow these steps:

1. Make sure you're still in the detail called Roof Taper Section.

2. On the Detail panel of the Annotate tab, click Region ➤ Masking Region, as shown in Figure 12.6.

3. The Line Style panel offers some choices in the subcategory. Choose <Invisible Lines>, as shown in Figure 12.7.

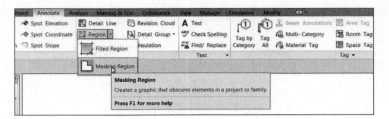

FIGURE 12.6:   Region a Masking Region on the Annotate tab

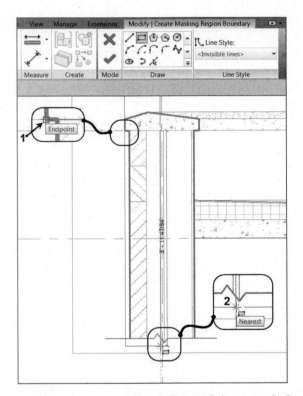

FIGURE 12.7:   Click the Rectangle button on the Draw panel, and place a masking region as shown.

 NOTE   By selecting <Invisible Lines>, you ensure that the perimeter of the masking region won't be visible when you exit Sketch Mode.

4. Again on the Draw panel, click the Rectangle button.

5. Draw a rectangle at the approximate points shown in Figure 12.7.

6. Click the Finish Edit Mode button on the Mode panel.

The area is now masked. The problem is, though, that some areas, such as the break, may be a little *too* masked. The next procedure walks through changing the display order of a detail's objects:

1. If the break line is behind the masking region, select the break line, as shown in Figure 12.8.

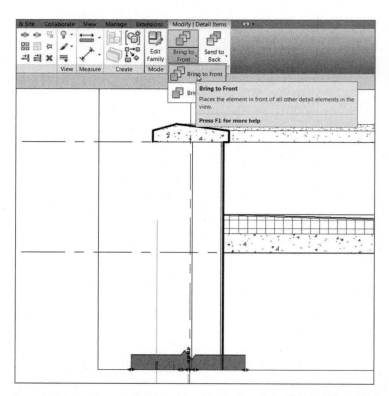

FIGURE 12.8:   Click the Bring To Front button on the Modify | Detail Items tab after selecting the break line.

2. On the Modify | Detail Items tab, click the Bring To Front button (see Figure 12.8).

Your detail should now look like Figure 12.9.

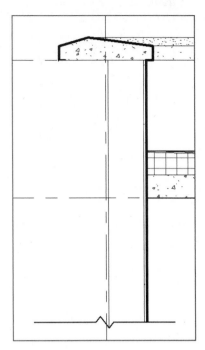

FIGURE 12.9:   The detail with the completed masking region

The next step is to add a brick face. Yes, Revit showed the brick before you masked it, but you need to show coursing, as well as how the façade is tied back to the wall. To do this, you'll use a function called a *repeating detail*.

Repeating Details

Revit has a technique that allows you to add a detail component as a group. You do this by basically drawing a line; Revit then adds the detail in an array based on the points you pick.

To learn how to add a repeating detail, follow this procedure:

1. On the Detail panel of the Annotate tab, select Component ➢ Repeating Detail Component, as shown in Figure 12.10.

2. In the Properties dialog, choose Repeating Detail : Brick from the Type Selector, as shown in Figure 12.10.

3. Pick the point labeled 1 in Figure 12.11.

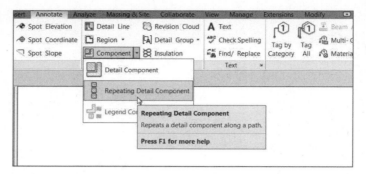

FIGURE 12.10: Select Component ➤ Repeating Detail Component.

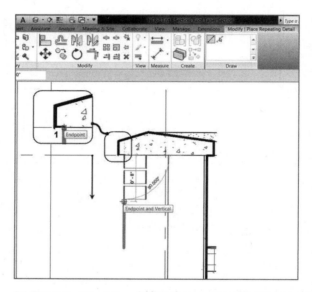

FIGURE 12.11: Adding the repeating detail based on the points shown

T I P   Picking that point will be a little harder now that it's not there! The objective is to draw an actual façade based on the existing points where the Revit-generated brick once resided. When you hover your mouse over where the brick was previously, the masked detail appears. When it does, you'll see the point you need to pick.

4. After you pick the first point, move your cursor down the view.

5. The brick is facing the wrong side. Press the spacebar to flip the brick into the wall (see Figure 12.11).

6. Pick the endpoint 8″ (203mm) down, as shown in Figure 12.11, so that three copies of the brick section are placed.

Your detail should look like Figure 12.12.

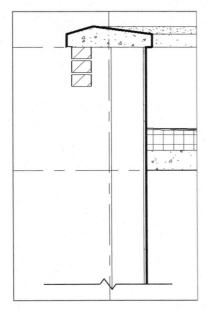

FIGURE 12.12:   The first repeating detail

Let's keep going with the repeating detail. The problem you're facing is that you need to deal with the soldier course in the exterior wall. You can add that in a moment. Right now, complete the brick down past the break line.

If you feel as though you're getting the hang of adding the repeating brick detail, go ahead and add the second repeating detail. If you would like some instruction, follow along:

1. Click the Component ➢ Repeating Detail Component button on the Detail panel on the Annotate tab.

2. Pick point 1, as shown in Figure 12.13.

3. Press the spacebar.

4. Pull the cursor straight down, and pick point 2 (see Figure 12.13). Make sure you pick the second point well past the break line, or the brick will stop short.

> Remember, you can add a second repeating brick detail by right-clicking the first one you added and selecting Create Similar.
>
>

5. Press Esc twice. Look at Figure 12.14. Does your detail look the same?

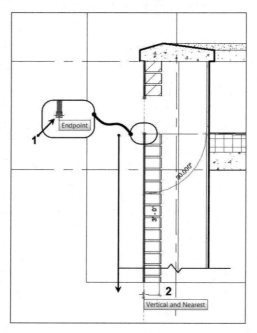

FIGURE 12.13: Picking two points

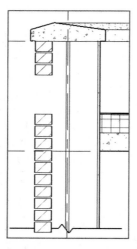

FIGURE 12.14: The bricks are being placed.

6. If the repeating detail is obscuring the break line, select the break line.

7. On the Arrange panel, click the Bring To Front button. The repeating detail is now behind the break line.

The next step is to add the soldier course. You'll do this the same way you added the break line. In this respect, Revit offers a good library broken down into the CSI format.

To add the soldier course, follow along:

1. On the Detail panel on the Annotate tab, click the Component ➢ Detail Component button.

2. In the Type Selector in the Properties dialog, select Brick Standard : Soldier & Plan.

3. Press the spacebar until it's flipped as shown in Figure 12.15, and place the new detail component into the model as shown.

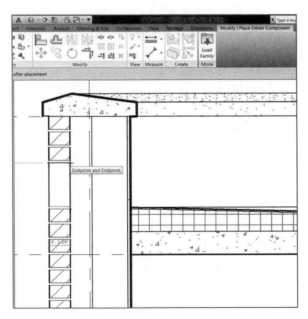

FIGURE 12.15:   Placing the new detail component

   TIP   If you haven't noticed, when you click the Component ➢ Repeating Detail Component button, you always go to the Families ➢ Detail Items directory in the Project Browser. This may go without saying, but it took a few months for me to understand this simple concept.

Well, the soldier course is in place, but that fat line weight is horrendous. It would be nice if everything that came out of the Revit box looked nice and met your specifications—but alas, that isn't the case. Let's modify this component to make it presentable.

Modifying a Detail Component

Right about now is when every CAD/BIM manager around the globe raises an eyebrow—for good reason. Revit allows you to modify a component by actually opening the file! But don't worry; you have to issue a Save As command to save the detail.

The objectives of the following procedure are to create a texture on the brick detail and to use a line weight that the user can control in the model:

1. If you still have a command running, click the Modify button to the left of the Ribbon, or press the Esc key.

2. Select the Bricks - Standard Soldier & Plan family that you just placed.

3. On the Modify | Detail Items tab, click the Edit Family button, as shown in Figure 12.16.

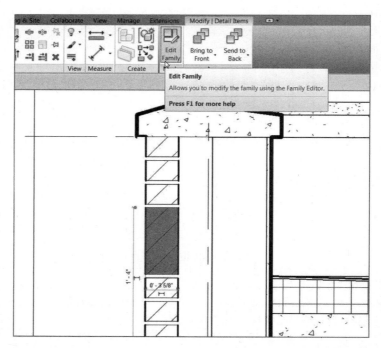

FIGURE 12.16: Open the family for editing after selecting the detail component.

4. The next dialog may ask you if you want to open this file to edit it. Click Yes if you get that message.

The detail component family is now open. It's time to operate, Doctor. The next set of procedures will focus on modifying the linework of the brick and adding what is called a *filled region*.

Modifying Filled Regions

A *filled region* is similar to a masking region in that you apply both in the same manner. A filled region, however, contains a hatch pattern that is visible when the region is completed. This is how you hatch in Revit. It takes the place of the conventional hatch command found in AutoCAD and MicroStation.

The objective of the next procedure is to modify the filled region that makes up the brick. You'll also use the region's outline to define the perimeter and the texture of the brick itself:

1. Go to the Revit application button, and Select Save As ➢ Family.

2. Call the new family **Brick - Soldier**.

3. Click the Family Types button, as shown in Figure 12.17.

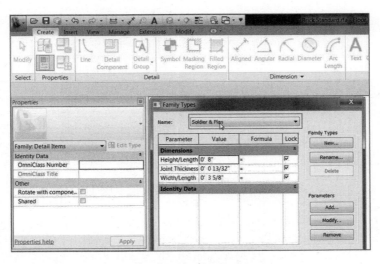

FIGURE 12.17: Cleaning out the extra types

4. In the Name menu, make sure Running Section is selected.

5. Click the Delete button at right in the dialog.

6. Select Rowlock from the list, and delete that type as well.

7. Click OK.

8. Select the line that is hovering over the top of the brick, and mirror it to the bottom so you have a line above and a line below the brick, as shown in Figure 12.18.

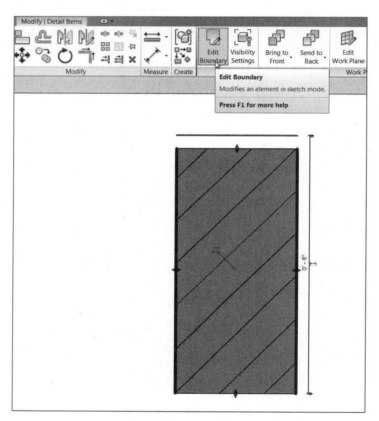

FIGURE 12.18:   Editing the boundary of the filled region

9. Select one of the heavy lines that form the outline of the brick (see Figure 12.18). Revit indicates that this is a filled region, as revealed in the tooltip that appears when you hover your pointer over one of the boundaries.

10. On the Mode panel of the Modify | Detail Items tab, click the Edit Boundary button (see Figure 12.18).

11. Delete the two thick, vertical lines.

 N O T E   As you may notice, changing a line's property is almost the same as in AutoCAD. You select the line and then change its line type in the Type Selector.

12. On the Draw panel, select the Line button, as shown in Figure 12.19.

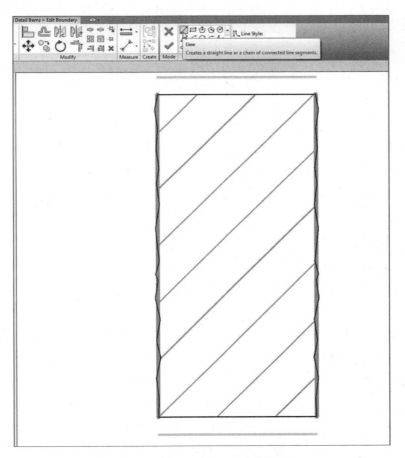

FIGURE 12.19: Adding a texture to the brick family

WHERE SHOULD YOU SAVE THIS?

When you clicked the Save icon, Revit didn't save over the original file. You're forced to perform a Save As. You have three choices:

▶ If the file isn't write-protected and you have administrative access to the original folder, you can save over the original file. (Do I need to mention that you had better make sure this is what you want to do?)

▶ Save the file as a different file, either in the same directory or somewhere else.

▶ Don't save the file at all, and load it into your project. Revit will still update the project with the changes even if you didn't save the family file.

You can even close out of the family file and not save any changes. Your model will still hold the changes. If you choose to edit the file at a later date, you can select the family in the model and click Edit Family. Revit will open a copy of the modified family.

13. In the Line Style panel that appears, select Detail Items.

14. Draw a series of jagged lines on the right and left of the brick, as shown in Figure 12.19.

15. After you finish sketching the texture, click Edit Type.

16. Change the background from Opaque to Transparent, as shown in Figure 12.20.

17. Click OK.

18. Click Finish Edit Mode. Your brick should resemble Figure 12.21.

Next you'll add a mortar joint to the bottom of the brick. You simply add drafting lines:

1. On the Create tab, click the Line button.

2. On the Draw panel, click the Start-End-Radius Arc button.

3. Draw two arcs to the left and right of the top of the brick, as shown in Figure 12.22.

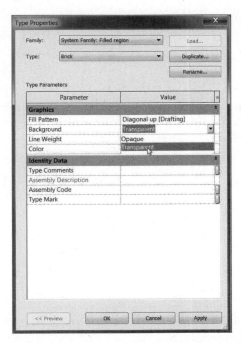

FIGURE 12.20:   Changing the background to Transparent

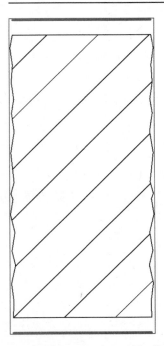

FIGURE 12.21:   The finished soldier

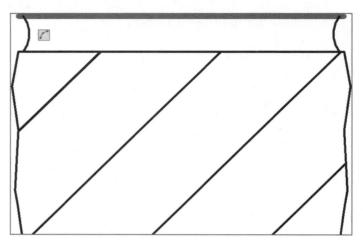

FIGURE 12.22:   Adding the mortar joint

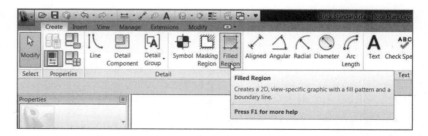

N O T E   By putting all the lines on the Detail Items line type, you tell Revit that you don't want to specify a line weight here. Rather, Revit should let you specify the line weight by changing the Detail Items in the Object Properties dialog after you load the detail back into the model.

The next step is to add shading underneath the brick pattern. To do this, you'll create an entirely new filled region and add it to the brick by tracing over the existing filled region:

1. On the Detail panel of the Create tab, click the Filled Region button, as shown in Figure 12.23.

2. In the Properties dialog, click the Edit Type button, and make sure Type is Solid Fill - Black, as shown in Figure 12.24.

FIGURE 12.23:   Click the Filled Region button on the Detail panel.

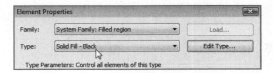

FIGURE 12.24:   Changing the region to Solid Fill - Black

3. Click Duplicate.

4. Call the new region **Light Shade**.

5. Click OK.

6. In the Fill Pattern row, click into the Solid Fill [Drafting] field. Click the […] button in the right corner.

7. You can select any hatch pattern you wish. Make sure Solid Fill is selected, as shown in Figure 12.25, and click OK.

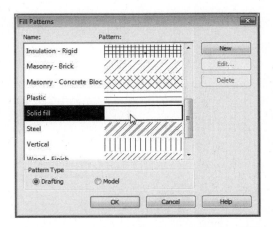

FIGURE 12.25:   Select the Solid Fill pattern, and click OK.

8. In the Color row is a button labeled Black. It includes a little black box icon. Pick the black box.

9. In the Color dialog, click the Gray tile, as shown in Figure 12.26. (The color is actually RGB 192-192-192.)

10. Click OK twice.

11. On the Draw panel, click the Pick Lines button, as shown in Figure 12.27.

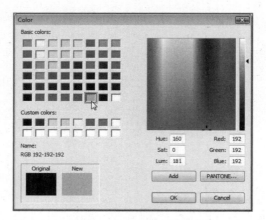

FIGURE 12.26: Selecting the gray color (RGB 192-192-192)

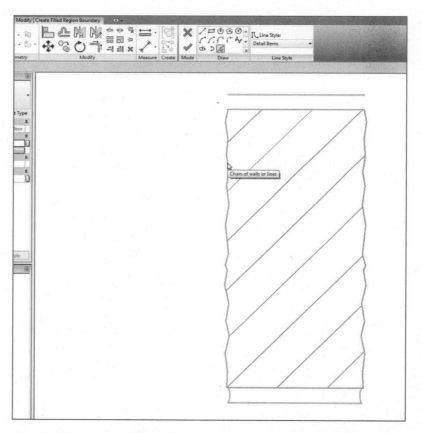

FIGURE 12.27: Press Tab to select the chain of lines, as shown here.

12. Hover your cursor over one of the jagged lines of the brick face, and press the Tab key. All the lines you're trying to trace are highlighted.

13. Pick any one of the lines (see Figure 12.27). Revit draws the region based on these points.

14. On the Mode panel, click Finish Edit Mode, and then press Esc. Your brick should look like Figure 12.28.

You may find that nothing happens when you press Tab. If this is the case, click any location in the view. Revit needs to focus on the view. You can also hold down the wheel button on your mouse to pan a little. This will also switch the focus from the Options bar to the view window.

FIGURE 12.28: The solid pattern covers the previous pattern. You'll fix this in a moment.

15. When the filled region is in place, select it by clicking the boundary.

16. On the Arrange panel, click the Send To Back button, as shown in Figure 12.29.

17. Press Esc. Your brick should now look like Figure 12.30.

18. Click the Save icon.

19. On the Family Editor panel on the Create tab, click the Load Into Project button, as shown in Figure 12.31.

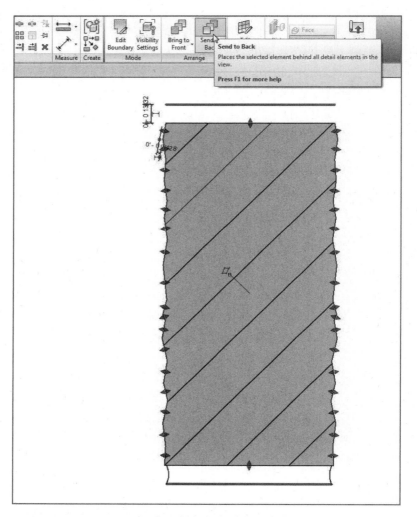

FIGURE 12.29: Sending the light shade to the back

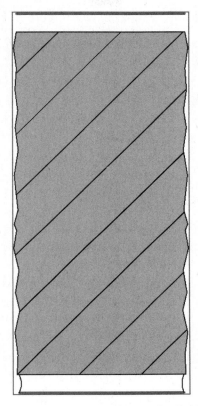

FIGURE 12.30: The finished brick

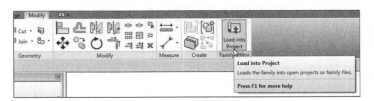

FIGURE 12.31: The Load Into Project button

20. Place the new soldier to the left of the wall.

21. Select the smooth, boring, existing soldier.

22. In the Type Selector, change it to Brick - Soldier: Soldier & Plan.

23. Delete the extra brick. Your wall should look like Figure 12.32.

24. Save the model.

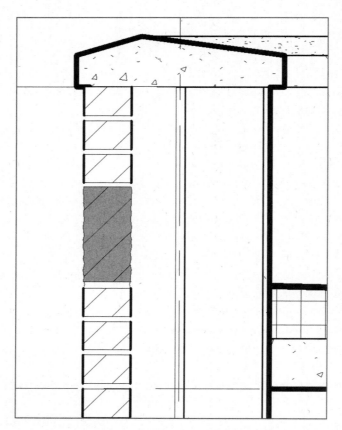

FIGURE 12.32:   The new soldier brick in the model

The next group of procedures focuses on editing the bricks used in the repeating detail. You certainly want the same face texture, and it would be nice if there was a mortar joint between them.

Before you modify the bricks, let's explore how a repeating detail is created. The objective of the next procedure is to discover how a repeating detail works and how you can create a new one:

1. Make sure you're in the detail called Roof Taper Section.

2. Select one of the repeating details, as shown in Figure 12.33.

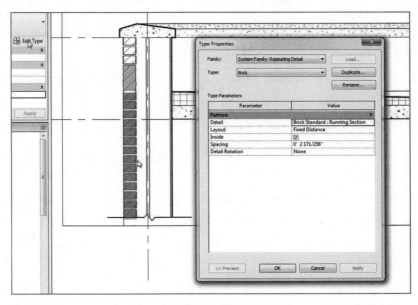

FIGURE 12.33: Click the Edit Type button after selecting one of the brick repeating details.

3. In the Properties dialog, click Edit Type, as shown at the upper left in Figure 12.33.

4. Click into the detail Value list. Every detail component listed in your model is available. The detail component being used here is Brick Standard : Running Section.

   You can change the spacing and the patterns of how the repeating detail will perform.

5. Click Cancel.

The next objective is to modify the specific detail component that the repeating detail is using. To do so, you must add an instance of the detail component (in this case, Brick Standard : Running Section) and then edit the family. After you load it back into the model, the repeating detail will be up to date.

If you would like to give it a shot and do it on your own, go ahead. If you would rather have some guidance, follow along:

1. On the Detail panel of the Annotate tab, click the Component ➤ Detail Component button.

2. In the Type Selector in the Properties dialog, pick the Brick Standard : Running Section detail component. (Remember, this was the component that you discovered the repeating detail was using.)

3. Place the detail component off to the side of the wall, as shown in Figure 12.34.

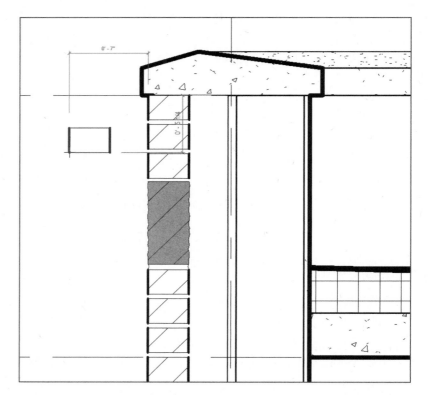

FIGURE 12.34: Place the Brick Standard : Running Section detail component off to the side. You'll delete this occurrence of the component later.

4. Press Esc twice, or click Modify.

5. Select the Brick Standard : Running Section that you just inserted.

6. On the Mode panel, click the Edit Family button.

7. Select the filled region.

8. On the Mode panel, click Edit Boundary.

9. Delete the right and left thick lines.

10. On the Draw panel, click the Line button.

11. In the Type Selector in the Properties dialog, click Detail Items.

12. Draw the jagged lines on both sides, as shown in Figure 12.35.

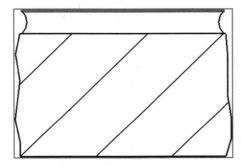

FIGURE 12.35: Draw the textured face while you're in the Edit mode for the filled region. Draw the arcs for the mortar joint using lines.

13. Click Finish Edit Mode on the Mode panel.

14. On the Create tab, click the Line button.

15. On the Draw panel, click the Start-End-Radius Arc button.

16. On the Subcategory panel, be sure Detail Items is chosen from the Type Selector list.

17. Draw an arc on both sides of the brick (see Figure 12.35).

18. When you're finished, save the new brick as **Brick Standard**. You can also find this brick on the book's web page in Chapter 12. It's called `Brick Standard.rfa`.

19. On the Family Editor panel, click Load Into Project.

20. In the project, click to overwrite the family.

21. Delete the stray detail component you placed. (You were only using it for access to the family.)

Compare your detail to the detail in Figure 12.36.

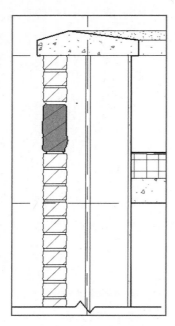

FIGURE 12.36:   The brick actually looks like brick!

Next, you'll anchor this façade back to the wall. You need to add two things: a structural relief angle above the soldier course, and a brick tieback to a lower course. Follow along:

1. On the Annotate tab, click the Component ➤ Detail Component button.

2. On the Mode panel, click the Load Family button.

3. Open the Detail items folder.

4. Select Div 05-Metals.

5. Select 051200-Structural Steel Framing.

6. Double-click the file AISC Angle Shapes-Section.rfa.

7. In the Type list, select L6×4×5/16 (152×102×8).

8. Click OK. You'll have to use the spacebar and flip controls to rotate and flip the instance.

9. Place it into the model, as shown in Figure 12.37.

10. Press Esc twice, or click Modify.

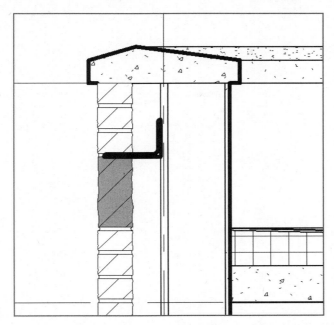

FIGURE 12.37: Placing the L6 × 4 × 5/16 (152 × 102 × 8) angle

Of course, the line weight is basically a blob, so you must modify the family in order for it to look accurate. The next procedure is almost a review of what you had to do to the bricks:

1. Select the angle.

2. On the Mode panel, click Edit Family.

3. In the Family Editor, select the filled region (the entire angle), and click Edit Boundary on the Mode panel.

4. Select all the lines that form the perimeter of the angle.

5. In the Type Selector in the Properties dialog, select Detail Items. (You're switching from Heavy Lines to Detail Items.)

6. On the Mode panel, click Finish Edit Mode.

7. On the Family Editor panel, click Load Into Project.

8. Click Overwrite The Existing Version.

9. Adjust the angle so it looks like Figure 12.38.

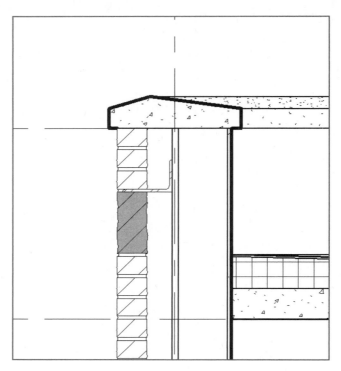

FIGURE 12.38: The angle in place and looking like an angle

The next step is to find a fastener to anchor the angle back to the wall's substrate. There is a problem, however. The type of bolt you need is a lag bolt that is power-driven from the exterior into the wall. Revit doesn't provide one out of the box. Luckily, the book you bought does! To find the lag bolt provided with the book, go to the book's web page, browse to the Chapter 12 folder, and find the file A307 Lag_Bolt-Side.rfa. Then follow along:

1. To load the lag bolt into your model, select the Insert tab and click the Load Family button. Browse to the directory where you put the A307 Lag_Bolt-Side.rfa file. Find the file, and click Open.

2. With the lag bolt loaded, click the Component ➢ Detail Component button on the Annotate tab.

3. Select A307 Lag_Bolt-Side : ¾″ from the Type Selector.

4. Insert the lag bolt into the angle, as shown in Figure 12.39.

5. Press Esc twice.

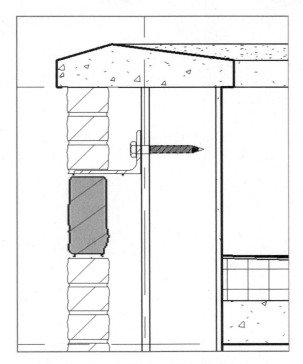

FIGURE 12.39: Inserting the lag bolt

Now you'll add a corrugated wall tie to the brick below the soldier course. Because the brick is a pretty good distance away from the wall, you first need to add some wood blocking to the model:

1. On the Insert tab, click the Load Family button.

2. Go to the `Detail Items` folder.

3. Select `Div 06-Wood And Plastic`.

4. Select `061100-Wood Framing`.

5. Click the file `Nominal Cut Lumber-Section.rfa`.

6. Select the 2×6 (51×152) type, and click OK.

7. Select the Annotate tab, click the Component ➤ Detail Component button, and place the 2×6 (51×152) into the wall, as shown in Figure 12.40.

8. Press Esc twice.

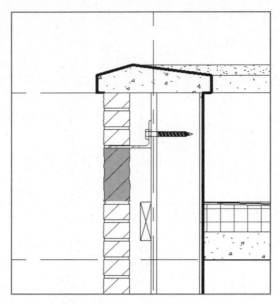

FIGURE 12.40: Adding the wood blocking

9. Select the blocking you just added, and right-click it.

10. Select Override Graphics In View ➤ By Element.

11. In the Projection Lines category, change the weight to 2.

12. Click OK. Your blocking should look like Figure 12.40.

The next step is to add the corrugated wall tie. You'll do this in the same manner, except that it's located in a different directory:

1. On the Insert tab, click the Load Family button.

2. Go to the Detail Items folder.

3. Select Div 04-Masonry.

4. Select 040500-Common Work Results For Masonry.

5. Select 040519-Masonry Anchorage And Reinforcing.

6. Select the file called Corrugated Wall Tie-Section.rfa.

7. Use the Detail Component button to place the wall tie into your model, as shown in Figure 12.41.

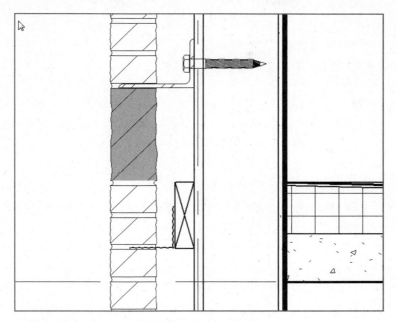

FIGURE 12.41:   Placing the corrugated wall tie

8. Press Esc twice, or click Modify.

Now you'll add some blocking along the concrete parapet cap. You also need additional blocking along the lag bolts. If you would like, go ahead and copy the 2×6 (51×152) blocking around the model to mimic the figure at the end of this series of steps. Or you can follow along:

1. Select the 2×6 (51×152) blocking.

2. On the Modify | Detail Items tab, click the Copy command.

3. Pick the base point of the upper-right corner.

4. Copy the blocking.

5. Select the new blocking and rotate it into position. (You'll also have to nudge the blocking, using the arrow keys to center it into the wall.)

6. Copy the blocking down to double it, as shown in Figure 12.43.

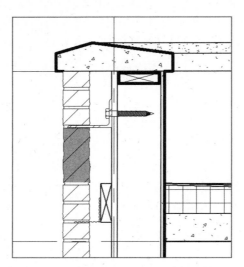

FIGURE 12.42:   Rotating the blocking after copying it

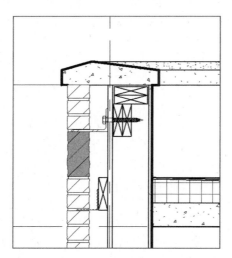

FIGURE 12.43:   Copy the blocking as shown.

7. Copy and rotate the blocking to the positions shown in Figure 12.43 to allow for support of the lag bolt.

8. Select all the blocking that has the heavy line weight, right-click, and choose Override Graphics In View ➢ By Element. Change the Projection Line Weight to 2.

9. Compare your detail to Figure 12.43.

When you're drafting over a true section of your model, it's always good to try to use as much of the graphical information from the actual model as possible. For example, the ¾" (16mm) void you see the bolt going through is actually ¾" (16mm) plywood sheathing. For some reason, the default plywood material has its cut pattern set to None. Let's fix this:

1. Select the wall.

2. Click Edit Type.

3. Click the Edit button in the Structure row.

4. Click into the Material column in row 5. It's the substrate row, and the material is –Plywood, Sheathing.

5. When you click –Plywood, Sheathing, you see a tiny […] button. Click it.

6. On the Graphics tab, click into the Pattern field in the Cut Pattern category, and change the pattern to Plywood, as shown in Figure 12.44.

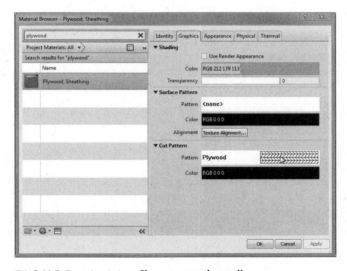

FIGURE 12.44:   Show us your plywood!

7. Double-click the plywood pattern (see Figure 12.44 for the location of the cursor).

8. Click the Edit button.

9. Select the Align With Element drop-down for the Orientation In Host Layers field.

10. Click OK three times to get back to the model.

Now that you have a good grasp of adding detail components, you need to learn how to control the line weight so that the outlines of the bricks look a little bolder.

If you remember, some of the detail components were modified based on the line weight of the filled region perimeter. This thickness was changed from Heavy Lines to Detail Items. You need to set Detail Items to a thickness you can live with:

1. On the Manage tab, click the Object Styles button.

2. Scroll down the list until you see Detail Items.

3. Change the Projection Line Weight to 2, as shown in Figure 12.45.

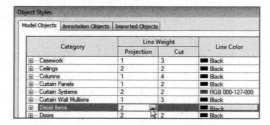

FIGURE 12.45: Changing the Detail Items Projection Line Weight to 2

4. Click OK. Your detail now has a bolder perimeter.

N O T E   It's a great idea to plot this detail right now. Although Revit does a nice job of letting you see the contrasting line weights on the screen, it may be a different story at the plotter. Do yourself a favor, and make sure this is the line weight you want.

Another item left to explore in terms of adding detail to a view is the simple concept of drawing lines.

Drawing Detail Lines

As I mentioned before, in Revit you can simply draw lines. You can only get so far with detail components, and then you need to pick up the pencil and add your lines.

The next set of procedures will focus on adding lines to your model. Then we'll look deeper into how these lines are created and modified:

1. In the Project Browser, make sure you're in Sections (Building Sections : Roof Taper Section).

2. On the Detail panel of the Annotate tab, click the Detail Line button, as shown in Figure 12.46.

3. In the Line Style menu, select Medium Lines, as shown in Figure 12.47.

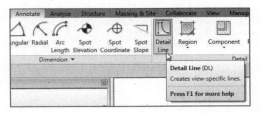

FIGURE 12.46: Click the Detail Line button on the Annotate tab.

FIGURE 12.47: Select the Medium Lines choice in the Line Style menu.

4. On the Options bar, deselect the Chain option.

N O T E   Does this seem familiar? If you're used to the AutoCAD method of drafting, this is the same as starting the Line command and choosing the correct layer.

5. Draw a line, as shown in Figure 12.48. Be sure to use your endpoint and perpendicular snaps.

6. With the Line command still running, click the Pick Lines icon on the Draw panel.

7. Change Offset to **1 1/2″** (38mm), as shown in Figure 12.49.

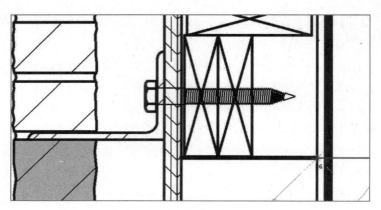

FIGURE 12.48: Drawing a medium line

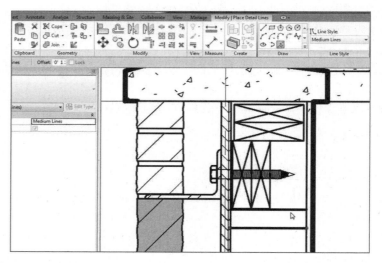

FIGURE 12.49: Offsetting the line down 1 1/2″ (38mm) to create a second line

8. Offset the line you just drew down 1 1/2″ (38mm) (see Figure 12.49).

9. With the Line command still running, change to Thin Lines in the Line Style panel.

10. In the Draw panel, click the Line button.

11. Change the offset to 0.

12. Draw the *X* for the blocking, as shown in Figure 12.50.

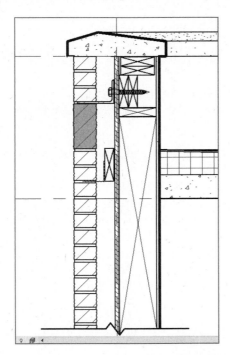

FIGURE 12.50: Adding the detail to indicate studs and plates by using detail lines

13. Copy the blocking down to form a double plate (see Figure 12.50).

14. Draw another *X* below the plates to indicate a stud (again, see Figure 12.50).

So what makes a Medium Line medium and a Thin Line thin? This is a part of Revit over which you need to have full control. After all, your biggest challenge will be getting your plotted sheets to match your old CAD-plotted sheets. Specifying line weights is crucial.

Specifying Drafting Line Weights

Just as in CAD, you wouldn't dare to draw even a single line if you didn't know the proper layer on which it was being drafted, right? Why should Revit be any different?

The objective of the next procedure is to investigate where the line weights are stored and how they relate to the lines you're drawing:

1. On the Manage tab, choose Additional Settings ➤ Line Styles.

2. In the Line Styles dialog, expand the Lines category by clicking the plus sign next to Lines.

   Some of the line styles were generated in AutoCAD. These line styles were imported when you brought in the legend back in Chapter 11, "Schedules and Tags."

3. Click into the Wide Lines category, and change the value from 5 to 4, as shown in Figure 12.51.

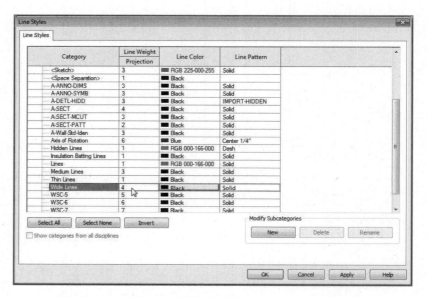

FIGURE 12.51: Changing Wide Lines from 5 to 4

4. Click OK. Wide Lines in all project views will now show the new line weight.

The next item to tackle is the fact that this detail looks naked without any text or dimensions added to it. Although you've applied both of these items in past chapters, you need to use them because they're relevant to detailing.

WHAT DO 5 AND 4 REPRESENT?

In Revit, line weights are sorted from thinnest to heaviest. You can add additional line weights, but I recommend that you stick to the 16 available. To see where these settings are stored, choose Additional Settings ➢ Line Weights. In the Line Weights dialog, the numbers 1 through 16 are listed. These numbers represent what you see in the Line Styles dialog. Also notice that the thicker line weights degrade in thickness as the scale is reduced (see the following graphic):

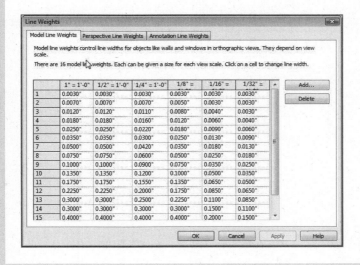

Adding Notes

In Revit, adding notes to a section can take on a whole different meaning than in CAD. You may remember back in Chapter 11 when you were able to specify materials and then tag them in a plan. Well, you can do the same thing in a detail.

Or, if you wish, adding notes to a detail can be exactly as it was back in CAD. Sometimes, sticking to the tried-and-true isn't such a bad thing.

The objective of the next set of procedures is to add notes by simply leadering in some text.

Adding Textual Notations

We're duplicating efforts with text to drive home the fact that Revit lets you add text regardless of the view and also regardless of the scale. Text in a plan is the same as text in a detail, and you'll prove it in the next procedure:

1. On the Annotate tab, click the Text button.

2. The next three steps use the Format panel of the Modify | Place Text tab (see Figure 12.52). Click the Align Right button.

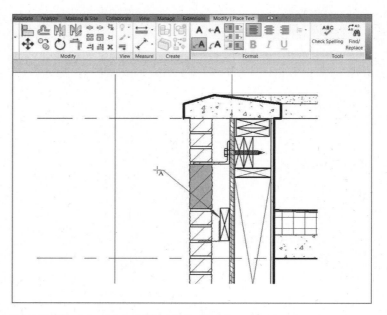

FIGURE 12.52: Adding the leadered text

3. Again, on the Modify | Place Text tab, click the Two Segments leader (the uppercase A in the lower-left corner of the Format panel; see Figure 12.52).

4. Also on the Format panel, click the Leader At Top Right button.

5. In the section, pick the first point of the leader at the top of the brick tie detail (shown in Figure 12.52).

6. Pick the second point above and to the left of the first point (shown in Figure 12.52).

7. Pick the third point for the second segment (as shown in Figure 12.52).

8. Type the note **CORRUGATED BRICK TIE ON 2X6 BLOCKING**.

9. Click off the text into another part of the model, and your text justifies to the leader.

10. Press Esc twice.

11. Select the text.

12. Pick the grip to the left, and drag the box to resemble Figure 12.53. The text wraps.

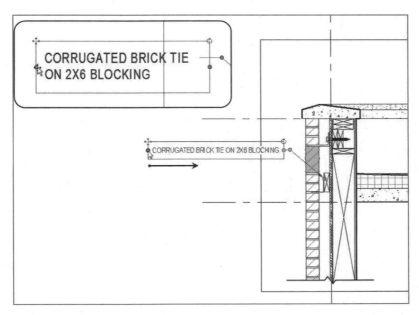

FIGURE 12.53: Wrapping the text

13. Save the model.

These steps are the most common procedure for adding detail to a model. In other words, take what you can from the model, and then add linework and detail components to the view. However, eventually you'll find yourself in a situation where you would rather draft your detail from scratch. You can do this as well, as you'll see in the next section.

Creating Blank Drafting Views

Over the years, Revit has been labeled as a "poor drafting application." This is unfortunate, because it can be a very good drafting application when given the chance. The only challenge is to figure out where to start!

The objective of the next procedure is to create a blank view and then simply learn how to draw lines:

1. On the View tab, click the Drafting View button, as shown in Figure 12.54.

FIGURE 12.54:   Click the Drafting View button on the View tab.

2. In the New Drafting View dialog, name the new view **TYPICAL WALL TERMINATION**.

3. Change the scale to 3/4″ = 1′–0″ (1:20 for the metric users). (See Figure 12.55.)

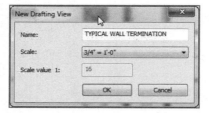

FIGURE 12.55:   Changing the view name and scale

4. Click OK.

You're now in a completely blank canvas. Anything you draw here is truly drafting, and it isn't tied back to the model at all.

The objective of the next procedure is to start adding lines and more detail components. The item you'll draft is a detail showing a flexible top track of a metal-stud partition:

1. On the Annotate tab, click the Detail Line button.

2. In the Properties dialog, click Medium Lines.

3. Draw a horizontal line about 4′–7″ (1375mm) long, as shown in Figure 12.56.

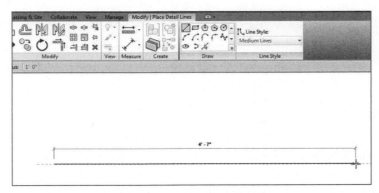

FIGURE 12.56: Drawing a detail line approximately 4′–7″ (1375mm)

4. With the Detail Lines command still running, change the Offset setting in the Options bar to 8″ (200mm).

5. Using the two endpoints of the first line, draw another line below.

GET DOWN THERE

Remember, if your line is above the first line you drew, press the spacebar to flip the line down below the first, as shown in this image:

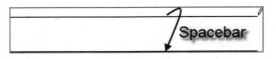

6. On the Draw panel, click the Pick Lines icon.

7. Again, on the Options bar, change Offset to **1 1/2"** (38mm).

8. Offset the bottom line down 1 1/2" (38mm). Your detail should look like Figure 12.57.

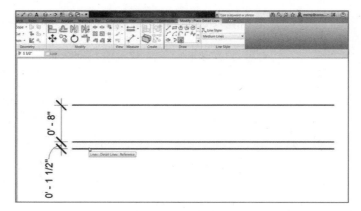

FIGURE 12.57: Using Pick Lines and adding an offset of 1 1/2" (38mm)

9. With the Detail Line command still running, click the Line button and set the Offset value to 3" (75mm).

10. On the Options bar, make sure the Chain option is deselected.

11. For the first point of the line, pick the midpoint of the bottom line, as shown in Figure 12.58.

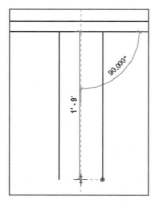

FIGURE 12.58: By setting an offset of 3" (75mm), you can draw two lines using a common centerline.

12. For the second point of the line, pick a point about 1′–9″ (525mm), straight down, as shown in Figure 12.59. (This draws a line offset 3″ [75mm] to the right from the center of the line above.)

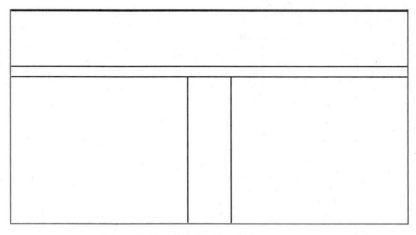

FIGURE 12.59: The detail up to this point

13. To draw the other line, pick the same midpoint you picked to draw the first line.

14. Move your cursor down the view, but this time tap the spacebar to flip the line to the other direction (see Figure 12.59).

15. Draw another line of the same length (again, see Figure 12.59).

16. Click Modify.

17. Compare your lines with the lines in Figure 12.59.

18. Click the Trim/Extend To Corner button on the Modify tab, as shown in Figure 12.60.

19. Trim the edges of the top of the wall (see Figure 12.60).

The next step is to add the track to the bottom of the floor. You'll do this by creating three wide lines. The trick is to do a good amount of offsetting. If you want to explore and try the procedure on your own, look ahead to Figure 12.63 and try to match it dimensionally. Remember, you're using wide lines for the track.

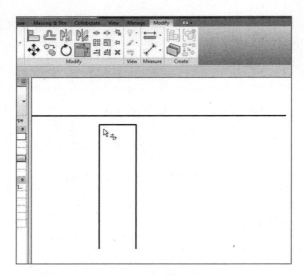

FIGURE 12.60:   Trimming the corners

If you would rather have guidelines, follow these steps:

1. On the Annotate tab, click the Detail Line button.

2. In the Properties dialog, click Wide Lines.

3. On the Draw panel, click the Pick Lines button.

4. On the Options bar, set Offset to 1/8″ (3mm).

5. Offset the bottom of the floor down 1/8″ (3mm). (It will look like the bottom line simply got thicker, but when you trim it up, it will look right.)

6. With the Detail Line command still running, set Offset to 3/8″ (9mm).

7. Offset the left and the right lines, as shown in Figure 12.61.

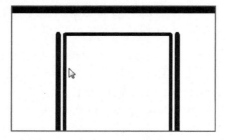

FIGURE 12.61:   Offsetting the heavy lines 3/8″ (9mm) to the right and the left

8. Offset the bottom of the "floor" down 3″ (75mm).

9. Extend the tops of the left and right thick vertical lines to the thick horizontal line.

10. Trim the bottoms of the thick vertical lines to the 3″ (75mm) horizontal line, as shown in Figure 12.62.

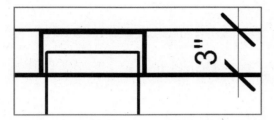

FIGURE 12.62:   Offsetting the thick lines

11. Trim the top horizontal line to the new vertical lines.

12. Delete the 3″ (75mm) horizontal line. Your detail should now look like Figure 12.63.

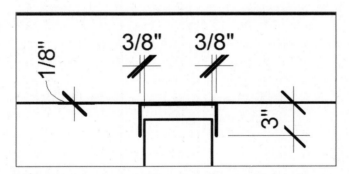

FIGURE 12.63:   The top track is now in place.

It's time to add the gypsum to both sides of the wall. By using the same method as you did before, you'll use thin lines to denote two layers of ⅝″ (15mm) gypsum on both sides of the stud. If you're ready to complete this task on your own, go ahead. (Remember, you're adding two layers of ⅝″ [15mm] gypsum to both sides of the wall, and you're using thin lines to denote this.)

If you would rather have some guidelines with which to practice, let's step through the procedure:

1. On the Annotate tab, click the Detail Line button.

2. Select Thin Lines in the Properties dialog.

3. On the Draw panel, click the Pick Lines icon, as shown in Figure 12.64.

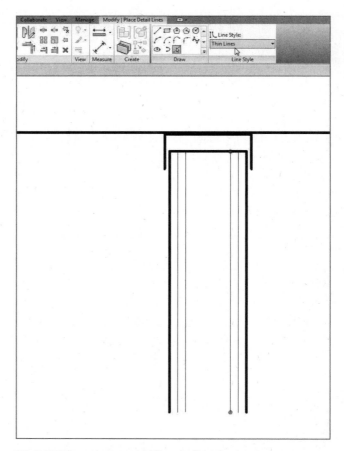

FIGURE 12.64:   Adding the lines for the gypsum

4. Type 5/8" (15mm) in the Offset field.

5. Offset two lines in from the right and the left (see Figure 12.64).

Look at this: the steps are getting shorter. You used only the Detail Line command but have successfully offset every line you needed without leaving the command that you were running at the time. Who says you can't draft in Revit?

The next procedure involves adding a filled region to the "floor." Although you don't want to be too specific about what you're calling out, you still need some contrasting hatch.

If you would like to venture out on your own, try to duplicate Figure 12.66. You'll need to add a filled region using diagonal lines. If you would rather follow the procedure, let's get started:

1. On the Annotate tab, click the Region ➤ Filled Region button.

2. In the Line Style panel, select <Invisible Lines>, as shown in Figure 12.65. On the Options bar, pick Chain.

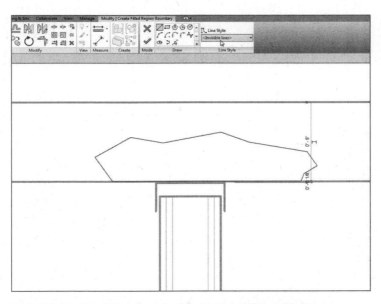

FIGURE 12.65: Draw the filled region with invisible lines.

3. Draw a boundary (see Figure 12.65), and press Esc.

4. In the Properties dialog, click the Edit Type button.

5. Click Duplicate.

6. Call the new region **ROOF**.

7. Change Fill Pattern to Diagonal Up-Small [Drafting].

N O T E   Remember to change the Fill pattern by clicking the [...] button after you click in the Value cell. You can then browse to find the pattern that you're looking for in the menu.

8. Click OK.

9. Click Finish Edit Mode on the Mode panel. Your pattern should look like Figure 12.66. (Remember, the loop must be completely closed, with no gaps or overlaps.)

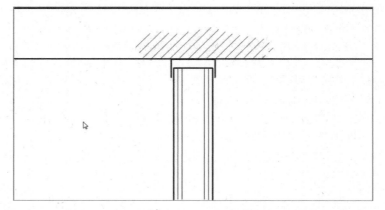

F I G U R E   1 2 . 6 6 :   The detail with the hatching included

This detail is looking good—so good that it would be nice to never have to draw it again. Let's proceed with creating a special group that you can drag onto another view.

Creating a Detail Group

Groups can be extremely advantageous to the drafting process. Although I mentioned earlier that details and drafting views aren't linked to the model, you can still provide some global control within the details themselves by creating a group. This will give you further control over every instance of this specific detail in the entire model.

The objective of the following procedure is to create a new group and add it to another view:

1. Select everything in the view by picking a window.

2. On the Modify | Multi-Select tab in the Create panel, click the Create Group button, as shown in Figure 12.67.

3. In the Create Detail Group dialog, call the new group **Typical Slip Track**. Click OK.

4. The group has been created. You see an icon similar to the UCS icon in AutoCAD; this is your origin. Pick the middle grip, and drag it to the left corner of the track (where it meets the floor), as shown in Figure 12.68.

5. Save the model.

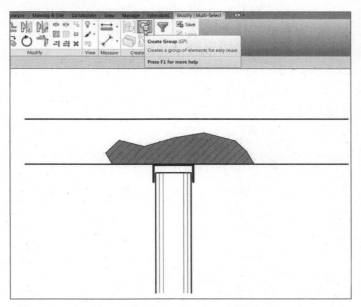

FIGURE 12.67: The Create Group button on the Create tab

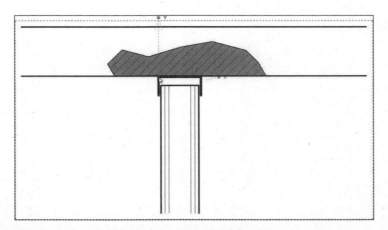

FIGURE 12.68: Move the origin to the location shown here.

With the group created, let's add it to another view. Because not every view shows exactly the same thing, you can alter the group's instance to conform to the detail into which it's being placed.

The objective of this next procedure is to add the new detail group physically to the Roof Taper Section:

1. In the Project Browser, find the Sections (Building Section) called Roof Taper Section, and open it.

2. On the Annotate tab, click Detail Group ➢ Place Detail Group, as shown in Figure 12.69.

3. Move your cursor over the underside of the roof. You get a snap; this is the origin point of the detail.

4. Pick a point along the bottom of the roof, similar to what is shown in Figure 12.70.

5. When the group is placed, press Esc.

FIGURE 12.69: Choose Place Detail Group.

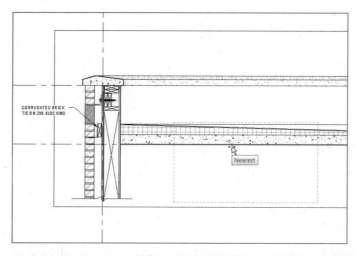

FIGURE 12.70: Picking a point along the bottom of the roof to place the group

The next step is to remove some of the extraneous hatch and lines. You can do this within a group, but you must be careful not to edit the group in a way that affects all other instances:

1. Hover your cursor over the bottom line of the filled region, as shown in Figure 12.71.

2. Press the Tab key. This allows you to select the filled region.

3. Pick the region (see Figure 12.71).

4. A small, blue group icon appears. When you hover your cursor over it, it says that you can exclude this member from the group. This is what you want to do, so click the button.

5. Repeat the process for the top floor line.

6. Repeat the process for the hatch.

7. Save the model. Your detail should now look like Figure 12.72.

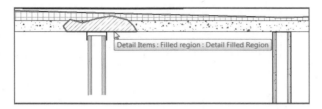

FIGURE 12.71: Excluding an element from the group

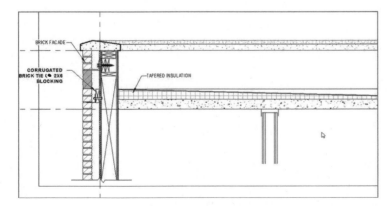

FIGURE 12.72: The slip track without the filled region

Now you'll open the original group and make modifications to it to see how each insertion of a group is influenced. This is where the advantage of using groups in a model comes into play. When the modifications are completed, the other groups will be updated:

1. In the Project Browser, find the TYPICAL WALL TERMINATION view under Drafting Views (Detail), and open it.

2. Select the group.

3. On the Modify | Detail Groups tab, click Edit Group.

4. On the Detail panel of the Annotate tab, click the Insulation button, as shown in Figure 12.73.

5. Place the insulation starting at the midpoint of the top of the stud, and terminate the insulation at the bottom of the stud, as shown in Figure 12.74. You're lucky the width fits perfectly. If it didn't, you could change the width on the Options bar.

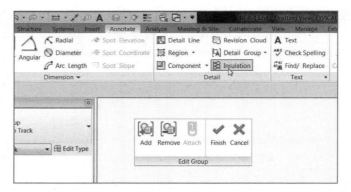

FIGURE 12.73: The Insulation button on the Detail panel of the Annotate tab

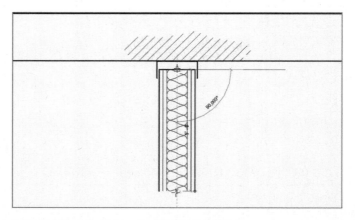

FIGURE 12.74: Drawing the insulation

6. Click the Finish button on the Edit Group toolbar, as shown in Figure 12.75.

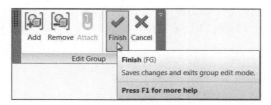

FIGURE 12.75:   The Finish button on the Edit Group toolbar

7. Open the Roof Taper Section, and observe that the insulation has been added.

You're starting to understand detailing pretty well. There are two issues left to discuss. First, it would be nice to reference these details from the plan, even knowing that they aren't physically tied into the model. Second, you need to know how to import CAD into a detail.

ALWAYS BE AWARE OF THE PROJECT BROWSER

You can add a group from the Project Browser as well. If you scroll down in the Project Browser, you'll see a category called Groups. Expand the Groups category, and locate the Detail category. Expand this, and find the Typical Slip Track group, as shown in the following graphic. All you need to do is click this group and drag it into the model.

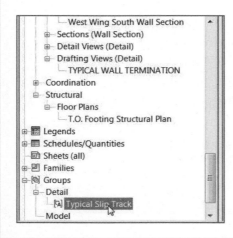

Adding a Section to Another View

You already know how to add a section marker in plan. What you may not know is how to tell Revit that you would rather specify the reference.

In this procedure, you'll go to the Level 1 ceiling plan and add a section pointing to your drafting view:

1. In the Project Browser, open the Level 1 floor plan.

2. Zoom in on the area of the east wing shown in Figure 12.76.

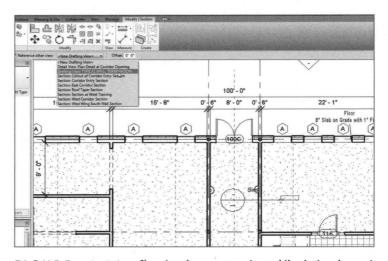

FIGURE 12.76:   Choosing the correct options while placing the section

3. On the View tab, click the Section button. Pick Detail in the Type Selector.

4. Before you place the section, click the Reference Other View button on the Options bar.

5. In the menu to the right of the Reference Other View label, expand the drop-down and select Drafting View: TYPICAL WALL TERMINATION.

6. Place the section into the model (see Figure 12.76).

7. Press Esc.

8. Double-click the section marker that you placed in the model. Doing so opens your drafting view.

9. Save the model.

 W A R N I N G   Be careful! In AutoCAD and MicroStation, you got used to doing this type of referencing daily. In Revit, your coworkers may not be accustomed to this inaccurate style. Be deliberate when you add sections referring to other views, and try not to do it too often.

Creating a drafting view is behind you. Now it's time to look at our old friend CAD. (Some may say that the new meaning of the acronym is Ctrl+Alt+Delete.) Regardless of the existing sentiment toward CAD, it did get us this far. And we still need it—more so in the drafting capacity. Yes, you can import CAD files into a detail.

Importing AutoCAD Files into a Drafting View

I'll go out on a limb and venture to guess that you have a handful of CAD details that you use on a daily basis. The question always is, "What do I do with this pile of details I spent years and thousands of dollars to create?" Well, you can still use them.

The objective of the next procedure is to create a new drafting view and import an AutoCAD detail. If you would like, you can attempt to import your own detail, or you can use the file provided. Just go to the book's web page at www.sybex.com/go/revit2014ner. Browse to the Chapter 12 folder, and find the base cabinet.dwg file. You can then place it on your system for later retrieval.

Follow along:

1. In the View tab, click the Drafting View button.

2. In the next dialog, name the new view **TYPICAL BASE CABINET**.

3. Set Scale to 1 1/2″ = 1′–0″, and then click OK.

4. On the Insert tab, click the Import CAD button.

5. Browse to the location where you placed your CAD file.

6. Select the file, but don't click Open yet.

7. At the bottom of the Import dialog, set Colors to Black And White.

8. Set Layers to All.

9. Set Import Units to Auto-Detect.

10. Set Positioning to Auto - Center To Center.

11. Click Open.

12. Type **ZA**. The detail should now be in full view.

13. Select the detail.

14. On the Modify | Base cabinet.dwg tab, click Explode ➤ Full Explode.

15. Select one of the filled regions.

16. In the Properties dialog, click Edit Type.

17. Change Fill Pattern to Sand - Dense, and select the Drafting radio button.

18. Click OK.

19. Click OK one more time to get back to the model.

20. Make sure your cabinet is hatched properly.

21. Save the model.

USE THE BUILDER BUTTON!

To change the pattern to Sand, make sure you click the [...] button next to the area that says Fill Pattern, as shown in this graphic. From there, you can choose the hatch pattern.

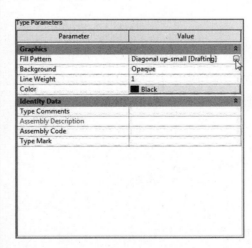

Up to this point, you've been using detail lines for your drafting. The one issue is that detail lines are visible only in the specific view in which you're working. Suppose you wanted linework to show up both in plan/elevation as well as a 3D view. In this situation, you should use the actual Lines tool.

Adding 2D and 3D Lines to the Model

Just because you're drafting, that doesn't mean you can't create lines in all views, such as in a 3D view in a 3D function. Revit has a tool that is simply called *Lines*, and you use it to project lines into multiple views. You apply the Lines tool just like a detail line—only it behaves the same as a Revit 3D family in that you can see it in every view (unless you turn it off).

In this procedure, you'll add detail lines to the west sloping roof. They're nothing fancy, but you'll quickly get the idea of how to use this feature:

1. In the Project Browser, find the West Roof floor plan and open it.

2. On the Architecture tab, click the Set button in the Work Plane panel, as shown in Figure 12.77.

FIGURE 12.77: The Set button on the Work Plane panel of the Architecture tab

3. In the Work Plane dialog, select the Pick A Plane radio button.

4. Click OK.

5. Pick the roof, as shown in Figure 12.78.

6. On the Model panel of the Architecture tab, click the Model Line button.

7. In the Line Style menu, select Medium Lines, as shown in Figure 12.79.

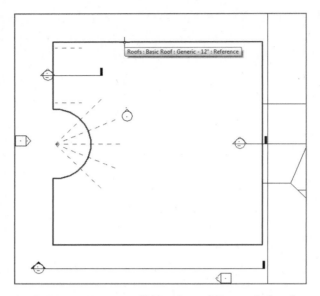

FIGURE 12.78: Picking the roof. Your work plane is now set to slope with the roof. Anything you draw will be on this sloping plane.

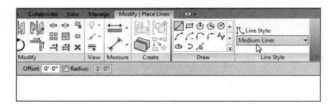

FIGURE 12.79: Select Medium Lines under Line Style.

8. On the Draw panel, click the Start-End-Radius Arc button, as shown in Figure 12.80.

9. Draw an arc from the two endpoints shown in Figure 12.80. Make the radius 80′–0″ (24000mm). Simply enter the numbers on the keyboard and press Enter, and they will fill in the radius field. Click Modify.

10. Go to an exterior 3D view. You can still see the arc.

11. Save the model.

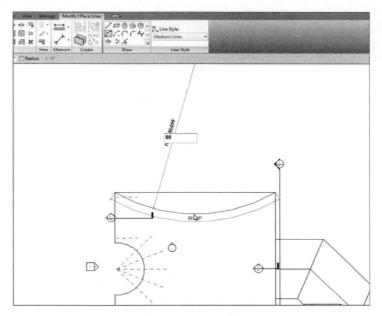

FIGURE 12.80:   Drawing an 80′–0″ (24m) radius arc

It's a good idea to keep this feature in mind. This drafting tool will become useful when it comes to sketching in 3D. There will be many situations in which you'll use this little nugget.

Are You Experienced?

Now you can...

☑ modify and add line weights to be used in both the 3D and 2D environments

☑ add linework in a drafting view as well as a 2D and 3D view

☑ create both masking regions and filled regions to provide hatching to a model

☑ mask an area so that you can draft over it

☑ add detail components to the model, and create repeating details

☑ modify detail families to suit your needs

☑ create a group to be used in multiple drafting views, change the group, and update each copy in each view

☑ create a new drafting view to draft from scratch, and import a CAD file into a drafting view

Creating Specific Views and Match Lines

As you can see, the Autodesk® Revit® Architecture platform is all about the views. In fact, by using Revit, not only are you replacing the application you use for drafting, but you're also replacing your existing file storage system. This is largely because you're now using one model, and you're using views of that model for your project navigation.

▶ **Duplicating views**

▶ **Creating dependent views**

▶ **Adding match lines**

▶ **Using view templates**

Duplicating Views

I wanted to dedicate an entire chapter to project navigation. Although you've steadily gained experience in this area, we can expand on it much more to round out your Revit expertise.

The first item we'll tackle in this chapter is the process of duplicating a view to create another. Although it's a straightforward procedure, a lot is riding on the hope that you proceed with this function correctly. As you're about to find out, this command isn't a simple copy-and-paste operation.

Revit will change how you organize a project. You'll no longer open a file and save it as another file so that you can make changes without affecting the original. As you know, Revit is all-inclusive in terms of files. There is only one. From that one file, there are views that reside in the Project Browser.

Of course, I'm not telling you anything you haven't learned already. If you've gone through the book from page 1, you've gained experience in creating views (especially in Chapter 3, "Creating Views"). If you're jumping to this chapter, you most certainly have had some exposure to view creation. This topic is broken into two chapters to help you gain a more in-depth understanding of how you can manipulate and organize views.

N O T E   Metric users should not type in mm or other metric abbreviations when entering amounts suggested in the exercises. Revit won't accept such abbreviations. Simply enter the number provided within the parentheses.

The difference between choosing Duplicate With Detailing and Duplicate is that Duplicate With Detailing also copies all the tags and annotations you have in the original view. Duplicate only copies the geometry.

Now let's duplicate some views! To begin, open the file on which you've been following along. If you didn't complete the previous chapter, go to the book's web page at www.sybex.com/go/revit2014ner. From there, you can browse to the Chapter 13 folder and find the file called NER-13.rvt.

The objective of the following procedure is to create a furniture plan of Level 1 and then turn off the furniture on the original Level 1. Follow along:

1. In the Project Browser, find the Level 1 floor plan, and right-click.

2. Select Duplicate View ➢ Duplicate With Detailing, as shown in Figure 13.1.

3. You now have a view called Copy of Level 1. Right-click it in the Project Browser.

4. Rename it **Level 1 Furniture Plan.**

5. Make sure you're in the Level 1 floor plan, not the new Furniture Plan. In the Level 1 view window, type **VG.** Doing so brings up the Visibility/Graphics Overrides window.

6. In the Visibility column, deselect Casework, Furniture, and Furniture Systems.

7. Click OK.

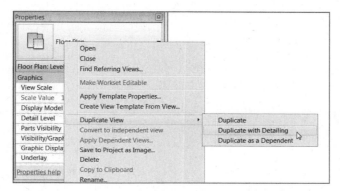

Now, any time you add furniture or casework, it will only appear in the furniture plan. You don't need to deal with layer or display configuration.

The ability to create a copy of a view and then modify its visibility graphics to display certain items is a critical function in Revit. Another similar task is also available: creating coordinated match-line divisions in a model by creating dependent views.

Creating Dependent Views

You create a dependent view in much the same way you duplicate a view. In fact, you *are* duplicating a view. The function of a dependent view is to nest a duplicate of a view within the host view (or the view of which you're making the duplicate). This nested view is dependent on the host view in terms of visibility graphics and View Properties. You can have multiple dependent views categorized under the host view.

You create dependent views in order to add match lines. Yes, you could simply duplicate a view and move its crop region, but when you have dependent views, as you'll see in Chapter 14, "Creating Sheets and Printing," you can tag those views in a specific way for Revit to track the sheets they're on. Dependent views also give the advantage of making your Project Browser much less cluttered, without unnecessary floor plans.

In the next procedure, you'll make a dependent view of the Level 1 floor plan:

1. In the Project Browser, right-click the Level 1 floor plan.

2. Select Duplicate View ➤ Duplicate As A Dependent. You now have a view that is nested under Level 1. As you can see, Level 1 is expanded to show its dependencies.

3. Right-click Level 1 again.

4. Select Duplicate View ➤ Duplicate As A Dependent. You now have two views nested under Level 1 (see Figure 13.2).

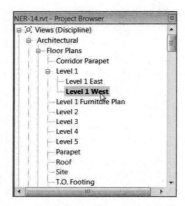

FIGURE 13.2: Creating the two views dependent on Level 1

5. Right-click Dependent (2) on the Level 1 dependent view.

6. Rename it **Level 1 East**.

7. Rename the other dependent view **Level 1 West** (see Figure 13.2).

Now that the views are duplicated and nested in the host view, it's time to divide the Level 1 floor plan. You'll do this by adjusting the crop region.

Adjusting the Crop Regions

Every view in Revit has a crop region. Crop regions play an important role when your plan is too large to fit on a sheet. All you need to do at this point is to slide the east and west crop regions to display the appropriate parts of the plan based on the name of the views:

1. Open the Level 1 West dependent view.

2. Select the crop region, as shown in Figure 13.3.

3. Drag the right side of the crop region to the position shown in Figure 13.3.

4. Open the Level 1 East view.

5. Select the crop region.

6. Drag the left side of the region to the right, as shown in Figure 13.4.

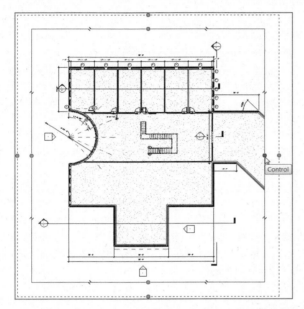

FIGURE 13.3:   Dragging the crop region in the Level 1 West view

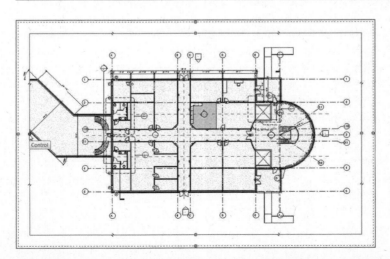

FIGURE 13.4:   Dragging the crop region to the right in the Level 1 East view

7. Select the crop region again, if it isn't selected already, and right-click.

8. Choose Go To Primary View to open the Level 1 floor plan.

9. In the Level 1 floor plan, turn on the crop region by clicking the Show Crop Region button on the View Control toolbar, as shown in Figure 13.5.

FIGURE 13.5: Turning on the crop region from the View Control toolbar

You can see the area where you need to draw the match line. The crop region should overlap in the corridor. If not, drag the crop regions so they match Figure 13.6.

STRETCH THAT VIEW

You'll notice that there are two stretch grips. One is for the actual crop region, and the other is for the annotation crop region. We'll cover what the annotation crop region means in a moment. For now, pick the stretch grip to the inside, as shown in this image.

 N O T E   If you want to turn a dependent view back into an independent view, you can right-click the dependent view and select Convert To Independent View. Doing so breaks the link to the host view.

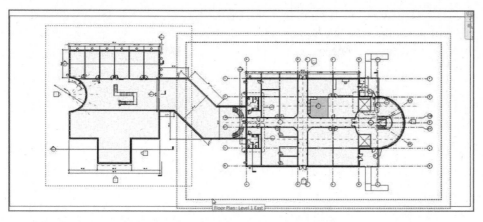

FIGURE 13.6:   Adjusting the crop regions to overlap in the corridor

Unfortunately, if you have a match-line situation in your project, you must follow this procedure with each floor plan separately. For multi-floor projects, doing so can become time consuming. Alternatively, you can right-click a view that has dependencies and select Apply Dependent Views. From there, you can select the views to which the dependent views will be added.

As you can see, adjusting the crop region is how you specify which part of the plan will appear on your sheet. This poses one issue: if you have text that you would like to lie outside the crop region—that is, if a leadered note is pointing to an item within the cropped boundary—you may not see the note. To fix this, you can adjust the annotation crop region.

Adjusting the Annotation Crop Region

Because the crop region cuts off the model at a specified perimeter, what is to become of text that needs to lie outside this boundary? This is where the annotation crop region comes in handy. You'll always have the situation where leadered text must be outside of the geometry it's labeling. You can make adjustments to ensure that this can happen.

Let's adjust an annotation crop region to clean up a plan. Follow along:

1. In the Project Browser, open the Level 1 West dependent view.

2. Select the crop region, as shown in Figure 13.7. Notice the two perimeters: one is a solid-line type, and the other is a dashed-line type.

3. In the corridor is a dimension that seems to be floating. This is because the crop region allows this dimension to show. With the

crop region still selected, pick the outside stretch grip, as shown in Figure 13.8, and stretch the annotation crop region in until the dimension disappears.

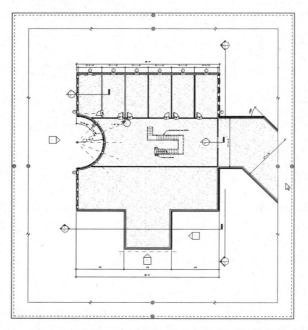

FIGURE 13.7: Selecting the plan's crop region. Notice the additional region on a dashed line type—this is the annotation crop region.

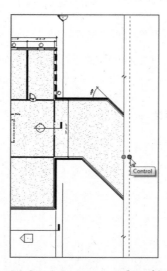

FIGURE 13.8: Stretching the annotation crop region to the left

N O T E The Annotation Crop feature is available in any view. This example uses a plan, but you can use the same procedure in a section or an elevation as well.

Now that you understand how to add crop regions and display them appropriately, let's add the match line.

THE SECOND LINE

If you don't see the second line, follow these steps:

1. In the Properties dialog, scroll down to the Extents area.

2. Make sure the Annotation Crop option is selected, as shown here:

Adding Match Lines

In CAD, adding a match line is nothing more than the simple practice of drawing a line. The same is true in Revit, except that in Revit, you draw that line in Sketch Mode and you can propagate it to other views. Also in Revit, after you place the line, it registers as having two sides of a model. In Chapter 14, when you drag your views onto sheets, Revit will know where each side of the model is located in terms of being placed on a sheet.

The objective of the next procedure is to place a match line into the model. Follow these steps:

1. Open the Level 1 floor plan.

2. On the Sheet Composition panel of the View tab, click the Matchline button, as shown in Figure 13.9.

3. In the Properties dialog, make sure the Top and Bottom constraints are set to Unlimited.

4. On the Draw panel, click the Line button.

5. Draw the match line as shown in Figure 13.10.

6. Click Finish Edit Mode on the Mode panel.

FIGURE 13.9: The Matchline button on the View tab

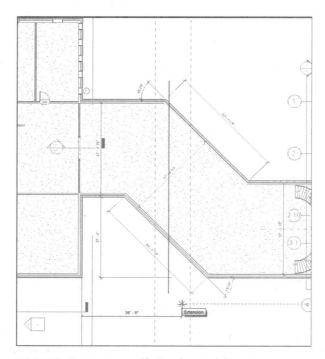

FIGURE 13.10: Placing the match line

Your match line appears as a bold, dashed line. Because the physical appearance of a match line never seems to be the same from firm to firm, you can adjust the line's appearance.

Match-Line Appearance

A match line isn't an actual line by definition; it's an object. Therefore, you can control its appearance by using the Object Styles dialog.

The next procedure focuses on changing the appearance of the match line:

1. On the Manage tab, click the Object Styles button.

2. Click the Annotation Objects tab, as shown in Figure 13.11.

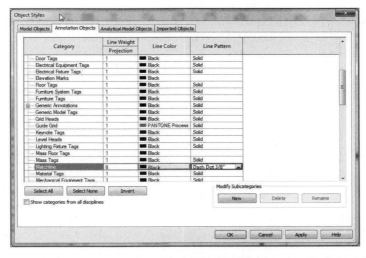

FIGURE 13.11:   Changing the Matchline line pattern to Dash Dot 3/8″

3. Scroll down to the Matchline category.

4. Click into Line Pattern (the Dash cell).

5. You see a menu arrow. Click it, and select Dash Dot 3/8″ (10mm) (see Figure 13.11).

6. Click OK. Your match line is now a different line type.

With the match line in place and the plan split into two halves, let's add an annotation to label the match line. For the match-line annotation, you'll place a piece of text that says MATCHLINE. But when you're referencing each side of the plan, you'll need to add view references.

Adding View References to a Match Line

After the plan is split and the match line is in place, you can tag each side of the match line. When you drag the view onto a drawing sheet, the tag will be filled out with the correct page name. It's important to note, however, that although this process is automatic, it isn't *fully* automatic. You do need to specify the correct view name as you're placing the tag.

In this procedure, you'll place a piece of text that says MATCHLINE along the match line, and add a view reference to each side of the match line. Follow along:

1. In the Project Browser, open the Level 1 floor plan view.

2. On the Annotate tab, click the Text button.

 N O T E   Unfortunately, when you're placing text, you can't rotate the text until after you've added it. In this procedure, place the note, rotate it, and then move it into position.

3. On the Modify | Place Text tab are leader options. Click the No Leader button (the A), as shown in Figure 13.12.

4. Pick a window near the match line for the text.

5. Type the word **MATCHLINE**, click off the text, and press Esc twice (see Figure 13.12).

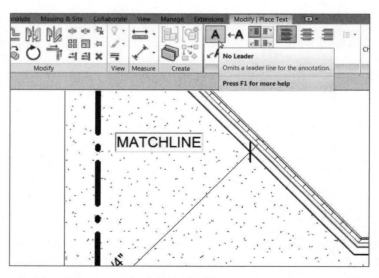

F I G U R E   1 3 . 1 2 :   Typing the text MATCHLINE

6. Select the text (if it isn't selected already).

7. Click the rotate grip, and rotate the text 90°.

8. Click the move grip, and drag the text over to the match line so it's positioned as shown in Figure 13.13.

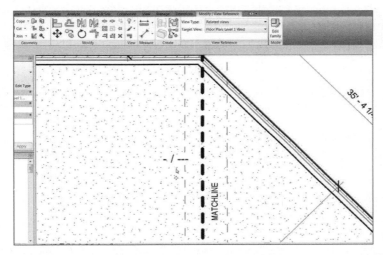

FIGURE 13.13: Adding a view reference includes choosing the correct target view.

9. On the Sheet Composition panel of the View tab, click the View Reference button.

10. In the View Reference panel is a Target View list. Make sure Floor Plan: Level 1 West is current (see Figure 13.13).

11. Pick a point to the left of the match line (again, see Figure 13.13).

12. With the View Reference command still running, change Target View to Floor Plan: Level 1 East.

13. Place a view reference to the right of the match line.

14. Press Esc. You have two view references, and you're ready to add these views to a drawing sheet in the next chapter. Once you do this, the tags will become populated with the sheets on which you placed the views.

One last item to discuss before we close this chapter is how to create and use settings from a single view, after you determine that you want to repeat the view settings.

Using View Templates

When you created the furniture plan in the beginning of the chapter, you manipulated the data in the Visibility/Graphics Overrides options to hide furniture in a specific plan. It would be nice to build settings like these into a template so you could simply apply that template to a view the next time the situation arose.

Let's create a view template and apply it to another view. Follow these steps:

1. In the Project Browser, right-click the Level 1 floor plan.

2. Select Create View Template From View.

3. In the Name dialog, call the template **Without Furniture or Casework**, and then click OK.

4. In the View Templates dialog, Revit allows you to further control the View Properties and visibility graphics. Because you don't need to make any other adjustments, click OK.

5. Right-click the Level 2 floor plan.

6. Select Apply Template Properties.

7. In the Apply View Template dialog, select the Without Furniture Or Casework template, as shown in Figure 13.14.

8. Click OK.

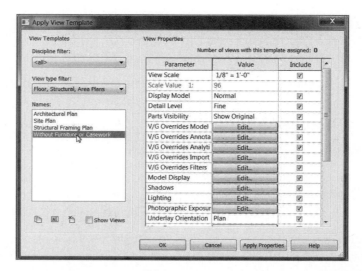

FIGURE 13.14:   Selecting the Without Furniture Or Casework template

As you can see, using view templates will help you immensely with maintaining company-wide standards. Use templates as often as possible.

Are You Experienced?

Now you can...

☑ create duplicates of views, and tell the difference between duplicating with detailing and simply duplicating a view

☑ create dependent views, allowing separate views to be nested under one host view

☑ add match lines and view reference tags

☑ create and use view templates

You can also select multiple items and apply the same template to many plans, if you desire.

Creating Sheets and Printing

Your deliverable product is a set of construction documents and specifications. So it stands to reason that the application you use to produce these construction documents is at its strongest in this area. Unfortunately, when you see marketing campaigns related to Autodesk® Revit® Architecture software, all they show are huge skyscrapers and realistic renderings. And, of course, you see the slide of the architect handing a model to the contractor and then the contractor handing it to the owner. Don't get me wrong—all that stuff is good, but the most powerful feature of Revit Architecture is its ability to create sheets. You wouldn't think this is the standout feature—but when it's 4:30 in the afternoon and the job is going out the door at 5:00, you'll never go back to a drafting application after you've used Revit at the eleventh hour.

▶ **Creating and populating sheets**

▶ **Modifying a viewport**

▶ **Adding revisions to a sheet**

▶ **Addressing project parameters**

▶ **Generating a cover sheet**

▶ **Printing from Revit Architecture**

Creating and Populating Sheets

The first part of the chapter will focus on creating a sheet and how to populate it with views. Although you completed this task back in Chapter 11, "Schedules and Tags," it's time to drill into the ins and outs of sheet creation.

Luckily, when you create and populate sheets, Revit holds true to form—that is, you don't have to start setting up different drawings or models simply to reference them together. You create sheets much as you create most other views, because that's all a sheet is: a view. But a sheet goes one step further. Look at a sheet as a view that collects other views for the purpose of printing.

 N O T E   Metric users should not type in mm or other metric abbreviations when entering amounts suggested in the exercises. Revit won't accept such abbreviations. Simply enter the number provided within the parentheses.

The objective of the following procedure is to create a new sheet. To get started, open the model on which you've been working. If you missed the previous chapter, go to the book's web page at www.sybex.com/go/revit2014ner. From there, you can browse to Chapter 14 and find the file called NER-14.rvt. Follow along:

1. In the Project Browser, scroll down until you see the Sheets category, as shown in Figure 14.1.

2. Right-click Sheets, and select New Sheet (see Figure 14.1).

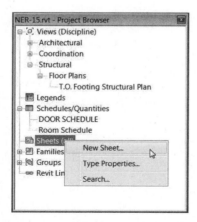

FIGURE 14.1:   Selecting a new sheet

3. In the Select Titleblocks area of the New Sheet dialog, select the E1 30 × 42 Horizontal title block. (It's probably the only one available.)

4. Click OK.

N O T E   You're using a standard Autodesk-supplied title block. Later in this chapter, you'll learn how to make custom title blocks. Also, your new sheet may be numbered differently from the example in the book. This is okay; you'll change the numbering in a moment.

Congratulations! You now have a blank sheet. Next you'll add views to it by using the click-and-drag method:

1. On the View tab, click Guide Grid, as shown in Figure 14.2.

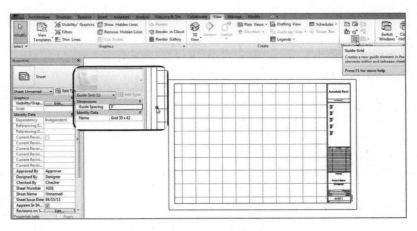

F I G U R E   1 4 . 2 :   Adding a guide grid to a sheet

2. In the Guide Grid Name dialog, call the guide **Grid 30 × 42 (750 × 1050)**, and click OK.

3. Select the guide grid, and drag it into place by using the blue grips (see Figure 14.2).

4. With the guide grid still selected, change Guide Spacing to 3″ (75mm) in the Properties dialog (see Figure 14.2).

 N O T E   You don't have to add a guide grid. The guide grid keeps your plans in the same spot from sheet to sheet, however, which can be a good idea.

   5. In the Project Browser, find the dependent view called Level 1 West, as shown in Figure 14.3.

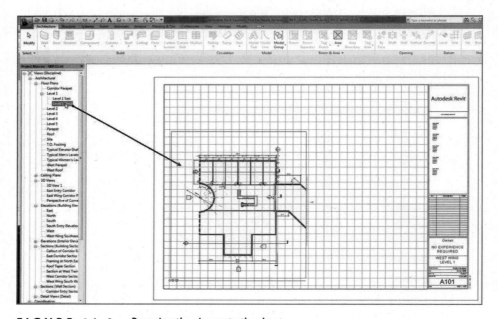

F I G U R E   1 4 . 3 :   Dragging the view onto the sheet

---

   6. Pick the view, and hold down the pick button.

   7. Drag the view onto the sheet (see Figure 14.3).

   8. When the view is centered in the sheet, let go of the pick button. The view follows your cursor. Try to align the lower-left corner of the viewport with a guide grid, and then click. Doing so places the view onto the sheet.

   This is how you populate a sheet using Revit—quite the departure from CAD. One nice detail is that the title is filled out, and the scale will never be incorrect. The next step is to begin renumbering sheets so that you can create a logical order.

Sheet Organization

If you've been following along with the book, you already have a sheet numbered A101. It would be nice if you could give this sheet a new number and start your sequence over. Revit lets you do just that.

The objective of the next procedure is to change the sheet numbering and to add more sheets, allowing Revit to number the sheets sequentially as they're created. Follow these steps:

1. In the Project Browser, find the sheet A101 - Unnamed, and right-click.

2. Select Rename, as shown in Figure 14.4.

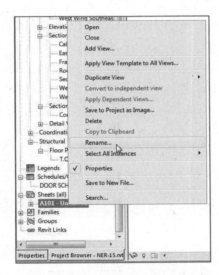

FIGURE 14.4: Renaming the sheet

3. Change the sheet name to **WEST WING LEVEL 1**.

4. Click OK.

5. Right-click Sheets (All), and create a new sheet.

6. Make sure the number is **A102**.

Your Project Browser should now resemble Figure 14.5.

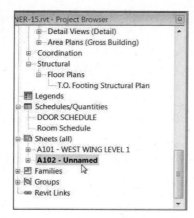

FIGURE 14.5: The reorganized Project Browser

You may notice a plus sign (+) next to A101. If you expand the tree by clicking the +, you can see the views that are included on this view. This can prove to be immensely useful, because you can't add a view to another sheet (or the same sheet, for that matter) if it's already included in a sheet.

With the sheets organized, you can now proceed to create more. As you do, you'll see that not only do the sheets number themselves, but all of the sections, elevations, and callouts begin reading the appropriate sheet designations:

1. In the Project Browser, drag the Level 1 East dependent view onto the new sheet.

2. Pick a point on the sheet to place the view aligned with the guide grid (see Figure 14.6).

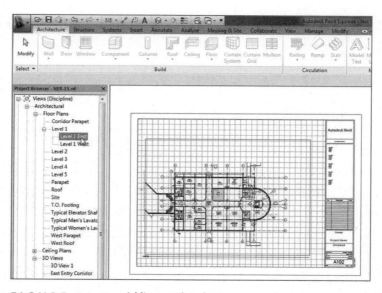

FIGURE 14.6: Adding another sheet

3. In the Project Browser, double-click the A101 sheet, opening the view. Notice that the view reference next to the match line is filled out with the appropriate designation.

4. Double-click A102 to open the view again.

In the Project Browser, sheet A102 is still unnamed. The next procedure describes a different way to rename and renumber a sheet:

1. With Sheet A102 open, zoom in to the right side of the view, as shown in Figure 14.7.

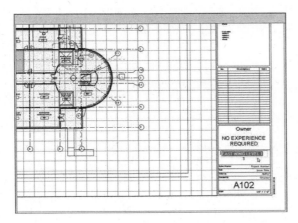

FIGURE 14.7: Changing the title-block information

2. Select the title block. A few items turn blue. If you remember, any item that turns blue can be modified.

3. Click into the text that says *Project Name*, and type NO EXPERIENCE REQUIRED.

4. Click into the text that says *Unnamed*, and type EAST WING LEVEL 1 (see Figure 14.7).

5. Create another sheet using the 30 × 42 Horizontal title block.

6. Number it A201.

7. Name it ENLARGED PLANS.

8. Add the 30 × 42 grid guide.

9. Drag the following views onto the sheet:

▶ Typical Elevator Shaft

▶ Typical Men's Lavatory

▶ Typical Women's Lavatory

10. Arrange them so that they're in a row, as shown in Figure 14.8.

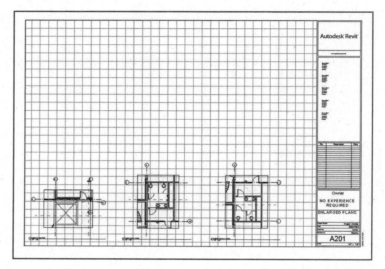

FIGURE 14.8: Creating a sheet and adding views in a row across the bottom of the page

 NOTE   The title block is filled out. The page number and the sheet name are filled out because you edited those names when you made the sheet, but the project name will appear on every new sheet that you create.

Now that the first floor plans and typical enlarged plans are placed on a sheet, let's move on to adding the details you've created.

If you feel as though you have enough experience creating a sheet and adding views, go ahead and proceed on your own. Your new sheet will be numbered A301 and will be called Building Sections, and you'll add the views East Corridor Section, West Corridor Section, Section at West Training, and West Wing South Wall Section. Your sheet should look like Figure 14.9.

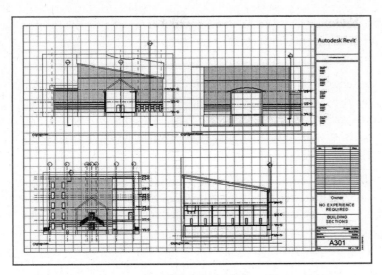

FIGURE 14.9: The completed sheet A301

If you'd like some assistance in putting the section sheet together, follow along with this procedure:

1. In the Project Browser, right-click the Sheets category.

2. Select New Sheet.

3. Select the E1 30 × 42 Horizontal title block, and click OK.

4. In the Project Browser, right-click the new sheet and select Rename.

5. Give the new sheet the number **A301** and the name **BUILDING SECTIONS**.

6. In the Properties dialog, add the 30 × 42 grid guide.

7. In the Project Browser, find the Sections (Building Sections) category.

8. Drag the section called East Corridor Section onto the lower-left corner of the sheet.

9. Drag the section called Section At West Training onto the sheet to the right of East Corridor Section.

10. Drag the section called West Corridor Section onto the sheet, and place it in the upper-left corner. Be sure you align it directly above East Corridor Section.

11. Drag the section called West Wing South Wall Section to the right of West Corridor Section and directly above Section At West Training. The alignment lines allow you to place the section accurately. After you have these four sections in place, your sheet A301 should look like Figure 14.9.

You've created a few sheets, and you may want to make some adjustments to the view without leaving the sheet. The next section of this chapter will focus on the properties of a viewport and how to make it *live* on the sheet so you can make modifications.

Modifying a Viewport

Wait a second, isn't a viewport AutoCAD® vernacular? Yes, it is. But a viewport in AutoCAD and a viewport in Revit are two completely different things.

In Revit, when you drag a view onto a sheet, a linked copy of that view becomes a viewport. This is what you see on the sheet. Any modification you make to the original view is immediately reflected in the viewport, and vice versa. See Figure 14.10 for a graphical representation.

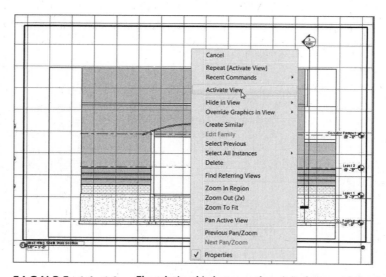

FIGURE 14.10:   The relationship between the original view and the viewport

In the next procedure, you'll activate a viewport to make modifications on the sheet, and you'll also explore the Element Properties of the viewport. Follow along:

1. Open sheet A301 (if it isn't open already).

2. Zoom in on the viewport West Wing South Wall Section, as shown in Figure 14.11.

3. Select the view.

4. Right-click, and select Activate View (see Figure 14.11).

5. With the view activated, you can work on it just as if you had opened it from the Project Browser. Select the crop region, as shown in Figure 14.12.

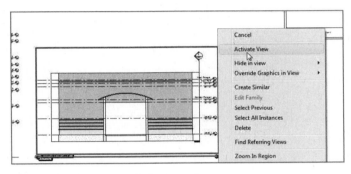

FIGURE 14.11:   Activating a view

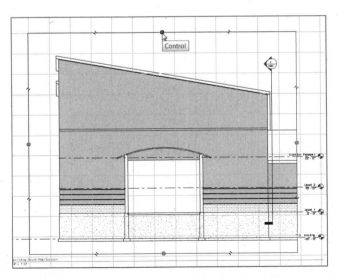

FIGURE 14.12:   Stretching the crop region so you can see the entire view

6. Stretch the top of the crop region upward so you can see the entire view.

 N O T E   By activating the view in this manner, you're essentially opening the view. The only difference between physically opening the view in the Project Browser and activating the view on the sheet is that by activating the view, you can see the title block, which helps in terms of layout.

7. On the View Control toolbar, select Hide Crop Region.

UNSIGHTLY CROP REGIONS BEGONE!

By selecting Hide Crop Region, as shown in this image, you're simply cleaning up the view. As we'll explore in this chapter, you can also keep the crop region on and tell Revit not to print it.

8. Right-click, and select Deactivate View.

9. Right-click the view to the left of West Wing South Wall Section (it's the view called West Corridor Section), and select Activate View.

10. Stretch the crop region downward so you can see the entire foundation.

11. Hide the crop region.

12. Right-click, and deactivate the view.

With the view widened, it's coming close to the actual title. You can move the viewport and the title independently of one another. The following procedure involves moving the viewport up and then moving the view title down to provide some more room:

1. Select the West Wing South Wall Section viewport.

2. Hold down the pick button, and move the entire viewport up. As you do so, an alignment line appears. This means the views are physically aligned. When you see the alignment line, release the pick button.

3. Press Esc.

4. Select the view title, as shown in Figure 14.13.

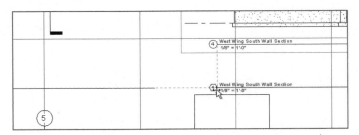

FIGURE 14.13: You can select the view title independently of the actual viewport.

5. Move it down. As you move the view title, it snaps in alignment to the view title to the left (see Figure 14.13).

Now that you have some experience creating sheets and making adjustments to the views and viewports, you can easily create one more sheet that contains sections.

The following procedure focuses on creating a detail sheet. If you feel as though you can create this sheet on your own, go ahead. The sheet will be number A401, it will be named DETAILS, and the views to be added are Corridor Entry Section, Callout of Corridor Entry Section, Roof Taper Section, and TYPICAL WALL TERMINATION. Your finished sheet should look like Figure 14.14.

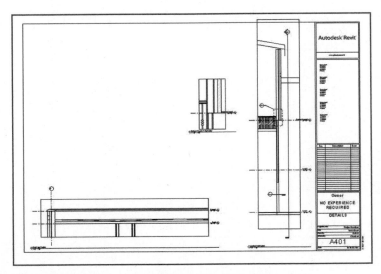

FIGURE 14.14: Building the A401 DETAILS sheet

If you'd rather have some assistance, follow along:

1. In the Sheets category in the Project Browser, right-click the Sheets title.

2. Select New Sheet.

3. Number it **A401**, and name it **DETAILS**.

4. In the Project Browser, drag the Sections (Wall Section) item Corridor Entry Section and place it in the sheet all the way to the right.

5. Right-click the new viewport, and select Activate View.

6. Stretch the section bubble down so that it fits into the sheet.

7. Right-click again, and select Deactivate View.

8. In the Project Browser, drag the Sections (Building Section) item Callout Of Corridor Entry Section onto the sheet to the top left of the previous section.

9. Drag the section called Roof Taper Section to the bottom left of the first view you added.

10. Zoom in on the view title for the Corridor Entry Section, as shown in Figure 14.15.

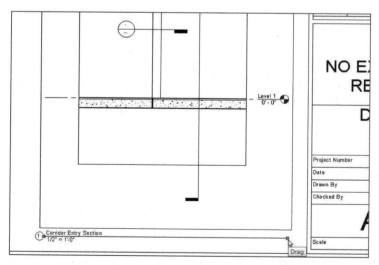

FIGURE 14.15: Stretching the view title line to the right using the blue grip

11. Select the Corridor Entry Section viewport. Notice the blue grips on the view title.

12. Extend the line by stretching the grip on the right to the right (see Figure 14.15).

13. Save the model.

Pan and zoom around to investigate all the reference markers. They're starting to fill themselves out based on the sheets where you placed the referring views.

N O T E   You can place only one instance of a view on a sheet. You also can't place a view on multiple sheets. This is how Revit keeps track of what view is on a page and which page the view is on. The only types of view that you can place on more than one sheet are legends and schedules. If you would like to place a model view on a sheet more than once, you'll need to duplicate the view in the Project Browser.

Now that you know how to manipulate a viewport, it's time to look at the viewport's properties. I think you'll be glad to see how familiar these properties are.

Viewport Properties

Just like anything else in Revit, viewports have associated properties. You can select the viewport and click the Properties button on the Ribbon if the Properties dialog isn't already open.

The objective of the following procedure is to look through the viewport's properties and make some minor modifications. Follow along:

1. Open the view A401 - DETAILS (if it isn't already open).

2. Select the Corridor Entry Section view (the tall section to the right of the sheet).

N O T E   Notice that the properties for the viewport are exactly the same as those for a typical view. When you change the properties of a viewport, you're actually changing the properties of the corresponding view.

3. In the Properties dialog, scroll down the list until you arrive at Title On Sheet, as shown in Figure 14.16.

4. Change Title On Sheet to **SECTION AT ENTRY CORRIDOR**.

5. Click Edit Type.

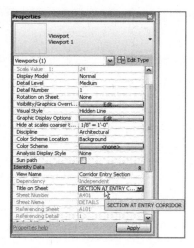

FIGURE 14.16: You can make the title on the sheet different from the view name.

6. In the Type Parameters, you can choose which view title you'll be using, or whether you want any view title at all. For now, click OK.

7. Zoom in on the detail, and notice that the name has changed.

You've pretty much exhausted creating and manipulating sheets. It's time to explore another sheet function: adding revisions.

When you select the viewport, the name and detail number turn blue. This means you can change the values right on the sheet.

Adding Revisions to a Sheet

An unfortunate reality in producing construction documents is that you must eventually make revisions. In CAD, you normally create a duplicate of the file, save that file into your project directory, and then create the revisions. The only way to keep track of them is to add a revision cloud and change the attribute information in the title block. In Revit, however, you're given a revision schedule and the means to keep track of your revisions.

In the next procedure, you'll add a revision cloud and populate a schedule that is already built into the sheet. Follow these steps:

1. In the Project Browser, open Sheet A101.

2. On the Annotate tab, click the Revision Cloud button, as shown in Figure 14.17. You're now in Sketch Mode.

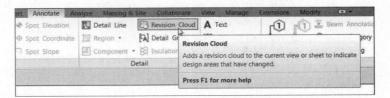

FIGURE 14.17: The Revision Cloud button on the Annotate tab

3. Place a revision cloud around the plan, as shown in Figure 14.18.

4. On the Modify | Create Revision Cloud Sketch tab, click Finish Edit Mode.

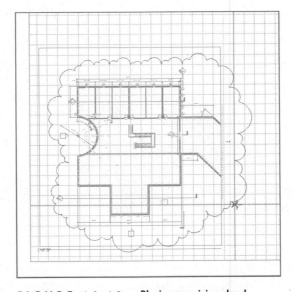

FIGURE 14.18: Placing a revision cloud

 TIP   To draw the revision cloud accurately, you must work in a clockwise manner. The shorter the distance you move your cursor between clicks, the smaller the arcs that Revit draws, so you have some control over the appearance of the cloud. Unfortunately, if you err in getting the cloud on the sheet, you should probably undo it and start over.

5. On the Annotate tab, click Tag By Category.

6. Pick the revision cloud.

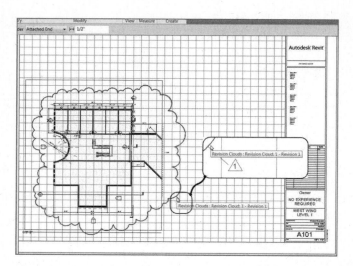

FIGURE 14.19: The revision tag has been added to the cloud. Also, notice that the title block has Revision 1 added to it.

7. You may get a dialog stating that you don't have a tag loaded for this category. If you see this dialog, click Yes to load one.

8. Select Annotations ➤ Revision Tag.rfa.

9. Pick the revision cloud. It's now tagged (see Figure 14.19).

Zoom closer to the title block. The revision schedule has the first revision added to it. Revit is keeping track of your revisions.

Next you'll modify the revision scheme so that you can better keep track of the revision schedule. Follow along:

1. On the View tab, click the Sheet Issues/Revisions button on the Sheet Composition panel. The dialog shown in Figure 14.20 opens.

2. In the Sheet Issues/Revisions dialog, change the date to today's date.

3. For the description, type **First Floor Revisions**.

4. Click the Add button (see Figure 14.20).

5. Give the new revision a date in the future.

6. For the description, enter **Revised Sections** (again, see Figure 14.20).

7. For Numbering, click the Per Project radio button.

8. Click OK.

9. In the Project Browser, open the sheet A301 - BUILDING SECTIONS.

10. On the Annotate tab, click the Revision Cloud button.

11. Place a cloud around the upper-right detail.

12. On the Mode panel, click Finish Edit Mode.

13. Select the cloud you just added.

14. On the Options bar, make sure Seq. 2 - Revised Sections is selected, as shown in Figure 14.21.

15. On the Annotate tab, select Tag By Category.

16. Place the revision tag on the cloud. The schedule in the title block is filled with only the appropriate revision relevant to this sheet.

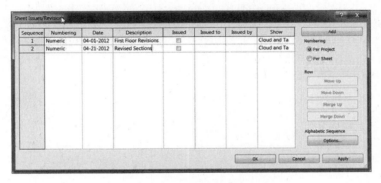

FIGURE 14.20: The Sheet Issues/Revisions dialog

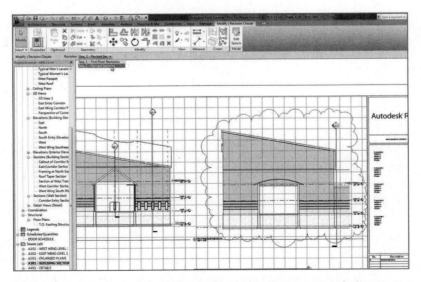

FIGURE 14.21: By selecting the revision cloud, you can specify the sequence from the Options bar.

Now that you have experience with the concept of how sheets and revisions come together, we need to explore one more avenue of populating sheet information. You may have noticed that the title blocks aren't yet complete. The empty fields relate to project information that needs to be included on each sheet. This is where project parameters come in.

Addressing Project Parameters

Because Revit is built on a database, it makes sense that items like Project Name and Project Number are added to the design in a different manner than in CAD. In CAD, you fill out attributes sheet by sheet, or you externally reference a title block with the sheet information. In Revit, you fill out the project information in one place. The information you add to the database propagates down to the sheets. When (or if) this information changes, it's done quickly and accurately.

The objective of the next procedure is to locate the project parameters and populate the model with the job information:

1. On the Manage tab, click Project Information, as shown in Figure 14.22.

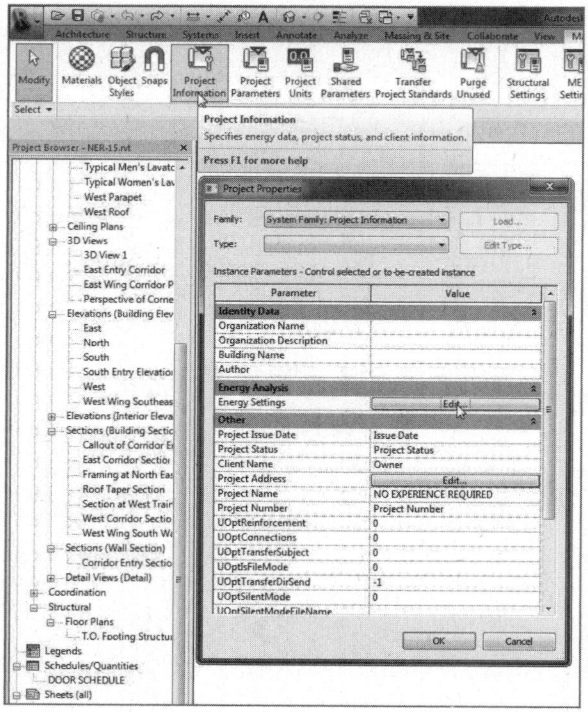

FIGURE 14.22: Filling out the project data

2. In the Project Properties dialog, click the Edit button next to Energy Settings, as shown to the right in Figure 14.22. The resulting dialog allows you to add the project's geographical information as well as energy data. This lets you export the information to gbXML as well as provide information so that your architectural model can be imported into Revit MEP.

SAVE THAT MODEL!

You may have noticed that a save reminder keeps popping up (as shown here). Revit likes to ask you if you want to save the model *before* you execute a command. This process has greatly reduced the number of crashes when compared to the number in AutoCAD.

3. Click OK.

4. You can fill out the rest of the information as follows (see Figure 14.22):

   ▶ Project Issue Date: **5/10/12**

   ▶ Project Status: **100%**

   ▶ Project Name: **NO EXPERIENCE REQUIRED**

   ▶ Project Number: **20090342**

   ▶ Owner: Your name

N O T E   The NO EXPERIENCE REQUIRED text has already been entered. This is because you added it to the appropriate field in the title block. Remember, when you're dealing with Revit, and databases in general, it's a two-way flow of information.

5. Click OK.

6. Open any sheet, and examine the title block. All of the information should be filled out.

You can now populate the information in a sheet. Before we jump into printing, we need to cover one more item quickly: adding a drawing list.

Generating a Cover Sheet

It goes without saying that this ingenious method of creating and managing sheets wouldn't be quite perfect unless you could generate a sheet list and put it on a cover sheet. Well, this is Revit. Of course you can do this! The best part is that you already have the experience necessary to carry out this procedure.

The objective here is to create a sheet list and add it to a cover sheet. Follow these steps:

1. On the View tab, click Schedules ➤ Sheet List, as shown in Figure 14.23.

2. In the Sheet List Properties dialog, add Sheet Number and Sheet Name, as shown in Figure 14.24.

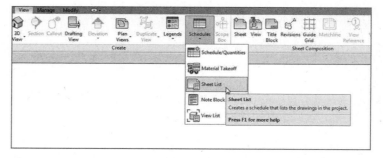

FIGURE 14.23: Selecting Schedules ➤ Sheet List on the View tab

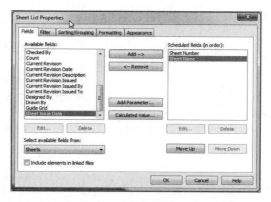

FIGURE 14.24: Adding Sheet Number and Sheet Name (in that order)

3. Click the Sorting/Grouping tab.

4. Sort by Sheet Number.

5. Select Ascending.

6. Click OK.

Wow! Creating a schedule is so easy, you'll probably be doing this on your lunch break instead of playing Internet games!

While you're still in the schedule, you can add a new row. This row will constitute a filler sheet that you can add to the Project Browser at a later date:

1. Make sure you're in the Sheet List schedule.

2. On the Rows panel, click the New button, as shown in Figure 14.25.

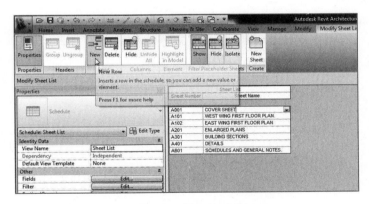

FIGURE 14.25: You can add a placeholder row.

3. Call the new row **COVER SHEET A001** (see Figure 14.25).

For now, let's keep this schedule in the Project Browser and create a cover sheet onto which you can drag it. You'll create a new title-block family, add it to the project, and then drag the drawing list onto the cover. Follow these steps:

1. Click the Application button, and choose New ➤ Title Block, as shown in Figure 14.26.

2. Select E1 - 42 x 30.rft (1050 × 750).

3. Click Open.

4. On the Text panel of the Create tab, click Label, as shown in Figure 14.27.

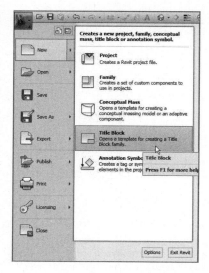

FIGURE 14.26: Creating a new title block

FIGURE 14.27: Clicking Label on the Create tab

5. In the Properties dialog, click Edit Type.

6. Click Duplicate.

7. Call the new tag **TITLE**, and click OK.

8. Make sure Text Font is set to Arial.

9. Change Text Size to 1″ (25mm).

10. Click Bold.

11. Click OK.

12. On the Format panel, click the Center Middle button.

13. Pick a point in the upper center of the sheet.

After you place the tag, you immediately see the Edit Label dialog. This dialog lets you add the label you wish. When you load this cover sheet into the project and add it to a new sheet, the project information will populate automatically.

Next, you'll add the correct tags to the sheet. Follow along:

1. Select Project Name, and click the Add Parameter(s) To Label button, as shown in Figure 14.28.

2. Click OK.

3. Click the label, and widen the grips. You may have to adjust the label so that it's centered in the sheet, as shown in Figure 14.29.

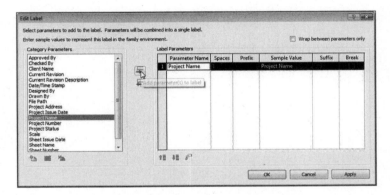

FIGURE 14.28:   Adding the project name to the label

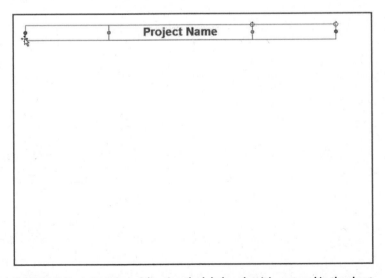

FIGURE 14.29:   Adjusting the label so that it's centered in the sheet

4. Click the Application button, and then click Save As ➤ Family.

5. Save the file somewhere that makes sense to you. Call it **Title Sheet**.

6. Click Load Into Project.

    If you have more than one project open, a dialog opens in which you can choose a project to load the sheet into. If this is the case, choose the No Experience Required project on which you're working. If the sheet appears under your cursor in a sheet view, press Esc.

7. In the Project Browser, right-click Sheets, and select New Sheet.

8. In the New Sheet dialog, select Title Sheet.

9. Also in the New Sheet dialog, select the placeholder sheet that you added to the schedule, as shown in Figure 14.30.

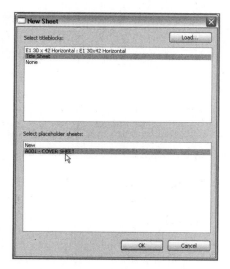

FIGURE 14.30: Adding the new sheet

10. Click OK. Your tag is populated with the project information.

11. In the Project Browser, find Sheet List (it's in the Schedules/ Quantities category), and drag it onto the sheet.

12. Select the schedule, and adjust it so that the text is readable. Your title sheet, although not very glorious, should look like Figure 14.31.

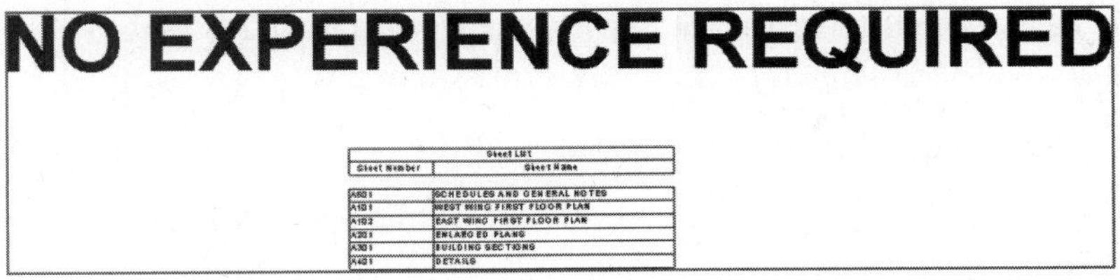

FIGURE 14.31:   The completed title sheet

In most cases, you don't want the actual cover sheet to be an item in the schedule. You can fix this. While still in the cover sheet, deselect Appears In Sheet List in the Properties dialog, as shown in Figure 14.32.

FIGURE 14.32:   Deselect the Appears In Sheet List option.

Perfect! You have a handful of sheets. The beauty is that you don't have to leave the model to see how these sheets are shaping up. In Revit, they're always just a click away.

You have these sheets, so let's explore how you send them to the plotter. After all, you're producing paper construction documents.

Printing from Revit Architecture

Luckily, printing is one of the easiest things you'll confront in Revit. However, you must consider some dangerous defaults when printing. I can go out on a limb and say that printing from Revit is too easy in some cases.

In this procedure, you'll print a set of drawings. Pay special attention to the warnings—they will steer you clear of danger. Follow along:

1. Click the Application button, and select Print.

2. For the printer name, select the printer to which you wish to print.

3. If you're printing to a file, you can choose to combine all files into one or create separate files. Choose to combine into one file. If you aren't printing to a file, ignore this choice.

4. For Print Range, you can print the current window, the visible portion of the current window, or you can choose Selected Views/Sheets. In this case, choose Selected Views/Sheets.

 T I P   When you choose to print the current window, you're printing the current view. When you choose to print the visible portion of the current window, you're printing the area into which you're currently zoomed. In Revit, you don't pick a window as you do in CAD.

5. Click the Select button, as shown at the lower left of Figure 14.33.

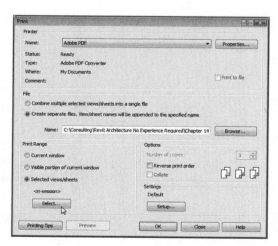

F I G U R E   1 4 . 3 3 :   Choosing the options to print the drawings

6. At the bottom of the View/Sheet Set dialog, deselect Views.

7. Only the sheets are listed. Click all the sheets.

8. Click OK.

9. Revit asks if you want to save the settings for a future print. Click No.

10. In the lower-right corner in the Settings area, click the Setup button, as shown in Figure 14.34.

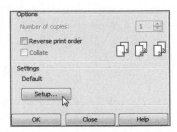

FIGURE 14.34: Clicking the Setup button

 TIP   Printing from Revit is similar to an AutoCAD paperspace or modelspace environment where you can print a specific view or print an entire sheet. The only difference is that you aren't bothered by scale. The sheets and views are printed at the scale specified in Revit.

 WARNING   Make a habit of clicking the Setup button before you print. You need to verify some crucial settings in the resulting dialog.

11. For Paper, choose the correct paper size to which you wish to print.

12. For Paper Placement, choose Center.

13. For Zoom, select Zoom: 100% Of Size.

 WARNING   The Fit To Page radio button should never be selected unless you know you aren't plotting to scale. If you want a reduced set of drawings, you can specify Zoom and then change to a smaller percentage (50% is a half-size set).

14. For the options, select Hide Ref/Work Planes.

15. Select Hide Unreferenced View Tags.

16. Hide Scope Boxes.

17. Hide Crop Boundaries.

18. Click OK.

19. Click OK again, and your plot is off.

20. Save the file.

There you have it.

The book doesn't create a sheet for every single view. If you feel as though you're still lacking experience in creating sheets and printing, go ahead and create more sheets and keep printing away until you're confident about moving on to Chapter 15, "Creating Rooms and Area Plans."

Are You Experienced?

Now you can...

- ☑ **create sheets by dragging views and creating viewports**

- ☑ **configure project parameters to populate the sheets**

- ☑ **create a drawing list for a cover sheet**

Creating Rooms and Area Plans

This chapter brings you to a great point in the Autodesk® Revit® Architecture platform. You're in a position where you can begin to build on what you've added to your model up to now. By creating rooms and areas, you're starting to merge the model with the database. In Chapter 11, "Schedules and Tags," you did the same thing; but by adding rooms and areas, you physically build your construction documents while at the same time adding crucial information to the model's database.

- ▶ **Creating rooms**

- ▶ **Adding a room schedule**

- ▶ **Adding a color fill plan**

- ▶ **Adding room separators**

- ▶ **Creating an area plan**

Creating Rooms

The first topic we'll tackle is the task of creating a room and adding it to the model. The procedures that follow will focus on finding where to launch the room and areas and the parameters Revit looks for while placing a room into the floor plan.

Because Revit draws from a database to gather information, the process of creating a room boils down to your adding some notes to an already-built form. When you place the room in the model, Revit automatically tags it. Unlike other drafting applications, however, Revit doesn't rely on the tag for its information. When a room is in the model, it can either contain or not contain a tag. This is a great way to organize the flow of room information.

To get started, open the model on which you've been working. If you skipped the previous chapter, go to the book's web page at www.sybex.com/go/revit2014ner. From there, you can browse to Chapter 15 and find the file called NER-15.rvt.

The objective of the following procedure is to find the Room & Area panel on the Architecture tab, and to configure and add some rooms to the model. Follow along:

1. In the Project Browser, find the dependent view called Level 1 East, and open it.

2. In the Room & Area panel on the Architecture tab, click the Room button, as shown in Figure 15.1.

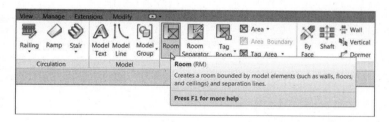

FIGURE 15.1: Clicking the Room button on the Room & Area panel of the Architecture tab

3. Hover your cursor over the southeast room, as shown in Figure 15.2. An X appears, along with the outline of a room tag.

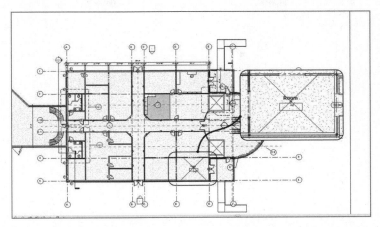

FIGURE 15.2: When you hover your mouse over the intended area of the room, you see an indication that Revit has found the bounding edges.

4. Pick a spot in the middle of the four walls.

5. Press Esc.

You've now added a room to the model. Of course, it's a nondescript room name with a nondescript room number. Let's correct that by changing the room name and number on the screen:

1. Select the room tag that you just added to the model.

NOTE   You may be sick of hearing this by now, but I'll say it again: when you select a component in Revit, the items that turn blue are always editable.

2. Click the Room text.

3. Change the name to **SOUTHEAST CORNER OFFICE**.

4. Click room number 1.

5. Change the number to **101** (see Figure 15.3).

Now that you have a room in place and it's named properly, you can start cooking in terms of adding more rooms. This is because Revit will begin to number the rooms sequentially as you place them into the model.

When you modify the fields in a tag in Revit, the best method to finalize the data is to click an area away from the tag. Doing so ensures that you don't inadvertently create an additional line in the tag's value.

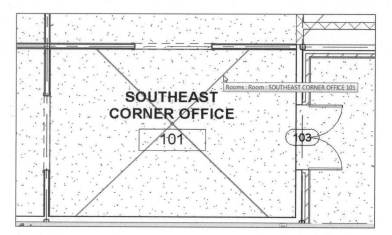

FIGURE 15.3: Changing the room name and number to SOUTHEAST CORNER OFFICE and 101, respectively

Next you'll populate the rest of the east wing with rooms. Follow these steps:

1. On the Room & Area panel of the Architecture tab, click the Room button.

 TIP If you get the Save reminder, be sure to save the model. In no situation is this ever a bad idea!

2. Place a room in the adjacent area, as shown at lower left in Figure 15.4.

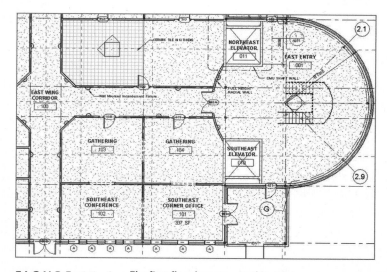

FIGURE 15.4: The first floor layout up to this point

3. Call the room **SOUTHEAST CONFERENCE** (see Figure 15.4).

> **N O T E**   Did you notice that the room tag tries to align itself with the adjacent tag? This is a fantastic feature in Revit Architecture.

4. On the Room & Area panel of the Architecture tab, click the Room button again.

5. Place a room in the radial entry area.

6. Rename the room **EAST ENTRY**.

7. Renumber the room **001**.

8. Place a room in the south elevator shaft.

9. Rename and renumber it **SOUTHEAST ELEVATOR** and **010**.

10. Place a room in the north elevator shaft.

11. Rename and renumber it **NORTHEAST ELEVATOR** and **011**.

12. Place a room in the corridor.

13. Call it **EAST WING CORRIDOR**, and number it **100**.

14. Just north of SOUTHEAST CONFERENCE and SOUTHEAST CORNER OFFICE, place two rooms, each called **GATHERING**. Number them **103** and **104**.

15. Zoom over to the west portion of the east wing, where the lavatories are located.

16. In the north lavatory, add a room named **MEN'S**, numbered **105**.

17. In the south lavatory, add a room named **WOMEN'S**, numbered **106**.

I think you're getting the concept of adding rooms. Although you've added a number of rooms to the east wing, you need to begin adding some plain old offices. The next procedure will involve adding offices to the rest of the spaces in the east wing of Level 1. From there, you can look at a room's properties and figure out how to alter the room information. Follow along:

1. Make sure you're in the east wing area of the model, on Level 1.

2. On the Room & Area panel of the Architecture tab, click the Room button.

3. Pick the large area to the right of the women's lavatory, as shown in Figure 15.5.

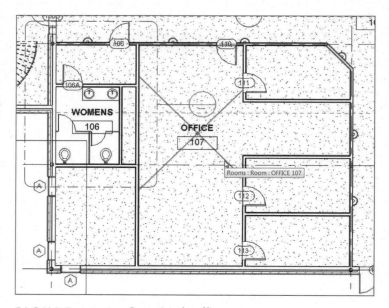

FIGURE 15.5: Renaming the office

4. Rename the room **OFFICE**, and change the number to **107** (see Figure 15.5).

N O T E   If the numbering starts to become inconsistent with the examples in the book, that's okay. This will happen from time to time in Revit. You can either accept the differences between the book and your model, or you can renumber the rooms to match. Either way, the numbering won't affect the outcome of the procedures.

5. Click the Room button.

6. Add rooms to the rest of the vacant areas, renaming them all **OFFICE**. (Skip the kitchen area and the room to the right of it, as shown in Figure 15.6.)

With all the rooms in (at least in this section of the building), you can begin examining specific properties to see how you can add functionality, and further populate the database information pertaining to each room.

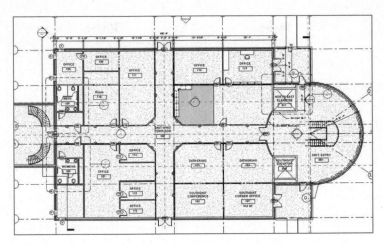

FIGURE 15.6: Adding rooms to the remainder of the spaces

Configuring Properties

Each room has specific properties associated with it. There are floor finishes and wall finishes as well as ceiling types and finishes. It would be nice if Revit picked up this information by "reading" the ceilings, walls, and floors, but it doesn't. And for good reason—imagine having to create a different wall type for each paint color, and then splitting each partition as it passed through each room. In Revit, you specify individual room finishes in the properties of the room itself.

In the next procedure, you'll generate additional room information in the properties of the room. Follow these steps:

1. Zoom in on the SOUTHEAST CORNER OFFICE 101 room.

2. Hover your cursor over the room until you see the X, as shown in Figure 15.7.

TIP   Any time you wish to view the properties of a room, you need to click the actual room, not the room tag. Sometimes, selecting a room can be difficult because the room is invisible until you hover over it. With some practice, this process will soon become second nature.

3. Pick the room, as shown in Figure 15.8.

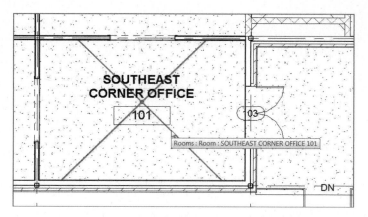

FIGURE 15.7: Hover the cursor over the room until the X appears.

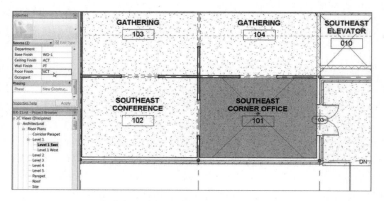

FIGURE 15.8: Adding values to the identity data

4. In the Properties dialog, scroll down to the Identity Data group.

5. Add **WD-1** to Base Finish.

6. Add **ACT** to Ceiling Finish.

7. Add **PT** to Wall Finish.

8. Add **VCT** to Floor Finish (see Figure 15.8).

9. Select the SOUTHEAST CONFERENCE room.

10. In the Properties dialog, click into the Base Finish field. Click the arrow for the pull-down menu, and select WD-1, as shown in Figure 15.9.

11. Change the rest of the fields using the previous entries.

12. Save the model.

FIGURE 15.9: When a field has been added to the database, it's available for the rest of the rooms.

Changing a room's properties is a simple task. There is, however, one more item to discuss. It pertains to a room that spans multiple floors, such as the east entry.

The objective of the next procedure is to change the height of the east entry room's properties:

1. Zoom in on the east entry area, and select the room, as shown in Figure 15.10.

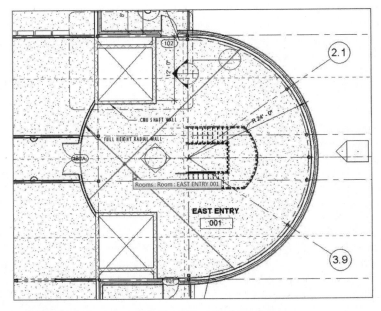

FIGURE 15.10: Selecting the east entry room

2. In the Properties dialog, change Upper Limit to Roof.

3. Change Limit Offset to 0. Doing so sets the east entry room to extend from Level 1 to the roof.

Now that you have experience changing the properties of the rooms, it's time to look at the properties of the walls that divide the rooms. You certainly noticed that when you placed the rooms in the lavatories, the rooms didn't fill the small entry areas. You can correct this by changing the walls' room-bounding properties.

Room-Bounding Properties

By default, each wall you add to the Revit model automatically defines a room boundary, and this is what you want 95 percent of the time. In some situations, however, you don't want a wall to separate the room. In such cases, you can modify the instance parameters of the wall to disallow the division of the room.

In this procedure, you'll turn off the room bounding in certain walls. Follow along:

1. In the East Wing floor plan, zoom in on the lavatory area.

2. Select the wall that divides the men's toilet area from the men's lavatory entry area, as shown in Figure 15.11.

3. In the Properties dialog, scroll down to the Room Bounding row.

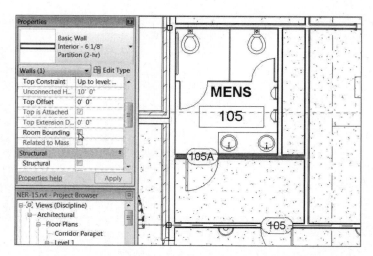

FIGURE 15.11: Selecting the partition within the men's lavatory

4. Deselect Room Bounding (see Figure 15.11).

5. Repeat the procedure in the women's lavatory.

6. Save the model.

Having the ability to add rooms and manipulate the information easily in the Revit database gives you a tremendous advantage as you move forward with the rest of the model. Also, that information is relayed into the room's tag, which is automatically added as you place rooms into the model.

This concept brings us to the next topic: how to change the tag to display the information you desire on the drawings.

Placing and Manipulating Room Tags

As mentioned earlier, the room tag is merely a vehicle to relay the room's data to the construction documents. As a default, a room tag is added automatically as you place the room into the model. A default room tag is included, but you aren't stuck with it.

Let's add an alternate room tag to the room and open the tag's Family Editor to investigate the composition of the tag:

1. Zoom in to SOUTHEAST CORNER OFFICE.

2. Select the room tag.

3. In the Type Selector, select Room Tag With Area. The tag displays the area, as shown in Figure 15.12.

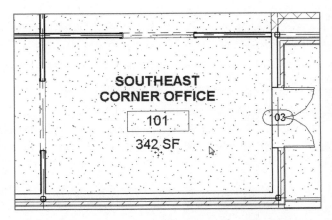

FIGURE 15.12: Change the type to Room Tag With Area.

That was way too easy! Let's take a closer look at what you just did. A room tag is nothing more than the cover sheet label you created back in Chapter 14, "Creating Sheets and Printing." All you need to do is open the file and place a tag into the family.

To open the tag's Family Editor, follow this procedure:

1. Select the room tag for SOUTHWEST CORNER OFFICE.

2. On the Modify | Room Tags tab, click the Edit Family button.

3. With the family file open, click the Room Name piece of text that is visible. (These pieces of text are actually labels.)

4. On the Modify | Label tab, click the Edit Label button.

5. In the Edit Label dialog, the list to the left displays all the parameters that you can add to the room tag (see Figure 15.13). Don't change anything; click OK.

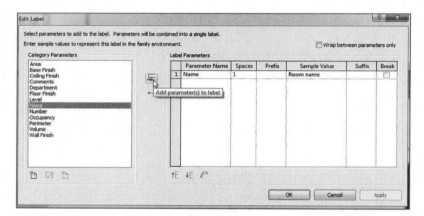

FIGURE 15.13: A list of available parameters that you can add to the room tag

---

 WARNING   If you're modifying the room tag, do yourself and the rest of your design team a huge favor and inform everyone that you're changing your company's standards! If you're the BIM manager, set the permissions to this network directory accordingly.

---

6. Close out of this file without saving any changes.

Now that you know what tag Revit uses when it places a room and how to manipulate that tag, let's tie the tag into something more robust. A tag is just a reflection of the room data. You can add another Revit object that does the same thing: a room schedule.

Adding a Room Schedule

Up to this point in your career, you've been adding room information twice, or sometimes three times. Why? Because you had to fill out the tag in the plan and then fill out the same information in the room schedule. If you were in the unfortunate situation of having an enlarged plan, then you added the information a third time. When you needed to change that information, you had to do so in multiple places. I'm not saying that Revit will end all your problems, but it sure will make life easier.

The objective of the next procedure is to create a room schedule. You'll then finish filling out the room information from the schedule, thus saving time and increasing accuracy. Follow along:

1. On the View tab, click Schedules, and then click the Schedule/ Quantities button.

2. In the New Schedule dialog, select Rooms from the list at left.

3. Click OK.

4. On the Fields tab of the Schedule Properties dialog that opens, add the following fields in the specified order (see Figure 15.14):

   ▶ Number

   ▶ Name

   ▶ Base Finish

   ▶ Wall Finish

   ▶ Floor Finish

   ▶ Ceiling Finish

   ▶ Comments

   ▶ Level

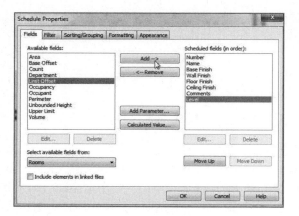

FIGURE 15.14: Adding fields to the schedule

---

5. Click the Sorting/Grouping tab.

6. Sort by number.

7. Click OK. Your schedule should look similar to Figure 15.15.

Room Schedule							
Number	Name	Base Finish	Wall Finish	Floor Finish	Ceiling Finish	Comments	Level
001	EAST ENTRY						Level 1
010	SOUTHEAST ELEVATOR						Level 1
011	NORTHEAST ELEVATOR						Level 1
100	EAST WING CORRIDOR						Level 1
101	SOUTHEAST CORNER OFFICE	WD-1	PT	VCT	ACT		Level 1
102	SOUTHEAST CONFERENCE	WD-1	PT	VCT	ACT		Level 1
103	GATHERING						Level 1
104	GATHERING						Level 1
105	MENS						Level 1
106	WOMENS						Level 1
107	OFFICE						Level 1
109	OFFICE						Level 1
110	OFFICE						Level 1
112	OFFICE						Level 1
113	OFFICE						Level 1
114	OFFICE						Level 1
115	OFFICE						Level 1
116	OFFICE						Level 1
117	OFFICE						Level 1
118	OFFICE						Level 1
119	OFFICE						Level 1

FIGURE 15.15: The room schedule

---

8. With the schedule still open, click into the EAST ENTRY Base Finish cell, and type **WD-2**.

9. Click into the Floor Finish cell, and type **TER** (for Terrazzo).

10. Click into the Wall Finish cell, and type **VINYL**.

11. Click into the Ceiling Finish cell, and type a hyphen (-).

TURNING OFF UNWANTED ROOMS

Your model may have an errant room that doesn't belong in the schedule. Because going step-by-step through a book doesn't give you a true feel for a real-world scenario, I can tell you that you'll wind up with some misplaced rooms. This is OK, because you can turn them off in the schedule. If you click the Not Placed/ Not Enclosed menu, you'll see that you can show, hide, or isolate unwanted data. For this example, choose Hide to remove the row (see the following graphic):

12. Click into the EAST WING CORRIDOR Base Finish cell. Click the menu arrow, as shown in Figure 15.16. You have a choice between two base finishes: choose WD-2.

		Room Schedule					
Number	Name	Base Finish	Wall Finish	Floor Finish	Ceiling Finish	Comments	Level
001	EAST ENTRY	WD-2	VINYL	TER	-		Level 1
010	SOUTHEAST ELEVATOR						Level 1
011	NORTHEAST ELEVATOR						Level 1
100	EAST WING CORRIDOR	WD-1	/INYL	TER	ACT		Level 1
101	SOUTHEAST CORNER OFFICE	WD-1	'T	VCT	ACT		Level 1
102	SOUTHEAST CONFERENCE	WD-1	PT	VCT	ACT		Level 1
103	GATHERING						Level 1
104	GATHERING						Level 1
105	MENS						Level 1
106	WOMENS						Level 1
107	OFFICE						Level 1
109	OFFICE						Level 1
110	OFFICE						Level 1
112	OFFICE						Level 1
113	OFFICE						Level 1
114	OFFICE						Level 1
115	OFFICE						Level 1
116	OFFICE						Level 1
117	OFFICE						Level 1
118	OFFICE						Level 1
119	OFFICE						Level 1

FIGURE 15.16: Filling out the room schedule

13. Change the other values to VINYL, TER, and ACT (see Figure 15.16).

With the rooms in place and a schedule filled out, let's move to a more colorful aspect of placing rooms in the model: adding a color-fill plan.

Adding a Color-Fill Plan

Another benefit of using the room feature in Revit is that you can add a color-fill plan at any time, and you can create virtually any type of color or pattern scheme you desire. Here's the best part: adding one is so easy, it's almost fun.

In this procedure you'll make a duplicate of the East Wing floor plan and create a color scheme based on room names. Follow these steps:

1. Right-click the Level 1 floor-plan view, and select Duplicate View ➢ Duplicate With Detailing, as shown in Figure 15.17. If you get an error pertaining to the view references, click the Delete button.

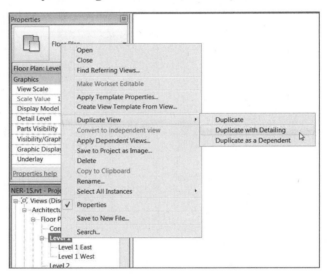

FIGURE 15.17:   Duplicating the view

2. Right-click the new view, and select Rename.

3. Rename the view **Level 1 Color Plan**.

4. Click OK.

5. Open the new plan if it isn't open already.

6. On the Analyze tab, click the Color Fill Legend button, as shown in Figure 15.18.

7. Change Space Type to Rooms and Color Scheme to Name (see Figure 15.19).

8. Place the color scheme into the model in the upper-right corner of the view (inside the crop region).

FIGURE 15.18:   Clicking the Color Fill Legend button

9. Click OK. You have a nice color plan.

10. Select the color scheme legend.

11. Click the Edit Scheme button on the Modify | Color Fill Legends tab, as shown in Figure 15.20.

12. In the Edit Color Scheme dialog that opens, you can alter the color and the fill pattern for each room. After you investigate this area, click OK.

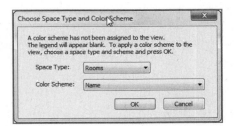

FIGURE 15.19:   Specifying the color scheme

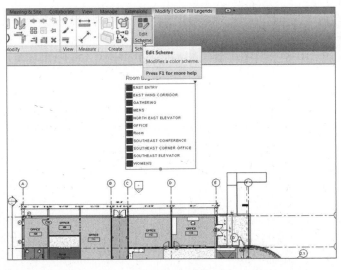

FIGURE 15.20:   Proceeding to edit the scheme

Pretty cool concept! You may notice that the two rooms you skipped are still white. It's time to look at this situation. The problem is, there are no walls dividing the two rooms, but it would be nice to have two separate rooms anyway. To do this, you can add a room separator.

Adding Room Separators

Although it seems like a small issue, adding room separators has been known to confuse people. In Revit, you can physically draw a room without any walls. Or you can draw a line in the sand between two rooms that aren't separated by an actual wall. This is known as adding a *room separator*.

Let's separate the kitchen from the break room by adding a room separator:

1. In the Level 1 floor plan, zoom in on the area shown in Figure 15.21.

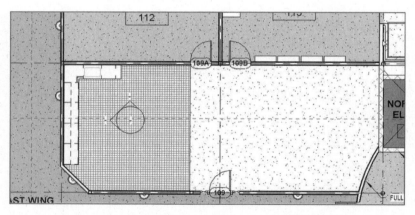

FIGURE 15.21: Place a room over the tiles (it will spill into the adjacent room).

2. On the Room & Area panel of the Architecture tab, click the Room button.

3. Place a room over the top of the tile flooring (see Figure 15.21).

4. On the Room & Area panel of the Architecture tab, choose Room ➢ Room Separator, as shown in Figure 15.22.

FIGURE 15.22:   Click the Room Separator button on the Room & Area panel of the Architecture tab.

5. On the Draw tab, click the Pick Lines icon.

6. Pick the edge of the flooring, as shown in Figure 15.23.

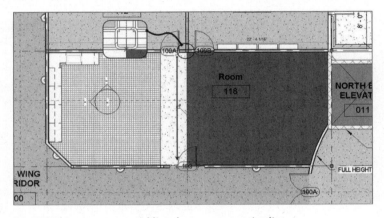

FIGURE 15.23:   Adding the room-separation line

7. Click the Room button.

8. Place a room to the right of the kitchen area.

9. Change the room to the left to **KITCHEN**.

10. Change the room to the right to **BREAK**.

You're really moving along. You now have a fully coordinated room schedule tied into a room color-fill plan that can be modified by simply changing a room tag. How did you ever live without Revit?

The next item we'll discuss is how to create a gross area plan. The process is similar to, but slightly more involved than, creating a room color plan.

Creating an Area Plan

Almost any job of considerable size will require an area plan at some point in the project's early development. This normally occurs in the programming phase, but the need for this type of plan can persist well into the later stages of the project.

The objective of the next procedure is to create a separate floor plan and then divide it into areas. Follow these steps:

1. On the Room & Area panel of the Architecture tab, select Area and click the Area Plan button, as shown in Figure 15.24.

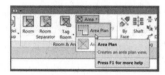

FIGURE 15.24: Clicking the Area Plan button

2. In the New Area Plan dialog, choose Gross Building from the Type list, and choose Level 1 for the Area Plan Views.

3. Click OK.

4. Click Yes to create area boundaries automatically. You now have a new floor plan with a blue boundary around the perimeter of the entire building.

5. On the Room & Area panel, click the Area Boundary button, as shown in Figure 15.25.

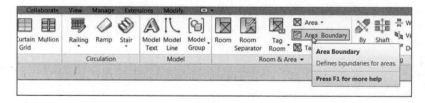

FIGURE 15.25: Clicking Area Boundary

6. Draw a line, as shown in Figure 15.26, separating the corridor from the east wing.

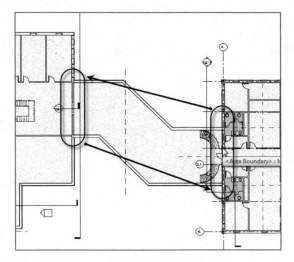

FIGURE 15.26: Separating the areas

7. Draw another similar separator between the west wing and the corridor.

NOTE If your lines aren't exactly snapping to the endpoints, it isn't a big deal. Unlike Sketch Mode, Revit is much more forgiving when it comes to creating area separations.

8. On the Room & Area panel, click the Area button, as shown in Figure 15.27.

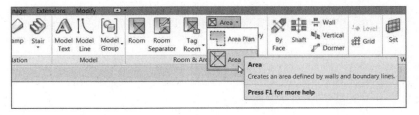

FIGURE 15.27: The Area button

9. If Revit says a tag isn't loaded, click Yes to load the family. Browse to Annotation ➤ Area Tag.rfa.

10. Place an area in the west wing, then in the corridor, and then in the east wing, as shown in Figure 15.28.

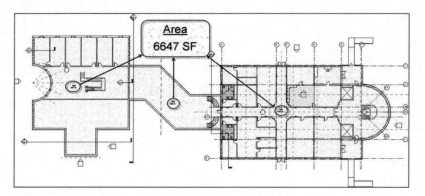

FIGURE 15.28: The plan is divided into three areas.

11. Select the tag in the west wing.

12. Rename it **WEST WING**.

13. Click the Corridor tag.

14. Rename it **LINK**.

15. Click the East Wing tag.

16. Rename it **EAST WING**.

17. On the Color Fill panel of the Annotate tab, click the Color Fill Legend button.

18. Place the legend in the upper-right corner of the view.

19. In the Choose Space Type And Color Scheme dialog, choose Areas (Gross Building) for Space Type and Gross Building Area for Color Scheme.

20. Click OK.

21. Select the color scheme legend.

22. Click the Edit Scheme button on the Modify | Color Fill Legends tab.

23. For Color, change Area Type to Name.

24. Click OK in the warning dialog.

25. Click OK to return to the model (see Figure 15.29).

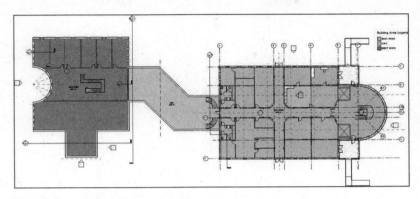

FIGURE 15.29: Adding an area legend

26. Save the model.

Great job! You now have experience with creating area plans. If you feel as though you could use some more practice before you begin a real project, there are five more floors in this model that you can work on. You can either work on your own, or step back through this chapter's procedures.

Are You Experienced?

Now you can...

☑ **add rooms to the model**

☑ **add room separators to the model**

☑ **create color-scheme plans**

☑ **create area plans**

☑ **create room schedules**

☑ **update the rooms in the model directly from a room schedule**

Advanced Wall Topics

More on walls? Really? It seems as though all we do is walls. Well, that's because buildings are composed mainly of walls. As you may have noticed, the exterior walls are compound wall structures with reveals and parapet caps. In the west wing, you have a staircase that is completely unsupported. It would be nice to add a wall to make those stairs less spongy. Given the fact that the west wing is a high-end architectural woodwork area, that wall could use some trims that can be added right to the wall's profile. Also, we haven't touched on a curtain wall of any kind.

▶ **Creating compound walls**

▶ **Adding wall sweeps**

▶ **Creating stacked walls**

▶ **Creating curtain walls**

▶ **Adding a wall to a massing object**

Creating Compound Walls

The first item to tackle is how to develop a wall with different materials. The exterior walls you've been using in this model are a prime example of compound walls. The bottom 3′ (900mm) of the wall consists of concrete block, and the rest of the wall is brick. When you cut a section through the wall, you can see that the wall has an airspace as well as a metal stud–wall backup.

Usually, these chapters start with a claim that "the following procedure is so easy...a child could do it" (or something of that nature). The development of compound walls isn't the easiest thing you'll tackle in the Autodesk® Revit® Architecture software. This procedure is somewhat touchy, and doing it well takes practice. In this section, you'll create an interior wall with a wood finish on the bottom along with different wood material on the top. You'll also extrude a chair rail along the wall.

 N O T E   Metric users should not type in mm or other metric abbreviations when entering amounts suggested in the exercises. Revit will not accept such abbreviations. Simply enter the number provided within the parentheses.

To get started, open the model on which you've been working. If you missed the previous chapter, go to the book's web page at www.sybex.com/go/revit2014ner. From there, you can browse to the Chapter 16 folder and find the NER-16.rvt file.

The objective of this procedure is to create a compound wall from a basic wall. Follow along:

1. Open the Level 1 West dependent floor plan view.

2. On the Architecture tab, click the Wall button.

3. In the Type Selector in the Properties dialog, choose Basic Wall : Generic - 6″ (152mm).

4. In the Properties dialog, click the Edit Type button.

5. Click Duplicate.

6. Call the new wall **West Stairwell support wall**, and click OK.

7. Click the Edit button in the Structure row.

8. Click into the Material cell for the Structure row, as shown in Figure 16.1.

9. Click the [...] button.

10. In the Material Browser, select Metal - Stud Layer, and click OK.

11. Change the thickness to **5 1/2″ (140mm)** (see Figure 16.1).

12. At the bottom of the Edit Assembly dialog, click the Preview button (see Figure 16.2).

13. With the preview open, change View to Section: Modify Type Attributes.

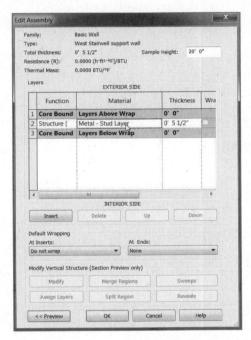

FIGURE 16.1:   Changing the structure to a 5 1/2″ (140mm) metal stud

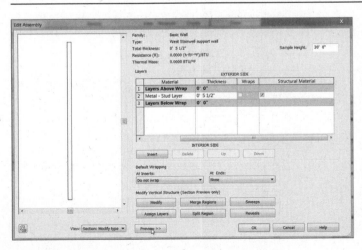

FIGURE 16.2:   Changing the view to a section

It doesn't seem as though you've done much, but you've set the stage to start building your wall. It's time now to focus back on the Layers field.

Adding Layers to the Compound Wall

If you're an Autodesk® AutoCAD® veteran, the term *layer* takes on a different meaning. In Revit, the term *layer*, as it pertains to a wall assembly, represents a material layer that is assigned an actual thickness as well as its own material.

As you can see in Figure 16.3, Revit understands the difference between interior and exterior. For the following procedure, you'll add materials to both the exterior and interior portion of the wall. Follow these steps:

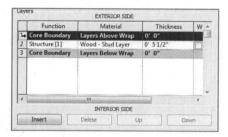

FIGURE 16.3:   Clicking row 1 to highlight the entire row

1. In the Layers area, click the number 1, as shown in Figure 16.3. (It's the row that holds the Layers Above Wrap field.)

TIP   Note that to highlight an entire row in the Layers area, you must click right on the actual number. A small black arrow will appear, indicating that you can click that spot to highlight the entire row.

2. Click the Insert button. Revit creates a new layer above the one you select. The new layer is always set to Function: Structure [1], Material: <By Category>, and Thickness: 0.

3. Change Function to Finish 1 [4].

4. Click into the Material cell, and click the [...] button.

5. Select Gypsum Wall Board.

Adding a preview to the Edit Assembly dialog is not only a nice feature; it's also absolutely necessary to continue with the editing of the wall. As you'll soon see, you won't have access to certain buttons without the preview being displayed in a sectional view.

6. Click OK in the Material Browser.

7. Change Thickness to 5/8″ (13mm).

8. Click row 4 (Layers Below Wrap).

9. Click the Insert button.

10. Click the Down button, as shown in Figure 16.4. It's located below the Layers area all the way to the right. Your new layer becomes 5.

The preview instantly adds the changes to the wall. This interaction will be of great benefit down the road.

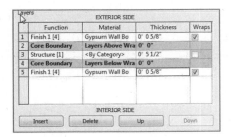

	Function	Material	Thickness	Wraps
1	Finish 1 [4]	Gypsum Wall Bo	0' 0 5/8"	☑
2	Core Boundary	Layers Above Wra	0' 0"	
3	Structure [1]	<By Category>	0' 5 1/2"	☐
4	Core Boundary	Layers Below Wra	0' 0"	
5	Finish 1 [4]	Gypsum Wall Bo	0' 0 5/8"	☑

FIGURE 16.4: Adding a 5/8″ gypsum layer to the interior side of the wall

11. Change Function to Finish 1 [4].

12. Click into the Material cell, and click the [...] button.

13. Find and select Gypsum Wall Board.

14. Click OK in the Material Browser.

15. Change Thickness to 5/8″ (13mm). Your Layers field should resemble Figure 16.4.

Now that the wall is wrapped with one layer of ⅝″ (13mm) gypsum on each side, let's start placing the veneered plywood layers on the exterior of the wall.

In the next procedure, you'll add a ¾″ (19mm) plywood layer to the exterior of the wall. Follow along:

1. Click 1 Finish 1 [4] (the top layer).

2. Click Insert.

3. Change Function to Finish 2 [5].

4. Change Material to Mahogany (it's the mahogany material that has Plywood for the cut pattern). Click OK.

5. Change the Thickness to 3/4" (19mm). Your wall's layers should resemble Figure 16.5.

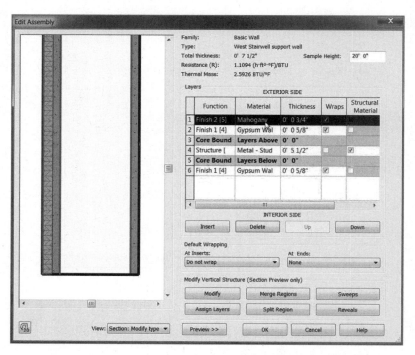

FIGURE 16.5: Adding the 3/4" (19mm) mahogany veneered plywood material

6. At the bottom of the dialog, click the OK button.

7. Click Apply.

In the preview, you can hold down the wheel button on your mouse and pan around. You can also spin the wheel in and out to zoom in and out of the preview.

WARNING   By clicking OK and then Apply, you're basically saving your work. In the Edit Assembly dialog, there is no Save or Apply button as you create the wall. Also, never press Esc—doing so will cancel every change you've made and will almost certainly result in costly repairs to your computer as you rain blows upon it.

Next, let's go back in and split the wall materials in two. It would be nice if you could have cherry at the top and mahogany at the bottom. Revit gives you the ability to do this.

Adding New Materials by Splitting a Region

If you want more than one material along the face of a wall, you can use the Split Region command in the Edit Assembly dialog. The objective of the following procedure is to add a new material and then apply it to the top half of the plywood face:

1. Click the Edit button in the Structure row.

2. Click Layer 1 (the top layer).

3. Click Insert.

4. Change Function to Finish 2 [5].

5. For Material, select Cherry, and click OK. (Don't give it a thickness. The next procedure takes care of that.)

6. Click the Split Region button, as shown in Figure 16.6.

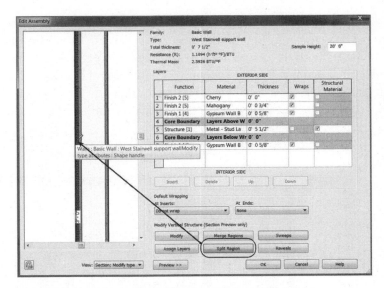

FIGURE 16.6: Cutting the plywood at a specific height

7. Move your cursor up the plywood face. The cursor turns into a knife. You also see a short, horizontal line within the plywood: this indicates where the region will be cut.

N O T E   Splitting the correct region can be extremely difficult even if you've done this procedure many times. Make sure you zoom in to the area, take a deep breath, and try again if you're getting frustrated.

8. When you see 3'–0" (900mm) in the temporary dimension, pick the point as shown in Figure 16.6. *Do not press Esc when you're finished!* If you place the split in the wrong place, click the Modify button and then select the split line you just created. You can then click the dimension field to edit the location. There is also a direction arrow that specifies whether the split is set from the bottom up (what you just did) or from the bottom down.

You've split the plywood. The only thing left to do is to apply a new material to the upper region. You can accomplish this by using the Assign Layers button.

Assigning Material to Different Layers

The Assign Layers command lets you choose where you would like to assign a layer. This is useful in the context of this dialog because you aren't stuck without the ability to move the layers around the wall as necessary. Of course, when you split the wall layer as you just did, notice that the thicknesses of the two wood layers are set to 0 and Variable. Revit needs you to assign an alternate layer at this point.

Next, you'll assign the cherry layer to the upper portion of the plywood. Follow along:

1. Pick the Layer 1 row (Cherry), as shown in Figure 16.7.

F I G U R E   1 6 . 7 :   Assigning the cherry layer to the upper portion of the wall

2. Click the Assign Layers button (see Figure 16.7).

3. Move your cursor over the upper region of the plywood layer, and pick. Cherry is assigned to the upper portion of the wall, and the thicknesses are set to 3/4″ (19mm) (again, see Figure 16.7).

4. At the bottom of the dialog, click OK.

5. Click Apply.

6. Click the Edit button in the Structure row to get back to the Edit Assembly dialog.

7. Pan to the top of the wall in the display, as shown in Figure 16.8.

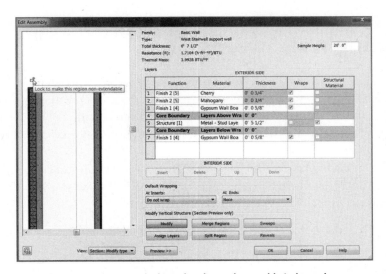

FIGURE 16.8: Unlocking the plywood to enable independent movement after the wall is placed into the model

8. Click the Modify button.

9. Hover your cursor over the top of the 3/4″ (19mm) plywood.

10. When the top of the plywood becomes highlighted, pick the line.

11. Unlock the blue padlock.

12. Click OK.

13. Click OK one more time to get back to the model.

14. Click the Modify button on the Architecture tab, or press Esc.

15. Save the model.

By unlocking the layer, you can move that layer up or down depending on what you need. Another good example of the usefulness of this functionality is when you need to slide a brick ledge down past a foundation.

Some people find splitting the regions in the Edit Assembly easy, whereas others consider it more difficult. I found the procedure difficult at first. If you're like me, this technique will require practice until you've done a few more walls. Don't worry—it gets easier as time passes.

Adding an automatic sweep along this wall would be nice. Come to think of it, a wood base and a chair rail would finish this wall perfectly.

Adding Wall Sweeps

The concept of adding a wall sweep is as close to actual construction as you can come without setting up a chop saw. That is because, when you want to add a specific profile to sweep along a wall, you need to go outside the model, find (or create) the profile, and then bring it into the model. This process is similar to ordering trim and installing it.

In the following procedure, you'll load a base and a chair rail trim into the model. You'll then include these items in the wall on which you've been working. Follow along:

1. On the Insert tab, click the Load Family button.

2. Go to the Profiles directory, and then go to Finish Carpentry.

3. Load the files Base 1.rfa and Casing Profile-2.rfa. (Use Ctrl to select both files.)

4. On the Manage tab, click the Materials button.

5. Right-click the material Cherry.

6. Click the Duplicate choice.

7. Call the new material **Cherry - Solid**.

8. Double-click the new material to open the Material Editor.

9. Change the cut pattern to **Wood 1**.

10. Select the material Mahogany.

11. Click the Duplicate button.

12. Change the name to **Mahogany Solid**.

13. In the Material Editor, change the cut pattern to **Wood 1**.

14. Click Done, and then click OK.

15. On the Architecture tab, click the Wall button.

16. Make sure the current wall is **West Stairwell support wall**.

17. In the Properties dialog, click Edit Type.

18. Click the Edit button in the Structure row.

19. Click the Sweeps button, as shown in Figure 16.9.

20. In the Wall Sweeps dialog, click the Add button, as shown in Figure 16.10.

FIGURE 16.9: Adding a sweep to the wall

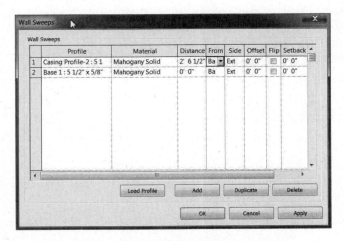

FIGURE 16.10: Configuring the two sweeps

21. For Profile, use Base 1 : 5 1/2″ × 5/8″ (140mm × 16mm).

22. For Material, use Mahogany Solid. Click OK.

23. Click the Add button again.

24. The new Profile is Casing Profile-2 : 5 1/2″ × 13/16″ (140mm × 21mm).

25. Set Material to Mahogany Solid.

26. Set Distance 2′–6 1/2″ (775mm) from the base (see Figure 16.10).

27. Click OK, and zoom in on the wall where the sweeps are located so that you can confirm they're placed as expected.

28. Click OK again.

29. Click OK one more time to get back to the model.

30. In the Properties panel, make sure Base Offset is set to 0′–0″.

31. In the Options bar, set Height to Unconnected with a height of 10′–0″ (3000mm).

32. Set Location Line to Finish Face: Exterior, and make sure the Chain option is on.

33. Set Offset to -1″ (-25mm).

34. Draw the wall by snapping to the inside of the stringers, as shown in Figure 16.11. You want to go in a clockwise direction, so start with the northern part of the staircase, marked 1 in Figure 16.11.

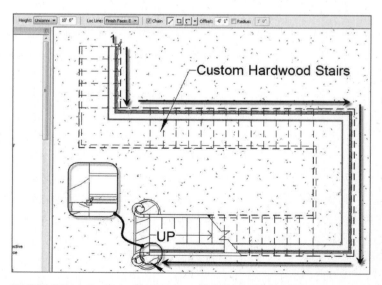

FIGURE 16.11: Placing the wall clockwise in the model

35. On the Geometry panel on the Modify | Place Wall tab, click the Wall Joins button.

36. Using the Wall Joins tool, go to each wall corner and make the join Mitered.

 T I P   If you receive a warning stating that a sweep can't be added, ignore it. This warning is sometimes generated when there is a sweep on the face of a wall.

The wall has been added to the model. Because you're placing it underneath a staircase, there will be issues with the wall's profile. This brings us to the next section of this chapter, which guides you through modifying a wall's shape after it has been placed into the model.

Modifying a Wall's Profile in Place

Although we touched on modifying a wall profile back in Chapter 2, "Creating a Model," in this section we'll take this technique to the next level. You can make a wall conform to any odd geometric shape you wish if you follow a few simple rules and procedures.

Let's edit the profile of the new walls to conform to the profile of the stairs. Follow these steps:

1. On the View tab, click the Elevation button.

2. Place an interior elevation, as shown in Figure 16.12.

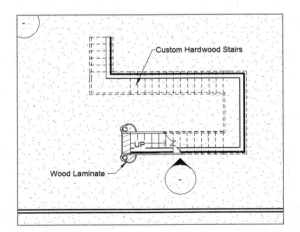

FIGURE 16.12: Placing an interior elevation

3. Open the elevation.

4. Select the wall, as shown in Figure 16.13.

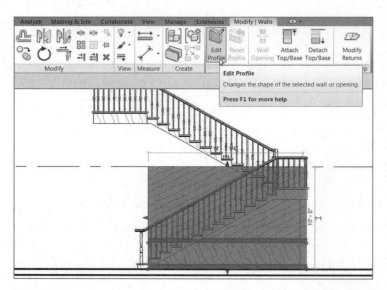

FIGURE 16.13: Selecting the wall to be modified, and clicking the Edit Profile button

5. On the Mode tab, click Edit Profile (see Figure 16.13).

6. On the Draw panel, click the Pick Lines icon.

7. Pick the underside of the stairs. Follow the profile exactly.

8. Delete the existing top magenta line and the existing left magenta line by selecting them and pressing the Delete key. All you should have left is the profile shown in Figure 16.14.

9. Use the Trim/Extend Single Element command to clean up all the corners. Revit won't allow you to continue if you don't.

10. Click Finish Edit Mode. Your wall is trimmed to the underside of the stairs.

N O T E   If your wall doesn't look right, select it again and click Edit Profile. Keep working on the wall until you're satisfied.

11. Repeat the procedure for each wall under the stairs. Remember to add elevations for each. Your finished walls should look like Figure 16.15.

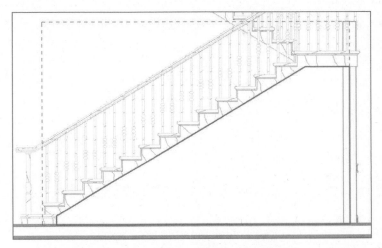

FIGURE 16.14: Cleaning up the lines so that they form a continuous loop

FIGURE 16.15: The finished walls should follow the profile of the stairs.

Now that you can create a compound wall and modify it to fit in an odd place, it's time to learn how to add some sweeps manually.

Manually Adding Host Sweeps

The problem with the wall scenario that you created in the previous procedure is that you have only horizontal wall sweeps. Suppose you need some vertical wall sweeps? This is where host sweeps come into play.

A host sweep is exactly like the sweeps you just added to the wall's properties, but by adding a host sweep, you can add sweeps manually. Next, you'll configure and add a host sweep to the model:

1. Go to the elevation shown in Figure 16.16 (the first one you placed, looking at the stairs).

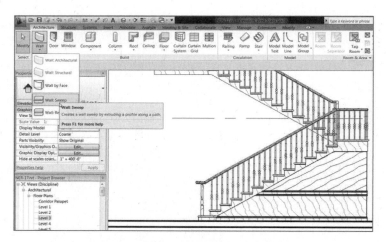

FIGURE 16.16:   Choosing the Wall Sweep command

2. On the Architecture tab, click the down arrow on the Wall button, and select Wall Sweep (see Figure 16.16).

3. In the Properties dialog, click Edit Type.

4. Click Duplicate.

5. Call the new sweep **Chair Rail Sweep**. Click OK.

6. For the profile, choose Casing Profile-2 : 5 1/2″ × 13/16″ (140mm × 21mm) from the list.

7. For Material, choose Mahogany Solid.

8. Click OK.

9. On the Modify | Place Wall Sweep tab, click Vertical on the Placement panel (see Figure 16.17).

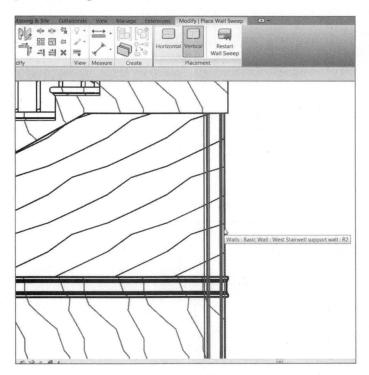

FIGURE 16.17: Adding the profile to the wall

10. Make sure your Chair Rail Sweep is current in the Type Selector menu.

11. Place a vertical rail in the right corner, as shown in Figure 16.18.

 NOTE   If you're having trouble placing the sweep on the corner, you need to go to the plan and select Edit Wall Joins from the Tools toolbar. Pick the corner of the walls, and select Mitered from the Options bar. If you need further assistance with this procedure, go back to Chapter 2 and read up on creating mitered wall joins.

12. After the trim is placed, press Esc.

13. Select the vertical trim. Notice the grips on the top and the bottom. Pick the bottom grip, and drag it up to meet the top chair rail, as shown in Figure 16.19.

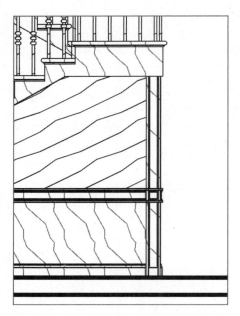

FIGURE 16.18: Placing the sweep on the corner

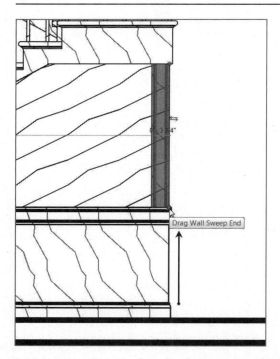

FIGURE 16.19: Dragging the sweep up to the chair rail

14. Add another sweep about 3′ (900mm) to the left of the first sweep.

15. When the sweep is in, select it. A temporary dimension appears. Change the dimension to 3′–0″ (900mm).

16. Drag the bottom up.

17. Repeat the procedure so that your elevation looks like Figure 16.20.

18. Add vertical rails at a 3′–0″ +/– (900mm) to the other walls, as well. Your walls should look like Figure 16.21.

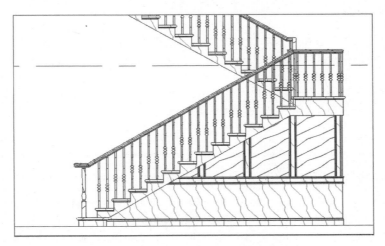

FIGURE 16.20: The finished south wall of the stairs

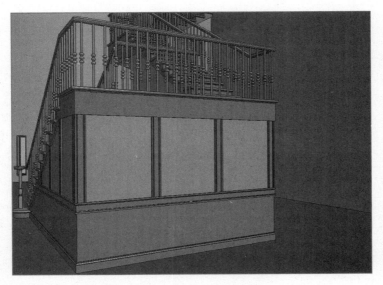

FIGURE 16.21: The final walls with the sweeps added

You can now make modifications to a simple wall in any direction. You have experience adding sweeps to the wall's composition, and you can add sweeps freehand when you need to.

One other type of wall that we should cover before we get to curtain walls is a stacked wall. When you need a compound wall, the outside face must always be in alignment. When you run into this situation, you have to construct an entirely new wall.

Creating Stacked Walls

A *stacked wall*, simply put, is a wall created by stacking two premade walls together. You can't have a stacked wall without at least two basic walls that you can join. The good thing about stacked walls is that you can stack as many as you like. I recommend that you use some restraint, though—these walls can use up memory if you get too carried away.

OPEN THIS DOOR ONLY IN CASE OF EMERGENCY!

Although it's true that a stacked wall is basically the only good way to create a wall system with an offset face, stacked walls are notoriously bad in terms of hosting items and joining to other walls. In addition, one of the biggest drawbacks of a stacked wall is the fact that it doesn't appear in a wall schedule—only the separate parts that form the wall will show up.

The objective of the following procedure is to join three basic walls together to create one stacked wall. The result will create an alcove for architectural casework. Follow these steps:

1. Go to Level 1 West, and, on the Architecture tab, click the Wall button.

2. In the Type Selector menu in the Properties dialog, select Basic Wall : Interior 6 1/8″ (156mm) Partition (2Hr).

3. Click Edit Type.

4. Click Duplicate.

5. Call the wall **18″ (450mm) Soffit Wall**, and click OK.

6. Change Wrapping At Inserts and Wrapping At Ends to Interior.

7. Click the Edit button in the Structure row.

8. In the Layers area, click 3 Core Boundary (Layers Above Wrap), and click Insert.

9. Set Function to Structure [1].

10. Set Material to Air Barrier - Air Infiltration Barrier.

11. Set Thickness to 8 1/4″ (210mm).

12. Click Insert (to insert another layer above).

13. Set Function to Structure [1].

14. Set Material to Metal - Stud Layer.

15. Set Thickness to 3 5/8″ (92mm) (see Figure 16.22).

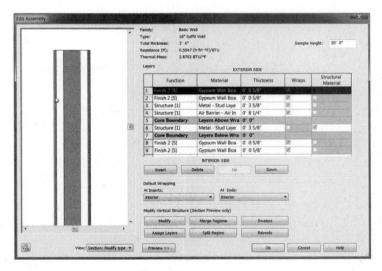

FIGURE 16.22: The wall layers

A good way to establish the overall thickness is to look at the top of the Edit Assembly dialog. There you can see the Total Thickness.

16. Click OK twice.

17. To the left of the Ribbon, click the Modify button (doing so clears the Wall command).

Let's begin building the stacked wall. Because you have two walls with which to work, you can specify them in the Edit Assembly dialog for the stacked wall.

The next procedure joins the 18″ (450mm) soffit wall with the 6 1/8″ (156mm) partition wall:

1. On the Architecture tab, click the Wall button if it isn't already running.

2. Scroll down the Type Selector until you arrive at Stacked Wall: Exterior – Brick Over CMU w Metal Stud, and select it.

3. Click Edit Type.

4. Click Duplicate.

5. Call the new wall **Recessed Wall**, and click OK.

6. Click Edit in the Structure row.

7. For Offset, select Finish Face: Interior.

8. In the Types area, change Wall 1 to 18″ (450mm) Soffit Wall.

9. Change Wall 2 to Interior - 6 1/8″ (156mm) Partition (2-Hr).

10. Change Height to 5′–6″ (1650mm).

11. Insert a wall below the Interior - 6 1/8″ (156mm) Partition (2-Hr) wall.

12. Change the third wall to 18″ (450mm) Soffit Wall.

13. Change the height to 3′–0″ (900mm).

14. At the top of the dialog, change Sample Height to 10′–0″ (3000mm) (see Figure 16.23).

15. Click the Preview button.

16. Click OK twice.

17. Draw the wall in the west wing, as shown in Figure 16.24. (If you wish, you can create an elevation or cut a section through the wall.)

With the concept of stacked walls behind us, we can move into the crazy world of curtain walls. Although curtain walls are complex in nature, Revit handles them quite well.

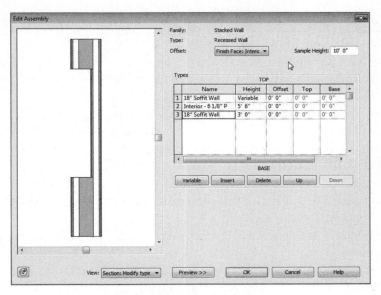

FIGURE 16.23: Creating the stacked wall

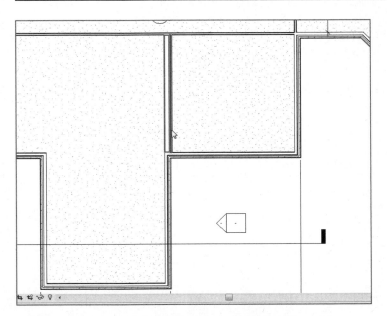

FIGURE 16.24: Adding the new stacked wall to the model

Creating Curtain Walls

The topic of curtain walls brings us away from the conventional mindset of walls. Curtain walls are placed into the model the same way as conventional walls, but curtain walls have many more restrictions and Element Properties that we should examine before you go throwing one into your model.

With that said, curtain walls also provide the most dramatic effect on your building. As this section will explain in detail, a curtain wall is not only composed of glass and aluminum extrusions but can also be constructed from building materials such as brick, CMU, and wood. You can also predefine the materials and the spacing, or you can create them grid by grid, depending on your situation.

The first part of this section will focus on adding a predefined curtain system to the model.

Adding a Predefined Curtain Wall

The quickest way to model a curtain wall is to use one that has already been created for you. The out-of-the-box curtain walls that are provided with Revit have enough instance and type parameters available to make the curtain wall conform to your needs for each situation.

In the next procedure, you'll add a predefined curtain-wall system to the radial east entry wall. Follow these steps:

1. In the Project Browser, open the Level 1 East plan view.

2. Zoom in on the east entry.

3. On the Architecture tab, click the Wall button.

4. In the Type Selector, select Curtain Wall: Storefront.

5. Click Edit Type.

6. Click Duplicate.

7. Call the new curtain wall **East Entry**, and click OK.

8. You can configure many parameters. Verify that Automatically Embed is selected. For Vertical Grid Pattern, change Spacing to 4′–0″ (1200mm).

9. Select Adjust For Mullion Size.

10. For Horizontal Grid Pattern, change Layout to Maximum Spacing, and change the spacing to 4′–0″ (1200mm). Also select Adjust For Mullion Size.

11. Click OK.

12. In the Instance Properties dialog, change Base Offset to 3′–7″ (1075mm).

13. Set Top Constraint to Up To Level: Roof.

14. Set Top Offset to -1′–0″ (that's minus 1′–0″) (-300mm).

15. On the Draw panel, click the Pick Lines icon.

16. Pick the radial entry wall, as shown in Figure 16.25. Make sure you're picking the wall centerline.

17. Go to a 3D view. Your curtain wall should resemble Figure 16.26.

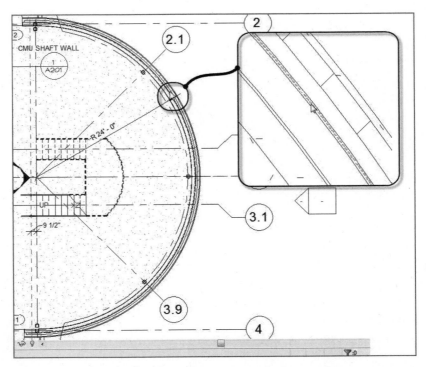

FIGURE 16.25:   Picking the radial entry wall to add the curtain wall

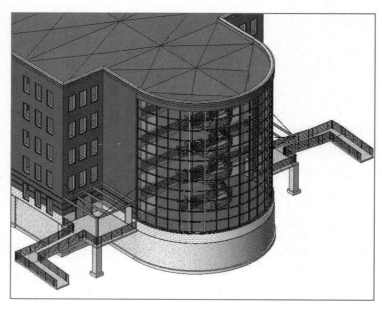

FIGURE 16.26: The curtain wall in 3D

REVIT CAN BE TOUCHY

You may receive a warning that says, "Could not create integral reveal for wall instance. Sweep position is outside of its wall. Please check sweep parameters." If you do, click the red X in the upper-right corner of the warning to dismiss it (as seen in the following graphic).

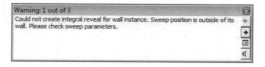

The ability to create an automatic curtain wall such as the radial one in the west entry way is quite an advantage when it comes to modeling a curtain system quickly. However, you won't always be presented with a perfectly square, vertical shape. This is where creating a blank curtain wall comes in handy. You can then add grids and mullions at spaces that are at odd intervals.

Adding a Blank Curtain Wall

A blank curtain wall is nothing but a giant chunk of glass. By adding a blank curtain wall, you tell Revit, "Don't bother spacing the panels—I'll do it myself."

Let's create a blank curtain wall and add it to the model. You'll then go to an elevation and edit the profile of the panel. Follow along:

1. In the Project Browser, open the Level 1 West view.

2. On the Work Plane panel of the Architecture tab, click Ref Plane, and then click Pick Lines on the Draw panel.

3. Offset a reference plane 2′–0″ (600mm) from the face of brick, as shown in Figure 16.27.

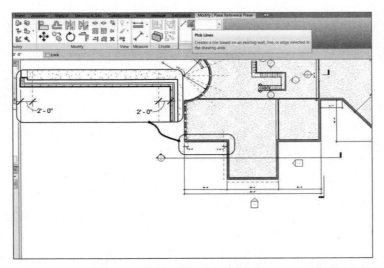

FIGURE 16.27: Offsetting two reference planes 2′–0″ (600mm) from the face of brick

4. On the Architecture tab, click the Wall button.

5. In the Type Selector, pick Curtain Wall: Curtain Wall 1 from the list.

6. Click Edit Type.

7. Click Duplicate.

8. Call the new curtain system **South West Entry**, and click OK.

9. Select the Automatically Embed check box.

10. Click OK.

11. For Base Offset, change the value to 0′–0″.

12. For Top Constraint, set the value to Up To Level: Level 5.

13. For Top Offset, change the value to 0′–0″.

14. Draw the wall at the centerline of the wall between each reference plane, as shown in Figure 16.28. Note that if you draw from left to right, the exterior face of the new wall will be to the inside.

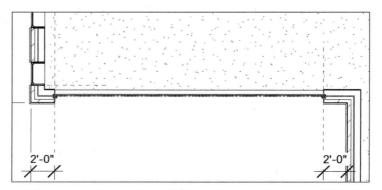

2'-0"   2'-0"

F I G U R E   1 6 . 2 8 : Drawing the curtain wall at the centerline of the wall between the two reference planes

15. In the Project Browser, open South Entry Elevation.

16. In the South Entry Elevation, change Visual Style to Shaded (so that you can see the glass wall better).

Now that you've drawn the wall and are looking at the elevation, you can begin to alter the profile and add some curtain grids of your own. To edit the curtain profile, follow these steps:

1. Select the curtain wall.

2. On the Modify | Walls tab, click Edit Profile.

3. On the Draw panel, click Pick Lines.

4. Using the Options bar, offset the roof down 2′–0″ (600mm), and trim the edges of the curtain wall to the offset line.

5. Delete the horizontal magenta line that is now floating.

6. Click Finish Edit Mode. Your curtain wall's profile should resemble Figure 16.29.

To select the curtain wall, you have to hover your pointer over an edge. When the curtain wall's perimeter becomes highlighted, select it.

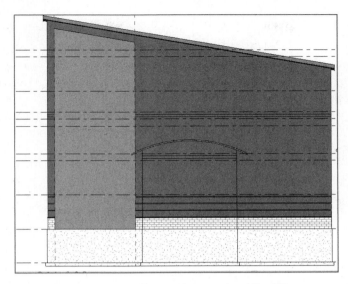

FIGURE 16.29: The complete curtain-wall profile

With the shape of the curtain wall finished, let's create some divisions along the vertical and horizontal plane of the wall. In Revit, these are called *curtain grids*.

Creating Curtain Grids

Because all you have is a single pane of glass, you need to dice it up. In this situation, you can begin dividing the glass panel by using the Curtain Grid command. When you've finished, you can add mullions, doors, and even materials to the panels.

Begin by adding curtain grids to the glass panel:

1. On the Build panel of the Architecture tab, click the Curtain Grid button, as shown in Figure 16.30.

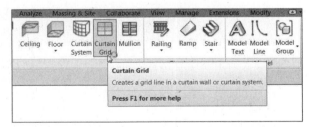

FIGURE 16.30: Click the Curtain Grid button on the Build panel of the Architecture tab.

2. On the Modify | Place Curtain Grid tab, click the All Segments button, as shown in Figure 16.31.

3. Move your cursor up the left side of the curtain wall, and pick a horizontal point that is 8'–0" (2400mm) up from the base of the wall (see Figure 16.31).

4. Press Esc twice, or click Modify.

5. Select the horizontal grid.

6. Click the Copy button on the Modify panel.

7. Copy the grid up 4'–0" (1200mm).

8. Copy the 4' grid up 2'–0" (600mm).

9. Repeat this pattern until you've reached the top of the wall (see Figure 16.32).

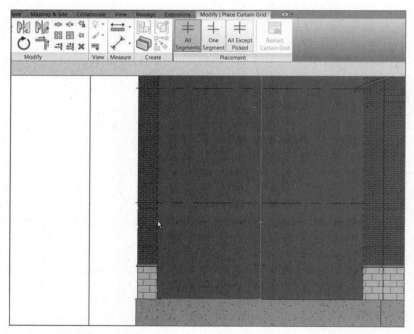

FIGURE 16.31: Picking a point 8'–0" (2400mm) up from the base of the wall

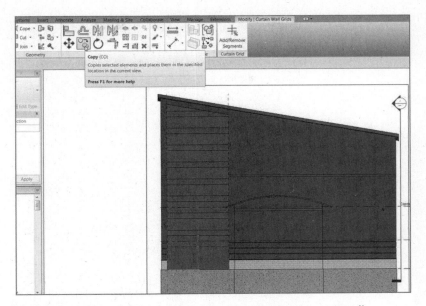

FIGURE 16.32: Copying the grids to form the custom curtain wall

10. Click the Curtain Grid button.

11. Slide your cursor along the base of the panel (the grid is extended in a vertical direction).

12. On the Placement panel, click the One Segment button.

13. Pick the midpoint of the panel. (You should have segmented only the bottom panel.)

14. Click Modify.

15. Select the vertical grid.

16. On the Modify toolbar, click the Move icon.

17. Move the grid to the left 3′–0″ (900mm).

18. Copy the grid to the right 6′–0″ (1600mm). Your wall should now look like Figure 16.33.

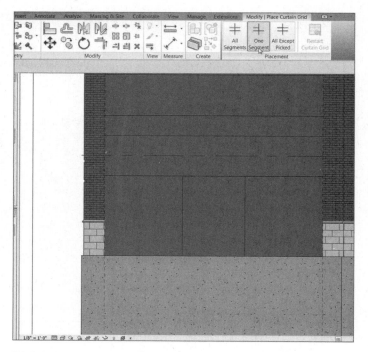

FIGURE 16.33: Chopping up the panel

With the panel broken up, you can begin adding materials. One material you may not think of is an actual door! Yes, in Revit curtain walls, you add a door to a curtain panel as a material.

Adding Materials

In addition to doors, you can add to a curtain wall any material that is present in the model. You can even add separate wall systems.

In this procedure, you'll add a door to the curtain system. Then you'll add brick belts that fill the 2′–0″ (600mm) sections. Follow these steps:

1. On the Insert tab, click the Load Family button.

2. Browse to Doors, and open the Curtain Wall-Store Front-Dbl .rfa file.

3. Zoom in to the 6′ × 8′ (1800mm × 2400mm) panel.

4. Hover your cursor at the top of the panel.

5. Press the Tab key twice. When the panel is highlighted, pick it (see Figure 16.34).

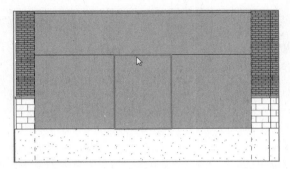

FIGURE 16.34: Selecting the 6' × 8' (1800mm × 2400mm) panel

6. In the Type Selector, pick Curtain Wall-Store Front-Dbl: Store Front Double Door. A door appears in the panel.

7. Select the 2'–0" (600mm) panel above the door.

8. In the Type Selector, pick Basic Wall: Generic - 12" (300mm) Masonry.

9. Press Esc.

10. Fill the rest of the 2'–0" (600mm) bands with the same Generic - 12" (300mm) Masonry.

HEY, THIS IS GRAY!

If the wall shows up backward (appears gray), then you need to flip the curtain wall physically. To do so, go to the Level 1 West plan, and select the curtain wall. Then click the little double arrow in the middle of the wall, as shown in this graphic. Doing so flips the direction of the entire curtain wall.

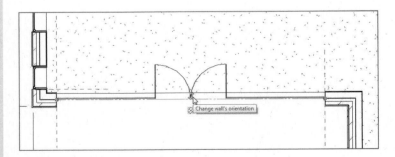

With the panels in place, you can start filling in the mullions. This brings us to the next step: adding mullions to the grid.

Adding Mullions to the Grid

The next logical step is to create the mullions that will be attached to the grid you just added. Because you have a few areas where there shouldn't be mullions, the job becomes more tedious.

The next example could go one of two ways. One technique adds mullions *piece by piece*, and the other procedure lets you add mullions all at once and then delete the mullions you don't need. This procedure takes the latter approach; you'll add the mullions all at once and then remove the superfluous mullions:

1. On the Build panel of the Architecture tab, click the Mullion button, as shown in Figure 16.35.

2. In the Properties dialog, choose Rectangular Mullion: 2.5″ × 5″ (64mm × 127mm) Rectangular.

3. On the Placement panel, click All Grid Lines.

4. Pick the grid above the door, as shown in Figure 16.36.

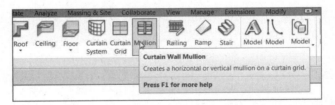

FIGURE 16.35: Click the Mullion button on the Architecture tab.

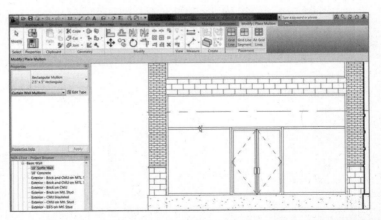

FIGURE 16.36: Place the 2.5″ × 5″ (64mm × 127mm) rectangular mullion above the door.

5. Pick anywhere on the grid. The mullions are added to the entire system.

6. Press Esc.

With the mullions added, you've actually gone too far! An aluminum extrusion separates the CMU from the adjacent brick. You also need to delete the mullion that appears under the door. Let's remove these pieces of mullion:

1. Zoom in to an area where the CMU meets the brick, as shown in Figure 16.37.

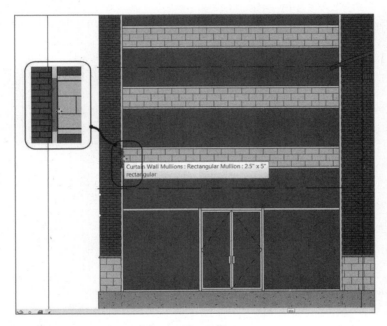

Curtain Wall Mullions : Rectangular Mullion : 2.5" x 5" rectangular

FIGURE 16.37: Selecting the mullion

2. Select the small mullion piece that lies between the brick and the CMU. (You'll have to press the Tab key several times to accomplish this.)

3. You can either modify the join (as shown in Figure 16.37) or press the Delete key and remove the mullion. In this case, delete the mullion. Repeat the procedure for other similar areas.

What have you accomplished? You've embedded a predefined curtain wall into a radial profile, and you've added a curtain system to a giant glass panel by hand. The only thing left to do is to apply a curtain wall to a sloping surface.

Adding a Wall to a Massing Object

Everything you've done up to this point has been within a perfectly plumb application. Not everything in architecture is perfectly plumb, however. Suppose you needed a wall that sloped in or out at an angle. Well, gentle readers, let's get into the world of massing.

Now that you're finally using 3D for the first time in the book, you need to think in those terms. You have to deal with two dimensions and then let Revit project the third. You first need to provide geometry in plan. Second, you provide geometry in elevation. When you have the plan and elevation geometry, you can blend the two together, creating the third dimension. Once this mass is created, you simply apply a wall system to the face of the mass. Let's get started:

1. Open the Level 1 West view.

2. Zoom in on the area shown in Figure 16.38.

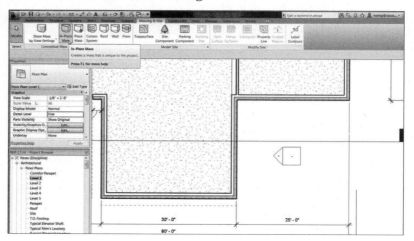

FIGURE 16.38: Massing up your model

3. On the Massing & Site tab, click the In-Place Mass button (see Figure 16.38). Revit may throw a warning stating that it's turning on the mass visibility. This is good, so click Close.

4. Call the new mass **West Wing Atrium**, and click OK.

5. On the Draw panel, click the Reference Line button, as shown in Figure 16.39.

6. Make sure the Draw On Work Plane button is active.

7. Draw a straight line from the corner of the building as shown, moving to the right 4′–2″ (1250mm). Be sure to pick face of brick as the start.

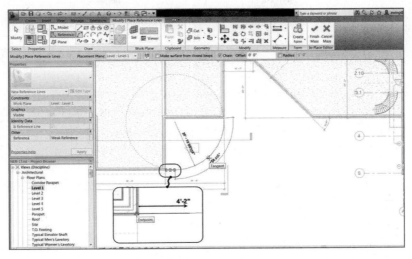

FIGURE 16.39: Creating the plan geometry

8. With the Reference command still running, click the Start - End - Radius Arc button.

9. Pick the corner of the building.

10. Move your cursor to the right until the arc snaps to the tangency, and then pick the third point (see Figure 16.39).

11. Click Modify. Your plan should look like Figure 16.40.

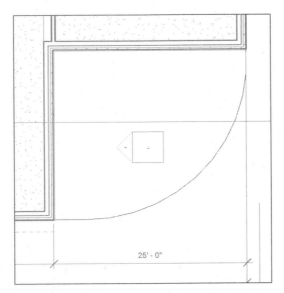

FIGURE 16.40: A simple line and an arc

Let's take a breather. You've satisfied the first criteria of creating a mass element by creating a simple line and arc. This line and arc will be the guide for your vertical geometry to ride along—that is, the path. It's time to move on to the second dimension: the vertical dimension. Follow these steps:

1. Open the section called West Corridor Section. You can double-click the section in plan, or you can open it from the Project Browser.

2. In the Draw panel, click the Reference Plane button, as shown in Figure 16.41.

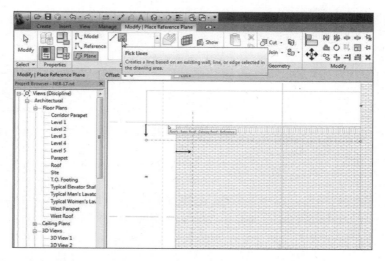

FIGURE 16.41: Creating some guides

3. Use Pick Lines, and offset the front face of the wall to the right 2′–0″ (600mm).

4. With the same command still running, offset another reference plane down 2′–0″ (600mm) from the bottom of the roof beyond (see Figure 16.41).

Now let's draw the actual shape:

1. In the Draw panel, click the Model line button (see Figure 16.42).

2. In the Work Plane dialog, select Pick A Plane, click OK, and select the wall.

3. On the Options bar, be sure that Make Surface From Closed Loops is unchecked and that the Chain button is selected.

4. Verify that Draw Line is the draw option. Draw a line from point 1 to point 2, as shown in Figure 16.43. (This line is from the bottom of the CMU wall to the bottom of the concrete ledge.)

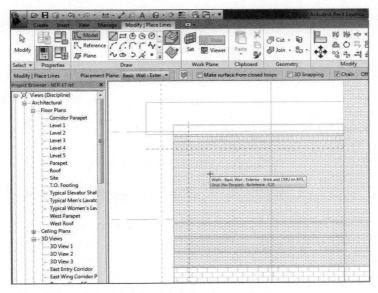

FIGURE 16.42: Setting the vertical work plane

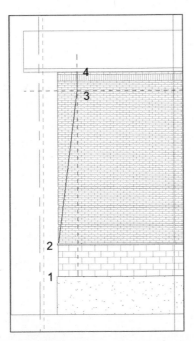

FIGURE 16.43: Drawing the face of the shape

5. Draw a line from point 2 to point 3 (see Figure 16.43).

6. Draw a line from point 3 to point 4 (see Figure 16.43).

7. Press Esc once (and only once).

8. Click the Pick Lines button.

9. Set Offset to 6″ (150mm).

10. Hover over the angled line.

11. Press the Tab key. When the three lines are highlighted, pick the wall. You may have to zoom in a little to tell Revit that you need to make a screen selection.

12. Offset the three lines to the right, as shown in Figure 16.44.

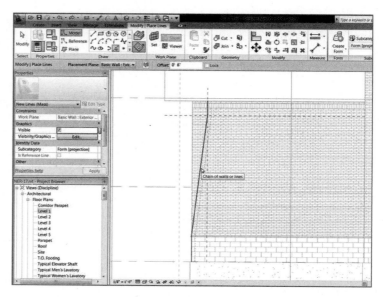

FIGURE 16.44: Creating the thickness

13. Change Offset to 0 on the Options bar.

14. Change the Pick Lines option to Draw Lines.

15. Draw a line at the top and the bottom, closing the loop. See Figure 16.45. Pick Modify.

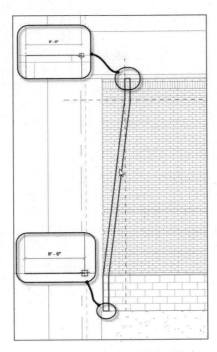

FIGURE 16.45: Closing the loop

Nice! Two out of the three requirements for 3D are completed: horizontal (plan) and vertical (elevation). The only thing left to do is tell Revit to blend the two together:

1. Go to the default 3D view.

2. Zoom in on the area in which you're working.

3. Hover your cursor over one of the lines of the shape you just drew.

4. Press the Tab key. Revit selects the entire perimeter of the shape.

5. With the vertical shape selected, hold the Ctrl key and pick the reference arc you drew.

6. Click the Create Form button, as shown in Figure 16.46.

7. When the form is placed, click the Finish Mass button. You should be looking at what is shown in Figure 16.47.

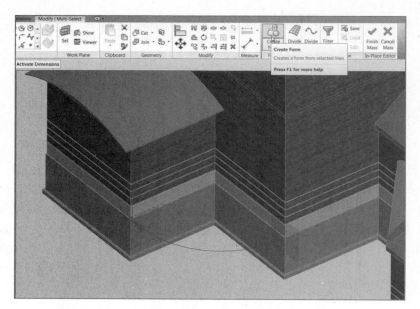

FIGURE 16.46: Selecting the objects, and creating the form

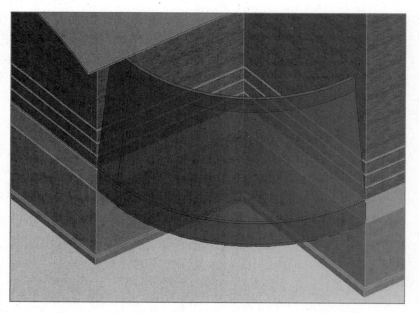

FIGURE 16.47: The finished mass

Now it gets fun! You'll begin adding walls to the shape. In Revit Architecture, there are three ways to add walls to a model: draw them in, pick lines to add them, or pick faces. You have some pretty sweet faces eager to host some walls, so let's dig in. Follow these steps:

1. On the Architecture tab, click the Curtain System button, as shown in Figure 16.48.

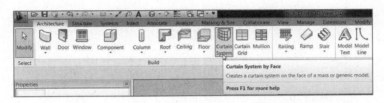

FIGURE 16.48: The Curtain System button on the Architecture tab

2. Click Edit Type.

3. Click Duplicate, and call the new system **Atrium Curtain System**.

4. For Curtain Panel, select System Panel : Glazed.

5. Set Join Condition to Border And Grid 1 Continuous.

6. Layout for Grid 1 pattern is Maximum Spacing, and Spacing is 2′–0″ (600mm).

7. Select Adjust For Mullion Size.

8. Repeat the settings for the Grid 2 pattern.

9. For the Grid 1 and Grid 2 mullions, select Circular Mullion : 2.5″ (50mm Radius) Circular for Interior Type as well as the Border 1 and 2 types, as shown in Figure 16.49.

10. Click OK.

11. Pick the two sloping faces of the mass, as shown in Figure 16.50.

12. Click the Create System button, and you have it! (See Figure 16.51.)

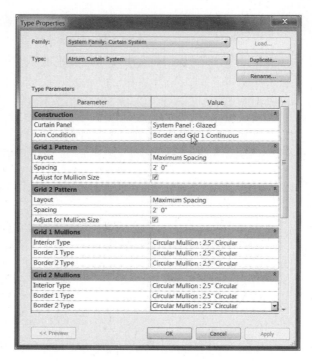

FIGURE 16.49: Configuring the curtain system

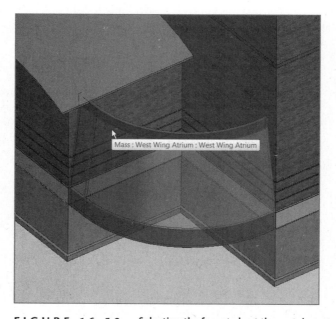

FIGURE 16.50: Selecting the faces to host the curtain system

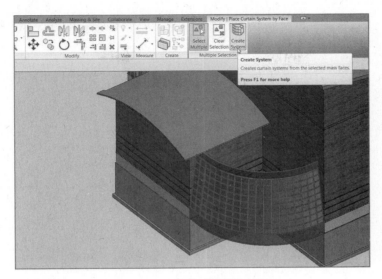

FIGURE 16.51:   The curtain wall in all its glory

Let's add some CMU and brick walls to the top and bottom:

1. Change Visual Style to Shaded.

2. On the Architecture tab, click the Wall button.

3. In the Type Selector in the Properties dialog, select Basic Wall Generic 12″ (300mm) Masonry.

4. On the Draw panel, click the Pick Faces button, as shown in Figure 16.52.

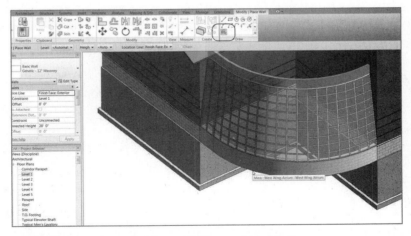

FIGURE 16.52:   Adding something on which to bear

5. On the Options bar, select Finish Face Exterior for Location Line.

6. Pick the bottom faces of the mass (see Figure 16.52).

7. In the Type Selector, select Generic 4″ Brick (Generic 102 Brick), and select the top faces.

8. Your wall system should look like Figure 16.53.

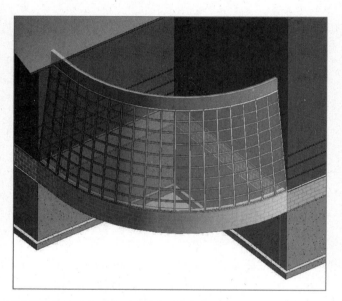

FIGURE 16.53:   The completed system

I think you'd better add a roof, just to close out the exercise. Although it's superfluous to this example, it will bother all of us throughout the rest of the book if you don't. Follow these steps:

1. Go to Floor Plan: Corridor Parapet.

2. Set Visual Style to Wireframe in the View Control bar.

3. On the Architecture tab, click the Roof button.

4. In the Type Selector, set the roof to Basic Roof: Canopy Roof.

5. Set Base Offset From Level to -4-1/2″ (-112mm).

6. Make sure the Defines Slope button is deselected on the Options bar.

7. Make sure the Pick Walls option is selected on the Draw panel.

8. Set the overhang to 1'–0" (300mm), and pick the walls of the atrium.

9. Set Offset to 0, and pick the walls of the building.

10. Clean up any overlapping corners. Your sketch should look like Figure 16.54.

11. Click Finish Edit Mode.

12. Go to the default 3D view.

13. Select the Massing & Site tab.

14. Click Show Mass By View Settings. Your new atrium should look like Figure 16.55.

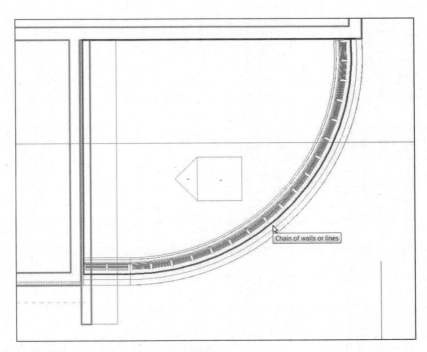

FIGURE 16.54: The roof footprint

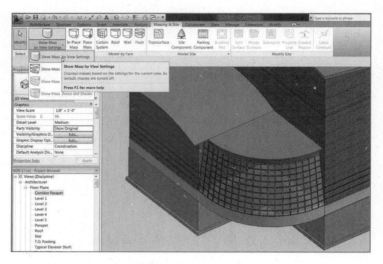

FIGURE 16.55:   The new funky atrium

As you can see, you're just at the doorway of massing. Literally. There is no way to get into the little portico you just created. In the next chapter, we'll discuss creating families, and we'll delve much deeper into the massing that makes up the components built in Revit Architecture 2014.

Are You Experienced?

Now you can...

- ☑ create custom compound walls by using the Edit Assembly dialog

- ☑ create stacked walls by joining compound walls together

- ☑ create sweeps in a wall's profile and freeform sweeps

- ☑ create curtain walls by using a predefined wall system and from a blank panel

- ☑ create vertically angled walls by applying a curtain system to a massing object

CHAPTER 17

Creating Families

As you're probably becoming acutely aware, having the right content makes or breaks an Autodesk® Revit® Architecture project. I'm sure you're also very aware that, other than the content Autodesk has provided and the content you downloaded from this book's web page, you don't have anywhere near the amount of content you need to start a project! That being said, it's time to buckle down and dig into how Revit works and see how having adjustable, parametric families will turn you into a Revit fan for life.

▶ **Creating a basic family**

▶ **Using a complex family to create an arched door**

▶ **Creating an in-place family**

Creating a Basic Family

The first item we'll tackle is how to create a basic family. We'll start with the creation of a wall sweep and then move on to creating an arched doorway. As you become fluent with these two basic family types, you'll start to be able to create families quite fast.

You have to start somewhere. To be honest, no good family is "basic," but some are easier to create than others. The concept is the same, however.

Essentially, a family has three fundamental components:

Reference Planes   Yes, reference planes drive the family. Look at these as the family's skeleton.

Constraints   *Constraints* are dimensions with a parameter associated with them to give the skeleton its flexibility.

3D Massing   3D massing is locked to the skeleton. We'll call this the skin. Corny, I know, but it gets the point across.

 N O T E   Metric users should not type in mm or other metric abbreviations when entering amounts suggested in the exercises. Revit will not accept such abbreviations. Simply enter the number provided within the parentheses.

First you need to figure out where to start. Any family that you want to insert into a Revit model must begin with a template. Choosing the correct template, as you'll soon discover, will make your life much simpler.

The objective of this procedure is to start a new family by choosing a template in Revit. Follow these steps:

1. Open Revit Architecture.

2. In the Recent Files screen, click the New link in the Families column, or click the Application button and select New ➢ Family.

3. Select Profile-Hosted.rft (Metric Profile-Hosted.rft), and then click Open.

As mentioned earlier, you'll notice the reference planes. A good family starts and ends with these. Next, you'll notice some text. Revit adds *advice* in each of its family templates. After you read the advice, you can delete it. You'll do that in a moment, but first let's add reference planes to the family.

Adding Reference Planes to a Family

The one bad thing about creating a family is that you can get away with doing so without using reference planes. This is unfortunate, because a family made with no (or not enough) reference planes will be faulty at best. I've learned that lesson the hard way. Although it may seem redundant to add reference planes, I strongly advise you to use them, and use them often.

In the following procedure, you'll offset some reference planes to create the wall sweep. Follow along:

1. On the Datum panel of the Create tab, click the Reference Plane button, as shown in Figure 17.1.

FIGURE 17.1:   The Reference Plane button on the Create tab

2. In the Draw panel, click the Pick Lines button.

3. On the Options bar, set Offset to 1'–0" (300mm).

4. Hover your cursor over the center, vertical reference plane. When the blue reference line appears to the right of the vertical plane (as shown in Figure 17.2), pick the center reference plane. You now have two vertical reference planes spaced 1'–0" (300mm) apart.

5. With the Reference Plane command still running, pick the horizontal reference plane, and offset it down using the same offset increment of 1'–0" (300mm). Your family should resemble Figure 17.3.

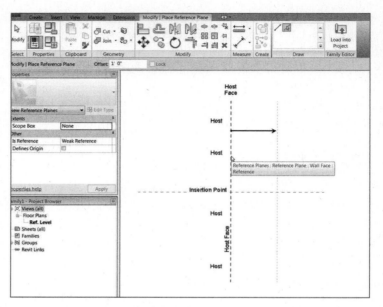

FIGURE 17.2: Adding a second vertical reference plane

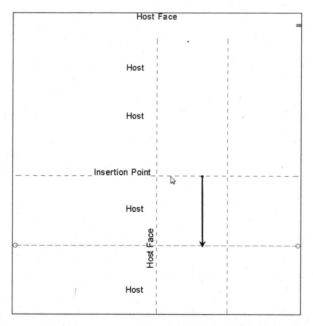

FIGURE 17.3: Adding a second horizontal reference plane downward

These two reference planes represent the body of the sweep. Next, let's add two more secondary reference planes for more control over the family:

1. Set Offset to 2″ (50mm).

2. Offset the top horizontal reference plane down.

3. Offset the left vertical reference plane to the right (see Figure 17.4).

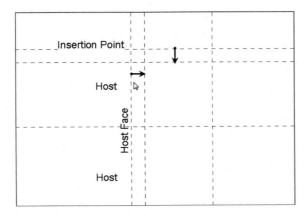

FIGURE 17.4: Offsetting two more reference planes

With the reference planes in place, you can move on to adding dimensions to them. After you add the dimensions, you'll add parameters to those dimensions to make your family flexible when you add it to the model.

Adding Dimensions and Parameters to a Family

We're now looking at one of the most outstanding features of Revit. Because you can create a parametric component easily and then allow the end user to change the dimensions, you can put your company into overdrive in terms of pushing BIM through and having success with Revit.

The next procedure involves adding dimensions to the reference planes you've already put in place. The procedure after that will add parameters to the dimensions you've added. Follow along:

1. On the Measure panel of the Modify | Place Reference Plane tab, click the Aligned Dimension button.

2. Add a horizontal dimension from the left reference plane to the right reference plane. The dimension should be 1′–0″ (300mm).

3. Add a second dimension from the top reference plane to the bottom reference plane. The dimension should be 1′–0″ (300mm).

4. Add a dimension from the left reference plane to the 2″ (50mm) reference plane to the right.

5. Add a dimension from the top reference plane to the reference plane 2″ (50mm) down (see Figure 17.5).

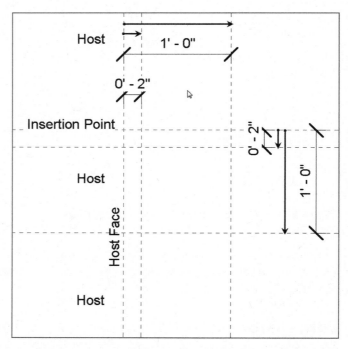

FIGURE 17.5:   Adding the dimensions to the reference planes

The next step is to make this family come alive! Because you're in the Family Editor, when you select a dimension you can choose to add a label to the dimension. This label is tied to a parameter that can be modified.

To add a label to a dimension, follow these steps:

1. Press Esc twice. Then, select the top, horizontal 1′–0″ (300mm) dimension.

2. On the Options bar, click the Label pull-down menu, and choose <Add Parameter> (see Figure 17.6).

3. In the Parameter Properties dialog, under Parameter Data (as shown in Figure 17.7), type **Width** for Name.

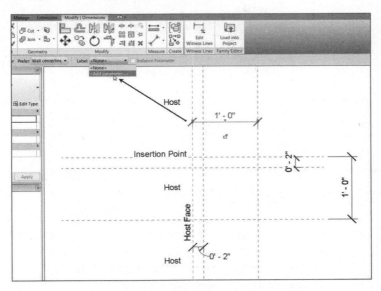

FIGURE 17.6: Choosing Add Parameter on the Options bar

FIGURE 17.7: Configuring the parameter

 NOTE When you add a name to the parameter, you're actually adding part of a formula. There is a chance that this name will be part of a mathematical expression. When you name parameters, be deliberate, and give the names some thought. Also keep in mind that the mathematical expressions built in to the parameters are case sensitive. If you capitalize the first letter of each word, be consistent.

4. Click OK. The parameter is added to the dimension.

5. Select the 1'–0" (300mm) vertical dimension.

6. On the Options bar, click the Label pull-down menu.

7. Select <Add Parameter>.

8. For Name, type **Height**.

9. Click OK.

10. Select the two 2" (50mm) dimensions.

CHOOSING INSTANCE OR TYPE

The decision to use Instance or Type may be the most important decision you make when creating family parameters. As you've noticed, when you're modifying a family in the model (such as a wall, door, or window), you can either make a change to the single instance of the component you've selected or click Type and change the component globally in the model.

When the parameter was created, either Instance or Type was selected. So, when you're creating a parameter, you need to ask yourself, "Do I want the user to modify only one instance of this family by changing this parameter, or do I want the user to change every instance of this family by changing this parameter?"

To complicate matters, if you plan to use this parameter in a mathematical expression, every parameter in that expression must be of the same type. For example, you can't add an instance parameter to a type parameter. Revit won't allow it.

Remember, if you hold the Ctrl key, you can select multiple items. The objective of selecting both the 2" (50mm) dimensions is that you're going to create one parameter and put both items on it.

11. On the Options bar, click the Label pull-down menu.

12. Select <Add Parameter>.

13. For Name, type **Reveal**.

14. Click OK.

15. Click anywhere to clear the selection.

The reference planes are in place, and the dimensions are set with the parameters. It's time to go behind the scenes and see how these families operate by examining the family types and adding formulas to the parameters.

The Type Properties Dialog

Within the Family Editor lies a powerful dialog that lets you organize the parameters associated with the family you're creating. The Type Properties dialog also allows you to perform calculations and to add increments in an attempt to test the flex of the family before it's passed into the model.

The objective of the following procedure is to open the Family Types dialog and configure some parameters. Follow along:

1. On the Properties panel, click the Family Types button, as shown in Figure 17.8.

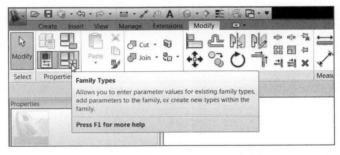

FIGURE 17.8: The Family Types button on the Properties panel

2. In the Family Types dialog, click into the Formula cell in the Height row.

3. Type **Width**, and press the Tab key (see Figure 17.9).

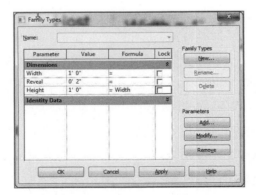

FIGURE 17.9: The Height parameter is now constrained to the Width parameter.

4. Click into the Width Value (the area in the Width row that has the 1′–0″ [300mm] increment).

5. Change Width from 1′–0″ (300mm) to 6″ (150mm). The Height value changes, too.

6. Click OK. The 1′–0″ (300mm) dimensions are reduced to 6″ (150mm).

7. Click the Family Types button.

8. Change Width back to 1′–0″ (300mm).

9. Click Apply. The dimensions update in the drawing area.

10. Click the New button in the Family Types area, as shown in Figure 17.10.

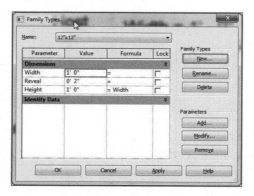

FIGURE 17.10:   Creating a new family type

11. Call the new type 12″×12″ (300mm×300mm), and click OK (see Figure 17.10).

12. Click the New button again.

13. Call the new type 6″×6″ (150mm×150mm), and click OK.

14. Change Width to 6″ (150mm).

15. Change Reveal to 1″ (25mm).

16. Click Apply. The reference planes and dimensions update.

17. Change Type back to 12″×12″ (300mm×300mm).

18. Click OK.

19. Click Save, and save the family somewhere you'll be able to retrieve it later. Name the file **Cove sweep.rfa**.

Now that the reference planes and parameters are in place, you can flex the family to make sure it will work properly when you load it into the project.

It's Time to Flex Your Family

With the family complete, you need to go back to the Type Properties dialog and change the parameters to see where the family will break. This testing is called *flexing* in the Revit world and should be done as often as possible.

The next step is to add the physical lines that form the perimeter of the sweep. Given that this was created using the hosted profile template, the actual family will merely be a 2D profile. The family won't become a 3D object until you pass it into the model and use it as a wall sweep.

In this procedure, you'll draw the perimeter of the cove sweep. Follow these steps:

1. On the Detail panel of the Create tab, click the Line button.

2. Draw a line from the intersection labeled 1 in Figure 17.11 to the intersection labeled 2.

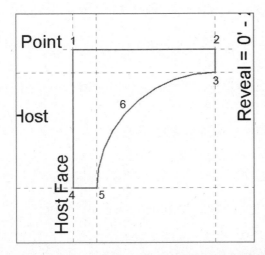

FIGURE 17.11: Drawing the boundary of the profile

3. Draw a line from point 2 to point 3.

4. Press Esc.

5. Draw a line from point 1 to point 4.

6. Draw a line from point 4 to point 5.

7. On the Draw panel, click the Start-End-Radius Arc button, and draw an arc from point 5 to point 3. When the two points are snapped in place, move your cursor to the left until the radius snaps into place (point 6). Your family should look like Figure 17.11.

Now you can load the family into the model and use it as a wall sweep. This is when you get to enjoy the fruits of your labor. To get started, open the building model on which you've been working. If you missed the previous chapter, go to the book's web page at www.sybex.com/go/revit2014ner. From there, you can browse to Chapter 17 and find the NER-17.rvt file. Follow along with these steps:

1. Open the Cove Sweep file (if you've closed it).

2. On the Family Editor panel, click the Load Into Project button.

3. In the NER-17 project, select one of the exterior walls in the east wing.

4. In the Properties dialog, click Edit Type.

5. Click the Edit button in the Structure row.

6. Make sure the preview is on and that it's showing a section.

7. Click the Sweeps button.

8. In the Wall Sweeps dialog, click the Add button.

9. For the Profile, select Cove Sweep: 12″×12″ (300mm×300mm) from the list (notice that 6″×6″ [150mm×150mm] is available too).

10. For Material, apply Concrete - Precast Concrete.

11. Set Distance to -1′–4″ (-400mm).

12. In the From column, make sure the value is Top.

13. In the Side column, make sure the choice is Exterior.

14. Click OK twice.

15. Click OK yet again.

16. Zoom in on the walls. There should be a sweep, as shown in Figure 17.12.

FIGURE 17.12: The new precast concrete wall sweep

You're getting a taste for what you can do with this powerful tool. And as you can see, you're only scratching the surface of the fun you can have. Now you're ready to try a real family!

The next section of this chapter will be spent on creating an opening with a radial header. Think about the lessons learned with the cove sweep, and let's dig in.

Using a Complex Family to Create an Arched Door

The "easy" family is out of the way, and next you'll begin blending the procedures of creating a parametric frame with actual 3D extrusions and sweeps. These 3D extrusions and sweeps will behave exactly like the cove family you just made. When you learn how to create one type of family, the knowledge transfers to the next.

This section of the chapter starts with a blank door template and proceeds with modifying a wall cut. Then you'll add casing, a jamb, and a door. Follow along:

1. Click the Application button, and select New ➤ Family.

2. Find the template called Door.rft (Metric Door.rft), and click Open.

3. Quite a bit of work has been done for you. This is great, but you don't need all the items in the template. Select the door jambs, as shown in Figure 17.13, and delete them from either side of the door.

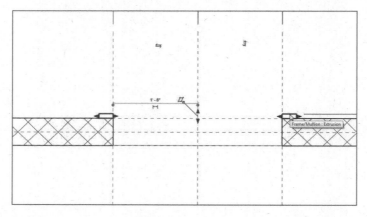

FIGURE 17.13:   Deleting the jambs from either side of the door

4. In the Project Browser, find the Exterior elevation under the Elevations (Elevation 1) category, and open it.

5. In this view, you see a wall and an opening. Select the bottom of the opening, as shown in Figure 17.14.

N O T E   The wall that you see is provided by Revit in order for you to design your opening to be flexible with any sized wall in the model after you load this family. After the door family is in the project, this wall is removed. It's provided merely for layout.

6. On the Options bar, click Transparent In: Elevation.

7. Click the Edit Sketch button on the Opening panel (see Figure 17.14).

8. By clicking Edit Sketch, you enter Sketch Mode. On the Draw panel, click the Start-End-Radius Arc button.

9. Draw an arc, as shown in Figure 17.15.

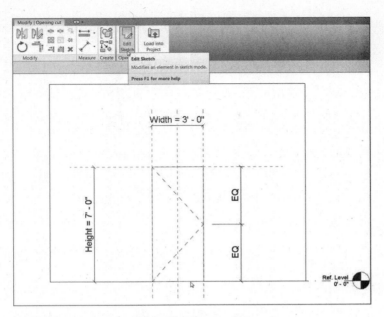

FIGURE 17.14: Editing the door opening

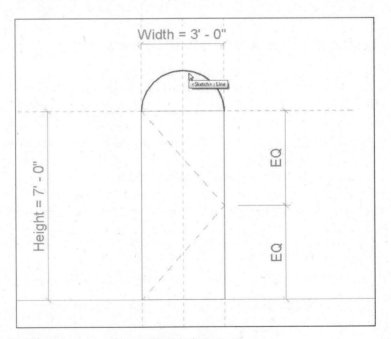

FIGURE 17.15: Rounding off the door top

10. Delete the leftover top line. Your door opening should be a continuous perimeter.

11. Click Finish Edit Mode.

With the opening in place, you can begin testing. Yes, you need to test the width to see if the actual radial top will behave as expected. Taking the time to do this now is an extremely small concession to the pain of deleting half the family later trying to find out what broke:

1. Click the Family Types button on the Properties panel.

2. Change the value for Width to 4′–0″ (1200mm).

3. Click OK.

4. Verify that the arc behaved as expected. If it didn't, you need to reedit the opening and make sure you're snapped to the correct points.

I told you that would be quick. That is all the time it takes to make sure your family is good to go up to this point.

Now let's add some components to the family. The first item you'll tackle is the door jamb. You'll do this by creating a solid form and then a solid extrusion.

Creating a 3D Extrusion in a Family

Other than the curtain wall you applied to a face of a mass in the previous chapter, you've been working in this huge 3D program without doing a single 3D operation. Well, that has come to an end. At some point, you'll need to deal with 3D and massing. When it comes to learning families, you can't avoid it.

But 3D in a family is slightly different than any 3D item you may have created in the past. The wonderful thing about creating 3D items in a family is that these items are fully adjustable after they're created.

The objective of the next procedure is to create a door jamb using solid extrusion. You'll then lock the faces of the extrusion to the walls so that the family will adapt to any wall thickness when passed into the model. Follow these steps:

1. Make sure you're in the exterior elevation.

2. On the Forms panel of the Create tab, click the Extrusion button.

3. In the Work Plane panel, click the Set button, as shown in Figure 17.16.

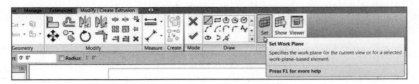

FIGURE 17.16: The Set button in the Work Plane panel

4. In the Work Plane dialog, click Pick A Plane, and then click OK.

5. Pick the face of the wall, as shown in Figure 17.17.

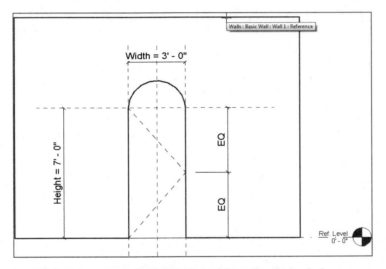

FIGURE 17.17: Setting the face of the wall as the work plane

6. Now that the work plane has been set, click the Pick Lines icon on the Draw panel.

 WARNING   Steps 3–5 have you set the work plane to the face of the wall. *This is of the utmost importance.* If you skip this step, your door won't respond to the change in the wall's thickness when you load it into the model.

7. On the Options bar, select the Lock toggle.

8. Pick the inside face of the opening (see Figure 17.18).

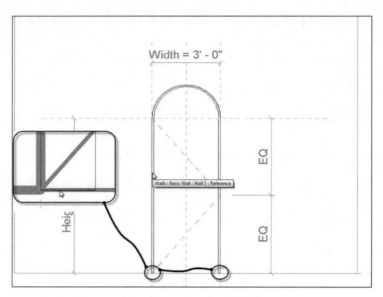

FIGURE 17.18:   Picking the frame for the jamb

9. Change Offset on the Options bar to **1″** (25mm).

10. Pick the same lines, offsetting the inside face of the jamb into the opening **1″** (25mm).

11. Zoom in to the bottom of the jambs.

LINE IS TOO SHORT

You may get an error at some point as you pick these lines, as shown in the following image. This is more of a nuisance than anything else. All you need to do is click OK, delete the line(s) that were set into the wrong spot, and redo the same command. You'll have more success the second time through.

12. Set Offset on the Options bar to 0.

13. Draw a line connecting the bottom of each jamb (see Figure 17.18).

14. In the Properties dialog, make sure the type is set to Extrusion, as shown in Figure 17.19.

FIGURE 17.19: Clicking the button to add a material parameter

15. Set Extrusion End to -3″ (-75mm), as shown in Figure 17.19.

16. Click the small button to the right of the Material row (see Figure 17.19).

17. Click Add Parameter at lower left in the dialog.

18. Name the parameter **Jamb Material**.

19. Keep it grouped under Materials And Finishes.

20. Keep it a Type parameter.

21. Click OK.

22. The Material field is no longer active. Click OK again, and then click Finish Edit Mode.

What did you just do? By not selecting the actual material in the properties of the extrusion, you created a parameter so that users can specify whatever material they deem necessary. This is a valuable step in family creation: it's called *flexibility*.

Speaking of flexibility, this jamb is held at a steady 3″ (75mm). This is an incorrect value and will remain static unless you do something about it. You'll do so right now.

The objective of the next procedure is to align the inside face of the jamb with the inside face of the wall and to lock that alignment in place. Follow along:

1. Go to a 3D view, and make sure you're spun around so that you can see the inside face of the wall where the jamb doesn't align.

2. Click the Align button on the Modify tab, as shown in Figure 17.20.

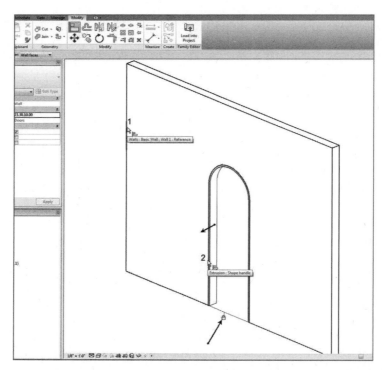

FIGURE 17.20:   Aligning and locking the inside face of the jamb to the wall

3. On the Options bar, select Wall Faces for Preference.

4. Pick the inside face of the wall.

5. Pick the inside face of the jamb.

6. Click the open padlock icon that appears (see Figure 17.20).

7. Press Esc.

8. Click the Save icon.

9. Save the door in a directory where you'll be able to find it.

10. Call it **Arched Door.rfa**.

11. Make sure your project is open.

12. In the Arched Door.rfa file, click Load Into Project.
    If you have more than one project or family open, Revit will make you choose a model to load the family into. Be sure to pick your project file.

13. In the model, open the Level 1 view.

14. On the Architecture tab, click the Door button.

15. Insert the new door in the wall, as shown in Figure 17.21. (Don't worry too much about placement.)

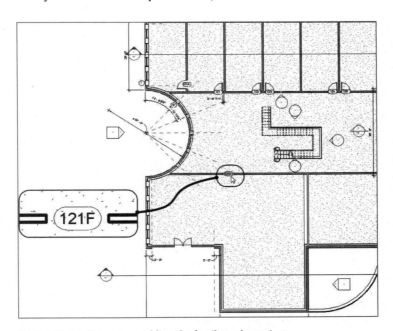

FIGURE 17.21: Adding the family to the project

16. Select the door.

17. In the Properties dialog, click Edit Type, and observe the parameters. Look familiar? You created them!

18. Click OK.

19. Go back to the door family.

Wow! This thing actually works. Good deal. The next trick is to add some casing to the outside of the frame. To do so, you'll have to use a solid sweep.

Creating a 3D Sweep in a Family

Going along the same lines (literally) as the extrusion, you can create a situation where you sketch a path and extrude a profile along that path. The trick is to make sure this sweep can flex along with the door.

The objective of the next procedure is to create the door casing by using a 3D sweep. Follow these steps:

1. Go to a 3D view (if you aren't there already), and position the view so that it looks like Figure 17.22.

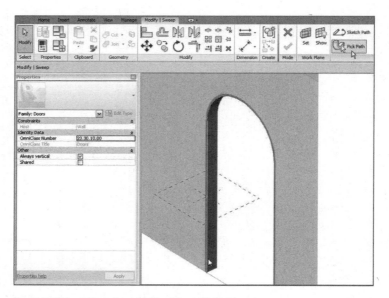

FIGURE 17.22: Picking the path for the sweep

2. On the Create tab, click the Sweep button.

3. On the Sweep panel, click the Pick Path button.

4. Pick the inside corner of the jamb starting with the left side (see Figure 17.22).

5. Click Finish Edit Mode on the Mode panel.

6. On the Sweep panel, click the Load Profile button.

7. Go to the Profiles ➢ Finish Carpentry folder, and select Casing Profile-2.rfa.

8. Click Open.

9. In the menu on the Sweep panel, click the Profile drop-down, and select Casing Profile 2: 5 1/2″ × 13/16″ (the red dot is replaced with the actual profile).

10. On the Options bar, type -0′–5 3/4″ (-144mm) for the Y offset. The profile is pushed back onto the wall with a ¼″ (6mm) reveal.

11. Click Finish Edit Mode. Select the new sweep.

12. In the Properties dialog, click the small button to the right of the Material category.

13. Click Add Parameter.

14. Call the parameter **Casing Material**.

15. Group it under Materials And Finishes.

16. Click OK twice.

17. Repeat steps 2 through 11 on the other side of the door. (Don't try to mirror the sweep—it won't work.)

18. Save the family.

19. Load it into the project. Select Overwrite Existing Version.

20. In your model, select the door.

21. In the Properties dialog, click Edit Type.

22. Change the Width value to 3′–0″ (900mm).

23. Click OK.

24. Load the door back into the model, and click Overwrite Existing Version.

Your door is still working properly and looks better, as shown in Figure 17.23.

FIGURE 17.23:   The finished sweep. If you'd like, go ahead and create a new camera view of this door.

Let's move forward and begin working on adding a door to the family. The biggest challenge here will be the plan swing representation, but with a few new items to learn, this won't be a problem.

In the next procedure, you'll add a door, a stop, and some plan symbolic line-work. Follow along:

1. Open the door family.

2. Go to the exterior elevation.

3. On the Create tab, click the Extrusion button.

4. On the Draw panel, click the Pick Lines icon.

5. Set Offset to 1/8″ (3mm).

6. Offset the two sides and the radial top of the jamb extrusion to the inside.

7. Set Offset to 1/2″ (12mm).

8. Offset the bottom up (see Figure 17.24).

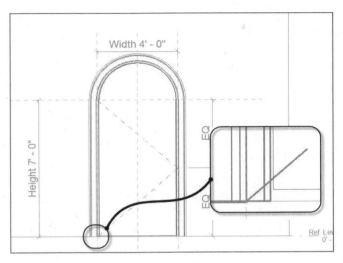

FIGURE 17.24: Adding the door

9. Trim the bottom corners so that the door is one panel.

10. In the Properties dialog, make sure Extrusion is current in the Type menu.

11. For the Extrusion end, type -1 3/8″ (-35mm).

12. For the material, click the button to the right of the Material field, and add a new parameter called **Door Material**.

13. Keep it categorized under Materials And Finishes.

14. Click OK twice.

15. Click Finish Edit Mode.

16. In the Project Browser, go to the Ref. Level floor plan view.

17. Your door should look like the one in Figure 17.25.

18. Load the door into your project. (Click Yes to overwrite the door that is there.) Verify that the door looks correct.

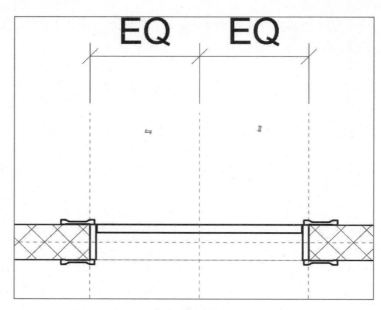

FIGURE 17.25: The finished door in plan

Now that you've created the door, you can fix up the plan view. You need to add a door swing. In addition, you don't want to see the door panel in any plan view, so you can create a view state to turn it off in the plan view. Follow these steps:

1. Go back to the door family in the Ref Plan view. On the Annotate tab, click the Symbolic Line button, as shown in Figure 17.26.

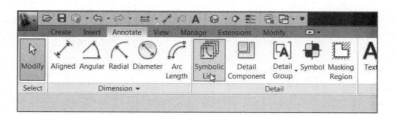

FIGURE 17.26: The Symbolic Line button

2. Draw a line straight up from the right corner of the jamb (on the exterior side of the wall) 4′–0″ (1200mm), as shown in Figure 17.27.

3. Draw another line to the left 1 ⅜″ (35mm).

4. Draw another line straight down 4′–0″ (1200mm).

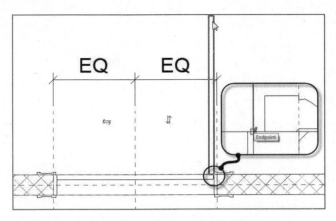

FIGURE 17.27: Drawing the symbolic door swing

5. Draw another line to the right 1 ⅜″ (35mm) (see Figure 17.27).

6. Click the Symbolic Line button again (if it isn't currently running).

7. Draw an arc from the left side of the jamb to the top of the symbolic swing, as shown in Figure 17.28. Click Modify.

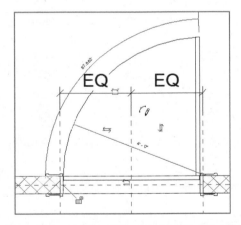

FIGURE 17.28: Drawing the plan swing arc

With the plan swing in place, you can turn off the actual door panel. This process is quick and painless:

1. Select the door panel.

2. On the Modify | Extrusion tab, click the Visibility Settings button on the Mode panel.

3. Deselect Plan/RCP.

4. Deselect When Cut In Plan/RCP (If Category Permits).

5. Click OK.

6. Save the family.

7. Load it into the project. Overwrite the existing version. If it didn't explode, your door is complete!

As you can see, it isn't that difficult to create a family. This topic could be a book within a book. Start experimenting with your own families. If you run into a snag, send me an email at ewing@cscos.com, and we can work on it.

The next type of family we'll study is one that literally can't be avoided. Eventually, you'll need the surrounding geometry of the model to create the family. This is called an *in-place family*.

Creating an In-Place Family

An in-place family gives you the best of both worlds. When you start the In-Place Family command, your model turns into the Family Editor. You can make a family exactly the same way you just did, except that it's native to the model. Many times, you'll need this flexibility when you have a family that you'll never use again in any other building. This also gives you the flexibility to create custom content that can't be created using the conventional Revit commands.

To create an in-place family, follow along with this procedure:

1. Open the model on which you've been working.

2. Open the section view called West Wing South Wall Section. You're in the atrium.

3. On the Architecture tab, click Component ➤ Model In-Place, as shown in Figure 17.29.

4. Set Family Category to Doors, and then click OK.

5. Call the new door **West Opening**.

6. Click OK.

7. On the Model panel of the Create tab, click the Opening button.

8. Pick the brick wall facing you.

9. Sketch an opening, as shown in Figure 17.30.

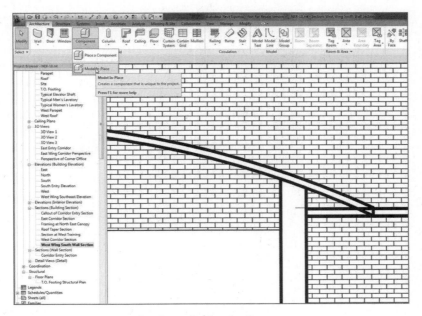

FIGURE 17.29:   Starting an in-place family

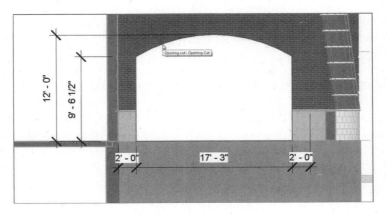

FIGURE 17.30:   The arched opening

10. Click Finish Edit Mode.

11. Go to a 3D view.

12. On the Forms panel of the Create tab, click the Sweep button.

13. On the Sweep panel, click the Pick Path button.

14. Pick the exterior corners of the opening forming the arc and the two straight lines to either side of the opening (see Figure 17.31).

When you're picking the lines for the path, you'll find that you can't pick the entire line on either of the two sides of the arc. All you need to do is pick any line on the three corners and then trim the lines to meet at the corners.

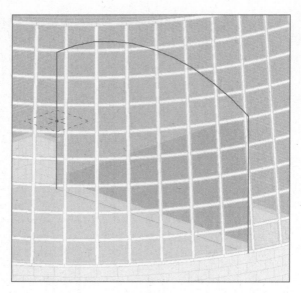

FIGURE 17.31:   Picking the exterior edge for the sweep's path

15. Click Finish Edit Mode on the Mode tab.

16. In the Project Browser, go to the Level 1 floor plan. Zoom in to the new opening.

17. Click the Select Profile button on the Sweep panel.

18. On the Sweep panel, click the Edit Profile button (see Figure 17.32).

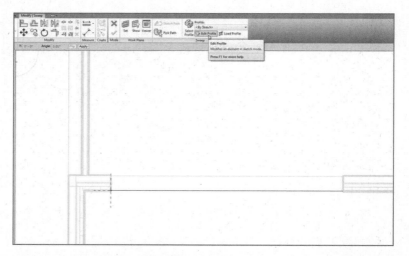

FIGURE 17.32:   Sketching the profile

19. Sketch a profile similar to that shown in Figure 17.32. Make it any size, shape, and complexity you wish.

20. Click Finish Edit Mode.

21. In the Properties dialog, make sure Sweep is current, and then click the little gray button to the left of the Materials row.

22. Add a parameter called **Casing Material**. Click OK.

23. At the bottom of the Properties palette, in the Other category, click Trajectory Segmentation.

24. Set Maximum Segment Angle to 1.

25. Click Finish Edit Mode.

26. Click Finish Model.

27. Go to a 3D view. Your opening should look like Figure 17.33.

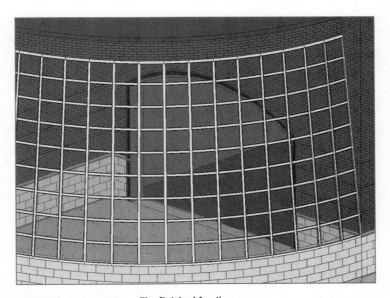

FIGURE 17.33: The finished family

The moral of the story is this: when you have a custom situation in the model that can't be created using the conventional Revit tools, create an in-place family. You should make it as flexible as possible and give the user some choices, such as materials, so that anyone can manipulate the family as if Autodesk provided it.

Are You Experienced?

Now you can...

☑ create a cove sweep family

☑ identify the family template you need to use to start a family

☑ create a door family

☑ add symbolic lines to a family

☑ create an in-place family

☑ create sweeps and extrusions

☑ create parameters

Site and Topography

When it comes to adding a site to a model, the Autodesk® Revit® Architecture software is well equipped to take on the challenge. However, in many cases Revit is dependent on Autodesk® AutoCAD® or MicroStation to provide a real-case scenario for a site that can be imported (similar to importing a plan or a detail). Fortunately, Revit provides tools to add a topographic surface to an imported CAD site.

▶ **Adding a site in Revit**

▶ **Splitting the surface**

▶ **Creating subregions**

▶ **Adding site components**

▶ **Adding building pads to displace earth**

▶ **Adding a property line**

▶ **Creating a toposurface by instance**

▶ **Creating a graded region**

Adding a Site in Revit

To get started, let's do something easy and then migrate into the more difficult areas, such as importing a CAD file. The first item you'll tackle will be to start a site using datum points that you'll manually pick using the Toposurface function on the Ribbon's Massing & Site tab.

> **N O T E**   Metric users should not type in mm or other metric abbreviations when entering amounts suggested in the exercises. Revit will not accept such abbreviations. Simply enter the number provided within the parentheses.

Let's get cracking. First, open the model on which you've been working. If you missed the previous chapter, go to the book's web page at www.sybex.com/go/revit2014ner. From there, you can browse to the Chapter 18 folder and find the NER-18.rvt file.

The objective of this procedure is to add a topographical surface by choosing datum points and elevations. Follow along:

1. In the Project Browser, find the Site floor plan and open it.

2. Type **VG** for Visibility Graphics.

3. On the Annotation Categories tab, deselect Callouts, Elevations, Grids, Matchline, Stairs, and Sections, and click OK.

4. On the Massing & Site tab, click the Toposurface button, as shown in Figure 18.1.

F I G U R E   1 8 . 1 :   Click the Toposurface button on the Massing & Site tab of the Ribbon.

5. On the Options bar, set the elevation to -2′–6″ (-750mm) (that's negative 2′–6″ [negative 750mm]).

6. Pick points in a pattern to the right half of the building, as shown in Figure 18.2.

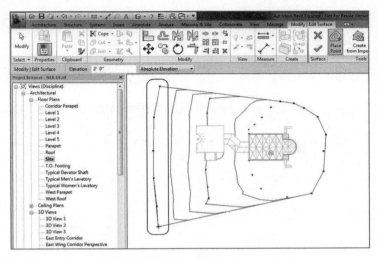

FIGURE 18.2: Adding the first contours

 NOTE   Notice that after you click the Toposurface button, Revit launches Sketch Mode. The Place Point button is selected by default in Toposurface Sketch Mode.

7. With the Place Point command still running, set Elevation on the Options bar to -1'–0' (-300mm).

8. Pick five or six points in a line, similar to Figure 18.3.

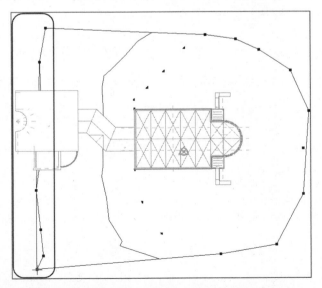

FIGURE 18.3: Adding the second contour to the site

9. With the Place Point command still running, set Elevation on the Options bar to **2′ (600mm)**.

10. Add a third contour line to the left of the second, as shown in Figure 18.4.

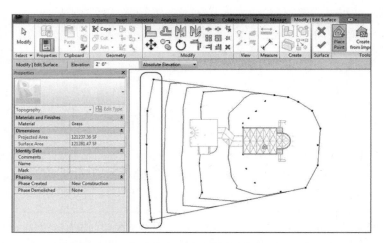

FIGURE 18.4:   Adding the third set of contours

11. Click Finish Surface (the green check mark).

12. Select the topographical surface; then, in the Properties dialog, click into the Material field, and click the […] button.

13. At the top of the Material Browser, enter the word **grass**, as shown in Figure 18.5.

14. When the Grass material appears in the search results window, select it.

15. Select the Graphics tab, and change Cut Pattern to Earth (see Figure 18.5).

16. Click OK.

17. Go to a 3D view, and check out your site.

Next let's see how you can modify a site after you create it. You'll have to deal with the fact that the ramps at the east entry are now buried in your site.

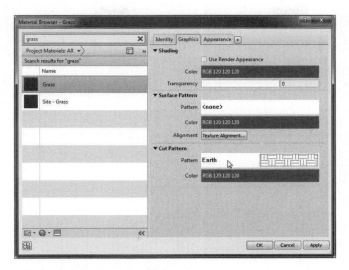

FIGURE 18.5: Finding some grass

Modifying a Toposurface

Because you must always make modifications to a toposurface, you need to learn how to do so. The method is basic. Select the site, click Edit, and away you go!

In this procedure, you'll modify the toposurface to allow for the ramps to land on earth. Follow these steps:

1. Go back to the Site plan.

2. Set Visual Style to Wireframe.

3. Zoom in on the west wing area where the slanted curtain wall resides, as shown in Figure 18.6.

4. Select the site (you may have to find an edge).

5. On the Modify | Topography tab, click Edit Surface.

6. On the Tools panel, click the Place Point button.

7. On the Options bar, set Elevation to 0.

8. Pick five points (see Figure 18.6).

9. Click Finish Surface on the Surface panel.

10. Change Visual Style to Realistic.

11. Go to a 3D view to make sure it looks correct.

12. Save the model.

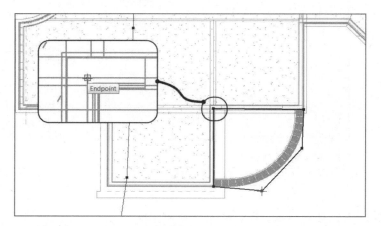

FIGURE 18.6: Adding the 0 elevation points

Excellent! You're getting the hang of this. Next you need to create some raised areas (small hills) where you can eventually add plantings and different materials. The problem is, to create a small hill, you need the site to rise sharply to the new elevation. To achieve this, you have to split the surface physically.

Splitting the Surface

When you need to make a drastic change to the surface's elevation without influencing the rest of the site, you must split the surface. Just to warn you up front, be deliberate about when and where you do this, because you're physically cutting a hole in the surface and adding a secondary toposurface to the void. Although you can merge these surfaces back together, in some situations it can be difficult to merge cleanly.

Let's split the toposurface and create smaller toposurfaces. Follow along:

1. In the Project Browser, go back to the Site plan.

2. On the Massing & Site tab, click the Split Surface button, as shown in Figure 18.7.

FIGURE 18.7: The Split Surface button

3. Select the toposurface.

4. Zoom in on the corridor area that links the east and west wings, as shown in Figure 18.8.

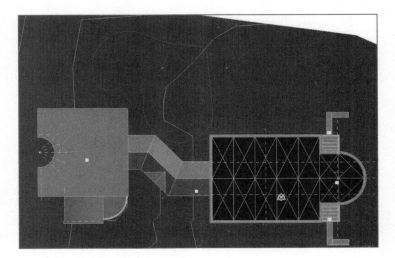

FIGURE 18.8: The split surface sketch

5. On the Draw panel, click the Start - End - Radius Arc button.

6. Sketch a perimeter similar to the one in Figure 18.8.

7. Click Finish Edit Mode. You have a new toposurface.

You can manipulate this surface without influencing the main topography. This is the ideal situation for creating bumps and berms.

Next you'll raise this toposurface to an elevation of 4′ (1200mm). You do this by using a point and placing the datum in the middle of the berm. Follow these steps:

1. Select the newly formed toposurface, as shown in Figure 18.9.

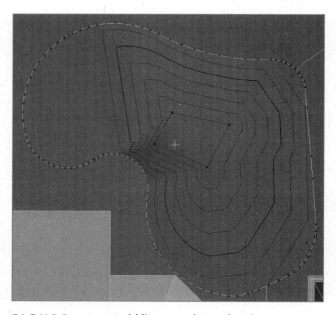

FIGURE 18.9:   Adding a new datum elevation

2. Click the Edit Surface button on the Modify | Topography tab.

3. On the Tools panel, click the Place Point button.

4. On the Options bar, enter a value of 4′–0″ (1200mm) in the Elevation field.

5. Pick four points near the center of the hill (see Figure 18.9).

6. Click Finish Surface.

7. Select the split surface again.

8. In the Properties dialog, change the material to Earth.

9. Deselect the topography. Your site should resemble Figure 18.10.

N O T E   Yes, you can copy these little hills just like anything else in Revit—I'm glad you asked! After you copy the hills, you can edit them like any other toposurface.

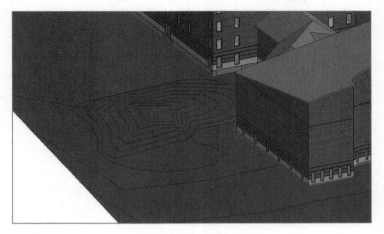

FIGURE 18.10:   The raised area of the site

Well, I think you can see where this is going. When you work with sites, it's good to have some kind of procedure. This takes us to our next perplexing situation. Suppose you want to keep the contours and the dips and hills intact, and you only want to specify a new material in a subregion of the main topography. Is this possible? Yes, it is!

Creating Subregions

The purpose of a *subregion* is to match two surface materials so that any change in elevation or lateral movement is reflected in both regions. You need this ability for walks and most roadways. When you divide the toposurface into subregions, you give yourself the freedom to manipulate two different materials in the same datum. Another benefit of subregions is that the file size remains as if there were still one toposurface. If you were to split the surface every time you needed a path or a roadway, your file size would bloat.

In the following procedure, you'll create a walkway path using the Subregion command. Follow along:

1. Go to the Site plan.

2. Zoom in on the east entry.

3. On the Massing & Site tab, click the Subregion button, as shown in Figure 18.11.

4. Change the view to Wireframe, and start sketching away.

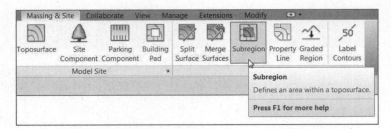

FIGURE 18.11: The Subregion button

5. Draw a region similar to the one shown in Figure 18.12. (It doesn't have to be exact.) This image shows a parking area with some pedestrian access. The inside of the parking area follows the building footprint. Pick Finish Edit Mode.

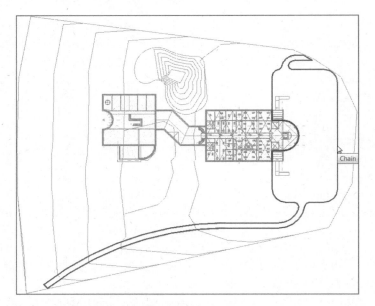

FIGURE 18.12: Sketching the subregion

6. In the Material row in the Properties dialog, change the material to Brick, Pavers from the AEC Materials list in the lower panels.

7. Change the view back to Realistic.

8. Go to a 3D view, and compare yours with Figure 18.13.

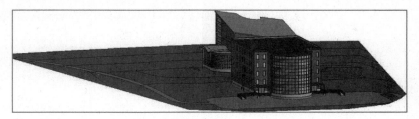

FIGURE 18.13: The sidewalks in 3D

 NOTE You can't cross over and exceed the extents of the original boundary. If you do, Revit won't allow you to finish the sketch. Also, this subregion must form a continuous loop with no gaps or overlapping lines. You need a straight line at each end of the path.

How did you do? If you aren't happy with your parking lot layout, go back and redo it. Not too shabby! There is definitely something missing from this parking lot, though. Perhaps some actual parking spaces would be nice. And a parking island or two would make the parking lot stand out.

Adding Site Components

Adding a site component to Revit is no different than adding a desk or a door. A component is a component, as far as Revit is concerned. As you've learned, a component is hosted by a system component. For example, when you're inserting a window, there needs to be a wall, or Revit won't allow such a foolish transaction to occur. In Revit, you can host a site component to a level, but it's a bad idea to do so. When you add a site component, you always want to host that component to the actual topography.

In this procedure, you'll add parking components and plantings to the Revit model. Follow these steps:

1. On the Insert tab, click the Load Family button.

2. Scroll to the Parking directory in the Site folder.

3. Load every file in the directory. If you get a Family Already Exists message about Parking Space, click Overwrite The Existing Version.

4. In the Project Browser, go to the Site plan.

5. In the View Control bar, set Visual Style to Realistic.

6. On the Massing & Site tab, click the Site Component button, as shown in Figure 18.14.

FIGURE 18.14:   The Site Component button

7. In the Type Selector, select Parking Island - Single Sided 15 Spaces per row.

8. In the Properties dialog, change Parking Width to 138′–8″ (41600mm).

9. Place the parking island in a location similar to that shown in Figure 18.15. Note that you'll have to press the spacebar to orient the component correctly. Click Modify.

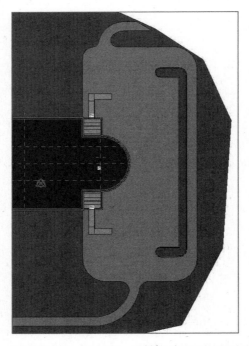

FIGURE 18.15:   Adding the component to the parking lot

10. Select the parking component.

11. Click the Edit Family button on the Modify | Site tab.

12. Select both the curb and the grass extrusions.

13. In the Properties dialog, click the Edit button in the Visibility/ Graphics Overrides row.

14. In the Display In 3D Views menu, select all four items.

15. Click OK.

16. Click the Load Into Project button. Click Overwrite The Existing Version if prompted to do so. Your model should resemble Figure 18.15.

Now that the island is in place, it's time to add the parking spots. You'll need an ADA (parking for disabled drivers, required by the Americans with Disabilities Act) space as well as some general parking spaces. Follow along:

1. On the Massing & Site tab, click the Parking Component button.

2. Select Parking Space - ADA 9′ × 18′ (5′ Aisle) (2743mm × 5486mm). Place an instance as shown in Figure 18.16. Use the spacebar to rotate it properly.

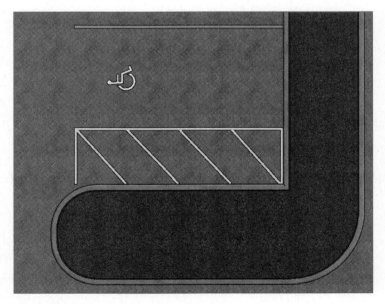

FIGURE 18.16: The ADA parking space

Chapter 18 · Site and Topography

3. Click the Site Component button.

4. Add Parking Symbol – ADA, and place it as shown in Figure 18.16.

5. Mirror the ADA space and the ADA symbol to the north of the parking island, as shown in Figure 18.17.

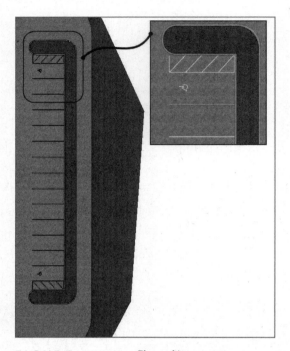

FIGURE 18.17: The parking spaces

6. Add a parking space 9′ × 18′ - 90 deg (2743mm × 5486mm), and copy it up to fill the island with parking (see Figure 18.17).

The parking lot is somewhat complete, so let's add some trees and shrubs to the site. This will be a lot easier! Follow these steps:

1. On the Insert tab, click the Load Family button.

2. Browse to the Planting folder.

3. Select everything available, and load it into the model. Overwrite any existing versions.

4. On the Massing & Site tab, click the Site Component button.

5. Place trees and shrubs on the parking island and on the berm you created. Notice that the plantings always follow the grade of your site. Be creative.

6. Go to a 3D view and check it out, as shown in Figure 18.18.

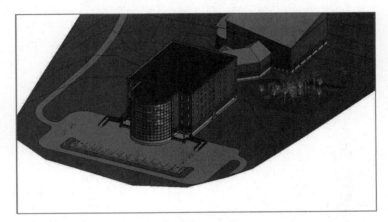

FIGURE 18.18: Adding the plantings

With all the contours and plantings in place, you need to knock out a small maintenance issue. There is a function that will allow you to add contour labels to the site automatically; this is a great feature in Revit Architecture.

Adding Contour Properties and Labels

Because nothing in Revit Architecture is dumb, you can take advantage of a topographic surface having some smarts as well. Even the contour lines of a site are smart.

The objective of this procedure is to examine some site settings and throw some labels into the contours. It's a quick set of steps, but important nonetheless:

1. Click the arrow in the lower-right corner of the Model Site panel, as shown in Figure 18.19.

2. In the Site Settings dialog that opens is a field that contains additional contours. In the Increment panel, change the value 1'–0" (300mm) to 6" (150mm) (see Figure 18.19).

3. Click OK. Notice that the contours are tighter.

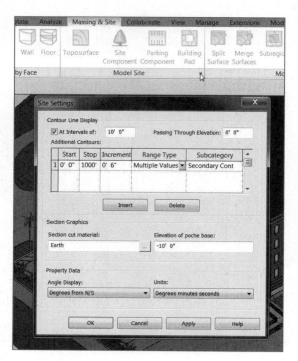

FIGURE 18.19:   Changing the additional contour increment

Now that the contours are in place, you can label them. Luckily, a function in Revit allows you to do this in one shot. All you need to do is draw a *line* specifying the alignment of the contours, and Revit will add the labels automatically.

Follow these steps to add contour labels to the site:

1. On the Massing & Site tab, click the Label Contours button, as shown in Figure 18.20.

2. Pick a point to the outside of the toposurface, labeled 1 in Figure 18.20.

3. Pick a second point near the building, labeled 2 in Figure 18.20. After you pick the second point, the contours are labeled.

Next you need to address a situation that has arisen unbeknownst to you. You see, you never defined any areas into which you may not want earth to spill, such as the basement. This will affect every section you have. You can place a *pad* to displace the earth in the basement.

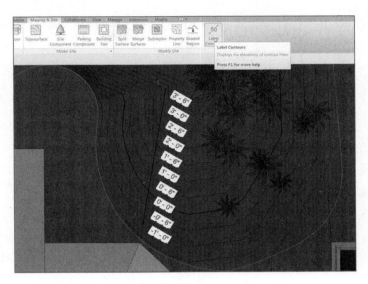

FIGURE 18.20: Labeling the contours

Adding Building Pads to Displace Earth

When you need to displace a volume of earth, you use a tool exclusive to the Massing & Site tab to do so. By placing a building pad into your model, you tell Revit that you want to cut the earth away from this area while still leaving the earth beneath at a certain elevation. For example, if you want to remove the earth from the basement (which you'll be doing), but you still need the earth to exist beneath the basement, you must place a building pad.

To place a building pad into the model, follow this procedure:

1. In the Project Browser, go to the T.O. Footing plan.

2. On the Massing & Site tab, click the Building Pad button, as shown in Figure 18.21.

FIGURE 18.21: The Building Pad button

3. In the Properties dialog, make sure Pads is current, and click Edit Type.

4. Click Duplicate.

5. Call the pad **Footprint**, and click OK.

6. For the Structure, click the Edit button.

7. Change Thickness to **6″ (150**mm).

8. Click OK twice.

9. Change Height Offset from Level to **6″** (150mm).

10. Set Offset to **1″** (25mm) on the Options bar, and pick walls to place the pad against the outside of the foundation wall underneath the entire model, as shown in Figure 18.22. Trim the sketch lines as necessary.

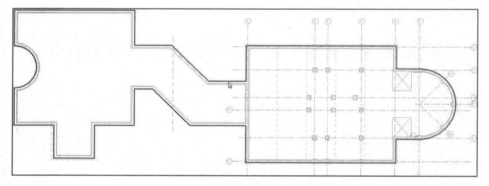

FIGURE 18.22: Place the pad 1″ (25mm) to the outside of the wall.

11. Click Finish Edit Mode.

12. In the Project Browser, open West Corridor Section. You may have to adjust the crop region to see the footings.

13. You can see the pad sitting on top of the footing extending past the wall, as shown in Figure 18.23. Select it.

14. Right-click, and select Hide In View ➢ Elements (see Figure 18.23).

15. Go to the Model Site panel, and click the Site Settings arrow.

16. In the Section Graphics area, change the Elevation Of Poche Base value to -15′–0″ (-4500mm).

17. Click OK. The earth hatch is now beneath the slab area.

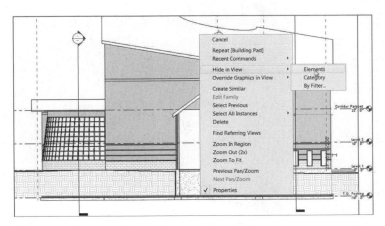

FIGURE 18.23:   Hiding the pad in the view

With the pad in place, you can rest assured that your sections are showing the earth where it's supposed to be.

The next item we'll cover is creating a property line. In most conventional drafting applications, this involves nothing more than adding a polyline around the site. In Revit, this approach is the same, but the property line can tell you much more about the boundary it's encasing.

Adding a Property Line

If you want to add a property line, Revit provides the tool you need. Of course, this is Revit, so you aren't just adding a dumb line to the model. When you start the Property Line command, Revit will ask if you want to create the property line either by using bearing distances or by sketching (a sketch can be converted to a bearing table after it has been placed).

To add a property line, follow this procedure:

1. In the Project Browser, go to the Site floor plan.

2. On the Massing & Site tab, click the Property Line button, as shown in Figure 18.24.

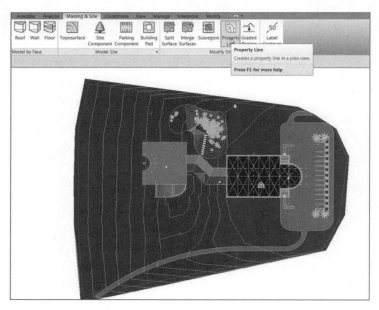

FIGURE 18.24: Adding a property line

3. In the Create Property Line dialog that appears, click the Create By Sketching option.

4. Draw a series of lines around the perimeter (see Figure 18.24). Close the sketch by returning to the starting point, but note that you don't have to close a property line.

5. Click Finish Edit Mode.

6. Select the property line.

7. On the Modify | Property Lines panel, click the Edit Table button.

8. Click Yes if you get a "Do you want to continue?" dialog.

9. Close the Property Lines dialog, and save the model.

You now have a table of deed data that can be modified as you see fit. If your property line is open, there is an option in the table to create a line to close it so that you can calculate area.

The next item on the agenda is a powerful tool when it comes to creating a site in Revit. As nice as it would be never to depend on CAD, most of your topographical information will come from the CAD world. Revit has a By Instance function that can facilitate this procedure.

Creating a Toposurface by Instance

Creating a toposurface by instance requires that you import a CAD file. After you do so, you can go to the Toposurface command, which offers the choice to use an imported instance to drape a surface from Revit.

To get started, you can either choose a site that was created in CAD and with which you want to experiment, or you can go to the book's web page at www.sybex .com/go/revit2014ner. From there, you can browse to the Chapter 18 folder and find the contours.dwg file.

The first thing you need to do is think about coordinates. That's right: coordinates. You're bringing in a file from AutoCAD, right? How do you know where this site will be placed? You must consider two things: where the project base point is in AutoCAD, and where the survey point is located. When you know these two things, you can work more logically between AutoCAD and Revit. The next set of procedures will show you how to coordinate your Revit site with an AutoCAD site:

1. Start a new Revit model.

2. Go to the Site plan.

3. Notice the two blue icons in the model. Pick a window around them, and click the Filter button.

4. Deselect Project Base Point, as shown in Figure 18.25.

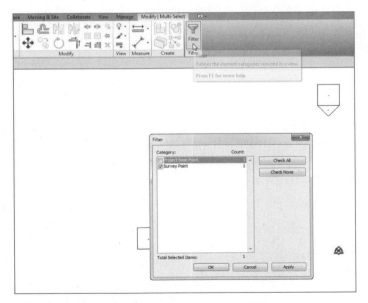

FIGURE 18.25: Selecting the project datum

5. Click OK.

6. Deselect the blue paperclip, as shown in Figure 18.26.

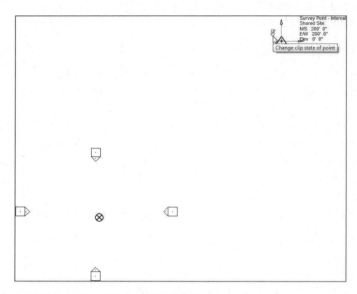

FIGURE 18.26: Altering the survey point

7. Change N/S to 200′ (60000mm).

8. Change E/W to 200′ (60000mm).

WHAT ARE YOU CHANGING, AND WHY?

What you're changing here is a survey point. You don't know the survey point of the practice file you're bringing into the model, so for now you're making one up. The project base point always wants to be 0,0.

9. Click the Survey Point - Internal link (see Figure 18.26).

10. In the Location Weather And Site dialog that opens, on the Site tab, click the Duplicate button.

11. Call the new location **Site Datum.** Click OK.

12. Click the Location tab.

13. Using the Internet Mapping Service, set the location for Syracuse, NY USA (see Figure 18.27). You can also use your own location.

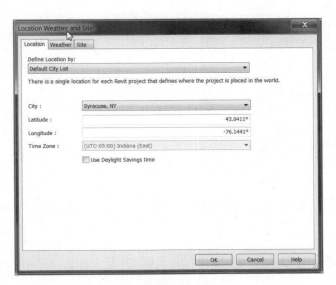

FIGURE 18.27: Setting the site

14. Click OK.

15. Press Esc.

Okay, great. Now you'll set the project orientation. In Revit, you can rotate the site plan to true north while leaving the other views oriented to project north. Let's do it:

1. In the Properties dialog for the view, change Orientation to True North, as shown in Figure 18.28.

2. On the Manage tab, click Position ➤ Rotate True North, as shown in Figure 18.29.

3. Pick the node on the Survey point, as shown in Figure 18.30.

4. Pick a second point at 45° left (which lands you straight up—see Figure 18.30). Your site view is now facing true north, and all your other views are project north.

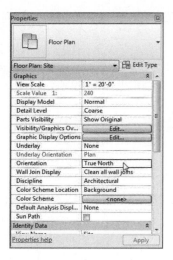

FIGURE 18.28: Orienting the site to true north

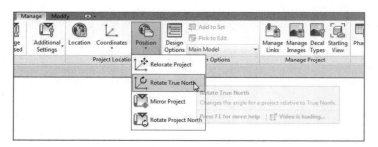

FIGURE 18.29: Rotating true north

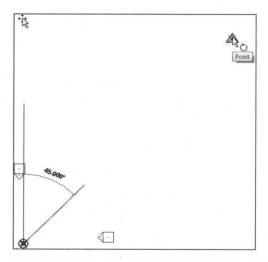

FIGURE 18.30: Finalizing the rotation

Next you'll import a site from CAD. To use an imported instance to create a toposurface, follow these steps:

1. Save your model as **Imported Site.rvt**.

2. In the Project Browser, go to the Site plan if you aren't there already.

3. On the Insert tab, click the Link CAD button.

4. Browse to the contours.dwg file you downloaded. (If you have your own site DWG file, that's fine, too.)

5. Before you click Open, change Colors to Black And White, Layers to All, and Import Units to Feet. Also, change Positioning to Auto - By Shared Coordinates. Be sure Current View Only is deselected.

6. Make sure Orient To View is selected. (See Figure 18.31.)

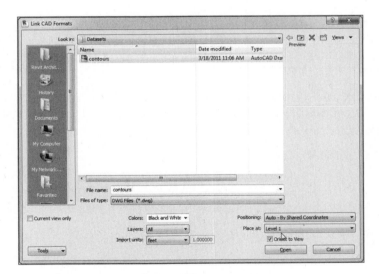

FIGURE 18.31: Changing the link settings

7. Click Open.

8. The Differing Coordinate Systems For Project And File dialog opens. Click Close.

9. Click the existing coordinate choice, and click OK.

10. Your site should be positioned as shown in Figure 18.32.

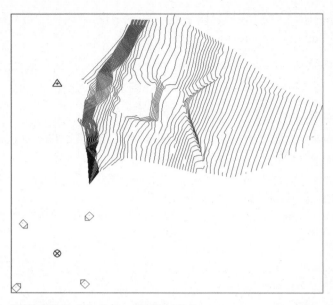

FIGURE 18.32:   The linked site

Because you didn't know the actual survey point of your site, AutoCAD gave you one. It's obviously off the grid. You can move the site to a specific point and create an actual survey point in the native AutoCAD file. Follow along:

1. Select the imported site.

2. Click the Move button.

3. Move the site to a position similar to that shown in Figure 18.33.

4. Save the file. A dialog opens, asking about your shared position.

5. Click Save. Doing so adds a new position in the site DWG file. You're now coordinated with your site people. (See Figure 18.33.)

It's time to add a Revit surface to the contours. This is pretty easy; follow these steps:

1. On the Massing & Site tab, click the Toposurface button.

2. On the Tools panel, click Create From Import ➤ Select Import Instance, as shown in Figure 18.34.

3. Select the imported CAD file.

4. Deselect Layer 0 and Defpoints in the Add Points From Selected Layers dialog.

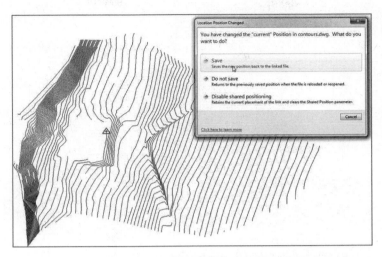

FIGURE 18.33: Saving the shared position back to the drawing

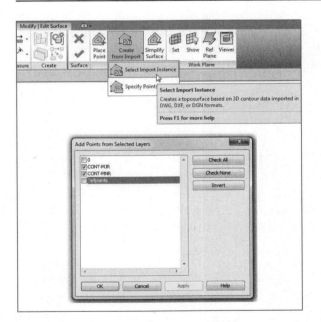

FIGURE 18.34: Adding the toposurface

5. Click OK.

6. In the Properties dialog, change Material to Grass.

7. Click OK to get back to the model.

8. Click Finish Surface.

9. Go to a 3D view. Your topography should look like Figure 18.35.

FIGURE 18.35:   The new toposurface in Revit

That would be a difficult toposurface to create entirely in Revit! The next item we need to explore is how to grade a surface, yielding areas of cuts and fills. The process is straightforward; but as you're about to learn, you need to first deal with *project phasing*.

Creating a Graded Region

This section of the chapter will focus on creating cuts and fills in a site. You do this by lowering and raising points that already exist in the topography. The problem is, after you alter the site, you don't know which part of the site is original or existing, and which part is new.

The objective of the following procedure is to move the site to an existing phase to prepare it for the grading process. Follow along:

1. Go to your Site plan, and type **VG**.

2. In the Visibility/Graphics Overrides dialog, click the Imported Categories tab.

3. Deselect contours.dwg.

4. Click OK.

5. Select the toposurface.

6. In the Properties dialog, change Phase Created to Existing.

7. On the Massing & Site tab, click the Graded Region button, as shown in Figure 18.36.

FIGURE 18.36:   The Graded Region button

8. In the next dialog, click Create A New Toposurface Exactly Like The Existing One.

9. Draw a selection window around the center of the site (doing so selects a bunch of points), as shown in Figure 18.37.

10. In the Properties dialog, enter a value of 0 for the elevation.

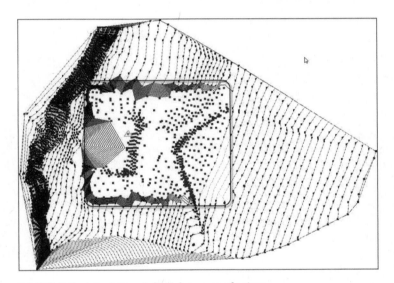

FIGURE 18.37:   Selecting a range of points

11. Click Finish Surface.

12. Verify that your site appears similar to Figure 18.38.

13. Select the newly graded surface, and notice in the Properties that you can get the volumes for Net Cut/Fill.

14. Save the model, and close it.

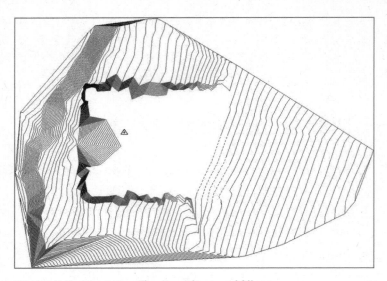

FIGURE 18.38: The site with cuts and fills

That's quite a bit of information regarding sites. It's nice that Revit allows some level of site manipulation, but it would be handy if there was a Revit Site application. I, for one, could see the value in that.

Are You Experienced?

Now you can...

- ☑ **add a topographical surface to your site by using points**
- ☑ **create a topographical surface in your site by using an imported CAD file**
- ☑ **add site components**
- ☑ **split and divide a site's topography**
- ☑ **rotate a project to true north**
- ☑ **relocate a project's datum elevation**

Rendering and Presentation

Well, here we are —the chapter you've probably been chomping at the bit to get into—and for good reason. The output that you create from this chapter will make your bosses and, better yet, your clients get behind your presentations. As I always say, none of this software is any good if you can't capture the work to begin with. That being said, in this chapter we'll focus on creating renderings, adding animations, and providing solar studies based on a project's geographical location.

▶ **Creating an exterior rendering**

▶ **Creating an interior rendering**

▶ **Creating walkthroughs**

▶ **Creating a solar study**

Creating an Exterior Rendering

The first item we need to tackle is how to go about creating an exterior rendering. Trying to address the subject of rendering as a whole would convolute the matter. The thing is, when you create a rendering, lighting obviously plays a major role. Day lighting and artificial lighting are two completely different beasts—one will influence the effect of the other. For example, if you're rendering an exterior scene, there are bound to be windows. If this rendering appears at night or at dusk, the interior lights will be turned on.

The objective of the first section of this chapter is to create a rendering from the exterior of a building using day-lighting scenes, sky, and shadowing to create the rendering you need.

In the previous chapter, you completed one of the most difficult tasks when it comes to creating a proper exterior rendering: rotating a building in terms of true north. It stands to reason that your rendering won't be accurate if you have a glass curtain wall that is facing north, but you still have sunlight pouring through it.

To get started, open the model on which you've been working. If you skipped the previous chapter, go to the book's web page at www.sybex.com/go/revit2014ner. From there, you can browse to Chapter 19 and find the file called NER-19.rvt.

 N O T E   Metric users should not type in mm or other metric abbreviations when entering amounts suggested in the exercises. Revit will not accept such abbreviations. Simply enter the number provided within the parentheses.

The objective of this procedure is to create a camera view that you can use for your first rendering. You'll then adjust the view controls and look at the sunlight effects. Follow along:

1. In the Project Browser, open the Level 1 floor plan.

2. Zoom in on the corridor area in the middle of the building.

3. Add some curtain walls to the corridors, as shown in Figure 19.1. (Come on, I know you can do it.) These are Level 1 to Level 3 with a -6″ (-150mm) offset from Level 3. You can use Curtain Wall Storefront.

4. On the View tab, select 3D View ➢ Camera.

5. Create a camera view of the area shown in Figure 19.1.

6. When the view opens, rename it **Rendering View Corridor**.

7. Open the Rendering View Corridor view (it should open automatically).

8. Select the crop region, and widen the view as shown in Figure 19.2.

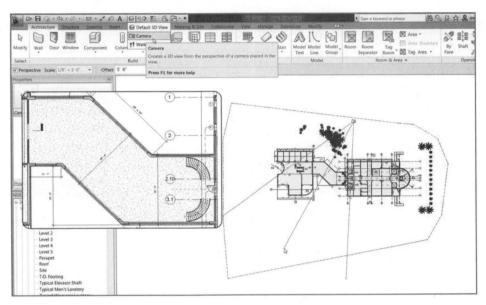

FIGURE 19.1:   Add the curtain walls, and create the camera view.

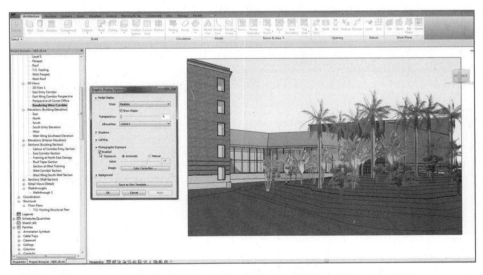

FIGURE 19.2:   Selecting Graphic Display Options, and changing the crop region

9. On the View Control bar, set Detail Level to Fine.

10. Change Visual Style to Realistic.

You can also access the Graphic Display Options dialog by clicking the small black arrow in the right corner of the Graphics panel, in the View tab.

11. In the Properties dialog, click the Edit button in the Graphic Display Options row (see Figure 19.2).

12. In the Graphic Display Options dialog, click into the Photographic Exposure section, and click the Enabled check box.

13. Turn on the Gradient background (at the bottom of the dialog).

14. Click OK.

15. In the Properties dialog, click the Edit button to the right of the Rendering Settings field (in the Camera group). Doing so brings up the Rendering Settings dialog.

16. Click the […] button to the right of the Sun Settings category, as shown in Figure 19.3.

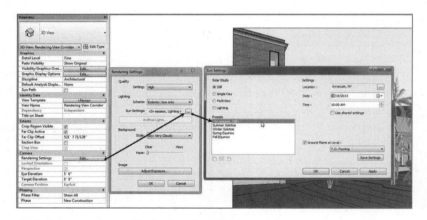

FIGURE 19.3: The Sun Settings dialog

17. Make sure the Still choice is selected for Solar Study, and choose appropriate settings and your geographic location for the settings Date, Time, and Location. (I chose Syracuse, NY, and my birthday [05/10 is the default].) You can change these settings if you would like (see Figure 19.3).

18. Make sure Ground Plane At Level is set to Level 1.

19. Click OK.

20. Click OK again to get back to the model.

21. Click the Show Render Dialog button on the View Control bar, as shown in Figure 19.4.

FIGURE 19.4: The Show Render Dialog button

In the Rendering dialog, you'll see quite a few choices. They vary depending on the scene you're trying to capture. The next procedure will move through the Rendering dialog from top to bottom.

At the top of the Rendering dialog is a Render button. This is the last button you'll click—it starts the rendering process. For the rest, follow these steps:

N O T E   The Region check box (to the right of the Render button) allows you to pick a window to be rendered. Because the scene in this example is somewhat small, you won't need to select this option. If you were rendering a much larger scene, you would render a region. That way, it wouldn't take hours upon hours to complete the rendering, and the resulting rendered scene would be a smaller size. Also, it is good practice to set the first rendering as a test and crank out a much lower DPI, perhaps 150. Once you've verified the rendering will work, let 'er rip at a higher DPI, such as 300.

1. For Output Settings, set Resolution to Printer and 300 DPI.

2. In the Lighting category, set Scheme to Exterior: Sun Only.

3. In the Background category, set Style to Sky: Very Cloudy (see Figure 19.5).

4. Click the Rendering button. After the scene is rendered, it should appear similar to Figure 19.6.

T I P   Before you click the Render button, find something else to do for two to three hours—at this resolution, Revit needs about that much time to render this scene. I recommend that you have Revit installed on another machine at your place of business. You don't want to watch the rendering process, because it's similar to gazing into a campfire. Plus, if your model is being rendered on another machine, you can get some work done at the same time. If you're trying to avoid work, disregard this statement.

FIGURE 19.5:   The Rendering dialog

FIGURE 19.6:   The 300 dpi rendering

So you waited half your day for this rendering to complete. If you're like me, you carefully move your mouse around, wondering how long it will be before something happens and you lose your rendering.

The next procedure will look at how to save the rendering to the model, and also how to export the rendering to an image. Follow these steps:

1. In the Rendering dialog, click the Save To Project button, as shown in Figure 19.7.

FIGURE 19.7: Saving the rendering to the project

2. Call the new rendering view **Exterior Rendering at Corridor**; then click OK.

3. Click the Export button.

THAT'S NOT A VERY GOOD IMAGE!

After you create a rendering that you like, export it immediately. That's how you get the best resolution in the external image you create. Also, you don't want a lot of trial renderings clunking around in your project—they will start to bog down the project. Unless that rendering is going on a sheet, throw it out.

4. Save the file somewhere you can retrieve it. You can choose whichever file format you prefer.

5. At the bottom of the Rendering dialog, in the Display section, click Show The Model. The rendering reverts back to the original graphic style.

6. Click the Show The Rendering button. The rendering reappears.

 WARNING   The ability to jump back and forth from the model to the rendering is a nice feature, but it's short-lived. After you close this project, the rendering is no longer available. Don't close this project until you've finished saving the view to the model and exporting it (if you wish to do so).

Let's try a really cool feature in Revit. The fact is, the sky in Revit just doesn't cut it. However, Revit allows you to add a background image to produce a realistic scene.

The objective of the next procedure is to create a perspective view and render it with a background that comes with the book. Follow along:

1. Go to the Site plan.

2. Create a camera, as shown in Figure 19.8.

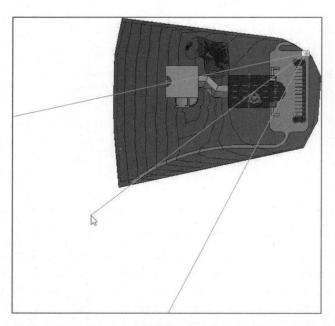

FIGURE 19.8:   Create a new camera view.

3. When the view opens, stretch the crop region generously to show more parking and site. The image shows some hills added to the background.

4. Click the Render button in the View tab under Graphics.

5. At the bottom, select Image from the Style menu in the Background field.

6. Change the background from Sky Cloudy to Image.

7. In the Background Image dialog, click the Image button to browse for the image.

8. Browse to where you put your datasets for this chapter. The file is called Background.tif. If you're using your own model, go to Google Earth and take a screenshot.

9. For Scale, pick Stretch.

10. Click OK.

11. Set the Quality setting to Draft. (When you aren't sure how your rendering will look, or whether it will even render, it's a good idea to render a simple view first and then go for high quality once you're sure your rendering will be accurate.)

12. Set Resolution to Screen.

13. Click the Render button.

14. Look at the rendering. If you like it, render it at a higher quality, as shown in Figure 19.9.

FIGURE 19.9:   Rendering a background image

With the first few renderings under your belt, it's time to create another exterior rendering. This time, however, you'll add some lighting and produce the rendering at night. There is nothing like a good before-and-after rendering to sell a project. Follow these steps:

1. In the Project Browser, go to the Level 1 ceiling plan (that's *ceiling plan*, in case you missed it).

2. In the Architecture tab, click the Component button.

3. On the Mode panel, click the Load Family button.

4. Go to the Lighting folder.

5. Go to Architectural and then to the Exterior folder.

6. Select the family called Wall Pack Light - Exterior.rfa [M-Wall Pack Light - Exterior.rfa], and click Open. If a dialog about loading tags opens, click No.

7. Place the lights at the locations shown in Figure 19.10.

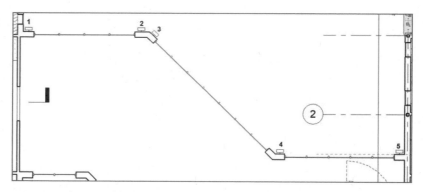

FIGURE 19.10:   Placing the exterior lights

8. In the Project Browser, open the Level 1 floor plan.

9. On the Architecture tab, click the Component button.

10. In the Properties dialog, choose the Sconce Light - Uplight 100W - 120V (or equivalent) family, as shown in Figure 19.11.

11. Place some lights in the link, as shown in Figure 19.12.

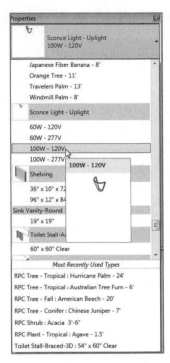

FIGURE 19.11: Choosing the sconce

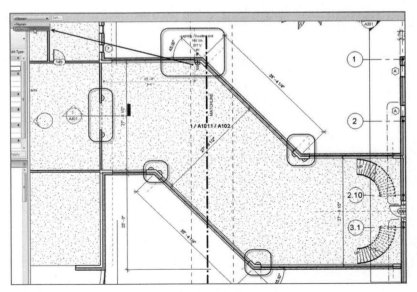

FIGURE 19.12: Adding the interior lighting to the link

With some lights in place, let's look at how you can efficiently group the various types of lighting fixtures to create a nice lighting scene.

Creating Lighting Groups

All too often, you render scenes with no real consideration for the lighting that has been added to the model. Because you lean heavily on Revit to produce accurate scenarios to present to clients, you should spend some time thinking through your lighting before you create a rendering.

In this procedure, you'll create two lighting groups and render the same view using a nighttime setting. Follow along:

Remember, some components are more fickle than others. Lighting fixtures sometimes require finesse. Make sure you're zoomed back enough to see a large portion of the wall, or Revit may not place the fixtures where you expect.

1. Select one of the sconces you just added to the model, as shown in Figure 19.13.

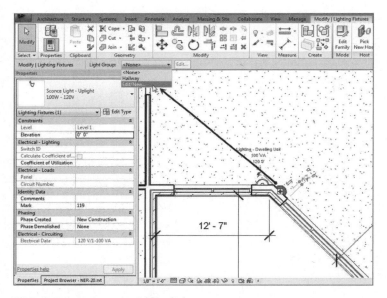

FIGURE 19.13: Adding lights

2. On the Options bar, click the Light Group menu, and select Edit/New (see Figure 19.13).

3. In the Artificial Lights - Level 1 dialog, click the New button in the Group Options area.

4. Call the new group **Lighting Link**, as shown in Figure 19.14.

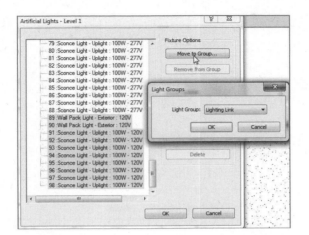

FIGURE 19.14: Creating a new group, and adding the proper lights

5. Scroll down to the bottom of the list, and locate the lights Sconce Light - Uplight : 100W - 120V. Select all of them (see Figure 19.14). Also find the wall packs and add them to the group.

6. Click the Move To Group button under Fixture Options.

7. Choose the Lighting Link group in the Light Groups dialog, and click OK.

8. Click OK to close the dialog.

9. In the Project Browser, go to the Rendering View Corridor view.

10. On the View Control bar, click the Sun Path button (it's the picture of the Sun with the small red x), and click Sun Settings.

11. Make sure Solar Study is set to Still, and change the time to 7:30 PM, as shown in Figure 19.15.

12. Click OK.

13. Click the Show Rendering Dialog button on the View Control bar (if the Rendering dialog isn't still open).

14. Set the Setting value to High.

15. Set Lighting Scheme to Exterior: Sun And Artificial.

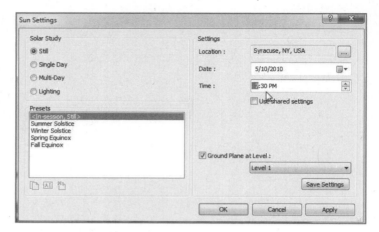

FIGURE 19.15: Changing the scene to dusk

16. Click the Artificial Lights button to make sure all your groups are present, and then click OK.

17. Click the Render button. Your scene should look like Figure 19.16.

FIGURE 19.16: The rendering at dusk

If you're in Syracuse during the winter, it would probably be a good idea to get inside! While you're there, you can bring the experience you just gained with you to create an interior rendering scene.

Creating an Interior Rendering

You create an interior rendering almost exactly the same way as an exterior rendering. Of course, you'll definitely use artificial lighting. You'll also use sunlight to make sure you account for any natural light that comes into the building.

In this procedure, you'll create an interior lighting scene using a premade 3D perspective of a hallway:

1. In the Project Browser, find the 3D view called East Wing Corridor Perspective.

2. On the View Control bar, click the Show Rendering Dialog button.

3. Set Quality to High.

4. Set Resolution to Printer and to 300 DPI.

5. Set Lighting Scheme to Interior: Sun And Artificial.

6. Set Sun to Sunlight From Top Right.

7. Make sure Background Style is set to Color.

8. Click the Render button. Your hallway should resemble Figure 19.17.

FIGURE 19.17: The interior corridor

This is getting almost too easy! I suppose you could keep rendering all week, but in the interest of saving some trees, I encourage you to render only a little more. If you run into any trouble during your foray into additional rendering, give me a shout at ewing@cscos.com and ask your question. The winding stairs heading up to the balcony in the west wing would make a nice scene to hang on your cubicle or office wall.

If you feel as though you have enough experience with rendering, let's jump to the next section and tackle creating a walkthrough for a presentation.

Creating Walkthroughs

For some reason, you can show a client a beautiful rendering of a space or building that you plan to design for them and still be met with a blasé, half-hearted reaction. But if you show them the same space as though you're walking through it … well then, the client perks right up!

Although this part of the chapter isn't crucial to your expertise in Revit, it's certainly worth a glance. Sometimes the special tools you pull out of your belt can win a job or impress your friends on a Saturday night.

A *walkthrough* is a series of points you pick in a sequence in a plan view. It's sort of like connecting the dots, but these dots will advance a frame as if you were walking to the points you picked.

The objective of this procedure is to create a walkthrough of the building and to export the walkthrough to an AVI file. Follow these steps:

1. Go to the Level 1 floor plan.

2. On the View tab, choose 3D View ➢ Walkthrough, as shown in Figure 19.18.

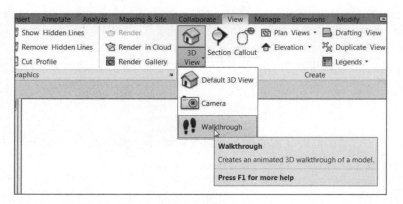

FIGURE 19.18: The Walkthrough command

3. Zoom in on the east entry.

4. Start picking points, as shown in Figure 19.19.

5. Keep picking points down the hallway, into the corridor, and into the west wing, as shown in Figure 19.20.

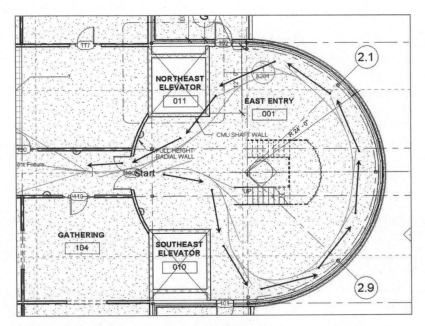

FIGURE 19.19: Picking the points in the floor plan

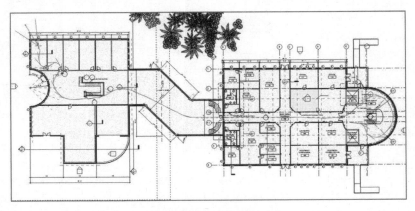

FIGURE 19.20: Sketching the walkthrough path

6. On the Modify | Walkthrough tab of the Ribbon, click Finish Walkthrough.

7. On the Modify | Cameras tab of the Ribbon, click the Edit Walkthrough button.

8. In the Project Browser, find the Walkthroughs category, open the Walkthrough 1 view, and select the crop region.

9. Click Edit Walkthrough.

10. On the Options bar, change the first frame to 1.

11. On the View Control bar, click Realistic.

12. Select the crop region.

13. On the Modify | Cameras tab, click the Edit Walkthrough button (again).

14. On the Modify | Cameras tab, click the Play button, as shown in Figure 19.21.

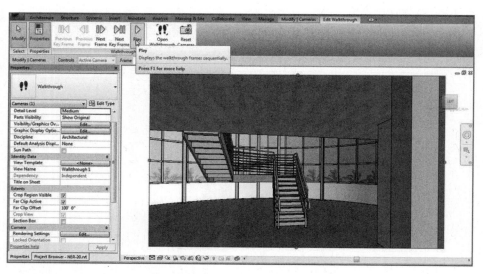

> Note that you can adjust the camera height on the Options bar. This is especially useful for walking up and down stairs.

FIGURE 19.21: Clicking the Play button to start the walkthrough

15. When the walkthrough is finished, click the button that contains the value 300 (the number of frames) on the Options bar, as shown in Figure 19.22.

16. In the Walkthrough Frames dialog, change the Frames Per Second value to 20. Click OK.

17. Run the walkthrough again. This time it's sped up.

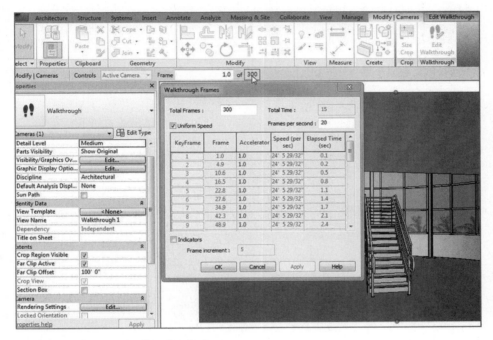

FIGURE 19.22:   Changing the frames

The walkthrough is complete. One thing you certainly will be asked is whether you can give the walkthrough to someone to use for a presentation. Luckily, the answer is yes, and the person presenting doesn't have to be Revit literate or even own the application.

Exporting an Animation

Exporting an animation is a great, but slightly hidden, feature. The Export function isn't located on the Ribbon—you'll find it in the Application menu, as shown in Figure 19.23. By exporting a walkthrough, you're creating an animated vector image (AVI) that will translate the native Revit walkthrough. It's quick and almost completely painless.

FIGURE 19.23: Choosing to export the walkthrough

To create an AVI of the walkthrough, follow these steps:

1. Make sure the walkthrough view is open, and click the Application button.

2. Choose Export ➢ Images And Animations ➢ Walkthrough (see Figure 19.23).

3. Select the defaults in the next dialog, and click OK.

4. Find a location for the file, and click Save.

5. Click OK in the Video Compression dialog. (You'll have to wait for Revit to go through the walkthrough as it creates the AVI.)

6. Find the AVI, and run it to make sure it works.

N O T E   In case you're wondering, yes, the size of this AVI is over a gigabyte. If necessary, you can attempt to compress the file as you export it, but the quality will probably degrade. Besides, memory is cheap these days.

With the walkthrough complete, there is one more animation we need to look at. It's not as cool as the walkthrough, but it's just as interesting. This animation is called a solar study.

Creating a Solar Study

A *solar study* is a shaded 3D view that provides a time-lapsed visual of how the building will cast shadows over the course of a day or multiple days. Let's create a single-day solar study by specifying the geographical location of your building. Follow along:

1. Go to the view {3D} in the Project Browser.

2. Right-click, and choose Duplicate View ➢ Duplicate With Detailing.

3. Rename the new 3D view **One Day Solar Study**.

4. On the View Control toolbar, click the Sun Path button, and choose Sun Settings.

5. In the Sun Settings dialog, click the Single Day radio button, as shown in Figure 19.24.

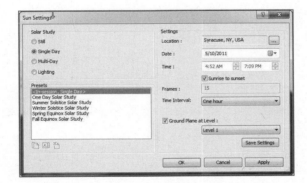

FIGURE 19.24: Setting up the solar study

6. Set Location to Syracuse, NY (or wherever you find yourself these days).

7. Change Date to **5/10/2013**. Select Sunrise To Sunset. Set Ground Plane At Level to Level 1.

8. Set Time Interval to One Hour (see Figure 19.24).

9. Click OK.

10. Click the Sun Path button again, and turn on the sun path.

11. On the View Control bar, click the Shadows button, and then select Preview Solar Study, as shown in Figure 19.25. (You can spin the view to check out the different sunlight effects on the building.)

12. On the Options bar, click the Play button, as shown in Figure 19.26.

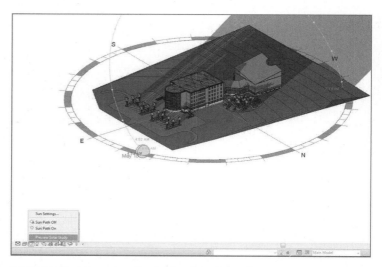

FIGURE 19.25: Previewing the solar study

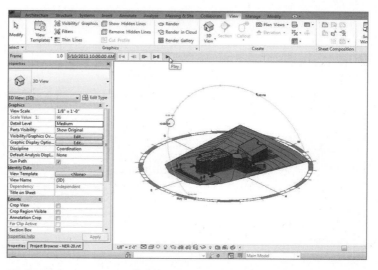

FIGURE 19.26: Clicking Play to start the solar study

Animations such as solar studies and walkthroughs are unique features of Revit that aid you in capturing your work. Keep these features in mind the next time you're working up a proposal or a presentation.

Are You Experienced?

Now you can...

- ☑ **create an exterior rendering by specifying a day-lighting scene based on your geographic location**

- ☑ **create an exterior rendering scene at dusk using lighting**

- ☑ **create an interior rendering using a mixture of day lighting and artificial lighting**

- ☑ **create a walkthrough, and export it to an AVI**

- ☑ **create a solar study that allows you to visualize the shadowing effect of your model**

CHAPTER 20

Importing and Coordinating Models

It's amazing that we're up to Chapter 20, and yet I'm sure many readers are still unclear about how BIM fits in here. Yes, most of the previous chapters showed how you benefit from BIM when you change an item in one place and it changes in another—yada, yada, yada…. But you were probably sold on the whole "coordinating with your consultants" thing back when you were considering purchasing the Autodesk® Revit® Architecture software. Well, here we are. It's time to tackle that mystical ideology that has put our industry in a loose headlock.

▶ **Linking a Revit Structure model**

▶ **Activating Copy/Monitor**

▶ **Running interference detection**

▶ **Importing and exporting AutoCAD®**

Linking a Revit Structure Model

The first section of this chapter will focus on the actual event of importing a Revit Structure model. As you start the process, you'll see that this procedure isn't unfamiliar if you have any CAD background whatsoever. If you don't have a CAD background, I think you'll find these procedures to be intuitive enough to get through importing Revit models.

As you proceed into design development, you must get your structural engineer on board. This consultant may be an external or an in-house resource. Either way, this individual will have a different model with which you need to coordinate.

This section will focus on the procedures involved with importing a Revit Structure model. We'll also cover the concept of creating a live monitoring system with the structure as well as interference detection.

N O T E   Metric users should not type in mm or other metric abbreviations when entering amounts suggested in the exercises. Revit will not accept such abbreviations. Simply enter the number provided within the parentheses.

To get started, open the model on which you've been working. If you missed the previous chapter, go to the book's web page at www.sybex.com/go/revit2014ner. From there, you can browse to the Chapter 20 folder and open the NER-20.rvt file. You'll also need to locate the model called NER-20_STRUCTURAL.rvt. Save both files in a location where you can retrieve them.

The objective of the following procedure is to import and link a Revit Structure model. Follow along:

1. In the Project Browser, go to the Level 1 floor plan.

2. Delete every structural column. (Keep the canopy framing intact. Don't delete the beams and columns in these two areas.)

N O T E   Why are you deleting these structural members you worked so hard to add? Because the structural consultant laid out their grid based on yours. You'll copy their grid back in and monitor any movement that may occur throughout the life of the project. As far as the columns go, you're going to use the structural engineer's columns for your elevations, plans, and sections from this point forward.

3. On the Link panel of the Insert tab, click the Link Revit button, as shown in Figure 20.1.

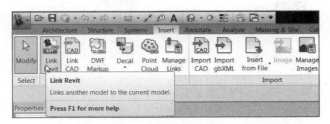

FIGURE 20.1: The Link Revit button on the Link panel of the Insert tab

4. Browse to the NER-20_STRUCTURAL.rvt file, but don't click Open just yet.

5. Select the file.

6. At the bottom of the dialog, you have a choice of Positioning. Select Auto - Origin To Origin, as shown in Figure 20.2.

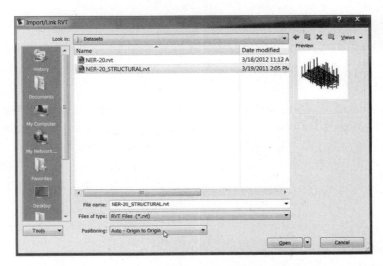

FIGURE 20.2: Pay attention to the choices provided before you click Open.

7. Click Open. Your structural model is now linked.

8. Because this structural model was created independent of your architectural model, you need to align the structural grid with the architectural grid. Use the Align function to do this.

9. Open the 3D view East Entry Corridor.

You can now see the wood framing the structural engineer added to support the cantilevered slab, as shown in Figure 20.3.

FIGURE 20.3:   The supporting framing under the cantilevered slab at the east link

Already you're seeing the benefits of a collaborative model, and you've done nothing more than insert one model into another. This isn't new technology, and you're certainly not doing anything profound. The real benefit comes from how you can keep track of what the structural model is doing underneath your model. You can copy items from the structural model and then monitor any changes made from the linked model. This is the definition of BIM.

Activating Copy/Monitor

I can almost sum up BIM in one command: Copy/Monitor. I hate to break down the most important acronym in our industry since CAD into such simple terms, but Building Information Modeling is the process of monitoring and tracking change, and that process starts right here.

In the next procedure, you'll copy the structural grids and apply a monitoring system that will alert you when the grids have moved. Although this chapter will focus solely on copying and monitoring the grids, your takeaway will be the experience required to recognize the procedure and the importance of this function.

To create a copying and monitoring system, follow these steps:

1. Go to the Level 1 floor plan.

2. On the Coordinate panel of the Collaborate tab, select Copy/
   Monitor ➢ Select Link, as shown in Figure 20.4.

3. Hover your pointer over one of the grids. You see an outline of
   the Revit Structure model that you've linked in. Pick the grid (see
   Figure 20.5).

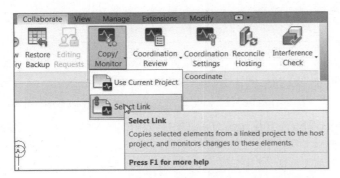

FIGURE 20.4: The Copy/Monitor button on the Coordinate panel of the
Collaborate tab

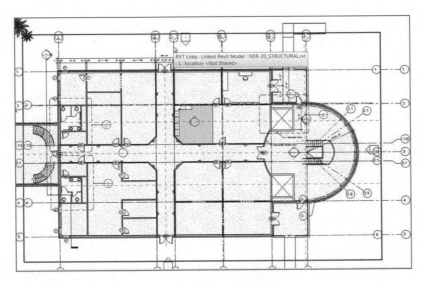

FIGURE 20.5: Selecting the link to Copy/Monitor

4. On the Copy/Monitor tab, click the Copy button, as shown in Figure 20.6.

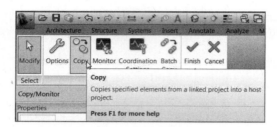

FIGURE 20.6: Clicking the Copy button

5. On the Options bar, select the Multiple option.

6. While pressing the Ctrl key, select all the grids in the linked model.

7. When you're finished, click Finish on the Options bar, as shown in Figure 20.7.

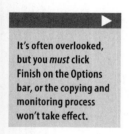

It's often overlooked, but you *must* click Finish on the Options bar, or the copying and monitoring process won't take effect.

FIGURE 20.7: The Finish button on the Options bar

8. You may get a warning saying, "The following types already exist but are different." Close the warning. Your grids should look like Figure 20.8.

9. Close out of any warnings stating that new items have been renamed. This is inconsequential information.

10. Click Finish, as shown in Figure 20.9.

You now have a relationship with the structural model. Next, you'll put this relationship to the test and generate a coordination alert. I suppose you could say that the honeymoon is over!

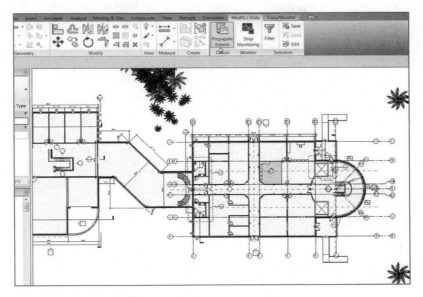

FIGURE 20.8:   The copied grids

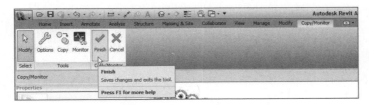

FIGURE 20.9:   Clicking Finish

Coordination Alert

Suddenly you've been thrust into a completely different way of working. You have a structural model inserted into your architectural model that will bark at you every time something changes. There's nothing wrong with that. Sure, occasionally there will be some annoyances, but these irritations are a small concession for being truly tied in with the structure.

When something changes in the structural model that is involved with an active monitor, you'll be alerted. This alert will occur either when you open your model or when you reload the linked Revit file.

To review the coordination alert, follow this procedure:

1. Save and close your model.

2. Open the NER-20_STRUCTURAL.rvt model.

3. Open the Level 1 structural view; and rename grid A to z, as shown in Figure 20.10.

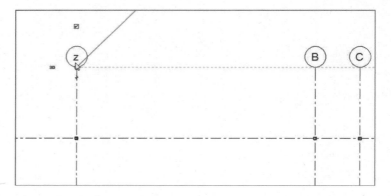

FIGURE 20.10:   Renaming grid A

4. Save the model and close it.

5. Open the architectural model. You may see the warning shown in Figure 20.11.

FIGURE 20.11:   Coordination alert

6. Click OK to continue opening the model.

7. Go to Level 1.

8. Select the link. (You may have to hover your mouse over one of the grids and press the Tab key.)

9. On the Monitor panel of the Modify | RVT Links tab, click the Coordination Review button, as shown in Figure 20.12.

10. In the Coordination Review dialog, expand the Grids category (under the New/Unresolved category), as shown in Figure 20.13.

11. Expand the Maintain Name category.

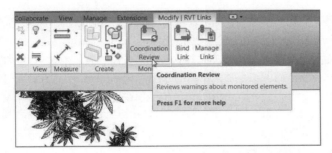

FIGURE 20.12: The Coordination Review button on the Monitor panel of the Modify | RVT Links tab

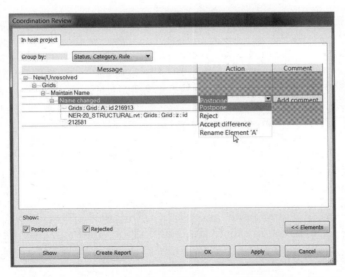

FIGURE 20.13: Telling Revit to rename the grid automatically

 TIP The category that says Grid Moved is the actual alteration that occurred in the structural model. Finally! Somebody is telling us what they changed without fear of us getting mad at them.

12. To the right of the Name Changed category is the Action column. Click into the cell that says Postpone, and look at the list. You'll see four categories:

Reject   Reject postpones the change. Each time you run a coordination review, this instance is listed as rejected. You'll have a chance to modify the instance at a later date.

Accept Difference   Accept Difference basically skips the error. You can change it at a later date.

Rename Element 'A'   This choice takes action. If the difference is the name (which it is in this case), Revit renames the grid. If the grid moves, or if it's deleted, Revit moves or removes the grid for you. (Basically, any necessary modification can be made automatically right here.)

Postpone   This allows you to wait until later to make a decision.

13. Select Rename Element 'A'.

14. Click Apply.

 N O T E   You can also add a comment pertaining to the change. Typically, it's a note to yourself; but in some situations, you'll need such a comment when you're involved in friendly discussions about who started a chain of events.

15. Click the Create Report button at the bottom of the dialog.

16. Save the HTML file to a location where you can find it.

17. Click OK in the Coordination Review dialog. (Notice that grid A is changed.)

18. Open Windows Explorer, find the HTML report, and open it. It's an uneditable report about the coordination effort that just occurred.

19. Close the report.

20. Save the model.

21. To check whether there are any more issues, select the structural link, and click the Coordination Review button on the Modify | RVT Links tab, as shown in Figure 20.14.

FIGURE 20.14:   Click the Coordination Review button.

22. Select the linked structural model. The report should be empty.

A coordination report is an excellent way to track changes, but you're alerted to these changes only if you have the elements copied and monitored. How are you supposed to know if other elements are colliding with one another? This question is answered by using the Interference Detection function built into Revit.

Running Interference Detection

What came first, the chicken or the egg? That's a tough call. Another tough call is whether the beam comes before the duct or wall. Ask a structural engineer and they will answer that the beam does in fact come before the wall, the door, or any other architectural appointment. On the other hand, an architect will ask the structural engineer to move or eliminate a structural component. But the fact is, if the architect and the structural engineer are having this argument, that means they know there is an interference, and their disagreement about the chicken and the egg is actually a good thing.

You can use interference detection in Revit to keep the contractor from asking such questions. If the contractor is asking questions, then you have a problem, don't you? It means a collision has occurred that nobody caught. Don't worry—you can still have the chicken argument, only now it's called litigation.

To use interference detection, you don't have to do anything more than open a single dialog. There, you can select specific elements that you're worried about colliding. And in true Revit form, you can create a report and even zoom in on the issue.

The objective of the following activity is to find some clashes between the architectural model and the structural model:

1. On the Coordinate panel of the Collaborate tab, select Interference Check ➢ Run Interference Check, as shown in Figure 20.15.

2. In the panel to the left of the Interference Check dialog that opens, select Current Project as the Categories From setting.

3. Select Doors and Stairs from the list, as shown in Figure 20.16.

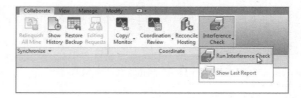

FIGURE 20.15:   Run Interference Check on the Coordinate panel of the Collaborate tab

FIGURE 20.16:   Selecting the components to find in the interference report

4. In the Categories From menu, select the NER-20_STRUCTURAL.rvt file.

5. Select Structural Framing and Structural Columns (see Figure 20.16).

6. Click OK.

7. The Interference Report dialog shows that you have a stair issue. Expand the first Structural Framing category under Stairs, and click Stairs ➤ Stairs: Assembled Stairs.

8. At the bottom of the dialog, click the Show button (see Figure 20.17). You may have to go through a couple of good views to find the interference (by clicking the Show button). Get used to this.

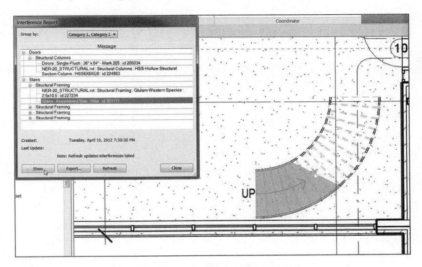

FIGURE 20.17: The offending items are discovered!

9. You can set the visual style any way you want it, but you may have to hide some items (as I did) to see the collision.

10. Revit zooms right in on the issue. Click the Export button.

11. Save the report in the same directory as the coordination report.

12. Click Close.

WHAT DO YOU MEAN, CLOSE? WE DIDN'T FIX ANYTHING!

Yes, that's right—you only identified the issue. Revit doesn't breach another model to fix your consultant's work. It does, however, give you a specific, detailed report for your meeting. Remember, using Revit doesn't negate the need for open discussion during a project.

That is some good stuff. Lucky for you, your consultants are all up and running on Revit. Oh, they aren't? What kind of world are you living in?

It's true. Your consultants won't all be on Revit. If you're lucky, 1 in 10 uses Revit in such a capacity that they're ready to share a model with you. This is okay—don't panic. You're still in a great position. You can easily import from AutoCAD (or MicroStation), and you can export your model just as easily.

Importing and Exporting CAD Formats

The first process we'll delve into is importing an AutoCAD structural floor plan. Although you've imported CAD in this book numerous times, you have yet to do so in the context of a coordinated floor plan. The mindset for this is a little different. And why is that? Because you now care about where this AutoCAD drawing lands in relation to your model; you care also about maintaining that relationship.

For the CAD file used in the following procedure, go to the book's web page, browse to the Chapter 20 folder, and find the NER-20_STRUCTURAL.dwg file. Save this file in a location where you can retrieve it.

Now, let's import an AutoCAD 2D floor plan and pin down its coordinates. Follow these steps:

1. Go to the Level 1 floor plan.

2. Right-click the Level 1 view in the Project Browser, and click Duplicate View ➢ Duplicate With Detailing, as shown in Figure 20.18.

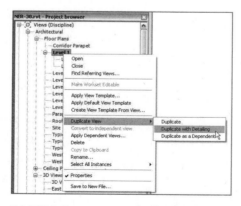

FIGURE 20.18: Duplicating the view

3. Rename the new view **Level 1 CAD Coordination**.

4. Open the new view.

5. Type **VG** (for Visibility Graphics).

6. Click the Revit Links tab.

7. Uncheck the `NER-20_STRUCTURAL.rvt` model.

8. Click OK.

9. On the Link panel of the Insert tab, click the Link CAD button, and then browse to the location where you saved the `NER-20_STRUCTURAL.DWG` file.

10. At the bottom of the Link CAD Formats dialog, select the Current View Only check box.

11. Set Colors to Black And White.

12. Set Layers/Levels to All.

13. Set Import Units to Auto-Detect.

14. Set Positioning to Auto - Origin To Origin (see Figure 20.19).

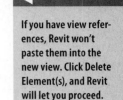

If you have view references, Revit won't paste them into the new view. Click Delete Element(s), and Revit will let you proceed.

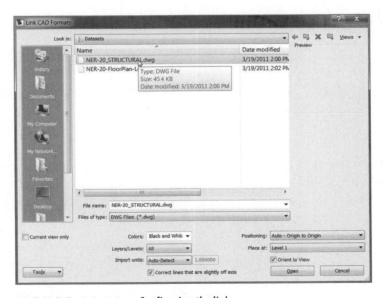

FIGURE 20.19: Configuring the link

15. Click Open.

16. On the View Control bar, click the Wireframe button so you can see the AutoCAD structure, as shown in Figure 20.20.

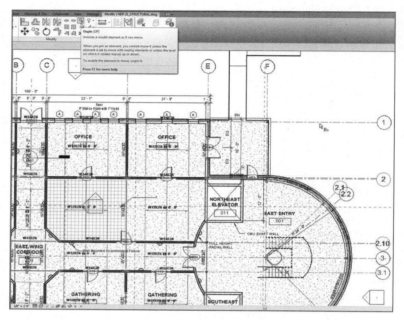

FIGURE 20.20: Unpinning and aligning the reference

17. As you can see, the underlay isn't positioned correctly. Select the linked CAD, and unpin it (see Figure 20.20).

18. Align column lines A and 1.

The next step is to make sure the coordinates in the Revit model stay true in the DWG file. With one simple procedure, you can publish the coordinates of the Revit model to the DWG file to ensure accuracy while importing because you had to move the link. Follow along:

1. On the Project Location panel of the Manage tab, click Coordinates ➤ Publish Coordinates, as shown in Figure 20.21.

2. Select the AutoCAD link by left-clicking it in the view.

3. On the Site tab of the Location Weather And Site dialog, click the Duplicate button.

4. Call the new location **Revit Position**, and click OK.

5. Click OK.

6. Press Esc, and then select the AutoCAD link.

7. In the Properties dialog, verify that Shared Site is now Revit Position.

8. Save the Revit model.

9. After you save the Revit model, you're prompted to save the new coordinates in the DWG file. Click the Save button, as shown in Figure 20.22.

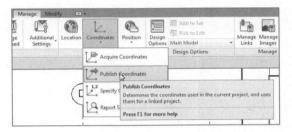

FIGURE 20.21: Publishing the coordinates

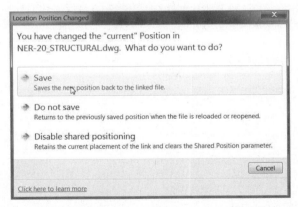

FIGURE 20.22: Saving the coordinates to the AutoCAD file

So that's importing. Now, suppose you need to send your model to clients and consultants who don't have Revit. This can be addressed quickly and deliberately.

Exporting a Model to CAD

For some of you, this is a nice-to-know subject. But for most of you, this is a need-to-know subject. Taking the plunge into Revit may be something you're doing alone. Even if you're using Revit, you may still need the ability to provide CAD drawings based on your models.

This section will focus on the process of exporting your Revit model to both 2D and 3D CAD.

Exporting a 2D Model

Most of the time, your deliverable to your clients will be a 2D model. If your consultants aren't on Revit, usually they aren't using 3D CAD either. The 2D CAD format is the lowest common denominator. Not that a 2D model is bad—it means you need to export your model in a way that the client can pick it up and run with it.

The objective of this procedure is to export your model to a 2D AutoCAD drawing file. Follow these steps:

1. In the Project Browser, open the Level 1 floor plan.

2. Click the Application button, and select Export ➤ CAD Formats ➤ DWG Files, as shown in Figure 20.23.

3. Click the [...] button to the right of the Select Export Setup drop-down, as shown in Figure 20.24.

FIGURE 20.23: Exporting the model to CAD

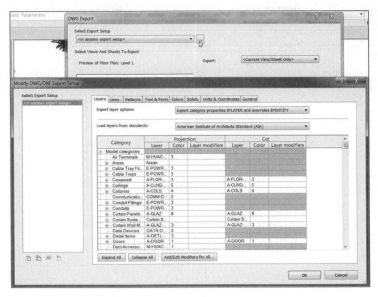

FIGURE 20.24: Look at all the CAD choices!

4. You have all sorts of CAD options. Click OK in this dialog.

5. Click OK.

6. Click the Next button, and save the file. You can open it and check it out if you wish.

Now that you can export to a flat 2D file, it's time to export your model as a full 3D entity. The process is similar to exporting as 2D.

Exporting the Model to 3D CAD

It's a shame to dumb down a 3D model to flat 2D CAD. It feels as though you're taking a step backward each time you do it. When you find yourself in a situation where your consultants are using CAD but are using 3D modeling, you can give them the gift of 3D. Follow along:

1. Go to the Default 3D view.

2. Select Export ➢ CAD Formats ➢ DWG Files.

3. Set the Export option to Current View/Sheet Only.

4. Click the Next button.

> The most important step in exporting to a 3D CAD format is to be in a 3D view.

5. Find a place to save the 3D model, and click OK.

6. Save the model.

As you can see, it's not a difficult process, but it's important to know. You'll often find yourself exporting all your hard work and data to a lesser CAD format as you wait for the rest of the industry to catch up to you!

Are You Experienced?

Now you can...

- ☑ **import a Revit Structure model**

- ☑ **copy and monitor the Revit model**

- ☑ **run interference checking on a linked Revit model**

- ☑ **export a Revit model to CAD formats (2D and 3D)**

CHAPTER 21

Phasing and Design Options

Of all the projects with which I have been involved over the years, I can remember only a handful that didn't involve some kind of existing condition. It would be nice if we could find a giant, flat field on which to construct our buildings, but those projects are few and far between.

▶ **Managing project phasing**

▶ **Examining graphic overrides**

▶ **Creating design options**

Managing Project Phasing

The term *phasing* in the Autodesk® Revit® Architecture platform is often taken literally, and it can be confused with construction sequencing. When we talk about phasing in a Revit context, we're talking about adding new construction to an existing building and demolishing the existing structure. Although you can use Revit to track all aspects of construction, the base use and purpose of phasing is dealing with existing conditions.

The first section of this chapter will focus on the setup of your phasing scheme. By default, Revit Architecture provides two phases: Existing and New Construction. As it stands, everything you've placed into your model in the last 20 chapters has been exclusively related to the New Construction phase. You'll now alter that.

I've seen this scenario played out more times than I would have liked. People get Revit, build a model, and then start clicking the Demolish button found on the Phasing panel on the Manage tab. Yes, doing so forces hidden lines, and now you're demolishing walls that were constructed in the same phase in which they're being removed. You can't do that!

FIGURE 21.1:   Clicking the Phases button

With some practice, and by following the procedures in this chapter, you'll be able to swing that hammer all you want. But for now, to get started, go to the book's web page at www.sybex.com/go/revit2014ner. From there, you can browse to the Chapter 21 folder and find the NER-21.rvt file. (If you prefer, you can follow along with your own model as well.)

N O T E   Metric users should not type in mm or other metric abbreviations when entering amounts suggested in the exercises. Revit will not accept such abbreviations. Simply enter the number provided within the parentheses.

The objective of the following procedure is to create a Demolition phase and insert it between the Existing phase and the New Construction phase. Follow along:

1. On the Manage tab, click the Phases button on the Phasing panel, as shown in Figure 21.1.

2. In the Phasing dialog, click the number 1. This is the control for the Existing phase row.

3. In the Insert section, click the After button, as shown in Figure 21.2.

4. Rename the phase that is now in the middle to **Demolition**.

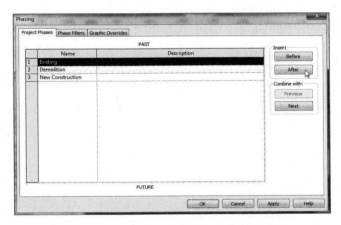

FIGURE 21.2: Starting to add the Demolition phase

5. Click OK.

6. Make sure you're in Level 1. On the View tab, click Duplicate View ➢ Duplicate View, as shown in Figure 21.3.

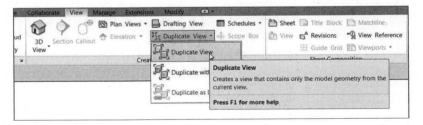

FIGURE 21.3: Duplicating the view

7. Right-click the new view, and rename it **Level 1 Demolition**.

8. Open the Level 1 Demolition plan.

9. Select every exterior wall in the east building, and change Phase Created to Existing at the bottom of the Properties dialog.

10. Press Esc.

11. Select the entire south ramp, floor slab, railings, and framing. Make sure you select the structural framing system that is spacing the beams for the canopy roof and not the beams themselves.

12. In the Properties dialog, set Phase Created to Existing and Phase Demolished to Demolition.

13. Go to the Level 1 floor plan (not the demolition). There is no longer a ramp. No sense living in the past. The demolition plan shows the items on a demo line type. Who needs layers, right?

14. Go back to the Level 1 Demolition floor plan.

15. In the Properties dialog for the Level 1 Demolition plan, scroll down to Phasing, and change Phase to Demolition, as shown in Figure 21.4. Change Phase Filter to Show All.

FIGURE 21.4:   Changing Phase to Demolition

16. Zoom in on the east entry, specifically where the ramp enters the building to the south, as shown in Figure 21.5. Revit automatically changes the line weight to Heavy, and the line type to Demolished.

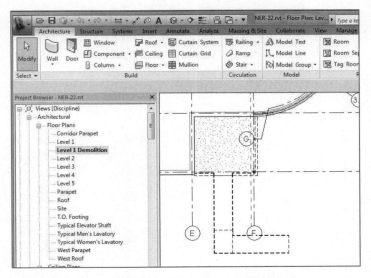

FIGURE 21.5: Seeing the results of demolishing an item

17. Go back to the Level 1 plan, and select the two doors shown in Figure 21.6.

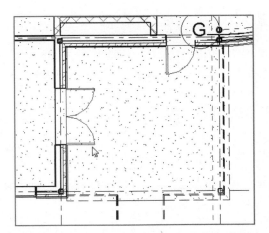

FIGURE 21.6: You no longer need these doors.

18. Set Phase Created to Existing.

19. In the properties, set Phase Demolished to Demolition. Revit removes the doors and infills the openings, as shown in Figure 21.7. (It's understood that the entire building should be existing. This is an example of how Revit behaves during the phasing process.)

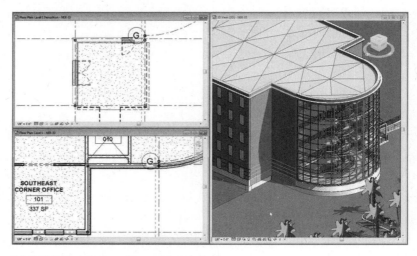

FIGURE 21.7: The completed phasing

Examining Graphic Overrides

After you've changed the phasing of an object's creation and demolition, Revit magically puts everything on the correct display. Well, as magical as it seems, there are some features driving this display. Let's take a look at them:

1. Click the Phases button on the Phasing panel of the Manage tab.

2. Click the Graphic Overrides tab.

3. In the Existing row, for the Lines column under the Cut heading, click the button that displays a shaded line, as shown in Figure 21.8.

4. Click the Color button.

5. Change the shading of the line to 75, 75, 75 (see Figure 21.8). Click OK to exit all dialogs. The existing walls update in the views.

Another function of Revit that we need to delve into is similar to phasing, but it has an entirely different meaning when it comes to tracking aspects of a project. This functionality is called *design options*.

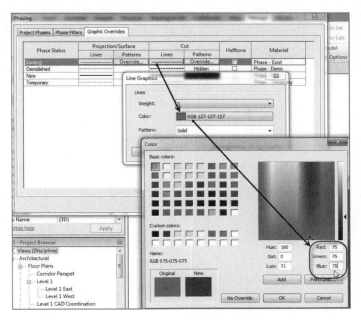

Creating Design Options

FIGURE 21.8: Making the existing shading darker

Creating Design Options

Revit is equipped with the functionality to allow you to model different options in one model, better known in the design world as *bid alternates*. The great thing about how Revit handles this functionality is that any alternate design is never—or, at least, is seldom—a completely new structure. Some items are in more than one option. Revit lets you keep like items intact while creating new or different items that belong to different options. This creates a situation in which you only need to model the common items once, so you can focus on the alternates.

That being said, there is a lot to be added to this functionality in future versions of Revit. To begin adding and implementing design options, follow these steps.

1. On the Manage tab, click the Design Options button, as shown in Figure 21.9.

FIGURE 21.9: Clicking the Design Options button

2. In the Design Options dialog, click the New button under Option Set.

 N O T E   You can have as many option sets as you choose. There will be cases in which you have other, unrelated options in other places in your model.

3. Select Option Set 1.

4. In the Option Set category, click the Rename button.

5. Call the option set **Ramp Options**.

6. Select Option 1 (Primary).

7. In the Option category, click Rename.

8. Rename the option set **L-Shaped Ramp**.

9. In the Option category, click the New button.

10. Rename the new option **Curved Ramp** (see Figure 21.10).

FIGURE 21.10:   Adding options

11. Click Close.

12. In the Project Browser, go to the Level 1 floor plan.

13. Select both the ramp and the railing, as shown in Figure 21.11.

14. Click the Add To Set button at the bottom of the Revit window (see Figure 21.11).

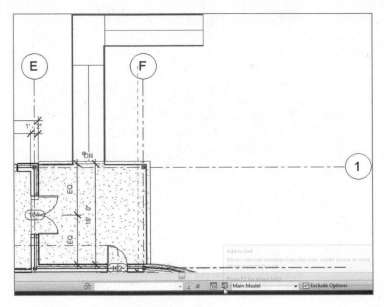

FIGURE 21.11:   Adding to a set

15. Deselect the Curved Ramp, and click OK.

IT'S HARD TO SELECT STUFF NOW

At the bottom of the screen, next to the Main Model text, is an Exclude Options check box. Revit forces you to be in an option to make edits to the model unless this check box is deselected.

It's time to create a new ramp. To do so, follow along:

1. Switch to the Curved Ramp option, as shown in Figure 21.12.

FIGURE 21.12:   Jumping into an option

2. The L-shaped items disappear. Draw a ramp and a railing similar to those shown in Figure 21.13. Remember, the ramp is from Level 1 to Level 1, with a -2′–6″ (-750mm) bottom offset.

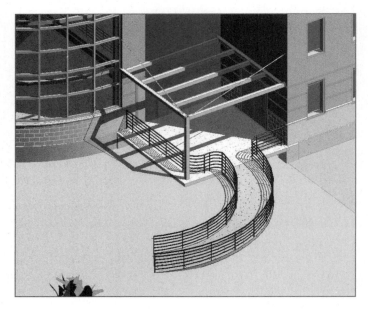

FIGURE 21.13:   The curved option

3. Change the option back to Main Model, as shown in Figure 21.14.

4. Find the {3D} view in the Project Browser.

5. Right-click it, and choose Duplicate With Detailing.

6. Rename the new view **L-Shape Option**.

7. Create another view, and rename it **Curved Ramp**.

8. Open the Curved Ramp view.

9. Type **VG** for Visibility Graphics.

10. Click the new Design Options tab.

11. Change Design Option to Curved Ramp, and click OK (see Figure 21.15).

FIGURE 21.14:   Switching back to Main Model

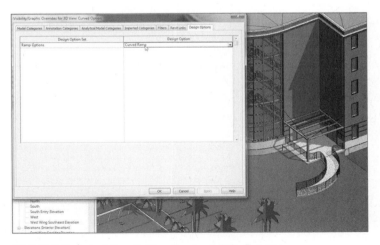

FIGURE 21.15:   Setting the view's default option

ACCEPTING THE PRIMARY OPTION

You'll notice that when you're working in design options, you can only edit items belonging to the current option, unless you deselect the Exclude Options check box on the status bar Design Options panel (it defaults to being selected in all views). If your options set is set to None, then you're actually in the Main Model option. When you've finished with the options and an alternative has been accepted, you can make the accepted option the primary option and click Accept Primary. Doing so deletes all other options, leaving just the one option. (Make sure you have a backup before you do this.)

As you can see, this is a powerful tool. Gone are the days of copying around several Autodesk® AutoCAD® files to accomplish the task of designing alternates. The great thing about the design options in Revit is that if you need to make a modification to the building, and it needs to be shown in all your options, you can simply make the Main Model option current and work away.

Are You Experienced?

Now you can...

☑ configure project phasing settings by adding new phases

☑ change and add phase filters, and create phasing graphical overrides

☑ create demo plans

☑ organize the Project Browser to reflect your phasing

☑ create design options

Project Collaboration

It's quite ironic that the last chapter of this book contains information that many of you'll need to get your first Autodesk® Revit® Architecture project off the ground. That is, how do you work on a project when multiple people need to be in the model? Revit is only one model, right?

▶ **Enabling and utilizing worksharing**

▶ **Working in the Revit shared environment**

Enabling and Utilizing Worksharing

You may be surprised, but the answer to the question posed in the chapter introduction and the procedure itself aren't as difficult as some make them out to be. I have seen many explanations on the subject of project collaboration that are far-reaching and convoluted, causing an air of uneasiness. Collaboration isn't as horrible as it sounds, and this chapter will explain project collaboration in the simplest terms possible.

N O T E   Metric users should not type in mm or other metric abbreviations when entering amounts suggested in the exercises. Revit will not accept such abbreviations. Simply enter the number provided within the parentheses.

First we'll establish exactly what you're trying to accomplish and how to go about doing it. The backbone of project collaboration is the functionality of *worksharing*.

The concept of worksharing in Revit, broken into its simplest form, is this:

1. Go to your project directory to open the model.

2. Find a file called the *central model*, make sure Create Local is selected, and click Open.

This process saves a linked copy to your C:\ drive under My Documents. Now you and your co-workers can all access the same model at the same time. What a productive way to get a job out the door! (See Figure 22.1.)

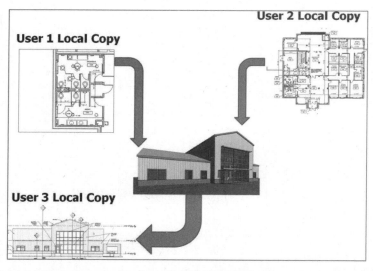

F I G U R E   2 2 . 1 :   The basic file-sharing configuration

Okay, so that's the concept of worksharing. It's now time to drill down and see how to activate this network of linked files. As mentioned earlier, Revit has a function called *worksets*. The worksets are the backbone of this entire concept.

Enabling Worksets

The worksets function in Revit influences your model and the way you go about working more than anything you can do. Using worksets is a mode you literally have to enter into.

Essentially, worksets are a way to divide your model. After you activate worksharing, every element in your model has a workset with which it's associated. Levels and grids are on their own workset, and everything else in the model is automatically assigned Workset1. This *assignment* is in the form of a parameter that you can see in the Properties dialog. You can change that parameter if necessary.

Why would you want to change it? Good question. Here's an example. Say you're modifying an interior partition, and your co-worker (who is working on a local model) tries to edit that same wall. Your co-worker will be denied access to the wall. But nothing is stopping your co-worker from working on another wall in the same area, one to which you intended to make the same modifications. This could get messy fast. To avoid this situation, you can add all your interior partitions to a workset called Interior Partitions and *lock* everybody else out of any item you've placed in this workset.

Now that's the way to work!

Obviously, this process isn't without its rules, quirks, and parts that need further explanation. To get started, go to the book's web page at www.sybex.com/go/revit2014ner. From there, you can browse to the Chapter 22 folder and find the NER-22.rvt file.

To enable worksets and start the worksharing process, follow these steps:

1. Open the NER-22.rvt file.

2. On the Collaborate tab, click the Worksets button on the Worksets panel, as shown in Figure 22.2. Note that the Worksharing button is also on the status bar at the bottom of the Revit window.

3. A Worksharing dialog welcomes you to the point of no return. Accept the default values—Shared Levels And Grids and Workset1—as shown in Figure 22.3, and click OK.

N O T E   Turning on worksets is a one-time activation process. You don't have to do this every time you want to work on the project.

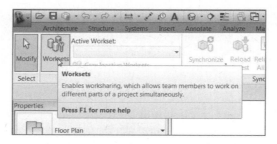

FIGURE 22.2:   Clicking the Worksets button

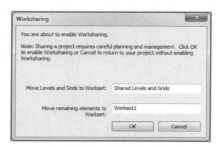

FIGURE 22.3:   The Worksharing dialog

4. The next dialog is named Worksets, as shown in Figure 22.4. Your two worksets are presented in a spreadsheet format that says they're both editable and you own them. Congratulations. There is plenty to explain here:

▶ Active Workset indicates the workset in which any new item will be either drawn or inserted (sort of like the current *layer* in Autodesk® AutoCAD®). There is also a Gray Inactive Workset Graphics check box. When selected, it shades items that aren't in the current workset.

▶ The Show area at the bottom of the Worksets dialog lets you add specific families, project standards, and views to the workset list (see Figure 22.4).

5. Click OK to get back to the model.

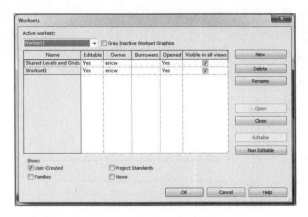

FIGURE 22.4:   The Worksets dialog

 N O T E   You can turn on additional items in the Show category. But unless there is a compelling reason to do so, *don't*—especially if this is the first project your team is taking on in Revit. Try to keep your worksets as simple and painless as possible. Just because you *can* assume ultimate control over your users doesn't mean you *have* to.

Now that you've activated the worksets and saved the model, it's time to create the central model. This will always be the next step in the process.

Creating a Central Model

Creating the central model is generally a one-time deal. You create it immediately after you enable your worksets. The individual who creates the central model needs to be your best Revit user. If not, and this procedure is done incorrectly, you'll have struggles for the entire life of the project.

Okay, best Revit user, follow this procedure to learn how to create the central model:

1. Click the Application button, and choose Save As ➤ Project, as shown in Figure 22.5.

2. In the Save As dialog, click the Options button in the lower-right corner.

3. In the File Save Options dialog, change Maximum Backups to **1** (see Figure 22.6).

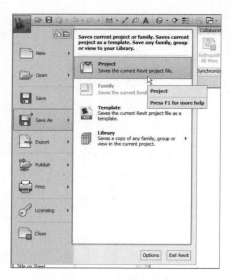

FIGURE 22.5: Saving the project using Save As

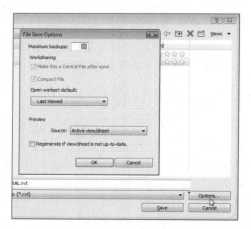

FIGURE 22.6: Modifying the settings before you save the file

NOTE Notice that the Worksharing area isn't active. This is because you're saving the file for the first time after activating worksharing. You have no choice but to make this the central model.

4. Click OK.

5. Call the file **NER-CENTRAL.rvt**.

6. Click Save.

7. On the Collaborate tab, choose Synchronize With Central ➢ Synchronize Now, as shown in Figure 22.7. Doing so saves any changes made.

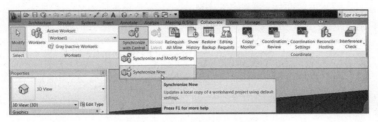

FIGURE 22.7: Choosing Synchronize Now

8. On the Worksets panel in the Collaborate tab, click the Worksets button.

9. Change both worksets by choosing No in the Editable column (see Figure 22.8).

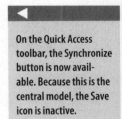

On the Quick Access toolbar, the Synchronize button is now available. Because this is the central model, the Save icon is inactive.

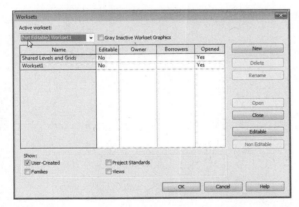

FIGURE 22.8: Releasing the worksets by clicking No for Editable

10. Click OK. (Don't worry—I'll explain what all this means in a moment.)

11. Click the Synchronize Now button.

You made these worksets not editable because, when you're working in the central file, you always want to leave it without editable worksets. That way, users don't have access to these worksets in their local models.

The next task you need to tackle in the creation of a central model is how to make a new workset and move some components onto it. In this procedure, you'll create a Site workset and move the topography and the site components to it. Follow these steps:

1. Click the Worksets button on the Collaborate tab.

2. In the Worksets dialog, click the New button, as shown in Figure 22.9.

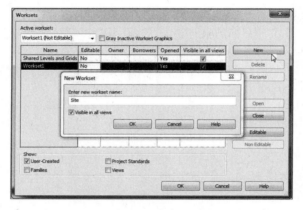

FIGURE 22.9:   Creating a new workset

3. In the New Workset dialog, call this workset **Site**, and then click OK.

4. Make sure Site has Yes in the Editable row.

5. Click OK.

6. Go to the default 3D view.

7. Select the toposurface.

8. In the Properties dialog, find the Identity Data category, locate the Workset row, and change the workset to Site.

9. Select the rest of the site components, including the split surfaces, the tree, and the shrubs.

10. Put these items in the Site workset.

11. On the Collaborate tab, click the Synchronize Now button.

12. On the Collaborate tab, click the Worksets button.

13. Make all worksets not editable, as shown in Figure 22.10, and then click OK.

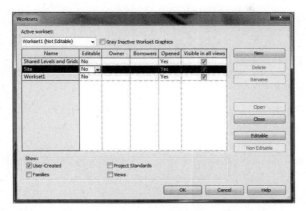

FIGURE 22.10:   Making all worksets not editable

14. Click the Synchronize Now button.

N O T E   You make sure all the worksets aren't editable because, in the central model, everything needs to be turned off. Look at the central model as a *hub* that serves as a conduit for passing data as your team collaborates on the project.

Next you'll create your local model. Luckily, you've done all the difficult work. Setting up the central file is the hardest part of the worksharing process, and it's usually done by the BIM manager or at least the BIM lead on the project. The act of creating a local file is as simple as issuing a Save As.

Creating a Local File

With the central model in place, you're ready for the rest of your team to have at it. Although I keep mentioning how easy most of this stuff is, there is one danger to look out for. Please, never open the central model and stay in it, if you don't want to be thrashed by your co-workers. When you're in the process of creating a local model, you select the central model and choose the Create New Local option. If you don't make sure this check box is selected, guess what?

You're sitting in the central model. If this occurs, nobody has access to synchronize with the central model. Shame on you.

This section of the chapter will guide you through the process of creating a local model. Follow along:

1. Close out of the central model. You'll never go back into it again.

2. In the Recent Files screen, click the Open button under the Files heading.

3. Browse to your NER_CENTRAL file.

4. Select it, but don't open it yet.

5. At the bottom of the dialog is a Create New Local check box. Make sure it's selected (see Figure 22.11).

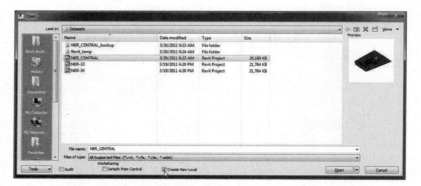

FIGURE 22.11:   Creating a new local model

6. Click Open.

Congratulations! You're the proud owner of a new Revit file that knows your name and everything.

Yes, it knows your name. You see, when you create the local model, it's yours to keep. This file resides in your personal documents folder on your C:\ drive, with your username. Not only does your local model keep a live link back to the central model, but it also knows to whom it belongs. Revit does this for a good reason: this file represents you within the team.

Working in the Revit Shared Environment

With the local model saved, you're free to work away. As you'll recall, you created the central model with three worksets: Shared Levels And Grids, Workset1, and Site. You, as a local user, can begin working. As you start editing the model, however, Revit makes a note that you're borrowing a workset. Revit also notes that you physically own the item you're editing.

Borrowing? Let's stop and look at what this means. In Revit worksharing, you can be either a borrower of a workset or an owner of a workset. If you're a borrower, the rest of the design team can make modifications to elements in the workset but not to the specific element on which you're working.

The objective of the next exercise is to make a modification to the site and investigate what happens in the Worksets dialog. Follow these steps:

1. Go to the default 3D view.

2. Delete one of the shrubs. (Remember, you put the shrubs on the Site workset.)

3. On the Collaborate tab, click the Worksets button.

4. In the Worksets dialog, notice that you're now borrowing the Site workset, as shown in Figure 22.12. Click OK.

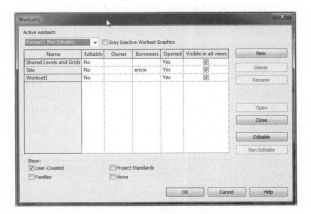

FIGURE 22.12: Borrowing a workset

Because there is no good way to have you go through this exercise, you can take your hand off the mouse and read for a few paragraphs. If you're at work and have another willing participant, have them create their own local model, and ask them to start making edits to the model.

The Site workset still says No for Editable. This means that if Cassidy begins working on the shrubs right next to the one you just deleted, she can do so. You don't own the workset—you're just borrowing it. If you change the shrub to a tree (or make any modifications whatsoever to the shrub), Cassidy can't make any edits to the new tree. When she tries to edit the tree, she gets the error shown in Figure 22.13. She can then place a request that Eric will see at the bottom of his screen.

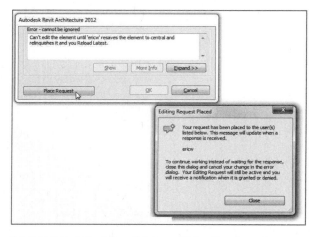

FIGURE 22.13: Eric is modifying the element.

GET IN SYNC

After you've created the local model, you can see what others are doing, as well as publish what you're doing for the other users. To do so, click the Synchronize Now button on the Quick Access toolbar: you and your users are now in sync.

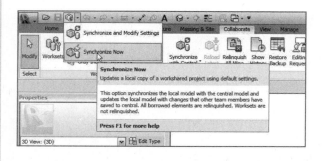

After the request is placed, Eric sees it pop up at the bottom of the screen, as shown in Figure 22.14.

FIGURE 22.14: Please release me.

When you see that someone is begging you to release an item, you get to do the right thing and grant the request. You do this by clicking the Relinquish All Mine button on the Collaborate tab, as shown in Figure 22.15.

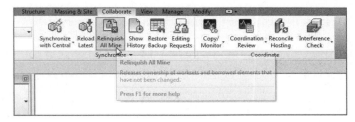

FIGURE 22.15: The Relinquish All Mine button

See? You *can* all get along! (Until you pull the next move.) Suppose you don't want anybody else on the team to modify anything in the entire Site workset. There are times when this will occur. To learn how to do this, follow along:

1. On the Collaborate tab, click the Worksets button.

2. In the Site workset, select Yes in the Editable field, as shown in Figure 22.16. Although Cassidy is a borrower, you can still take over the workset.

3. Click OK.

 NOTE   If Cassidy is in the middle of an active edit on any items in the workset, you can't take over. You have to place an editing request to her. See? You should have given her the shrub when she asked for it earlier!

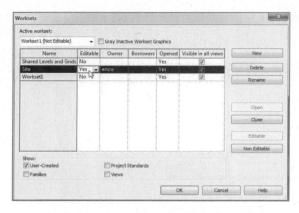

FIGURE 22.16: Occupying the entire workset

ERIC A.K.A. CASSIDY

If Eric decides to not relinquish an item to Cassidy and then decides to close his model and go on vacation (ignoring repeated warnings), you have a situation, don't you? His office door is locked, and you don't know his password. What you can do in these trying times is click the Options button at the bottom of the Application menu. Then select the General tab, and change the username to the offender's name. You can now open Eric's local file and relinquish the worksets, as shown in the following graphic:

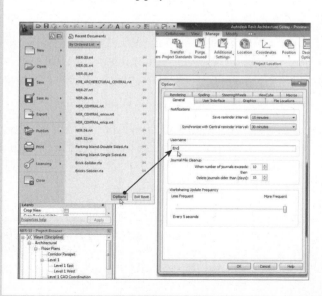

And so the workday goes in an environment of sharing and getting along. Speaking of environment, suppose you could not care less about the site. There is a good chance that you don't even want to see it. Well, you're in luck. Because you have worksets enabled, you can make it so that Revit doesn't even load the site into your local model.

Loading or Not Loading a Workset

I'm making a big deal out of a simple task only because it can speed up your performance—nothing can bog down a Revit model more than a huge site complete with landscaping and maybe an image.

Switching the Opened status to No in a workset forces Revit not to load the workset into your model. If you make an edit that has an influence on the site, don't worry: Revit will take care of that in the central model.

To turn off the site, follow this procedure:

1. Click the Worksets button on the Collaborate tab.

2. In the Site workset, change the Opened status to No, as shown in Figure 22.17.

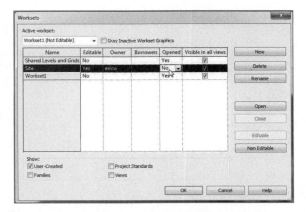

FIGURE 22.17: Changing the Opened status to No

3. Click OK. Notice something missing?

Having the ability to turn off large portions of a model can be a tremendous advantage as you move forward in Revit. You need to exercise caution, however. You could easily deceive yourself into thinking that some portions of the model haven't been created yet.

Detaching from Central

You can also detach a model from central. This is sometimes useful when things run amok—and they will, from time to time. Detaching from central allows you to strip a model of all its owners and borrowers. You can then save back over the top of the existing central model so that everyone can get back to enjoying their Revit experience.

Let's look at some maintenance procedures:

1. Synchronize with Central, and close out of any model you may be in currently.

2. In Revit, click the Open button.

3. Browse to the central model.

4. Instead of selecting Create New Local, click Detach From Central, as shown in Figure 22.18.

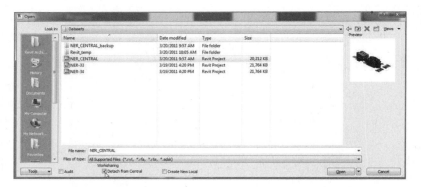

FIGURE 22.18: Detaching from Central

5. Click Open.

6. You can turn off all file sharing and put the model back into a single-user state. In this instance, however, click Detach And Preserve Worksets, as shown in Figure 22.19.

7. On the Quick Access toolbar, click the Save button.

8. Revit doesn't know what to save the file as, so it gives you the choice. Click the Options button in the lower-right corner.

9. Make This A Central File After Save is selected and grayed out. This is what you want to see.

10. Click OK.

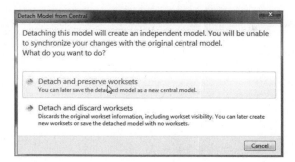

FIGURE 22.19:   Preserving the worksets

11. Save right over the top of NER_CENTRAL.rvt.

12. You've just safely saved the day.

13. Tell *all* users that they need to make new local models.

MAKE IT A HABIT!

Every time you close your local file, you should make a new one the next time you go into the model. Look at your local model as a disposable one-time-use kind of thing. Don't keep reopening the same local file, or it will start causing difficulties. You'll find that your local model becomes incompatible with the central model. Worse yet, sometimes if you synchronize an old local model, you run the risk of reverting the central model back to an earlier version. When you create a new local, Revit will warn you that you're about to overwrite the existing local file. This is fine, and you should do so.

Here we are at the end of the book! As I mentioned at the beginning, this book is meant to serve as a step-by-step tutorial as well as a desk reference. There are also classroom-style datasets and training materials on the book's web page. As always, please feel free to contact me directly at ewing@csos.com.

Are You Experienced?

Now you can...

- ☑ activate worksharing in a Revit project
- ☑ create a central file
- ☑ create a local file
- ☑ manipulate worksets

INDEX

Note to the Reader: Throughout this index **boldfaced** page numbers indicate primary discussions of a topic. *Italicized* page numbers indicate illustrations.